A People and a Nation

Brief Edition

A PEOPLE AND A NATION

A History of the United States

Volume 1 • To 1877

BRIEF SIXTH EDITION

Mary Beth Norton
Cornell University

David M. Katzman
University of Kansas

David W. Blight
Amherst College

Howard P. Chudacoff
Brown University

Thomas G. Paterson
University of Connecticut

William M. Tuttle, Jr.
University of Kansas

Paul D. Escott
Wake Forest University

and

William J. Brophy
Stephen F. Austin State University

Houghton Mifflin Company   Boston   New York

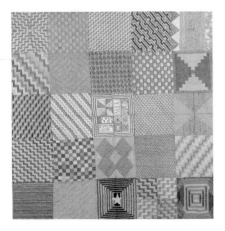

The icons used throughout Chapters 1–16 are details from "Sampler Block Quilt" by Evelyn Derr. National Museum of American Art, Smithsonian Institution, Washington, D.C./Art Resource, N.Y.

Sponsoring Editor: Mary Dougherty
Development Editor: Leah Strauss
Senior Project Editor: Christina M. Horn
Editorial Assistant: Talia M. Kingsbury
Senior Production/Design Coordinator: Carol Merrigan
Senior Manufacturing Coordinator: Marie Barnes
Senior Marketing Manager: Sandra McGuire

Cover image: *Mrs. James Smith and Grandson*, Charles Willson Peale, 1775. National Museum of American Art, Washington, D.C.

Printed in the U.S.A.

Library of Congress Control Number: 2001097962

ISBN: 0-618-21469-0

3 4 5 6 7 8 9-DOC-06 05 04 03

BRIEF CONTENTS

CONTENTS

MAPS

CHARTS

PREFACE TO THE BRIEF SIXTH EDITION

Almost two decades have passed since the publication of the first brief edition of *A People and a Nation*. In that initial brief edition, as well as each subsequent one, the intent was to preserve the uniqueness and integrity of the complete work while condensing it. This Brief Sixth Edition once again reflects the scholarship, readability, and comprehensiveness of the full-length version. It also maintains the integration of social, cultural, political, economic, and foreign relations history that has been a hallmark of *A People and a Nation*.

Creation of the Brief Edition

William J. Brophy has again prepared the brief text. As in the past, he worked closely with the authors. This collaboration ensured that the changes in content and organization incorporated in the full-length Sixth Edition were retained in the condensation. By reviewing each line, the authors attained reductions by paring down details rather than deleting entire sections. The Brief Sixth Edition thus contains fewer statistics, fewer quotations, and fewer examples than the unabridged version. A sufficient number of quotations and examples were retained, however, to maintain the richness in style created by the authors.

The Brief Sixth Edition is available in both one-volume and two-volume formats. The two-volume format is divided as follows: Volume 1 contains Chapters 1 through 16, beginning with a discussion of three cultures—American, African, and European—that intersected during the exploration and colonization of the New World and ending with a discussion of the Reconstruction era. Volume 2 contains Chapters 16 through 33, beginning its coverage at Reconstruction and extending the history of the American people to the present. The chapter on Reconstruction appears in both volumes to provide greater flexibility in matching a volume to the historical span covered by a specific course.

While the following Preface to the full-length Sixth Edition elaborates on specific content changes,

Changes in This Edition

we note briefly that the authors paid increased attention to the following: the interaction of the private sphere of everyday life with the public sphere of politics and government; grassroots movements; religion; the emerging cultural globalism of American foreign relations; the development of the American West; and the relationship of the people to the land, including conflict over access to natural resources. These new emphases, as well as the up-to-date scholarship on which they are based, are retained in the Brief Sixth Edition.

Although each author feels answerable for the whole of *A People and a Nation*, we take primary responsibility for particular chapters: Mary Beth Norton, Chapters 1–8; David M. Katzman, Chapters 9–12; David Blight, Chapters 13–16; Howard P. Chudacoff, Chapters 17–21 and 24; Thomas G. Paterson, Chapters 22–23, 26, 29, 31, and shared responsibility for 33; William M. Tuttle, Jr., Chapters 25, 27, 28, 30, 32, and shared responsibility for 33.

A number of useful learning and teaching aids accompany the Brief Sixth Edition of *A People and a Nation*. They are designed to help instructors and students achieve their teaching and learning goals. *@history: an interactive American history source* is a multimedia teaching/learning package that combines a variety of material on a cross-platformed CD-ROM—primary sources (text and graphic), video, and audio—with activities that can be used to analyze, interpret, and discuss primary sources; to enhance collaborative learning; and to create multimedia lecture presentations.

Study and Teaching Aids

American History GeoQuest is a CD-ROM designed to improve students' geographical literacy. The program consists of thirty interactive historical maps, each of which provides background information and a series of self-correcting quizzes so that students can master the information on their own.

The *Online Study Guide*, prepared by George Warren and Cynthia Ricketson of Central Piedmont Community College, includes an introductory chapter on studying history that focuses on interpreting historical facts, test-taking hints, and critical analysis. The guide also includes learning objectives, a thematic guide, lists of terms, multiple-choice and essay questions for each chapter, as well as map exercises and sections on organizing information of some chapters. An answer key alerts students to the correct response and also explains why the other choices are wrong. This *Online Study Guide* is free to students and may be found at **college.hmco.com/students.**

An *Online Instructor's Resource Manual*, also created by George Warren, will now be downloadable from Houghton Mifflin's web site. For each chapter, the manual includes a content overview, a brief list of learning objectives, a comprehensive chapter outline, ideas for classroom activities, discussion questions, and ideas for paper topics.

A *Test Bank*, also prepared by George Warren, provides multiple-choice questions, identification questions, and essay questions. This content is also available in a *Computerized Test Bank* for both Windows and Macintosh platforms.

An *Instructor's Web Site* includes the *Online Instructor's Resource Manual*, interactive Legacy activities, online primary sources with teaching instructions, and annotated links to other sites. The *Student's Web Site* includes ACE self-quizzes; online primary sources, including text, photo, and audio resources; an annotated guide of the top historical research web sites; and interactive Legacy activities.

The *HM ClassPrep CD-ROM with HM Testing* is a complete electronic resource for instructors that features the text's maps and charts in PowerPoint for presentations, and other documents in Word, such as lecture outlines. Also included is *HM Testing* for Macintosh and Windows. This computerized version of the printed *Test Bank* allows instructors to create customized tests by editing and adding questions. Most electronic resources can be customized to complement the way you teach your course.

There is also a set of full-color *American History Map Transparencies*, available in two-volume sets upon adoption.

Please visit us on the Web at **college.hmco.com** or contact your local Houghton Mifflin representative for more information about the ancillary items or to obtain desk copies.

Author teams rely on review panels to help create and execute successful revision plans. Many historians advised us on the revision of this Brief Sixth Edition, and the book is better because of their thoughtful insights and recommendations. We heartily thank

Acknowledgments

S. Carol Berg, *College of St. Benedict*
Trace' Etienne-Gray, *Southwest Texas State University*
Irene Guenther, *Houston Community College*
Martin Haas, *Adelphi University*
Andrew C. Holman, *Bridgewater State College*
Eric Juhnke, *Southwest Missouri State University*
Eric Mogren, *Northern Illinois University*
Seth Wigderson, *University of Maine–Augusta*

Finally, we want to thank the many people who have contributed their thoughts and labors to this work, including the talented staff at Houghton Mifflin.

For the authors, WILLIAM J. BROPHY

PREFACE TO THE FULL-LENGTH SIXTH EDITION

"What? Another edition?" asked one of our friends. "History hasn't changed that much in the last few years!" Wrong. "History" *has* changed, in several ways. More of "history's" story has been told in new books and articles and revealed in newly released documents. Our interpretation of "history" has changed because new perspectives on familiar topics have continued to emerge from the prolific writings of historians, anthropologists, and other scholars. And, last, our understanding of "history" has changed as our engagement with current events reshapes how we remember the past.

Like other teachers and students, we are always recreating our past, restructuring our memory, rediscovering the personalities and events that have influenced us, inspired us, and bedeviled us. This book represents our rediscovery of America's history—its diverse people and the nation they created and have nurtured. As this book demonstrates, there are many different Americans and many different memories. We have sought to present all of them, in both triumph and tragedy, in both division and unity.

Although much is new in this Sixth Edition in coverage, interpretation, and organization, we have sustained the qualities that have marked

About *A People and a Nation*

A People and a Nation from the beginning: our approach of telling the story of all the people; our study of the interaction of the private sphere of everyday life with the public sphere of politics and government; our integration of political and social history; our spirited narrative based on diaries, letters, oral histories, and other sources; and our effort to challenge readers to think about the meaning of American history, not just to memorize facts. Students and instructors have commented on how enjoyable the book is to read. Scholars have commended the book for its up-to-date scholarship.

Readers have also told us that we have demonstrated, in section after section and in the "How Do

Historians Know?" feature, how the historian's mind works asking questions and teasing conclusions out of vast and often conflicting evidence. Each chapter's highlighted "How Do Historians Know?" explains how historians go about using sources—such as artifacts, cartoons, census data, medical records, and popular art—to arrive at conclusions. This feature also helps students understand how scholars can claim knowledge about historical events and trends. Chapter-opening vignettes, dramatically recounting stories of people contending with their times, continue to define the key questions of each chapter. Succinct introductions and summaries still frame each chapter. As before, myriad illustrations, maps, tables, and graphs tied closely to the text encourage visual and statistical explorations. Readability, scholarship, critical thinking, clear structure, instructive illustrative material—these strengths have been sustained in this edition.

Guided by Houghton Mifflin's excellent editorial and design staffs, by instructors' thorough reviews, by the authors' ongoing research, and

What's New in This Edition

by our frank and friendly planning sessions and critical reading of one another's chapters, we worked to improve every aspect of the book. We added a distinguished new author, David W. Blight, whose expertise on the antebellum period, slavery, the Civil War, and historical memory has strengthened these topics in the book. To reflect new scholarship and to satisfy instructors' needs for improved chronological flow, we substantially reorganized the chapters that cover the antebellum and post-1945 periods. We have expanded our treatment of slavery, women, religion in America's social and political life, race theory and the social construction of racial identity, the West, the South's relationship to the nation, cultural expansion as a dimension of foreign relations, and the globalization of the U.S. economy. Throughout the book, we reexamined every sentence, interpretation, map, chart, illustration, and caption, refining the narrative, presenting new examples, and rethinking and labeling the Summary section for each chapter. More than half of the chapter-opening vignettes are new to this edition, as are more than one-third of the "How Do Historians Know?" entries. The "Important Events" tables have been trimmed for easier reference. The "Suggestions for Further Reading" have been revised to include new literature and conveniently consolidated at the end of the book.

Eager to help students link the past to the present, to identify the origins of issues of current interest, we have introduced in each chapter a new feature: "Legacy for a People and a Nation." Appearing after each chapter's Summary, the Legacy feature spotlights a specific contemporary topic; examples include Columbus Day, women's education, Bible Belt, revolutionary violence, Fourteenth Amendment, ethnic food, intercollegiate athletics, Peace Corps, atomic waste, and the Internet. After exploring the subject's beginnings, a few tightly focused paragraphs trace its important history to the present, inviting students to think about the historical roots of their world today and to understand the complexity of issues that on the surface seem so simple. For students who ask what history has to do with the immediate events and trends that swirl around them—or who wonder why we study history at all—these timely legacies provide telling answers.

New "Legacy for a People and a Nation"

As in previous editions, several themes and questions stand out in our concerted effort to incorporate the most recent scholarship that integrates political, social, and cultural history. We study the many ways Americans have defined themselves—gender, race, class, region, ethnicity, religion, sexual orientation—and the many subjects that have reflected their multidimensional experiences: social, political, economic, diplomatic, military, environmental, intellectual, cultural, technological, and more. We highlight the remarkably diverse everyday life of the American people—in cities and on farms and ranches, in factories and in corporate headquarters, in neighborhood meetings and in powerful political chambers, in love relationships and in hate groups, in recreation and in work, in the classroom and in mil-

Themes in This Book

itary uniform, in secret national security conferences and in public foreign relations debates, in church and in prison, in polluted environments and in conservation areas. We pay particular attention to lifestyles, diet and dress, family life and structure, labor conditions, gender roles, and childbearing and child rearing. We explore how Americans have entertained and informed themselves by discussing their music, sports, theater, print media, film, radio, television, graphic arts, and literature, in both "high" culture and "low" culture. We study how technology has influenced Americans' lives, such as through the internal combustion engine and the computer.

The private sphere of everyday life always interacts with the public sphere of politics and government. To understand how Americans have sought to protect their different ways of life and to work out solutions to thorny problems, we emphasize their expectations of governments at the local, state, and federal levels; governments' role in providing answers; the lobbying of interest groups; the campaigns and outcomes of elections; and the hierarchy of power in any period. Because the United States has long been a major participant in world affairs, we explore America's descent into wars, interventions in other nations, empire-building, immigration patterns, images of foreign peoples, cross-national cultural ties, and international economic trends.

Mary Beth Norton, who had primary responsibility for Chapters 1–8, expanded and revised her coverage of the peopling of the Americas and early settlements, the Salem witchcraft crisis, and masculinity and public rituals in the colonial period. She reorganized Chapter 3 to highlight new scholarship identifying the 1670s as a crucial turning point in the relationships of Europeans and Indians in several regions of North America, and to emphasize the key role of the slave trade in the economy of all the colonies. In Chapter 4, she added a discussion of regional differences in African American family life. Chapters 3, 4, and 8, moreover, all incorporate recent scholarship on the complex relationship between the development of the slave system and the creation of racial categories.

Section-by-Section Changes in This Edition

David M. Katzman, who had primary responsibility for Chapters 9–12, substantially reorganized the early-nineteenth-century chapters. Chapters 9–11 now have a more focused chronological narrative, integrating political events with related social, economic, and cultural developments. The antebellum chapters give added emphasis to regional interconnections in the emerging market economy, Indian–white relations and Native American adaptations to the market economy, demographic changes, internal migration, popular culture, and the formation of racial ideas. Katzman also gives new attention to the Barbary captives, the Lewis and Clark expedition, early Texas settlement, and population movements. He also explores anew immigration, ethnicity and race, frontier communities in the West, and the links between reform politics and religion.

David W. Blight, who had primary responsibility for Chapters 13–16, brought fresh perspectives to the antebellum South and its relation to the nation's cultural life and market revolution. He added new material on slave culture and resistance, slavery's intersection with westward expansion, the War with Mexico, and the Underground Railroad. In his discussion of the South, he increased coverage of free blacks and social reform movements. In the Civil War and Reconstruction chapters, Blight has revised the history of military battles, women and nursing, emancipation, wartime reconstruction, the meanings of freedom for former slaves, and the Fourteenth Amendment. He has introduced the problem of memory—especially Americans' difficulty in confronting the Reconstruction period of their history. Replacing Paul D. Escott, who brought distinction to *A People and a Nation* for five editions and whose fine writing and scholarship remain evident throughout, Blight has worked with co-author Katzman to reorganize all the antebellum period chapters.

Howard P. Chudacoff, who had primary responsibility for Chapters 17–21 and 24, reconfigured material throughout these chapters. Chapter 17 now focuses solely on the West, with additions on Indian economic and cultural life, women in frontier communities, mining, irrigation, and transportation. In his other chapters, he has increased the coverage of southern industrialization, immigrants and migrants in southern cities, and southern Progressivism. He also presents new discussion of the characteristics of the industrial revolution, race and ethnicity in urban bor-

derlands, Mexican American farmers, religion and science, technology, the clash between modernism and fundamentalism, women's political activities, and the causes of the Great Depression.

Thomas G. Paterson, who had primary responsibility for Chapters 22–23, 26, 29, and 31, and shared responsibility for 33, and who served as the book's coordinating author, offers new material throughout on cultural expansion and on the influence of ideology and images of foreign peoples on foreign policy decisions. He has augmented coverage of religious missionaries, Anglo-American cooperation, and navalism. Labor issues, Indian soldiers, weapons technology, and gas warfare receive new treatment for World War I. As part of the restructuring of the post-1945 chapters, Chapters 29 and 31 are newly designed to parallel chapters on domestic history. Paterson reexamines the Korean War, U.S. Information Agency activities, and popular fears of nuclear war. For the Vietnam War, he has revisited presidential leadership, the war's impact on domestic reform, and military experiences. The last chapter newly explores environmental diplomacy, the globalization of U.S. culture, intrastate wars, and humanitarian intervention.

William M. Tuttle, Jr., had primary responsibility for Chapters 25, 27, 28, 30, and 32, and shared responsibility for 33. In Chapter 25, he expanded treatment of New Deal cultural programs, unionism, and the question of "whiteness." For World War II, he added new material on the cultural history of the home front, the wartime economy, technological research, and homosexuals in the armed forces. In his post-1945 chapters, Tuttle has revised his coverage of McCarthyism, race relations, the New Left and counterculture, Indian protest, immigration legislation, the Reagan presidency, AIDS, and the anti-abortion movement. In the last chapter, Tuttle has expanded his discussion of political violence and public dissatisfaction with government, and he has included new material on school shootings and the presidential impeachment crisis.

The multidimensional Appendix, prepared by Thomas G. Paterson, has been brought up to date. Once again, the Appendix includes a guide to reference works on key subjects in American history. Students may wish to use this updated and enlarged list of encyclopedias, atlases, chronologies, and other books, for example, when they start to explore topics for research papers, when they seek precise definitions or dates, when they need biographical profiles, or when they chart territorial or demographic changes. The tables of statistics on key features of the American people and nation also have been updated, as have the tables on the states (and the District of Columbia and Puerto Rico), presidential elections, presidents and vice presidents, party strength in Congress, and the justices of the Supreme Court. Other information, including the Articles of Confederation and a complete table of the cabinets by administration, is available on the *A People and a Nation* web site.

A People and a Nation continues to be supported by an extensive supplements package. For this edition, many more resources will be available to students and instructors online and on CD-ROM. We have also revised and updated all elements of our existing package.

Study and Teaching Aids

A new version of *@history*, Houghton Mifflin's CD-ROM featuring nearly one thousand primary source materials, including video, audio, visual, and textual resources, has been keyed to the organization of the Sixth Edition of *A People and a Nation*. Available in both instructor's and student's versions, *@history* is an interactive multimedia tool that can improve the analytical skills of students and introduce them to historical sources.

American History GeoQuest is a CD-ROM designed to improve students' geographical literacy. The program consists of thirty interactive historical maps, each of which provides background information and a series of self-correcting quizzes so that students can master the information on their own.

The *A People and a Nation* web site has been redesigned, updated, and augmented for users of the Sixth Edition. An *Instructor's Web Site* includes the *Online Instructor's Resource Manual* (see below), downloadable PowerPoint lecture outline slides, interactive Legacy activities, online primary sources with teaching instructions, and annotated links to other sites. The *Student's Web Site* includes ACE reading self-quizzes; online primary sources, including text, photo, and audio resources; an annotated guide of the top historical research Web sites; and interactive Legacy activities.

The *Study Guide*, prepared by George Warren of Central Piedmont Community College, includes an introductory chapter on studying history that focuses on interpreting historical facts, test-taking hints, and critical analysis. The guide also includes learning objectives, a thematic guide, lists of terms, multiple choice and essay questions with answer keys, and map exercises.

A new *Online Instructor's Resource Manual*, also created by George Warren, will now be downloadable from Houghton Mifflin's web site. For each chapter, the manual includes a content overview, a brief list of learning objectives, a comprehensive chapter outline, ideas for classroom activities, discussion questions, and ideas for paper topics.

A *Test Bank*, also prepared by George Warren, provides approximately 1,700 new multiple choice questions, more than 1,000 identification questions, and approximately 500 essay questions. This content is also available in a *Computerized Test Bank* for both Windows and Macintosh platforms.

A set of *American History Map Transparencies* is also available to instructors upon adoption.

At each stage of this revision, a sizable panel of historian reviewers read drafts of our chapters. Their suggestions, corrections, and pleas helped guide us through this momentous revision. We could not include all of their recommendations, but the book is better for our having heeded most of their advice. We heartily thank

Acknowledgments

Patrick Allitt, *Emory University*
Cara Anzilotti, *Loyola Marymount University*
Felix Armfield, *Western Illinois University*
Robert Becker, *Louisiana State University*
Jules Benjamin, *Ithaca College*
Roger Bromert, *Southwestern Oklahoma State University*
Jonathan Chu, *University of Massachusetts at Boston*
Nathaniel Comfort, *George Washington University*
Mary DeCredico, *U.S. Naval Academy*
Judy DeMark, *Northern Michigan University*

Jonathan Earle, *University of Kansas*

Alice Fahs, *University of California, Irvine*

Neil Foley, *University of Texas*

Colin Gordon, *University of Iowa*

Robert Gough, *University of Wisconsin at Eau Claire*

Brian Greenberg, *Monmouth University*

Harland Hagler, *University of North Texas*

Elizabeth Haiken, *University of British Columbia*

Benjamin Harrison, *University of Louisville*

Elizabeth Cobbs Hoffman, *San Diego State University*

Marianne Holdzkom, *Ohio State University*

John Inscoe, *University of Georgia*

Frank Lambert, *Purdue University*

David Rich Lewis, *Utah State University*

Nancy Mitchell, *North Carolina State University*

Patricia Moore, *University of Utah*

John Neff, *University of Mississippi*

James Reed, *Rutgers University*

Joseph Rowe, *Sam Houston State University*

Sharon Salinger, *University of California, Riverside*

Richard Stott, *George Washington University*

Daniel B. Thorp, *Virginia Polytechnic Institute and State University*

Marilyn Westerkamp, *University of California, Santa Cruz*

John Wigger, *University of Missouri, Columbia*

John Scott Wilson, *University of South Carolina*

The authors once again thank the extraordinary Houghton Mifflin people who designed, edited, produced, and nourished this book. Their high standards and acute attention to both general structure and fine detail are cherished in the publishing industry. Many thanks, then, to Colleen Shanley Kyle, sponsoring editor; Ann Hofstra Grogg, freelance development editor; Christina Horn, senior project editor; Jean Woy, editor-in-chief; Sandra McGuire, senior marketing manager; Pembroke Herbert, photo researcher; Charlotte Miller, art editor; and Michael Kerns, editorial assistant.

The authors also extend their thanks to the following for helping us: Sandra Greene, Karin Beckett, Nancy Board, Frank Couvares, Jan D. Emerson, Alice Fahs, Jeffrey Ferguson, Irwin Hyatt, Steven Jacobson, Andrea Katzman, Eric Katzman, Henry W. Katzman, Julie Stephens Katzman, Sharyn Katzman, Ariela Katzman-Jacobson, Elizabeth Mahan, Terri Rockhold, Martha Sandweiss, Martha Saxton, Barry Shank, John David Smith, Kathryn Nemeth Tuttle, and Samuel Watkins Tuttle.

We welcome comments from instructors and students about this new edition of *A People and a Nation*, which can be communicated through its accompanying web site, found at **http://college.hmco.com.**

For the authors, Thomas G. Paterson

A People and a Nation

Brief Edition

Three Old Worlds Create a New

1492–1600

American Societies
North America in 1492
African Societies
European Societies
Early European Explorations
The Voyages of Columbus, Cabot, and Their Successors
Spanish Exploration and Conquest
The Columbian Exchange
Europeans in North America
LEGACY FOR A PEOPLE AND A NATION
Columbus Day

As they neared the village called Cofitachequi on May 1, 1540, the band of Spanish explorers led by Hernán de Soto beheld a surprising scene. Villagers came to meet the Europeans, carrying their female chief, or *cacica*. The Lady of Cofitachequi, a Spanish chronicler recorded, welcomed the weary Spaniards to her domain in today's western South Carolina, giving Soto a string of pearls from her neck. Later, she gave the hungry men huge quantities of corn and, seeing that they especially valued pearls, suggested they take the ones they would find in nearby burial chambers.

The Spanish explorers had landed at Tampa Bay, Florida, about a year earlier. They would wander through what is now the southeastern United States for three more years, encountering many different peoples, whom they often treated with great cruelty. Always they sought gold and silver. The people of Cofitachequi told the Spaniards they might find these treasures in another ruler's domain, about twelve days' travel away. When Soto left, he took the Lady with him as a captive, but she escaped and presumably returned home.

Why had the Lady greeted Soto's force so kindly? Perhaps she did not have enough men to resist the Europeans. Her people had been devastated by an unknown "pestilence" two years earlier. Or possibly messengers had informed the Lady about Soto's vicious

1

treatment of villages he had previously encountered. Whatever her reasoning, the strategy worked: Soto and his men moved on, and Cofitachequi survived to be recorded by Spanish, French, and finally English visitors in the course of the next 130 years.

For thousands of years before 1492, human societies in the Americas had developed in isolation from the rest of the world. The era that began in the Christian fifteenth century brought that long-standing isolation to an end. As Europeans sought treasure and trade, peoples from different cultures came into regular contact for the first time. All were profoundly changed. The brief encounter between Soto and the Lady of Cofitachequi illustrates many of the elements of those contacts and changes: cruelty and kindness, greed and deception, trade and theft, surprise and sickness, captivity and enslavement. By the time Soto and his men landed in Florida in 1539, the age of European expansion and colonization was already well under way. The history of the tiny colonies that would become the United States must be seen in this broad context of European exploration and exploitation.

The continents that European sailors reached in the late fifteenth century had their own history. The residents of the Americas were the world's most skillful plant breeders; they had developed vegetable crops more nutritious and productive than those grown in Europe, Asia, or Africa. They had invented systems of writing and mathematics and had created calendars as accurate as those used on the other side of the Atlantic. In the Americas, as in Europe, states rose and fell as leaders succeeded or failed in expanding their political and economic power. The arrival of Europeans immeasurably altered the Americans' struggles with one another.

After 1400, European nations tried to acquire valuable colonies and trading posts elsewhere in the world. While they were initially interested primarily in Asia and Africa, many Europeans eventually focused their attention on the Americas. Their contests for trade and conquest changed the course of history on four continents. Even as Europeans slowly achieved dominance, their fates were shaped by the strategies of Americans and Africans. In the Americas of the fifteenth and sixteenth centuries, three old worlds came together to produce a new. ∎

American Societies

 Human beings originated on the continent of Africa, where humanlike remains about 3 million years old have been found in what is now Ethiopia. Over many millennia, the growing population slowly dispersed to the other continents. Scholars have long believed that all the earliest inhabitants of the Americas crossed a land bridge known as Beringia (at the site of the Bering Strait) approximately 12,000 to 14,000 years ago. Yet striking new archaeological discoveries in both North and South America suggest that some parts of the Americas may have been settled much earlier, perhaps by seafarers crossing from northern Europe by island-hopping from Iceland to Greenland to Baffin Island, much as the Vikings did many millennia later (see Map 1.1 on page 6).

The first Americans are called Paleo-Indians. Nomadic hunters of game and gatherers of wild plants, they spread throughout North and South America, probably moving as bands composed of extended families. By about 11,500 years ago the Paleo-Indians were making fine stone projectile points, which they attached to wooden spears and used to kill the large mammals then living in the Americas. But as the Ice Age ended and the human population increased, all the large American mammals except the bison (buffalo) disappeared. As their meat supply decreased, the Paleo-Indians found new ways to survive.

Paleo-Indians

By approximately 9,000 years ago, the residents of what is now central Mexico began to cultivate food crops, especially maize (corn), squash, beans, and peppers. In the Andes Mountains of South America, people started to grow potatoes. As knowledge of agricultural techniques improved and spread throughout the Americas, vegetables and maize proved a more reliable source of food than hunting and gathering. Thus most Americans started to adopt a more sedentary style of life so that they could tend their fields regularly. Some established permanent settlements; others moved several times a year among fixed sites. All the American cultures emphasized producing sufficient food to support them-

Importance of Agriculture

IMPORTANT EVENTS

15,000–10,000 B.C.E.	Paleo-Indians begin migrating from Asia to North America across the Beringia land bridge
7000 B.C.E.	Cultivation of food crops begins in America
c. 1000 B.C.E.	Olmec civilization appears
c. 300–600 C.E.	Height of influence of Teotihuacán
c. 600–900 C.E.	Classic Mayan civilization
1000 C.E.	Anasazi settlements in modern states of Arizona and New Mexico flourish as trading centers
1001	Norse establish settlement in "Vinland"
1050–1250	Height of influence of Cahokia; prevalence of Mississippian culture in midwestern and southeastern United States
14th century	Aztec rise to power
1450s–80s	Portuguese explore and colonize islands in the Mediterranean Atlantic and São Tomé in Gulf of Guinea
1477	Publication of Marco Polo's *Travels*, describing China
1492	Columbus reaches Bahamas
1494	Treaty of Tordesillas divides land claims between Spain and Portugal in Africa, India, and South America
1496	Last Canary Island falls to Spain
1497	Cabot reaches North America
1513	León explores Florida
1518–30	Smallpox epidemic devastates Indian population of West Indies and Central and South America
1519	Cortés invades Mexico
1521	Tenochtitlán surrenders to Cortés; Aztec Empire falls to Spaniards
1524	Verrazzano sails along Atlantic coast of United States
1534–35	Cartier explores St. Lawrence River
1539–42	Soto explores southeastern United States
1540–42	Coronado explores southwestern United States
1587–90	Raleigh's Roanoke colony vanishes
1588	Harriot publishes *A Briefe and True Report of the New Found Land of Virginia*

selves. Trade existed, but no society ever became dependent on another group for items vital to its survival.

Wherever agriculture dominated the economy, complex civilizations flourished. Such societies, assured of steady supplies, were able to accumulate wealth, produce ornamental objects, trade with other groups, and create elaborate rituals and ceremonies. In North America, the successful cultivation of nutritious crops seems to have led to the growth and development of all the major civilizations: first the large city-states of Mesoamerica (modern Mexico and Guatemala), and then the urban clusters known collectively as the Mississippian culture and located in the present-day United States. Each of these societies reached its height of population and influence only after achieving success in agriculture. Each later collapsed after reaching the limits of its food supply.

The earliest major Mesoamerican civilization was that of the Olmecs, who about 3,000 years ago lived near the Gulf of Mexico in large cities dominated by temple pyramids.

Mesoamerican Civilizations

More than 1,000 years later, the Mayan civilization developed on the Yucatán Peninsula, in today's eastern Mexico. The Mayas built large urban centers containing tall pyramids and temples. They studied astronomy, created the first writing system in the Americas, and developed a richly symbolic religious life in which rituals of bloodletting played a major role. By the fifth century C.E. (Common Era), or about 1,500 years ago, the kings of the Mayan city-states started to war with one another. But no king or city could win total victory. Eventually, the constant fighting combined with an inadequate food supply to cause the collapse of the most powerful cities, ending the classic era of Mayan civilization by 900 C.E.

Some of the more than 100,000 residents of Teotihuacán, the largest Mesoamerican metropolis, traded regularly with the Mayas. That city, founded in the Valley of Mexico about 300 B.C.E. (Before the Common Era)—some 2,300 years ago—was one of the most heavily populated urban areas in the world in the fifth century C.E. The rulers of Teotihuacán gained their position chiefly through commerce; their trading network extended hundreds of miles in all directions. Teotihuacán also served as a religious center; pilgrims must have come long distances to visit the impressive Pyramid of the Sun, Pyramid of the Moon, and the great temple of Quetzalcoatl—the feathered serpent, the primary god of central Mexico.

Moundbuilders, Anasazi, and Mississippians

Teotihuacán's influence was felt so widely in Mesoamerica before its decline in the eighth century C.E. that some scholars have argued that this Mexican city-state also influenced societies in what is now the United States. The Moundbuilders of the Ohio River region, who flourished about 2,000 years ago, just as Teotihuacán rose to prominence, constructed earthen mounds. But the Ohioan mounds were used as burial sites, not as bases for temple pyramids. Also, the Moundbuilders' economy, which was based on hunting and gathering, bore little resemblance to that of Mesoamerica. Trade goods from the Gulf of Mexico have been found in the mounds, but direct evidence of contact with Teotihuacán is lacking.

Nor is there evidence of contact with Teotihuacán in sites inhabited by the Anasazi peoples in the modern states of Arizona and New Mexico. Pueblo Bonito, one of nine "Great Houses" in Chaco Canyon, by 1100 C.E. consisted of a series of large adobe buildings constructed along the sides of the canyon. The Anasazi constructed extensive irrigation systems in order to cultivate maize and other Mesoamerican crops in an arid environment, but they did not construct temple

pyramids, nor did their towns resemble those built by their contemporaries in what is now Mexico.

It is more likely that Teotihuacán had an impact on the development of the Mississippian culture, which flourished around 1000 C.E. in what is now the midwestern and southeastern United States. This civilization, like those to the south, depended on the cultivation of maize, beans, and squash. The introduction of agriculture (about 800 C.E.) made possible the growth of large cities, many of which included plazas and earthen pyramids. The largest of the urban centers was the City of the Sun (now called Cahokia), near modern St. Louis. At its peak (in the twelfth century), the City of the Sun had a population of about twenty thousand—small by Mesoamerican standards but larger than any other northern community. Like Teotihuacán and Chaco Canyon, Cahokia was a religious and trading center. Its main pyramid, today called Monks Mound, was at the time of its construction the third largest structure of any description in the Western Hemisphere.

Aztecs

The Aztecs' histories tell of the long migration of their people (who called themselves Mexica) into the Valley of Mexico during the twelfth century. The uninhabited ruins of Teotihuacán, which by then had been deserted for at least two hundred years, awed and mystified the migrants. The Aztecs' primary god, Huitzilopochtli, was a god of war represented by an eagle. The chronicles record that Huitzilopochtli directed the Aztecs to establish their capital at the spot on an island where they saw an eagle eating a serpent (thus symbolizing Huitzilopochtli's triumph over the traditional deity, Quetzalcoatl). That island city became Tenochtitlán, the center of a rigidly stratified society composed of hereditary classes of warriors, merchants, priests, common folk, and slaves.

The Aztecs conquered their neighbors, forcing them to pay tribute, including human beings who could be sacrificed to Huitzilopochtli. The war god's taste for blood was not easily quenched. At the 1502 coronation of Motecuhzoma II (Montezuma to the Spaniards), five thousand people are thought to have been sacrificed by having their still-beating hearts torn from their bodies.

The Aztecs believed that they lived in the age of the Fifth Sun. Four times previously, they wrote, the

Pueblo Bonito in Chaco Canyon in what is now the state of New Mexico. More than six hundred buildings were present on the well-defended site. The circular structures were kivas, used for food storage and for religious rituals.   (David Muench photography)

earth and all the people who lived on it had been destroyed. They predicted that their own world would end in earthquakes and hunger. In the Aztec year Thirteen Flint, volcanoes erupted, sickness and hunger spread, and an eclipse of the sun darkened the sky. Did some priest wonder whether the Fifth Sun was approaching its end? In time, the Aztecs learned that Thirteen Flint was called 1492 by the Europeans.

North America in 1492

 Over the centuries, the Americans who lived north of Mexico adapted their once-similar ways of life to very different climates and terrains, thus creating the diverse cultures that the Europeans encountered when they first arrived (see Map 1.1). Scholars often refer to such cultures by language group (such as Algonquian or Iroquoian), since neighboring Indian nations commonly spoke related languages. Bands that lived in environments not well suited to agriculture followed a nomadic lifestyle. Within the area of the present-day United States, these groups included the Paiutes and

Shoshones, who inhabited the Great Basin (now Nevada and Utah). Because of the difficulty of finding sufficient food for more than a few people, such hunter-gatherer bands were small. The men hunted small animals, and the women gathered seeds and berries. Where large game was more plentiful and food supplies were therefore more certain, as in present-day central and western Canada and the Great Plains, bands of hunters were somewhat larger.

In more favorable environments, larger groups combined agriculture with gathering, hunting, and fishing. Those who lived near the seacoasts, like the Chinooks of present-day Washington and Oregon, consumed fish and shellfish in addition to growing crops and gathering seeds and berries. Residents of the interior (for example, the Arikaras of the Missouri River valley) hunted large animals while also cultivating maize, squash, and beans. The peoples of what is now eastern Canada and the northeastern United States also combined hunting and agriculture.

Societies that relied primarily on hunting large animals assigned that task to men and allotted food preparation, clothing production, and child rearing to

Map 1.1 Native Cultures of North America The natives of the North American continent effectively used the resources of the regions in which they lived. As this map shows, coastal groups relied on fishing, residents of fertile areas engaged in agriculture, and other peoples employed hunting (often combined with gathering) as a primary mode of subsistence.

Sexual Division of Labor in North America

women. Agricultural societies, by contrast, differed in their assignments of work to the sexes. In what is now the southwestern United States, the Pueblo peoples defined agricultural labor as men's work. In the east, large clusters of peoples speaking Algonquian, Iroquoian, and Muskogean languages allocated most agricultural chores to women. In all the farming societies, women gathered wild foods, prepared food for consumption or storage, and cared for children, while men were responsible for hunting.

The southwestern and eastern agricultural peoples had similar social organizations. The Pueblos, descendants of the Anasazi, lived in large, multistory buildings constructed on terraces along the sides of cliffs or other easily defended sites. Northern Iroquois villages (in modern New York State) were composed of large, rectangular, bark-covered structures, or long houses. In the present-day southeastern United States, Muskogeans and southern Algonquians lived in large houses made of thatch. Most of the eastern villages were surrounded by wood palisades and ditches to aid in fending off attackers.

Social Organization

In all the agricultural societies, each dwelling housed an extended family defined matrilineally (through a female line of descent). Mothers, their married daughters, and their daughters' husbands and children all lived together. Matrilineal descent did not imply matriarchy, or the wielding of power by women, but rather served as a means of reckoning kinship. Extended families were linked into clans defined by matrilineal ties. The nomadic bands of the Great Plains, by contrast, were most often related patrilineally (through the male line).

War and Politics

Long before Europeans arrived, residents of the continent fought one another for control of the best hunting and fishing territories, the most fertile agricultural lands, or the sources of essential items like salt (for preserving meat) and flint (for making knives and arrowheads). People captured by the enemy in such wars were sometimes enslaved, but slavery was never an important source of labor in pre-Columbian America.

American political structures varied considerably. Among Pueblo and Muskogean peoples, the village council was the highest political authority; no government structure connected the villages. Nomadic hunters also lacked formal links among separate bands. The Iroquois, by contrast, had an elaborate political hierarchy incorporating villages into nations and nations into a confederation; a council comprising representatives from each nation made crucial decisions concerning war and peace for the entire confederacy. In all the North American cultures, political power was divided between civil and war leaders, who wielded authority only so long as they retained the confidence of the people. Women assumed leadership roles more often among agricultural peoples than among nomadic hunters. Female sachems (rulers) led Algonquian villages in what is now Massachusetts, but women never became heads of Great Plains hunting bands. Iroquois women did not become chiefs, yet the clan matrons of each village chose its chief and could both start wars (by calling for the capture of prisoners to replace dead relatives) and stop them (by refusing to supply warriors with necessary foodstuffs).

Religion

Americans' religious beliefs varied even more than did their political systems, but all the peoples were polytheistic, worshiping a multitude of gods. Each group's most important beliefs and rituals were closely tied to its means of subsistence. The major deities of agricultural peoples like the Pueblos and Muskogeans were associated with cultivation. The most important gods of hunters (such as those living on the Great Plains) were associated with animals. A band's economy and women's role in it helped to determine women's potential as religious leaders. Women held the most prominent positions in those agricultural societies (like the Iroquois) in which they were also the chief food producers, whereas in hunting societies men took the lead in religious as well as political affairs.

A wide variety of cultures, comprising more than 5 million people, thus inhabited mainland North America when Europeans arrived. The diverse inhabitants of North America spoke well over one thousand different languages. For obvious reasons, they did not consider themselves one people, nor did they—for the most part—think of uniting to repel the European invaders.

African Societies

 Fifteenth-century Africa also housed a variety of cultures adapted to different terrains and climates (see Map 1.2). In the north, along the Mediterranean Sea, lived the Berbers, a Muslim people. (Muslims are adherents of Islam, founded by the prophet Mohammed in the seventh century C.E.) On the east coast of Africa, Muslim city-states engaged in extensive trade with India, the Moluccas (part of modern Indonesia), and China. Through the East African city-states passed waterborne commerce between the eastern Mediterranean and East Asia; the rest followed the long land route across Central Asia known as the Silk Road.

South of the Mediterranean coast in the African interior lie the great Saharan and Libyan deserts. Below the deserts, much of the continent is divided between tropical rain forests (along the coasts) and grassy plains (in the interior). People speaking a variety of languages and pursuing different subsistence strategies lived in a wide belt south of the deserts. South of the Gulf of Guinea, the grassy landscape came to be dominated by Bantu-speaking peoples, who left their homeland in modern Nigeria about 2,000 years ago and slowly migrated south and east across the continent.

West Africa was a land of tropical forests and savanna grasslands where fishing, cattle herding, and agriculture supported the inhabitants. The northern region of West Africa, or Upper Guinea, was heavily influenced by the Islamic culture of the Mediterranean. Trade via camel caravans between Upper Guinea and the Muslim Mediterranean was sub-Saharan Africa's major connection to Europe and West Asia. In return for salt, dates, silk, and cotton cloth, Africans exchanged ivory, gold, and slaves with northern merchants. Most of the enslaved people carried to North America came from this region, which Europeans called Guinea.

West Africa (Guinea)

The people of Upper Guinea's northernmost region, the so-called Rice Coast (present-day Gambia, Senegal, and Guinea), fished and cultivated rice. The Grain Coast, the next region to the south, was thinly populated and not readily accessible from the sea because it had only one good harbor (modern Freetown, Sierra Leone). Its people concentrated on farming and raising livestock. Both the Rice Coast and the Grain Coast—especially the former—supplied slaves destined for sale in the Americas, but even more enslaved people came from Lower Guinea.

West African law recognized both individual and communal land ownership, but men seeking to accumulate wealth needed access to labor, including slaves. Africans held in slavery on their own continent (primarily criminals, debtors, or wartime captives, and their descendants) were therefore essential components of the economy. The degree to which slaves in Africa were exploited varied greatly. Some slaves were held as chattel; others could engage in trade, retaining a portion of their profits; and still others achieved prominent political or military positions. All, however, found it difficult to overcome the social stigma of enslavement.

Slavery in West Africa

Many of the first slaves destined for sale across the Atlantic came from the Gold Coast, composed of thirty little kingdoms known as the Akan States. By the eighteenth century, though, the area farther east and south—the modern nations of Togo, Benin, Nigeria, and Angola—supplied most of the slaves sold in the English colonies. The Adja kings of the Slave Coast encouraged the founding of slave-trading posts and served as middlemen in the trade. Access to valuable European trade goods enhanced their positions in their own societies and improved their kingdoms' standing relative to their neighbors. When Europeans in America increasingly demanded slave labor, Africans responded by selling male prisoners of war.

The societies of West Africa, like those of the Americas, assigned different tasks to men and women. In general, the sexes shared agricultural duties. Men also hunted, managed livestock, and did most of the fishing. Women were responsible for childcare, food preparation, and cloth manufacture. Everywhere in West Africa women were the primary local traders.

Sexual Division of Labor in West Africa

Despite their different economies and the rivalries among states, the peoples of Lower Guinea had similar social systems organized on the basis of what anthropologists have called the dual-sex principle. In Lower Guinea, each sex handled its own affairs: just as male political and religious leaders governed men, so

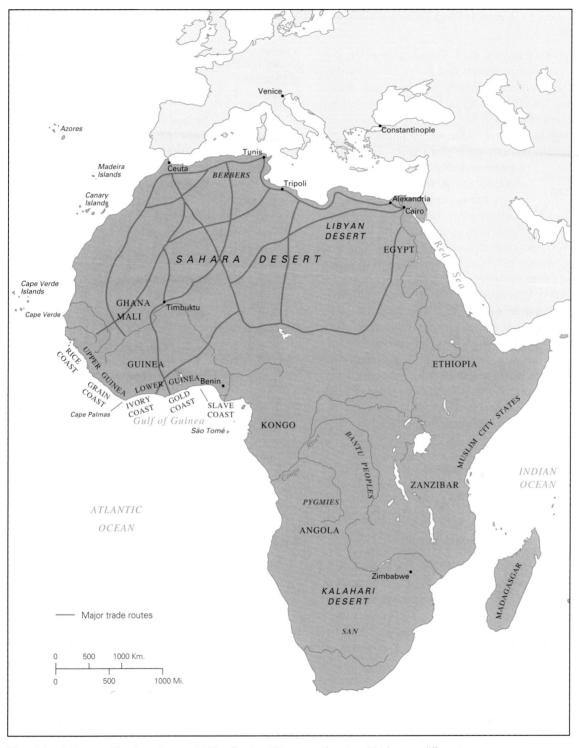

Map 1.2 Africa and Its Peoples, c. 1400 On the African continent resided many different peoples in a variety of ecological settings and political units. Even before Europeans began to explore Africa's coastlines, its northern regions were linked to the Mediterranean (and thus to Europe) by a network of trade routes.

females ruled women. In the Dahomean kingdom, for example, every male official had his female counterpart; in the Akan States, chiefs inherited their status through the female line, and each male chief had a female assistant who supervised other women.

Throughout Upper Guinea, religious beliefs stressed complementary male and female roles. Both women and men served as heads of the cults and secret societies that directed the spiritual life of the villages. Young women were initiated into the Sandé cult, young men into Poro. Although West African women rarely held formal power over men, female religious leaders did govern other members of their sex within the Sandé cult.

West African Religion

The West Africans carried to the Americas, then, were agricultural peoples, skilled at tending livestock, hunting, fishing, and manufacturing cloth from plant fibers and animal skins. Both men and women were accustomed to working communally, alongside other members of their own sex or in family groups. They were also accustomed to a relatively egalitarian relationship between the sexes, especially within the context of religion. In the Americas, they entered societies that used their labor but had little respect for their cultural traditions.

European Societies

 In the fifteenth century, Europeans, too, were agricultural peoples. Split into numerous small, warring countries, Europe was divided linguistically, politically, and economically, yet in social terms Europeans' lives were more similar than different. European societies were hierarchical: a few families wielded autocratic power over the majority of the people. At the base of such hierarchies were people held in a variety of forms of bondage. Although Europeans were not subjected to perpetual slavery, Christian doctrine permitted the enslavement of "heathens" (all non-Christians), and serfdom tied some Europeans to the land if not to specific owners. In short, Europe's kingdoms resembled those of Africa or Mesoamerica but differed greatly from the more egalitarian societies found in America north of Mexico.

Most Europeans, like most Africans and Americans, lived in small villages. European farmers, who were called peasants, owned or leased separate landholdings, but they worked the fields communally. Because fields had to lie fallow (unplanted) every second or third year to regain fertility, a family could not ensure itself a regular food supply unless the work and the crops were shared annually by all the villagers. Men did most of the fieldwork; women helped out chiefly at planting and harvest time. In some areas men concentrated on herding livestock. Women's duties consisted primarily of childcare and household tasks, including preserving food, milking cows, and caring for poultry. Since Europeans kept domesticated animals (pigs, goats, sheep, and cattle) for meat, hunting had little economic importance in their cultures.

Sexual Division of Labor in Europe

Unlike in African and American societies, in which women often played prominent roles in politics and religion, men dominated all areas of life in Europe. A few women—notably Queen Elizabeth I of England—achieved status or power by right of birth, but the vast majority were excluded from positions of political authority. In the Roman Catholic Church and later in the new Protestant denominations, leadership roles were reserved for men. Simply put, European women generally held inferior social, economic, and political positions.

When the fifteenth century began, European nations were slowly recovering from the devastating epidemic of plague known as the Black Death. Bubonic plague, spread by rats and fleas as well as by human contact, arrived in Europe from China, traveling with long-distance traders along the Silk Road to the eastern Mediterranean. From 1346 through the 1360s and 1370s, the plague killed an estimated one-third of Europe's people. That decimation led to a precipitous economic decline and to severe social, political, and religious disruption because of the deaths of clergymen and other leading figures.

Black Death

As plague ravaged the population, England and France waged the Hundred Years War (1337–1453), initiated because the English monarchy claimed the French throne. The war interrupted overland trade routes through France that connected England and the Netherlands to the Italian city-states and thence to Central

Political, Economic, and Technological Change

Asia. Merchants in the eastern Mediterranean thus had to find new ways of reaching their northern markets. They solved that dilemma by forging a regular maritime link with the Netherlands to replace the overland route. The use of a triangular, or lateen, sail (rather than the then-standard square rigging) improved the maneuverability of ships. Also of key importance was the perfection of navigational instruments like the astrolabe and the quadrant, which allowed oceangoing sailors to estimate their position (latitude) by measuring the relationship of the sun, moon, or certain stars to the horizon.

In the aftermath of the Hundred Years War, European monarchs forcefully consolidated their previously diffuse political power and raised new revenues through increased taxation of an already hard-pressed peasantry. In England, Henry VII in 1485 founded the Tudor dynasty and began uniting a previously divided land. In France, the successors of Charles VII unified the kingdom. Most successful of all were Ferdinand of Aragón and Isabella of Castile. In 1469 they married and combined their kingdoms, thereby creating the foundation of a strongly Catholic Spain. In 1492 they defeated the Muslims, who had lived in Spain and Portugal for centuries, and thereafter expelled all Jews and Muslims from their domain.

The fifteenth century also brought technological change to Europe. Movable type and the printing press, invented in Germany in the 1450s, made information more accessible than ever before. Printing stimulated the Europeans' curiosity about fabled lands across the seas, lands they could now read about in books. The most important such work was Marco Polo's *Travels*, first published in 1477, which recounted a Venetian merchant's adventures in thirteenth-century China and, most intriguing, described that nation as being bordered on the east by an ocean. Polo's account led many Europeans to believe that they could trade directly with China in oceangoing vessels instead of relying on the Silk Road or the route through East Africa.

Technological advances and the growing strength of newly powerful national rulers made possible the European explorations of the fifteenth and sixteenth centuries. Each country craved easy access to desirable African and Asian goods—spices like pepper, cloves, cinnamon, and nutmeg (to season the bland European diet), silk, dyes,

Motives for Exploration

perfumes, jewels, sugar, and gold. A secondary concern for spreading Christianity around the world supplemented the economic motive. This linking of materialist and spiritual goals might seem contradictory today, but fifteenth-century Europeans saw no necessary conflict between the two.

Early European Explorations

 Before European mariners could discover new lands, they had to explore the oceans. To reach Asia, seafarers needed not just maneuverable vessels and navigational aids, but also knowledge of the sea, its currents, and especially its winds. How did the winds run? Where would Atlantic breezes take their ships?

Europeans learned the answers to these questions in the region that has been called the Mediterranean Atlantic: the expanse of the Atlantic Ocean that is south and west of Spain and is bounded by the island groups of the Azores (on the west) and the Canaries (on the south), with the Madeiras in their midst. Europeans reached all three sets of islands during the fourteenth century. The Canaries proved a popular destination for mariners from Iberia, the peninsula that includes Spain and Portugal. Sailing to the Canaries from Europe was easy because strong winds known as the Northeast Trades blow southward along the Iberian and African coastlines. The problem was getting back. The very winds that had brought the Iberian sailor to the Canaries now blew directly at him.

Sailing in the Mediterranean Atlantic

What could be done? Some unknown seafarer figured out the answer: sailing "around the wind." If a mariner could not sail against the trade winds, he had to sail as close as possible to the direction from which the wind was coming without being forced to tack. In the Mediterranean Atlantic, that meant pointing his vessel northwest into the open ocean, away from land, until—weeks later—he reached the winds that would carry him home, the so-called Westerlies. Those winds blow (we now know, though the mariners at first did not) northward along the coast of North America before heading east toward Europe.

This solution became the key to successful exploration of both the Atlantic and the Pacific Oceans. Once a sailor understood the winds and their allied currents, he no longer feared leaving Europe without being able to return. Faced with a contrary wind, all he had to do was sail around it until he found a wind to carry him in the proper direction.

During the fifteenth century, armed with knowledge of the winds and currents of the Mediterranean Atlantic, Iberian seamen regularly visited the three island groups, all of which they could reach in two weeks or less. By the 1450s Portuguese colonists in the Madeiras were employing slaves (probably Jews and Muslims brought from Iberia) to grow large quantities of sugar for export to the mainland. By the 1470s Madeira had developed into the world's first colonial plantation economy.

Islands of the Mediterranean Atlantic

Meanwhile, the Guanche people of the Canary Islands fought the assaults of the French, Portuguese, and Spanish. However, the Guanches were weakened by European diseases, and one by one the islands fell and the Guanches were carried off as slaves to the Madeiras or the Iberian Peninsula. Spain conquered the last island in 1496 and subsequently devoted the land to sugar cultivation. Collectively, the Canaries and Madeira became known as the Wine Islands because much of their sugar production was directed to making sweet wines. For Portugal's Prince Henry the Navigator, the islands were steppingstones to Africa. He knew that vast wealth awaited the first European nation to tap the riches of Africa and Asia directly. Each year he dispatched ships southward along the African coast, attempting to discover an oceanic route to Asia. But not until after Prince Henry's death did Bartholomew Dias round the southern tip of Africa (1488) and Vasco da Gama finally reach India (1498).

Long before that, West African states had allowed the Portuguese to establish trading posts along their coasts. Charging the traders rent and levying duties on goods they imported, the African kingdoms set the terms of exchange and benefited considerably from their new, easier access to European manufactures. The Portuguese gained too, for they no longer had to rely on trans-Saharan camel caravans. Their vessels earned immense profits by swiftly transporting African gold, ivory, and slaves to Europe. When they carried previ-

Portuguese Trading Posts in Africa

ously enslaved Africans back to Iberia, the Portuguese introduced black slavery into Europe.

An island off the African coast, previously uninhabited, proved critical to Portuguese success. São Tomé, located in the Gulf of Guinea (see Map 1.2), was colonized in the 1480s. The soil of São Tomé proved ideal for raising sugar, and plantation agriculture there expanded rapidly. Planters imported large numbers of slaves from the mainland to work in the cane fields, thus creating the first economy based primarily on the bondage of black Africans.

By the 1490s, Europeans had learned three key lessons of colonization in the Mediterranean Atlantic. First, they had learned how to transplant their crops and livestock successfully to exotic locations. Second, they had discovered that the native peoples of those lands could be either conquered (the Guanches) or exploited (the Africans). Third, they had developed a viable model of plantation slavery—an exploitative economy based on the labor of large numbers of people held in perpetual bondage—and a system for supplying nearly unlimited quantities of such workers. The stage was set for a pivotal moment in world history.

Lessons of Early Colonization

The Voyages of Columbus, Cabot, and Their Successors

Christopher Columbus was well schooled in the lessons of the Mediterranean Atlantic. Born in 1451 in the Italian city-state of Genoa, Columbus was by the 1490s an experienced sailor and mapmaker. Like many mariners of the day, he was drawn to Portugal and its islands, especially Madeira, where he commanded a merchant vessel. At least once he voyaged to the Portuguese outpost on the Gold Coast. There he acquired an obsession with gold, and there he came to understand the economic potential of the slave trade.

Like all accomplished seafarers and most educated people, Columbus knew the world was round. However, he differed from other cartographers in his estimate of the earth's size: he thought that China lay only 3,000 miles from the southern European coast. Thus, he argued, it would be easier to reach Asia by sailing west than by making the difficult voyage around the southern tip of Africa. Experts scoffed at this crackpot notion, accurately predicting that the two continents lay 12,000 miles apart. When Columbus in 1484 asked the Portuguese authorities to back his plan to sail west to Asia, they rejected the proposal.

Columbus's Voyage

Ferdinand and Isabella of Spain, ruling a newly united kingdom and jealous of Portugal's successes in Africa, were more receptive to Columbus's ideas. Urged on by some Spanish noblemen and a group of Italian merchants residing in Castile, the monarchs agreed to finance the risky voyage. And so, on August 3, 1492, in command of the *Pinta*, the *Niña*, and the *Santa Maria*, Columbus set sail from the Spanish port of Palos.

On October 12, he and his men landed on an island in the Bahamas, which he renamed San Salvador. Later he went on to explore the islands now known as Cuba and Hispaniola, which their residents, the Taíno people, called Colba and Bohío. Because he thought he had reached the Indies, Columbus referred to the inhabitants of the region as Indians.

Columbus's Observations

Three themes predominate in Columbus's log. First, he insistently asked the Taínos where he could find gold, pearls, and valuable spices. Each time, his informants replied (largely via signs) that such products could be obtained on other islands, on the mainland, or in cities in the interior. Second, he wrote repeatedly of the strange and beautiful plants and animals. Columbus's interest was more than aesthetic. "I believe that there are many plants and trees here that could be worth a lot in Spain for use as dyes, spices, and medicines," he observed, adding that he was carrying home to Europe "a sample of everything I can," so that experts could examine them.

The Taíno People

Third, Columbus also described the islands' human residents, and he seized some to take back to Spain. The Taínos were, he said, very handsome, gentle, and friendly. Columbus believed the Taínos to be likely converts to Catholicism. But he also thought the islanders "ought to make good and skilled servants."

Thus the records of the first encounter between Europeans and America and its residents revealed the themes that would be of enormous significance for centuries to come. Above all, Europeans wanted to extract profits from North and South America by exploiting their natural resources, including plants, animals, and peoples alike.

Naming of America

Christopher Columbus made three more voyages to the west, exploring most of the major Caribbean islands and sailing along the coasts of Central and South America. Until the day he died in 1506 at the age of fifty-five, Columbus believed that he had reached Asia. Even before his death, however, others knew better. Because the Florentine Amerigo Vespucci, who explored the South American coast in 1499, was the first to publish the idea that a new continent had been discovered, Martin Waldseemüller in 1507 labeled the land "America." By then, Spain, Portugal, and Pope Alexander VI had signed the Treaty of Tordesillas (1494), confirming Portugal's dominance in Africa—and later Brazil—in exchange for Spanish preeminence in the rest of the Americas.

Northern Voyages

The mariners who explored the region of North America that was to become the United States and Canada followed a very different route. Some historians argue that European sailors may have found the rich Newfoundland fishing grounds in the 1480s, but kept their discoveries a secret so that they alone could exploit the sea's bounty. Whether or not fishermen crossed the entire width of the Atlantic, however, they thoroughly explored its northern reaches. In the same way that the Portuguese traveled regularly in the Mediterranean Atlantic, fifteenth-century seafarers voyaged among the European continent, England, Ireland, and Iceland.

Norse Seafarers

Five hundred years before Columbus, about the year 1001, the Norseman Leif Ericsson and other Viking explorers sailed to North America across the Davis Strait, which separated their villages in Greenland from Baffin Island (see Map 1.1), settling at a site they named Vinland (now L'Anse aux Meadows, Newfoundland). Attacks by local residents forced them to depart after just a few years. Thus the European generally credited with "discovering" North America is John Cabot. More precisely, Cabot brought to Europe the first formal knowledge of the northern coastline of the continent.

Cabot, a master mariner from the Italian city-state of Genoa, was in Spain when Columbus returned from

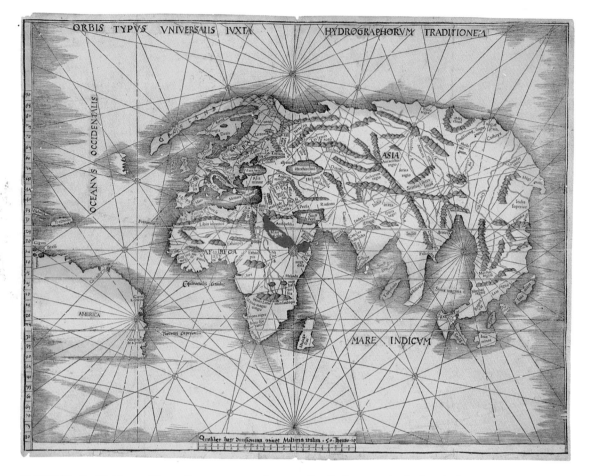

In 1507 Martin Waldseemüller, a German mapmaker, was the first person to designate the newly discovered southern continent as "America." He named the continent after Amerigo Vespucci, the Italian explorer who realized that he had reached a "new world" rather than islands off the coast of Asia.   (John Carter Brown Library at Brown University)

John Cabot's Explorations

his first trip to America. Calculating that England—which traded with Asia only through a long series of middlemen stretching from Belgium to Venice to the Muslim world—would be eager to sponsor exploratory voyages, Cabot sought and won the support of King Henry VII. He set sail from Bristol in late May 1497, reaching his destination on June 24. Scholars disagree about the location of his landfall (some say it was Cape Breton Island, others Newfoundland), but all recognize the importance of his month-long exploration of the coast.

The voyages of Columbus, Cabot, and their suc-cessors finally brought the Eastern and Western Hemispheres together. The Portuguese explorer Pedro Alvares Cabral reached Brazil in 1500; John Cabot's son Sebastian followed his father to North America in 1507; France financed Giovanni da Verrazzano in 1524 and Jacques Cartier in 1534; and in 1609 and 1610 Henry Hudson explored the North American coast for the Dutch West India Company (see Map 1.3). Although these men were primarily searching for the legendary, nonexistent "Northwest Passage" through the Americas, their discoveries interested European nations in exploring North and South America.

Spanish Exploration and Conquest

Only in the areas that Spain explored and claimed did colonization begin immediately. On his second voyage in 1493, Columbus brought to Hispaniola seventeen ships loaded with twelve hundred men, seeds, plants, livestock, chickens, and dogs—along with microbes, rats, and weeds. The settlement named Isabela (in the modern Dominican Republic) and its successors became the staging area for the Spanish invasion of America.

At first, Spanish explorers fanned out around the Caribbean basin. In 1513 Juan Ponce de León reached Florida and Vasco Núñez de Balboa crossed the Isthmus of Panama to the Pacific Ocean. In the 1530s and 1540s, conquistadors traveled farther, exploring many regions claimed by the Spanish monarchs: Francisco Vásquez de Coronado journeyed through the southwestern portion of what is now the United States at approximately the same time as Hernán de Soto explored the southeast and encountered the Lady of Cofitachequi. Juan Rodriguez Cabrillo sailed along the California coast; and Francisco Pizarro, who ventured into western South America, acquired the richest silver mines in the world by conquering and enslaving the Incas. But the most important conquistador was Hernán Cortés.

Cortés, an adventurer who first arrived in the West Indies in 1504, embarked for the mainland in 1519 in search of the wealthy cities rumored to exist there. As he moved his force inland from the Gulf of Mexico, local Mayas presented him with a gift of twenty young female slaves. One of them, Malinche, who had been sold into slavery by the Aztecs and raised by the Mayas, became Cortés's translator and mistress. Malinche bore Cortés

Hernán Cortés and Malinche

Map 1.3 European Explorations in America In the century following Columbus's voyages, European adventurers explored the coasts and parts of the interior of North and South America.

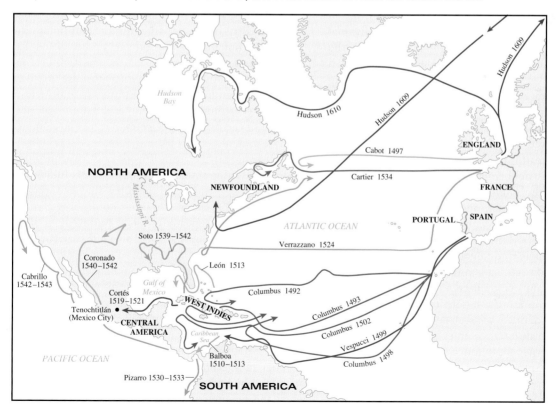

a son, Martín—one of the first *mestizos*, or mixed-blood children—and eventually married one of his officers. When the Aztec capital Tenochtitlán fell to the Spaniards in 1521, Cortés and his men seized a fabulous treasure of gold and silver. Thus, not long after Columbus's first voyage, the Spanish monarchs controlled the richest, most extensive empire Europe had known since ancient Rome.

Spain established the model of colonization that other countries later attempted to imitate, a model with three major elements. First, the

Spanish Colonization

Crown maintained tight control over the colonies, imposing a hierarchical government that allowed little autonomy to New World jurisdictions. Second, most of the colonists sent from Spain were male. They took Indian—and later African—women as their sexual partners, thereby creating the racially mixed population that characterizes much of Latin America to the present day.

Third, the colonies' wealth was based on the exploitation of both the native population and slaves imported from Africa. The *encomienda* system, which granted tribute from Indian villages to individual conquistadors as a reward for their services to the Crown, in effect legalized Indian slavery. Yet in 1542 a new code of laws reformed the system, forbidding Spaniards from enslaving Indians. In response, the conquerors, familiar with slavery in Spain, began to import Africans in order to increase the labor force under their direct control.

Spanish wealth derived from American suffering. The Spaniards deliberately leveled American cities, building cathedrals and monasteries on sites once occupied by Aztec, Incan, and Mayan temples. Some conquistadors sought to erase all vestiges of the great Indian cultures by burning the written records they found. With their traditional ways of life in disarray, devastated by disease, and compelled to labor for their conquerors, many demoralized residents of Mesoamerica accepted the Christian religion brought to New Spain by friars of the Franciscan and Dominican orders.

The friars devoted their energies to persuading Mesoamerican people to move into new towns and to build Roman Catholic churches. In such towns, Indians were exposed to European customs and religious rituals designed to assimilate Catholic and pagan be-

Christianity in New Spain

liefs. Friars deliberately juxtaposed the cult of the Virgin Mary with that of the corn goddess, and the Indians adeptly melded aspects of their traditional world-view with Christianity, in a process called syncretism. Thousands of Indians residing in Spanish territory embraced Catholicism, at least partly because it was the religion of their new rulers.

The Columbian Exchange

A broad mutual transfer of diseases, plants, and animals (called the Columbian Exchange by the historian Alfred Crosby) resulted directly from the European voyages of the fifteenth and sixteenth centuries and from Spanish colonization (see Figure 1.1). The two hemispheres had evolved separately for thousands of years, developing widely different forms of life. Many large mammals like cattle and horses were native to the connected continents of Europe, Asia, and Africa, but the Americas contained no domesticated beasts larger than dogs and llamas. The vegetable crops of the Americas—particularly corn, beans, squash, cassava, and potatoes—were more nutritious and produced higher yields than those of Europe and Africa, such as wheat, millet, and rye. In time, native peoples learned to raise and consume European livestock, and Europeans and Africans became accustomed to planting and eating American crops. The diets of all three peoples were consequently vastly enriched.

Diseases carried from Europe and Africa, though, had a devastating impact on the Americas. Indians fell victim to microbes that had long infested the other continents and had repeatedly killed hundreds of thousands but had also left survivors with some measure of immunity. The statistics are staggering. When Columbus landed on Hispaniola in 1492, approximately half a million people resided there. Fifty years later, fewer than two thousand native inhabitants were still alive.

Smallpox and Other Diseases

The greatest killer was smallpox, spread primarily by direct human contact. One epidemic began on Hispaniola in December 1518 and was carried to the mainland by Spaniards in 1520. There it fatally weakened the defenders of Tenochtitlán. As an old Aztec

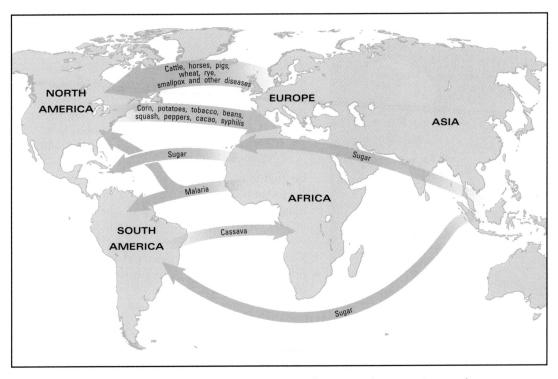

Figure 1.1   Major Items in the Columbian Exchange   As European adventurers traversed the world in the fifteenth and sixteenth centuries, they initiated the "Columbian Exchange" of plants, animals, and diseases. These events changed the lives of the peoples of the world forever, bringing new foods and new pestilences to both sides of the Atlantic.

man recalled, "It spread over the people as great destruction." Largely as a consequence, Tenochtitlán surrendered, and the Spaniards built Mexico City on its site.

Far to the north, where smaller American populations encountered only a few Europeans, disease also ravaged the countryside. A great epidemic, probably smallpox coupled with measles, swept through the villages along the coast north of Cape Cod from 1616 to 1618. Again the mortality rate may have been as high as 90 percent. Because of this dramatic depopulation of the area, just a few years later English colonists were able to establish settlements virtually unopposed.

The Americans, though, took a revenge of sorts. They gave the Europeans syphilis, a virulent venereal disease. The first recorded European case of the new ailment occurred in Barcelona, Spain, in 1493, shortly

Syphilis

after Columbus's return from the Caribbean. Carried by soldiers, sailors, and prostitutes, it spread quickly through Europe and Asia, reaching as far as China by 1505.

The exchange of three commodities had significant impacts on Europe and the Americas. Sugar, which was first domesticated in the East Indies, was being grown on the islands of the Mediterranean Atlantic by 1450. The insatiable European demand for sugar led Columbus to take Canary Island sugar canes to Hispaniola on his 1493 voyage. By the 1520s, plantations in the Greater Antilles worked by African slaves regularly shipped cargoes of sugar to Spain. Half a century later, the Portuguese colony in Brazil (founded in 1532) was

Sugar, Horses, and Tobacco

A male effigy dating from 200–800 C.E., found in a burial site in Nayarit, Mexico. The lesions covering the figurine suggest that the person it represents is suffering from syphilis, which, untreated, produces these characteristic markings on the body in its later stages. Such evidence as this pre-Columbian effigy has now convinced most scholars that syphilis originated in the Americas—a hypothesis in dispute for many years.   (Private Collection)

nation with gathering and agriculture, became one focused almost wholly on hunting buffalo.

In America, Europeans encountered tobacco, which at first they believed to have beneficial medicinal effects. Smoking and chewing the "Indian weed" became a fad in Europe. Despite the efforts of such skeptics as King James I of England, who in 1604 pronounced smoking "harmfull to the brain, [and] dangerous to the Lungs," tobacco's popularity climbed.

The European and African invasion of the Americas therefore had a significant biological component, for the invaders carried plants and animals with them. Some creatures, such as livestock, they brought deliberately. Others, including rats, weeds, and diseases, arrived unexpectedly. And upon their return home, the Europeans deliberately took back such crops as corn, potatoes, and tobacco, along with that unanticipated stowaway, syphilis.

Europeans in North America

Northern Europeans, denied access to the wealth of Mesoamerica by the Spanish and beaten to South America by the Portuguese, were initially more interested in exploiting North America's abundant natural resources than in the difficult task of establishing colonies on the mainland. Following John Cabot's report of a plentiful supply of fish along the North American coast, Europeans rushed to reap the sea's bounty. By the 1570s, more than 350 ships, primarily from France and England, were capitalizing on the fisheries of the Newfoundland Banks each year.

European fishermen soon learned that they could augment their profits by exchanging cloth and metal goods like pots and knives for the native trappers' beaver pelts, which Europeans used to make fashionable hats. At first the Europeans conducted their trading from ships sailing along the coast, but later they established permanent outposts on the mainland to centralize and control the traffic in furs.

Trade Among Indians and Europeans

The Europeans' demand for furs, especially beaver, was matched by the Indians' desire for European goods that could make their lives easier and es-

producing sugar on an even larger scale for the European market, and after 1640, sugar cultivation became the crucial component of English and French colonization in the Caribbean.

Horses, which like sugar were brought to America by Columbus in 1493, fell into the hands of North American natives during the seventeenth century. Through trade and theft, horses spread among the peoples of the Great Plains, reaching most areas by 1750. Sioux, Comanches, and Crows, among others, came to use horses for transportation and hunting, calculated their wealth in the number of horses owned, and waged wars primarily from horseback. Women no longer had to carry the bands' belongings on their backs. Moreover, a mode of subsistence that had been based on hunting several different animals, in combi-

tablish their superiority over their neighbors. Some bands began to concentrate so completely on trapping for the European market that they abandoned their traditional economies. The intensive trade in pelts also had serious ecological consequences. In some regions, beavers were completely wiped out. The disappearance of their dams led to soil erosion, especially when combined with the extensive clearing of forests by later European settlers.

Although their nation reaped handsome profits from fishing, English merchants and political leaders watched enviously as Spain's American possessions enriched Spain immeasurably.

Contest of Spain and England

In the mid-sixteenth century, English "sea dogs" like John Hawkins and Sir Francis Drake began to raid Spanish treasure fleets sailing home from the West Indies. Their actions helped to foment a war that in 1588 culminated in the defeat of a huge invasion force—the Spanish Armada—off the English coast. As a part of the contest with Spain, English leaders started to think about planting colonies in the Western Hemisphere, thereby gaining better access to valuable trade goods and simultaneously preventing their enemy from dominating the Americas.

The first English colonial planners hoped to reproduce Spanish successes by dispatching to America men who would similarly exploit the native peoples for their own and their nation's benefit.

Sir Walter Raleigh's Roanoke Colony

In the mid-1570s, a group that included Sir Humphrey Gilbert and his younger half-brother Sir Walter Raleigh began to promote a scheme to establish outposts that could trade with the Indians and provide bases for attacks on New Spain. Approving the idea, Queen Elizabeth I authorized first Gilbert, then Raleigh, to colonize North America.

Gilbert failed to plant a colony in Newfoundland, and Raleigh was only briefly more successful. After two preliminary expeditions, in 1587 he sent 117 colonists to the territory he named Virginia, after Elizabeth, the "Virgin Queen." They established a settlement on Roanoke Island, in what is now North Carolina, but in 1590 a resupply ship—delayed in leaving England because of the Spanish Armada—could

not find them. The colonists had vanished, leaving only the name of a nearby island carved on a tree.

Thus England's first attempt to plant a permanent settlement on the North American coast failed, as had similar efforts by Portugal on Cape Breton Island (in the early 1520s) and France in northern Florida (in the mid-1560s). All three enterprises collapsed because of the hostility of their neighbors and their inability to be self-sustaining in foodstuffs.

The explanation for these failures becomes clear in Thomas Harriot's *A Briefe and True Report of the New Found Land of Virginia*, published in 1588 to publicize Raleigh's colony.

Thomas Harriot's *Briefe and True Report*

Harriot, a noted scientist who sailed with the second of the preliminary voyages to Roanoke, described the animals, plants, and people of the region for an English readership. His account revealed that although the explorers depended on nearby villagers for most of their food, they needlessly antagonized their neighbors by killing some of them for what Harriot himself admitted were unjustifiable reasons. The scientist advised later colonizers to deal with the native peoples of America more humanely than his comrades had.

Harriot's *Briefe and True Report* depicted for his English readers a bountiful land full of opportunities for quick profit. The people already residing there would, he thought, "in a short time be brought to civilitie" through conversion to Christianity, admiration for European superiority, or conquest—if they did not die from disease, the ravages of which he witnessed. Thomas Harriot's prediction was far off the mark. European dominance of North America would be difficult to achieve.

Summary

The process of initial contact between Europeans and Americans that ended near the close of the sixteenth century had begun approximately 250 years earlier when Portuguese sailors first set out to explore the Mediterranean Atlantic and to settle on its islands. That region of the Atlantic so close to European and African shores nurtured the mariners who, like Christopher

Columbus, ventured into previously unknown waters. When Columbus first reached the Americas, he thought he had found Asia, his intended destination. Later explorers knew better but, except for the Spanish, regarded the Americas primarily as a barrier that prevented them from reaching their long-sought goal of an oceanic route to the riches of China and the Moluccas. Ordinary European fishermen were the first to realize that the northern coasts had valuable products to offer: fish and furs, both much in demand in their homelands.

The wealth of the north could not compare to that of Mesoamerica. The Aztec Empire, heir to the trading networks of Teotihuacán as well as to the intellectual sophistication of the Mayas, dazzled the conquistadors with the magnificence of its buildings and its seemingly unlimited wealth. The Aztecs believed that their Fifth Sun would end in earthquakes and hunger. Hunger they surely experienced after Cortés's invasion; and, if there were no earthquakes, the great temples tumbled to the ground nevertheless, as the Spaniards used their stones (and Indian laborers) to construct cathedrals honoring their God and his son Jesus rather than Huitzilopochtli. The conquerors employed first American and later enslaved African workers to till the fields, mine the precious metals, and herd the livestock that earned immense profits for themselves and their mother country.

The initial impact of Europeans on the Americas proved devastating. Flourishing civilizations were, if not entirely destroyed, markedly altered in just a few short decades. By the end of the sixteenth century, fewer people resided in North America than had lived there before Columbus's arrival, even taking into account the arrival of many Europeans and Africans. And the people who did live there—Indian, African, and European—resided in a world that was indeed new—a world engaged in the unprecedented process of combining foods, religions, economies, styles of life, and political systems that had developed separately for millennia. Understandably, conflict and dissension permeated that process.

LEGACY FOR A PEOPLE AND A NATION

Columbus Day

Each year, the United States celebrates the second Monday in October as a tribute to Christopher Columbus's landing in the Bahamas in 1492. The first known U.S. celebration of Columbus's voyage occurred in New York City on October 12, 1792, when a men's social club gave a dinner to mark its three hundredth anniversary. In the late 1860s, Italian American communities in New York City and San Francisco began to celebrate October 12, but not until 1892 did a congressional resolution order a one-time national commemoration. Columbus Day was first observed as a national holiday in 1971.

Today, the annual observances can arouse strong emotions. The American Indian Movement (AIM), founded in 1968, has declared that "from an indigenous vantage point, Columbus' arrival was a disaster" and that he "deserves no recognition or accolades." At the same time, people of Hispanic descent have claimed Columbus as their own, insisting that his voyage was "a thoroughly Spanish event." In some cities—most notably New York—their celebrations rival those long organized by Italian Americans; in others, such as Miami, Hispanics control the official commemorations. Still other Latinos, especially those of Mexican descent living in Los Angeles, call October 12 Día de la Raza and use it as an occasion to protest current U.S. immigration policy.

As ethnic diversity has increased in the nation, and as peoples of different origins have sought to claim a share of the American heritage, holidays have unsurprisingly become the occasion for heated contests. Each fall, the American people and nation therefore continue to confront the controversial legacy of Columbus's 1492 voyage.

For Further Reading, see the Appendix. For Web resources, go to history.college.hmco.com/students.

EUROPEANS COLONIZE NORTH AMERICA

1600–1640

In August 1630, Fray Alonso de Benavides brought thrilling news to Madrid. Franciscan priests in the remote territory called New Mexico had successfully converted at least eighty thousand heathens to Roman Catholicism. Even the nomadic Apaches and Navajos had eagerly embraced baptism in the new faith. Moreover, the priests' missionary activities had repeatedly benefited from God's "wonders and miracles." For example, when an old woman from Taos tried to convince four others to renounce their Christian marriages, "a bolt of lightning flashed from a clear untroubled sky, killing that infernal agent of the demon."

Fray Alonso supervised the New Mexico missions from 1626 to 1629. His account of the Franciscans' successes created a sensation in Europe. Alonso's *Memorial* not only was immediately published in Spanish but also was quickly translated into Latin, French, Dutch, and German. Fray Alonso undertook an arduous and successful journey to Spain to convince the king to increase his financial and administrative support of the Franciscan missions. Yet even Fray Alonso's enthusiastic and optimistic report contained a troubling undercurrent. Only about 250 Spaniards (along with another 750 Pueblos and *mestizos*) inhabited the colonial capital at Santa Fe. The soldiers were "few and poorly equipped," and not all the local Indians had been receptive to the priests' message. The residents of Picurís, for instance, were "treacherous" and "on various occasions" had tried to murder the priests stationed there.

21

So, while praising the Spaniards' stunning successes in New Mexico, Fray Alonso revealed their equally striking weaknesses: many Native Americans resisted their proselytizing; both priests and soldiers lacked adequate financial resources; and the one tiny, impoverished European settlement was surrounded by tens of thousands of potentially troublesome Pueblos, Apaches, and Navajos. Fray Alonso furthermore failed to identify an additional problem: royal governors often clashed with the Franciscans in a struggle for control of the region.

By the time Fray Alonso arrived in Madrid in 1630, England, France, and the Netherlands had also founded permanent colonies in North America. No longer were the Spaniards the only Europeans on that vast continent. Just as Franciscans played a major role in the Spanish settlements, so too Jesuit priests were active in New France. The French and Dutch colonies, like the Spanish outposts, were settled largely by European men. Like the conquistadors, the French and Dutch merchants hoped to make a quick profit and then perhaps return to their homelands.

In contrast to other Europeans, most of the English settlers came to America intending to stay. Especially in the area that came to be known as New England, they arrived in family groups. They recreated European society and family life to an extent not possible in the other colonies, where migrant men found their sexual partners within the Native American or African populations. Among the English colonies, those in the Chesapeake region and on the Caribbean islands most closely resembled colonies founded by other nations. Their economies, like those of Hispaniola or Brazil, soon came to be based on large-scale production for the international market by a labor force composed of bonded servants and slaves.

Wherever they settled, the English, like other Europeans, prospered only after they learned to adapt to the alien environment. The first permanent English colonies survived because nearby Indians assisted the newcomers. The settlers had to learn to grow unfamiliar American crops. They also had to develop extensive trading relationships with Native Americans and with colonies established by other European countries. Needing laborers for their fields, they first used English indentured servants, then later began to import African slaves. Thus the early history of the region that became the United States and the English Caribbean is best understood not as an isolated story of English colonization, but rather as a series of complex interactions among a variety of European, African, and American peoples and environments. ■

New Spain, New France, and New Netherland

 Spaniards were the first Europeans to establish a permanent settlement within the boundaries of the modern United States, but they were not the first to attempt that feat. Twice in the 1560s groups of French Protestants (Huguenots) sought to escape from persecution in their homeland by planting colonies on the south Atlantic coast. The first colony, in present-day South Carolina, collapsed, and its starving inhabitants had to be rescued by a passing ship. The second, near modern Jacksonville, Florida, was destroyed in 1565 by a Spanish expedition under the command of Pedro Menéndez de Avilés. To ensure Spanish domination of the strategically important region (located near sea-lanes used by Spanish treasure ships bound for Europe), Menéndez set up a small fortified outpost, which he named St. Augustine—now the oldest continuously inhabited European settlement in the United States. Franciscan missionaries soon followed, and by the end of the sixteenth century a chain of Franciscan missions stretched across northern Florida.

More than thirty years after the founding of St. Augustine, Juan de Oñate, a Mexican-born adventurer, led

New Mexico

a group of about five hundred soldiers and settlers to New Mexico. The year was 1598, and at first the Pueblos greeted the newcomers cordially. When the Spaniards began to use torture, murder, and rape to extort food and clothing from the villagers, however, the residents of Acoma killed several soldiers. The invaders responded ferociously, killing more than eight hundred people and capturing the remainder. Not surprisingly, the other Pueblo villages surrendered.

Because New Mexico held little wealth and was too far from the Pacific coast to assist in protecting Spanish sea-lanes, many of the Spaniards returned to Mexico, and officials considered abandoning the isolated colony. Instead, in 1609, the authorities decided to maintain a small military outpost and a few Chris-

IMPORTANT EVENTS

1533 Henry VIII divorces Catherine of Aragon; English Reformation begins

1558 Elizabeth I becomes queen

1565 Founding of St. Augustine (Florida), oldest permanent European settlement in present-day United States

1598 Oñate conquers Pueblos in New Mexico for Spain

1603 James I becomes king

1607 Jamestown founded, first permanent English settlement in North America

1608 Quebec founded by the French

1609 Hudson explores Hudson River for the Dutch

1610 Founding of Santa Fe, New Mexico

1611 First Virginia tobacco crop

1614 Fort Orange (Albany) founded by the Dutch

1619 Virginia House of Burgesses established, first representative assembly in the English colonies

1620 Plymouth colony founded, first permanent English settlement in New England

1622 Powhatan Confederacy attacks Virginia colony

1624 Dutch settle on Manhattan Island (New Amsterdam)
English colonize St. Kitts, first island in Lesser Antilles to be settled by Europeans
James I revokes Virginia Company's charter

1625 Charles I becomes king

1630 Massachusetts Bay colony founded

1634 Maryland founded

1636 Williams expelled from Massachusetts Bay; founds Providence, Rhode Island
Connecticut founded

1637 Pequot War in New England

1638 Hutchinson expelled from Massachusetts Bay colony; goes to Rhode Island

c. 1640 Sugar cultivation begins on Barbados

1642 Montreal founded by the French

1646 Treaty ends hostilities between Virginia and Powhatan Confederacy

---

tian missions in the area, with the capital at Santa Fe (founded in 1610). This was the constricted world of Fray Alonso de Benavides.

After Spain's destruction of France's Florida settlement in 1565, the French turned their attention north-

Quebec and Montreal

ward. In 1608 Samuel de Champlain set up a trading post at an interior site the local Iroquois had called Stadacona; Champlain renamed it Quebec.

He had chosen well: Quebec was the most easily defended spot in the entire St. Lawrence River valley, a stronghold that controlled access to the heartland of the continent. In 1642 the French established a second post, Montreal, at the falls of the St. Lawrence (and thus at the end of navigation by ocean-going vessels).

Before the founding of these settlements, French fishermen had served as the major transporters of North American beaver pelts to France, but the new

posts quickly took over control of the lucrative trade in furs (see Table 2.1). In the hope of attracting settlers, the colony's leaders gave land grants along the river to wealthy seigneurs (nobles), who then imported tenants to work their farms. Even so, more than twenty-five years after Quebec's founding, it had just sixty-four resident families, along with traders and soldiers.

One other important group that composed part of the population of New France was missionaries of the Society of Jesus (Jesuits), a Roman

Jesuit Missions in New France

Catholic order dedicated to converting nonbelievers to Christianity. First arriving in Quebec in 1625, the Jesuits, whom the Indians called Black Robes, initially tried to persuade indigenous peoples to live near French settlements and to adopt European agricultural methods as well as the Europeans' religion. When that effort failed, the Black Robes learned Indian languages and traveled to remote regions of the

Table 2.1   The Founding of Permanent European Colonies in North America, 1565–1640

Colony	Founder(s)	Date	Basis of Economy
Florida	Pedro Menéndez de Avilés	1565	Farming
New Mexico	Juan de Oñate	1598	Livestock
Virginia	Virginia Company	1607	Tobacco
New France	France	1608	Fur trading
New Netherland	Dutch West India Company	1614	Fur trading
Plymouth	Pilgrims	1620	Farming, fishing
Maine	Sir Ferdinando Gorges	1622	Fishing
St. Kitts, Barbados, et al.	European immigrants	1624	Sugar
Massachusetts Bay	Massachusetts Bay Company	1630	Farming, fishing, fur trading
Maryland	Cecilius Calvert	1634	Tobacco
Rhode Island	Roger Williams	1636	Farming
Connecticut	Thomas Hooker	1636	Farming, fur trading
New Haven	Massachusetts migrants	1638	Farming
New Hampshire	Massachusetts migrants	1638	Farming, fishing

interior, where they lived in twos and threes among hundreds of potential converts.

Using a variety of strategies, Jesuits sought to undermine the authority of village shamans (the traditional religious leaders) and to gain the confidence of leaders who could influence others. Trained in rhetoric, they won admirers by their eloquence. Immune to smallpox (for all had survived the disease already), they explained epidemics among the Indians as God's punishment for sin. Perhaps most important, they amazed the villagers by communicating with each other over long distances and periods of time by employing marks on paper. The Indians' desire to learn how to harness the extraordinary power of literacy was one of the critical factors making them receptive to the missionaries' spiritual message.

The Jesuits slowly gained thousands of converts, some of whom moved to reserves set aside for Christian Indians. In those communities the converts replaced their own culture's traditional equal treatment of men and women with notions more congenial to the Europeans' insistence on male dominance and female subordination. Further, they altered their practice of allowing premarital sexual relationships and easy divorce because Catholic doctrine prohibited both customs.

Jesuit missionaries faced little competition from other Europeans for Native Americans' souls, but French fur traders had to confront a direct challenge. In 1614, only five years after Henry Hudson sailed up the river that now bears his name, his sponsor, the Dutch West India Company, established an outpost (Fort Orange) on that river at the site of present-day Albany, New York. Like the French, the Dutch sought beaver pelts. Because the Dutch were interested primarily in trade rather than colonization, New Netherland remained small. The colony's southern anchor was New Amsterdam (see Map 2.1), a town founded in 1624 on Manhattan Island.

New Netherland

As the Dutch West India Company's colony in North America, New Netherland was a relatively unimportant part of a vast commercial empire. The colony was ruled autocratically, and settlers felt little loyalty to their nominal leaders. Migration was sparse. Even a company policy of 1629 that offered a large land grant, or patroonship, to anyone who would bring fifty settlers to the province failed to attract takers. As late as the mid-1660s, New Netherland had only about five thousand inhabitants. Some of those were Swedes and Finns, who resided in the former colony of New

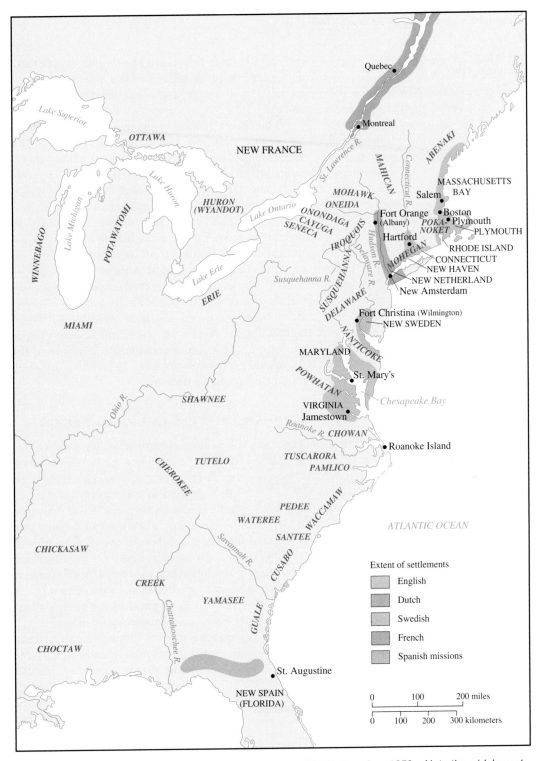

Map 2.1   European Settlements and Indians in Eastern North America, 1650   Note the widely scattered European settlements along the ocean and riverbanks, while America's native inhabitants controlled
the vast interior.

Sweden (founded in 1638 on the Delaware River), which was taken over by the Dutch in 1655.

The Native American allies of New France and New Netherland came into armed conflict with each other in part because of fur-trade rivalries. In the 1640s, the Iroquois, who traded chiefly with the Dutch and lived in modern upstate New York, went to war against the Hurons, who traded primarily with the French and lived in present-day Ontario. Using guns supplied by the Dutch, the Iroquois largely exterminated the Hurons, whose population had already been decimated by a smallpox epidemic. The Iroquois thus established themselves as a major force in the region, one that Europeans could ignore only at their peril.

The Caribbean

 In the Caribbean, France, the Netherlands, and England clashed openly in the first half of the seventeenth century. The Spanish concentrated their efforts on colonizing the Greater Antilles—Cuba, Hispaniola, Jamaica, and Puerto Rico—and on exploiting the mainland's wealth. They left many smaller islands alone. But other European nations saw the tiny islands both as bases from which to attack Spanish vessels loaded with American gold and silver and as sources of valuable tropical products such as spices, dyes, and fruits.

England was the first northern European nation to establish a permanent foothold in the smaller West Indian islands (the Lesser Antilles). English people settled on St. Christopher (St. Kitts) in 1624, then later on other islands such as Barbados (1627). France was able to colonize Guadeloupe and Martinique, and the Dutch gained control of St. Eustatius (strategically located near St. Kitts). Because of conflict among the European powers, most of the islands were attacked at least once during the course of the century, and some changed hands.

Why did other Europeans devote so much energy to gaining control of these tiny bits of land neglected by Spain? The primary answer to that question is sugar. Early in the 1640s, English residents of Barbados discovered that the island's soil and climate were ideally suited for culti-

The Importance of Sugar

vating sugar cane. Europeans loved sugar; it gave them a quick energy boost and served as a sweetener for two stimulating, addictive, and bitter Asian drinks: coffee and tea.

The Dutch helped to introduce sugar cane into the newly colonized Lesser Antilles. In 1630 they seized control of northeastern Brazil, holding the region until 1654. There the Dutch learned how to grow the canes and to process them. When they taught those skills to Barbadians, they were not being altruistic. They expected to sell African slaves to West Indian planters and to carry to Europe barrels of molasses and rum, which was distilled from sugar. The results must have exceeded their wildest dreams. The Barbados sugar boom in the 1640s earned immense profits for planters, slave traders, and Dutch shipping interests alike. Sugar remained the most valuable American commodity for more than one hundred years. Yet, in the long run, the future economic importance of the Europeans' American colonies lay on the mainland rather than in the Caribbean.

English Interest in Colonization

 The failure of Raleigh's Roanoke colony ended English efforts to settle in North America for nearly two decades. When the English decided in 1606 to try once more, they again planned colonies that imitated the Spanish model. Success came only when they abandoned that model and sent large numbers of men and women to set up agriculturally based colonies on the mainland. Two major developments prompted approximately 200,000 ordinary English men and women to move to North America in the seventeenth century and led their government to encourage their emigration.

The first impetus that led English folk to move to North America was the onset of dramatic social and

Social Change in England

economic change caused by a population boom. In the 150-year period after 1530, largely as a result of the introduction of nutritious American crops into Europe, England's population doubled. All those additional people needed food, clothing, and other goods. The competition for goods led to high inflation, coupled with a fall in real wages as the number of workers increased. The enhanced de-

London in 1616, with London Bridge at center right. Overcrowding in the city led many observers to conclude that American colonization could remove "excess" population and provide new employment for poverty-stricken persons. The rapidly growing community of London merchants also sought to develop new sources of overseas profits.   (Trustees of the British Library)

mand for food and wool for clothing benefited those with sizable landholdings, but drove landless peasants and those with small amounts of land into unremitting poverty.

Well-to-do English people reacted with alarm as they saw landless and homeless people fill the streets and highways. Obsessed with the problem of maintaining order, officials came to believe that England was overcrowded. They concluded that colonies established in North America could siphon off England's "surplus population," thus easing social strains at home. For similar reasons, many English people decided that they could improve their circumstances by migrating to a large, land-rich, apparently empty continent. Such economic considerations were rendered even more significant in light of the second development, a major change in English religious practice.

The sixteenth century witnessed a religious transformation that eventually led large numbers of English dissenters to leave their homeland. In 1533 Henry VIII, wanting a male heir and infatuated with Anne Boleyn, sought to annul his marriage to his Spanish-born queen, Catherine of Aragon. When the pope refused to approve the annulment, Henry left the Roman Catholic Church. He founded the Church of England and—with Parliament's concurrence—proclaimed himself its head. At first the reformed Church of England differed little from Catholicism in its practices, but under Henry's daughter Elizabeth I (the child of his marriage to Anne Boleyn), new currents of religious belief that had originated on the European continent early in the sixteenth century dramatically affected the English church.

The English Reformation

The leaders of the continental Protestant Reformation were Martin Luther, a German monk, and John Calvin, a French cleric and lawyer. Contradicting the Catholic doctrine that priests must serve as intermediaries between laypeople and God, Luther and Calvin insisted that people could interpret the Bible for themselves. Both Luther and Calvin rejected Catholic rituals and denied the need for an elaborate church hierarchy. They also asserted that salvation rested on faith alone, rather than—as Catholic teaching had it—on a combination of faith and good works. Calvin, though, went further than Luther in stressing God's omnipotence and emphasizing the need for people to submit totally to God's will.

Elizabeth I tolerated religious diversity among her subjects as long as they generally acknowledged her authority as head of the Church of England. Accordingly, during her long reign (1558–1603), Calvin's ideas gained influence within the English church. By the late sixteenth century, many English Calvinists—those who came to be called Puritans because they wanted to purify the Church of England—believed that the English Reformation had not gone far enough. Henry had simplified the church hierarchy; they wanted to abolish it altogether. Henry had subordinated the church to the interests of the state; they wanted a church free from political interference. And whereas the Church of England continued to include all English people, the Puritans wanted to confine church membership to persons they believed to be "saved"—those God had selected for salvation before birth.

Puritans

Paradoxically, though, a key article of the Puritans' faith insisted that people could not know for certain if they were "saved" because mere mortals could not comprehend or affect their predestination to heaven or hell. Thus pious Puritans daily confronted a serious dilemma: if one was predestined for heaven or hell and could not alter one's fate, why should one attend church or do good works? Puritans resolved this conundrum by reasoning that God gave the elect the ability to accept salvation and to lead a good life. Therefore, piety and good works could indicate one's place in the ranks of the saved.

Elizabeth I's Stuart successors, her cousin James I (1603–1625) and his son Charles I (1625–1649), were less tolerant of Puritans than she. As Scots, they had

The First Stuart Monarchs

little respect for the traditions of representative government that had developed in England under the Tudors and their predecessors. As adherents of the theory of the divine right of kings, the Stuarts insisted that a monarch's power came directly from God and that his subjects had a duty to obey him. A king's authority was absolute, they argued.

Both James I and Charles I believed that their authority included the power to enforce religious conformity among their subjects. Because Puritans were challenging many of the most important precepts of the English church, the monarchs authorized the removal of Puritan clergymen from their pulpits. In the 1620s and 1630s a number of English Puritans decided to move to America, where they hoped to put their religious beliefs into practice unmolested by the Stuarts or the church hierarchy.

The Founding of Virginia

The initial impulse that would lead to England's first permanent colony in the Western Hemisphere came not from the Puritans but from a group of merchants and wealthy gentry. In 1606, envisioning the possibility of earning great profits by finding precious metals and opening new trade routes, the men established a joint-stock venture, the Virginia Company, to plant colonies in America.

Joint-stock companies had been developed in England during the sixteenth century as a mechanism for pooling the resources of many small investors, primarily to finance trading voyages. For that purpose they worked well: no one risked too much money, and investors usually received quick returns. But joint-stock companies turned out to be a poor way to finance colonies because the early settlements required enormous amounts of capital and, with rare exceptions, failed to return much immediate profit. Colonies founded by joint-stock companies consequently suffered from a chronic lack of capital.

Joint-Stock Companies

The Virginia Company was no exception. Chartered by James I in 1606, the company tried but failed to start a colony in Maine and barely succeeded in planting one in Virginia. In May 1607, the company sent 104 men and boys, who established the settlement called

Jamestown

Jamestown. Ill-equipped for survival in the unfamiliar environment, the colonists were afflicted by dissension and disease. Moreover, through sheer bad luck they arrived in the midst of a severe drought (now known to be the worst in the region for nearly eight hundred years). The lack of rainfall not only made it difficult for them to cultivate crops but also polluted their drinking water.

By January 1608, only thirty-eight of the original colonists remained alive. Many of the first immigrants were gentlemen unaccustomed to working with their hands or artisans with irrelevant skills like glassmaking. Having come to Virginia expecting to make easy fortunes, they resisted hard labor, retaining elaborate English dress and casual work habits despite their desperate circumstances. Such attitudes, combined with the effects of chronic malnutrition and epidemic disease, took a terrible toll. Only when Captain John Smith, one of the colony's founders, imposed military discipline on the colonists in 1608 was Jamestown saved from collapse. But after Smith's departure the settlement experienced a severe "starving time" (the winter of 1609–1610). Although more settlers (including a few women and children) arrived in 1608 and 1609 and living conditions slowly improved, as late as 1624 only 1,300 of approximately 8,000 English immigrants to Virginia remained alive.

The Powhatan Confederacy

The survival of Jamestown may be attributed not to the English, but rather to a group of six Algonquian tribes known as the Powhatan Confederacy (see Map 2.1). Powhatan was aggressively consolidating his authority over some twenty-five smaller bands when the Europeans arrived. Fortunately for the colonists, Powhatan at first viewed them as potential allies. He found the English colony a reliable source of useful items such as steel knives and guns, which gave him a technological advantage over his Indian neighbors. In return, Powhatan's people traded their excess corn and other foodstuffs to the starving settlers. The initially cordial relationship soon deteriorated, however. The English colonists kidnapped Powhatan's daughter, Pocahontas, holding her as a hostage in retaliation for Powhatan's seizure of several settlers. In captivity, she agreed in 1614 to marry a colonist, John Rolfe.

The Jamestown colony and the coastal Indians had an uneasy relationship. English and Algonquian

Algonquian and English Cultural Differences

peoples had much in common: deep religious beliefs, a lifestyle oriented around agriculture, clear political and social hierarchies, and sharply defined gender roles. Yet the two groups focused on their cultural differences. English men regarded Indian men as lazy because they did not cultivate crops and spent much of their time hunting (a sport, not work, in English eyes). Indian men thought English men effeminate because they did "women's work" of cultivation.

Other differences between the two cultures caused serious misunderstandings. Among the East Coast Algonquians, people were not born to positions of leadership, nor were political power and social status necessarily inherited through the male line. Members of the English gentry inherited their position from their fathers, and English leaders tended to rule autocratically. By contrast, the authority of Algonquian leaders rested on consensus. Accustomed to the European concept of powerful kings, the English sought such figures in native villages. Often (for example, when negotiating treaties) they willfully overestimated the ability of chiefs to make independent decisions for their people.

Furthermore, the Algonquians and the English had very different notions of property ownership. In most Algonquian villages, land was held communally by the entire group. It could not be bought or sold absolutely, although certain rights to use the land (for example, for hunting or fishing) could be transferred. English people, in contrast, were accustomed to individual farms and to buying and selling land. The English also refused to accept the validity of Indians' claims to traditional hunting territories, insisting that only land that was intensively cultivated could be regarded as owned or occupied. Above all, the English settlers believed unwaveringly in the superiority of their civilization.

The Cultivation of Tobacco

The spread of tobacco cultivation upset the balance of power in early Virginia. In tobacco, the settlers and the Virginia Company found the salable commodity for which they had been searching. John Rolfe planted the first crop in 1611. By the late 1620s, shipments totaled 1.5 million pounds. The great tobacco boom had begun, fueled by high prices and substantial profits for planters. Although the price of tobacco fluctuated wildly from year to year, the crop made Virginia prosper. Soon the once all male outpost was inhabited by both men and women.

Successful tobacco cultivation required abundant land, since the crop quickly drained the soil of its nutrients. Farmers soon learned that a field could produce only about three satisfactory crops before it had to lie fallow for several years to regain its fertility. Thus the once-small English settlements began to expand rapidly: eager applicants asked the Virginia Company for large land grants on both sides of the James River and its tributary streams.

To attract more settlers to the colony, the Virginia Company in 1617 developed the "headright" system.

Virginia Company Policies

Every new arrival paying his or her own way was promised a land grant of 50 acres; those who financed the passage of others received similar headrights for each person. To ordinary English farmers, many of whom owned little or no land, the headright system offered a powerful incentive to move to Virginia. To wealthy gentry, it promised the possibility of establishing vast agricultural enterprises worked by large numbers of laborers. Two years later, the company introduced a second reform, authorizing the landowning men of the major Virginia settlements to elect representatives to an assembly called the House of Burgesses. Although England was a monarchy, English landholders had long been accustomed to electing members of Parliament and controlling their own local governments; therefore, they expected the same privilege in the nation's colonies.

Opechancanough, Powhatan's brother and successor, watched the English colonists steadily encroaching on the confederacy's lands and

Indian Uprisings

attempting to convert its members to Christianity. Recognizing the danger his brother had overlooked, the war leader launched coordinated attacks all along the James River on March 22, 1622. By the end of the day, 347 colonists (about one-quarter of the total) lay dead. Virginia reeled from the blow but did not collapse, and an uneasy peace prevailed. Two decades later Opechancanough tried one last time to repel the invaders. He failed, losing his life in the war that ensued. After this defeat and a 1646 treaty subordinating the Powhatan

Confederacy to English authority, the Indians' efforts to resist the spread of European settlement ended.

The 1622 Powhatan uprising that failed to destroy the colony succeeded in killing its parent. The Virginia Company had never made any

End of the Virginia Company

profits from the enterprise, for all its earnings were offset by the heavy cost of supporting the settlers and by internal corruption. In 1624 James I revoked the charter, transforming Virginia into a royal colony—a colony ruled by the king through appointed officials. James continued the headright policy but abolished the assembly. Virginians protested so vigorously, however, that by 1629 the House of Burgesses was functioning once again. Because Virginians successfully insisted on governing themselves at the local level, the political structure of England's American possessions came to differ from that of New Spain, New France, and New Netherland, all of which were ruled autocratically.

Life in the Chesapeake

By the 1630s, tobacco was firmly established as the staple crop and chief source of revenue in Virginia. It quickly became just as important in the second English colony planted on Chesapeake Bay: Maryland, given by Charles I to George Calvert, first Lord Baltimore, as a personal possession (proprietorship), which was settled in 1634. The Calverts intended the colony to serve as a haven for their fellow Roman Catholics, then being persecuted in England. Cecilius Calvert, second Lord Baltimore, became the first colonizer to offer freedom of religion to all Christian settlers; he understood that protecting the Protestant majority could also ensure Catholics' rights.

In everything but religion the two Chesapeake colonies resembled each other. In Maryland as in Virginia, tobacco planters spread out along the river banks, establishing isolated farms instead of towns. The region's deep, wide rivers offered dependable water transportation, and each farm or group of farms had its own wharf, where oceangoing vessels could take on or discharge cargo. As a result, Virginia and Maryland had few towns, for their residents did not need commercial centers in order to buy and sell goods.

Because the planting, cultivation, and harvesting of tobacco were labor-intensive, successful Chesapeake tobacco farms required laborers. But where and how could they be obtained? Nearby Indians, their numbers reduced by war and disease, could not supply the needed workers. Nor were enslaved Africans readily available: merchants could more easily and profitably sell those slaves to Caribbean sugar planters. In the first half of the seventeenth century, therefore, only a few people of African descent, some of them free or indentured laborers rather than slaves, arrived in the Chesapeake. By 1650 about three hundred blacks lived in Virginia.

Need for Laborers

Chesapeake tobacco farmers thus looked primarily to England to supply their labor needs. Under the headright system (which Maryland also adopted in 1640), a tobacco farmer anywhere in the Chesapeake could simultaneously obtain both land and labor by importing workers from England. Good management would make the process self-perpetuating: a farmer could use his profits to pay for the passage of more workers and thereby gain title to more land.

Because men did the agricultural work in European societies, colonists assumed that field laborers should be men. Such male laborers, along with a few women, immigrated to America as indentured servants—that is, in return for their passage they contracted to work for farmers for periods ranging from four to seven years. Indentured servants accounted for 75 to 85 percent of the approximately 130,000 English immigrants to Virginia and Maryland during the seventeenth century.

Indentured Servant Immigrants

Males between the ages of fifteen and twenty-four composed roughly three-quarters of these servants; only one immigrant in five or six was female. Most of these young men came from farming or laboring families and were what their contemporaries called the "common sort."

For such people the Chesapeake appeared to offer good prospects. Servants who fulfilled the terms of their indentures earned "freedom dues" consisting of clothes, tools, livestock, casks of corn and tobacco, and sometimes even land. Yet immigrants' lives were difficult. Servants typically worked six days a week, ten to fourteen hours a day. Their masters could discipline or sell them, and they faced severe penalties for running away. Even so, the laws did offer them some protection. For example, their masters were supposed to supply them with sufficient food, clothing, and shelter, and cruelly treated servants could turn to the courts for assistance.

Conditions of Servitude

Servants and their masters alike had to contend with epidemic disease. Immigrants first had to survive the process the colonists called "seasoning"—a bout with disease (probably malaria) that usually occurred during their first Chesapeake summer. They then had to endure recurrences of malaria, along with dysentery, typhoid fever, and other diseases. As a result, approximately 40 percent of male servants did not survive long enough to become freedmen.

For those who survived the term of their indentures, however, the opportunities for advancement were real. Until the last decades of the seventeenth century, former servants were usually able to become independent farmers ("freeholders") and to live a modest but comfortable existence. Some even assumed positions of political prominence. But after 1670 tobacco prices declined and good land grew increasingly scarce and expensive, and in 1681 Maryland dropped its legal requirement that servants receive land as part of their freedom dues. By 1700 the Chesapeake was no longer the land of opportunity it once had been.

Life in the early Chesapeake was hard for everyone, regardless of sex or status. Farmers (and sometimes their wives) toiled in the fields alongside servants. Most people rose and went to bed with the sun, lived in one- or two-room ramshackle houses, and consumed a filling but not especially nutritious diet based on pork and corn. Colonists devoted their income to improving their farms, buying livestock, and purchasing more laborers rather than to improving their standard of living.

Standard of Living

The predominance of males, the incidence of servitude, and the high mortality rates combined to produce unusual patterns of family life. Female servants normally could not marry during their terms of indenture because masters did not want pregnancies

Chesapeake Families

to deprive them of workers. Many male ex-servants could not marry at all because of the scarcity of women. In contrast, nearly every adult free woman in the Chesapeake married. Yet because of high infant mortality and because almost all marriages were delayed by servitude or broken by death, Chesapeake women commonly reared only one to three healthy children, in contrast to English women, who normally had at least five.

Thus Chesapeake families were few, small, and short-lived. Parents often died while their children were still young. In one Virginia county, for example, more than three-quarters of the children had lost at least one parent by the time they either married or reached age twenty-one. Indeed, the large number of orphaned children prompted a legal innovation: the establishment of orphans' courts to oversee the management of orphans' property.

Because of the low rate of natural increase, throughout the seventeenth century immigrants composed a majority of the Chesapeake population. Thus most of the members of Virginia's House of Burgesses and Maryland's House of Delegates (established in 1635) were immigrants; they also dominated the governor's council, which was simultaneously each colony's highest court, part of the legislature, and executive adviser to the governor. In the early eighteenth century a native-born ruling elite emerged. Until then the Chesapeake's immigrant leaders engaged in power struggles, often for personal economic advantage.

Chesapeake Politics

The Founding of New England

The economic motives that prompted English people to move to the Chesapeake colonies also drew men and women to New England. But because Puritans organized the New England colonies, and also because of environmental differences between the two regions, the northern settlements turned out very differently from those in the South. The northern climate was too cold and the soil too infertile to raise tobacco on a large scale or to raise sugar cane at all. Accordingly, diversified small farms dominated the landscape.

Except for the few Catholics who moved to Maryland, immigrants to the Chesapeake seem to have been little affected by religious motives. However, religion motivated many of the people who colonized New England. Puritan congregations quickly became key institutions in colonial New England, whereas neither the Church of England nor Roman Catholicism had much impact on the settlers or the early development of the Chesapeake colonies.

Contrasting Regional Religious Patterns

Religion was a constant presence in the lives of pious Puritans, who regularly reassessed the state of their souls. Many devoted themselves to self-examination and Bible study, and families prayed together each day under the guidance of the husband and father. Yet because even the most pious could never be certain that they were numbered among the elect, anxiety about their spiritual state troubled devout Puritans.

Some Puritans (called Congregationalists) wanted to reform the Church of England rather than abandon it. Other groups, known as Separatists, thought the Church of England too corrupt to be salvaged. Only by starting anew could the church be purified, they argued, and so they established their own religious bodies, with membership restricted to the saved, as nearly as they could be identified.

Congregationalists and Separatists

In 1620 some Separatists, many of whom had earlier migrated to Holland in quest of the right to freely practice their religion, received permission from the Virginia Company to colonize the northern part of its territory. That September more than one hundred people, only thirty of them Separatists, set sail from England on the old and crowded *Mayflower*. Two months later they landed in America, but farther north than they had intended. Still, given the lateness of the season, they decided to stay where they were. They established their settlement on a fine harbor and named it Plymouth.

Plymouth

Even before they landed, the Pilgrims had to surmount their first challenge—from the "strangers," or non-Puritans, who sailed with them to America. Because they landed outside the jurisdiction of the Virginia Company, some of the strangers questioned the authority of the colony's leaders. In response, the Mayflower Compact, signed in November 1620 while everyone was still on board the ship, established a "Civil Body Politic" and a rudimentary legal authority for the colony. The settlers elected a governor and at first made all decisions for the colony at town meetings. Later, after more towns had been founded and the population increased, Plymouth, like Virginia and Maryland, created an assembly to which the landowning male settlers elected representatives.

A second challenge facing the Pilgrims was simple survival. Like the Jamestown settlers before them, they were poorly prepared to subsist in their new environment. Winter quickly descended, compounding their difficulties. Only half the *Mayflower*'s passengers were still alive by spring. But, again like the Virginians, the Pilgrims benefited from the political circumstances of nearby Indians.

Pokanokets

The Pokanokets (a branch of the Wampanoags) controlled the area in which the Pilgrims settled. Their villages had suffered terrible losses in the epidemic of 1616–1618, so to protect themselves from the powerful Narragansetts of the southern New England coast, the Pokanokets decided to ally themselves with the newcomers. In the spring of 1621, their leader, Massasoit, signed a treaty with the Pilgrims, and during the colony's first difficult years the Pokanokets supplied the English with essential foodstuffs. The settlers were also assisted by Squanto, a Pokanoket who had earlier been captured by fishermen and taken to Europe, where he learned to speak English. Squanto became the Pilgrims' interpreter and a major source of information about the unfamiliar environment.

Massachusetts Bay Company

Before the 1620s ended, a group of Congregationalist Puritans launched the colonial enterprise that would come to dominate New England. Charles I, who became king in 1625, was more hostile to Puritans than his father had been. In response to Charles's attempts to suppress Puritanism, a group of Congregationalist merchants, concerned about their long-term prospects in England, sent out a body of colonists to Cape Ann (north of Cape Cod) in 1628. The following year the merchants obtained a royal charter, constituting themselves as the Massachusetts Bay Company.

The new joint-stock company quickly attracted the attention of Puritans of the "middling sort," who were becoming increasingly convinced that they would no longer be able to practice their religion freely in their homeland. They remained committed to the goal of reforming the Church of England but concluded that they should pursue that aim in America. In a dramatic move, the Congregationalist merchants boldly decided to transfer the Massachusetts Bay Company's headquarters to New England. The settlers would then be answerable to no one in the mother country and would be able to handle their affairs as they pleased.

Governor John Winthrop

The most important recruit to the new venture was John Winthrop. In October 1629, the Massachusetts Bay Company elected Winthrop as its governor. It fell to Winthrop to organize the initial segment of the great Puritan migration to America. In 1630 more than one thousand English men and women moved to Massachusetts—most of them to Boston, which soon became the largest town in English North America. By 1643 nearly twenty thousand of their compatriots had followed them.

Winthrop's was a transcendent vision. He foresaw in Puritan America a true commonwealth, a community in which each person put the good of the whole ahead of his or her private concerns. Although, as in England, that society would be characterized by social inequality and clear hierarchies of status and power, Winthrop hoped that its members would live according to the precepts of Christian love. Such an ideal was beyond human reach, but it persisted well into the third and fourth generations of the immigrants' descendants.

Ideal of the Covenant

The Puritans expressed their communal ideal chiefly in the doctrine of the covenant. They believed God had made a covenant—that is, an agreement or contract—with them when they were chosen for the special mission to America. In turn, they covenanted with one another, promising to work together toward their goals. The founders of churches and towns in the new land often drafted formal documents setting forth the principles on which these institutions would be based. The same was true of the colonial governments of New England.

The leaders of Massachusetts Bay likewise transformed their original joint-stock company charter into the basis for a covenanted community based on mutual consent. Under pressure from landowning male settlers, they gradually changed the General Court—officially the company's small governing body—into a colonial legislature. They also granted the status of freeman, or voting member of the company, to all property-owning adult male church members. Less than two decades after the first large group of Puritans arrived in Massachusetts Bay, the colony had a functioning system of self-government composed of a governor and a two-house legislature. The General Court also established a judicial system modeled on England's.

The colony's method of distributing land helped to further the communal ideal. Groups of men—often from the same region of England—applied together to the General Court for grants of land on which to establish towns (novel governance units that did not exist in England).

New England Towns

The men receiving such a grant determined how the land would be distributed. First they laid out lots for houses and a church. Then they gave each family parcels of land scattered around the town center: a pasture here, a woodlot there, an arable field elsewhere. Every man obtained land, but the best and largest plots were reserved for the most distinguished among them (including the minister).

Thus New England settlements initially tended to be more compact than those of the Chesapeake. Town centers grew up quickly, developing in three distinctly different ways. Some, chiefly isolated agricultural settlements in the interior, tried to sustain Winthrop's vision of harmonious community life based on diversified family farms. A second group, the coastal towns like Boston and Salem, became bustling seaports. The third category, commercialized agricultural towns, grew up in the Connecticut River valley, where easy water transportation made it possible for farmers to sell surplus goods readily.

When migrants began to move beyond the territorial limits of the Massachusetts Bay colony into Connecticut (1636), New Haven (1638), and New Hampshire (1638), the same pattern of land grants was maintained. (Only Maine, with coastal regions thinly populated by fishermen and their families, deviated from the standard practice.) The migration to the Connecticut valley ended the

Internal Migration

Puritans' relative freedom from clashes with nearby Indians. The first English people in the valley moved there from Massachusetts Bay under the direction of their minister, Thomas Hooker. Although their new settlements were remote from other English towns, the wide river promised ready access to the ocean. The site had just one problem: it fell within the territory controlled by the powerful Pequots.

The Pequots' dominance stemmed from their role as primary middlemen in the trade between New England Indians and the Dutch in New Netherland. The arrival of English settlers signaled the end of the Pequots' power over such regional trading networks, for previously subordinate bands could now trade directly with Europeans. Clashes between Pequots and English colonists began even before the establishment of settlements in the Connecticut valley, but the founding of these settlements tipped the balance toward war. After two English traders were killed (not by Pequots), the English raided a Pequot village. In return, the Pequots attacked the new town of Wethersfield in April 1637, killing nine and capturing two of the colonists. To retaliate, a Massachusetts Bay expedition the following month attacked and burned the main Pequot town on the Mystic River. At least four hundred Pequots, mostly women and children, were slaughtered.

Pequot War

For the next thirty years, the New England Indians accommodated themselves to the spread of European settlement. They traded with the newcomers and sometimes worked for them, but for the most part they resisted acculturation or incorporation into English society. Native Americans persisted in using traditional farming methods. The one European practice they adopted was keeping livestock, for domesticated animals provided excellent sources of meat once the territories where they had earlier hunted had been turned into English farms and wild game had consequently disappeared.

Although the official seal of the Massachusetts Bay colony showed an Indian crying "Come over and help us," most colonists showed little interest in converting the Algonquians to Christianity. Only a few Massachusetts clerics, most notably John Eliot, seriously undertook missionary activities. Eliot insisted that con-

John Eliot and the Praying Towns

Father Claude Chauchetière, a Jesuit in New France, sketched scenes of life in the colony's missions. His drawing of Indian women worshiping at a shrine of the Virgin Mary includes (at the rear) a view of one woman cutting her hair to conform more closely to European fashion. The other female converts show no evidence of having adopted European dress or hairstyles.   (Archives Départmentales de la Gironde, France)

verts reside in towns, farm the land in English fashion, assume English names, wear European-style clothing and shoes, cut their hair, and stop observing a wide range of their own customs. He understandably met with little success. At the peak of Eliot's efforts, only eleven hundred Indians lived in the fourteen "Praying Towns" he established.

The Jesuits' successful missions in New France contrasted sharply with the Puritans' failure to win many converts. Initially, Catholicism had several advantages over Puritanism. The Catholic Church employed beautiful ceremonies, instructed converts that through good works they could help to earn their own salvation, and offered Indian women an inspiring role

Puritan and Jesuit Missions Compared

model—the Virgin Mary. In Montreal and Quebec, communities of nuns taught Indian women and children and ministered to their needs. Furthermore, the few French colonists on the St. Lawrence did not alienate potential converts by encroaching steadily on their lands (as did New Englanders). Perhaps most important, the Jesuits understood that Christian beliefs could be compatible with Native American culture. Unlike Puritans, Jesuits accepted converts who did not wholly adopt European styles of life.

What attracted Indians to these religious ideas? Conversion often alienated the new Christians (both Catholic and Puritan) from their relatives and traditions—a likely outcome that must have caused many potential converts to think twice about making such a commitment. But surely many hoped to use the Europeans' religion as a means of coping with the dramatic changes the intruders had wrought. The combination of disease, alcohol, new trading patterns, and loss of territory disrupted customary ways of life to an unprecedented extent. Shamans had little success in restoring traditional ways. Many Indians must have concluded that the Europeans' own ideas could provide the key to survival in the new circumstances.

Life in New England

 New England's colonizers adopted lifestyles that differed considerably from those of both their Indian neighbors and their European counterparts in the Chesapeake. Unlike the Algonquian bands, who usually moved four or five times each year to take full advantage of their environment, English people lived in the same location year-round. And unlike residents of the Chesapeake, New Englanders constructed sturdy dwellings intended to last. They used the same fields again and again, believing it was less arduous to employ manure as fertilizer than to clear new fields every few years. Furthermore, they fenced their croplands to prevent them from being overrun by the cattle, sheep, and hogs that were their chief sources of meat.

Because Puritans commonly moved to America in family groups, the age range in early New England was wide; and because many more women went to New England than to the tobacco colonies, the population

In 1664 an eight-year-old girl, Elizabeth Eggington, became the subject of the earliest known dated New England painting. Her mother died shortly after her birth, perhaps because of childbirth complications; the girl's rich clothing, elaborate jewelry, and feather fan not only reveal her family's wealth but also suggest that she was much loved by her father, a merchant and ship captain. Unfortunately, Elizabeth died about the time this portrait was painted; perhaps it—like some other colonial portraits of young children—was actually painted after her death to memorialize her.   (Wadsworth Atheneum, Hartford. Gift of Mrs. Walter H. Clark. Endowed by her daughter, Mrs. Thomas L. Archibald)

size, the demographic characteristics of New England made families there numerous and large. If seventeenth-century Chesapeake women could expect to rear one to three healthy children, New England women could anticipate raising five to seven.

The nature of the population had other major implications for family life. New England in effect created grandparents, since in England people rarely lived long enough to know their children's children. And whereas early Chesapeake parents commonly died before their children married, New England parents exercised a good deal of control over their adult offspring. Young men could not marry without acreage to cultivate, and because of the communal land-grant system they had to depend on their fathers to give them that land. Daughters, too, needed a dowry of household goods supplied by their parents. Yet parents relied on their children's labor and often were reluctant to see them marry and start their own households. These needs at times led to considerable conflict between the generations.

Another important difference lay in the influence of religion on New Englanders' lives. Puritans controlled their governments. Congregationalism was the only officially recognized religion; except in Rhode Island, founded by dissenters from Massachusetts, members of other sects had no freedom of worship. Some non-Puritans voted in town meetings, but in Massachusetts Bay and New Haven, church membership was a prerequisite for voting in colony elections. All the early colonies taxed residents to build meetinghouses and pay ministers' salaries, but Puritan colonies in particular attempted to enforce strict codes of moral conduct. Colonists there were frequently tried for drunkenness, card playing, even idleness. Couples who had sex during their engagement—as revealed by the birth of a baby less than nine months after their wedding—were fined and publicly humiliated. More harshly treated were men—and a handful of women—who engaged in behaviors that today would be called homosexual. (The term did not then exist.) Several men who had consenting same-sex relationships were hanged.

Puritans objected to secular interference in religious affairs but at the same time expected the church to influence the conduct of politics and the affairs of society. They also believed that the state was obliged to

Impact of Religion

New England Families

could immediately begin to reproduce itself. Also, New England was much healthier than the Chesapeake. Once Puritan settlements had survived the difficult first few years and established self-sufficiency in foodstuffs, New England proved to be even healthier than the mother country. Adult male migrants to the Chesapeake lost about ten years from their English life expectancy of fifty to fifty-five years; their Massachusetts counterparts gained five or more years. Consequently, while Chesapeake population patterns gave rise to families that were few in number and small in

support and protect the one true church—theirs. As a result, although they came to America seeking freedom to worship as they pleased, they saw no contradiction in refusing to grant that freedom to others.

Roger Williams, a Separatist who immigrated to Massachusetts Bay in 1631, quickly ran afoul of that Puritan orthodoxy. He told his fellow settlers that the king of England had no right to grant them land already occupied by Indians, that church and state should be kept entirely separate, and that Puritans should not impose their religious beliefs on others. Because Puritan leaders placed a heavy emphasis on achieving consensus in both religion and politics, they could not long tolerate significant dissent.

Roger Williams

Banished from Massachusetts, Williams journeyed in early 1636 to the head of Narragansett Bay, where he founded the town of Providence. Because Williams believed that government should not interfere with religion in any way, Providence and other towns in what became Rhode Island adopted a policy of tolerating all religions, including Judaism. Along with Maryland (see page 30), the tiny colony founded by Williams thus presaged the religious freedom that eventually became one of the hallmarks of the United States.

A dissenter who presented a more sustained challenge to Massachusetts Bay colony leaders was Mistress Anne Marbury Hutchinson. A skilled medical practitioner popular with the women of Boston, she greatly admired John Cotton, a minister who stressed the covenant of grace, or God's free gift of salvation to unworthy human beings. By contrast, most Massachusetts clerics emphasized the need for Puritans to engage in good works, study, and reflection in preparation for receiving God's grace. After spreading her ideas for months in the context of childbed gatherings—when no men were present—Hutchinson began holding women's meetings in her home to discuss Cotton's sermons. She emphasized the covenant of grace more than did Cotton himself, and she even adopted the belief that the elect could be assured of salvation and communicate directly with God. Such ideas had an immense appeal for Puritans. Anne Hutchinson offered them certainty of salvation instead of a state of constant anxiety.

Anne Hutchinson

Hutchinson's ideas posed a dangerous threat to Puritan orthodoxy. So in November 1637, officials charged her with having maligned the colony's ministers by accusing them of preaching the covenant of works (the idea that one could earn salvation). For two days Hutchinson defended herself cleverly, but then she boldly declared that God had spoken to her directly, explaining that he would curse the Puritans' descendants for generations if they harmed her. That assertion assured her banishment to Rhode Island.

The authorities in Massachusetts Bay perceived Anne Hutchinson as doubly dangerous to the existing order: she threatened not only religious orthodoxy but also traditional gender roles. Puritans believed in the equality before God of all souls, including those of women, but they considered actual women (as distinct from their spiritual selves) inferior to men. Christians had long followed Saint Paul's dictum that women should keep silent in church and be submissive to their husbands. Hutchinson did neither. A minister told her bluntly: "You have stept out of your place, you have rather bine a Husband than a Wife and a preacher than a Hearer; and a Magistrate than a Subject."

The New England authorities' reaction to Anne Hutchinson reveals the depth of their adherence to European gender-role concepts. To them, an orderly society required the submission of wives to husbands as well as the obedience of subjects to rulers.

Summary

 By the middle of the seventeenth century, Europeans had unquestionably come to North America to stay, a fact that signaled major changes for the peoples of both hemispheres. Europeans killed Indians with their weapons and diseases and had but limited success in converting them to European religions. Contacts with the Native Americans taught Europeans to eat new foods, speak new languages, and recognize—however reluctantly—the persistence of other cultural patterns. The prosperity and even survival of many of the European colonies depended heavily on the cultivation of American crops (maize and tobacco) and an Asian crop (sugar), thus attesting to the importance of post-Columbian ecological change.

In America, Spaniards reaped the benefits of their South and Central American gold and silver mines, while French people earned their primary profits from Indian trade (in Canada) and cultivating sugar cane (in the Caribbean). Sugar also enriched the Portuguese. The Dutch, by contrast, concentrated on commerce—trading in furs and sugar as well as carrying human cargoes of enslaved Africans to South America and the Caribbean. Of these nations, only France and Spain went beyond the economic relationships they established with native peoples to attempt to Christianize them.

Although the English colonies, too, at first sought to rely on trade, they quickly took another form altogether when many English people of the "middling sort" decided to migrate to North America. To a greater extent than their European counterparts, the English transferred the society and politics of their homeland to a new environment. Their sheer numbers, coupled with their need for vast quantities of land on which to grow their crops and raise their livestock, inevitably brought them into conflict with their Native American neighbors. Ultimately New England and the Chesapeake would also be drawn into the increasingly fierce rivalries besetting the European powers. Those rivalries would continue to affect Americans of all races until after France and England in the mid-eighteenth century fought the greatest war yet known, and the Anglo-American colonies had won their independence.

LEGACY FOR A PEOPLE AND A NATION

The Foxwoods Casino and the Mashantucket Pequot Museum

In 1992 the Mashantucket Pequots opened the enormously successful Foxwoods Resort Casino on their small reservation in southeastern Connecticut. Just six years later, in August 1998, the Pequots proudly inaugurated a new museum (built with some of their substantial profits) presenting their people's story. Both developments surprised many Americans, who did not realize that Native Americans still lived in New England.

The existence of the Pequots was particularly startling, because histories had long recorded that the nation was destroyed in the Pequot War of 1637.

Survivors of the Mystic River massacre had regrouped in the Mashantucket swamps, building lives as farmers, laborers, and craftspeople. Some left the area, but a few Pequots remained: the 1910 census, the source today for determining Pequot tribal membership, counted sixty-six residents of a reservation just 213 acres in size. By the 1970s, the residents had been reduced to two, and the state of Connecticut threatened to turn the reservation into a park. But an elder, Elizabeth George, persuaded several hundred people tracing descent from those listed in 1910 to return to live on the reservation. In 1983 the determined Pequots won formal federal recognition, and in turn that allowed them to build the profitable casino, a hotel, and several restaurants, and to begin purchasing more land.

Now the museum introduces the history of the Pequots and of eastern Algonquian peoples to hundreds of thousands of visitors each year. At its heart is a re-creation of a Pequot village as it would have looked shortly before Europeans first arrived on Connecticut's shores, complete with sounds and smells controlled by state-of-the-art computers. Exhibits detail the origins of the Pequot War, and a film narrates the tale of the massacre.

The Pequots' success has helped to embolden other eastern Algonquian nations to reassert publicly their long-suppressed Indian identities. The Pequot people's dedication to preserving their culture and reaffirming their history has created a remarkable legacy for the nation.

For Further Reading, see the Appendix. For Web resources, go to history.college.hmco.com/students.

3

AMERICAN SOCIETIES TAKE SHAPE
1640–1720

The Restoration Colonies
1670–1680: A Decade of Crisis
The Introduction of African Slavery
The Web of Empire and the Atlantic Slave Trade
Enslavement in North America
Colonial Political Development, Imperial Reorganization, and the Witchcraft Crisis

LEGACY FOR A PEOPLE AND A NATION
"Witch Hunts"

The *Seaflower*, Captain Thomas Smith, master, lay at anchor in Boston harbor in early September 1676, awaiting official documents signed by the governors of Massachusetts and Plymouth. Smith expected to sell the cargo in his hold in the West Indies. But that cargo differed from most: it comprised human beings, nearly two hundred "heathen Malefactors—men, women, and Children."

The certificates from the governors explained "To all People" the origins of Captain Smith's human cargo: "Philip an heathen Sachem . . . with others his wicked complices and abettors have treacherously and perfidiously rebelled against" these colonies. "By due and legall procedure" the captives on board the *Seaflower* were "Sentenced & condemned to perpetuall

Servitude." The Pokanoket leader King Philip (called Metacom at birth and later renamed "Philip" by New Englanders) had been killed a month earlier in the war that bore his name. His young son seems to have been sold into slavery, along with many shiploads of Philip's followers.

Only one prominent New Englander objected on moral grounds to the policy of selling the vanquished Algonquians into West Indian slavery. The Reverend John Eliot reminded the authorities that the colonists had a solemn duty to "inlarge the kingdom of Jesus Christ"; "to sell [the Indians] away for slaves, is to hinder the inlargement of his kingdom." If the Indians deserved to die, then "godly governors" should ensure that they died "penitently," rather than depriving them of "all meanes of grace" by selling them as slaves. It was the subversion of God's plan for Massachusetts, not enslavement itself, that concerned Eliot.

The tale of Thomas Smith (see the illustration on page 51) and the *Seaflower*'s human cargo illustrates not only the English colonists' willingness to enslave "heathen" peoples and their increasingly contentious relationship with Native Americans, but also the participation of the mainland colonies in a growing international network. North America, like England itself, was becoming embedded in a worldwide matrix of trade and warfare. The web woven by oceangoing vessels now crisscrossed the globe, carrying European goods to America and Africa, West Indian sugar to New England and Europe, Africans to the Americas, and New England fish and wood products—and occasionally Indian slaves—to the Caribbean.

Three developments shaped life in the mainland English colonies between 1640 and 1720: the introduction of a system of slavery, changes in the colonies' political and economic relationships with England, and escalating conflicts with Indians and other European colonies in North America.

The explosive growth of the slave trade significantly altered the Anglo-American economy. Carrying human cargoes paid off handsomely. At first primarily encompassing Indians and already enslaved Africans from the Caribbean, the trade soon came to focus almost exclusively on cargoes brought to the American mainland directly from Africa. The arrival of large numbers of West African peoples dramatically reshaped colonial society and fueled the international trading system. Moreover, the burgeoning North American economy attracted new attention from colonial administrators in London, who attempted to supervise the American settlements more effectively in order to ensure that the mother country benefited from their economic growth.

Neither English colonists nor London administrators could ignore other peoples living on the North American continent. As the English settlements expanded, they came into violent conflict not only with powerful Indian nations but also with the Dutch, the Spanish, and especially the French. By 1720, war had become an all-too-familiar feature of American life. No longer isolated from each other or from Europe, the people and products of the North American colonies had become integral to the world trading system and inextricably enmeshed in its conflicts. ◼

The Restoration Colonies

In 1642 England erupted into civil war. Disputes over taxation, religion, and other issues led to armed conflict between supporters of the Stuart King Charles I and the Puritan-dominated Parliament. After four years of warfare, Parliament triumphed. Following the execution of Charles I in 1649, the parliamentary army's leader, Oliver Cromwell, assumed control of the government. Yet after Cromwell's death in 1658 Parliament decided to restore the monarchy if Charles I's son and heir would agree to restrictions on his authority. In 1660, Charles II ascended the throne, having promised to support the Church of England and to seek Parliament's consent for any new taxes. Thus ended the tumultuous chapter in English history known as the Interregnum (Latin for "between reigns") or the Commonwealth period.

The English Civil War, the Interregnum, and the reign of Charles II (1660–1685) had far-reaching significance for the Anglo-American colonies. During the Civil War and the Commonwealth period, when Puritans controlled the English government, the migration to New England largely ceased. The subsequent reign of Charles II saw the founding of six of the thirteen colonies that eventually would form the American nation: New York, New Jersey, Pennsylvania (including Delaware), and North and South Carolina (see Map 3.1). All were proprietorships; in each of them, as in Maryland, one man or several men held title to the soil and controlled the government. Charles II gave these vast American holdings as rewards to men who had supported his family during the Civil War. Collectively, these became known as the Restoration colonies because they were created by the restored Stuart monarchy.

Proprietorships

Charles's younger brother James, the duke of York, quickly benefited from his brother's generosity. In 1664, Charles II gave James the region between the Connecticut and Delaware Rivers, including the Hud-

New York

IMPORTANT EVENTS

1642–46	English Civil War
1649	Charles I executed
1651	First Navigation Act passed to regulate colonial trade
1660	Stuarts restored to throne; Charles II becomes king
1663	Carolina chartered
1664	English conquer New Netherland; New York founded New Jersey established
1670s	Marquette, Jolliet, and La Salle explore the Great Lakes and Mississippi valley for France
1675–76	King Philip's War devastates New England
1676	Bacon's Rebellion disrupts Virginia government; Jamestown destroyed
1680–92	Pueblo revolt temporarily drives Spaniards from New Mexico
1681	Pennsylvania chartered
1685	James II becomes king
1686–89	Dominion of New England established, superseding all charters of colonies from Maine to New Jersey
1688–89	James II deposed in Glorious Revolution; William and Mary ascend throne
1689–97	King William's War fought on northern New England frontier
1692	Witchcraft crisis in Salem
1696	Board of Trade and Plantations established to coordinate English colonial administration
1701	Iroquois adopt neutrality policy toward France and England
1702–13	Queen Anne's War fought by French and English
1711–13	Tuscarora War (North Carolina) leads to capture or migration of most Tuscaroras
1715	Yamasee War nearly destroys South Carolina
1718	New Orleans founded in French Louisiana

son valley and Long Island. James immediately organized an invasion fleet. In August James's warships anchored off Manhattan Island and demanded New Netherland's surrender. The colony complied without resistance.

Thus James acquired a heterogeneous possession, which he renamed New York (see Table 3.1). An appreciable minority of English people already lived there, along with sizable numbers of Indians, Africans, and Germans and a smattering of other European peoples. The Dutch West India Company had actively imported slaves into the colony. Indeed, almost one-fifth of Manhattan's approximately fifteen hundred inhabitants were of African descent.

Recognizing the population's diversity, the duke of York's representatives moved cautiously in their efforts to establish English authority. The Duke's Laws, a legal code proclaimed in 1665, at first applied solely to the English settlements on Long Island, only later be-

The Duke's Laws

ing extended to the rest of the colony. Dutch forms of local government were maintained, Dutch land titles confirmed, and Dutch residents allowed to maintain customary legal practices. Each town was permitted to decide which church (Dutch Reformed, Congregational, or Church of England) to support with its tax revenues. Much to the dismay of English residents of the colony, the Duke's Laws made no provision for a representative assembly. Like other Stuarts, James distrusted legislative bodies, and not until 1683 did he agree to the colonists' requests for an elected legislature. The English takeover thus had little immediate effect on the colony. Its population grew slowly, barely reaching eighteen thousand by the time of the first English census in 1698.

A primary reason for New York's slow growth was that in 1664 the duke of York regranted the land between the Hudson and Delaware Rivers—East and

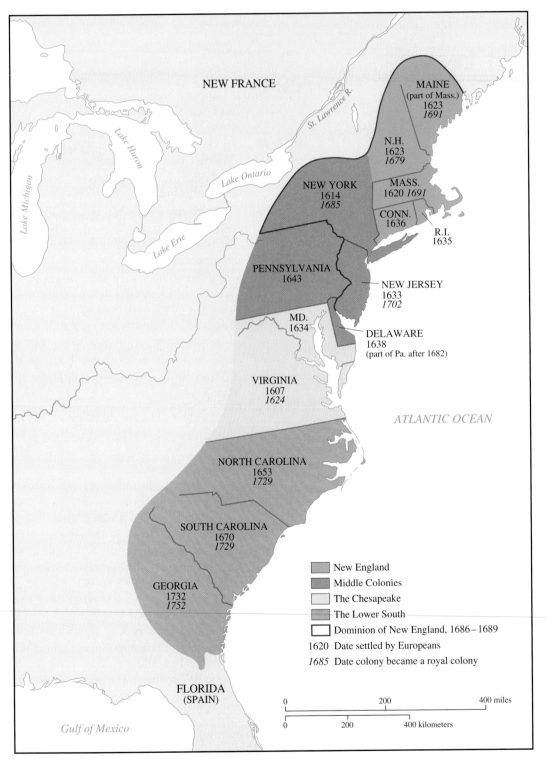

NEW FRANCE

Lake Huron

Lake Michigan

Lake Ontario

Lake Erie

St. Lawrence R.

MAINE
(part of Mass.)
1623
1691

N.H.
1623
1679

NEW YORK
1614
1685

MASS.
1620 *1691*

CONN.
1636

R.I.
1635

PENNSYLVANIA
1643

NEW JERSEY
1633
1702

MD.
1634

DELAWARE
1638
(part of Pa. after 1682)

VIRGINIA
1607
1624

ATLANTIC OCEAN

NORTH CAROLINA
1653
1729

SOUTH CAROLINA
1670
1729

GEORGIA
1732
1752

FLORIDA
(SPAIN)

Gulf of Mexico

New England
Middle Colonies
The Chesapeake
The Lower South
Dominion of New England, 1686–1689
1620 Date settled by Europeans
1685 Date colony became a royal colony

0		200		400 miles
0	200		400 kilometers	

Map 3.1   The Anglo-American Colonies in the Early Eighteenth Century   The colonies' formal boundary lines are deceiving because the western reaches of each colony were still largely unfamiliar to Europeans and because much of the land was still inhabited by Native Americans.

Table 3.1   The Founding of English Colonies in North America, 1664–1681

Colony	Founder(s)	Date	Basis of Economy
New York (formerly New Netherland)	James, duke of York	1664	Farming, fur trading
New Jersey	Sir George Carteret, John Lord Berkeley	1664	Farming
North Carolina	Carolina proprietors	1665	Tobacco, forest products
South Carolina	Carolina proprietors	1670	Rice, indigo
Pennsylvania	William Penn	1681	Farming

Founding of New Jersey

West Jersey—to his friends Sir George Carteret and John Lord Berkeley. That grant deprived New York of much fertile land and hindered its economic growth. Meanwhile, the Jersey proprietors acted rapidly to attract settlers, promising generous land grants, limited freedom of religion, and—without authorization from the Crown—a representative assembly. As a result, New Jersey grew quickly; in 1726, at the time of its first census as a united colony, it had 32,500 inhabitants, only 8,000 fewer than New York.

Within twenty years, Berkeley and Carteret sold their interests in the Jerseys to separate groups of investors. The purchasers of all of Carteret's share (West Jersey) and portions of Berkeley's (East Jersey) were members of the Society of Friends, seeking a refuge from persecution in England. The Society of Friends, also called Quakers, denied the need for intermediaries between individuals and God. They believed that anyone could be saved by the "inner light" and that all people were equal in God's sight. With no formally trained clergy, Quakers allowed anyone, male or female, to speak in meetings or become a "public Friend" and travel to spread God's word. The Quaker message of radical egalitarianism was unwelcome in both England and Puritan New England.

The Quakers obtained their own colony in 1681, when Charles II granted the region between Maryland and New York to his close friend William Penn, a prominent member of the sect. Although Penn held the colony as a personal proprietorship, he saw his province not merely as a source of revenue but also as a

Pennsylvania: A Quaker Haven

haven for persecuted coreligionists. Penn offered land to all comers on liberal terms, promised toleration of all religions (although only Christians were given the vote), guaranteed English liberties such as the right to bail and trial by jury, and pledged to establish a representative assembly. He also publicized the ready availability of land in Pennsylvania throughout Europe.

Penn's activities and the Quakers' attraction to his lands gave rise to a migration whose magnitude equaled the Puritan exodus to New England in the 1630s. By mid-1683, more than three thousand people—among them Welsh, Irish, Dutch, and Germans—had already moved to Pennsylvania, and within five years the population reached twelve thousand. Philadelphia, carefully planned to be the major city in the province, drew merchants and artisans from throughout the English-speaking world, including some with well-established trading connections. Pennsylvania's plentiful and fertile lands soon enabled its residents to begin exporting surplus flour and other foodstuffs to the West Indies. Practically overnight Philadelphia acquired more than two thousand citizens and started to challenge Boston's commercial dominance.

A pacifist with egalitarian principles, Penn attempted to treat Native Americans fairly. He learned to

William Penn's Indian Policy

speak the language of the Delawares (or Lenapes), from whom he purchased tracts of land to sell to European settlers. Penn also established strict regulations for trade and forbade the sale of alcohol to Indians. His policies attracted

William Penn, later the proprietor of Pennsylvania, as he looked during his youth in Ireland. In such pamphlets as the one shown here, Penn spread the word about his new colony to thousands of readers in England and its other colonial possessions.   (Historical Society of Pennsylvania)

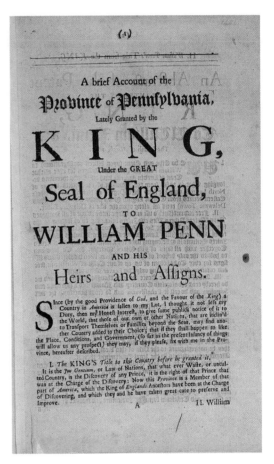

native peoples, who moved to Pennsylvania near the end of the seventeenth century to escape repeated clashes with English colonists. Most important were the Tuscaroras, Shawnees, and Miamis. By a supreme irony, however, the same toleration that attracted Native Americans also brought non-Quaker Europeans who showed little respect for Indian claims to the soil. In effect, Penn's policy was so successful that it caused its own downfall.

The southernmost proprietary colony, granted by Charles II in 1663, encompassed a huge tract of land stretching from the southern boundary of Virginia to Spanish Florida. The area had great strategic importance: a successful English settlement there would prevent the Spaniards from pushing farther north. The proprietors named

Founding of Carolina

their new province Carolina in honor of Charles, whose Latin name was Carolus. The "Fundamental Constitutions of Carolina," which they asked the political philosopher John Locke to draft for them, set forth an elaborate plan for a colony governed by a hierarchy of landholding aristocrats and characterized by a carefully structured distribution of political and economic power.

However, Carolina quickly developed two distinct population centers, which in 1729 split into separate colonies. Virginia planters settled the Albemarle region that became North Carolina. They established a society much like their own, with an economy based on cultivating tobacco and exporting such forest products as pitch, tar, and timber. Because North Carolina lacked a satisfactory harbor, its planters relied on Virginia's ports and merchants to conduct their trade, and the colonies remained tightly linked. The other population center, which eventually formed the core of South Carolina, developed at Charles Town, founded in 1670 near the juncture of the Ashley and Cooper Rivers.

Many of South Carolina's early residents were from Barbados. After unsuccessfully attempting to grow tropical plants, they began to raise corn and herds of cattle, which they sold to Caribbean sugar planters hungry for foodstuffs. They also depended on trade with nearby Indians to supply the only commodity for which they found a ready market in Europe: deerskins, which were almost as valuable as beaver pelts. During the first decade of the eighteenth century, South Carolina exported an average of 54,000 skins annually.

1670–1680: A Decade of Crisis

 As the Restoration colonies were extending the range of English settlement in North America, existing English colonies and French and Spanish settlements in North America faced new crises caused primarily by their changing relationships with America's indigenous peoples. Between 1670 and 1680, New England, Virginia, New France, and New Mexico experienced bitter conflicts as their interests collided with those of America's original inhabitants. All the early colonies changed irrevocably as a result.

In the mid-1670s, Louis de Buade de Frontenac, the governor-general of Canada, decided to expand New France's reach to the south and
New France and the Iroquois
west, hoping to establish a trade route to Mexico and to gain direct control of the valuable fur trade on which the prosperity of the colony rested. Accordingly, he encouraged the explorations of Father Jacques Marquette, Louis Jolliet, and Robert Cavelier de La Salle in the Great Lakes and Mississippi valley regions. His goal, however, brought him into conflict with the powerful Iroquois Confederacy, comprising not one Indian nation but five—the Mohawks, Oneidas, Onondagas, Cayugas, and Senecas. (In 1722 the Tuscaroras became the sixth.)

Under the terms of a unique defensive alliance forged early in the sixteenth century, a representative council made decisions of war and peace for the entire Iroquois Confederacy, although each nation still retained some autonomy and could not be forced to comply with a council directive against its will. Before the arrival of Europeans, the Iroquois waged wars primarily to acquire captives to replenish their population. The Europeans' presence created an economic motive for warfare: the desire to dominate the fur trade and to gain unimpeded access to European goods. The war with the Hurons in the 1640s (see page 26) was but the first of a series of conflicts with other Indians known as the Beaver Wars, in which the Iroquois fought to achieve control of the lucrative peltry trade.

In the mid-1670s, as Iroquois dominance grew, the French stepped in, for an Iroquois triumph would have destroyed France's plans to trade directly with western Indians. Over the next twenty years the French launched repeated attacks on Iroquois villages. The English offered little assistance other than weapons to their trading partners. Its people and resources depleted by constant warfare, the Confederacy in 1701 finally negotiated a neutrality treaty with France and other Indians. For the next half-century the Iroquois nations maintained their power through trade and skillful diplomacy rather than warfare.

The wars against the Iroquois initiated in the 1670s were crucial components of French Canada's plan to penetrate the heartland of North America. Unlike the Spaniards,
French Expansion into the Mississippi Valley
French adventurers did not attempt to subjugate the Indians they encountered or to formally claim large territories for France. And by tolerating the French presence, Indians gained access to European goods.

When France decided to strengthen its presence near the Gulf of Mexico by founding New Orleans in 1718—to counter both westward thrusts of the English colonies and eastward moves of the Spanish—the Mississippi posts became the glue of empire (see Map 3.2). At most such sites lived a small military garrison and a priest, surrounded by powerful nations such as the Choctaws, Chickasaws, and Osages. In all the French outposts, the shortage of European women led to interracial unions between French men and Indian women and to the creation of mixed-race people known as *metís*.

In New Mexico, too, events of the 1670s led to a crisis with long-term consequences. Over the years under Spanish domination, the Pueblo peoples had added Christianity to their religious beliefs while still

Map 3.2 Louisiana, c. 1720 By 1720 French forts and settlements dotted the Mississippi River and its tributaries in the interior of North America. Two isolated Spanish outposts were situated near the Gulf of Mexico. (Source: Adapted from *France in America*, by William J. Eccles. Copyright © 1972 by William J. Eccles. Reprinted by permission of HarperCollins Publishers, Inc.)

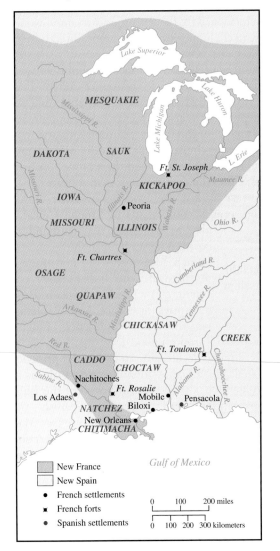

Pope and the Pueblo Revolt

retaining traditional rituals. But decade by decade Franciscans adopted increasingly brutal and violent tactics in order to erase all traces of the native religion. Priests and secular colonists who held *encomiendas* also placed heavy labor demands on the population. In 1680 the Pueblos revolted under the leadership of Popé, a respected shaman, successfully driving the Spaniards out of New Mexico (see Map 3.3). After Spanish authority was restored in 1692, Spanish governors no longer attempted to reduce the Pueblos to bondage or to violate their cultural integrity. The Pueblo revolt of 1680 instigated the most successful and longest-sustained Indian resistance movement in colonial North America.

When the Spanish expanded their territorial claims to the east and north, they followed the same strategy they had adopted in New Mexico, establishing their presence through military outposts and Franciscan missions. The army's role was to maintain order among the subject Indians and to guard the boundaries of the New Spain from possible incursions, especially by the French. The friars concentrated on conversions. By the late eighteenth century, Spain claimed a vast territory that stretched from California (first colonized in 1769) through Texas (settled after 1700) to the Gulf Coast.

Spain's North American Possessions

In the more densely settled English colonies, hostilities developed in the decade of the 1670s over land. In both New England and Virginia—though for different reasons—settlers began to encroach on territories that until then had remained in the hands of Native Americans.

By the 1670s, New England's population had more than tripled to reach approximately seventy thousand. Such a rapid increase placed great pressure on available land. Many members of the third and fourth generations had to migrate—north to New Hampshire or Maine, south to New York or New Jersey, west beyond the Connecticut River—to find sufficient farmland for themselves and their children. Others abandoned agriculture and learned such skills as blacksmithing or carpentry.

Population Pressures in New England

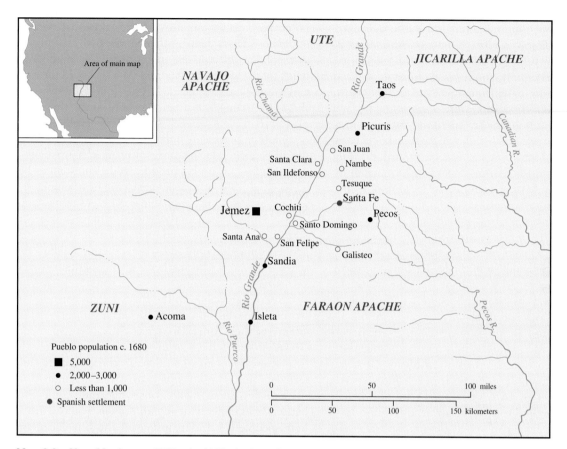

Map 3.3   New Mexico, c. 1680   In 1680, the lone Spanish settlement at Santa Fe was surrounded and vastly outnumbered by the many Pueblo villages nearby.   (Source: Adapted from *Apache, Navaho, and Spaniard,* by Jack D. Forbes. Copyright © 1960 by the University of Oklahoma Press. Used by permission.)

Colonial settlements eventually surrounded the ancestral lands of the Pokanokets (Wampanoags) on Narragansett Bay. The Pokanoket chief, King Philip, troubled by the loss of Pokanoket lands and concerned about the impact of European culture and Christianity on his people, led his warriors in attacks on nearby communities in June 1675. Other Algonquian peoples, among them Nipmucks and Narragansetts, soon joined King Philip's forces. In the fall, the Indian nations jointly attacked settlements in the northern Connecticut River valley. In early 1676, they devastated well-established villages and even attacked Plymouth and Providence. Altogether, the alliance wholly or partially destroyed twenty-five of the ninety Puritan towns and attacked forty others.

King Philip's War

Still, the tide turned in the summer of 1676. The Indian coalition ran short of food and ammunition, and after King Philip's death that August, the alliance crumbled. Many surviving Pokanokets, Nipmucks, and Narragansetts were captured and sold into slavery, and still more died of starvation and disease. New Englanders had broken the power of the coastal tribes. Thereafter the Indians lived in small clusters, subordinated to the colonists and often working as servants or sailors. But the settlers paid a terrible price for their victory: an estimated one-tenth of the able-bodied adult male population was killed or wounded. Proportional to population, it was the most costly conflict in American history.

Not coincidentally, conflict with Indians wracked Virginia at precisely the same time. By the early 1670s,

Bacon's Rebellion

Virginians were eagerly eying the rich lands north of the York River reserved for Native Americans by early treaties. Using as a pretext the July 1675 killing of an English servant by some Doeg Indians, settlers attacked not only the Doegs but also the powerful Susquehannocks. In retaliation, Susquehannock bands raided outlying farms in the winter of 1676. Governor William Berkeley resisted starting a major war. Dissatisfied land-hungry colonists then rallied behind the leadership of a recent immigrant, the wealthy Nathaniel Bacon, who like other new arrivals had found that all the desirable land in settled areas was already claimed by earlier residents.

Berkeley and Bacon soon clashed. After Bacon held members of the House of Burgesses hostage until they authorized him to attack the Indians, Berkeley declared Bacon and his men to be in rebellion. As the chaotic summer of 1676 wore on, Bacon alternately pursued Indians and battled the governor's supporters. In September Bacon marched on Jamestown itself, burning the capital to the ground. But when Bacon died the following month, the rebellion began to collapse. Even so, a new treaty signed in 1677 opened much of the disputed territory to English settlement.

The war, a turning point in Virginia's relationship with nearby Indians, also marked a turning point in the colony's internal race relations. After Bacon's Rebellion, Virginia landowners began to purchase large numbers of imported African slaves for the first time. By 1700 Anglo-Americans in the Chesapeake had irrevocably altered the racial composition of their labor force.

The Introduction of African Slavery

In the 1670s and 1680s, the prosperity of the Chesapeake rested on tobacco, and successful tobacco cultivation depended on an ample labor supply. But fewer and fewer English men and women proved willing to indenture themselves for long terms of service in Maryland and Virginia. That posed a problem for wealthy Chesapeake tobacco growers, whose farms had by then developed into plantations—large enterprises encompassing a number of fields worked by many laborers. Where could they obtain the workers they needed? They found the answer in the Caribbean sugar islands, where since the 1640s planters had eagerly purchased African slaves.

Slavery had been practiced in Europe (although not in England) for centuries. European Christians—

Why African Slavery?

both Catholics and Protestants—believed that enslaving heathen peoples was justifiable in religious terms. Consequently, when Portuguese mariners reached the sub-Saharan African coast and encountered non-Christian societies holding enslaved prisoners of war, they did not hesitate to buy such slaves.

Some were taken to the Iberian Peninsula; others to the Wine Islands. Iberians then exported African slavery to their American possessions, New Spain and Brazil. Because the Catholic Church prevented the formal enslavement of Indians in those domains and free laborers saw no reason to work voluntarily in mines or on sugar plantations when they could earn better wages under easier conditions elsewhere, African bondspeople became mainstays of the Caribbean and Brazilian economies. Sugar planters on English islands, who had the same problems of labor supply as did their French, Dutch, and Spanish counterparts, also purchased slaves.

Yet that slave system—well-established in the West Indies by the mid-1650s—did not immediately take root in the English mainland

Atlantic Creoles in Societies with Slaves

colonies. Before the 1660s, the few residents of African descent on the mainland varied in status: some were free, some indentured, some enslaved. All came from a population that the historian Ira Berlin has termed Atlantic creoles. Often of mixed race, many came to the English colonies from elsewhere in the Americas. Already familiar with Europeans, the Atlantic creoles fitted easily into established niches in the many-faceted hierarchical social structures of the early colonies. Berlin has characterized all the early mainland colonies as "societies with slaves"—that is, societies in which some people were held in perpetual bondage but that did not rely wholly on slave labor. He usefully contrasts such communities with "slave societies," or societies in which slavery served as the fundamental basis of the economy.

The many ambiguities of status in societies with slaves are evident in early laws adopted by the Chesapeake assemblies. In several Virginia statutes the term *Christian* was used to mean "free person"; when at least one slave therefore claimed freedom as a consequence of conversion to Christianity, the House of Burgesses provided (in 1667) that "the blessed sacrament of baptism" would not liberate bondspeople from perpetual servitude. And in 1670 the House of Burgesses declared that "all servants not being christians imported into this colony by shipping shalbe slaves for their lives," but similar servants that "shall come by land" would serve only for a term of years. The awkward phrases attempted to differentiate Africans from Indians; Virginians clearly saw both groups as distinguishable from English people, but expressed those distinctions in terms of religion and geography rather than race.

Yet just a few years later, Chesapeake legislators started to employ racial terminology. As increasing numbers of slaves arrived each year,

The Beginnings of Mainland Slave Societies

first from the Caribbean and then directly from Africa, the majority of the enslaved population changed from acculturated creole to newly imported African. Virginia in 1682 altered its definition of who could be enslaved, declaring bluntly that "Negroes, Moors, Mollatoes or Indians" arriving "by sea or land" could all be held in bondage for life if their "parentage and native country are not christian." Most of the English colonies, even those without many bondspeople, adopted detailed codes to govern slaves' behavior. By 1700 African slavery was firmly established as the basis of the economy in the Chesapeake and South Carolina as well as in the Caribbean. Under Berlin's definition, those colonies had become "slave societies."

English enslavers evidently had few moral qualms about these actions. Few at the time questioned the decision to hold Africans and their descendants in perpetual bondage. Initially the colonists lacked clear conceptual categories defining both "race" and "slave." They developed such categories and their meanings over time, through their experience with the institution of African (and Indian) slavery, which they originally adopted for economic reasons.

Between 1492 and 1770 more Africans than Europeans came to the Americas. Most went to Brazil or the Caribbean: of at least 10 million enslaved people brought to the Americas during the existence of slavery, only about 260,000 by 1775 were imported into the region that later became the United States. This massive trade in human beings is best understood within the context of the Atlantic trading system that developed during the middle years of the seventeenth century.

The Web of Empire and the Atlantic Slave Trade

The elaborate Atlantic economic system is commonly called the triangular trade. In that context, the traffic in slaves from Africa to the Americas has become known as the middle passage because it constituted the middle leg of such a theoretical triangle. But the terms *triangular trade* and *middle passage* fail to convey the complexities of late-seventeenth-century commercial relationships. Trade involving Europe, Africa, and the Americas did not move across the ocean in easily diagrammed patterns. Instead, there existed a complicated web of exchange that inextricably tied the peoples of the Atlantic world together (see Map 3.4).

The traffic in enslaved human beings served as the linchpin of the system. The expanding network of trade between Europe and its colonies was

Atlantic Trading System

fueled by the sale and transport of slaves, the exchange of commodities produced by slave labor, and the need to feed and clothe so many bound laborers. The profits from Chesapeake tobacco and Caribbean and Brazilian sugar sold in Europe paid for both the African laborers who grew these crops and European manufactured goods. The African coastal rulers who ran the entrepots where European slavers acquired their human cargoes received their payment in European manufactures. Europeans purchased slaves from Africa for resale in their colonies and acquired sugar and tobacco from America, in exchange dispatching their manufactures everywhere.

New England had the most complex relationship to the trading system. The region produced only one item England wanted: tall trees to serve as masts for sailing vessels. To buy English manufactures, New Englanders

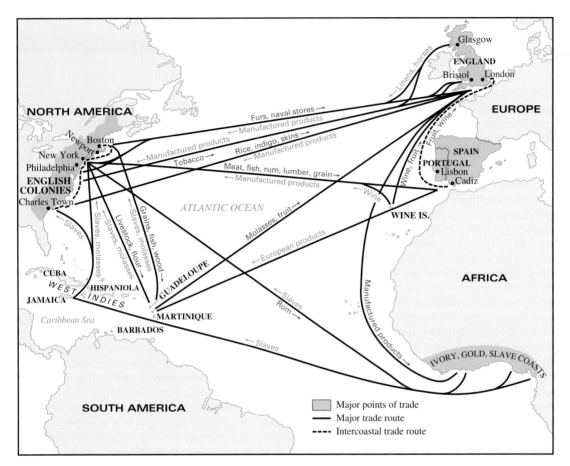

Map 3.4   Atlantic Trade Routes   By the late seventeenth century, an elaborate trade network linked the countries and colonies bordering the Atlantic Ocean. The most valuable commodities exchanged were enslaved people and the products of slave labor.

New England and the Caribbean

therefore needed profits earned elsewhere—the Wine Islands and such English islands as Barbados and St. Kitts. Those islands lacked precisely the items that New England could produce in abundance: cheap food (corn and salt fish) to feed the slaves and wood for barrels to hold wine and molasses (the liquid form in which sugar was shipped). By the late 1640s, New England's economy rested on consumption by slaves and their owners. After the founding of Pennsylvania, New York, and New Jersey, those colonies too participated in the lucrative West Indian trade.

Shopkeepers in the interior of New England and the middle colonies bartered with local farmers for

grains, livestock, and barrel staves, then traded those items to merchants located in port towns. Such merchants then dispatched their ships to the West Indies, where they sailed from island to island, exchanging their cargoes for molasses, fruit, spices, and slaves. Once they had a full load, the ships returned to Boston, Newport, New York, or Philadelphia to dispose of their cargoes. Americans then distilled West Indian molasses into rum, which was shipped to Africa and traded for slaves.

Tying the system together was the voyage that brought Africans to the Americas. That voyage was always traumatic and sometimes fatal. An average of 10 to 20 percent of the newly enslaved died en route. In

The Human Tragedy of the Slave Trade

addition, some slaves died either before the ships left Africa or shortly after their arrival in the Americas. Their European captors also died at high rates, chiefly through exposure to such diseases as yellow fever and malaria, which were endemic to Africa. Just 10 percent of the men sent to run the Royal African Company's forts in Lower Guinea lived to return home to England.

The slave trade had political and economic consequences for the nations of West Africa. Coastal rulers

West Africa and the Slave Trade

served as middlemen, allowing the establishment of permanent slave-trading posts in their territories and supplying resident Europeans with slaves to fill their ships. Such rulers controlled European traders' access to slaves and at the same time controlled inland peoples' access to desirable European goods. The centralizing tendencies of the slave trade helped to create such powerful eighteenth-century kingdoms as Dahomey and Asante.

The trade in human beings did not uniformly depopulate Guinea, a fertile and densely inhabited region. Instead, the slave trade affected African societies unevenly. Because they primarily bartered prisoners of war with European slavers, coastal rulers' participation in the trade depended on their involvement in warfare. Because American planters preferred to purchase male slaves, the trade did have an impact on the sex ratio of the remaining population. The relative shortage of men increased work demands on women, encouraged polygyny, and opened new avenues for advancement to women and their children.

This traffic in slaves chiefly benefited Europeans. The European economy, previously oriented toward the Mediterranean and Asia, shifted

European Rivalries and the Slave Trade

its emphasis to the Atlantic Ocean. By the late seventeenth century commerce in slaves and the products of slave labor constituted the basis of the European economic system. The irony of Columbus's discoveries thus became complete: seeking the wealth of Asia, Columbus instead found the lands that—along with Africa—ultimately replaced Asia as the source of European prosperity.

European nations fought bitterly to control the

Captain Thomas Smith, a Boston mariner who transported slaves, painted this remarkable self-portrait in the late seventeenth century. It links his sailing career—illustrated in the background battle scene, which is thought to represent a combined Anglo-Dutch assault on a North African fort in 1670—with his pious Puritan faith. The skull under his hand serves to remind viewers of the brevity of life, which the poem underscores. "Why, why should I the World be minding?" the poet asks, looking forward to a future in which "The Eternall" would "Crowne me (after Grace) with Glory." (Worcester Art Museum, Worcester, Massachusetts, Museum purchase)

slave trade. The Portuguese, who at first dominated the trade, were supplanted by the Dutch in the 1630s. The Dutch, in turn, lost out to the English, who controlled the trade through the Royal African Company, a joint-stock company chartered by Charles II in 1672. Holding a monopoly on all English trade with sub-Saharan Africa, this company transported about 100,000 slaves to England's Caribbean colonies. Yet even before the company's monopoly expired in 1712, many individual English traders had illegally entered the market for slaves. By the early eighteenth century, such independent traders carried most of the Africans imported into the colonies, earning huge profits from successful voyages.

English officials, seeking a new source of revenue after the disruptions of the Civil War, decided to tap into the profits produced by the expanding Atlantic trading system. Chesapeake tobacco and West Indian sugar had obvious value, but other colonial products also had considerable potential. Additional tax revenues could put England back on a sound financial footing, and English merchants wanted to ensure that they—not their Dutch rivals—reaped the benefits of trading with English colonies. Parliament accordingly began to draft laws designed to confine the proceeds of the English imperial web of trade primarily to the mother country.

Like other European nations, England based its commercial policy on a series of assumptions about the operations of the world's economic system. Collectively, these assumptions are usually called mercantilism.

Mercantilism

The theory viewed the economic world as a collection of national states, whose governments actively competed for shares of a finite amount of wealth. Each nation sought to become as economically self-sufficient as possible while maintaining a favorable balance of trade with other countries by exporting more than it imported. Colonies were important because they could supply the mother country with valuable raw materials and serve as a market for the mother country's manufactured goods.

Parliament applied mercantilist thinking to the American colonies in laws known as the Navigation Acts. The major acts—passed between 1651 and 1673—established three main principles. First, only English or colonial merchants and ships could engage in trade in the colonies. Second, certain valuable American products could be sold only in the mother country or in other English colonies. At first, these "enumerated" goods included wool, sugar, tobacco, indigo, ginger, and dyes; later acts added rice, naval stores (masts, spars, pitch, tar, and turpentine), copper, and furs to the list. Third, all foreign goods destined for sale in the colonies had to be shipped by way of England, paying English import duties. Some

Navigation Acts

years later, a new series of laws established a fourth principle: the colonies could not export items (such as wool clothing, hats, or iron) that competed with English products.

The Navigation Acts aimed at forcing American trade to center on England. The mother country would benefit from both colonial imports and exports. England had first claim on the most valuable colonial exports, and all foreign imports into the colonies had to pass through England first, enriching its customs revenues in the process. The laws adversely affected some colonies, like those in the West Indies and the Chesapeake, because planters there could not seek new markets for their staple crops. In others, the impact was minimal or even positive. Builders and owners of ships benefited from the monopoly on American trade given to English and colonial merchants. And the northern and middle colonies produced many unenumerated goods (fish and flour, for example) that could be traded directly to foreign buyers as long as they were carried in English or American ships.

The English authorities soon learned that writing mercantilist legislation was far easier than enforcing it. The many harbors of the American coast provided ready havens for smugglers, and colonial officials often looked the other way when illegally imported goods were offered for sale. Consequently, Parliament in 1696 enacted another Navigation Act. This law established in America a number of vice-admiralty courts, which operated without juries. Because American juries tended to favor local smugglers over customs officers, Parliament decided to remove Navigation Act cases from the regular colonial courts.

England took another major step in colonial administration in 1696 by creating the fifteen-member Board of Trade and Plantations, which thereafter served as the chief organ of government concerned with the American colonies. (Previously, no single body had that responsibility.) It gathered information, reviewed Crown appointments in America, scrutinized legislation passed by colonial assemblies, supervised trade policies, and advised successive ministries on colonial issues. Still, the Board of Trade did not have any direct powers of enforcement. It also shared jurisdiction over American affairs not only with the customs service and the navy but also with the

Board of Trade and Plantations

secretary of state for the southern department, the member of the ministry responsible for the colonies. In short, supervision of the American provinces remained decentralized and haphazard.

Enslavement in North America

 Typical slave ships leaving Africa followed the Northeast Trades to the Caribbean before heading north to the Chesapeake. So many Africans were imported into Virginia and Maryland so rapidly that by 1710 people of African descent composed one-fifth of the region's population. Even so, a decade later American-born slaves already outnumbered their African-born counterparts in the Chesapeake, and the native-born continued to grow thereafter as a proportion of the slave population.

Slaves brought from Africa tended to be assigned to outlying parts of the plantations (called quarters), at least until they learned some English and the routines of tobacco cultiva-

Enslavement in the Chesapeake

tion. They often lived in quarters composed of ten to fifteen workers housed together in one or two buildings and supervised by an Anglo-American overseer. Each man was expected to cultivate about two acres of tobacco a year. On Sundays, planters allowed them a day off. Many used that time to cultivate their own gardens or to hunt or fish to supplement their meager diets. Only rarely could they form families because of the scarcity of women among newly imported Africans.

Such slaves usually cost about two and a half times as much as indentured servants, but they repaid the greater investment with a lifetime of service. Planters with enough money could acquire slaves, accumulate wealth, and establish large planta-

Impact of Slavery on the Anglo-American Chesapeake

tions. Other planters could afford neither slaves nor indentured servants, whose cost had risen because of their scarcity. Anglo-American society in the Chesapeake thus became more and more stratified—that is, the gap between rich and poor steadily widened.

Africans who had lived in the Caribbean came with their masters to South Carolina from Barbados in 1670, composing one-quarter to one-third of the early

Enslavement in South Carolina

population. The Barbadian slaveowners quickly discovered that African-born slaves had a variety of skills well suited to the semitropical environment of South Carolina. African-style dugout canoes became the chief means of transportation in the colony, which was crossed by rivers. Fishing nets copied from African models proved more efficient than those of English origin. Africans' skill at killing crocodiles equipped them to handle alligators. Finally, Africans adapted their traditional techniques of cattle herding for use in America. Since meat and hides numbered among the colony's chief exports in its earliest years, Africans contributed significantly to South Carolina's prosperity.

The similarity of the South Carolinian and West African environments, coupled with the large proportion of Africans in the population, ensured that more aspects of West African culture survived in that colony than elsewhere on the North American mainland. Only in South Carolina did enslaved parents continue to give their children African names; only there did a dialect develop that combined English words with African terms. (Known as Gullah, it has survived to the present day in isolated areas.) African skills remained useful, so techniques lost in other regions when the migrant generation died were instead passed down to the migrants' children. And in South Carolina African women became the primary petty traders, dominating the markets of Charles Town as they did those of Guinea.

The importation of large numbers of Africans coincided with the successful introduction of rice as a staple crop in South Carolina. Eng-

Rice and Indigo

lish people knew little about the techniques of growing and processing rice, but people from Africa's Rice Coast (see page 8) had spent their lives working with the crop. It seems likely that the Africans' expertise assisted their English masters in cultivating the crop profitably. Slaves on rice plantations were each expected to cultivate three to four acres of rice a year and to grow part of their own food. A universally adopted task system of predefined work assignments provided that after bondspeople had finished their set "tasks" for the day, they could then relax or work in their own garden plots or on other projects. Experienced slaves could often complete their tasks by early afternoon;

after that, as on Sundays, their masters had no legitimate claim on their time.

When South Carolina developed a second staple crop, its planters too used the task system and drew on slaves' specialized skills. Indigo was much prized in Europe as a source of blue dye for cloth. In the early 1740s, Eliza Lucas, a young woman managing her father's plantations, began to experiment with indigo cultivation. Drawing on the knowledge of slaves and overseers from the West Indies, she developed the planting and processing techniques later adopted throughout the colony. Indigo grew on high ground, and rice was planted in low-lying swamps; rice and indigo also had different growing seasons. Thus the two crops complemented each other.

Among the many people held in slavery in both the Carolinas were Indians. In South Carolina a wide-spread traffic in Indian slaves devel-

Indian Enslavement in North and South Carolina

oped, as some Indian nations (for example, the Creeks and the Tuscaroras) sold their captives to the colonists, who either retained them or exported them to other colonies. There are no reliable statistics on the extent of the trade in Indian slaves, but in 1708 they composed 14 percent of the South Carolina population.

Bitter conflicts between North Carolina settlers and indigenous peoples produced not only Indian slaves but also mass migrations. In 1711 the Tuscaroras, an Iroquoian people, attacked a Swiss-German settlement at New Bern that had expropriated their lands without payment. Because the Tuscaroras had been avid slavers, their Algonquian neighbors took the opportunity to settle old scores, joining with the English colonists to defeat their enemy in a bloody two-year war. In the end, more than a thousand Tuscaroras were themselves sold into slavery, and the remnants of the group drifted northward, where they joined the Iroquois Confederacy.

The slave trade's abuses led as well to another Indian war in South Carolina. Colonial traders were well known for cheating Native Americans, physically abusing them, and selling friendly peoples into slavery.

Yamasee War

In the spring and summer of 1715, the Yamasees, aided by Creeks and others, retaliated by attacking English settlements. Refugees by the

hundreds streamed into Charles Town; the Creek-Yamasee offensive came close to driving the colonists from South Carolina. But reinforcements arrived from the north and the Cherokees joined the English settlers to fight the Creeks, their ancient foes. In the end, the Creeks were forced to retreat to villages in the west and the Yamasees moved south into Florida, seeking refuge among the Spanish.

Indian or African slavery was never of great importance in the economy of Spain's North American territories. But as slavery took

Slaves in Spanish North America

deeper root in South Carolina, Florida officials in 1693 offered freedom to fugitives who would convert to Catholicism. Hundreds of South Carolina runaways took advantage of the offer. Many settled in a town founded for them near St. Augustine, Gracia Real de Santa Teresa de Mose, which was led by a former slave and militia captain.

In early Louisiana, too, slaves—some Indians, some Atlantic creoles—at first composed only a tiny proportion of the residents. But a

Slaves in French Louisiana

growing European population demanded that the French government supply them with slaves, and in 1719 officials finally acquiesced, dispatching more than six thousand Africans (most from Senegal) over the next decade. The residents failed to develop a successful crop, but they did succeed in angering the Natchez Indians, whose lands they had usurped. In 1729 the Natchez, assisted by newly arrived slaves, attacked northern reaches of the colony, killing more than 10 percent of its European people. The French struck back, slaughtering the Natchez and their enslaved allies.

Atlantic creoles from the West Indies composed almost all the bondspeople in the northern mainland colonies. Some bondspeople resided

Enslavement in the North

in urban areas, especially New York, which in 1700 had a larger black population than any other mainland city. Women tended to work as domestic servants, men as unskilled laborers, and one or two slaves were commonly found in the households of well-to-do families. Some slaves also worked for ironmasters at forges and foundries.

Colonial Political Development, Imperial Reorganization, and the Witchcraft Crisis

 The crises of the 1670s in Virginia and New England focused the attention of reform-minded English officials on the mainland colonies. In the early 1680s, London administrators confronted a bewildering array of colonial governments. Massachusetts Bay (including Maine) functioned under its original charter. Neighboring Connecticut (including a formerly separate New Haven) and Rhode Island were granted charters by Charles II in 1662 and 1663, respectively, but Plymouth remained autonomous. Virginia, a royal colony, was joined in that status by New Hampshire in 1679, and by New York in 1685 when its proprietor ascended the throne as James II. All the other mainland settlements were proprietorships.

Still, the colonies shared characteristic political structures. A governor and a legislature ruled most. In

Colonial Political Structures

New England, property-holding men or the legislature elected the governors; in other regions, the king or the proprietor appointed such leaders. A council, either elected or appointed, advised the governor on matters of policy and sometimes served as the colony's highest court. The councils also served as upper houses of colonial legislatures. At first, councilors and elected representatives met jointly to debate and adopt laws affecting the colony. But as time passed, the fundamental differences between the two legislative groups' purposes and constituencies led them to separate. Thus developed the two-house legislature still used in all but one of the states.

Meanwhile, local political institutions took shape. In New England, elected selectmen initially governed the towns, but by the end of the seventeenth century, town meetings—held at least annually and attended by most free adult male residents—handled matters of local concern. In the Chesapeake colonies and both of the Carolinas, appointed justices of the peace ran local governments. At first the same was true in Pennsylvania, but by the early eighteenth century elected county officials began to take over some government func-

tions. And in New York, local elections were the rule even before the establishment of the colonial assembly in 1683.

By late in the seventeenth century, therefore, Anglo-American colonists everywhere had become accustomed to exercising a considerable degree of local political autonomy.

A Tradition of Autonomy Challenged

Free adult men who owned more than a minimum amount of property (which varied from place to place) expected to have an influential voice in their governments—and especially in decisions concerning taxation. Such expectations clashed with those of the monarch. James II and his successors sought to bring order to the apparently chaotic state of colonial administration by tightening the reins of government and by reducing the colonies' political autonomy. Administrators began to chip away at the privileges granted in colonial charters and to reclaim proprietorships for the Crown. Massachusetts (1691), New Jersey (1702), and the Carolinas (1729) all became royal colonies. The charters of Rhode Island, Connecticut, Maryland, and Pennsylvania were temporarily suspended but ultimately were restored to their original status.

The most drastic reordering of colonial administration targeted Puritan New England, which English

Dominion of New England

officials saw as a hotbed of smuggling. Moreover, Puritans refused to allow freedom of religion to non-Congregationalists and insisted on maintaining laws that ran counter to English practice. New England thus seemed an appropriate place to exert English authority with greater vigor. The charters of all the colonies from New Jersey to Maine were revoked, and a Dominion of New England was established in 1686. Sir Edmund Andros, the governor, had immense power: Parliament dissolved all the assemblies, and Andros needed only the consent of an appointed council to make laws and levy taxes.

New Englanders endured Andros's autocratic rule for more than two years. Then came the dramatic news that James II had been over-

Glorious Revolution in America

thrown in a bloodless coup known as the Glorious Revolution and had been replaced on the throne by his daughter Mary and her husband, the

Dutch prince William of Orange. James II had levied taxes without parliamentary approval and announced his conversion to Roman Catholicism. When Parliament offered the throne to the Protestants William and Mary, the Glorious Revolution affirmed the supremacy of both Parliament and Protestantism.

Upon hearing the news, New Englanders jailed Andros and his associates, proclaimed their loyalty to William and Mary, and wrote to England for instructions about the form of government they should adopt. In other colonies, too, the Glorious Revolution emboldened people for revolt. In Maryland the Protestant Association overturned the government of the Catholic proprietor, and in New York a militia officer of German origin, Jacob Leisler, assumed control of the government. Like the New Englanders, the Maryland and New York rebels allied themselves with the supporters of William and Mary. They saw themselves as carrying out the colonial phase of the English revolt against Stuart absolutism.

William and Mary, however, like James II, believed that England should exercise tighter control over its unruly American possessions. Consequently, only the Maryland rebellion received royal sanction, primarily because of its anti-Catholic thrust. In New York, Jacob Leisler was hanged for treason, and Massachusetts (including the formerly independent jurisdiction of Plymouth) became a royal colony with an appointed governor. The province retained its town meeting system of local government and continued to elect its council, but the new charter issued in 1691 eliminated the traditional religious test for voting and officeholding. A parish of the Church of England appeared in the heart of Boston.

A war with the French and their Algonquian allies compounded New England's difficulties in a time of political upheaval and economic un-

King William's War

certainty. King Louis XIV of France allied himself with the deposed James II, and England declared war on France in 1689. In Europe, this conflict was known as the War of the League of Augsburg, but the colonists called it King William's War. Indian attacks wholly or partially destroyed several English settlements in New York, Maine, and New Hampshire. Even the Peace of Ryswick (1697), which formally ended the war in Europe, failed to bring much of a respite from warfare to the northern frontiers.

Early in the conflict, New Englanders understandably feared a repetition of the devastation of King

The 1692 Witchcraft Crisis

Philip's War. For eight months in 1692, witchcraft accusations spread like wildfire through the rural communities of northeastern Massachusetts— precisely the area most threatened by the Indian attacks in southern Maine and New Hampshire. Like their contemporaries elsewhere, seventeenth-century New Englanders believed in the existence of witches. Before 1689, about one hundred New Englanders, most of them middle-aged women, had been charged with practicing witchcraft, chiefly by neighbors who attributed their misfortunes to the suspected witch. Only a few of the accused were convicted, and fewer still were executed.

The crisis began in late February 1692 when several girls in Salem Village (an outlying precinct of the bustling port of Salem) accused some older female neighbors of having bewitched them. Soon other accusers chimed in, many of them female domestic servants who had been orphaned in the Indian attacks on Maine. (One, for example, lost her grandparents in King Philip's War and her parents in King William's War.) These traumatized young women, perhaps the most powerless people in a region apparently powerless to affect its fate, offered their fellow New Englanders a compelling explanation for the seemingly endless chain of troubles afflicting them: their province was under direct attack not only by the Indians but also by the Devil and his allied witches. Before the crisis ended, fourteen women and five men were hanged, one man was pressed to death with heavy stones, and more than one hundred fifty people were jailed, some for many months.

In October, the crisis ended rapidly. Several prominent ministers expressed serious reservations about the validity of the evidence used to convict many of the accused, and opponents of the trials gained the ear of the new governor, publicly blaming the crisis on "hysterical girls."

With the end of the witchcraft crisis and with colonial administration firmly in place, Massachusetts and the rest of the English colonies in America accommodated themselves to the new imperial order. Most

Accommodation to Empire colonists resented the alien officials who arrived in America determined to implement the policies of king and Parliament, but they adjusted to their demands and to the trade restrictions imposed by the Navigation Acts. They fought another imperial war—the War of the Spanish Succession, or Queen Anne's War—from 1702 to 1713 without enduring the stresses of the first. Colonists who allied themselves with royal government received patronage in the form of offices and land grants and composed "court parties" that supported English officials. Others, who were either less fortunate in their friends or more principled in defense of colonial autonomy, made up the opposition, or "country" interest. By the end of the first quarter of the eighteenth century, most men in both groups had been born in America and were members of elite families.

Summary

 The eighty years from 1640 to 1720 established the basic economic and political patterns that were to structure subsequent changes in mainland colonial society. In 1640 just two isolated centers of English population, New England and the Chesapeake, existed along the seaboard, along with the tiny Dutch colony of New Netherland. In 1720 nearly the entire east coast of North America was in English hands, and Indian control east of the Appalachian Mountains had been broken. What had been an immigrant population was now mostly American-born, except for the many African-born people in South Carolina; economies originally based on trade in fur and skins had become far more complex and more closely linked with the mother country; and a wide variety of political structures had been reshaped into a more uniform pattern. Yet at the same time the introduction of large-scale slavery into the Chesapeake and the Carolinas differentiated those societies from the societies of the colonies to the north. They had become true slave societies, heavily reliant on a system of perpetual servitude. Although the northern colonies were not slave societies, their economies rested on profits derived from the Atlantic trading system, the key element of which was traffic in enslaved humans.

Meanwhile, from a small outpost in Santa Fe, New Mexico, and missions in Florida, the Spanish had expanded their influence throughout the Gulf Coast region and as far north as California. The French had come to dominate the length of the Mississippi River and the entire Great Lakes region. Both groups of colonists lived near Indian nations and depended on the indigenous people's labor and goodwill. The extensive Spanish and French presence to the south and west of the English settlements meant that future conflicts among the European powers in North America were nearly inevitable.

By 1720, the essential elements of the imperial administrative structure that would govern the English colonies until 1775 had been put firmly in place. The regional economic systems originating in the late seventeenth and early eighteenth centuries also continued to dominate North American life until after independence had been won. And Anglo-Americans had developed the commitment to autonomous local government that later would lead them into conflict with Parliament and the king.

LEGACY FOR A PEOPLE AND A NATION
"Witch Hunts"

Since the eighteenth century, the Salem witchcraft crisis has fascinated Americans. Movies, plays, television shows, and innumerable books and articles have examined the episode from a variety of perspectives. Some authors attribute the hysteria to food poisoning; some accuse a "girl gang" of delinquents of making mischief because they were repressed by Puritan culture (or perhaps because they were simply bored); one historian even asserts that there really *were* practicing witches in Salem in 1692.

Yet everyone today agrees that what happened in northeastern Massachusetts in 1692 was a "witch hunt." Americans now regularly apply that term to a misguided search for scapegoats on whom to blame assorted troubles. Because seventeenth-century people believed that those who allied themselves with the Devil could thereby gain the power to harm individuals and animals, they singled out some of their unpopular neighbors as witches and jailed or hanged them.

During the last half-century, some Americans have likewise used the term "witch hunt" as a code phrase to describe searches for scapegoats of various sorts. In the early 1950s it was employed with respect to Senator Joseph McCarthy's campaign against reputed Communists in the State Department and the Army, and the House Un-American Activities Committee's attack on prominent stage and film professionals for Communist Party membership. Democrats charged that the 1999 impeachment of President Bill Clinton by the House of Representatives was yet another "witch hunt." Always the term is used pejoratively by opponents of the actions in question, for because of the episode commonly known simply as "Salem," the phrase "witch hunt" has become an American byword for unjustified and unfair legal proceedings that appear to result from communal hysteria. The accusations of 1692 so shook the people of northeastern Massachusetts that they left an indelible legacy for the nation.

For Further Reading, see the Appendix. For Web resources, go to history.college.hmco.com/students.

A WORLD TRANSFORMED
1720–1770

Population Growth and Ethnic Diversity
Economic Growth and Development
Colonial Cultures
Colonial Families
Politics: Stability and Crisis in British America
A Crisis in Religion
LEGACY FOR A PEOPLE AND A NATION
Anti-Immigrant Sentiments

aturina, a free black resident of New Orleans, awoke with a start at 3 A.M. on June 2 to the shouts of her neighbor, a slave woman named Louisa. "Maturina, someone has stolen your hens!" Louisa yelled. Leaping from her bed, Maturina ran to investigate. She knew where to look for missing chickens. At dawn, Maturina, her son, and her brother Nicolas went to the city market on the levee (riverbank), where they encountered a man carrying three fowls they recognized as hers. By threatening him with prosecution, they extracted the information that he had purchased the hens from a French grocer named La Rochelle. So the three confronted La Rochelle at his hut. Under their questioning, the grocer reluctantly admitted that "it was a negro who had brought them to him to sell." Suspicious, Maturina searched La Rochelle's own hut, roust-

ing out the thief, who was hiding within. When brought before the authorities, the thief proved to be Juan, a runaway slave from the countryside.

That much of the action in the story took place on the Mississippi River levee is not surprising. In the mid-eighteenth century, the crude market centered there was a focal point of New Orleans. To the levee came Indian traders, French and German farmers, free and enslaved Africans—all intent on buying and selling.

The lively markets in New Orleans and Anglo-American cities such as Boston, Charles Town, and Philadelphia illuminate several key themes of colonial development in the mid-eighteenth century: population growth, ethnic diversity, the increasing importance of colonial urban centers, the creation of an urban elite that purchased food and clothing from other colonists, rising levels of consumption for all social ranks, and the new significance of internal markets. In the French and English mainland colonies, exports continued to dominate the economy. Yet expanding local populations demanded greater quantities and types of goods, and Europe could not supply all those needs. Therefore, colonists came increasingly to depend on exploiting and consuming their own resources.

Ethnic diversity was especially pronounced in the small colonial cities, but even the countryside attracted settlers from many European nations. The Spanish Borderlands and rural New England were the only exceptions; they attracted few new immigrants of any description. The middle and southern Anglo-American

"Rachel Weeping," by Charles Willson Peale, conveys as few other colonial portraits can the affection of eighteenth-century parents for their children and the grief they felt when those children died (as was so often the case) at an early age. Peale movingly revealed his wife's sorrow at the death of their daughter; thus his painting helps to refute the interpretation—advanced by some historians—that high levels of infant mortality led colonists to avoid becoming too attached to their young children. (Philadelphia Museum of Art, the Barra Foundation)

colonies attracted by far the largest number of newcomers. Their arrival not only swelled the population but also altered political balances and affected the religious climate by introducing new sects.

Intermarried networks of wealthy families developed in each of Europe's American possessions by the 1760s. These well-off, educated colonists participated in transatlantic intellectual life, such as the movement known as the Enlightenment, whereas many colonists of the "lesser sort" could neither read nor write. The elites lived in comfortable houses and enjoyed leisure-time activities. In contrast, most colonists, whether free or enslaved, struggled just to survive. Such divisions were most pronounced in British America, where by 1750 the social and economic distance among different ranks of Anglo-Americans had widened noticeably.

In 1720 much of the North American continent still fell under Indian control. By 1770, settlements of Europeans and Africans ruled by Great Britain filled almost all of the region between the Appalachian Mountains and the Atlantic Ocean; and the British, thanks to their victory over France in the Seven Years War (see pages 77–80), dominated the extensive system of rivers and lakes running through the heart of the continent. Spanish missions extended in a great arc from present-day northern California to the Gulf Coast. Such geographical, economic, and social changes transformed the character of Europe's North American possessions. ■

Population Growth and Ethnic Diversity

 Dramatic population growth characterized the English mainland colonies in the eighteenth century. Only about 250,000 European and African Americans resided in the colonies in 1700; by 1775, 2.5 million lived there. Such rapid expansion appears even more remarkable when it is compared with the modest changes that occurred in Louisiana, New Mexico, California, and Texas. By the last quarter of the eighteenth century, Texas contained only about 2,500 Spanish residents and California even fewer; the largest Spanish colony, New Mexico, included just 20,000 or so. The total European population of New France was about 70,000 in the 1760s.

Although migration accounted for a considerable share of the growth in English America, most of the

IMPORTANT EVENTS

1720–40 Black population of Chesapeake begins to grow by natural increase, contributing to rise of large plantations

1732 Founding of Georgia

1739 Stono Rebellion (South Carolina) leads to increased white fears of slave revolts

George Whitefield arrives in America; Great Awakening broadens

1739–48 King George's War disrupts American economy

1741 New York City "conspiracy" reflects whites' continuing fears of slave revolts

1760s Baptist congregations take root in Virginia

1760–75 Peak of eighteenth-century European and African migration to English colonies

1765–66 Hudson River land riots pit tenants and squatters against large landlords

1767–69 Regulator movement (South Carolina) tries to establish order in backcountry

1771 North Carolina Regulators defeated by eastern militia at Battle of Alamance

gain resulted from natural increase. Once the difficult early decades of settlement had passed, the American population doubled approximately every twenty-five years. Such a rate of growth, unparalleled in human history until very recent times, had a variety of causes, chief among them women's youthful age at the onset of childbearing. Since married women became pregnant every two or three years, women normally bore five to ten children. Because the colonies were relatively healthful places to live (especially north of Virginia), a large proportion of children who survived infancy reached maturity and began families of their own. As a result, about half of the American population was under sixteen years old in 1775.

Africans (about 260,000) constituted the largest racial or ethnic group that came to the mainland English colonies during the eighteenth

Newcomers from Africa and Europe

century. In the slaveholding societies of South America and the Caribbean, a surplus of males over females and appallingly high mortality rates meant that only a large, continuing flow of enslaved Africans could maintain the captive work force at constant levels. South Carolina, where rice cultivation was difficult and unhealthy and where planters preferred to purchase men, bore some resemblance to such colonies. But in the Chesapeake the number of black residents grew especially rapidly because the new imports were added to an African American population that began to sustain itself through natural increase after 1740.

The offspring of slaves were also slaves, whereas the children of servants were free. The consequences of this important difference between enslaved and indentured labor first became clear when the enslaved population began to grow primarily through natural increase. A planter who owned adult female slaves could watch the size of his labor force increase steadily through the births of their children. Not coincidentally, the first truly large Chesapeake plantations appeared in the 1740s.

In addition to the new group of Africans, about 585,000 Europeans moved to North America during the eighteenth century, most of them after 1730. Late in the seventeenth century, English officials decided to recruit foreign Protestant colonists in order to prevent further large-scale emigration from England itself, for, influenced by mercantilist thought, they had come to regard a large, industrious population at home as an asset rather than a liability. Thus they ordered the deportation to the colonies of "undesirables"—convicts and Jacobite rebels (supporters of the deposed Stuart monarchs)—but otherwise discouraged emigration. They offered foreign Protestants free lands and religious toleration, even financing the passage of some groups.

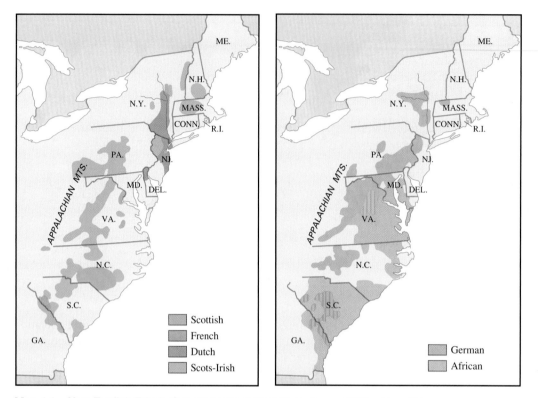

Map 4.1   Non-English Ethnic Groups in the British Colonies, c. 1775   Non-African immigrants arriving in the years after 1720 were pushed to the peripheries of settlement, as is shown by these maps. Scottish, Scots-Irish, French, and German newcomers had to move to the frontiers. The Dutch remained where they had originally settled in the seventeenth century. Africans were concentrated in coastal plantation regions.

One of the largest groups of immigrants—nearly 150,000—came from Ireland or Scotland. About 66,000 Scots-Irish descendants of Presbyterian Scots who had settled in the north of Ireland during the seventeenth century joined some 35,000 people who came directly to America from Scotland. Another 43,000 migrated from southern Ireland. Fleeing economic distress and (in Ireland) religious discrimination, they hoped to obtain their own land. Scots, Irish, and Scots-Irish immigrants usually landed in Philadelphia. They moved west and south, settling chiefly in Pennsylvania, Maryland, Virginia, and the Carolinas. Frequently unable to afford any acreage, they settled illegally on land belonging to Indians, land speculators, or colonial governments.

Migrants from Germany numbered about 85,000.

Scots-Irish, Germans, and Scots

Most emigrated from the Rhineland between 1730 and 1755, also usually arriving in Philadelphia. Late in the century they and their descendants accounted for one-third of Pennsylvania's residents. But many other Germans moved west and then south along the eastern slopes of the Appalachian Mountains, eventually finding homes in western Maryland and Virginia. Others landed in Charles Town and settled in the southern interior. The Germans belonged to a wide variety of Protestant sects and therefore added to the already substantial religious diversity of Pennsylvania and New York.

The most concentrated period of immigration to the colonies fell between 1760 and 1775. Tough economic times in Germany and the British Isles led many to decide to seek a better life in America; simultaneously, the slave trade burgeoned. In those fifteen years alone more than 220,000 persons arrived—nearly 10 percent of the entire population of British North America in 1775. Late-arriving free immigrants had little choice but to remain in the cities or move to the edges of settlement; land elsewhere was fully occupied (see Map 4.1).

Because of these migration patterns and the concentration of slaveholding in the South, half the colonial population south of New England had non-English origins by 1775.

Maintaining Ethnic Identities

Whether the migrants assimilated readily into Anglo-American culture depended on patterns of settlement, the size of the group, and the strength of the migrants' ties to their common culture. For example, the Huguenots—French Protestants who fled religious persecution in their homeland after 1685—settled in tiny enclaves in American cities but were unable to sustain either their language or their religious practices. By contrast, the equally small group of colonial Jews maintained a distinct identity. In a few cities—notably New York and Newport, Rhode Island—they established synagogues and worked actively to preserve their culture. As a general rule, members of the larger groups of migrants (Germans, Irish, and Scots) found it easier to sustain Old World ways.

Recognizing the benefits of keeping other racial and ethnic groups divided, the English elites on occasion deliberately fostered ethnic antagonisms. When the targets of these policies were European migrants, the elites hoped to maintain their political and economic power. When they targeted Indians and Africans, as in South Carolina, the stakes were considerably higher. South Carolinians of English origin, a minority of the population, wanted to prevent Indians and Africans from making common cause against them. To keep slaves from running away to join the Indians, Anglo-Americans hired Indians as slave catchers. To keep Indians from trusting Africans, slaves were employed as soldiers in Indian wars.

The elites probably would have preferred to ignore the English colonies' growing racial and ethnic diversity, but they could not do so for long and still maintain their power. When such men decided to lead a revolution in the 1770s, they recognized that they needed the support of non-English Americans. Quite deliberately, they began to speak of "the rights of man," rather than "English liberties," when they sought recruits for their cause.

Economic Growth and Development

 The dramatic increase in the population of Anglo America served as one of the few sources of stability for the colonial economy, which was primarily driven by the vagaries of international markets. A comparison to French and Spanish America reveals significant differences. The population and economy of New Spain's Borderlands both stagnated. The isolated settlements produced few items for export (notably, hides and skins, most obtained through trade with Indians). French Canada exported large quantities of furs and fish, but monopolistic trade practices ensured that most of the profits ended up in the home country. The Louisiana colony required substantial government subsidies to survive, despite its active internal trade and some agricultural exports. Of France's American possessions, only the Caribbean islands flourished economically.

In British North America, by contrast, each year the rising population generated ever-greater demands for goods and services, which led to

Overview of the Anglo-American Economy

the development of small-scale colonial manufacturing and a complex network of internal trade. As the area of settlement expanded, roads, bridges, mills, and stores were built to serve the new communities, and a lively coastal trade developed. Ships involved in the coastal trade not only collected goods for export and distributed imports but also sold items made in America. The colonies thus began to move away from their earlier pattern of near total dependence on Europe for manufactured goods. The largest indigenous industry was iron making; by 1775, American furnaces and forges produced more iron than did England itself.

The major energizing, yet destabilizing, influence on the colonial economy nevertheless remained foreign trade. Colonial prosperity still depended heavily on overseas demand for American products like tobacco, rice, indigo, fish, and barrel staves. The sale of such items earned the colonists the credit they needed to purchase English and European imports. If demand for American exports slowed, the colonists' income dropped and so did their ability to buy imported goods.

Despite fluctuations, the economy slowly grew during the eighteenth century. That growth produced better standards of living for all property-owning Americans. In the first two decades of the century, households began to acquire amenities such as chairs and earthenware dishes. Diet also improved as trading networks brought access to more varied foodstuffs. Thus the colonists became consumers, in the sense that for the first time they could make choices among a wide variety of products and also could afford to buy items not absolutely essential for survival and subsistence.

Growth of Consumption

Yet the benefits of economic growth were unevenly distributed: wealthy Americans improved their position relative to other colonists. The native-born elite families who dominated American political, economic, and social life by 1750 had begun the century with sufficient capital to take advantage of the changes caused by population growth. They were the urban merchants, the large landowners, the slave traders, and the owners of rum distilleries. Their rise helped to make the social and economic structure of mid-eighteenth-century America more stratified than before.

New arrivals did not have the opportunities for advancement that had greeted their predecessors. Even so, there seems to have been relatively little severe poverty among free settlers in rural areas, where over 90 percent of the colonists lived. But in the cities, families of urban laborers lived on the edge of destitution. In Philadelphia, for instance, a male laborer's average annual earnings fell short of the amount needed to supply his family with the bare necessities. Even in a good year, his wife or children had to do wage work; in a bad year, the family could be reduced to beggary. By the 1760s public urban poor-relief systems were overwhelmed with applicants for assistance, and some cities began to build workhouses or almshouses to shelter the growing number of poor people.

Urban Poverty

Within this overall picture, it is important to distinguish among the various regions: New England, the middle colonies (Pennsylvania, New York, and New Jersey), the Chesapeake (including North Carolina), and the Lower South (South Carolina and Georgia). Each region of the colonies had its own economic rhythm derived from the nature of its export trade.

In New England, three elements combined to influence economic development: the nature of the landscape, New England's leadership in colonial shipping, and the impact of imperial wars. New England's poor soil did not produce surpluses other than livestock, so wood products constituted important salable commodities. Farms were worked primarily by family members; the region had relatively few hired laborers. It also had the lowest average wealth per freeholder in the colonies. But New England had many wealthy men: merchants and professionals whose income was drawn from trade with the West Indies.

Boston, by the 1730s a major shipbuilding center, soon felt the effects when warfare between European powers resumed in 1739. British vessels clashed with Spanish ships in the Caribbean, setting off a conflict that became known in America as King George's War. Nominally the war (called the War of the Austrian Succession in Europe) concerned who would sit on the Austrian throne. At first, the war had a positive impact on Boston's economy. New England privateers seized enemy shipping, and area merchants profited from military supply contracts.

New England and King George's War

But New England suffered heavy losses of manpower in Caribbean battles and forays against Canada. In 1745 the most successful and expensive expedition captured the French fortress of Louisbourg (in modern Nova Scotia), which guarded the sea-lanes leading to New France. Afterward, though, Massachusetts had to levy heavy taxes on its residents to pay for the costly effort, and Boston was left with unprecedented numbers of widows and children on its relief rolls. The boom in shipbuilding ended when the war did, and taxes remained high. As a final blow to the colony, Britain gave Louisbourg back to France in the Treaty of Aix-la-Chapelle (1748).

King George's War and its aftermath affected the middle colonies more positively because of the greater fertility of the soil in New York and Pennsylvania, where commercial farming prevailed. With the outbreak of hostilities, the middle colonies were able to profit from the wartime demand for grain and meat, especially in the West Indies. After the war, poor grain harvests

Prosperity of the Middle Colonies

in Europe caused flour prices to rise rapidly. Philadelphia and New York became leaders in the foodstuffs trade, but Boston, lacking a fertile hinterland, found its economy stagnating.

Increased European demand for grain had a significant impact on the Chesapeake as well. After 1745, some Chesapeake planters began to convert tobacco fields to wheat and corn. By diversifying their crops, they could avoid dependency on one product for their income. Tobacco still ruled, but the conversion to grain cultivation brought about the first significant change in Chesapeake settlement patterns by encouraging the development of port towns (like Baltimore) to house the merchants who marketed the new products.

Change in the Chesapeake

Like the Chesapeake, the Lower South depended on staple crops and an enslaved labor force, but in contrast to tobacco prices, which rose slowly through the middle decades of the century, rice prices climbed steeply, doubling by the late 1730s, primarily because of heavy demand for rice in southern Europe. After Parliament removed rice from the list of enumerated products in 1730, South Carolinians did what colonial tobacco planters could never do: trade directly with continental Europe. But dependence on European sales had its drawbacks. King George's War in 1739, for instance, disrupted trade, causing a decade-long depression in South Carolina. Still, prosperity returned by the 1760s. Indeed, the Lower South experienced more rapid economic growth in that period than did the other regions of the colonies. Partly as a result, it had the highest average wealth per freeholder in Anglo America by the time of the American Revolution.

Trade and the Lower South

Closely linked to South Carolina geographically, demographically, and economically was the newest colony on the mainland, Georgia, chartered in 1732 as a haven for English debtors. Its founder, James Oglethorpe, envisioned Georgia as a garrison province peopled by sturdy farmers who would defend the southern flank of English settlement against Spanish Florida, and so its charter prohibited slavery. But Carolina rice planters successfully won the removal of the restriction in 1751. Thereafter, they es-

Georgia

sentially invaded Georgia, which—despite remaining politically independent and becoming a royal colony in 1752—developed into a rice-planting slave society resembling South Carolina.

The differing economic impact of King George's War on the English mainland colonies points up a crucial fact about those colonies: they did not compose a unified whole. Although linked economically into regions, they had few political or social ties beyond or even within those regions. Despite the growing coastal trade, the individual colonies' economic fortunes depended not on their neighbors in America but rather on the shifting markets of Europe and the West Indies.

Colonial Cultures

A seventeenth-century resident of England's American possessions miraculously transported to 1750 would have been surprised by what one historian has termed "the refinement of America." Wealthy colonists spent their money ostentatiously. Most notably, they built large houses containing rooms specifically designed for such forms of socializing as dancing, cardplaying, or drinking tea. Sufficiently well-off to enjoy "leisure" time, they attended concerts and the theater, gambled at horse races, and played billiards and other games. They also cultivated polite manners. Elite families in New Mexico, Louisiana, and Quebec also set themselves off from the "lesser sort."

Men from such families prided themselves not only on their possessions and on their positions in the colonial political, social, and economic hierarchy, but also on their level of education and their intellectual connections to Europe. Many had been tutored by private teachers; some even attended college in Europe or America. (Harvard, the first colonial college, was founded in 1636.) In the seventeenth century, studies focused heavily on ancient languages and theology. But by the mid-eighteenth century, colleges broadened their curricula to include courses on mathematics, the natural sciences, law, and medicine. Accordingly, young men from elite or upwardly mobile families enrolled in college to study for careers other than the ministry. American women were mostly excluded from advanced education.

Education

The intellectual current known as the Enlightenment deeply affected the learned clergymen who headed colonial colleges and their students. Around the middle of the seventeenth century, some European thinkers began to analyze nature in an effort to determine the laws that govern the universe. They employed experimentation and abstract reasoning to discover general principles behind phenomena such as the motions of planets and stars, the behavior of falling objects, and the characteristics of light and sound. Above all, Enlightenment philosophers emphasized acquiring knowledge through reason.

The Enlightenment

The Enlightenment had an enormous impact on educated, well-to-do people in Europe and America. It supplied them with a common vocabulary and a unified view of the world, through which they endeavored to make sense of God's orderly creation. Thus American naturalists like John and William Bartram supplied European scientists with information about New World plants and animals so that they could be included in newly formulated universal classification systems. A prime example of America's participation in the Enlightenment was Benjamin Franklin, who retired from a successful printing business in 1748 when he was just forty-two, thereafter devoting himself to scientific experimentation and public service. His *Experiments and Observations on Electricity* (1751) established the terminology and basic theory of electricity still used today.

The Enlightenment had its greatest impact on the lives of ordinary Americans through advances in medicine—specifically, the treatment of smallpox. The Reverend Cotton Mather, a prominent Puritan cleric, read in a British publication about the benefits of inoculation (deliberately infecting a person with a mild case of a disease) as a protection against smallpox. When Boston in 1720–1721 suffered a major smallpox epidemic, Mather urged the adoption of inoculation despite fierce opposition from the city's leading physician. Mortality rates eventually supported Mather—of those inoculated, just 3 percent died; of others, 15 percent. Enlightenment science thus provided colonial Americans with a means of preventing the greatest killer disease of all.

Enlightenment rationalism affected politics as well as science. John Locke's *Two Treatises of Government*

Contract Theory of Government

(1691) challenged previous concepts of a divinely sanctioned political order. Men created governments and so could alter them, Locke declared. A ruler who broke his contract with the people and failed to protect their rights could legitimately be ousted from power by peaceful—or even violent—means. Government should aim at the good of the people. A proper political order could prevent the rise of tyrants; God's natural laws governed even the power of monarchs.

The world in which such ideas were discussed was that of the few, not the many. Most residents of North America did not know how to read or write, and books were scarce and expensive. No colony required children to attend school; European American youngsters who learned to read usually did so in their own homes. A few months at a private "dame school" run by a literate local widow might complete their education by teaching them the basics of writing and simple arithmetic. Few Americans other than some Church of England missionaries in the South tried to teach enslaved children even the rudiments. And only the most zealous Indian converts learned Europeans' literacy skills.

Oral Cultures

Thus the cultures of colonial North America were primarily oral, communal, and—at least through the first half of the eighteenth century— intensely local. Different areas developed divergent cultural traditions, and racial and ethnic variations heightened those differences. Public rituals served as the chief means through which the colonists forged their cultural identities.

Religious Rituals

Attendance at church was perhaps the most important such ritual. In Congregational (Puritan) churches, church leaders assigned seating to reflect standing in the community. By the mid-eighteenth century, wealthy men and their wives sat in privately owned pews; their children, servants, and the less fortunate sat in sex-segregated fashion at the rear or sides of the church. In eighteenth-century Virginia, seating in Church of England parishes also conformed to the local status hierarchy. In Quebec city, formal processions of men into the parish church celebrated Catholic feast days; each participant's rank determined his placement in the procession. By contrast, Quaker meetinghouses in Pennsylvania and elsewhere used an egalitarian but sex-segregated seating system.

Civic Rituals

Communal culture also centered on the civic sphere. In New England, colonial governments proclaimed official days of thanksgiving and days of fasting and prayer. Everyone was expected to participate in the public rituals held in churches on such occasions. Monthly militia musters (known as training days) also brought the community together, since all able-bodied men between the ages of sixteen and sixty participated in the militia. In the Chesapeake, important cultural rituals occurred on court and election days. When the county court met, men came from miles around to file suits, appear as witnesses, serve as jurors, or observe the goings-on. Attendance at court functioned as a method of civic education; from watching the proceedings, men learned what behavior their neighbors expected of them.

Everywhere in colonial North America, the public punishment of criminals served not just to humiliate the offender but also to remind the community of proper standards of behavior. Public hangings and whippings expressed the community's outrage about crimes. Penalties often shamed miscreants in especially appropriate ways. When a New Mexico man assaulted his father-in-law, he was directed not merely to pay medical expenses but also to kneel before him and to beg his forgiveness publicly, in front of the entire community.

Rituals of Consumption

The wide availability of consumer goods after the early years of the eighteenth century fostered new rituals centered on consumption. The rituals began with the acquisition of desirable and often nonessential items. By 1750 specialized shops selling nonessentials had proliferated in cities such as Boston, New York, Philadelphia, and New Orleans, and even small and medium-size towns had one or two retail establishments. A colonist with money to spend would set aside time to "go shopping," a novel and pleasurable activity. The purchase of a desired object—for example, a ceramic bowl or a mirror—marked only the beginning of consumption rituals.

Consumers would then deploy their purchases in an appropriate manner: hanging the mirror promi-

nently on a wall of the house, displaying the bowl on a table or sideboard. Individual colonists took pleasure in owning lovely objects, but they also could take pride in displaying their acquisitions publicly to kin and neighbors.

Importance of Tea

Tea drinking played an especially important role in Anglo-American consumption rituals. From early in the eighteenth century, households with aspirations to genteel status sought to acquire the items necessary for the proper consumption of tea: not just pots and cups but also strainers, sugar tongs, bowls, and even special tables. Because of its cost, tea served as a crucial marker of status. Although poor households also consumed tea, they could not afford the fancy equipment used by their better-off neighbors.

Rituals on the "Middle Ground"

Other sorts of rituals allowed the disparate cultures of colonial North America to interact with one another. Particularly important rituals developed on what the historian Richard White has termed the "middle ground"—that is, the psychological and geographical space in which Indians and Europeans encountered each other.

When Europeans sought to trade with Indians, they came into contact with an indigenous system of exchange that stressed gift giving rather than formalized buying and selling. Although French and English traders complained constantly about the need to present Indians with gifts prior to negotiating for furs and skins, successful bargaining required such a step. Over time, an appropriate ritual developed. A European trader arriving at a village would give gifts (cloth, rum, gunpowder, and other items) to Indian hunters. Eventually, those gifts would be reciprocated. To the detriment of Indian societies, rum became a crucial component of these intercultural trading rituals. Traders soon concluded that drunken Indians would sell their furs more cheaply.

Intercultural rituals also developed to deal with murders. Europeans sought to punish, perhaps even kill, a murderer. To Indians, such "eye for an eye" revenge was just one of many possible responses to murder. Compensation could also be accomplished by capturing someone who could take the dead person's place or by "covering the dead"—providing the family of the deceased with goods that compensated for the loss. Eventually, the French and the Algonquians in particular evolved an elaborate ritual for handling frontier murders—a ritual that encompassed elements of both societies' traditions: murders were investigated and murderers identified, but by mutual agreement deaths were usually "covered" by trade goods rather than by blood revenge.

Colonial Families

 Families (rather than individuals) constituted the basic units of colonial society. People living together as families, commonly under the direction of a marital pair, were everywhere the chief mechanisms for both production and consumption. Yet family forms and structures varied widely in the mainland colonies, and not all were headed by couples.

As Europeans consolidated their hold on the North American continent during the first three-quarters of the eighteenth century, Native Americans had to adapt to novel circumstances. Bands that had been reduced in numbers by disease and warfare recombined into new units; for example, the group later known as the Catawbas emerged in the 1730s in the western Carolinas from the fragmentary remains of several earlier Indian nations. Likewise, Indian family forms were reshaped under pressure from European secular and religious authorities. Whereas many Indian societies had permitted easy divorce, Christian missionaries frowned on such practices; and those societies that had allowed polygynous marriages (including New England Algonquians) redefined such relationships, designating one wife as "legitimate" and others as "concubines."

Indian Families

Continued high mortality rates created Indian societies in which extended kin took on new importance, for when parents died, relatives assumed child-rearing responsibilities. Furthermore, European dominance meant that Indians could no longer pursue traditional modes of subsistence. That in turn altered family life. In New England, for instance, Algonquian husbands and wives often could not live together, for adults supported themselves by working separately for Anglo-Americans (perhaps wives as domestic servants, hus-

bands as sailors). And in New Mexico, detribalized Navajos, Pueblos, and Apaches employed as servants by Spanish settlers clustered in the small towns of the Borderlands. Known collectively as *genizaros*, they lost contact with Indian cultures.

Wherever the population contained relatively few European women, sexual liaisons occurred between European men and Indian women. The resulting mixed-race population of *mestizos* and *métis* worked as a familial "middle ground" to ease other cultural interactions. In New France and the Anglo-American backcountry, such families frequently resided in Indian villages and were enmeshed in trading networks; often, children of these unions became prominent leaders of Native American societies. By contrast, in the Spanish Borderlands the offspring of Europeans and *genizaros* were treated as degraded individuals.

Mixed-Race Families

Eighteenth-century Anglo-Americans used the word *family* to mean all the people who occupied one household (including any resident servants or slaves). Family life among the many European migrants to North America was far more stable than that among Indian and *mestizo* peoples. European men or their widows headed households considerably larger than American families today. Typical households were nuclear—that is, they included only parents and children. The head of the household represented it to the outside world, managing the finances and holding legal authority over the rest of the family, including his servants or slaves.

European American Families

In English, French, and Spanish America alike, the vast majority of European families supported themselves through agriculture. The scale and nature of the work varied: the production of indigo in Louisiana required different sorts of labor from subsistence farming in New England or cattle ranching in Texas. As in other societies, household tasks were allocated by sex.

The mistress took responsibility for what Anglo-Americans called "indoor affairs." She and her female helpers prepared food, cleaned the house, did laundry, and often made clothing. Preparing food alone involved planting and cultivating a garden, harvesting and preserving vegetables, salting and smoking meat, drying apples and pressing cider, milking cows and making butter and cheese, not to mention cooking and baking. The head of the household and his male helpers were responsible for "outdoor affairs." They planted and cultivated the fields, built fences, chopped wood for the fireplace, harvested and marketed crops, cared for livestock, and butchered cattle and hogs to provide the household with meat.

Most African American families lived as components of European American households. More than 95 percent of colonial African Americans were held in perpetual bondage.

African American Families

Although many African Americans lived on farms with only one or two other slaves, others had the experience of living and working in a largely black setting. In South Carolina, a majority of the population was of African origin; in Georgia, about half; and in the Chesapeake, 40 percent.

The setting in which African Americans lived determined the shape of their family lives. In the North, the scarcity of other blacks often made it difficult for bondspeople to form stable family units. In the Chesapeake, men and women who regarded themselves as married (slaves could not legally wed) frequently lived on different quarters or even on different plantations. Children generally resided with their mothers, seeing their fathers only on Sundays. On large Carolina and Georgia rice plantations, however, enslaved couples usually lived together with their children.

Because all the English colonies legally permitted slavery, bondspeople had few options if they considered running away. Some recently

Running Away and Other Forms of Resistance

arrived Africans stole boats to try to return home or ran off in groups to frontier regions to join the Indians or to establish independent communities. Among American-born slaves, family ties strongly affected such decisions. South Carolina planters soon learned, as one wrote, that slaves "love their families dearly and none runs away from the other." Thus many owners sought to keep families together for purely practical reasons.

Although colonial slaves rarely rebelled collectively, they often resisted enslavement in other ways. Bondspeople uniformly rejected any attempts by their owners to commandeer their labor on Sundays without compensation. Extended-kin groups protested excessive punishment of relatives and sought to live near each other. The links that developed among African

One of the few extant depictions of a mixed-race family in eighteenth-century North America, by the Mexican artist Miguel Cabrera, 1763. The Spanish father and Indian mother have produced a *mestiza* daughter. Families such as this would have been frequently seen in New Mexico as well.   (Private Collection)

American families who had lived on the same plantation for several generations served as insurance against the uncertainties of existence under slavery. If parents and children were separated by sale, other relatives could help with child rearing and similar tasks. Among African Americans, just as among Indians, the extended family thus served a more important function than it did among European Americans.

Most slave families managed to carve out a small measure of autonomy, especially in their working and spiritual lives. Enslaved Muslims often clung to their Islamic faith. Some African Americans preserved traditional beliefs; others converted to Christianity, finding comfort in the assurance that all people would be free and equal in heaven. South Carolina and Georgia slaves jealously guarded their customary ability to control their own time after the completion of their "tasks." Late in the century, some Chesapeake planters with a surplus of laborers began to hire out slaves to others, often allowing the workers to keep a small part of their earnings. Such accumulated property could buy desired goods or serve as a legacy for children.

Just as African and European Americans lived together on plantations, so too both groups were found side by side in cities. (Indeed, in 1760s Philadelphia one-fifth of the work force was enslaved, and by 1775 blacks composed nearly 15 percent of the population of New York City.) Yet colonial cities were nothing but large towns by today's standards. In 1750 the largest, Boston, had just seventeen thousand inhabitants. Life in the cities differed considerably

Life in the Cities

from that in rural areas. City dwellers everywhere purchased foodstuffs and wood at markets and cloth in shops instead of laboriously producing such items themselves. They also had much more contact with the world beyond their own homes than did their rural counterparts.

By the 1750s, most major cities had at least one weekly newspaper that printed the latest "advices from London," news from other English colonies, and local reports. Newspapers were available at taverns and inns, so people who could not afford to buy them could catch up on the news. Even illiterates could do so, since literate customers often read the papers aloud. Contact with the outside world, however, had its drawbacks. Sailors sometimes brought exotic and deadly diseases into port.

In 1713 the colony of Massachusetts constructed its impressive State House in Boston. Here met the assembly and the council. The solidity and imposing nature of the building must have symbolized for its users the increasing consolidation of power in the hands of the Massachusetts legislature.   (The Bostonian Society)

Politics: Stability and Crisis in British America

 In the first decades of the eighteenth century, Anglo-American political life exhibited a new stability. By then, most residents of the mainland had been born in America. Men from genteel families dominated the political structures in each province, for voters (free male property holders) tended to defer to their well-educated "betters."

Throughout the Anglo-American colonies, political leaders sought to increase the powers of elected assemblies relative to the powers of the governors and other appointed officials. Assemblies began to claim privileges associated with the British House of Commons, such as the rights to initiate all tax legislation and to control the militia. The assemblies also developed effective ways of influencing British appointees, especially by threatening to withhold their salaries. In some colonies (Virginia and South Carolina, for example), elite members of the assemblies usually presented a united front to royal officials, but in others (such as New York), they fought among themselves long and bitterly. To win hotly contested elections, New York's genteel leaders began to appeal to "the people," competing openly for the votes of ordinary voters. Yet in 1733 that same New York government imprisoned a newspaper editor, John Peter Zenger, who had too vigorously criticized its actions. Defending Zenger against the charge of "seditious libel," his lawyer argued that the truth could not be defamatory, thus helping to establish a free-press principle now found in American law.

Rise of the Assemblies

Eighteenth-century assemblies bore little resemblance to twentieth-first-century state legislatures. Only on rare occasions did they formulate new policies or pass laws of real importance. Members of the assemblies saw themselves as defenders rather than initiators. In their minds, their primary function was to prevent governors from imposing oppressive taxes.

By midcentury, politically aware colonists commonly linked their own governmental structures to Great Britain's balance of king, lords, and commons—a combination thought to produce a stable polity. Drawing rough analogies, political leaders equated their governors with the monarch, their councils with the aristocracy, and their assemblies with the House of Commons. All three were believed essential to good government, but Americans did not regard them with the same degree of approval. They viewed governors and appointed councils as potential threats to colonial freedoms. They saw the assemblies, however, as the people's protectors. And in turn the assemblies regarded themselves as representatives of the people.

Interpretations of the Assemblies

Again, though, such beliefs should not be equated with modern practice. The assemblies, firmly controlled by dominant families whose members were reelected year after year, rarely responded to the concerns of their poorer constituents. Although settlements continually expanded, assemblies failed to reapportion themselves to provide adequate representation for newer communities—a lack of action that led to serious grievances among frontier dwellers. The colonial ideal of the assembly as the defender of the people's liberties must therefore be distinguished from the colonial reality: the most dearly defended were the wealthy colonists, particularly the assembly members themselves.

At midcentury, the political structures that had stabilized in a period of relative calm confronted a series of crises. None affected all the mainland provinces, but no colony escaped wholly untouched. The crises of various descriptions exposed the internal tensions building in the pluralistic American society. Most important, they demonstrated that the political accommodations arrived at in the aftermath of the Glorious Revolution were no longer adequate to govern Britain's American empire.

One of the first and greatest crises occurred in South Carolina. Early one morning in September 1739, about twenty South Carolina slaves gathered near the Stono River south of Charles Town. Seizing guns and ammunition from a store, they killed the storekeepers and some nearby planter families. Then, joined by other local slaves, they headed toward Florida in hopes of finding refuge. Later that day, however, a troop of militia attacked the fugitives who then numbered about a hundred, killing some a dispersing the rest. More than a week later, most of t

Stono Rebellion

remaining conspirators were captured. Those not killed on the spot were later executed.

The Stono Rebellion shocked slaveholding South Carolinians as well as residents of other colonies.

New York Conspiracy

Throughout British America, laws governing the behavior of African Americans were stiffened. In New York City, the news from the South, coupled with fears of Spain generated by the outbreak of King George's War, set off a reign of terror in the summer of 1741. Hysterical whites suspected a biracial gang of conspiring to foment a slave uprising under the guidance of a supposed priest in the pay of Spain. By summer's end, thirty-one blacks and four whites had been executed for participating in the alleged plot. The Stono Rebellion and the New York conspiracy not only exposed and confirmed Anglo-Americans' deepest fears about the dangers of slaveholding but also revealed the assemblies' inability to prevent serious internal disorder. Events of the next two decades confirmed that pattern.

By midcentury most of the fertile land east of the Appalachians had been purchased or occupied. As a result, conflicts over land titles and

Land Riots in New Jersey and New York

conditions of landholding grew in number and frequency as colonists competed for control of land good for farming. In 1746, for example, some New Jersey farmers clashed violently with agents of the East Jersey proprietors. The proprietors claimed the farmers' land as theirs and demanded annual payments, called quit-rents, for the use of the property.

The most serious land riots of the period took place along the Hudson River in 1765–1766. Late in the seventeenth century, the governor of New York had granted huge tracts in the lower Hudson valley to prominent colonial families. The proprietors in turn divided these estates into small farms, which they rented chiefly to poor Dutch and German migrants. After 1740, though, increasing migration from New [England] brought conflict to the great New York es-[tates. T]he New Englanders did not want to become [tenants. M]any squatted on vacant portions of the [land, and] they rebelled violently when proprietors [evicted th]em in the mid-1760s, resisting success-[fully until] troops finally captured their leaders.

Violent conflicts of a different sort erupted just a few years later in the Carolinas. The Regulator movements of the late 1760s (South Carolina) and early 1770s (North Carolina) pitted backcountry farmers against wealthy eastern planters who controlled the provincial governments. Frontier dwellers, most of Scots-Irish origin, protested their lack of an adequate voice in colonial political affairs. South Carolinians for months policed the countryside in vigilante bands, complaining of lax and biased law enforcement. North Carolinians, who primarily objected to heavy taxation, fought and lost a battle with eastern militiamen at Alamance in 1771.

Regulators in the Carolinas

A Crisis in Religion

The most widespread crisis was religious. From the mid-1730s through the 1760s, waves of religious revivalism—today known collectively as the First Great Awakening—swept over various parts of the colonies, primarily New England (1735–1745) and Virginia (1750s and 1760s). Orthodox Calvinists sought to combat Enlightenment rationalism, which denied innate human depravity. In addition, many recent immigrants and residents of the backcountry had no prior religious affiliation, thus presenting evangelists with a potential source of converts.

The Great Awakening began in New England, where descendants of the Puritan founding generation still composed the membership of Congregational churches. During 1734 and 1735, Reverend Jonathan Edwards, a noted preacher and theologian, noticed a remarkable reaction among the youthful members of his church in Northampton, Massachusetts, to a message based squarely on Calvinist principles. Individuals could attain salvation, Edwards contended, only through recognition of their own depraved natures and the need to surrender completely to God's will. Such surrender came to be seen as a single identifiable moment of conversion.

New England and the Great Awakening

The effects of such conversions remained isolated until 1739, when George Whitefield, a Church of England clergyman, arrived in America. For fifteen

George Whitefield

months he toured the British colonies, preaching to large audiences from Georgia to New England. A gripping orator, Whitefield in effect generated the Great Awakening. Everywhere he traveled, his fame preceded him. Thousands of free and enslaved folk turned out to listen—and to experience conversion. Regular clerics initially welcomed Whitefield and the American-born itinerant evangelist preachers who sprang up to imitate him. Soon, however, many clergymen began to realize that although "revived" religion filled their churches, it ran counter to their own approach to doctrine and matters of faith.

Opposition to the Awakening heightened rapidly, causing congregations to splinter. "Old Lights"—traditional clerics and their followers—engaged in bitter disputes with the "New Light" evangelicals. Already characterized by numerous sects, American Protestantism became further divided as the major denominations split into Old Light and New Light factions and as new evangelical sects—Methodists and Baptists—gained adherents. Paradoxically, the angry fights and the rapid rise in the number of distinct denominations eventually led to an American willingness to tolerate religious diversity.

Most significantly, the Awakening challenged traditional modes of thought, for the revivalists' message directly contested the colonial tradition of deference. Itinerant preachers, only a few of whom were ordained clergymen, claimed they understood the will of God better than did elite college-educated clerics. The Awakening's emphasis on emotion rather than learning undermined the validity of received wisdom, and New Lights questioned not only religious but also social and political orthodoxy.

Impact of the Awakening

Nowhere was this trend more evident than in Virginia, where the Church of England was the established religion. By the 1760s Baptists had gained a secure foothold in Virginia; inevitably, their beliefs and behavior clashed with the way most genteel families lived. They rejected as sinful the horseracing, gambling, and dancing that occupied much of the gentry's leisure time. They addressed one another as "brother" and "sister" regard-

Virginia Baptists

less of social status, and they elected the leaders of their congregations.

Strikingly, almost all the Virginia Baptist congregations included both free and slave members. Church rules applied equally to all members; interracial sexual relationships, divorce, and adultery were off limits to all. In addition, congregations forbade masters from breaking up slave couples through sale. Biracial committees investigated complaints about church members' misbehavior. Churches excommunicated slaves for stealing from their masters, but they also excommunicated masters for physically abusing their slaves. Some Baptists decided that owning slaves was "unrighteous" and freed their bondspeople.

Summary

The Great Awakening thus injected an egalitarian strain into Anglo-American life at midcentury. Although primarily a religious movement, the Awakening had important social and political consequences, calling into question habitual modes of behavior in the secular as well as the religious realm. In short, the Great Awakening helped to break Anglo-Americans' ties to their seventeenth-century origins. So, too, did the newcomers from Germany, Scotland, Ireland, and Africa, who brought their languages, customs, and religions to British North America.

The economic life of all Europe's North American colonies proceeded simultaneously on two levels. On the farms, plantations, and ranches on which most colonists resided, chores dominated people's lives while providing the goods consumed by households and sold in the markets. Simultaneously, the British, French, and Spanish colonies were enmeshed in an international network of trade that affected their local economic circumstances. The bitter wars fought by European nations during the eighteenth century inevitably involved the colonists by creating new opportunities for overseas sales or by disrupting their traditional markets. The volatile colonial economy fluctuated for reasons beyond Americans' control.

A century and a half after European peoples first settled in North America, the colonies mixed diverse European, American, and African traditions into a novel cultural blend that owed much to Europe but just as much to North America itself. Europeans who interacted regularly with peoples of African and American origin—and with Europeans who came from nations other than their own—had to develop new methods of accommodating intercultural differences in addition to creating ties within their own potentially fragmenting communities. Yet at the same time the dominant colonists continued to identify themselves as French, Spanish, or British rather than as Americans. In the 1760s, however, some Anglo-Americans began to realize that their interests did not necessarily coincide with those of Great Britain or its monarch. For the first time, they offered a direct challenge to British authority.

LEGACY FOR A PEOPLE AND A NATION
Anti-Immigrant Sentiments

In 1751 Benjamin Franklin tried to convince British authorities to halt immigration from Germany to the colonies. In *Observations Concerning the Increase of Mankind*, he contended that Britain's mainland possessions would be peopled by natural increase alone, so immigration was unnecessary. Pennsylvania would soon become "a Colony of Aliens," he warned, who would "Germanize us instead of our Anglifying them"; and, he predicted, they "will never adopt our Language or Customs."

Such sentiments have a familiar ring, because policymakers and others today make similar comments about recent arrivals from South and Central America

and Asia. As the twenty-first century opens, the United States is grappling once again with immigration policy. State legislators, members of Congress, the courts, and public interest groups vie over such questions as how many immigrants to admit each year, what services and rights immigrants are entitled to, and how to deal with illegal aliens. Nativist groups argue for new controls on immigration, opposed by immigrants' rights organizations urging more lenient policies.

These current controversies have deep roots in American soil. Ever since the nation's founding, immigration policy has periodically caused vitriolic debates, as Americans argued over the admission of French and Haitian immigrants in the 1790s, Irish immigrants in the 1840s and 1850s, Chinese and Japanese in the 1870s and 1880s, and eastern and southern Europeans around the end of the nineteenth century. Often, these debates ended with the passage of restrictive legislation—for example, Asian exclusion acts in the 1880s and laws setting immigration quotas for foreign countries in 1921 and 1924 (not removed until 1965).

Franklin's fears have thus been voiced repeatedly during the intervening 250 years. The first substantial wave of foreign immigration to the colonies and reactions to it have thereby left an enduring legacy to the American people.

For Further Reading, see the Appendix. For Web resources, go to history.college.hmco.com/students.

SEVERING THE
BONDS OF EMPIRE
1754–1774

The two men must have found the occasion remarkable. The artist customarily painted portraits of the wealthy and high born, not of artisans. Moreover, the political sympathies of the artist, John Singleton Copley, lay primarily with Boston's conservatives, whereas the sitter, Paul Revere, was a noted leader of resistance to British policies. Yet sometime in 1768 Revere commissioned Copley to paint his portrait, and the result is one of the greatest works of American art.

Copley portrayed Revere, a silversmith, surrounded by the tools of his trade and contemplating a teapot he was crafting. Revere's pose and apparel convey an impression of thoughtfulness, virtuous labor, and solidity. The teapot too carries a message, especially in the year 1768. Simultaneously a reflection of a craftsman's skills and a prominent emblem of the new "empire of goods" in British America, it resonated with symbolism because, as shall be seen later in this chapter, tea boycotts were an important component of colonial resistance to Great Britain.

In retrospect, John Adams identified the years between 1760 and 1775 as the era of the true American Revolution. The Revolution, Adams declared, ended before the fighting started, for it was "in the Minds of the people," involving not the actual winning of independence but a fundamental shift of allegiance from Britain to America. Today, not all historians would concur with Adams that the shift he identified constituted the Revolution. But none would deny the importance of the events of those crucial years.

The story of the 1760s and early 1770s describes

an ever-widening split between Great Britain and Anglo America. In the long history of British settlement in the Western Hemisphere, considerable tension had occasionally marred the relationship between individual provinces and the mother country. Still, that tension had rarely persisted for long, nor had it been widespread, except during the crisis following the Glorious Revolution in 1689. In the 1750s, however, a series of events caused the colonists to examine their relations with Great Britain. It all started with the Seven Years War.

Britain's overwhelming victory in that war, confirmed by treaty in 1763, forever altered the balance of power in North America. France was ousted from the continent and Spain from Florida, events that had major consequences for both the indigenous peoples of the interior and the residents of the British colonies. Indians could no longer play off European powers against one another and so lost one of their major diplomatic tools. Anglo-Americans, for their part, no longer had to fear the French threat on their northern and western borders or the Spanish in the Southeast.

The British victory in 1763, then, dramatically affected all the residents of North America. That victory also had a significant impact on Great Britain. Britain's massive war-related debt needed to be paid, and so Parliament for the first time imposed revenue-raising taxes on the colonies in addition to the customs duties

that had long regulated trade. That decision exposed differences in the political thinking of Americans and Britons.

During the 1760s and early 1770s, a broad coalition of the residents of Anglo America resisted new tax levies and attempts by British officials to tighten their control over provincial governments. The colonies' elected leaders became ever more suspicious of Britain's motives as the years passed. They laid aside old antagonisms to coordinate their responses to the new measures, and they slowly began to reorient their political thinking. As late as the summer of 1774, though, few harbored thoughts of independence. ■

Renewed Warfare Among Europeans and Indians

 The English colonies along the Atlantic seaboard were surrounded by hostile, or potentially hostile, neighbors: Indians everywhere, the Spanish in Florida and along the coast of the Gulf of Mexico, the French along the great inland system of rivers and lakes that stretched from the St. Lawrence to the Mississippi. The Spanish outposts posed little direct threat, for Spain's days as a major power had passed. The French were another matter. Their long chain of forts and settlements dominated the

Table 5.1	**The Colonial Wars, 1689–1763**				
American Name	**European Name**	**Dates**	**Participants**	**American Sites**	**Dispute**
King William's War	War of the League of Augsburg	1689–97	England, Holland versus France, Spain	New England, New York, Canada	French power
Queen Anne's War	War of Spanish Succession	1702–13	England, Holland, Austria versus France, Spain	Florida, New England	Throne of Spain
King George's War	War of Austrian Succession	1739–48	England, Holland, Austria versus France, Spain, Prussia	West Indies, New England, Canada	Throne of Austria
French and Indian War	Seven Years War	1756–63	England versus France, Spain	Ohio country, Canada	Possession of Ohio country

IMPORTANT EVENTS

1754 Albany Congress meets to try to forge colonial unity
Fighting breaks out with Washington's defeat at Fort Necessity

1756 Britain declares war on France; Seven Years War officially begins

1759 British forces take Quebec

1760 American phase of war ends with fall of Montreal to British troops
George III becomes king

1763 Treaty of Paris ends Seven Years War
Pontiac's allies attack British forts in West
Proclamation of 1763 attempts to close land west of Appalachians to English settlement

1764 Sugar Act lays new duties on molasses, tightens customs regulations
Currency Act outlaws paper money issued by the colonies

1765 Stamp Act requires stamps on all printed materials in colonies
Sons of Liberty formed

1766 Stamp Act repealed
Declaratory Act insists that Parliament can tax the colonies

1767 Townshend Acts lay duties on trade within the empire, send new officials and judges to America

1768–70 Resistance to Townshend duties takes form of boycotts and public demonstrations but divides merchants and urban artisans

1770 Lord North becomes prime minister
Townshend duties repealed, except for tea tax
Boston Massacre kills five colonial rioters

1772 Boston Committee of Correspondence formed

1773 Tea Act aids East India Company
Boston Tea Party protests the Tea Act

1774 Coercive Acts punish Boston and Massachusetts as a whole
Quebec Act reforms government of Quebec

North American interior, facilitating trading partnerships and alliances with the Indians. In none of the three wars fought between 1689 and 1748 was England able to shake France's hold on the American frontier. Under the Peace of Utrecht, which ended Queen Anne's War in 1713, the English won control of such peripheral northern areas as Newfoundland, Hudson's Bay, and Nova Scotia (Acadia). But Britain made no territorial gains in King George's War (see Table 5.1).

During both Queen Anne's War and King George's War, the Iroquois Confederacy maintained the policy of neutrality it had first developed in 1701. The Iroquois fought only their southern enemies, the Catawbas. Since France repeatedly urged them to attack the Catawbas, who were allied with Britain, the Iroquois achieved desirable goals: they appeased the French while simultaneously consolidating their control over the entire interior region north of Virginia. The cam-

Iroquois Neutrality

paign against a common enemy also enabled the confederacy to cement its alliance with the Shawnees and Delawares.

But even careful Iroquois diplomats could not prevent the region inhabited by the Shawnees and Delawares (now western Pennsylvania and eastern Ohio) from providing the spark that set off a major war. That conflict spread from America to Europe and proved decisive in the contest for North America. Trouble began in 1752 when Anglo-American fur traders ventured into the area known as the Ohio country. The French could not permit their rivals to gain a foothold in that region. A permanent British presence in the Ohio country could challenge France's control of the western fur trade and even threaten its prominence in the Mississippi valley. Accordingly, in 1753 the French pushed southward from Lake Erie, building fortified outposts at strategic points.

In response to the French threat to their western frontiers, delegates from seven northern and middle

An eighteenth-century Iroquois warrior as depicted by a European artist. Such men of the Six Nations confederacy dominated the North American interior before the Seven Years War. Lines drawn on maps by colonizing powers and the incursions of traders made little impact on their power.   (Library of Congress, Rare Book and Special Collections Division)

Albany Congress

colonies gathered in Albany, New York, in June 1754. With the backing of administrators in London, they sought two goals: to persuade the Iroquois to abandon their traditional neutrality and to coordinate the defenses of the colonies. They succeeded in neither. The Iroquois saw no reason to change a policy that had served them well for half a century. And although the Albany Congress delegates adopted a Plan of Union (which would have established an elected intercolonial legislature with the power to tax), the provincial governments uniformly rejected the plan—primarily because those governments feared a loss of autonomy.

While the Albany Congress delegates deliberated,

the war they sought to prepare for was already beginning. Virginia claimed the Ohio country, and its governor sent a small militia force westward to counter the French. But the Virginia militiamen arrived too late, for the French were already engaged in constructing Fort Duquesne at the strategic point—now Pittsburgh—where the Allegheny and Monongahela Rivers meet to form the Ohio (see Map 5.1). The inexperienced young officer who commanded the Virginians attacked a French detachment and then allowed himself to be trapped in his crudely built Fort Necessity at Great Meadows, Pennsylvania. After a day-long battle (on July 3, 1754), twenty-two-year-old George Washington surrendered. He and his men were allowed to return to Virginia.

Washington had blundered grievously, setting off a war that eventually would encompass nearly the entire world. He also ensured that the Ohio Indians would support France in that conflict. The Indians took Washington's mistakes as an indication of Britain's weakness, and nothing that occurred in the next four years made them alter that judgment. In July 1755, a few miles south of Fort Duquesne, a combined force of French and Indians ambushed British and colonial troops led by General Edward Braddock; Braddock was killed and his surviving soldiers were demoralized. After news of the debacle reached London, Britain declared war on France in 1756, thus formally beginning the conflict known as the Seven Years War.

Seven Years War

For three more years one disaster followed another. British officers tried without much success to coerce the colonies into supplying men and materiel to the army. The war went so badly that Britain began to fear that France would try to retake Nova Scotia. As a result, Britain forced about half of the approximately twelve thousand French residents of Nova Scotia from their homeland—the first large-scale modern deportation. Ships crammed with Acadians sailed to each of the mainland colonies, where the dispirited exiles encountered hostility, discrimination, and disease.

In 1757, William Pitt, a civilian official, was placed in charge of the war effort. Under Pitt, Britain finally pursued a successful military strategy. He agreed to reimburse the colonies for their wartime expenditures and placed troop recruitment wholly in local hands, thereby gaining wholehearted American support for

Lake Superior

CHIPPEWA

NEW FRANCE

Quebec

Montreal

St. Lawrence R.

Ft. Western
(Augusta)

MAINE
(Part of Mass.)

Falmouth
(Portland)

N.H.

Portsmouth

Lake Huron

CHIPPEWA

MOHAWK

Lake Ontario

ONEIDA
TUSCARORA
ONONDAGA
CAYUGA

Ft. Stanwix

Albany

Boston

MASS.

Lake Michigan

OTTAWA

Ft. Niagara

SENECA

NEW
YORK

Hartford

CONN.

Providence

R.I.

Ft. Detroit

Lake Erie

Allegheny R.

1720–1760

POTAWATOMI

MIAMI

WYANDOT

DELAWARE

PENNSYLVANIA

Ft. Duquesne
(Pitt)

Philadelphia

New York

N.J.

ILLINOIS CONFEDERATION

WEA

OHIO COUNTRY

SHAWNEE

Monongahela R.

Ft.
Necessity

Tuscarora Migration

New Castle

Baltimore

M.D.

DEL.

Ohio R.

Richmond

VIRGINIA

Williamsburg

Mississippi R.

CHEROKEE

Proclamation Line of 1763

Hillsboro

Salem

NORTH CAROLINA

New Bern

CATAWBA

Wilmington

ATLANTIC OCEAN

CHICKASAW

Camden

SOUTH CAROLINA

Ft. Augusta
(Augusta)

Charleston

GEORGIA

CREEK

Savannah

CHOCTAW

NEW SPAIN

St. Augustine

Total population of
English colonies: c. 1.5 million

Extent of settlement

0		100		200 miles

0	100	200	300 kilometers

Map 5.1 European Settlements and Indians, 1754   By 1754, Europeans had expanded the limits of the
English colonies to the eastern slopes of the Appalachian Mountains.

the war. In July 1758, British forces recaptured the fortress at Louisbourg, winning control of the entrance to the St. Lawrence River and cutting the major French supply route. Then, in a stunning attack in September 1759, General James Wolfe's soldiers defeated the French on the Plains of Abraham and took Quebec. Sensing a British victory, the Iroquois abandoned their traditional neutrality and allied themselves with Britain. A year later the British captured Montreal, and the American phase of the war ended.

In the Treaty of Paris (1763), France ceded its major North American holdings to Britain. Spain, an ally of France toward the end of the war, gave Florida to the victors. France, meanwhile, ceded Louisiana west of the Mississippi to Spain, in partial compensation for its ally's losses elsewhere. The British thus gained control of the continent's fur trade. No longer would the English seacoast colonies have to worry about the threat to their existence posed by France's extensive North American territories.

Because most of the fighting occurred in the Northeast, the war had especially pronounced effects on New Englanders. Wartime service left a lasting impression on those who served in the provincial army. For the first time, ordinary Americans came into extended contact with Britons— and they did not like what they saw. The provincials regarded the British troops as haughty, profane Sabbath-breakers who arbitrarily imposed overly harsh punishments on anyone who broke the rules.

American Soldiers

The New England soldiers also learned that British troops did not share their adherence to principles of contract and consensus—the values that governed their lives at home. Colonial regiments mutinied or rebelled en masse if they believed they were being treated unfairly, as happened, for instance, when they were not allowed to leave when their enlistments expired. One private in these circumstances grumbled in his journal in 1759, "Although we be Englishmen born, we are debarred Englishmen's liberty." Such men would later recall their personal experience of British "tyranny" when they decided to support the Revolution.

The overwhelming British triumph stimulated some Americans to think expansively. People like the Philadelphia printer Benjamin Franklin, who had long touted the colonies' wealth and potential, predicted a glorious new future for British North America. Such individuals uniformly opposed any laws that would retard America's growth and persistently supported steps to increase Americans' control over their own destiny.

1763: A Turning Point

 The great victory over France had an irreversible impact on North America, felt first by the indigenous peoples of the interior. With France excluded from the continent altogether and Spanish territory now confined to west of the Mississippi, the diplomatic strategy that had served the Indians well for so long was now obsolete. The consequences were immediate and devastating.

Even before the Treaty of Paris, southern Indians had to adjust to the new circumstances. After Britain gained the upper hand in the American war in 1758, Creeks and Cherokees lost their ability to force concessions by threatening to turn instead to France or Spain. In desperation, and in retaliation for British atrocities, Cherokees attacked the Carolina and Virginia frontiers in 1760. Though initially victorious, the Indians were defeated the following year. Late in 1761 the two sides concluded a treaty under which the Cherokees allowed the construction of British forts in their territories and opened a large tract of land to European settlement.

In the Ohio country, the Ottawas, Chippewas, and Potawatomis reacted angrily when Great Britain, no longer facing French competition, raised the price of trade goods and ended traditional gift-giving practices. Britain also allowed settlers to move onto Delaware and Iroquois lands. A shaman named Neolin (also known as the Delaware Prophet) urged Indians to resist. If all Indians west of the mountains united to reject the invaders, Neolin declared, the Great Spirit would replenish the depleted deer herds and once again look kindly upon his people.

Neolin and Pontiac

Pontiac, the war chief of an Ottawa village near Detroit, became the leader of a movement based on Neolin's precepts. In the spring of 1763, Pontiac forged an unprecedented alliance among many Indian nations. He then laid siege to Fort Detroit while war parties attacked other British outposts in the Great Lakes region. Detroit withstood the siege, but by late June all the other forts west of Niagara and north of

Fort Pitt (formerly the French Fort Duquesne) had fallen to the alliance. Indians then raided the Virginia and Pennsylvania frontiers at will throughout the summer, killing at least two thousand settlers. Still, they failed to take the strongholds of Niagara, Fort Pitt, and Detroit. In early August, colonial militiamen soundly defeated a combined Indian force at Bushy Run, Pennsylvania. A treaty ending the war was finally negotiated three years later.

The uprising showed Great Britain that the huge territory just acquired from France would not be easy to govern. In October, the ministry issued the Procla-

Benjamin West, the first well-known American artist, engraved this picture of a prisoner exchange at the end of Pontiac's Uprising, with Colonel Henry Bouquet supervising the return of settlers abducted during the war. In the foreground, a child resists leaving the Indian parents he had grown to love. Many colonists were fascinated by the phenomenon West depicted—the reluctance of captives to abandon their adoptive Indian families. (Ohio Historical Society)

Proclamation of 1763

mation of 1763, which declared the headwaters of rivers flowing into the Atlantic from the Appalachian Mountains to be the temporary western boundary for colonial settlement (see Map 5.1). The proclamation was intended to prevent clashes by forbidding colonists to move onto Indian lands until tribes had given up their territory by treaty. But many Anglo-Americans had already established farms or purchased property west of the proclamation line, and from the outset the unenforceable policy was doomed to failure.

The hard-won victory in the Seven Years War had cost Britain millions of pounds and created an immense war debt.

George III

The problem of paying this debt bedeviled George III, who succeeded his grandfather, George II, on the British throne in 1760. The twenty-two-year-old king, a man of mediocre intellect, was also an erratic judge of character. During the crucial years between 1763 and 1770, when the rift with the colonies grew ever wider and he faced a series of political crises in England, the king replaced ministries with bewildering rapidity. Moreover, he often substituted stubbornness for cleverness, and he regarded adherence to the status quo as the hallmark of patriotism.

The man he selected as prime minister in 1763, George Grenville, confronted a financial crisis: England's burden of indebtedness had nearly doubled since 1754. Grenville's ministry had to find new sources of funds, and the British people themselves were already heavily taxed. Since the colonists had benefited greatly from the wartime expenditures, Grenville concluded that Anglo-Americans should be asked to pay a greater share of the cost of running the empire.

Grenville did not question Great Britain's right to levy taxes on the colonies. Like all his countrymen,

Theories of Representation

he believed that the government's legitimacy derived ultimately from the consent of the people, but he defined consent far more loosely than did the colonists. Americans had come to believe that they could be represented only by men who lived nearby and for whom they or their property-holding neighbors had actually voted. Grenville and his English contemporaries, however, believed that Parliament—king, lords, and commons acting together—by definition represented all British subjects, even colonists who could not vote.

According to this theory of government, called virtual representation, the colonists were seen as virtually, if not actually, represented in Parliament. Thus their consent to acts of Parliament could be presumed. In the colonies, by contrast, members of the lower houses of the assemblies were viewed as specifically representing the regions that had elected them. Before Grenville proposed to tax the colonists, the two notions had coexisted because no major conflict had arisen to expose the central contradiction.

Events in the 1760s threw into sharp relief Americans' attitudes toward political power. The colonists had become accustomed to a central gov-

Real Whigs

ernment that wielded only limited authority over them, affecting their daily lives very little. Consequently, they believed that a good government was one that largely left them alone, a view in keeping with the theories of a group of British writers known as the Real Whigs. These writers warned the people to guard constantly against government's attempts to encroach on their liberty and seize their property. Political power, they wrote, was always to be feared. Only the perpetual vigilance of people and their elected representatives could preserve their precious yet fragile liberty, which was closely linked to their right to hold private property.

Britain's attempts to tighten the reins of government and to raise revenues from the colonies in the 1760s and early 1770s convinced many Americans that the Real Whigs' reasoning applied to their circumstances, especially because of the link between liberty and property rights. Excessive and unjust taxation, they believed, could destroy their freedoms. They began to interpret British measures in light of the Real Whigs' warnings and to see oppressive designs behind the actions of Grenville and his successors. In the mid-1760s, however, colonial leaders did not immediately accuse Grenville of conspiring to oppress them. They at first merely questioned the wisdom of the laws he proposed.

Parliament passed the first such measures, the Sugar and Currency Acts, in 1764. The Sugar Act revised existing customs regulations, laid new duties on some foreign imports into the colonies, and aimed at stopping the widespread smuggling of molasses, one

Sugar and Currency Acts

of the chief commodities in American trade. It also established a vice-admiralty court at Halifax, Nova Scotia. (Vice-admiralty courts considered cases arising under maritime law and operated without juries.) Although the Sugar Act appeared to resemble the Navigation Acts, which the colonies had long accepted as legitimate, it broke with tradition in being explicitly designed to raise revenue, not to channel American trade through Britain. The Currency Act effectively outlawed colonial issues of paper money. (British merchants had long complained that Americans were paying their debts in inflated local currencies.) Americans could accumulate little sterling, since they imported more than they exported; thus the act seemed to the colonists to deprive them of a useful medium of exchange.

Because the Sugar and Currency Acts were imposed on an economy already in the midst of depression, it is not surprising that individual American essayists and incensed colonial governments protested the new policies. But, lacking any precedent for a united campaign against acts of Parliament, Americans in 1764 took only hesitant and uncoordinated steps. Eight colonial legislatures sent separate petitions to Parliament requesting the Sugar Act's repeal. They argued that its commercial restrictions would hurt Britain as well as the colonies and that they had not consented to its passage. The protests had no effect. The law remained in force, and Grenville proceeded with another revenue plan.

The Stamp Act Crisis

 The Stamp Act (1765), Grenville's most important proposal, was modeled on a law that had been in effect in Great Britain for almost a century. It touched nearly every colonist by requiring tax stamps on most printed materials, but it placed the heaviest burden on merchants and other members of the colonial elite, who used printed matter more frequently than did ordinary folk. Anyone who purchased a newspaper, made a will, transferred land, bought dice, applied for a liquor license, accepted a government appointment, or borrowed money would have to pay the tax. Never before had a revenue measure of such scope been proposed for the colonies. The act also required that tax stamps be paid for with sterling, which was scarce, and that violators be tried in vice-admiralty courts. Finally, such a law would break decisively with the colonial tradition of self-imposed taxation.

The most important colonial pamphlet protesting the Sugar Act and the proposed Stamp Act was

James Otis's Rights of the British Colonies

The Rights of the British Colonies Asserted and Proved, by James Otis, Jr., a brilliant young Massachusetts attorney. Otis starkly exposed the ideological dilemma that confounded the colonists for the next decade. How could they justify their opposition to certain acts of Parliament without questioning Parliament's authority over them? On the one hand, Otis asserted, Americans were "entitled to all the natural, essential, inherent, and inseparable rights" of Britons, including the right not to be taxed without their consent. On the other hand, Otis was forced to admit that under the British system, "the power of parliament is uncontrollable but by themselves, and we must obey."

Otis's first contention implied that Parliament could not constitutionally tax the colonies because Americans were not represented in its ranks. Yet his second point both acknowledged political reality and accepted the prevailing theory of British government: that Parliament was the sole, supreme authority in the empire. Even unconstitutional laws enacted by Parliament had to be obeyed until Parliament decided to repeal them. Otis tried to find a middle ground by proposing colonial representation in Parliament, but his idea was never taken seriously on either side of the Atlantic. The British believed that the colonists were already virtually represented in Parliament, and Anglo-Americans quickly realized that a handful of colonial delegates to London would simply be outvoted.

Otis published his pamphlet before the Stamp Act was passed. When Americans first learned of the act's adoption in the spring of 1765, they reacted indecisively. Few colonists publicly favored the law, but colonial petitions had already failed to prevent its adoption, and further lobbying appeared futile. Perhaps Otis was correct: the only course open to Americans was to pay the stamp tax, reluctantly but loyally.

Not all the colonists shared Otis's view. One who did not was a twenty-nine-year-old lawyer serving his

Patrick Henry and the Virginia Stamp Act Resolves

first term in the Virginia House of Burgesses. Appalled by the unwillingness of his fellow legislators to oppose the Stamp Act, Patrick Henry decided to act. "Alone, unadvised, and unassisted, on a blank leaf of an old law book," he wrote the Virginia Stamp Act Resolves.

Patrick Henry introduced his seven proposals near the end of the legislative session, when many burgesses had already departed for home. Henry's fiery speech led the Speaker of the House to accuse him of treason. (Henry denied the charge.) The few burgesses remaining in Williamsburg adopted five of Henry's resolutions by a bare majority. Although they repealed the most radical of the five the next day, their action had far-reaching effects.

The four propositions adopted by the burgesses repeated Otis's arguments, asserting that the colonists had never forfeited the rights of British subjects, among which was consent to taxation. The other three resolutions went much further. The one that was repealed claimed for the burgesses "the only exclusive right" to tax Virginians, and the final two (those never considered) asserted that residents of Virginia need not obey tax laws passed by other legislative bodies (namely Parliament).

The burgesses' decision to accept only the first four of Henry's resolutions anticipated the position most Americans would adopt through-

Continuing Loyalty to Britain

out the following decade. Though willing to contend for their rights, the colonists did not seek independence. They rather wanted some measure of self-government. Accordingly, they backed away from the assertions that they owed Parliament no obedience and that only their own assemblies could tax them.

Over the next ten years, America's political leaders searched for a formula that would enable them to control their internal affairs, especially taxation, but remain under British rule. The chief difficulty lay in British officials' inability to compromise on the issue of parliamentary power. The notion that Parliament could exercise absolute authority over all colonial possessions was inherent in the British theory of government. In effect, the Americans wanted British leaders to revise their fundamental understanding of the workings of their government. And that was simply too much to expect.

The ultimate effectiveness of Americans' opposition to the Stamp Act derived not from ideological arguments over parliamentary power but from the decisive and inventive actions of some colonists. In August 1765 the Loyal Nine, a Boston social club of printers, distillers, and other artisans, organized a demonstration against the Stamp Act. Hoping to show that people of all ranks opposed the act, they approached the leaders of the city's rival laborers' associations, based in Boston's North End and South End neighborhoods. The Loyal Nine convinced them to lay aside their differences to participate in the demonstration.

Loyal Nine

Early on August 14, the demonstrators hung an effigy of Andrew Oliver, the province's stamp distributor, from a tree on Boston Common. That night a large crowd led by a group of about fifty well-dressed tradesmen paraded the effigy around the city and threw stones at officials who tried to disperse them. In the midst of the melée, the North End and South End leaders drank a toast to their successful union. The Loyal Nine achieved success when Oliver publicly promised not to fulfill the duties of his office. Twelve days later a mob reportedly led by the South End leader Ebenezer MacIntosh attacked the homes of several customs officers. The crowd then completely destroyed Lieutenant Governor Thomas Hutchinson's elaborately furnished townhouse, an action that drew no praise from Boston's respectable citizens.

The differences between the two Boston mobs of August 1765 exposed divisions that would continue to characterize subsequent colonial protests. Few residents of the colonies sided with Great Britain during the 1760s, but various colonial groups had divergent goals. The skilled craftsmen who composed the Loyal Nine and merchants, lawyers, and other members of the educated elite preferred orderly demonstrations confined to political issues. For the city's laborers, by contrast, economic grievances may have been paramount. Certainly, their wrecking of Hutchinson's house suggests resentment against his ostentatious display of wealth.

Americans' Divergent Interests

Colonists, like Britons, had a long tradition of crowd action in which disfranchised people took to the streets to redress deeply felt local grievances. But the Stamp Act controversy drew ordinary urban folk into the vortex of transatlantic politics for the first time. Matters that previously had been of concern only to the gentry or to members of colonial legislatures were now discussed on every street corner.

The entry of unskilled workers, slaves, and women into the realm of imperial politics both threatened and aided the elite men who wanted to mount effective opposition to British measures. On the one hand, crowd action could have a stunning impact. Anti–Stamp Act demonstrations occurred in cities and towns stretching from Halifax in the north to the Caribbean island of Antigua in the south. They were so successful that by November 1, when the law was scheduled to take effect, not one stamp distributor was willing to carry out his official duties. Thus the act could not be enforced. But on the other hand, wealthy men recognized that mobs composed of the formerly powerless could endanger their own dominance of the society. What would happen, they wondered, if the crowd turned against them?

They therefore attempted to channel resistance into acceptable forms by creating an intercolonial association, the Sons of Liberty. New Yorkers organized the first such group in early November, and branches spread rapidly through the coastal cities. Composed of merchants, lawyers, and prosperous tradesmen, the Sons of Liberty by early 1766 linked protest leaders from Charleston, South Carolina, to Portsmouth, New Hampshire.

Sons of Liberty

The Sons of Liberty could influence events but could not control them. In Charleston in October 1765, an informally organized crowd forced the resignation of the South Carolina stamp distributor. But the new Charleston chapter of the Sons of Liberty was horrified when in January 1766 local slaves paraded through the streets crying "Liberty!" Freedom from slavery was not the sort of liberty elite slaveowners had in mind.

In Philadelphia, too, resistance leaders were dismayed when an angry mob threatened to attack Benjamin Franklin's house. The city's laborers believed Franklin to be partly responsible for the Stamp Act, since he had obtained the post of stamp distributor for a close friend. But Philadelphia's artisans—the backbone of the opposition movement there and elsewhere—were fiercely loyal to Franklin, and they gathered to protect his home and family from the crowd. The resulting split between the better-off tradesmen and the common laborers prevented the establishment of a successful workingmen's alliance like that of Boston.

During the fall and winter of 1765–1766, opposition to the Stamp Act proceeded on three separate fronts. Colonial legislatures petitioned Parliament to repeal the hated law, and courts closed because they could not obtain the stamps now required for all legal documents. In October nine colonies sent delegates to a general congress. The Stamp Act Congress met in New York to draft a unified but conservative statement of protest. At the same time, the Sons of Liberty held mass meetings, attempting to rally public support for the resistance movement. Finally, American merchants organized nonimportation associations to pressure British exporters. By the 1760s, one-quarter of all British exports went to the colonies, and American merchants reasoned that London merchants whose sales suffered severely would lobby for repeal. Since times were bad, American merchants believed that nonimportation would also help reduce their bloated inventories.

In March 1766, Parliament repealed the Stamp Act. The nonimportation agreements had had the anticipated effect, creating allies for the colonies among wealthy London merchants. But boycotts, formal protests, and crowd actions were less important in winning repeal than was the appointment of a new prime minister. Lord Rockingham, who replaced Grenville in the summer of 1765, had opposed the Stamp Act, not because he believed Parliament lacked the power to tax the colonies but because he thought the law unwise and divisive. Thus, although Rockingham proposed repeal, he linked it to passage of a Declaratory Act, which asserted Parliament's authority to tax and legislate for Britain's American possessions "in all cases whatsoever." Colonists celebrated the Stamp Act's repeal; few of them saw the implications of the Declaratory Act.

Repeal of the Stamp Act

Resistance to the Townshend Acts

 The colonists had accomplished their immediate aim, but the long-term prospects were unclear. In the summer of 1766, another change in the ministry in London revealed how fragile their victory had been. The new prime minister, William Pitt, was ill much of the time, and another minister, Charles Townshend, became the dominant force in the ministry. An ally of Grenville, Townshend decided to renew the attempt to obtain additional funds from Britain's American possessions.

The duties Townshend proposed in 1767 were to be levied on trade goods like paper, glass, and tea, and thus seemed to be nothing more than extensions of the existing Navigation Acts. But the Townshend duties differed from previous customs levies in two ways. First, they applied to items imported into the colonies from Britain, not from foreign countries. Thus they violated mercantilist theory (see page 52). Second, they were designed to raise money to pay the salaries of some royal officials in the colonies. That posed a direct challenge to the colonial assemblies, which derived considerable power from threatening to withhold officials' salaries. In addition, Townshend's scheme provided for the creation of an American Board of Customs Commissioners and of vice-admiralty courts at Boston, Philadelphia, and Charleston. Both moves angered merchants, whose profits would be threatened by more vigorous enforcement of the Navigation Acts.

The passage of the Townshend Acts drew a quick response. One series of essays in particular, *Letters from a Farmer in Pennsylvania* by the prominent lawyer John Dickinson, expressed a broad consensus. Dickinson contended that Parliament could regulate colonial trade but could not exercise that power to raise revenue.

John Dickinson's Farmer's Letters

By drawing a distinction between trade regulation and unacceptable commercial taxation, Dickinson avoided the sticky issue of consent and how it affected colonial subordination to Parliament. But his argument created a different, and equally knotty, problem. In effect it obligated the colonies to assess Parliament's motives in passing any law pertaining to trade before deciding whether to obey it. That was in the long run an unworkable position.

The Massachusetts assembly responded to the Townshend Acts by drafting a letter to circulate among the other colonial legislatures, calling

Massachusetts Assembly Dissolved

for unity and suggesting a joint petition of protest. Not the letter itself but the ministry's reaction to it united the colonies. When Lord Hillsborough, the first secretary of state for America, learned of the circular letter, he ordered Governor Francis Bernard of Massachusetts to insist that the assembly recall it. He also directed other governors to prevent their assemblies from discussing the letter. Hillsborough's order gave colonial assemblies the incentive they needed to join forces to oppose this new threat to their prerogatives. In late 1768 the Massachusetts legislature met, debated, and resoundingly rejected recall. Bernard immediately dissolved the assembly, and other governors followed suit when their legislatures debated the circular letter.

During the campaign against the Townshend duties, the Sons of Liberty and other American leaders made a deliberate effort to involve ordinary folk in the resistance movement. Most important, they urged colonists of all ranks and both sexes to sign agreements not to purchase or consume British products. The new consumerism that previously had linked the colonists economically now linked them politically as well, supplying them with a ready method of displaying their allegiance.

As the primary purchasers of textiles and household goods, women played a central role in the non-consumption movement. In Boston

Daughters of Liberty

more than three hundred matrons publicly promised not to buy or drink tea, "Sickness excepted." The women of Wilmington, North Carolina, burned their tea after walking through town in a solemn procession. The best known of the protests, the so-called Edenton Ladies Tea Party, actually had little to do with tea. It was a meeting of prominent North Carolina women who pledged formally to work for the public good and to support resistance to British measures.

Women also encouraged home manufacturing. In many towns, young women calling themselves Daughters of Liberty met to spin in public in an effort to persuade other women to make homespun, thereby ending the colonies' dependence on British cloth. When young ladies from well-to-do families sat publicly at spinning wheels all day, eating only American food and drinking local herbal tea, they were serving as political instructors. Many women took great satisfaction in their newfound role.

But the colonists were by no means united in support of nonimportation and nonconsumption. If the

Divided Opinion over Boycotts

Stamp Act protests had occasionally revealed a division between artisans and merchants on the one side and common laborers on the other, resistance to the Townshend Acts exposed new splits in American ranks. The most significant—which arose from a change in economic circumstances—divided urban artisans and merchants, allies in 1765 and 1766.

The Stamp Act boycotts had helped to revive a depressed economy by creating a demand for local products and reducing merchants' inventories. But in 1768 and 1769, merchants were enjoying boom times and had no financial incentive to support a boycott. As a result, merchants signed the agreements only reluctantly. In contrast, artisans supported nonimportation enthusiastically, recognizing that the absence of British goods would create a ready market for their own manufactures. Tradesmen also used coercion to enforce boycotts.

Such tactics were effective: colonial imports from England dropped dramatically in 1769. But they also aroused heated opposition. Some Americans who supported resistance to British measures began to question the use of violence to force others to join the boycott. In addition, wealthier and more conservative colonists were frightened by the threat to private property inherent in the campaign. Moreover, political activism by ordinary colonists challenged the ruling elite's domination.

Americans were relieved when news arrived in April 1770 that the Townshend duties had been repealed, with

Repeal of the Townshend Duties

the exception of the tea tax. A new prime minister, Lord North, had persuaded Parliament that duties on trade within the empire were ill advised. Although some colonial leaders argued that nonimportation should continue until the tea tax was repealed, merchants quickly resumed importing. The rest of the Townshend Acts remained in force, but repealing the duties made the other provisions appear less objectionable.

Confrontations in Boston

 On the very day Lord North proposed repeal of the Townshend duties, a confrontation between civilians and soldiers in Boston led to the death of five Americans. The origins of the event that patriots called the Boston Massacre lay in repeated clashes between customs officers and the people of Massachusetts. The decision to base the American Board of Customs Commissioners in Boston was the source of the problem.

Mobs targeted the customs commissioners from the day they arrived in November 1767. In June 1768 their seizure of the patriot leader John Hancock's sloop *Liberty* on suspicion of smuggling caused a riot in which customs officers' property was destroyed. The riot in turn helped to convince the British that they needed to assign troops to maintain order in the unruly port. Bostonians saw the troops as a constant reminder of the oppressive potential of British power. Guards on Boston Neck, the entrance to the city, checked all travelers and their goods. Redcoat patrols roamed the city day and night, questioning and sometimes harassing passersby. Parents began to fear for the safety of their daughters, who were subjected to soldiers' coarse sexual insults. But the greatest potential for violence lay in the uneasy relationship between the soldiers and Boston laborers. Many redcoats sought employment in their off-duty hours, competing for unskilled jobs with the city's ordinary workingmen.

Early on the evening of March 5, 1770, a crowd of laborers began throwing hard-packed snowballs at soldiers guarding the Customs House.
Boston Massacre
Goaded beyond endurance, the sentries acted against express orders to the contrary and fired on the crowd, killing four and wounding eight, one of whom died a few days later. Resistance leaders idealized the dead rioters as martyrs for the cause of liberty, holding a solemn funeral and later commemorating March 5 annually with patriotic orations.

Leading patriots wanted to ensure that the soldiers did not become martyrs as well. Thus when the soldiers were tried for the killings in November, John Adams and Josiah Quincy, Jr., both unwavering patriots, acted as their defense attorneys. All but two of the accused men were acquitted, and those convicted were released after being branded on the thumb. Undoubtedly the favorable outcome of the trials prevented London officials from taking further steps against the city.

For the next few years a superficial calm descended on the colonies. The most outspoken colonial newspapers published essays drawing
A British Plot?
on Real Whig ideology and accusing Great Britain of deliberately scheming to oppress the colonies. After the Stamp Act's repeal, the patriots had praised Parliament; following repeal of the Townshend duties, they warned of impending tyranny. What had seemed to be an isolated mistake, a single ill-chosen stamp tax, now appeared to be part of a plot against American liberties. Essayists pointed to the stationing of troops in Boston and the growing number of vice-admiralty courts as evidence of plans to enslave the colonists. Indeed, patriot writers played repeatedly on the word *enslavement*. Most white colonists had direct knowledge of slavery, and the threat of enslavement by Britain must have hit them with peculiar force.

Still, no one yet advocated complete independence from the mother country. Although the patriots were becoming increasingly convinced that they should seek freedom from parliamentary authority, they continued to acknowledge their British identity and their allegiance to George III. They began, therefore, to envision a system that would enable them to be ruled by their own elected legislatures while remaining loyal to the king. But any such scheme violated Britons' conception that Parliament wielded sole undivided sovereignty over the empire.

Then, in the fall of 1772, the North ministry began to implement the Townshend Act that provided for governors and judges to be paid from customs revenues. In early November, voters at a Boston town meeting established a Committee of Correspondence to publicize the decision by exchanging letters with other Massachusetts towns. Heading the committee was the man who had proposed its formation, Samuel Adams.

Fifty-one in 1772, Samuel Adams had been a Boston tax collector, a member and clerk of the Massachusetts assembly, an ally of the Loyal Nine, and a

Paul Revere's masterful portrayal of the Boston Massacre. The label "Butcher's Hall" on the Customs House merely reinforces the patriot view of the incident on March 5, 1770. The British soldiers are shown firing on an unresisting crowd, not the aggressive, angry mob described at the soldiers' trial. Even worse, a gun with smoke drifting up from its barrel emerges from a window above the redcoats, suggesting the complicity of civilian officials in what the patriots interpreted as an outrageous act.   (Photo: Courtesy of the John Carter Brown Library, Brown University)

Samuel Adams member of the Sons of Liberty. An experienced political organizer, Adams continually stressed the necessity of prudent collective action. His Committee of Correspondence thus undertook the task of creating an informed consensus among all the residents of Massachusetts.

Such committees, which were eventually established throughout the colonies, represented the next logical step in the organization of American resistance. Until 1772, the **Boston Committee of Correspondence** protest movement was largely confined to the seacoast and primarily to major cities and towns. Adams realized that the time had come to widen the movement's geographic scope by involving the residents of the interior in the struggle. Accordingly, the Boston town meeting directed the Committee of Correspondence "to state the Rights of the Colonists and of this Province in particular," to list "the Infringements and Violations thereof that have been, or from time to time may be made," and to send copies to the other towns in the province.

The statement of colonial rights declared that Americans had absolute rights to life, liberty, and property. The idea that "a British house of commons, should have a right, at pleasure, to give and grant the property of the colonists" was "irreconcileable" with "the first principles of natural law and Justice . . . and of the British Constitution in particular." The list of grievances complained of taxation without representation, the presence of unnecessary troops and customs officers on American soil, the use of imperial revenues to pay colonial officials, the expanded jurisdiction of vice-admiralty courts, and even the nature of the instructions given to American governors by their superiors in London. No mention was made of obedience to Parliament. Patriots—at least in Boston—placed American rights first, loyalty to Great Britain a distant second.

In their response, most towns aligned themselves with the city. From Braintree came the assertion that "all civil officers are or ought to be Servants to the people and dependent upon them for their official Support, and every instance to the Contrary from the Governor downwards tends to crush and destroy civil liberty." The town of Holden declared that "the People of New England have never given the People of Britain any Right of Jurisdiction over us." And the citizens of Petersham commented that resistance to tyranny was "the first and highest social Duty of this people." Beliefs like these made the next crisis in Anglo-American affairs the final one.

Tea and Turmoil

 The tea tax was the only Townshend duty still in effect by 1773. In the years after 1770, some Americans continued to boycott English tea, while others resumed drinking it. Tea figured prominently in the colonists' social lives, so observing the boycott required them not only to forgo a favorite beverage but also to alter habitual forms of socializing. Tea thus retained an explosively symbolic character even though the boycott began to fall apart after 1770.

In May 1773, Parliament passed an act designed to save the East India Company from bankruptcy. The

Tea Act

company, which held a monopoly on British trade with the East Indies, was critically important to the British economy. According to the Tea Act, legal tea would henceforth be sold in America only by the East India Company's designated agents, which would enable the company to avoid middlemen in both England and the colonies and to price its tea competitively with that offered by smugglers. The net result would be cheaper tea for American consumers. Resistance leaders, however, interpreted the new measure as a pernicious device to make them admit Parliament's right to tax them, for the less-expensive tea would still be taxed under the Townshend law. Others saw the Tea Act as the first step in the establishment of an East India Company monopoly of all colonial trade. Residents of the four cities designated to receive the first shipments of tea accordingly prepared to respond to what they perceived as a new threat to their freedom.

In New York City, the tea ships failed to arrive on schedule. In Philadelphia, the governor of Pennsylvania persuaded the captain to turn around and sail back to Britain. In Charleston, the tea was unloaded and stored; some was destroyed, and the rest was sold in 1776 by the new state government. The only confrontation occurred in Boston, where both the town meeting and Governor Thomas Hutchinson rejected compromise.

The first of three tea ships entered Boston harbor on November 28. The customs laws required cargo to

The Boston Tea Party

be landed and the appropriate duty paid by its owners within twenty days of a ship's arrival. After a series of mass meetings, Bostonians voted to post guards on the wharf to prevent the tea from being unloaded. Hutchinson refused to permit the vessels to leave the harbor. John Singleton Copley, whose father-in-law was a tea agent, tried to mediate the dispute.

On December 16, one day before the cargo would have been confiscated, more than five thousand people (nearly a third of the city's population) crowded into Old South Church. The meeting, chaired by Samuel Adams, made a final attempt to persuade Hutchinson to send the tea back to England. But the governor remained adamant. In the early evening Adams reportedly announced "that he could think of nothing further to be done—that they had now done all they could for the Salvation of their Country." Cries then rang out from the back of the crowd: "Boston harbor a tea-pot tonight! The Mohawks are come!" Within a few minutes, about sixty men of all social rank crudely disguised as Indians assembled at the wharf, boarded the three ships, and dumped the cargo into the harbor. By 9 P.M. their work was done: 342 chests of tea worth approximately £10,000 floated in splinters on the water.

While resistance leaders rejoiced, the North administration reacted with considerably less enthusiasm. In March 1774, Parliament adopted the first of four laws that became known as the Coercive, or Intolerable, Acts. It ordered the port of Boston closed until the tea was paid for, prohibiting all but coastal trade in food and firewood. Later in the spring, Parliament passed three other punitive measures. The Massachusetts Government Act altered the province's charter, substituting an appointed council for the elected one, increasing the governor's powers, and forbidding most town meetings. The Justice Act provided that a person accused of committing murder in the course of suppressing a riot or enforcing the laws could be tried outside the colony where the incident had occurred. Finally, the Quartering Act allowed military officers to commandeer privately owned buildings to house their troops. Thus the Coercive Acts punished not only Boston but also Massachusetts as a whole, alerting other colonies that their residents, too, could be subject to retaliation if they opposed British authority.

Coercive and Quebec Acts

After passing the last of the Coercive Acts, Parliament turned its attention to reforming the government of Quebec. The Quebec Act granted greater religious freedom to Catholics—thereby alarming Protestant colonists—and reinstated French civil law. Most important, the act annexed to Quebec the area east of the Mississippi River and north of the Ohio River. That region, parts of which were claimed by individual seacoast colonies, was thus removed from their jurisdiction.

Members of Parliament who voted for the punitive legislation believed that the acts would be obeyed. But to patriots the Coercive Acts and the Quebec Act proved what they had feared since 1768: that Great Britain had embarked on a deliberate plan to oppress them. If the port of Boston could be closed, why not the ports of Philadelphia or New York? If the royal charter of Massachusetts could be changed, why not the charter of South Carolina? If troops could be forcibly quartered in private houses, did not that action pave the way for the occupation of all of America? If the Roman Catholic Church could receive favored status in Quebec, why not everywhere?

Implications of the Coercive Acts

The Boston Committee of Correspondence urged all the colonies to join in an immediate boycott of British goods. But the other provinces hesitated. Rhode Island, Virginia, and Pennsylvania each suggested that another intercolonial congress be convened to consider an appropriate response. Few people wanted to take hasty action; even the most ardent patriots remained loyal to Britain and hoped for reconciliation with its leaders. So the colonies agreed to send delegates to Philadelphia in September to attend a Continental Congress.

Summary

 Just twenty years earlier, at the outbreak of the Seven Years War in the wilderness of western Pennsylvania, no one could have predicted that the future would bring such swift and dramatic change to Britain's mainland colonies. Yet that conflict—which simultaneously removed France from North America and created a huge war debt Britain had to find ways to pay—set in motion the process leading to the convening of the First Continental Congress.

In the years after the war ended in 1763, momentous changes occurred in the ways colonists thought about themselves and their allegiances. Once linked unquestioningly to Great Britain, they began to develop a sense of their own identity as Americans. They started to realize that their concept of the political process differed from that held by people in the mother country. They also came to understand that their economic interests did not necessarily coincide with those of Great Britain. Colonial political leaders reached such conclusions only after a long train of events.

By the late summer of 1774, the Americans were committed to resistance but not to independence. Even so, they had started to sever the bonds of empire. During the next decade, they would forge the bonds of a new American nationality to replace those rejected Anglo-American ties.

LEGACY FOR A PEOPLE AND A NATION
The Census and Reapportionment

When in the prerevolutionary years American colonists argued that "they were not represented in" Parliament, they developed a definition of *representation* very different from the understanding traditionally accepted in Great Britain. There, numbers did not matter: the entire British population was seen as being "virtually" represented in Parliament.

Americans, by contrast, placed great emphasis on the importance of being represented in government by someone for whom they—or at least their better-off male neighbors—had actually voted. And that carried with it the related desire for election districts that were regularly reapportioned in accordance with the movements and increase of the population. Article 1, Sec-

tion 2, of the U.S. Constitution thus provides for an "actual enumeration" of the nation's residents every ten years so that "representatives and direct taxes shall be apportioned among the several States . . . according to their respective numbers." Each decade, from 1790 to 2000, the government has tried to count the nation's residents accurately—although, according to historians and demographers, it has often failed to achieve that goal.

The planning for the year 2000 census led to heated debates in Congress and to a Supreme Court decision outlining appropriate techniques for conducting the mandated "actual enumeration" of the American population. In other years as well (especially 1920, near the close of an era of dramatic demographic change), planning and conducting the census proved extremely contentious. The origin of such contests lies in Americans' prerevolutionary experience, for the clause the Founding Fathers incorporated into the Constitution stemmed from ideological battles of the 1760s.

Thus every ten years the nation must still wrestle with an enduring legacy of the colonial period: the need to enumerate the American people and to alter the boundaries of electoral districts according to the results.

For Further Reading, see the Appendix. For Web resources, go to history.college.hmco.com/students.

6

A REVOLUTION, INDEED

1774–1783

The Shawnee chief Blackfish named his new captive Sheltowee, or Big Turtle, and adopted him as his son. Blackfish's warriors had easily caught the lone hunter, who was returning with a slaughtered buffalo to an encampment of men. The captive then persuaded his fellow frontiersmen to surrender. It was February 1778. The hunter was Daniel Boone, who less than three years earlier had moved his family from North Carolina to the western region of Virginia known as Kentucke. Some historians have wondered about Boone's allegiance during the American Revolution, for he moved to the frontier just as the war began. His encounter with the Shawnees highlights many of the ambiguities of revolutionary-era loyalties.

The Shawnees were seeking captives to cover the death of their chief Cornstalk (see pages 67–68). Of the twenty-six men taken with Boone, about half were adopted into Shawnee families; the others were dispatched as prisoners to the Shawnees' British allies. Boone, who assured Blackfish that he would later negotiate the surrender of the women and children remaining at his home settlement of Boonesborough, watched and waited. In June 1778 he escaped, hurrying home to warn the Kentuckians of impending attack.

When Blackfish's Shawnees and their British allies appeared outside the Boonesborough stockade in mid-September, Boone proved amenable to negotiations. Fragmentary evidence suggests that the settlers agreed to swear allegiance to the British in order to avert a bloody battle. But the discussions dissolved into a melee, and the Indians then besieged the fort for a week before withdrawing. With that threat gone,

IMPORTANT EVENTS

1774 First Continental Congress meets in Philadelphia, adopts Declaration of Rights and Grievances
Continental Association implements economic boycott of Britain; committees of observation established to oversee boycott

1774–75 Provincial conventions replace collapsing colonial governments

1775 Battles of Lexington and Concord; first shots of war fired
Second Continental Congress begins
Dunmore's proclamation offers freedom to patriots' slaves who join British forces

1776 Paine publishes *Common Sense*
British evacuate Boston

Declaration of Independence adopted
New York City falls to British

1777 British take Philadelphia
Burgoyne surrenders at Saratoga

1778 French alliance brings vital assistance to the United States
British evacuate Philadelphia

1779 Sullivan expedition destroys Iroquois villages

1780 British take Charleston

1781 Cornwallis surrenders at Yorktown

1782 Peace negotiations begin

1783 Treaty of Paris signed, granting independence to the United States

---

Boone was charged with treason and court-martialed by Kentucky militia. Although he was cleared, questions remained.

Where did Daniel Boone's loyalties lie? Had he betrayed the settlers to the Shawnees and sought to establish British authority in Kentucky? Had he—as he later claimed—deceived the Shawnees? Or had he rather made the survival of the fragile frontier settlements his highest priority?

Daniel Boone was not the only American of uncertain or shifting allegiance in the 1770s. The American Revolution uprooted thousands of families, disrupted the economy, reshaped society by forcing many colonists into permanent exile, led Americans to develop new conceptions of politics, and created a nation from thirteen separate colonies.

The struggle for independence required revolutionary leaders to accomplish three separate but closely related tasks. The first was political and ideological: transforming a consensus favoring loyal resistance into a coalition supporting independence. The second involved foreign relations. To win independence, patriot leaders knew they needed international recognition and aid, particularly from France. Thus they dispatched to Paris the most experienced American diplomat, Benjamin Franklin.

Only the third task directly involved the British. George Washington, commander-in-chief of the American army, soon recognized that his primary goal should be not to win battles but to avoid losing them decisively. The outcome of any one battle was less important than ensuring that his army survived to fight another day. Consequently, the story of the Revolutionary War reveals British action and American reaction, British attacks and American defenses and withdrawals. The American war effort was aided by Britain's focus on winning battles rather than on the primary goal of retaining the colonies' allegiance. ■

Government by Congress and Committee

 When the fifty-five delegates to the First Continental Congress convened in Philadelphia in September 1774, they knew that many Americans would support any measures they adopted. That summer, open meetings held throughout

the colonies had endorsed the idea of another nonimportation pact. Committees of correspondence publicized these meetings so effectively that Americans everywhere knew about them. Most of the congressional delegates were selected by extralegal provincial conventions, since governors had forbidden regular assemblies to conduct formal elections. Thus the very act of designating delegates to attend the Congress involved Americans in open defiance of British authority.

The colonies' leading political figures—most of them lawyers, merchants, and planters representing

First Continental Congress

every colony but Georgia—attended the Philadelphia Congress. The Massachusetts delegation included both Samuel Adams and his younger cousin John, an ambitious lawyer. Among others, New York sent John Jay, a talented young attorney. From Pennsylvania came the conservative Joseph Galloway and his long-time rival, John Dickinson. Virginia elected Richard Henry Lee and Patrick Henry, both noted for their patriotic zeal, as well as George Washington.

The congressmen faced three tasks when they convened on September 5, 1774. The first two were explicit: defining American grievances and developing a plan for resistance. The third—articulating their constitutional relationship with Great Britain—proved troublesome. The most radical congressmen, like Lee of Virginia, argued that the colonists owed allegiance only to George III and that Parliament was nothing more than a local legislature for Great Britain with no authority over the colonies. The conservatives—Joseph Galloway and his allies—proposed a formal plan of union that would have required Parliament and a new American legislature to consent jointly to all laws pertaining to the colonies. The delegates narrowly rejected Galloway's proposal but also refused to embrace the radicals' position.

Finally, they accepted a compromise position worked out by John Adams. The crucial clause that

Declaration of Rights and Grievances

Adams drafted in the Congress's Declaration of Rights and Grievances read in part: "From the necessity of the case, and a regard to the mutual interest of both countries, we cheerfully consent to the operation of such acts of the British parliament, as are bona fide, restrained to the regulation of our external commerce."

Notice the key phrases. "From the necessity of the case" declared that Americans would obey Parliament only because they thought that doing so was in the best interest of both countries. "Bona fide, restrained to the regulation of our external commerce" made it clear to Lord North that they would continue to resist taxes in disguise. Most striking of all was that such language—which only a few years before would have been regarded as irredeemably extreme—could be presented and accepted as a compromise in the fall of 1774.

With the constitutional issue resolved, the delegates readily agreed on the laws they wanted repealed (notably the Coercive Acts) and decided to implement an economic boycott while petitioning the king for relief. They adopted the Continental Association, which called for nonimportation of British goods (effective December 1, 1774), nonconsumption of British products (effective March 1, 1775), and nonexportation of American goods to Britain and the British West Indies (effective September 10, 1775, so that southern planters could market their 1774 tobacco crop).

To enforce the Continental Association, Congress recommended the election of committees of observa-

Committees of Observation

tion and inspection in every American locality. By specifying that committee members be chosen by all persons qualified to vote for members of the lower house of the colonial legislatures, Congress guaranteed the committees a broad popular base. The seven to eight thousand committeemen became the local leaders of American resistance.

Though officially charged only with overseeing implementation of the boycott, the committees soon became de facto governments. They examined merchants' records and published the names of those who continued to import British goods. They also promoted home manufactures, encouraging Americans to adopt simple modes of dress and behavior to symbolize their commitment to liberty and virtuous conduct. Since expensive leisure-time activities were believed to reflect vice and corruption, Congress urged Americans to forgo dancing, gambling, horseracing, cockfighting, and other forms of "extravagance and dissipation."

Thus the committees gradually extended their authority over many aspects of American life. They attempted to identify opponents of American resistance, developing elaborate spy networks, circulating copies of the Continental Association for signatures, and investigating reports of dissident remarks and activities. Suspected dissenters were first urged to support the colonial cause; if they failed to do so, the committees had them watched, restricted their movements, or tried to force them to leave the area. People engaging in casual political exchanges with friends one day could find themselves charged with "treasonable conversation" the next.

While the committees of observation were expanding their power during the winter and early spring of 1775, the regular colonial governments were collapsing. Only a few legislatures continued to meet without encountering patriot challenges to their authority. In most colonies, popularly elected provincial conventions took over the task of running the government, sometimes entirely replacing the legislatures and at other times holding concurrent sessions. In late 1774 and early 1775, these conventions approved the Continental Association, elected delegates to the Second Continental Congress (scheduled for May), organized militia units, and gathered arms and ammunition. Unable to stem the tide of resistance, the British-appointed governors and councils watched helplessly as their authority crumbled.

Provincial Conventions

Throughout the colonies British rule became paralyzed. Courts were prevented from holding sessions; taxes were paid to the conventions' agents rather than to provincial tax collectors; sheriffs' powers were challenged; and militiamen would muster only when committees ordered. In short, during the six months preceding the battles at Lexington and Concord, independence was being won at the local level. Not many Americans fully realized what was happening. The vast majority still proclaimed their loyalty to Great Britain, denying that they sought to leave the empire. Among the few who clearly recognized the trend toward independence were those who opposed it.

Choosing Sides: Loyalists, African Americans, and Indians

 The first protests against British measures in the mid-1760s won the support of most colonists. Only in the late 1760s and early 1770s did a significant number of Americans begin to question both the aims and the tactics of the resistance movement. By 1774 and 1775 such people found themselves in a difficult position. Most of them objected to parliamentary policies, favoring some kind of constitutional reform. Nevertheless, if forced to a choice, these colonists sympathized with Great Britain rather than with an independent America. Their objections to violent protest, their desire to uphold legally constituted government, and their fears of anarchy combined to make them especially sensitive to the dangers of resistance.

Some conservatives thus began to publish essays and pamphlets critical of the Congress and its allied committees. In Pennsylvania, Joseph Galloway published a tract attacking the Continental Congress for rejecting his plan of union. In Massachusetts the young attorney Daniel Leonard, writing under the pseudonym Massachusettensis, engaged in a prolonged newspaper debate with Novanglus (John Adams). Leonard and others realized that what had begun as a dispute over the nature of American subordination to Parliament was now raising the question of whether the colonies would remain linked to Great Britain at all.

Loyalists

Some colonists did heed the conservative pamphleteers' warnings. About one-fifth of the European American population remained loyal to Great Britain, firmly rejecting independence. Most loyalists had one thing in common: they had long opposed the men who became patriot leaders, though for varying reasons. British-appointed government officials; Anglican clergy everywhere and lay Anglicans in the North, where their denomination was in the minority; tenant farmers, particularly those whose landlords sided with the patriots; members of persecuted religious sects; many of the backcountry southerners who had rebelled against eastern rule in the late 1760s and early 1770s; and non-English ethnic minorities, especially Scots: all these groups feared the power wielded by those who controlled the colonial assemblies and who had shown little concern for their welfare in the past. Joined by merchants whose trade depended on imperial connections and by former officers and enlisted men from the British army who had settled in America after 1763, they formed a loyalist core.

Active revolutionaries, who accounted for about two-fifths of the population, came chiefly from the groups that had dominated colonial society, either

Patriots and Neutrals

numerically or politically. Among them were yeoman farmers, members of dominant Protestant sects, Chesapeake gentry, merchants dealing mainly in American commodities, city artisans, elected office-holders, and people of English descent. Wives usually but not always adopted their husbands' political beliefs. Although all these patriots supported the Revolution, they pursued divergent goals within the broader coalition, as they had in the 1760s. Some sought limited political reform, others extensive political change, and still others social and economic reforms.

Between the patriots and the loyalists, there remained in the middle perhaps two-fifths of the European American population. Some of those who tried to avoid taking sides were sincere pacifists, such as Quakers. Others opportunistically shifted their allegiance to whatever side happened to be winning at the time. Still others simply wanted to be left alone. The latter group made up an especially large proportion of the population in the southern backcountry (including Boone's Kentucky), where Scots-Irish settlers had little love for either the patriot gentry or the English authorities.

To patriots, apathy or neutrality was a crime as heinous as loyalism. By the winter of 1775–1776, the Second Continental Congress was recommending that all "disaffected" persons be disarmed and arrested. State legislatures passed laws prescribing severe penalties for suspected loyalists or neutrals. Many began to require all voters (or, in some cases, all free adult men) to take oaths of allegiance; the penalty for refusal was usually banishment or extra taxes. As a consequence of such treatment, perhaps 100,000 people left their homeland. Many migrated to the Canadian provinces of Nova Scotia, New Brunswick, and Ontario. After 1777 many states confiscated the property of banished persons, using the proceeds for the war effort.

The patriots' policies helped to ensure that their scattered and persecuted opponents could not band together to threaten the revolutionary cause. But loyalists and neutrals were not the patriots' only worry; they also feared that Indians and slaves might join the forces arrayed against them. Early in the war, free blacks from New England enthusiastically enlisted in local patriot militias, but the revolutionaries could not assume that *enslaved* African Americans would also support the struggle for independence.

Bondspeople faced a dilemma: how could they best pursue their goal of escaping slavery? Should they fight with or against their masters?

The Slaves' Dilemma

African Americans made different decisions, but to most slaves, supporting the British appeared more promising. Thus news of slave conspiracies surfaced in different parts of the colonies in late 1774 and early 1775. All shared a common element: a plan to assist the British army in return for freedom. The most serious incident occurred in 1775 in Charleston, where Thomas Jeremiah, a free black harbor pilot, was brutally executed after being convicted of attempting to foment a slave revolt.

Although the Caribbean islands too had protested British taxation in the 1760s, sugar planters in the British West Indies were more cautious in opposing parliamentary policies than were residents of the mainland. On most of the Caribbean islands, slaves outnumbered their masters by six or seven to one. With the ever-present threat of slave revolt or foreign attack hanging over their heads, planters could not afford to risk opposing Britain, their chief protector.

Slavery affected politics on the mainland as well. In New England, with few resident slaves, revolutionary fervor reached a peak. In Virginia and Maryland, where free people constituted a safe majority, the potential for slave revolts raised occasional but not disabling fears. By contrast, South Carolina and Georgia, where slaves composed more than half of the population, were noticeably less enthusiastic about resistance. Georgia sent no delegates to the First Continental Congress and reminded its representatives at the second one to consider its circumstances, "with our blacks and tories [loyalists] within us," when voting on the question of independence.

Slavery and Revolutionary Fervor

The slaveowners' worst fears were realized in November 1775, when Lord Dunmore, the governor of Virginia, offered to free any slaves and indentured servants who would leave their patriot masters to join the British forces. Dunmore hoped to use African Americans in his fight against the revolutionaries and to disrupt the economy by depriving planters of their labor force. But at most only two thousand African Americans rallied to the British standard. Even so, Dunmore's proclamation led Congress in January 1776 to modify an earlier policy that had prohibited the enlistment of African Americans in the regular American army.

Although slaves did not pose a serious threat to the revolutionary cause in its early years, the patriots turned rumors of slave uprisings to their own advantage. In South Carolina resistance leaders argued that unity under the Continental Association would protect masters from their slaves at a time when royal government was unable to muster adequate defense forces. The strategy drew many fearful whites into the patriot camp.

Similarly, the threat of Indian attacks helped persuade some reluctant westerners to support the struggle against Great Britain. In the years since the Proclamation of 1763, British officials had won the Indians' trust by attempting to protect them from land-hungry European Americans. The British-appointed superintendents of Indian affairs, John Stuart in the South and Sir William Johnson in the North, lived among and understood the Indians. In 1768 Stuart and Johnson negotiated separate agreements modifying the proclamation line and trying to draw realistic, defensible boundaries between tribal holdings and European American settlements. The treaties supposedly established permanent western borders for the colonies. But a few years later, the British pushed the southern boundary even farther west to accommodate the demands of settlers in western Georgia and Kentucky.

Indians' Grievances

By 1775 many Indian groups were provoked beyond endurance by the aggressive pressure on their lands. Such grievances and the tribes' confidence in Stuart and Johnson predisposed most Indians toward an alliance with Great Britain. Even so, the latter hesitated to make full and immediate use of these potential allies, because the Indians' war aims and fighting style were incompatible with those of the British. Accordingly, the British at first sought from native peoples only a promise of neutrality.

Recognizing that their standing with native peoples was poor, the patriots also sought the Indians' neutrality. In 1775 the Second Continental Congress sent a general message to Indian communities describing the war as "a family quarrel between us and Old England" and requesting that they "not join on either side." A group of Cherokees led by Chief Dragging Canoe nevertheless decided that the "family quarrel" would allow them to settle some old scores. They attacked settlements along the western borders of the Carolinas and Virginia in the summer of 1776. But a militia campaign destroyed many of their towns. Dragging Canoe and his diehard followers fled to the west; the rest of the Cherokees agreed to a treaty that ceded still more of their land.

Indians During the Revolution

Bands of Shawnees and Cherokees continued to attack frontier settlements in Kentucky and elsewhere throughout the war, but dissent in their own ranks crippled their efforts. The British victory over France in 1763 had destroyed the Indian nations' most effective means of maintaining their independence: their ability to play European powers off against one another. Successful strategies were difficult to envision under these new circumstances, and Indian leaders could no longer concur on a unified course of action. Communities split asunder as older and younger men, or civil and war leaders, disagreed vehemently over what policy to adopt. Only a few communities unwaveringly supported the American revolt; most other native villages either tried to remain neutral or at least partly aligned themselves with the British.

Although patriots could never completely ignore the threats posed by loyalists, neutrals, slaves, and Indians, only rarely did fear of these groups seriously hamper the revolutionary movement. In general, the practical impossibility of a large-scale slave revolt, coupled with dissension in Indian communities and the patriots' successful campaign to disarm and neutralize loyalists, ensured that the revolutionaries would by and large remain firmly in control of the countryside.

War and Independence

On January 27, 1775, Lord Dartmouth, secretary of state for America, addressed a fateful letter to General Thomas Gage in Boston. Expressing his belief that American resistance was nothing more than the response of a "rude rabble without plan," Dartmouth urged Gage to take a decisive step.

Dartmouth's letter did not reach Gage until April 14. He responded by sending an expedition to con-fiscate provincial military supplies stockpiled at Concord. Bostonians dis-patched two messengers, William Dawes and Paul Revere (later joined by Dr. Samuel Prescott), to rouse the countryside. So when the British vanguard of several hundred men approached Lexing-ton at dawn on April 19, they found a ragtag group of seventy militiamen. The Americans' commander or-dered his men to withdraw, realizing they could not halt the redcoats' advance. But as they began to dis-perse, a shot rang out; the British soldiers then fired several volleys. When they stopped, eight Americans lay dead. The British moved on to Concord, 5 miles away.

Battles of Lexington and Concord

There the contingents of militia were larger, Con-cord residents having been joined by groups of men from nearby towns. An exchange of gunfire at the North Bridge spilled the first British blood of the Rev-olution: three men were killed. Thousands of militia-men then fired from houses and from behind trees and bushes at the British forces as they retreated to Boston. By the end of the day, the redcoats had suffered 272 ca-sualties, including 70 deaths. The patriots suffered just 93 casualties.

By the evening of April 20, perhaps twenty thou-sand American militiamen had gathered around Bos-ton. Many did not stay long, since they were needed at home for spring planting, but those who remained dug in along siege lines encircling the city. For nearly a year the two armies sat and stared at each other across those lines. The redcoats attacked their besiegers only once, on June 17, when they drove the Americans from trenches atop Breed's Hill in Charlestown. In that misnamed Battle of Bunker Hill, the British incurred their greatest losses of the entire war: over 800 wounded and 228 killed. The Americans, though forced to abandon their position, lost less than half that number.

First Year of War

During the same eleven-month period, patriots captured Fort Ticonderoga, a British fort on Lake Champlain, acquiring much-needed cannon. Trying to bring Canada into the war on the American side, they also mounted an uncoordinated northern cam-paign that ended in disaster at Quebec in early 1776. Most significant, the lull in the fighting at Boston gave both sides a chance to regroup, organize, and plan their strategies.

Lord North and his new American secretary, Lord George Germain, made three central assumptions about the war they faced. First, they concluded that patriot forces could not withstand the assaults of trained British regulars. Accordingly, they dispatched to America the largest force Great Britain had ever assembled anywhere: 370 transport ships car-rying 32,000 troops and tons of supplies, accompanied by 73 naval vessels and 13,000 sailors. Such an extraor-dinary effort, they thought, would ensure a quick vic-tory. Among the troops were mercenaries from the German state of Hesse.

British Strategy

Second, British officials and army officers treated this war as comparable to wars they had fought suc-cessfully in Europe. They adopted a conventional strategy of capturing major American cities and de-feating the rebel army decisively without suffering se-rious casualties themselves. Third, they assumed that a clear-cut military victory would automatically bring about their goal of retaining the colonies' allegiance.

All these assumptions proved false. North and Germain vastly underestimated Americans' commit-ment to armed resistance. Battlefield defeats did not lead patriots to abandon their political aims and sue for peace. The ministers in London also failed to recog-nize the significance of the American population's dis-persal over an area 1,500 miles long. Although Great Britain would control each of the most important American ports at one time or another during the war, less than 5 percent of the population lived in those cities. Furthermore, the coast offered so many excel-lent harbors that essential commerce was easily rerouted. In other words, the loss of cities did little to damage the American cause.

Most of all, British officials did not at first under-stand that military triumph would not necessarily lead to political victory. Securing the colonies permanently would require hundreds of thousands of Americans to return to their original allegiance. Great Britain needed to both overpower and convert the patriots. After 1778 the ministry adopted a strategy designed to achieve that goal through the expanded use of loyalist forces and the restoration of civilian authority in occupied areas. But the new policy came too late. Britain's leaders never fully realized that they were fighting an entirely new kind of conflict: the first modern war of national liberation.

Great Britain at least had a bureaucracy ready to supervise the war effort. The Americans had only the Second Continental Congress, originally planned as a brief gathering to consider the ministry's response to the Continental Association. Instead, the delegates who convened in Philadelphia on May 10, 1775, had to assume the mantle of intercolonial government. As the summer passed, Congress authorized the printing of money with which to purchase necessary goods, established a committee to supervise relations with foreign countries, and took steps to strengthen the militia. Most important, it created the Continental Army and appointed its generals.

Second Continental Congress

Until Congress met, the Massachusetts provincial congress had taken responsibility for organizing the militiamen encamped at Boston. However, the cost of maintaining that army was a burden, and so Massachusetts asked the Continental Congress to assume the task of directing it. As a first step, Congress had to choose a commander-in-chief, and many delegates recognized the importance of naming someone who was not a New Englander. John Adams proposed the appointment of a Virginian "whose Skill and Experience as an Officer, whose . . . great Talents and excellent universal Character, would command the Approbation of all America": George Washington. The Congress unanimously concurred.

Washington was no fiery radical, nor had he played a prominent role in the prerevolutionary agitation. But his devotion to the American cause was unquestioned. He was dignified, conservative, and respectable—a man of unimpeachable integrity. Though unmistakably an aristocrat, he was unswervingly committed to representative government. He had other desirable traits as well. His stamina was remarkable, and he both looked and acted like a leader.

George Washington: A Portrait of Leadership

Washington needed all the coolness and caution he could muster when he took command of the army outside Boston in July 1775. It took him months to impose hierarchy and discipline on the unruly troops and to bring order to the supply system. But by March 1776, when the arrival of cannon from Ticonderoga finally enabled him to put direct pressure on the redcoats in the city, the army was prepared to act. As it happened, an assault on Boston proved unnecessary. Sir William Howe, who had replaced Gage, wanted to transfer his troops to New York City. The patriots' new cannon decided the matter. On March 17, the British and more than a thousand of their loyalist allies abandoned Boston forever.

British Evacuation of Boston

That spring of 1776, as the British fleet left Boston for the temporary haven of Halifax, Nova Scotia, the colonies were moving inexorably toward a declaration of independence. Even months after fighting began, American leaders still denied seeking a break with Great Britain. But in January 1776 there appeared a pamphlet by a man who advocated such a step.

Thomas Paine's *Common Sense* exploded on the American scene like a bombshell. Within three months of publication, it sold 120,000 copies. The author, a radical English printer who had lived in America only since 1774, called stridently for independence. Paine also challenged many common American assumptions about government and the colonies' relationship to Britain. Rejecting the notion that a balance of monarchy, aristocracy, and democracy was necessary to preserve freedom, he advocated the establishment of a *republic*, a government by the people with no king or nobility. Instead of acknowledging the benefits of links to the mother country, Paine insisted that Britain had exploited the colonies unmercifully. And for the frequently heard assertion that an independent America would be weak and divided, he substituted an unlimited confidence in America's strength once freed from European control.

Thomas Paine's *Common Sense*

There is no way of knowing how many people were converted to the cause of independence by reading *Common Sense*. But by late spring in 1776 independence had become inevitable. On May 10, the Second Continental Congress formally recommended that individual colonies "adopt such governments as shall, in the opinion of the representatives of the people, best conduce to the happiness and safety of their constituents in particular, and America in general." From that source stemmed the first state constitutions.

Then on June 7 Richard Henry Lee of Virginia, seconded by John Adams of Massachusetts, introduced the crucial resolution: "that these United Colonies are, and of right ought to be, free and independent States, that they are absolved of all allegiance to the British Crown, and that all political connection between them and the State of Great Britain is, and ought to be, totally dissolved." Congress debated but did not immediately adopt Lee's resolution. Instead, it postponed a vote until early July and appointed a five-man committee—including Thomas Jefferson, John Adams, and Benjamin Franklin—to draft a declaration of independence. The committee assigned primary responsibility for writing the declaration to Jefferson, who was well known for his apt and eloquent style.

The thirty-four-year-old Thomas Jefferson, a Virginia lawyer, had been educated at the College of William and Mary. A member of the House of Burgesses, he had read widely in history and political theory. That broad knowledge was evident not only in the declaration but also in his draft of the Virginia state constitution, completed just a few days before his appointment to the committee.

Thomas Jefferson and the Declaration of Independence

The draft of the declaration was laid before Congress on June 28, 1776. The delegates officially voted for independence four days later, then debated the wording of the declaration for two more days, adopting it with some changes on July 4. Since Americans had long ago ceased to see themselves as legitimate subjects of Parliament, the Declaration of Independence concentrated on George III (see the appendix). The document accused the king of attempting to destroy representative government in the colonies and of oppressing Americans through the unjustified use of excessive force.

The declaration's chief long-term importance, however, did not lie in its lengthy catalogue of grievances against George III. It lay instead in the ringing statements of principle that have served ever since as the ideal to which Americans aspire: "We hold these truths to be self-evident: That all men are created equal; that they are endowed by their Creator with certain unalienable rights; that among these are life, liberty and the pursuit of happiness; that, to secure these rights, governments are instituted among men, deriving their just powers from the consent of the governed; that whenever any form of government becomes destructive of these ends, it is the right of the people to alter or to abolish it, and to institute new government." These phrases have echoed down through American history like no others.

When the delegates in Philadelphia adopted the declaration, they risked their necks: they were committing treason. Therefore, when they concluded the declaration with the assertion that they "mutually

A statue of George III standing in the Bowling Green in New York City was one of the first casualties of the American Revolution, as colonists marked the adoption of the Declaration of Independence by pulling it down. Much of the metal was melted to make bullets, but in the twentieth century the head—largely intact—was unearthed in Connecticut. (Lafayette College Art Collection, Easton, Pennsylvania)

pledge[d] to each other our lives, our fortunes, and our sacred honor," they spoke no less than the truth.

The Long Struggle in the North

 In late June 1776, the first ships carrying Sir William Howe's troops from Halifax appeared off the coast of New York (see Map 6.1). On July 2, the day Congress voted for independence, redcoats landed on Staten Island. Washington marched his army of seventeen thousand from Boston to defend Manhattan. Because Howe waited until more troops arrived from England before attacking, the American army was able to prepare to defend the city.

But Washington and his men, still inexperienced in fighting and maneuvering, made major mistakes,

Loss of New York

losing battles at Brooklyn Heights and on Manhattan Island. The city fell to the British, who captured nearly three thousand American soldiers. During the autumn months, Washington retreated across New Jersey, with Howe in leisurely pursuit. The British took control of most of the state, and hundreds of New Jerseyites and Pennsylvanians accepted pardons for their "treasonous" activities. Occupying troops met little opposition, and the revolutionary cause appeared to be in disarray.

The British let their advantage slip away as redcoats stationed in New Jersey went on a rampage of rape and plunder. Because the invad-

Battles in New Jersey

ing troops failed to distinguish between loyalists and patriots, families on both sides suffered. Redcoats looted and burned houses and desecrated churches and public buildings. The murder and rape of innocent civilians alienated potentially loyal New Jerseyites whose allegiance the British could ill afford to lose. It also spurred Washington's determination to strike back. Moving quickly, he attacked a Hessian encampment at Trenton early in the morning of December 26, while the redcoats were still reeling from their Christmas celebration. A few days later, Washington attacked again at Princeton. Having gained command of the field and buoyed American spirits with the two swift victories, Washington set up winter quarters at Morristown, New Jersey.

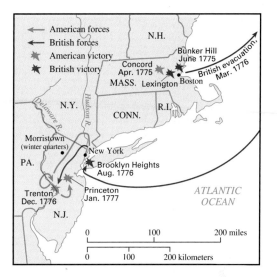

Map 6.1   The War in the North, 1775–1777
The early phase of the Revolutionary War was dominated by British troop movements in the Boston area, the redcoats' evacuation to Nova Scotia in the spring of 1776, and the subsequent British invasion of New York and New Jersey.

The 1776 campaign established patterns that persisted throughout much of the war, despite changes in British leadership and strategy. The British forces usually outnumbered and were often better led than the Americans. But their ponderous style of maneuvering, lack of familiarity with the terrain, and inability to live off the land without antagonizing the populace partially offset those advantages. Furthermore, although Washington always seemed to lack regular troops— the Continental Army never numbered more than 18,500 men—he could usually count on the militia to join him at crucial times. American militiamen preferred not to enlist for long terms of service or to fight far from home; but when their homes were threatened, they rallied to the cause.

As the war dragged on, the Continental Army and the militia took on decidedly different characters.

The American Army

State governments, responsible for filling military quotas, discovered that most men willing to enlist for long periods in the regular army were young, single, and footloose. Farmers with families tended to prefer short-term militia duty. As the

At the Battle of Princeton in early 1777, American forces under George Washington cemented the victory they had won a few days earlier at Trenton. This view was painted in 1787 by James Peale, who fought in the battle.   (Princeton University Library)

supply of men willing to join the Continentals dwindled, recruiters in northern states turned increasingly to African Americans, both slave and free. Approximately five thousand blacks eventually served in the army, most of them winning their freedom as a result. Also attached to the American forces were a number of women, the wives and widows of poor soldiers. Such camp followers worked as cooks, nurses, and launderers in return for rations and low wages. While the American army was unwieldy and difficult to manage, its shapelessness reflected an almost unlimited reservoir of manpower and womanpower.

The flashy "Gentleman Johnny" Burgoyne planned the major British effort in 1777. A subordinate of Howe, Burgoyne spent the winter in London,

Planning the 1777 Campaign

where he gained the ear of Lord George Germain. Burgoyne convinced Germain that he could lead an invading force of redcoats and Indians down the Hudson River from Canada, cutting off New England from the rest of the states. He proposed to rendezvous near Albany with a similar force that would move east along the Mohawk River valley. The combined forces would then presumably link up with Sir William Howe's troops in New York City.

That Burgoyne's scheme would give "Gentleman Johnny" all the glory did not escape Sir William's notice. While Burgoyne plotted in London, Howe prepared his own plans to take Philadelphia. Just as Burgoyne omitted Howe from his plans, so too Howe omitted Burgoyne. Thus the two major British armies in America would operate independently in 1777; the result would be a disaster.

Howe captured Philadelphia, but he did so in an inexplicable fashion, taking six weeks to transport his troops by sea instead of marching them overland. That maneuver cost him at least a month, debilitated his men, depleted his supplies, and placed him only 40 miles closer to Philadelphia than when he started. By the time Howe advanced on Philadelphia, Washington had had time to prepare its defenses. Twice, at Brandywine Creek and again at Germantown, the two armies clashed near the patriot capital. Although the British won both engagements, the Americans handled themselves well. The redcoats took Philadelphia in late September, but to little effect. The campaign season was nearly over, and far to the north Burgoyne was going down to defeat.

Howe Takes Philadelphia

Burgoyne and his men set out from Montreal in mid-June 1777, floating down Lake Champlain into New York in canoes and flat-bottom boats. They easily captured Fort Ticonderoga, but problems began when Burgoyne started an overland march. Because Burgoyne's clumsy artillery carriages and baggage wagons foundered in the heavy forests and ravines, his troops took twenty-four days to travel 23 miles. In August the campaign suffered two sharp blows—the first when the redcoats and Indians marching east along the Mohawk River turned back after a battle at Oriskany, New York; the second when in a clash near Bennington, Vermont, American militiamen nearly wiped out eight hundred of Burgoyne's German mercenaries. Yet the general continued to dawdle, giving the Americans more than enough time to prepare for his coming. After several skirmishes with an American army commanded by General Horatio Gates, Burgoyne was surrounded near Saratoga, New York. On October 17, 1777, he surrendered his entire force of more than six thousand men.

Burgoyne's Campaign in New York

The battle at Oriskany divided the Iroquois Confederacy. In 1776 the Six Nations formally pledged to remain neutral in the Anglo-American struggle. But two influential Mohawk leaders worked tirelessly to persuade their fellow Iroquois to join the British. Both

Split of the Iroquois Confederacy

Mary Brant, a powerful tribal matron and the widow of the Indian superintendent Sir William Johnson, and her younger brother Joseph, a renowned warrior, strongly believed that the Six Nations should ally themselves with the British in order to prevent American encroachment on their lands. The Brants won over to the British the Senecas, Cayugas, and Mohawks. But the Oneidas preferred the American side and brought the Tuscaroras with them. The Onondagas split into three factions, one on each side and one supporting neutrality. The wartime division shattered the Iroquois' three-hundred-year league of friendship.

The collapse of Iroquois unity and the confederacy's abandonment of neutrality had significant consequences. In 1778 Iroquois warriors allied with the British raided frontier villages in Pennsylvania and New York. To retaliate, an American expedition under General John Sullivan burned Iroquois crops, orchards, and settlements. The resulting devastation forced many bands to leave their ancestral homeland. A large number of Iroquois settled permanently in British Canada.

Burgoyne's surrender at Saratoga brought joy to patriots, discouragement to loyalists and Britons. It also prompted Lord North to authorize a peace commission to offer the Americans what they had requested in the Declaration of Rights and Grievances in 1774—in effect, a return to the imperial system of 1763. That proposal came far too late: the patriots rejected the overture.

Most important, the American victory at Saratoga drew France formally into the conflict. Ever since 1763, the French had sought to avenge their defeat in the Seven Years War, and the American Revolution gave them that opportunity. Even before Benjamin Franklin arrived in Paris in late 1776, France was covertly supplying the revolutionaries with military necessities.

Benjamin Franklin worked tirelessly to strengthen ties between the two nations. By presenting himself as a representative of American simplicity, Franklin played on the French image of Americans as virtuous yeomen. His efforts culminated in 1778 when the countries signed two treaties. In the Treaty of Amity and Commerce,

Franco-American Alliance of 1778

A British cartoon published in 1780. Even after Spain and the Netherlands had joined
France in supporting the Americans' quest for independence, this artist had confidence in
Britain's ability to outweigh the alliance in "The Ballance of Power." (Print Collection,
Miriam and Ira D. Wallach Division of Art, Prints and Photographs. The New York Public
Library, Astor, Lenox, and Tilden Foundations)

France recognized American independence, establishing trade ties with the new nation. In the Treaty of Alliance, France and the United States promised—assuming that France would go to war with Britain, which it soon did—that neither would negotiate peace with the enemy without consulting the other. France also formally abandoned any claim to Canada and to North American territory east of the Mississippi River.

The French alliance had two major benefits for the patriot cause. First, France began to aid the Americans openly, sending troops and naval vessels in addition to arms, ammunition, clothing, and blankets. Second, Great Britain could no longer focus solely on the American mainland, for it had to fight France in the Caribbean and elsewhere. Spain's entry into the war in 1779 as an ally of France (but not of the United States) further magnified Britain's problems, for the Revolution then became a global war.

The Long Struggle in the South

 In the aftermath of the Saratoga disaster, Lord George Germain and British military officials reassessed their strategy. Maneuvering in the North had done them little good; perhaps shifting the field of battle southward would bring success.

Sir Henry Clinton, Howe's replacement, became convinced that a southern strategy would succeed. In

British Victories in South Carolina

late 1779 he sailed down the coast from New York to besiege Charleston (formerly Charles Town), the most important city in the South (see Map 6.2). The Americans held out for months, but on May 12, 1780, General Benjamin Lincoln surrendered the entire southern army. The redcoats then spread throughout South Carolina, organizing loyalist regiments.

Yet the triumph was less complete than it appeared. The success of the southern campaign depended on control of the seas, for only by sea could the widely dispersed British armies coordinate their efforts. For the moment, the Royal Navy safely dominated the American coastline, but French naval power posed a threat to the entire southern enterprise. Moreover, the redcoats never managed to establish full control of the areas they seized. Patriot bands operated freely throughout the state, and loyalists could not be guaranteed protection against their enemies. Last but not least, the fall of Charleston spurred the patriots to greater exertions.

Nevertheless, the war in South Carolina went badly for the patriots throughout most of 1780. At Camden in August, forces under Lord Cornwallis, the new British commander in the South, crushingly defeated a reorganized southern army led by Horatio Gates. Hundreds, even thousands, of enslaved African Americans joined the redcoats, seeking freedom on the basis of Lord Dunmore's 1775 proclamation. Their actions disrupted planting and harvesting in the Carolinas, and thus had the effect that Dunmore sought.

After the Camden defeat, Washington appointed General Nathanael Greene to command the southern campaign. In the dire circumstances that he faced, Greene had to move cautiously.

Greene and the Southern Campaign

Adopting a conciliatory policy toward loyalists and neutrals, he persuaded the governor of South Carolina to pardon those who had fought for the British if they would now join the patriot militia. He also ordered his troops to treat captives fairly and not to loot loyalist property. Greene recognized that the patriots could win only by convincing the populace that they could bring stability to the region.

Since he had so few regulars (only sixteen hundred when he took command), Greene had to rely on west-

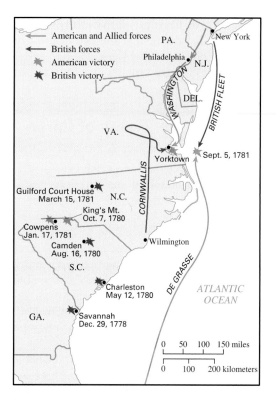

Map 6.2   The War in the South   The southern war—after the British invasion of Georgia in late 1778—was characterized by a series of British thrusts into the interior, leading to battles with American defenders in both North and South Carolina. Finally, after promising beginnings, Cornwallis's foray into Virginia ended with disaster at Yorktown in October 1781.

ern volunteers and could not afford to have frontier militia companies occupied in defending their homes from Indian attack. He accordingly pursued diplomacy aimed at keeping the Indians out of the war. His policy worked; by war's end, only the Creeks remained allied with Great Britain.

Even before Greene took command of the southern army in December 1780, the tide had begun to turn. In October, at King's Mountain, a force from the settlements west of the Appalachians defeated a large party of redcoats and loyalists. Then in January 1781 Greene's trusted aide Daniel Morgan brilliantly routed the crack British regiment Tarleton's Legion at Cowpens. Greene himself confronted the main body of British troops under Lord Cornwallis at Guilford

Court House, North Carolina, in March. Although Cornwallis controlled the field at the end of the day, most of his army had been destroyed. He had to retreat to the coast to receive supplies and fresh troops from New York.

Yorktown and the Treaty of Paris

 Cornwallis headed north into Virginia, where he joined forces with a detachment of redcoats commanded by the American traitor Benedict Arnold. Instead of acting decisively with his new army of 7,200 men, Cornwallis withdrew to the peninsula between the York and James Rivers, where he fortified Yorktown and awaited more supplies and reinforcements. Seizing the opportunity, Washington quickly moved more than 7,000 troops south from New York City. When a French fleet defeated the Royal Navy vessels sent to relieve Cornwallis, the British general was trapped. On October 19, 1781, Cornwallis surrendered.

When news of the surrender reached London, Lord North's ministry fell. Parliament voted to cease offensive operations in America, authorizing peace negotiations. Washington returned with the main army to the environs of New York, where his underpaid— and, they thought, underappreciated—officers grew restive; in March 1783 they threatened to mutiny unless Congress compensated them adequately. Washington, warned in advance of the so-called Newburgh Conspiracy, met the challenge brilliantly. Summoning his officers, he defused the crisis with a well-reasoned but emotional speech drawing on their patriotism. When, fumbling for glasses, he remarked that "I have grown gray in your service and now find myself growing blind," eyewitnesses reported that many of the rebellious officers began to cry. At the end of the year, Washington stood before Congress and formally resigned his commission as commander-in-chief. Through this action, Washington established an enduring precedent: civilian control of the American military.

The war had been won, but at terrible cost. More than twenty-five thousand American men died in the war. In the South, years of guerrilla warfare and the loss of thousands of runaway slaves shattered the economy. Indebtedness soared, and local governments were crippled for lack of funds, since few people could afford to pay their taxes.

The Cost of Victory

Americans rejoiced when they learned of the signing of the preliminary peace treaty at Paris in November 1782. The American diplomats—Benjamin Franklin, John Jay, and John Adams—ignored their instructions from Congress to be guided by France and instead negotiated directly with Great Britain. Their instincts were sound: the French government was more an enemy to Britain than a friend to the United States. In fact, French ministers worked secretly behind the scenes to try to prevent the establishment of a strong and unified government in America. But the American delegates proved adept at power politics; and, weary of war, the new British ministry, headed by Lord Shelburne, made numerous concessions.

Treaty of Paris

The treaty, signed formally on September 3, 1783, granted the Americans unconditional independence. Generous boundaries delineated the new nation: to the north, approximately the present-day boundary with Canada; to the south, the 31st parallel (about the modern northern border of Florida); to the west, the Mississippi River. Florida, which Britain had acquired in 1763, reverted to Spain. The Americans also gained unlimited fishing rights off Newfoundland. In ceding so much land to the United States, Great Britain ignored the territorial rights of its Indian allies, sacrificing their interests to the demands of European politics. British diplomats also poorly served loyalists and British merchants. The treaty's ambiguously worded clauses pertaining to the payment of prewar debts and the postwar treatment of loyalists caused trouble for years to come.

Summary

 With the long war finally over, the victorious Americans could look back on their achievement with satisfaction and awe. They had taken on the greatest military power in the world and won. In winning the war, the Americans reshaped the physical and mental landscapes in which they lived. They abandoned the British identity once so important to them and began the process of creating loyalty to a new nation. They also established a claim to most of the territory east of the Mississippi River and south of the Great Lakes, thereby greatly expanding the land potentially open to their settlements.

In achieving independence, Americans surmounted formidable challenges. But in the future they faced perhaps even greater ones: establishing stable republican governments at the state and national levels and ensuring their government's continued existence in a world of bitter rivalries among the major powers—Britain, France, and Spain.

LEGACY FOR A PEOPLE AND A NATION
The Black Patriots' Memorial

The Black Patriots Foundation has been actively soliciting private funds to build a memorial to the approximately five thousand African Americans who fought in the revolutionary army. The National Capital Planning Commission has approved a site on the mall in Washington, D.C., and a commemorative silver dollar, authorized by Act of Congress, is being sold to raise money. A sculptor has been selected, a design chosen. The black soldiers of the Revolution, declared a foundation supporter at a 1996 Memorial Day ceremony, "have been tragically overlooked by history. It's time—past time—that we right this historical wrong by honoring their noble service with a fitting memorial."

Although historians of the American Revolution appreciate the impulse behind the campaign, many find the project ironic. A prime example of what scholars have termed "contribution history"—that is, the notion that a people's history is important primarily insofar as it has contributed to the history of the nation—the Black Patriots' Memorial would enshrine in bronze the story of only approximately 10 percent of the African Americans who fought in the Revolutionary War. With good reason, the other 90 percent aligned themselves with the British.

Enslaved African Americans understandably sought their own personal freedom during the Revolution. The British held out that prospect to *any* slave of a rebel—man, woman, or child—who joined them during the conflict. Only a few African American men received similar promises from the patriot side. Black loyalists, who at the end of the war emigrated to the Bahamas, England, or Nova Scotia, and some of whom later founded Sierra Leone on the African continent, represented the vast majority of black participants in the Revolution.

The Black Patriots' Memorial ignores the fact that—judging by the number of slaves who seized freedom by joining the British forces—the Revolution was by far the most successful slave revolt in American history. Through their devotion to personal liberty and their open challenge to enslavement, the black people who chose loyalism have left at least as great a legacy to the nation today as did the much smaller number of black patriots.

For Further Reading, see the Appendix. For Web resources, go to history.college.hmco.com/students.

7

FORGING A NATIONAL REPUBLIC

1776–1789

On December 26, 1787, a group of Federalists—supporters of the proposed Constitution—gathered in Carlisle, a town on the Pennsylvania frontier. The men planned to fire a cannon to celebrate their state convention's ratification vote two weeks earlier, but a large crowd of Antifederalists prevented them from doing so. After forcing the Federalists to flee, the angry Antis publicly burned a copy of the Constitution.

The next day, the Federalists returned in force to fire their cannon and to read the convention's ratification proclamation. Choosing not to create another violent confrontation, Antifederalists instead paraded around the town effigies of two supporters of the Constitution, then burned them. When Federalist officials later arrested several Antifederalists on riot charges, the Antifederalist-dominated militia mustered to break the men out of jail. Only a flaw in the warrant—which freed the arrestees legally—prevented another bloody brawl.

The Carlisle riots presaged violent disputes over the new Constitution in Albany (New York), Providence (Rhode Island), and other cities. What happened in Carlisle in late 1787 was one incident in an ongoing struggle that began in 1775 and continued until the end of the century. In that contest, Americans argued continually over how to implement republican principles and who represented the people's will. Easterners debated with westerners; elites contended with ordinary folk. Public celebrations played an important part in the struggle, because in a world in which only relatively few property-holding men had the right to vote, other people expressed their political opinions in the streets.

Republicanism—the idea that governments should be based wholly on the consent of the people—originated with political theorists in ancient Greece and Rome. Republics, the theorists declared, were desirable yet fragile forms of government. Unless their

108

IMPORTANT EVENTS

1776 Second Continental Congress directs states to draft constitutions

1777 Articles of Confederation sent to states for ratification

Vermont becomes first state to abolish slavery

1781 Articles of Confederation ratified

1786 Annapolis Convention meets, discusses reforming government

1786–87 Shays's Rebellion in western Massachusetts raises questions about future of the republic

1787 Northwest Ordinance organizes territory north of Ohio River and east of Mississippi River

Constitutional Convention

1788 Hamilton, Jay, and Madison write *The Federalist*

Constitution ratified

1794 Wayne defeats Miami Confederacy at Fallen Timbers

1795 Treaty of Greenville opens Ohio to white settlement

---

citizens were especially virtuous—that is, sober, moral, and industrious—and largely in agreement on key issues, republics were doomed to failure. When Americans left the British Empire, they abandoned the idea that the best system of government required participation by a king, the nobility, and the people. They substituted a belief in the superiority of republicanism, in which the people, not Parliament, were sovereign. That decision raised several interrelated questions. How could Americans best ensure political stability? How could they foster consensus among the populace? How could they create and sustain a virtuous republic?

America's political and intellectual leaders worked hard to inculcate virtue in their fellow countrymen and countrywomen. After 1776, American literature, theater, art, architecture, and education all pursued explicitly moral goals. The education of women was considered particularly important, for as the mothers of the republic's children, they were primarily responsible for ensuring the nation's future. On such matters Americans could agree, but they disagreed on many other critical issues. Almost all white men assumed that women, Indians, and African Americans should have no formal role in politics, but they found it difficult to reach a consensus on how many of their own number should be included, how often elections should be held, or how their new governments should be structured.

Especially troublesome were Thomas Jefferson's words in the Declaration of Independence: "all men are created equal." Given that bold statement of principle, how could white republicans justify holding African Americans in perpetual bondage? Some answered that question by freeing their slaves or by voting for state laws that abolished slavery. Others responded by denying that blacks were "men" in the same sense as whites.

The most important task facing Americans in these years was the construction of a genuinely national government. Before 1765 the British mainland colonies had rarely cooperated on common endeavors, but fighting the Revolutionary War had brought them together and created a new nationalistic spirit. During the war, Americans began the process of replacing loyalties to state and region with loyalties to the nation.

Still, forging a national republic was neither easy nor simple. America's first such government, under the Articles of Confederation, proved too weak and decentralized. But some of the nation's political leaders learned from their experiences and tried another approach when they drafted the Constitution in 1787. Although some historians have argued that the Constitution represents an "aristocratic" counterrevolution against the "democratic" Articles, the two documents are more accurately viewed as successive attempts to solve the same problems—for instance, the relationship of states and nation and the extent to which authority should be centralized. ■

Creating a Virtuous Republic

 When the colonies declared their independence from Great Britain, John Dickinson recalled many years later, "there was no question concerning forms of Government, no enquiry whether a Republic or a limited Monarchy was best. . . . We knew that the people of this country must unite themselves under some form of Government and that this could be no other than the republican form." But how should that goal be implemented?

Three different definitions of *republicanism* emerged in the new United States. Ancient history and political theory informed the first,
Varieties of Republicanism
held chiefly by members of the educated elite. The histories of popular governments in Greece and Rome suggested that republics could succeed only if they were small in size and homogeneous in population. Unless a republic's citizens were willing to sacrifice their own private interests for the good of the whole, the government would collapse. In return for sacrifices, though, a republic offered its citizens equality of opportunity. A republic's government would be in the hands of a "natural aristocracy" of men whose rank had been attained by merit rather than inheritance.

A second definition, advanced by other members of the elite but also by some skilled craftsmen, drew more on economic theory than on political thought. Instead of perceiving the nation as an organic whole composed of people nobly sacrificing for the common good, this version of republicanism followed the Scottish theorist Adam Smith in emphasizing individuals' pursuit of rational self-interest. When republican men sought to improve their own economic and social circumstances, the entire nation would benefit. Republican virtue would be achieved through the pursuit of private interests, rather than through subordination to some communal ideal.

The third notion of republicanism was less influential but more egalitarian than the other two. Many of its illiterate or barely literate proponents could write little to promote their beliefs. Men who advanced the third version of republicanism called for widening men's participation in the political process. They also wanted government to respond directly to the needs of ordinary folk, rejecting any notion that the "lesser sort" should automatically defer to their "betters." They were, indeed, democrats in more or less the modern sense.

Despite their differences, the three strands of republicanism shared many of the same assumptions. All three contrasted the industrious virtue of America to the corruption of Britain and Europe. In the first version, that virtue manifested itself in frugality and self-sacrifice; in the second, it would prevent self-interest from becoming vice; in the third, it was the justification for including even propertyless free men in the ranks of voters.

As citizens of the United States set out to construct their republic, they believed they were embarking on an unprecedented enterprise.
Virtue and the Arts
With great pride in their new nation, they expected to replace the vices of monarchical Europe with the sober virtues of republican America. They wanted to embody republican principles not only in their governments but also in their society and culture. They looked to painting, literature, drama, and architecture to convey messages of nationalism and virtue to the public.

Americans faced a crucial contradiction at the very outset of their efforts. To some republicans, the fine arts themselves were manifestations of vice. What need did a frugal yeoman have for a painting—or, worse yet, a novel? The first American artists, playwrights, and authors thus confronted an impossible dilemma. They wanted to produce works embodying virtue, but those very works were viewed by many as corrupting.

Still, they tried. William Hill Brown's *The Power of Sympathy* (1789), the first novel written in the United States, was a lurid tale of seduction intended as a warning to young women, who made up a large proportion of America's fiction readers. In Royall Tyler's *The Contrast* (1787), the first successful American play, the virtuous conduct of Colonel Manly was contrasted (hence the title) with the reprehensible behavior of the fop Billy Dimple. The most popular book of the era, Mason Locke Weems's *Life of Washington* (1800), was intended by its author to "hold up his great Virtues . . . to the imitation of Our Youth."

Painting and architecture, too, were expected to embody high moral standards. Two of the most prominent artists of the period, Gilbert Stuart and Charles Willson Peale, painted innumerable portraits of upstanding republican citizens. John Trumbull's vast canvases depicting milestones of American history such as Cornwallis's capitulation at Yorktown were intended to instill patriotic sentiments in their viewers. Architects likewise hoped to convey in their buildings a sense of the young republic's ideals. When the Virginia government asked Thomas Jefferson for advice on the design of the state capitol in Richmond, Jefferson unhesitatingly recommended copying a Roman building. Jefferson set forth ideals that would guide American architecture for a generation to come: simplicity of line, harmonious proportions, a feeling of grandeur.

Despite the artists' efforts, some Americans began to detect signs of luxury and corruption by the mid-1780s. The resumption of European trade after the war brought a return to fashionable clothing and abandonment of the simpler homespun garments patriots had once worn with pride. Elite families again attended balls and concerts. Parties no longer seemed complete without gambling and cardplaying. Especially alarming to fervent republicans was the establishment in 1783 of the Society of the Cincinnati, a hereditary association for Revolutionary War officers and their descendants. Opponents feared that the group would become the nucleus of a native-born aristocracy.

Americans' deep-seated concern for the future of the republic focused their attention on their children, the "rising generation." Education

Educational Reform

had previously been seen as a private means to personal advancement, a concern only for individual families. Now, though, schooling would serve a public purpose. If young people were to become useful citizens prepared for self-government, they would need a better education. In fact, the very survival of the nation depended on it. The 1780s and 1790s thus witnessed two major changes in educational practice.

First, in contrast to the colonies, where nearly all education had been privately financed, some northern states began to use tax money to support public elementary schools. In 1789 Massachusetts became one of the first states to require towns to offer their citizens free public elementary education. Second, schooling

for girls was improved. Americans' recognition of the importance of the rising generation led to the realization that mothers would have to be properly educated if they were to instruct their children adequately. Therefore, Massachusetts insisted in its 1789 law that town elementary schools be open to girls as well as boys. Throughout the United States, private academies were founded to give teenage girls from well-to-do families an opportunity for advanced schooling. No one yet proposed opening colleges to women, but a few fortunate girls could study history, geography, rhetoric, and mathematics.

The chief theorist of women's education in the early republic was Judith Sargent Murray of Massachusetts. In a series of essays published in

Judith Sargent Murray and Women's Education

the 1780s and 1790s, Murray argued that women and men had equal intellectual capacities, that boys and girls should be offered equivalent scholastic training, and that girls should be taught to support themselves by their own efforts.

Murray's theories were part of a general rethinking of women's position that occurred as a result of the Revolution. Male patriots who enlisted in the army or served in Congress were away from home for long periods of time. In their absence their wives, who previously had handled only the "indoor affairs" of the household, shouldered the responsibility for "outdoor affairs" as well. As the wife of a Connecticut militiaman later recalled, her husband "was out more or less during the remainder of the war [after 1777], so much so as to be unable to do anything on our farm. What was done, was done by myself." Both men and women realized that female patriots had made vital and important contributions to winning the war through their work at home and that their notions of proper gender roles had to be rethought. Americans began to develop new ideas about the role women should play in a republican society.

The best-known expression of those new ideas appears in a letter Abigail Adams addressed to her husband

Abigail Adams: "Remember the Ladies"

John in March 1776. "In the new Code of Laws which I suppose it will be necessary for you to make I desire you would Remember the Ladies," she wrote. "If perticuliar care and attention is not paid to the Laidies [*sic*] we are determined to foment a Rebellion, and will not hold ourselves bound by any Laws in which we have no voice, or Representation." With these words, Abigail Adams took a step that was soon to be duplicated by other disfranchised Americans. She deliberately applied the ideology developed to combat parliamentary supremacy to purposes revolutionary leaders had never intended.

Abigail Adams did not ask that women be allowed to vote, but others claimed that right. The men who drafted the New Jersey state constitution in 1776 defined voters carelessly as "all free inhabitants" who met certain property qualifications. They thereby unintentionally gave the vote to property-holding white spinsters and widows, as well as to free black landowners. Qualified women and African Americans regularly voted in New Jersey's local and congressional elections until 1807, when they were disfranchised by the state legislature. Yet the fact that women voted at all was evidence of their altered perception of their place in the political life of the country.

Such dramatic episodes were unusual. After the war, European Americans continued to believe that women's primary function was to be good wives, mothers, and mistresses of households. They perceived significant differences between male and female characters. That distinction eventually enabled Americans to resolve the conflict between the two most influential strands of republican thought. Because wives could not own property or participate directly in economic life, women in general came to be seen as the embodiment of self-sacrificing, disinterested republicanism. Through new female-run charitable associations founded after the war, better-off women assumed public responsibilities, in particular through caring for poor widows and orphaned children. Thus men were freed to pursue economic self-interest (that other republican virtue), secure in the knowledge that their wives and daughters were fulfilling the family's obligation to the common good. The ideal republican man, therefore, was an individualist, seeking advancement for himself and his family. The ideal republican woman, by contrast, always put the well-being of others ahead of her own.

Together European American men and women established the context for the creation of a virtuous

Women's Role in the Republic

republic. But how did approximately 700,000 African Americans fit into the developing national plan?

The First Emancipation and the Growth of Racism

 Revolutionary ideology exposed one of the primary contradictions in American society. Both European and African Americans saw the irony in slaveholders' claims that they sought to prevent Britain from "enslaving" them. In 1773 Dr. Benjamin Rush of Philadelphia, an ardent patriot, warned that liberty "cannot thrive long in the neighborhood of slavery."

African Americans did not need revolutionary ideology to tell them that slavery was wrong, but they quickly took advantage of that ideology. In 1779 a group of slaves from Portsmouth, New Hampshire, asked the state legislature "from what authority [our masters] assume to dispose of our lives, freedom and property." The same year several bondspeople in Fairfield, Connecticut, petitioned the legislature for their freedom, characterizing slavery as a "dreadful Evil" and "flagrant Injustice."

Both legislatures responded negatively, but the postwar years witnessed the gradual abolition of slavery in the North, a process that has become known as "the first emancipation." Vermont abolished slavery in its 1777 constitution. Massachusetts courts decided in the 1780s that a clause in the state constitution prohibited slavery. Most of the other northern and middle states adopted gradual emancipation laws between 1780 (Pennsylvania) and 1804 (New Jersey). No southern state adopted similar general emancipation laws, but the legislatures of Virginia (1782), Delaware (1787), and Maryland (1790 and 1796) altered laws that earlier had restricted slaveowners' ability to free their bondspeople. South Carolina and Georgia never considered adopting such acts, and North Carolina insisted that all manumissions (emancipations of individual slaves) be approved by county courts.

Emancipation and Manumission

Revolutionary ideology thus had limited impact on the well-entrenched economic interests of large slaveholders. Only in the North, where slaves were less common, could state legislatures vote to abolish slavery. Even there, legislators' concern for property rights led them to favor gradual emancipation. Most states provided only for the freeing of children born after passage of the law, not for the emancipation of adults. And even those children were to remain slaves until reaching adulthood. Still, by 1840 only one northern state—New Jersey—permitted holding African Americans in bondage.

Despite the slow progress of abolition, the number of free people of African descent in the United States grew dramatically in the first years after the Revolution. Before the war they had been few in number. But wartime disruptions radically augmented the freed population. Slaves who had escaped from plantations during the war, others who had served in the American army, and still others who had been emancipated by their owners or by state laws were now free. By 1790 nearly 60,000 free people of color lived in the United States; ten years later they numbered more than 108,000, nearly 11 percent of the total African American population.

Growth of Free Black Population

In the 1780s and thereafter, freed people from rural areas often made their way to northern port cities. Boston and Philadelphia, where slavery was abolished sooner than in New York City, were popular destinations. Women outnumbered men among the migrants by a margin of three to two, for they had better employment opportunities in the cities, especially in domestic service. Some freedmen also worked in domestic service, but larger numbers were employed as unskilled laborers and sailors. A few of the women and a sizable proportion of men were skilled workers or retailers. As soon as possible they established independent two-parent nuclear families instead of continuing to live in their employers' households. They also began to occupy distinct neighborhoods, probably as a result of discrimination.

Migration to Northern Cities

Emancipation did not bring equality. Laws discriminated against freed people as they had against slaves. South Carolina, for example, did not permit free blacks to testify against whites in court. Public schools often refused to educate their children. Freedmen found it difficult to purchase property and find good jobs. And though in many areas African Americans were accepted as members—even ministers—of evangelical churches, they were rarely allowed an equal voice in church affairs.

Gradually, freed people developed their own institutions. In Charleston mulattos formed the Brown Fellowship Society, which provided insurance coverage for its members, financed a school, and helped to support orphans. In 1794 former slaves in Philadelphia and Baltimore founded societies that eventually became the African Methodist Episcopal (AME) denomination. AME churches later sponsored schools in a number of cities and, along with African Baptist, African Episcopal, and African Presbyterian churches, became cultural centers of the free black community.

Freed People's Churches and Associations

Their endeavors were all the more important because the postrevolutionary years witnessed the development of a formal racist theory in the United States. European Americans had long regarded their slaves as inferior, but the most influential writers had argued that African slaves' seemingly debased character derived from their enslavement, rather than enslavement being the consequence of inherited inferiority. In the Revolution's aftermath, though, slaveowners needed to defend holding other human beings in bondage against the notion that "all men are created equal." Consequently, they began to argue that the principles of republican equality applied only to European Americans. To avoid having to confront the contradiction between their practice and the egalitarian implications of revolutionary theory, they redefined the theory.

Development of Racist Theory

Simultaneously, the very notion of "race" appeared in coherent form, applied to groups defined by skin color as "whites" and "blacks." The rise of egalitarian thinking among European Americans both downplayed status distinctions within their own group and differentiated all "whites" from people of color—Indians and African Americans. (That differentiation soon manifested itself in new miscegenation laws adopted in both northern and southern states to forbid intermarriage among whites and blacks or Indians.) Meanwhile, a generation or two of experience as slaves on American soil forged the identity "African" or

Liberty Displaying the Arts and Sciences: In 1792 the Library Company of Philadelphia, a private lending library founded in the mid-eighteenth century, commissioned the artist Samuel Jennings to produce a depiction of slavery and abolitionism showing the "figure of Liberty (with her Cap and proper Insignia) displaying the arts." The painting, probably the first to celebrate emancipation, shows the blonde goddess presenting books (symbolizing knowledge and freedom) to several suppliant and grateful blacks, while in the background former slaves dance joyfully around a liberty pole. Although the theme is abolition and the African Americans in the foreground have realistic features, the portrayal of blacks in passive roles and diminutive sizes portended future stereotypes. Thus the picture linked emancipation and the growth of racism.   (The Library Company of Philadelphia)

"black" from the various ethnic and national affiliations of people who had survived the transatlantic crossing. Strikingly, among the first to term themselves "Africans" were black oceanic sailors—men whose wide-ranging contacts with Europeans caused them to construct a separate, unified identity for themselves. Thus in the revolutionary era "whiteness" and "blackness"—along with the superiority of the former, the inferiority of the latter—developed as contrasting terms in tandem with each other.

Such racism had several intertwined elements. First came the assertion that, as Thomas Jefferson insisted in 1781, blacks were "inferior to the whites in the endowments both of body and mind." There followed the belief that blacks were congenitally lazy, dishonest, and uncivilized (or uncivilizable). Third, and of crucial importance, was the notion that all blacks were sexually promiscuous and that African American men lusted after European American women. The specter of interracial sexual intercourse involving black men and white women haunted early American racist thought. Significantly, the more common reverse circumstance—the sexual exploitation of enslaved women by their masters—aroused little comment or concern.

African Americans did not allow these developing racist notions to go unchallenged. Benjamin Banneker, a free black surveyor, astronomer, and mathematical genius, directly disputed Thomas Jefferson's belief in Africans' intellectual inferiority. In 1791 Banneker sent Jefferson a copy of his latest almanac (which included his astronomical calculations) as an example of blacks' mental powers. Jefferson's response admitted Banneker's capability but indicated that he regarded Banneker as an exception.

At its birth, then, the republic was defined by its leaders as an exclusively white male enterprise. Indeed, some historians have argued that the

A Republic for White Men Only

subjugation of blacks and women was a necessary precondition for theoretical equality among white men. They have pointed out that identifying a common racial antagonist helped to create white solidarity and to lessen the threat to gentry power posed by the enfranchisement of poorer white men. Some scholars have pointed out that it was less dangerous to allow white men with little property to participate formally in politics than to open the possibility that they might join with former slaves to question the rule of elites. That was perhaps one reason why after the Revolution the division of American society between slave and free was transformed into a division between blacks—some of whom were free—and whites. The white male wielders of power ensured their continued dominance in part by substituting race for enslavement as the primary determinant of African Americans' status.

Designing Republican Governments

In May 1776, the Second Continental Congress directed states to devise new republican governments to replace the provincial congresses and committees that had met since 1774. Thus American men initially concentrated on drafting state constitutions and devoted little attention to their national government.

They immediately faced the problem of defining a "constitution." Americans wanted to create tangible documents specifying the fundamental structures of government. Beginning with Vermont in 1777 and Massachusetts in 1780, the states decided that specially elected conventions—not their regular legislative bodies—should draft the constitutions. Accordingly, states sought direct authorization from the people— the theoretical sovereigns in a republic—before establishing new governments. After preparing new constitutions, delegates submitted them to voters for ratification.

Drafting of State Constitutions

The framers of state constitutions concerned themselves primarily with outlining the distribution of and limitations on government power. Through their experience under British rule, Americans had learned to fear the power of the governor and to see the legislature as their defender. Accordingly, the first state constitutions typically provided for the governor to be elected annually (commonly by the legislature), limited the number of terms he could serve, and gave him little independent authority. Simultaneously, the constitutions expanded the legislature's powers. Every state except Pennsylvania and Vermont retained a two-house structure, with members of the upper house having longer terms and being required to meet higher property-holding standards than members of the lower house. But they also redrew electoral districts to reflect population patterns more accurately, and they increased the number of members in both houses. Finally, most states lowered property qualifications for voting. Thus the revolutionary era witnessed the first deliberate attempt to broaden the base of American government, a process that has continued into our own day.

The constitutions also included explicit limitations on government authority. In an attempt to protect what they regarded as the inalienable rights of individual citizens, seven of the constitutions contained formal bills of rights, and the others had similar clauses. Most guaranteed citizens freedom of the press and of religion, the right to a fair trial, the right of consent to taxation, and protection against general search warrants. An independent judiciary was charged with upholding such rights.

Limits on State Governments

In sum, the constitution makers put far greater emphasis on preventing state governments from becoming tyrannical than on making them effective wielders of political authority. Their approach to shaping governments was understandable, given the American experience with Great Britain. But establishing such weak political units, especially in wartime, practically ensured that the constitutions soon would need revision.

Rewriting the State Constitutions

Invariably, the revised versions increased the powers of the governor and reduced the scope of the legislature's authority. In the mid-1780s, some American political leaders started to develop a theory of checks and balances as the primary means of controlling government power. They sought to balance the powers of the legislative, executive, and judicial branches against one another.

The constitutional theories Americans applied at the state level did not at first influence their conception of national government. Since American officials initially focused on organizing the military struggle against Britain, the powers and structure of the Continental Congress evolved by default early in the war. Not until late 1777 did Congress send the Articles of Confederation to the states for ratification.

Articles of Confederation

The chief organ of national government was a unicameral (one-house) legislature in which each state had one vote. Its powers included conducting foreign relations, mediating disputes between states, controlling maritime affairs, regulating Indian trade, and valuing state and national coinage. The Articles did not give the national government the ability to raise revenue effectively or to enforce a uniform commercial policy. The United States of America was described as "a firm league of friendship" in which each state "retains its sovereignty, freedom and independence, and every Power, Jurisdiction and right, which is not by this confederation expressly delegated to the United States, in Congress assembled."

The Articles required unanimous consent of state legislatures for ratification or amendment, and a clause concerning western lands proved troublesome. The draft accepted by Congress allowed states to retain all land claims derived from their original charters. Because Maryland feared being overpowered by states that could grow in size and power through western land claims, it refused to accept the Articles until 1781, when Virginia finally promised to surrender its western holdings to national jurisdiction. Other states followed suit, establishing the principle that unorganized lands would be held by the nation as a whole.

The capacity of a single state to delay ratification for three years portended the fate of American government under the Articles of Confederation. The Articles' authors had not given adequate thought to the distribution of power within the national government or to the relationship between the Confederation and the states. The Congress they created was simultaneously a legislative body and a collective executive (there was no judiciary), but it had no independent income and no authority to compel the states to accept its rulings.

Trials of the Confederation

Finance posed the most persistent problem faced by both state and national governments. Because legislators at all levels levied taxes only reluctantly, both Congress and the states at first tried to finance the war simply by printing currency. Even though the money was backed by nothing but good faith, it circulated freely and without excessive depreciation during 1775 and most of 1776.

But in late 1776, as the American army suffered reverses in New York and New Jersey, prices began to rise and inflation set in. The currency's value rested on Americans' faith in their government, a faith that was sorely tested during the dark days of early British triumphs in the South

Inflation and Taxation

(1779 and 1780). By early 1780 it took forty paper dollars to purchase one silver dollar. Soon, Continental currency was worthless (see Figure 7.1).

In 1781, faced with total collapse of the monetary system, the congressmen undertook ambitious reforms. After establishing a department of finance under the wealthy Philadelphia merchant Robert Morris, they asked the states to amend the Articles of Confederation to allow Congress to levy a duty of 5 percent on imported goods. Morris put national finances on a

solid footing, but the customs duty was never adopted. First Rhode Island and then New York refused to agree to the tax. The states' resistance reflected fear of a too-powerful central government.

Inability to Regulate Commerce

Because the Articles denied Congress the power to establish a national commercial policy, the realm of foreign trade also exposed the new government's weaknesses. Immediately after the war, Britain, France, and Spain restricted American trade with their colonies. Members of Congress watched helplessly as British manufactured goods flooded the United States while American produce could no longer be sold in the British West Indies, once its prime market. Although Americans reopened commerce with other European countries and started a profitable trade with China in 1784, neither substituted for access to closer and larger markets.

Figure 7.1   Depreciation of Continental Currency, 1777–1780   The depreciation of Continental currency accelerated in 1778, as is shown in this graph measuring its value against one hundred silver dollars. Thereafter, its value dropped almost daily.   (Source: Data from John J. McCusker, "How Much Is That in Real Money? A Historical Price Index for Use as a Deflator of Money Values in the Economy of the United States," *Proceedings of the American Antiquarian Society*, Vol. 101, Pt. 2 [1991], Table C-1.)

Relations with Spain and Britain

Congress furthermore had difficulty dealing with the Spanish presence on the nation's southern and western borders. Determined to prevent the republic's expansion, Spain in 1784 closed the Mississippi River to American navigation, thereby depriving the growing settlements west of the Appalachians of their access to the Gulf of Mexico. Congress opened negotiations with Spain in 1785, but even John Jay, one of the nation's most experienced diplomats, could not win the necessary concessions. The talks collapsed the following year after Congress divided sharply: southerners and westerners insisted on navigation rights on the Mississippi; northerners were willing to abandon that claim in order to win commercial concessions in the West Indies.

Provisions of the 1783 Treaty of Paris also caused serious problems. Article Four, which promised the repayment of prewar debts (most of them owed by Americans to British merchants), and Article Five, which recommended that states allow loyalists to recover their confiscated property, aroused considerable opposition. States passed laws denying British subjects the right to sue for recovery of debts or property in American courts, and town meetings decried the loyalists' return.

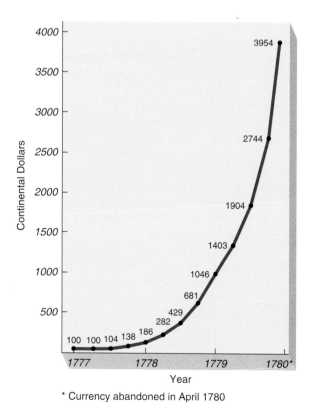

* Currency abandoned in April 1780

The refusal of state and local governments to comply with Articles Four and Five gave Britain an excuse to maintain military posts on the Great Lakes

Because of their citizens' resistance to taxation, the early state governments found it hard to raise sufficient revenues. Some, like Massachusetts, turned to state-run lotteries to make up the shortfall. Here a New Englander proudly poses with a lottery ticket, demonstrating his support for the state. (Milwaukee Art Museum Purchase, Layton Art Collection)

long after its troops were supposed to have withdrawn. Furthermore, Congress's inability to convince the states to implement the treaty disclosed its lack of power. Concerned nationalists argued publicly that enforcement of the treaty, however unpopular, was a crucial test of the republic's credibility in foreign affairs.

Order and Disorder in the West

 Congressmen also confronted knotty problems when they considered the status of land beyond the Appalachians. Although British and American diplomats did not discuss tribal claims, the United States assumed that the Treaty of Paris cleared its title to all land east of the

Mississippi except the area still held by Spain. Still, recognizing that land cessions should be obtained from the most powerful tribes, Congress initiated negotiations with both northern and southern Indians (see Map 7.1).

At Fort Stanwix, New York, in 1784, American diplomats negotiated a treaty with chiefs who said they represented the Iroquois; and at Hopewell, South Carolina, in late 1785 and early 1786, they did the same with emissaries from the Choctaw, Chickasaw, and Cherokee nations. In 1786 the Iroquois formally repudiated the Fort Stanwix treaty, denying that the men who attended the negotiations had been authorized to speak for the Six Nations. The confederacy threatened new attacks on frontier settlements, but everyone knew the threat was empty; the flawed treaty stood by default. At intervals until the end of the decade New York State purchased large tracts of land from individual Iroquois nations. By 1790 the once-dominant confederacy was confined to a few scattered reservations. In the South as well the United States took the treaties as confirmation of its sovereignty, authorizing settlers to move onto the territories in question. European Americans poured over the southern Appalachians, provoking the Creeks—who had not agreed to the Hopewell treaties—to defend their territory by declaring war. Only in 1790 did they come to terms with the United States.

Western nations such as the Shawnees, Chippewas, Ottawas, and Potawatomis previously had allowed the Iroquois to speak for them. After the collapse of Iroquois power, they formed their own confederacy and demanded direct negotiations with the United States. They intended to present a united front so as to avoid the piecemeal surrender of land by individual bands and villages.

At first the national government ignored the western confederacy. Shortly after state land cessions were completed, Congress began to organize the Northwest Territory, bounded by the Mississippi River, the Great Lakes, and the Ohio River. Ordinances passed in 1784, 1785, and 1787 outlined the process through which the land could be sold to settlers and formal governments could be organized.

Relations with the Indians

Ordinances of 1784 and 1785

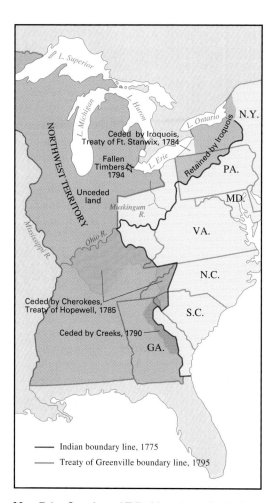

Map 7.1   Cession of Tribal Lands to the United States, 1775–1790   The land claims of the United States meant little as long as Indian nations still controlled vast territories within the new country's formal boundaries. A series of treaties in the 1780s and 1790s opened some lands to white settlement.   (Source: From Lester J. Cappon et al., eds., *Atlas of Early American History: The Revolutionary Era, 1760–1790.* Copyright © 1976 by Princeton University Press. Reprinted by permission of Princeton University Press.)

To ensure orderly development, Congress in 1785 directed that the land be surveyed into townships 6 miles square, each divided into thirty-six sections of 640 acres (1 square mile). Revenue from the sale of the sixteenth section of each township was to be reserved for the support of public schools—the first instance of federal aid to education in American history. One dollar was the minimum price per acre; the minimum sale was one section. The resulting $640 minimum outlay was beyond the reach of ordinary Americans. Proceeds from western land sales constituted the first independent revenues available to the national government.

The most important of the three land policies—the Northwest Ordinance of 1787—contained a bill of rights guaranteeing settlers freedom of religion and the right to a jury trial, forbidding cruel and unusual punishments, and nominally prohibiting slavery. As some residents of the territory already had slaves, the prohibition had little immediate effect. Moreover, the ordinance contained a provision allowing slaveowners to "lawfully reclaim" runaway bondspeople who took refuge in the territory—the first national fugitive slave law. Still, the prohibition eventually became an important symbol for antislavery northerners. It was not until 1848, however, that enslavement was abolished throughout the region, now known as the Old Northwest.

Northwest Ordinance

The ordinance of 1787 also specified the process by which residents of the territory could organize state governments and seek admission to the Union "on an equal footing with the original States." Early in the nation's history, therefore, Congress laid down a policy of admitting new states on the same basis as the old and assuring residents of the territories the same rights held by citizens of the original states.

In a sense, though, in 1787 the ordinance was purely theoretical. The Miamis, Shawnees, and Delawares refused to acknowledge American sovereignty. They opposed settlement violently, attacking unwary pioneers who ventured too far north of the Ohio River. In 1788 the Ohio Company, to which Congress had sold a large tract of land at reduced rates, established the town of Marietta at the juncture of the Ohio and Muskingum Rivers. But Indians prevented the company from extending settlement very far into the interior. After General Arthur St. Clair, the Northwest Territory's first governor, failed to negotiate a meaningful treaty with the Indians in early 1789, the United States could not avoid clashing with the Miami-led western confederacy.

Little Turtle, the able war chief of the Miami Confederacy, defeated first General Josiah Harmar (1790) and then St. Clair himself (1791) in major battles near the present border between Indiana and Ohio. More than six hundred of St. Clair's men died, and scores more were wounded, in the United States' worst defeat in the entire history of the American frontier. In 1793 the Miami Confederacy declared that peace could be achieved only if the United States recognized the Ohio River as its northwestern boundary. But the national government refused and a new army under the command of General Anthony Wayne, a Revolutionary War hero, attacked and defeated the confederacy in August 1794 at the Battle of Fallen Timbers. Peace negotiations began after the victory.

War in the Old Northwest

The Treaty of Greenville (1795) gave each side a portion of what it wanted. The United States gained the right to settle much of what was to become Ohio, the indigenous peoples retaining only the northwest corner of the region. Indians, though, received the acknowledgment they had long sought: American recognition of their rights to the soil. At Greenville, the United States formally accepted the principle of Indian sovereignty, by virtue of residence, over all lands the native peoples had not ceded. Never again would the United States government claim that it had acquired Indian territory solely through negotiation with a European or North American country.

The problems the United States encountered in ensuring safe settlement of the Northwest Territory revealed the basic weakness of the Confederation government. Not until after the Articles of Confederation were replaced with a new constitution could the United States muster sufficient force to implement the Northwest Ordinance.

From Crisis to the Constitution

The most obvious deficiencies of the Articles involved finance, overseas trade, and foreign affairs. Congress could not levy taxes, nor could it impose its will on the states to establish a uniform commercial policy or to ensure the enforcement of treaties. Partly as a result, the American economy slid into a depression less than a year after the war's end. Exporters of staple crops (especially tobacco and rice) and importers of manufactured goods suffered from the postwar restrictions European powers imposed on American commerce. Although recovery began by 1786, the war's effects proved impossible to erase.

The war, indeed, wrought permanent change in the American economy. The near total cessation of foreign commerce in nonmilitary items during the war stimulated domestic manufacturing. Consequently, despite the influx of European goods after 1783, the postwar period witnessed the stirrings of American industrial development. For example, the first American textile mill began production in Pawtucket, Rhode Island, in 1793. Moreover, foreign trade patterns shifted from Europe and toward the West Indies. Foodstuffs shipped to the French and Dutch Caribbean islands became America's largest single export.

Economic Change

Recognizing the Confederation Congress's inability to deal with commercial matters, representatives of Virginia and Maryland met in March 1785 to negotiate an agreement about trade on the Potomac River. The successful meeting led to an invitation to other states to discuss trade policy at a convention in Annapolis, Maryland. Although nine states named representatives to the meeting in September 1786, only five delegations attended. Those present realized that so few people could not have any significant impact on the political system. They issued a call for another convention, to be held in Philadelphia nine months later, "to devise such further provisions as shall . . . appear necessary to render the constitution of the federal government adequate to the exigencies of the Union."

Annapolis Convention

The other states did not respond immediately. But then an armed rebellion in Massachusetts did what a polite invitation to convene could not: convince doubters that reform was needed. Farmers from the western part of the state, many of them veterans, violently opposed high taxes (levied by the eastern-dominated legislature to pay off war debts) and an allied policy of foreclosing on the lands of tax defaulters. Daniel Shays, a former officer in the Continental Army, assumed the nominal

Shays's Rebellion

leadership of the disgruntled western farmers. On January 25, 1787, he led about 1,500 men in an assault on the federal armory at Springfield. The militiamen mustered to defend the armory fired on their former comrades in arms, who then withdrew. The westerners did not confine to the battlefield their challenge to the legitimacy of a government controlled by eastern merchants. Terming Massachusetts "tyrannical," they insisted that "whenever any encroachments are made either upon the liberties or properties of the people, if redress cannot be had without, it is virtue in them to disturb government." They thereby explicitly linked their rebellion to the earlier independence struggle.

To some, the rebellion confirmed the need for a much stronger federal government. After most of the states had already appointed delegates, the Confederation Congress belatedly endorsed the convention, "for the sole and express purpose of revising the Articles of Confederation." In mid-May 1787, fifty-five men, representing all the states but Rhode Island, assembled in Philadelphia to begin their deliberations.

The vast majority of delegates to the Constitutional Convention were men of property and substance. Their ranks included merchants, planters,

Constitutional Convention in Philadelphia

physicians, generals, governors, and especially lawyers—twenty-three had studied the law. Most had been born in America. In an era when only a tiny proportion of the population had any advanced education, more than half of the delegates had attended college. A few had been educated in Britain, but most had graduated from American institutions. The youngest delegate was twenty-six, the oldest—Benjamin Franklin—eighty-one. Like George Washington, whom they elected their presiding officer, most were in their vigorous middle years. A dozen men did the bulk of the convention's work. Of these, James Madison of Virginia was by far the most important; he deserves the title "Father of the Constitution."

Madison stood out among the delegates for his systematic preparation for the Philadelphia meeting. Through Jefferson in Paris he bought more than two hundred books on history and government, carefully analyzing their accounts of past confederacies and republics. A month before the Constitutional Convention began, he summed up the results of his research in

James Madison: Father of the Constitution

a lengthy paper entitled "Vices of the Political System of the United States." In this paper Madison set forth the principle of checks and balances. The government, he believed, had to be constructed in such a way that it could not become tyrannical or fall wholly under the influence of a particular faction. He regarded the large size of a potential national republic as an advantage in that respect. Rejecting the common assertion that republics had to be small to survive, Madison argued that a large, diverse republic should be preferred. Because the nation would include many different factions, no one of them would be able to control the government. Political stability would result from compromises among the contending parties.

The so-called Virginia Plan, introduced on May 29 by Edmund Randolph, embodied Madison's conception of national government. The

Virginia and New Jersey Plans

plan provided for a two-house legislature, the lower house elected directly by the people and the upper house selected by the lower; representation in both houses proportional to property or population; an executive elected by Congress; a national judiciary; and congressional veto over state laws. The Virginia Plan gave Congress the broad power to legislate "in all cases to which the separate states are incompetent." Had it been adopted intact, it would have created a government in which national authority reigned unchallenged and state power was greatly diminished. Proportional representation in both houses would also have given large states a dominant voice in the national government.

The convention included many delegates who recognized the need for change but believed the Virginia Plan went too far in the direction of national consolidation. Disaffected delegates—particularly those from small states—united under the leadership of William Paterson of New Jersey, who presented an alternative scheme; the New Jersey Plan called for strengthening the Articles rather than completely overhauling the government. Although the convention initially rejected Paterson's position, he and his allies won a number of victories in the months that followed.

The delegates began their work by discussing the structure and functions of Congress. They readily

In August 1787 a first draft of the Constitution was secretly printed in Philadelphia for the use of convention members. Wide margins left room for additions and amendments, such as those made on this copy by the South Carolina delegate Pierce Butler. Note that in this early version the preamble does not yet read "We the people of the United States," but instead begins by listing the individual states. (The Gilder Lehrman Collection, on deposit at the Pierpont Morgan Library/Art Resource, N.Y.)

The Debates: Houses of Congress

agreed that the new national government should have a two-house (bicameral) legislature. But they discovered that they differed widely in their answers to three key questions: Should representation in *both* houses of Congress be proportional to population? How was representation in either or both houses to be apportioned among the states? And, finally, how were the members of the two houses to be elected?

The last issue proved the easiest to resolve. To quote John Dickinson, the delegates thought it "essential" that members of the lower branch of Congress be elected directly by the people and "expedient" that members of the upper house be chosen by state legislatures. Since state legislatures had selected delegates to the Confederation Congress, they would expect a similar privilege in the new government.

The possibility of representation proportional to population in the Senate caused considerably greater disagreement. The delegates accepted without much debate the principle of proportional representation in the House of Representatives. But small states argued for equal representation in the Senate, while large states supported a proportional plan for the upper house. For weeks the convention deadlocked. A committee appointed to work out a compromise recommended equal representation in the Senate, coupled with a proviso that all appropriation bills originate in the lower house. But not until the convention accepted a suggestion that a state's two senators vote as individuals rather than as a unit was a breakdown averted.

One critical question remained: how was representation in the lower house to be apportioned among states? Delegates from states with

The Debates: Slavery and Representation

large numbers of slaves wanted African and European inhabitants to be counted equally; delegates from states with few slaves wanted only free people to be counted. The delegates resolved the dispute by using a formula developed by the Confederation Congress in 1783 to allocate financial assessments among states: three-fifths of slaves would be included in population totals. (The formula reflected the delegates' judgment that slaves were less efficient producers of wealth than free people, not that they were 60 percent human and 40 percent property.) The three-fifths compromise on representation won unanimous approval.

Although the words *slave* and *slavery* do not appear in the Constitution (the framers used euphemisms such as "other persons"), the document con-

Constitutional Protections for Slavery

tained both direct and indirect protections for slavery. The three-fifths clause, for example, assured white southern male voters not only congressional representation out of proportion to their numbers but also a disproportionate influence on the selection of the president, since the number of each state's electoral votes was determined by the size of its congressional delegation. The Constitution prohibited Congress from outlawing the slave trade for at least twenty years, and the fugitive slave clause required all states to return runaways to their masters. By guaranteeing that the national government would aid any states threatened with "domestic violence," the Constitution promised aid in putting down future slave revolts.

Once agreement was reached on the problems of slavery and representation, the delegates readily achieved consensus on the other issues. All agreed that the national government needed the authority to tax and to regulate commerce. And while delegates enumerated congressional powers, they then provided for flexibility by granting Congress all authority "necessary and proper" to carry out those powers. They further provided that the Constitution plus national laws and treaties would constitute "the supreme law of the land; and the judges in every state shall be bound thereby." As another means of circumscribing state powers, delegates drafted a long list of actions forbidden to states. Finally, the convention established the electoral college and a four-year term for the chief executive, who could seek reelection. Foreign affairs were placed in the hands of the president, who was also made the commander-in-chief of the armed forces.

The key to the Constitution was the distribution of political authority—that is, separation of powers among executive, legislative, and ju-

Separation of Powers

dicial branches of the national government, and division of powers between states and nation. The systems of checks and balances would make it difficult for the government to become tyrannical. At the same time, though, the elaborate system would sometimes prevent the government from acting quickly and decisively. Furthermore, the Constitution drew such a vague line between state and national powers that the United States fought a civil war in the next century over that very issue.

The convention held its last session on September 17, 1787. Of the forty-two delegates still present, only three refused to sign the Constitution, two of them in part because of the lack of a bill of rights. Although the delegates had accepted the Constitution, a key question remained: would the states ratify it?

Opposition and Ratification

 The ratification clause provided for the new system to take effect once it was approved by special conventions in at least nine states, with delegates being elected by qualified voters. Thus the national Constitution, unlike the Articles of Confederation, would rest directly on popular authority.

As states began to elect delegates to the special conventions, discussion of the proposed government grew more heated. Newspaper essays and pamphlets vigorously defended or attacked the Philadelphia convention's decisions. The extent of the debate was unprecedented, and it quickly became apparent that the disputes within the Constitutional Convention had been mild compared to the divisions of opinion within the populace as a whole.

Those supporting the proposed Constitution called themselves Federalists. They argued that the carefully

Federalists

structured government would preclude the possibility of tyranny. A republic could be large, they declared, if the government's design prevented any one group from controlling it. The separation of powers among legislative, executive, and judicial branches, and the division of powers between states and nation, would accomplish that goal. People did not need to be protected from the powers of the new government in a formal way. Instead, their liberties would be guarded by elected officials of the "better sort" whose only goal (said George Washington) was "to merit the approbation of good and virtuous men."

The Federalists termed those who opposed the Constitution Antifederalists. Antifederalists feared a too-powerful central government.

Antifederalists

They saw the states as the chief protectors of individual rights; consequently, weakening the states could bring the onset of arbitrary power. Heirs of the Real Whig ideology of the late 1760s and early 1770s, Antifederalists stressed the need for constant popular vigilance to avert oppression. Indeed, some of the Antifederalists had originally promulgated those ideas—Samuel Adams, Patrick Henry, and Richard Henry Lee led the opposition to the Constitution. Joining them were small farmers preoccupied with guarding their property against excessive taxation, and ambitious, upwardly mobile men who would benefit from an economic and political system less tightly controlled than that the Constitution envisioned. Federalists denigrated such men as disorderly, licentious, and even "unmanly" and "boyish" because they would not follow the elites' lead in supporting the Constitution.

As public debate continued, Antifederalists focused on the Constitution's lack of a bill of rights.

Importance of a Bill of Rights

Even if the new system weakened the states, Antis believed, people could still be protected from tyranny by specific guarantees of rights. *Letters of a Federal Farmer*, perhaps the most widely read Antifederalist pamphlet, listed the rights that should be protected: freedom of the press and religion, trial by jury, and guarantees against unreasonable searches. Thomas Jefferson added his voice to the chorus, expressing his concern over "the omission of a bill of rights."

As state conventions considered ratification, the lack of a bill of rights loomed ever larger. Four of the first five states to ratify did so unani-

Ratification of the Constitution

mously, but serious disagreements then surfaced. Massachusetts, in which Antifederalist forces had been bolstered by a backlash against the state government's heavy-handed treatment of the Shays rebels, ratified by a majority of only 19 votes out of 355 cast. In June 1788, when New Hampshire ratified, the requirement of nine states was satisfied. But New York and Virginia had not yet voted, and everyone realized the new Constitution could not succeed unless those key states accepted it.

Despite a valiant effort by the Antifederalist Patrick Henry, pro-Constitution forces won by 10 votes in the Virginia convention. In New York, James Madison, John Jay, and Alexander Hamilton campaigned for ratification by publishing *The Federalist*, a political tract that explained the theory behind the Constitution and masterfully answered its critics. Their reasoned arguments, coupled with Federalists' promise to add a bill of rights to the Constitution, helped win the battle. On July 26, 1788, New York ratified the Constitution by the slim margin of 3 votes. Although the last states—North Carolina and Rhode Island—did not join the Union until November 1789 and May 1790, respectively, the new government was a reality.

Americans in many cities celebrated ratification (somewhat prematurely) with a series of parades on July 4, 1788. The carefully planned

Celebrating Ratification

processions dramatized the history and symbolized the unity of the new nation, seeking to counteract memories of the dissent that had so recently engulfed such cities as Carlisle, Pennsylvania. Like pre-Revolution protest meetings, the parades served as political lessons for literate and illiterate Americans alike. The processions aimed to educate men and women about the significance of the new Constitution and to instruct them about political leaders' hopes for industry and frugality on the part of a virtuous American public.

Summary

 During the 1770s and 1780s the nation took shape as a political union. It began to develop an economy independent of the British Empire and attempted to chart its own course in the world in order to protect the national interest. An integral part of the formation of the Union was the systematic formulation of American racist thought. Emphasizing race as a determinant of African Americans' standing in the nation, and defining women as nonpolitical, allowed men who now termed themselves "white" to define *republicanism* to exclude all people but themselves and to ensure their control of the country.

The experience of fighting a war and of struggling for survival as an independent nation altered the political context of American life in the 1780s. At the outset of the war, most Americans believed that "that government which governs best governs least," but by the late 1780s many had changed their minds. They were the drafters and supporters of the Constitution, who concluded from the republic's vicissitudes under the Articles of Confederation that the United States needed a more powerful central government. They contended during ratification debates that their proposed solution to the nation's problems was just as "republican" in conception as the Articles (if not more so). Ratification created the constitutional republic; the decade of the 1790s would witness the first hesitant steps toward the creation of a true nation, the United States of America.

LEGACY FOR A PEOPLE AND A NATION
Women's Education

In the early years of the twenty-first century, women comprise a slim majority of the students enrolled in U.S. colleges and universities. Because women were denied all access to collegiate education in this country until the middle of the nineteenth century, that is a remarkable development. Its roots lie deep, in the republican ideology of the 1770s and 1780s.

Once the United States had established republican forms of government at both state and national levels, its citizens began to worry about sustaining those governments. The future, everyone knew, lay in the hands of the nation's children, especially its sons. And theorists concluded that those sons could successfully perpetuate the republic only if they learned the lessons of patriotism from their mothers. Male and female reformers therefore began to argue that women in the United States should be better educated than those who lived under other forms of government.

Some of those reformers accordingly founded private academies (roughly equivalent to modern high schools) to teach young women from leading families such subjects as history, geography, mathematics, and languages. Some of the women who attended those academies later started educational establishments of their own—including Mary Lyon, who in 1837 founded Mt. Holyoke College in western Massachusetts, the first institution of higher education for women in the United States. A few years later, some colleges for men (such as Oberlin, in Ohio) and state universities (for example, Michigan) admitted women as students, and a number of women's colleges were established. Not until the second half of the twentieth century, however, did American women gain truly equal access to higher education. In the 1970s such Ivy League universities as Yale and Princeton finally opened their doors to women students, and others (such as Cornell) that had sharply restricted women's enrollment through admissions quotas removed all constraints.

Along with the existence of the nation itself, increased educational opportunity for women is therefore one of the most important legacies of the revolutionary era for the American people.

For Further Reading, see the Appendix. For Web resources, go to history.college.hmco.com/students.

8

The Early Republic: Conflicts at Home and Abroad

1789–1800

The twenty-eight-year-old guest on the Georgia plantation, a recent graduate of Yale College, had already proved himself to be good with his hands. His hostess, Catherine Greene (the widow of the Revolutionary War general Nathanael Greene), had complained that her embroidery frame was poorly designed—and so he quickly constructed a replacement. Thus, when some neighboring planters discussed in Mrs. Greene's presence the seemingly insurmountable problem of extracting seeds from cotton fibers, she told them, "apply to my young friend, Mr. Whitney, he can make any thing."

Catherine Greene's "young friend," Eli Whitney, attacked the planters' challenge. Within ten days, he later recalled, he produced a small working model of the machine that would become known as the cotton gin. When Whitney invented his cotton gin in 1793, the only cotton that would grow widely in the United States had fibers that twisted tightly around its seeds. His invention was able to process cotton fifty times faster than hand workers could. With this device, it became economically feasible for cotton to become a primary staple crop. Whitney's device thus changed the lives of millions of people, for good and ill.

Cotton exports became one of the mainstays of the American economy in the nineteenth century. The surge in cotton cultivation revived the institution of slavery, which in the immediate postrevolutionary period had appeared to be losing its reason for being as Chesapeake tobacco planters switched to less labor-intensive grains, indigo cultivation collapsed, and new markets for rice had to be established. Southern

IMPORTANT EVENTS

1789 Washington inaugurated as first president
Judiciary Act of 1789 organizes federal
court system
French Revolution begins

1790 Hamilton's *Report on Public Credit* proposes
assumption of state debts

1791 First ten amendments (Bill of Rights)
ratified
First national bank chartered

1793 France declares war on Britain, Spain, and
the Netherlands
Washington's neutrality proclamation
Democratic-Republican societies founded

1794 Whiskey Rebellion in western
Pennsylvania

1795 Jay Treaty with England
Pinckney's Treaty with Spain

1796 First contested presidential election: Adams
elected president, Jefferson vice president

1798 XYZ affair
Sedition Act penalizes dissent
Virginia and Kentucky resolutions

1798–99 Quasi-War with France

1800 Franco-American Convention
Jefferson elected president
Gabriel's Rebellion

planter families and New England capitalists gained a great deal by Whitney's invention, but enslaved people lost much more.

In the 1790s, before the full impact of Whitney's invention, the American economy still rested in large part on traditional exports. Americans found their vital commerce disrupted once more in 1793, when England and France again went to war. The fight over ratifying the Constitution turned out to presage an even wider division over the major political, economic, and diplomatic questions confronting the young republic: the extent to which authority should be centralized in the national government; the relationship of national power and states' rights; the formulation of foreign policy in an era of continual warfare in Europe; and the limits of dissent. Americans did not anticipate the acrimonious disagreements that rocked the 1790s. And no one predicted the difficulties that would develop as the United States attempted to deal with Indian nations now wholly encompassed within its borders.

Most important of all, perhaps, Americans could not understand or fully accept the division of the country's political leaders into two factions—not yet political parties—known as Federalists and Democratic-Republicans, believing that only monarchies should experience such factional disputes. In republics, they believed, the rise of factions signified decay and corruption. ■

Building a Workable Government

The nationalistic spirit expressed in the processions celebrating ratification of the Constitution carried over to the first session of Congress. Only a few Antifederalists ran for office in the congressional elections held late in 1788, and even fewer were elected. Thus the First Congress consisted chiefly of men who supported a strong national government. The drafters of the Constitution had deliberately left many key issues undecided, so the nationalists' domination of Congress meant that their views on those points quickly prevailed.

Congress faced four immediate tasks when it convened in April 1789: raising revenue to support the new government, responding to states' calls for a bill of rights, setting up executive departments, and organizing the federal judiciary. The last task was especially important. The Constitution established a Supreme Court but left it to Congress to decide whether to have other federal courts as well.

James Madison, who had been elected to the House of Representatives, soon became as influential in Congress as he had been at the Constitutional Convention. A few months into the first session, he persuaded Congress to adopt the Revenue Act of 1789, imposing a 5 percent tariff on certain imports. Thus the First Congress quickly

Madison and the First Congress

achieved what the Confederation Congress never had: an effective national tax law. The new government would have problems in its first years, but lack of revenue was not one of them.

Madison also took the lead with respect to constitutional amendments. He placed nineteen proposed amendments before the House. The states soon ratified ten, which officially became part of the Constitution on December 15, 1791 (see the appendix for the Constitution and all amendments). Their adoption defused Antifederalist opposition and rallied support for the new government.

The First Amendment specifically prohibited Congress from passing any law restricting the right to freedom of religion, speech, press, peaceable assembly, or petition. The next two amendments arose directly from the former colonists' fear of standing armies as a threat to freedom. The Second Amendment guaranteed the right "to keep and bear arms" because of the need for a "well-regulated Militia." Thus the constitutional right to bear arms was based on the expectation that most able-bodied men would serve the nation as citizen-soldiers, and so there would be little need for a standing army. The Third Amendment limited the conditions under which troops could be quartered in private homes. The Fourth Amendment prohibited "unreasonable searches and seizures"; the Fifth and Sixth established the rights of accused persons; the Seventh specified the conditions for jury trials in civil (as opposed to criminal) cases; and the Eighth forbade "cruel and unusual punishments." The Ninth and Tenth Amendments reserved to the people and the states other unspecified rights and powers. In short, the amendments' authors made it clear that in listing some rights, they did not mean to preclude the exercise of others.

Bill of Rights

While debating the proposed amendments, Congress also considered the organization of the executive branch. It readily agreed to continue the three administrative departments established under the Articles of Confederation: War, Foreign Affairs (renamed State), and Treasury. Congress also instituted two lesser posts: the attorney general—the nation's official lawyer—and the postmaster general. And by agreeing that the president alone could dismiss officials whom he had originally appointed with the consent of the Senate, Congress established the principle that the heads of executive departments are accountable solely to the president.

Aside from constitutional amendments, the most far-reaching piece of legislation enacted by the First Congress was the Judiciary Act of 1789, which defined the jurisdiction of the federal judiciary and established a six-member Supreme Court, thirteen district courts, and three circuit courts of appeal. Its most important provision, Section 25, allowed appeals from state courts to federal courts when cases raised certain types of constitutional issues. Section 25 thus implemented Article VI of the Constitution, which stated that federal laws and treaties were to be considered "the supreme Law of the Land."

Federal Judiciary

During its first decade, the Supreme Court handled few cases of any importance. But in a significant 1796 decision, *Ware v. Hylton*, the Court for the first time declared a state law unconstitutional. That same year it also reviewed the constitutionality of an act of Congress, upholding its validity in the case of *Hylton v. U.S.* The most important case of the decade, *Chisholm v. Georgia* (1793), established that citizens of other states could sue states in federal courts. The Eleventh Amendment to the Constitution overruled this decision, which was unpopular with state governments, five years later.

Domestic Policy Under Washington and Hamilton

In 1783 George Washington returned to Mount Vernon eager for the peaceful life of a Virginia planter. But his fellow countrymen never regarded Washington as just another private citizen. When the new Constitution was adopted, Americans concurred that only George Washington had sufficient stature to serve as the republic's first president. The unanimous vote of the electoral college merely formalized that consensus.

Washington acted cautiously during his first months in office, knowing that whatever he did would set precedents for the future. When the title by which he should be addressed aroused controversy, Washington said nothing. The accepted title soon became a

Washington's First Steps

plain "Mr. President." By using the heads of the executive departments collectively as his chief advisers, he created the cabinet. As the Constitution required, he sent Congress an annual State of the Union message. Washington also concluded that he should exercise his veto power over congressional legislation very sparingly—only, indeed, if he became convinced a bill was unconstitutional.

Early in his term, Washington undertook elaborately organized journeys to all the states. At each stop, he was ritually welcomed by uniformed militia units, young women strewing flowers in his path, local leaders, groups of Revolutionary War veterans, and respectable citizens who presented him with formal addresses reaffirming their loyalty to the United States. The president thus personally came to embody national unity, simultaneously drawing ordinary folk into the sphere of national politics.

Washington's first major task as president was to choose the heads of the executive departments. For the War Department he selected an old comrade-in-arms, Henry Knox of Massachusetts. His choice for the State Department was his fellow Virginian Thomas Jefferson, who had just returned to the United States from his post as minister to France. And for the crucial position of secretary of the treasury, the president chose the brilliant, intensely ambitious Alexander Hamilton.

Two traits distinguished Hamilton from most of his contemporaries. First, he displayed an undivided loyalty to the nation as a whole. A

Alexander Hamilton

West Indian who had lived on the mainland only briefly before the war, Hamilton had no ties to a particular state. He showed little sympathy for, or understanding of, demands for local autonomy. Thus the aim of his fiscal policies was always to consolidate power at the national level. Further, he never feared the exercise of centralized executive authority, as did older counterparts who had clashed repeatedly with colonial governors, nor was he afraid of maintaining close political and economic ties with Britain.

Second, Hamilton regarded his fellow human beings with unvarnished cynicism. Perhaps because of his difficult early life (he was the illegitimate son of an aristocrat and had lived in poverty) and his own overriding ambition, Hamilton believed people to be

John Trumbull, known primarily for his larger-than-life portraits of patriot leaders, painted this miniature (c. 1792–1794) of George Washington, who posed for it during his presidency. (Division of Political History, Smithsonian Institution, Washington, D.C.)

motivated primarily by self-interest—particularly economic self-interest. He placed no reliance on people's capacity for virtuous and self-sacrificing behavior. This outlook set him apart from those Americans who foresaw a rosy future in which public-spirited citizens would pursue the common good rather than their own private advantage.

In 1789, Congress ordered the new secretary of the treasury to assess the public debt and to submit

National and State Debts

recommendations for supporting the government's credit. Hamilton found that the country's remaining war debts fell into three categories: those owed by the nation to foreign governments and investors, mostly to France (about $11 million); those owed by the national government to merchants, former soldiers, holders of revolutionary bonds, and the like (about $27 million); and, finally, similar debts owed by state governments (roughly $25 million). With respect to the national debt, few Americans disagreed: they recognized that if their new government was to succeed, it would have to repay at full face value those financial obligations incurred by the nation while winning independence.

The state debts were another matter. Some states—notably Virginia, Maryland, North Carolina, and Georgia—already had paid off most of their war debts. They would oppose the national government's assumption of responsibility for other states' debts. Massachusetts, Connecticut, and South Carolina, by contrast, still had sizable unpaid debts and would welcome a system of national assumption. The possible assumption of state debts also had political implications. Consolidating the debt in the hands of the national government would help to concentrate economic and political power at the national level. A contrary policy would reserve greater independence of action for the states.

Hamilton's first *Report on Public Credit*, sent to Congress in January 1790, stimulated lively debate.

Hamilton's Financial Plan

The treasury secretary proposed that Congress assume outstanding state debts, combine them with national obligations, and issue new securities covering both principal and accumulated unpaid interest. Hamilton thereby hoped to ensure that holders of the public debt—many of them wealthy merchants and speculators—had a significant financial stake in the new government's survival. The opposition coalesced around James Madison, who was against the assumption of state debts for two reasons: first, his state had already paid off most of its obligations, and second, he wanted to avoid rewarding wealthy speculators who had purchased debt certificates at a small fraction of their face value from needy veterans and farmers.

The House initially rejected the assumption of state debts. The Senate, however, adopted Hamilton's plan largely intact. A series of compromises followed, in which the assumption bill became linked with the location of the permanent national capital. The legend that Hamilton and Madison agreed over Jefferson's dinner table to exchange assumption of state debts for

a southern site is not supported by the surviving evidence, but a political deal was undoubtedly struck. The Potomac River was designated as the site for the capital, and the first part of Hamilton's financial program became law in August 1790.

Four months later Hamilton submitted to Congress a second report on public credit, recommending the chartering of a national bank.

First Bank of the United States

The Bank of the United States was to be capitalized at $10 million, of which only $2 million would come from public funds. Private investors would supply the rest. The bank's charter would run for twenty years, and the government would name one-fifth of the directors. The bank's notes would circulate as the nation's currency. The bank would also act as collecting and disbursing agent for the Treasury and would lend money to the government. Most political leaders recognized that such an institution would be beneficial, but another issue arose: did the Constitution give Congress the power to establish such a bank?

James Madison answered that question with a resounding *no*. He pointed out that Constitutional Convention delegates had specifically rejected a clause authorizing Congress to issue corporate charters.

Strict and Broad Constructions of the Constitution

Consequently, he argued, that power could not be inferred from other parts of the Constitution. Madison's contention disturbed President Washington, who decided to request other opinions before signing the bill into law. Thomas Jefferson, the secretary of state, agreed with Madison. Jefferson referred to Article I, Section 8, of the Constitution, which gave Congress the power "to make all Laws which shall be necessary and proper for carrying into Execution the foregoing Powers." The key word, Jefferson argued, was *necessary*: Congress could do what was needed, but without specific constitutional authorization could not do what was merely desirable. Thus Jefferson formulated the strict-constructionist interpretation of the Constitution.

Washington asked Hamilton to reply to the negative assessments of his proposal. Hamilton's *Defense of the Constitutionality of the Bank* (1791) brilliantly expounded a broad-constructionist view of the Constitution. Hamilton argued forcefully that Congress could choose any means not specifically prohibited by the Constitution to achieve a constitutional end. He reasoned thus: if the end was constitutional and the means was not unconstitutional, then the means was constitutional. Washington concurred and the bill became law.

In December 1791, Hamilton presented to Congress his *Report on Manufactures*, the third and last of his prescriptions for the American economy. In it he outlined an ambitious plan for encouraging and protecting the United States's infant industries. Hamilton argued that the nation could never be truly independent as long as it relied heavily on Europe for manufactured goods. He thus urged Congress to promote the immigration of technicians and laborers and to support industrial development through a limited use of protective tariffs. Many of Hamilton's ideas were implemented in later decades, but few congressmen in 1791 could see much merit in his proposals. They firmly believed that America's future lay in agriculture and the carrying trade and that the mainstay of the republic was the virtuous small farmer. Therefore, Congress rejected the report.

Hamilton's Report on Manufactures

That same year Congress accepted Hamilton's proposed tax on whiskey produced within the United States. Although proceeds from the Revenue Act of 1789 covered the interest on the national debt, the decision to fund state debts meant that the national government required additional income. A tax on whiskey affected relatively few farmers—those west of the mountains who sold their grain in the form of distilled spirits as a means of avoiding the high cost of transportation. Moreover, Hamilton knew that those western farmers were Jefferson's supporters, and he saw the benefits of taxing them rather than the merchants who supported his own policies.

News of the tax set off protests in frontier areas of Pennsylvania. Unrest continued for two years on the frontiers of Pennsylvania, Maryland, and Virginia. President Washington responded with restraint until violence erupted in July 1794, when western Pennsylvania farmers resisted a federal marshal and a tax collector trying to enforce the law. Three rioters were killed and several militiamen wounded. About seven thousand rebels convened on August 1 to plot the destruction of Pitts-

Whiskey Rebellion

burgh but decided not to face the heavy guns of the fort guarding the town. Washington then took decisive action to prevent a crisis reminiscent of Shays's Rebellion. On August 7, he called on the insurgents to disperse and summoned almost thirteen thousand militia from Pennsylvania and neighboring states. By the time federal forces marched westward in October and November, the disturbances had ceased.

The chief importance of the Whiskey Rebellion's suppression lay in the message it conveyed to the American people. The national government, Washington had demonstrated, would not allow violent resistance to its laws. In the republic, change would be effected peacefully, by legal means.

The French Revolution and the Development of Partisan Politics

 By 1794, some Americans were already beginning to seek change systematically through electoral politics. At the time, though, traditional political theory regarded organized opposition as illegitimate. In a republic, serious and sustained disagreement was taken as a sign of corruption and subversion.

Thomas Jefferson and James Madison became convinced as early as 1792 that Hamilton's policy of favoring wealthy commercial interests at the expense of agriculture was aimed at imposing a corrupt, aristocratic government on the United States. Characterizing themselves as the true heirs of the Revolution, they charged that Hamilton was plotting to subvert republican principles. To dramatize their point, Jefferson, Madison, and their followers in Congress began calling themselves Democratic-Republicans. Hamilton, in turn, accused Jefferson and Madison of the same crime: attempting to destroy the republic. Hamilton and his supporters began calling themselves Federalists, to legitimize their claims and link themselves with the Constitution. Each group accused the other of being an illicit faction working to sabotage the republican principles of the Revolution. (By traditional definition, a faction was opposed to the public good.)

Democratic-Republicans and Federalists

At first, President Washington tried to remain aloof from the political dispute that divided Hamilton and Jefferson, his chief advisers. Yet the growing controversy helped persuade him to seek a second term of office in 1792 in hopes of promoting political unity. But in 1793 and thereafter, developments in foreign affairs magnified the disagreements.

In 1789 Americans welcomed the news of the French Revolution and France's move toward republicanism. But by the early 1790s the reports from France were disquieting. Outbreaks of violence continued, ministries succeeded each other with bewildering rapidity, and execution mounted—even the king was beheaded. Although many Americans, including Jefferson and Madison, retained a sympathetic view of the revolution, Hamilton and others began to cite France as a prime example of the perversion of republicanism.

The French Revolution

When France declared war on Britain, Spain, and Holland in 1793, the Americans faced a dilemma. The 1778 Treaty of Alliance with France bound them to that nation "forever," and a mutual commitment to republicanism created ideological bonds. Yet the United States was connected to Great Britain as well. Beyond the shared history and language, Great Britain was America's most important trading partner. Indeed, the financial system of the United States depended heavily on import tariffs levied on goods from the former mother country.

The political and diplomatic climate grew even more complicated in April 1793, when Citizen Edmond Genêt, a representative of the French government, landed in Charleston, South Carolina. As Genêt made his way north to New York City, he recruited Americans for expeditions against British and Spanish colonies in the Western Hemisphere, freely distributing privateering commissions. Genêt's arrival raised troubling questions for President Washington. Should he receive Genêt, thus officially recognizing the French revolutionary government? Should he acknowledge an obligation to aid France under the terms of the 1778 Treaty of Alliance? Or should he proclaim American neutrality?

Citizen Genêt

For once, Hamilton and Jefferson saw eye to eye. Both told Washington that the United States could not afford to ally itself with either side. Washington agreed. He received Genêt but also issued a proclamation informing the world that the United States would

adopt "a conduct friendly and impartial toward the belligerent powers."

Genêt himself was removed from politics when his faction fell from power in Paris, but his disappearance from the diplomatic scene did not diminish the impact of the French Revolution in America. The domestic divisions Genêt helped to widen were perpetuated by clubs called Democratic-Republican societies, formed by Americans sympathetic to the French Revolution and worried about the policies of the Washington administration.

More than forty Democratic-Republican societies were organized between 1793 and 1800. Their members saw themselves as heirs of the Sons of Liberty, seeking the same goal as their predecessors: protection of people's liberties against encroachments by corrupt and self-serving rulers. To that end, they publicly protested government fiscal and foreign policy and repeatedly proclaimed their belief in the rights to free speech, free press, and assembly. Like the Sons of Liberty, the Democratic-Republican societies chiefly comprised artisans and craftsmen, although professionals, farmers, and merchants also joined.

Democratic-Republican Societies

The rapid growth of such groups deeply disturbed Hamilton and eventually Washington himself. Some newspapers charged that the societies were subversive agents of a foreign power. The counterattack climaxed in the fall of 1794, when Washington accused the societies of having fomented the Whiskey Rebellion.

In retrospect, Washington and Hamilton's reaction to the Democratic-Republican societies seems disproportionately hostile. But at the time, factions were seen as dangerous and the idea that a loyal opposition was part of a free government had not yet been accepted.

Partisan Politics and Relations with Great Britain

 In 1794 George Washington dispatched Chief Justice John Jay to London to negotiate four unresolved questions in Anglo-American relations. The first point at issue was recent British seizures of American merchant ships trading in the French West Indies. The United States wanted to establish the principle of freedom of the seas and to assert its right, as a neutral nation, to trade freely with both combatants. Second, in violation of the 1783 peace treaty, Great Britain had not yet evacuated its posts in the American Northwest. The Americans also hoped for a commercial treaty and sought compensation for the slaves who left with the British army at the end of the war.

The negotiations in London proved difficult, since Jay had little to offer in exchange for the concessions he sought. Britain did agree to

Jay Treaty

evacuate the western forts and ease restrictions on American trade with England and the West Indies. The treaty established two arbitration commissions—one to deal with prewar debts Americans owed to British creditors and the other to hear claims for captured American merchant ships—but Britain adamantly refused slaveowners compensation for their lost bondspeople. Under the circumstances, Jay did remarkably well: the treaty averted war with England. Nevertheless, most Americans, including the president, were dissatisfied.

The Senate debated the Jay Treaty in secret, so members of the public did not learn its provisions until after Senate ratification (by a vote of 20 to 10) in June 1795. The Democratic-Republican societies led protests against the treaty. Especially vehement opposition arose in the South, as planters criticized the failure to obtain compensation for runaway slaves and objected to the commission on prewar debts, which might require them to pay off sizable obligations to British merchants dating back to the 1760s. Once President Washington had signed the treaty, though, there seemed little the Democratic-Republicans could do to prevent it from taking effect. Just one opportunity remained: Congress had to appropriate funds to carry out the treaty provisions.

When the House debated the issue in March 1796, members opposing the treaty tried to prevent approval of the appropriations. To that end, they asked Washington to submit to the House all documents pertinent to the negotiations. In successfully resisting the House's request, Washington established the doctrine of executive privilege—the power of the president to withhold information from Congress if he believes circumstances warrant doing so.

The treaty's opponents initially appeared to be in the majority, but pressure for appropriating the neces-

sary funds built as time passed. Frontier residents eagerly sought Britain's evacuation of its remaining outposts, and merchants wanted to reap benefits from expanded trade. Furthermore, Thomas Pinckney of South Carolina had negotiated a treaty with Spain giving the United States navigation privileges on the Mississippi River, which would be an economic boost to the West and South. The popularity of Pinckney's Treaty helped to overcome opposition to the Jay Treaty. For all these reasons, the House appropriated the money.

Analysis of the vote reveals both the regional nature of the division and the growing cohesion of the Democratic-Republican and Federalist factions in Congress. Voting for the appropriations were 44 Federalists and 7 Democratic-Republicans; voting against were 45 Democratic-Republicans and 3 Federalists. The final tally also divided by region. Southerners cast the vast majority of votes against the bill, and almost all supporters hailed from New England and the middle states.

Partisan Divisions in Congress

The small number of defectors on both sides reveals a new force at work in American politics: partisanship. Voting statistics from the first four Congresses show the ever-increasing tendency of members of the House of Representatives to vote as cohesive groups, rather than as individuals. The growing division cannot be explained in the terms used by Jefferson and Madison (aristocrats versus the people) or by Hamilton and Washington (true patriots versus subversive rabble). Simple economic differences between agrarian and commercial interests do not provide the answer either.

Yet certain distinctions can be made. Democratic-Republicans, especially prominent in the southern and middle states, tended to be self-assured, confident, and optimistic about both politics and the economy. Southern planters, firmly in control of their region and of a class of enslaved laborers, foresaw a prosperous future based partly on continued westward expansion, a movement they expected to dominate. Democratic-Republicans employed democratic rhetoric to win the allegiance of small farmers south of New England. Members of non-English ethnic groups—especially Irish, Scots, and

Bases of Partisanship

Germans—found the Democratic-Republicans' words attractive. Democratic-Republicans of all descriptions emphasized developing America's own resources, worrying less than Federalists did about the nation's place in the world. Democratic-Republicans also remained sympathetic to France in international affairs.

By contrast, Federalists, concentrated in New England, came mostly from English stock. Insecure and uncertain of the future, they drew considerable support from commercial interests. They stressed the need for order, authority, and regularity in the political world. Federalists had no grassroots political organization and put little emphasis on involving ordinary people in government. Wealthy New England merchants aligned themselves with the Federalists, but so too did the region's farmers, who, prevented from expanding agricultural production because of New England's poor soil, gravitated toward the more conservative party. Federalists, like Democratic-Republicans, assumed that southern and middle-state interests would dominate the land west of the mountains, so they had little incentive to work actively to develop that potentially rich territory. In Federalist eyes, potential enemies—both internal and external—perpetually threatened the nation, which required a continuing alliance with Great Britain for its own protection.

The presence of the two organized groups made the presidential election of 1796 the first serious contest for the position. Wearied by the criticism to which he had been subjected, George Washington decided to retire from office. In September Washington published his Farewell Address. In it he outlined two principles that guided American foreign policy at least until the late 1940s: to maintain commercial but not political ties to other nations and to enter no permanent alliances. He thus encouraged the nation to follow the path of unilateralism (independent action in foreign affairs).

Washington's Farewell Address

To succeed Washington, the Federalists in Congress put forward Vice President John Adams, with the diplomat Thomas Pinckney as his running mate. Congressional Democratic-Republicans met and chose Thomas Jefferson as their presidential candidate; Aaron Burr of New York agreed to run for vice president.

Election of 1796

That the election was contested does not mean that the people decided its outcome. Voters could cast their ballots only for electors, not for the candidates themselves, and not all electors publicly declared their preferences. State legislatures, not a popular vote, selected more than 40 percent of the members of the electoral college. Moreover, the method of voting in the electoral college did not take into account the possibility of party slates. The Constitution's drafters had not foreseen the development of competing national political organizations, so the Constitution provided no way to express support for one person for president and another for vice president. The electors simply voted for two people. The man with the highest total became president; the one with the second highest, vice president. Thus Adams, the Federalist, won the presidency with 71 votes, and Jefferson, the Democratic-Republican, with 68 votes, became the vice president.

John Adams and Political Dissent

 John Adams took over the presidency peculiarly blind to the partisan developments of the previous four years. As president he never abandoned an outdated notion discarded by George Washington as early as 1794: that the president should be above politics, an independent and dignified figure who did not seek petty factional advantage. Thus Adams kept Washington's cabinet intact, despite its key members' allegiance to his chief rival, Alexander Hamilton. Adams often adopted a passive posture, letting others (usually Hamilton) take the lead when the president should have acted decisively. As a result, his administration gained a reputation for inconsistency. When Adams's term ended, the Federalists were severely divided, and the Democratic-Republicans had won the presidency. But Adams's detachment from Hamilton's maneuverings did enable him to weather the greatest international crisis the republic had yet faced: the Quasi-War with France.

The Jay Treaty improved America's relationship with Great Britain, but it provoked French retaliation. Angry that the United States had reached agreement with its enemy, the French government ordered its ships to seize American vessels carrying British goods. In response, Congress increased military spending, and President Adams sent three commissioners to Paris to negotiate a settlement. For months, the American commissioners sought talks with Talleyrand, the French foreign minister, but Talleyrand's agents demanded a bribe of $250,000 before negotiations could begin. The Americans reported the incident in dispatches that the president received in early March 1798. Adams informed Congress of the impasse and recommended further increases in defense appropriations.

Convinced that Adams had deliberately sabotaged the negotiations, congressional Democratic-Republicans insisted that the dispatches be turned over to Congress. Adams complied, aware that releasing the reports would work to his advantage. He withheld only the names of the French agents, referring to them as X, Y, and Z. The revelation that the Americans had been treated with contempt stimulated a wave of anti-French sentiment in the United States. Cries for war filled the air. Congress formally abrogated the Treaty of Alliance and authorized American ships to seize French vessels.

XYZ Affair

Thus began an undeclared war with France. U.S. warships and French privateers seeking to capture American merchant vessels fought the Quasi-War in Caribbean waters. Although Americans initially suffered heavy losses of merchant shipping, by early 1799 the U.S. Navy had established its superiority in the West Indies, easing the threat to America's vital Caribbean trade.

Quasi-War with France

The Democratic-Republicans, who opposed war and continued to sympathize with France, could do little to stem the tide of anti-French feelings. Since Agent Y had boasted of the existence of a "French party in America," Federalists flatly accused Democratic-Republicans of traitorous designs. And Federalists saw the political climate of opinion as an opportunity to deal a death blow to their Democratic-Republican opponents. Now that the country seemed to see the truth of what they had been saying ever since the Whiskey Rebellion in 1794—that Democratic-Republicans were subversive foreign agents—Federalists sought to codify that belief into law. In 1798 the Federalist-controlled Congress adopted a set of four laws known as the Alien and Sedition Acts, intended to suppress dissent and to prevent further growth of the Democratic-Republican faction.

Alien and Sedition Acts

Three of the acts targeted recently arrived immigrants, whom Federalists accurately suspected of being Democratic-Republican in their sympathies. The Naturalization Act lengthened the residency period required for citizenship and ordered all resident aliens to register with the federal government. The two Alien Acts provided for the detention of enemy aliens in time of war and gave the president authority to deport any alien he deemed dangerous to the nation's security. Neither act was implemented during the Adams administration, however.

The fourth statute, the Sedition Act, sought to control both citizens and aliens. It outlawed conspiracies to prevent the enforcement of federal laws, setting the maximum punishment for such offenses at five years in prison and a $5,000 fine. The act also tried to control speech. Writing, printing, or uttering "false, scandalous and malicious" statements against the government or the president "with intent to defame . . . or to bring them or either of them, into contempt or disrepute" became a crime punishable by as much as two years' imprisonment and a fine of $2,000.

The Sedition Act led to fifteen indictments and ten convictions. Most of the accused were outspoken Democratic-Republican newspaper editors. But the first victim was a hot-tempered Democratic-Republican congressman from Vermont, Matthew Lyon. The Irish-born Lyon was convicted, fined $1,000, and sent to prison for four months for declaring in print that John Adams had displayed "a continual grasp for power" and "an unbounded thirst for ridiculous pomp, foolish adulation, and selfish avarice." Lyon was reelected while serving his jail term.

Faced with prosecutions of their supporters, Jefferson and Madison sought an effective means of combating the acts. In doing so, they turned to constitutional theory and the state legislatures. Carefully concealing their own role—it would not have been desirable for the vice president to be indicted for sedition—Jefferson and Madison each drafted a set of resolutions. Introduced into the Kentucky and Virginia legislatures, respectively, in the fall of 1798, the resolutions differed somewhat but had the same import. Since a compact among the states created the Constitution, they contended, people speaking through their states had a legitimate right to judge the constitutionality of

Virginia and Kentucky Resolutions

actions taken by the federal government. Both sets of resolutions pronounced the Alien and Sedition Acts unconstitutional and asked other states to join in a concerted protest against them.

Although no other state endorsed them, the Virginia and Kentucky resolutions nevertheless had considerable influence. First, they constituted superb political propaganda, rallying Democratic-Republican opinion throughout the country and simultaneously placing the party in the revolutionary tradition of resistance to tyrannical authority. Second, the theory of union they proposed inspired southern states' rights advocates in the 1830s and thereafter. Jefferson and Madison had identified a key constitutional issue: how far could states go in opposing the national government? How could a conflict between the two be resolved?

Meanwhile, the Federalists split over the course of action the United States should take toward France. Hamilton and his supporters called for a declaration legitimizing the undeclared naval war. But Adams received a number of private signals that the French government regretted its treatment of the American commissioners. Acting on such assurances, he dispatched the envoy William Vans Murray to Paris. The United States sought two goals: compensation for ships the French had seized since 1793 and abrogation of the treaty of 1778. The Convention of 1800, which ended the Quasi-War, provided for the latter but not the former. The results of the negotiations did not become known in the United States until after the presidential election of 1800. By then divisions within the Federalist party had already cost Adams the election.

Convention of 1800

The Democratic-Republicans entered the 1800 presidential race firmly united behind Jefferson and Burr. Although they won the election, their lack of foresight almost cost them dearly. All Democratic-Republican electors voted for both Jefferson and Burr, giving each 73 votes (Adams had 65). Because neither man had a plurality, the Constitution required that the contest be decided in the House of Representatives, with each state's congressmen voting as a unit. Since the new House, dominated by Democratic-Republicans, would not take office for some months, Federalist congressmen decided the

Election of 1800

election. It took them thirty-five ballots to decide that Jefferson would be a lesser evil than Burr. In response to the tangle, the Twelfth Amendment to the Constitution (1804) changed the method of voting in the electoral college to allow for a party ticket.

Race Relations at the End of the Century

 As the nation anticipated the inauguration of a new president, it had added three states (Vermont, Kentucky, and Tennessee) to the original thirteen and more than 1 million people to the nearly 4 million counted by the 1790 census. Nine-tenths of the approximately 1 million resident African Americans—most still enslaved—lived in the Chesapeake or the Lower South. And by 1800, all the Indian nations residing in U.S. territory east of the Mississippi River had made peace with the republic.

The new nation's policymakers, all of European American descent, could not ignore such large proportions of the population. How should the republic deal with eastern Indians, who no longer posed a military threat to the country? Did the growing population of bondspeople present new hazards? The second question took on added significance after 1793, when a bloody revolt of mulattoes and blacks led by Toussaint L'Ouverture overthrew French rule in Saint Domingue (Haiti).

In 1789 Henry Knox, Washington's secretary of war, proposed that the new national government assume the task of "civilizing" America's indigenous population. The first step in such a project, Knox suggested, should be to introduce to Indian peoples "a love for exclusive property"; to that end, he proposed that the government give livestock to individual Indians. Four years later, the Indian Trade and Intercourse Act of 1793 codified Knox's plan, promising Indians federally supplied animals, agricultural implements, and instructors.

"Civilizing" the Indians

This well-intentioned plan reflected federal officials' blindness to the realities of native peoples' lives. It ignored both the Indians' traditional commitment to communal notions of landowning and the centuries-long agricultural experience of eastern Indian peoples. The policymakers focused only on Indian *men*: since they hunted, male Indians were "savages" who had to be "civilized" by being taught to farm. That in these societies *women* traditionally did the farming was irrelevant because in the eyes of the officials, Indian women—like those of European descent—should properly confine themselves to child rearing, household chores, and home manufacturing.

Indian nations at first responded cautiously to the "civilizing" plan. By the 1790s the Iroquois Confederacy had been relegated to small reservations increasingly

Iroquois and Cherokees

surrounded by Anglo-American farmlands. Quaker missionaries started a demonstration farm among the Senecas, intending to teach men to plow, but they quickly learned that women showed greater interest in their message. The same was true among the Cherokees of Georgia. As their southern hunting territories were reduced, Cherokee men did begin to raise cattle and hogs, but they startled the reformers by treating livestock like wild game, allowing the animals to run free in the woods and simply shooting them when needed, in the same way they had once killed deer. Men also

In 1805, an unidentified artist painted Benjamin Hawkins, a trader and U.S. agent to the Indians of the Southeast, at the Creek agency near Macon, Georgia. Hawkins introduced European-style agriculture to the Creeks, who are shown here with vegetables from their fields. Throughout the eastern United States, Indian nations had to make similar adaptations of their traditional lifestyles in order to maintain their group identity. (Collection of the Greenville County Art Museum, South Carolina)

started to plow the fields, although Cherokee women continued to bear primary responsibility for cultivation and harvest.

Iroquois men became more receptive to the Quakers' lessons after the spring of 1799, when a Seneca named Handsome Lake experienced a remarkable series of visions. Like other prophets stretching back to Neolin (see page 80), Handsome Lake preached that Indian peoples should renounce alcohol, gambling, and other destructive European customs. Handsome Lake aimed above all to preserve Iroquois culture. He recognized that, since men could no longer obtain meat through hunting, only by adopting a sexual division of labor that had originated in Europe could the Iroquois retain an autonomous existence.

African Americans had long been forced to conform to European American notions of proper gender roles and had embraced Christianity. Yet, just as Cherokees and Iroquois adapted the reformers' plans to their own purposes, so too enslaved blacks found new meanings in the dominant society's ideas. African Americans (both slave and free) became familiar with concepts of liberty and equality during the Revolution. They also witnessed the benefits of fighting collectively for freedom, rather than resisting individually or running away. And, as white evangelicals by the end of the century began to back away from the earlier racial egalitarianism of their movement, African Americans increasingly formed their own separate Baptist and Methodist congregations.

African Americans and Ideas of Freedom

Such congregations near Richmond became the seedbeds of revolt. Gabriel, an enslaved blacksmith who argued that African Americans should fight for their freedom, carefully planned a large-scale revolt. Often accompanied by his brother Martin, a preacher, he visited Sunday church services, where blacks gathered outside of the watchful eyes of their owners. Gabriel first recruited to his cause other skilled African Americans who like himself lived in semifreedom under minimal supervision. Next he enlisted rural slaves (see Map 8.1). The conspirators planned to attack Richmond on the night of August 30, 1800, set fire to the city, seize the state capitol, and capture the governor. At that point, Gabriel believed, other slaves and sympathetic poor whites would join in.

Gabriel's Rebellion

The plan showed considerable political sophistication, but heavy rain forced a postponement. Several planters then learned of the plan from slave informers and spread the alarm. Gabriel avoided arrest for some weeks, but militia troops quickly apprehended and interrogated most of the other leaders of the rebellion. Twenty-six conspirators, including Gabriel himself, were hanged, but that did not end the unrest among Virginia's slaves.

Map 8.1 African American Population, 1790: Proportion of Total Population   The first census clearly indicated that the African American population was heavily concentrated in just a few areas of the United States, most notably in coastal regions of South Carolina, Georgia, and Virginia. Although there were growing numbers of blacks in the backcountry—presumably taken there by migrating slaveowners—most parts of the North and East, with the exception of the immediate vicinity of New York City, had few African American residents.   (Source: From Lester J. Cappon et al., eds., *Atlas of Early American History: The Revolutionary Era, 1760–1790.* Copyright © 1976 by Princeton University Press. Reprinted by permission of Princeton University Press.)

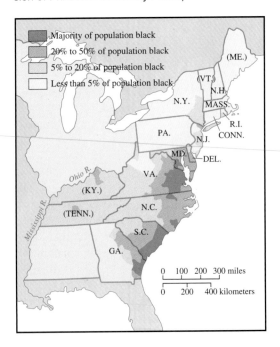

At his trial, one of Gabriel's followers made explicit the links that so frightened Chesapeake slaveholders. He told his judges that, like George Washington, "I have adventured my life in endeavouring to obtain the liberty of my countrymen, and am a willing sacrifice in their cause." Southern state legislatures responded to such claims by increasing the severity of the laws regulating slavery. Before long, all talk of emancipation (gradual or otherwise) ceased, and slavery became even more firmly entrenched as an economic institution and way of life.

Summary

 As the nineteenth century began, inhabitants of the United States faced changed lives in the new republic. Indian peoples east of the Mississippi River found that they had to give up some parts of their traditional culture to preserve others. Some African Americans struggled unsuccessfully to free themselves from the inhuman bonds of slavery, then subsequently confronted more constraints than ever because of increasingly restrictive laws.

European Americans too adjusted to changed circumstances. The first eleven years of government under the Constitution established many enduring precedents for congressional, presidential, and judicial action—among them the establishment of the cabinet, the interpretations of key clauses of the Constitution, and the stirrings of judicial review of state and federal legislation. Building on successful negotiations with Spain, Britain, and France, the United States developed its diplomatic independence, striving to avoid entanglement with European powers. The 1790s also spawned vigorous debates over foreign and domestic policy and saw the beginnings of a system of organized political factionalism.

At the end of the 1790s, after more than a decade of struggle, the Jeffersonian view of the future of republicanism prevailed over Hamilton's approach. In the years to come the country would be characterized by a decentralized economy, minimal government, and maximum freedom of action and mobility for individual white men. Jeffersonians failed to extend to white women, Indian peoples, and African Americans the freedom and individuality they recognized as essential for themselves.

LEGACY FOR A PEOPLE AND A NATION
Dissent During Wartime

The Quasi-War with France in 1798 and 1799, the nation's first overseas conflict, brought the first attempt to suppress dissent. The Sedition Act of 1798 tried to quiet the Democratic-Republicans' criticism of the war and President John Adams. Ten men were fined and jailed after being convicted under the statute's provisions.

Although Americans might assume that their right to free speech under the First Amendment, more fully accepted now than it was two hundred years ago, would today protect dissenters in the event of another war, the history of the nation suggests otherwise. Each major conflict fought under the Constitution—the Civil War, World War I, World War II, and Vietnam—has stimulated efforts by both government and individual citizens to suppress dissenting voices. For example, during the Civil War, the Union jailed civilian Confederate sympathizers, holding them under martial law for long periods. During the First World War, a later Sedition Act allowed the government to deport immigrant aliens who too vocally criticized the war effort. Moreover, citizens who objected to government policies were subjected to a variety of formal and informal sanctions by their neighbors. World War II brought the silencing of isolationists' voices, as those who had opposed American entry into the war were denied public outlets for their ideas. The consequences of antiwar protests in the Vietnam era still affect the nation today. And during the Gulf War in the early 1990s, military officials restricted reporters' access to the battlefront to forestall potential criticism.

Freedom of speech is never easy to maintain, and wartime conditions make it much more difficult. When the nation comes under attack from a foreign power, many patriotic Americans argue that the time for dissent has ceased. Others contend that, if freedom in the nation is to mean anything, people must have the right to speak their minds freely at all times. Tracing the history of wartime dissent in the United States suggests that this legacy will remain extremely contentious.

For Further Reading, see the Appendix. For Web resources, go to history.college.hmco.com/students.

"A WISE AND FRUGAL GOVERNMENT": THE DEMOCRATIC-REPUBLICANS IN POWER

1801–1815

The Jefferson Presidency and Marshall Court
Louisiana and Lewis and Clark
Political Factionalism and Jefferson's Reelection
Indian Resistance
American Neutrality Imperiled by a World at War
Commerce and Industry
The War of 1812
Peace and Consequences

LEGACY FOR A PEOPLE AND A NATION
The Peaceful Transfer of Power

John Foss, captured by "pirates" off the Barbary Coast of North Africa in the 1790s, wrote of the "hellish tortures and punishments" inflicted "on the unfortunate Christians." Marched through Algiers, the party of nine ragged sailors heard shouts from the Islamic crowds praising the victories over "Christian dogs," and in prison they learned of ten other recently captured American vessels. In Algiers they became white slaves under African masters.

In the early nineteenth century, the Barbary captivity stories had the drama of modern gothic novels. In telling of white slaves with black masters, the tales turned American assumptions of the natural order on their heads. Firsthand descriptions of Africa projected negative images of a despotic, depraved people, so very different from Americans. In the end, the Americans—at least those who survived to tell their stories—prevailed, and so the stories became epic affirmations of Western culture over "barbarians."

In reality, the "pirates"—from what Europeans called the Barbary states and Africans the Maghreb—had challenged the United States in a most fundamental way: was this new nation an independent, sovereign state that could protect its citizens and commerce abroad?

The issue was money. In 1801 the *bashaw* of Tripoli, angry over the United States's refusal to pay tribute for safe passage of its ships, sailors, and passen-

IMPORTANT EVENTS

1801 Marshall becomes chief justice of the United States
Jefferson inaugurated as first Democratic-Republican president

1801–05 United States defeats Barbary pirates in Tripoli War

1803 *Marbury v. Madison* establishes judicial review
United States purchases Louisiana Territory from France

1804 Burr kills Hamilton in a duel
Jefferson reelected

1804–06 Lewis and Clark explore Louisiana Territory

1805 Prophet emerges as Shawnee leader

1807 *Chesapeake* affair
Embargo Act halts foreign trade

1808 Congress bans importation of slaves into the United States
Madison elected president

1808–13 Prophet and Tecumseh organize Native American tribal resistance

1808–15 Embargoes and war stimulate domestic manufacturing

1812–15 United States and Great Britain fight the War of 1812

1813 Death of Tecumseh ends effective pan-Indian resistance
New England capitalists form Boston Manufacturing Company

1814 Jackson's defeat of Creeks at Battle of Horseshoe Bend begins Indian removal from the South
Treaty of Ghent ends the War of 1812

1814–15 Hartford Convention

1815 Battle of New Orleans

1816 James Monroe elected president

gers through the Mediterranean, declared war on the United States. President Thomas Jefferson responded by sending a naval squadron to protect American ships in the area. After two years of stalemate, Jefferson ordered a blockade of Tripoli, but the American frigate *Philadelphia* ran aground in its harbor and three hundred American officers and sailors were taken captive. Jefferson refused to ransom them. With the blockade still in place, seven marines and four hundred soldiers of fortune marched overland from Egypt to seize the port of Derne, on the shores of Tripoli. Finally, by treaty with Tripoli in 1805, the United States paid $60,000 to free the *Philadelphia* prisoners, and the war was over. But the United States continued to pay tribute to the other three Barbary states until 1815.

American independence and stability passed a political test at home when the presidential succession in 1801 took place by ballot rather than by arms, which some had feared. Despite the bitterness of the campaign and the ensuing political intrigue, Thomas Jefferson replaced John Adams as president. The Con-

stitution withstood the test, but the transfer of power to the Democratic-Republicans from the Federalists intensified political conflict. Democratic-Republican presidents sought to restrain the national government, believing that limited government would foster republican virtue. Federalists advocated a strong national government with centralized authority to promote economic development. As the two factions competed for popular support, they laid the basis for the evolution of party politics.

Events abroad and in the West both encouraged and threatened Americans. Seizing one opportunity, the United States purchased the Louisiana Territory. But as American interests turned westward, events in Europe and on the high seas of the Atlantic forced an about-face. Caught between the warring British and French, the United States found its ships seized, its foreign commerce interrupted, and its sailors impressed (forcibly drafted), all in violation of its rights as a neutral and independent nation. In what some have called the second war for independence, the United

States fought Great Britain to a standoff, while on another front routing Indian resistance and shattering Native American unity. A peace treaty restored the prewar status quo, but the war and the treaty reaffirmed U.S. sovereignty and strengthened America's determination to steer clear of further European conflicts. The war also stimulated industry and nationalism. ■

The Jefferson Presidency and Marshall Court

 In later years Thomas Jefferson would always refer to his taking office as the "Revolution of 1800." He viewed his victory that year as a revolution that restored government to its limited role, restrained and frugal. To Jefferson, society should reflect the republican virtues of independence, self-reliance, and equality. His presidency followed a bitter election campaign. The animosity of the contest was reflected in a letter from Jefferson to a British scientist in which the president described his victory as defeating "the Barbarians."

Yet in public, Jefferson sought unity by reaching out to his opponents. Unity and nation building were the order of the day and the theme of his inaugural address. Standing in the Senate chamber, he declared: "We are all republicans, we are all federalists." He thus appealed to the electorate not as party members but as citizens who shared common beliefs in republicanism and federalism. Jefferson called for a "wise and frugal government, which shall restrain men from injuring one another, which shall leave them free to regulate their pursuits of industry and improvement, and shall not take from the mouth of labor the bread it has earned."

Jefferson's Inaugural

To implement the restoration of republican values, Jefferson aggressively extended the Democratic-Republicans' grasp on the national government. Virtually all of the six hundred or so officials appointed during the administrations of Washington and Adams had been loyal Federalists. To bring into his administration men who shared his vision of an agrarian republic and individual liberty, Jefferson refused to recognize

Democratic-Republican Ascendancy

appointments that Adams had made in the last days of his presidency and dismissed Federalist customs collectors from New England ports. He awarded vacant treasury and judicial offices to Democratic-Republicans. By July 1803, Federalists held only 130 of 316 presidentially controlled offices.

The Democratic-Republican Congress proceeded to affirm its belief in limited government. Albert Gallatin, secretary of the treasury, and Representative John Randolph of Virginia translated ideology into policy, putting the federal government on a diet. Congress repealed all internal taxes, including the whiskey tax. Gallatin cut the army budget in half and reduced the 1802 navy budget by two-thirds. He then moved to reduce the national debt from $83 million to $57 million, as part of a plan to retire it altogether by 1817.

More than frugality, however, distinguished Democratic-Republicans from Federalists. Before Jefferson's election, opposition to the Alien and Sedition Acts of 1798 had helped unite Democratic-Republicans. Jefferson now declined to use the acts against his opponents, and Congress let them expire in 1801 and 1802. Congress also repealed the Naturalization Act of 1798, which had required fourteen years of residency for citizenship. The 1802 act that replaced it required only five years of residency, loyalty to the Constitution, and the forsaking of foreign allegiance and titles.

The Democratic-Republicans turned next to the judiciary, the last stronghold of Federalist power. During the 1790s not a single Democratic-Republican had occupied the federal bench; thus the judiciary became a battlefield following the revolution of 1800. The first skirmish erupted over repeal of the Judiciary Act of 1801, which had been passed in the final days of the Adams administration. The act created fifteen new judgeships, which Adams filled by signing "midnight" appointments until his term was just hours away from expiring. The act also reduced by attrition the number of justices on the Supreme Court from six to five. Since that reduction would have denied Jefferson a Supreme Court appointment until two vacancies occurred, the new Democratic-Republican–dominated Congress repealed the 1801 act.

War on the Judiciary

Partisan Democratic-Republicans created another front in the war for control of the judiciary by targeting opposition judges for removal. Republicans were

This portrait of President Thomas Jefferson was painted by Rembrandt Peale in 1805. Charles Willson Peale (Rembrandt's father) and his five sons helped establish the reputation of American art in the new nation. Rembrandt Peale achieved fame for his presidential portraits; here he has captured Jefferson in a noble pose without the usual symbols of office or power, befitting the Republican age. (© Collection of The New-York Historical Society)

dicial misconduct. A staunch Federalist, Chase had repeatedly denounced Jefferson's administration from the bench. The Democratic-Republicans, however, failed to muster the two-thirds majority of senators necessary to convict him. Chase's acquittal preserved the Court's independence and established the precedent that criminal actions, not political disagreements, were the only proper grounds for impeachment. In his tenure as president, Jefferson appointed three new Supreme Court justices. Nonetheless, the Court remained a Federalist stronghold under Chief Justice John Marshall.

In his last weeks as a lame-duck president, President Adams, in an act especially galling to Jefferson, appointed Marshall as chief justice. A

John Marshall

Virginia Federalist, Marshall was an autocrat by nature but possessed a grace and openness of manner that complemented the new Republican political style. Under Marshall's domination, the Supreme Court retained a Federalist outlook even after Democratic-Republican justices achieved a majority in 1811. Throughout his tenure (1801–1835), the Court consistently upheld federal supremacy over the states and protected the interests of commerce and capital.

Marshall made the Court an equal branch of government in practice as well as theory. Judicial service became a coveted honor for ambitious and talented men. Previously people had regarded it lightly. Marshall also unified the Court, influencing the justices to issue joint majority opinions rather than a host of individual concurring judgments. Marshall himself became the voice of the majority: from 1801 through 1810 he wrote 85 percent of the opinions, including every important one.

Marshall significantly increased the Supreme Court's power in the landmark case of *Marbury v. Madison* (1803). William Marbury,

Marbury v. Madison

one of Adams's midnight appointees, had been named a justice of the peace in the District of Columbia. James Madison, Jefferson's new secretary of state, declined to certify Marbury's appointment so that the president could instead appoint a Democratic-Republican. Marbury sued, requesting a writ of mandamus (a court order forcing the president to appoint him). The case presented a political dilemma. If the Supreme Court ruled in favor of Marbury and issued a

especially infuriated with the Federalist judges who had refused to review the Sedition Act, under which Federalists had prosecuted critics of the Adams administration. At Jefferson's prompting, the House impeached (indicted) Federal District Judge John Pickering of New Hampshire, an emotionally disturbed alcoholic. In 1805 the Senate convicted him, removing him from office.

The day Pickering was ousted, the House impeached Supreme Court Justice Samuel Chase for ju-

writ, the president probably would not comply with it, and the Court had no way to force him to do so. But if the Federalist-dominated bench refused to issue the writ, it would be handing the Democratic-Republicans a victory.

Marshall brilliantly avoided both pitfalls. Speaking for the Court, he ruled that Marbury had a right to his appointment but that the Supreme Court could not compel Madison to honor the appointment because the Constitution did not grant the Court power to issue a writ of mandamus. In the absence of any specific mention in the Constitution, Marshall ruled, the section of the Judiciary Act of 1789 that authorized the Court to issue such writs was unconstitutional. In *Marbury v. Madison*, the Supreme Court denied itself the power to issue writs of mandamus but established its far greater power to judge the constitutionality of laws passed by Congress.

In succeeding years Marshall fashioned the theory of judicial review, the power of the Supreme Court to decide the constitutionality of legislation and presidential acts. Since the Constitution was the supreme law, he reasoned, any federal or state act contrary to the Constitution must be null and void. The Supreme Court, whose duty it was to uphold the law, would decide whether or not a legislative act contradicted the Constitution. The power of judicial review established in *Marbury v. Madison* permanently enhanced the independence of the judiciary.

Louisiana and Lewis and Clark

Louisiana

Democratic-Republicans and Federalists divided sharply over other issues; the acquisition of the Louisiana Territory in 1803 was another point of contention. Jefferson shared with many other Americans the belief that the United States was destined to expand its "empire of liberty."

By 1800 hundreds of thousands of Americans in search of land had settled in the rich Mississippi and Ohio River valleys, intruding on Indian lands. These settlers floated their farm goods down the Mississippi and Ohio Rivers to New Orleans for export. Whoever controlled the port of New Orleans thus had a hand on the throat of the American economy. Spain had owned Louisiana since the end of the Seven Years War in 1763, but rumors of a transfer back to France concerned the United States.

As a result of secret pacts with Spain in 1800 and 1801, France had reacquired the territory. The United States learned of the transfer only in 1802, when Napoleon seemed poised to rebuild a French empire in the New World. "Every eye in the United States is now focused on the affairs of Louisiana," Jefferson wrote to Robert R. Livingston, the American minister in Paris. Then, on the eve of ceding control to the French, Spain violated Pinckney's Treaty by denying Americans the privilege of storing their products at New Orleans prior to transshipment to foreign markets. Western farmers and eastern merchants thought a devious Napoleon had closed the port; they grumbled and talked war.

Jefferson personally took charge. To relieve the pressure for war and to win western farm support, he prepared for war while sending Virginia governor James Monroe as his personal envoy to join Robert Livingston in France. Their mission: to buy the port of New Orleans and as much of the Mississippi valley as possible. Meanwhile, Congress authorized the call-up of eighty thousand militiamen in case war became necessary. Arriving in Paris in April 1803, Monroe was astonished to learn that France already had offered to sell all 827,000 square miles of Louisiana to the United States for a mere $15 million. Napoleon had lost interest in the New World. On April 30 Monroe and Livingston signed a treaty buying the vast territory, whose exact borders were not yet mapped and whose land was uncharted (see Map 9.1).

Louisiana Purchase

The Louisiana Purchase doubled the size of the nation and opened the way for continental expansion. But was this most popular achievement of Jefferson's presidency constitutional? The Constitution nowhere authorized the president to acquire new territory and incorporate it into the nation. Jefferson considered proposing a constitutional amendment to allow the purchase but decided against it. He believed that the president's implied powers to protect the nation justified the purchase. His long-standing interest in Louisiana and the West also allayed his constitutional concerns. (As a naturalist and scientist, Jefferson had long had an interest in the geography, people, plants,

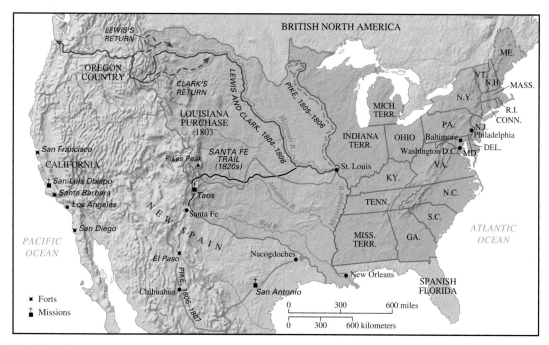

Map 9.1   Louisiana Purchase   The Louisiana Purchase (1803) doubled the area of the United States and opened the trans-Mississippi West for American settlement.

and animals found in the West. He was also interested in finding "the shortest & most convenient route of communications between the U.S. & the Pacific Ocean.")

In 1803 Jefferson sent an expedition headed by Meriwether Lewis and William Clark to the Pacific coast via the Missouri and Columbia Rivers. Lewis and Clark officially started their journey in May 1804. They traveled up the Missouri River and wintered at Fort Mandan in present-day North Dakota. Here they selected their twenty-nine-member corps and were joined by Indian guides. In April 1805 they resumed their journey. At times they lost their way, tumbled down steep mountain trails, and slept in the snow. In November 1805 they reached the Pacific Ocean in present-day Oregon, where they wintered, and the following March they began the return trek. Lewis and Clark split up to explore alternate routes and reunited in August 1806. They arrived home in St. Louis on September 23, 1806.

Lewis and Clark

The original Corps of Discovery was a diverse group. It included army regulars and young adventurers from Kentucky. Clark's slave York came along, as did two men who were half-French and half-Omaha. Immigrants included an Irishman and a German. Later, at the Mandan villages, the French Canadian trader Toussaint Charbonneau and his pregnant fifteen-year-old Shoshone wife, Sacagawea, joined the expedition. Lewis and Clark took Charbonneau because they wanted Sacagawea, who knew the languages of the mountain Indians, and she proved invaluable as a guide and translator.

Corps of Discovery

Headed by army officers, the expedition followed military rules. But it also was, at times, much more informal and democratic than army regulations or even civilian society allowed. When trouble arose, Lewis and Clark held courts-martial to discipline corps members for such infractions as drunkenness. Contrary to army rules, enlisted men sat on the court. And in November 1805, when the expedition voted where to locate its winter quarters on the Pacific coast, all voted, including the slave York and the Indian woman Sacagawea. Yet issues of race and gender were present. At the end of the journey, the names of York and Sacagawea did not appear on the roster Lewis submitted to the War Department. Neither received pay for their work, though their assistance had been indispensable.

Although some Americans still believed that the lands in the West were uninhabited, Lewis and Clark knew better. They anticipated a crowded wilderness and hoped to cement U.S. relations with Indians. The explorers carried gifts for Native American leaders, both to establish goodwill and to stimulate interest in trading for American manufactured goods. They brought back stories not only of various peoples, but also of fauna and flora unknown to the western scientific community; they encountered the grizzly bear, bighorn sheep, and mountain goats. Lewis sent boxes of natural-history specimens to Jefferson, including plant and tree cuttings. The two also mapped the West and, with their reports and specimens, furthered dreams of a continental empire.

Other explorations followed Lewis and Clark's. In 1805 and 1806 Lieutenant Zebulon Pike sought the source of the continent-cutting river and a navigable water route to the Far West. When Pike and his men wandered into Spanish territory to the south, the Spanish held them captive for several months in Mexico. After his release, Pike wrote an account of his experiences that set commercial minds spinning. Over the next few decades, Americans avidly read accounts of western exploration. The vision of a road to the Southwest became a reality with the opening of the Santa Fe Trail in the 1820s, and settlement followed the trail.

Exploration of the West

New Spain's *Tejas* (Texas) province bordered the Louisiana Territory. Provincial officials welcomed Americans, some of whom fought as volunteers with Indians and Mexican rebels in a twelve-year war with Spain that ended with Mexican independence in 1821. The establishment of an independent Mexico inspired these Americans to dream of an independent Texas nation—a place for Americans, not for Mexicans. It seems there was no place for people of color, including Mexicans—a mix of European, Indian, and African peoples—in the "empire of liberty."

Political Factionalism and Jefferson's Reelection

Prior to the Republican victory in 1800, most Federalists had disdained popular campaigning. They believed in government by the "best" people—those whose education, wealth, and experience qualified them to be leaders. For candidates to debate their own merits in front of their inferiors—the voters—was utterly demeaning, they thought.

After the resounding Federalist defeat in 1800, however, a younger generation of Federalists began to imitate the Democratic-Republicans. Led by such men as Josiah Quincy, a Massachusetts congressman, the Younger Federalists campaigned for popular support. Quincy cleverly presented the Federalists as the people's party, attacking Democratic-Republicans as autocratic planters and slaveholders. In attacking frugal government, the Federalists played on fears of a weakened army and navy. Eastern merchants depended on a strong navy to protect ocean trade; westerners looked to the army to defend them as they encroached on Indian territory.

A New Style of Campaigning

In states where both factions organized and ran candidates, people became more active in politics. In some states about 90 percent of the eligible voters cast ballots between 1804 and 1816. But the base of eligible voters remained restricted: property qualifications for voting and holding office persisted. Fearing the divisiveness of partisanship, some Democratic-Republicans restrained their organizational efforts, and most leaders shied away from formal, cohesive political organizations.

Yet political competition and a vigorous partisan press prompted grassroots electioneering. Political barbecues symbolized the new style of campaign. At these barbecues, guests washed down their meals with beer and punch and listened to the lengthy orations of candidates. The speeches often contained wild accusations, which—given the slow speed of communications—might go unanswered until after the election.

Grassroots Electioneering

The Federalists never mastered the art of campaigning. Older Federalists remained opposed to blatant appeals. And though strong in Connecticut, Delaware, and a few other states, the Federalists were weak at the national level and never offered the Democratic-Republicans sustained competition. Moreover, the extremism of some Older Federalists discredited most of the rest. Timothy Pickering, a Massachusetts congressman and former secretary of state, for instance, opposed the Louisiana Purchase, feared Jefferson's reelection, and urged the secession of New England in 1803 and 1804. He won some support, but most Federalists balked at his plan for secession. Ever the opportunist, Vice President Aaron Burr, intrigued with Pickering's idea, fantasized about leading New York into secession, with other states following. But when Burr lost his bid to become governor of New York in 1804, dreams of a northern confederacy evaporated.

Where Federalists were too weak to pose a threat, Democratic-Republicans fought among themselves. Politics suffered from divisiveness and personal animosities that were as strong a force as ideology. Although the United States was beginning to build a tradition of nonviolent politics, it had not yet taken hold. Thus there were times when political disagreements erupted into violence. The most famous was the Burr-Hamilton duel, involving a former vice president and a former secretary of the treasury.

Aaron Burr and Alexander Hamilton had long despised each other. Hamilton relentlessly blocked Burr's path. He thwarted Burr's attempt to steal the election of 1800

Hamilton-Burr Duel

from Jefferson, and in the mudslinging 1804 New York gubernatorial race, Burr lost to a rival Democratic-Republican faction backed by the Federalist Hamilton. Both Burr and Hamilton held grudges, and when Hamilton made derogatory remarks about him, Burr challenged his nemesis to a duel. Hamilton accepted even though he found dueling repugnant. Because New York had outlawed dueling, the two men met across the Hudson River at Weehawken, New Jersey. Hamilton did not fire, and he paid for that decision with his life. Burr was indicted for murder.

His political career in ruins, Burr plotted to create in the Southwest a new empire carved out of the Louisiana Territory. With the collusion of General James Wilkinson, the U.S. commander in the Missis-

sippi valley, Burr planned to raise a private army to grab land from the United States or from Spain (his exact plans remain unknown). However, Wilkinson switched sides and informed President Jefferson of Burr's devious intention. Jefferson personally assisted the prosecution in Burr's 1807 trial for treason, over which Chief Justice Marshall presided. The jury acquitted Burr, who fled to Europe.

Campaigning for reelection in 1804, Jefferson took credit for the restoration of republican values and

Jefferson's Reelection

the acquisition of the Louisiana Territory. Jefferson and the Democratic-Republicans claimed they ended the Federalist threat to liberty by repealing the Alien and Sedition and Judiciary Acts and boasted of reducing the size of government by cutting spending. Despite his opponents' charges, Jefferson had demonstrated that Democratic-Republicans supported commerce and promoted free trade. American trade with Europe was flourishing.

Jefferson's opponent in 1804 was Charles Cotesworth Pinckney, a wealthy South Carolina lawyer and former Revolutionary War aide to George Washington. As Adams's vice-presidential running mate in 1800, Pinckney had inherited the Federalist leadership. Jefferson and his running mate George Clinton of New York easily won the election.

Indian Resistance

 Lewis and Clark's account testified to the Indian presence in the West, and most Americans viewed Native Americans, no matter where they lived, as obstacles to American settlement. Violations of treaties and coerced new ones forced Indians to cede ever more land, continually shrinking Indian territory.

In the early 1800s two Shawnee brothers, Prophet (1775–1837) and Tecumseh (1768–1813), led a revolt against further American encroachment by fostering a pan-Indian federation that stretched from the Old Northwest to the South. Prophet's early life typified the experiences of the Indians of the Old Northwest. Born in 1775 a few months after his father's death in battle, Prophet, called Lalawethika ("Noisemaker"), as a young man was expelled to Ohio along with other Shawnees under the 1795 Treaty of Greenville (see page 120), and he later moved to Indiana. Within Prophet and Tecumseh's own lifetimes the Shawnees had lost most of their Ohio land. Displacement left Lalawethika forlorn, and he turned to whiskey for escape. He also turned to traditional folk knowledge and remedies and in 1804 became a tribal medicine man. His medicine, however, could not stop the white man's diseases from ravaging his village.

Lalawethika emerged from his own battle with illness in 1805 as a new man, called Tenskwatawa ("the Open Door"), or "the Prophet."

The Prophet

Claiming to have died and been resurrected, he traveled widely in the Ohio River valley as a religious leader, attacking the decline of moral values among Native Americans, warning of damnation for those who drank whiskey, condemning intertribal battles, and stressing harmony and respect for elders. He urged Indians to return to the old ways and abandon white customs. Prophet's outspoken opposition to federal Indian policy drew others into his camp, and as his message spread to southern tribes, the federal government and white settlers became alarmed.

By 1808 Prophet and his older brother Tecumseh were talking less about spiritual renewal and more about resisting American aggression. Tecumseh was turning Prophet's religious movement into a political one. They encouraged Indians to resist eviction from lands claimed by the U.S. government. In repudiating land cessions to the government under the Treaty of Fort Wayne (1809), Tecumseh told Indiana's governor William Henry Harrison at Vincennes in 1810 that "the only way to check and stop this evil is, for all the red men

Tecumseh

The Shawnee chiefs Tecumseh *(left)* and Prophet *(right).* The two brothers led a revival of traditional Shawnee culture and preached Native American federation against white encroachment. In the War of 1812 they allied themselves with the British, but Tecumseh's death at the Battle of the Thames (1813) and British indifference thereafter caused Native Americans' resistance and unity to collapse.   (Tecumseh: Field Museum of Natural History, Chicago, FMNH Neg. #A93851; Prophet: National Museum of American Art, Smithsonian Institution, Washington, D.C.)

to unite in claiming a common and equal right in the land, as it was at first, and should be yet; for it . . . belongs to all, for the use of each. . . . No part has a right to sell, even to each other, much less to strangers."

Tecumseh, a towering six-foot warrior and charismatic orator, soon overshadowed his brother as Shawnee leader. He sought to unify northern and southern Indians by traveling widely, preaching Indian resistance. And he warned Harrison that Indians would resist white occupation of the 2.5 million acres on the Wabash River that they had ceded in the Treaty of Fort Wayne.

American Neutrality Imperiled by a World at War

 "Peace, commerce, and honest friendship with all nations, entangling alliance with none," President Jefferson had proclaimed in his first inaugural address. Jefferson's efforts to stand aloof from European conflict were successful until 1805. Thereafter the United States could not escape the web of European hostilities.

The root of America's problems lay in the May 1803 renewal of the Napoleonic wars between France and Britain. Initially American commerce benefited from the conflict. As the world's largest neutral carrier, the United States became the chief supplier of food to Europe. American merchants also gained control of most of the West Indian trade. But after defeating the French and Spanish fleets at the Battle of Trafalgar in October 1805, Britain's Royal Navy tightened its control of the oceans. Two months later Napoleon crushed Britain's allies, the Russians and Austrians, at Austerlitz. Stalemated, France and Britain launched a commercial war, blockading each other's trade. As a trading partner of both countries, the United States paid a high price.

All tension focused on the high seas, as Britain suffered a severe shortage of sailors. Too few men enlisted, and those in service frequently deserted, demoralized by harsh treatment. The Royal Navy resorted to stopping American vessels and seizing British deserters, British-born naturalized American seamen, and other unlucky sailors suspected of being British. Perhaps six to eight

Impressment of American Sailors

thousand Americans were impressed in this way between 1803 and 1812.

The British violated other American rights as well. They interfered with U.S. trade with the West Indies by blocking goods the United States believed were part of neutral trade. They also searched and seized U.S. vessels within American territory offshore.

In February 1806 Americans denounced British impressment. In protest, Congress passed the Non-Importation Act, barring British manufactured goods from entering American ports. Since the act exempted most cloth or metal articles, it had little impact on British trade; instead, it was a warning to the British of what to expect if they continued to violate American rights. In November Jefferson suspended the act temporarily while William Pinckney, a Baltimore lawyer, joined James Monroe in London to negotiate a settlement. But the treaty Monroe and Pinckney carried home violated their instructions—it did not so much as mention impressment—and Jefferson never submitted it to the Senate for ratification.

Anglo-American relations steadily deteriorated. Then in June 1807, the forty-gun frigate U.S.S. *Chesapeake* left Norfolk, Virginia, and while still inside American territorial waters met the fifty-gun British frigate *Leopard*. When the *Chesapeake* refused to be searched for deserters, the *Leopard* repeatedly fired its cannon broadside into the American ship. Three Americans were killed and eighteen wounded, including the ship's captain. The British seized four deserters from the Royal Navy—three of them American citizens. Damaged and humiliated, the *Chesapeake* returned to port.

Chesapeake Affair

Had the United States been better prepared militarily, the ensuing howl of public indignation might have brought about a declaration of war. But the still-fledgling country was no match for the British navy. With Congress in recess, Jefferson was able to avoid hostilities. In July the president closed American waters to British warships to prevent similar incidents, and soon thereafter he increased military and naval expenditures. In December 1807 Jefferson again put economic pressure on Great Britain by invoking the Non-Importation Act, followed eight days later by a new restriction, the Embargo Act.

The Embargo Act forbade all exports from the United States to any country, an action that Jefferson

Embargo Act perceived as a short-term measure to avoid war. Exports dropped by some 80 percent in 1808. Mercantile New England was especially hard hit. New England was a bastion of Federalist opposition to Jefferson, and in the winter of 1808–1809 talk of secession spread from one port to another.

Few American policies were as well intentioned and as unpopular and unsuccessful as Jefferson's embargo. Moreover, the embargo had little impact on Britain, and France used the policy as an excuse to set privateers against American ships that had evaded the embargo. The French cynically claimed that such ships were British vessels in disguise because the embargo prevented American ships from sailing.

In the election of 1808, the Democratic-Republicans faced not only the Federalists but also factional dissent and dissatisfaction in seaboard states **Election of 1808** hobbled by the embargo. Jefferson followed Washington's lead in renouncing a third term. He supported James Madison, his secretary of state, as the Democratic-Republican standard-bearer. Madison won the endorsement of the party's congressional caucus and with his running mate, Vice President George Clinton, defeated the Federalist ticket.

Under the pressure of domestic opposition, the embargo eventually collapsed. In its place, the Non-Intercourse Act of 1809 reopened **Non-Intercourse Act** trade with all nations except Britain and France, and it authorized the president to resume trade with Britain or France if either of them ceased to violate neutral rights. Although the new law solved the problems created by the embargo, it did not prevent further British and French interference with American commerce.

When the Non-Intercourse Act expired in 1810, Congress substituted a variant, Macon's Bill Number 2, that exchanged the proverbial stick for a carrot. The bill reopened trade with both Great Britain and France but provided that when either nation stopped violating American commercial rights, the president could suspend American commerce with the other. Madison, eager to avoid war, fell victim to French duplicity. When Napoleon accepted the offer, Madison declared nonintercourse with Great Britain in 1811. Napoleon, however, tricked him. The French continued to seize American ships, and nonintercourse failed a second time. But because the Royal Navy dominated the seas, Britain, not France, became the main focus of American hostility.

Commerce and Industry

 The economy of the early republic relied heavily on shipping, and the commercial fleet played a significant role in extending American trade around the world. American ships carried cotton, lumber, sugar, and other commodities to Europe, and brought back manufactured goods. The slave trade lured American sailing ships to Africa. Boston, Salem, and Philadelphia merchants opened trade with China, sending cloth and metal to swap for furs with Chinook Indians on the Oregon coast, then sailing to China to trade for porcelain, tea, and silk. Greater profits could be made by importing manufactured goods than by producing them at home.

After 1807, however, embargoes and war boosted domestic manufacturing. The disruptions in commerce made domestic manufactures profitable, and merchants began to shift their capital from shipping to manufacturing. In 1807 there were twenty cotton and woolen mills in New England; by 1813 there were more than two hundred.

Samuel Slater set up the first American textile mill in Rhode Island in the 1790s. It used water-powered spinning machines that English immigrant Slater had built from memorized British models. The construction **Waltham or Lowell System** of the first American power loom and the chartering of the Boston Manufacturing Company in 1813, however, radically transformed textile manufacturing. Francis Cabot Lowell and other Boston merchants capitalized the corporation at $400,000—ten times the amount behind the first Rhode Island mills. The owners erected their factories in Waltham, Massachusetts, bringing all the manufacturing processes to a single location. They employed a resident manager to run the mill, thus separating ownership from management. Workers received wages, and the inexpensive cloth they produced was sold throughout the United States.

The managers could not find enough hands in rural Waltham to staff the mill, so they recruited New England farm daughters. As inducements they offered cash wages, company-run boarding houses, and cultural events such as evening lectures. This paternalistic approach, called the Waltham or Lowell system, spread to other mills.

The early mills, dependent on waterpower, sprung up in rural areas. By erecting dams and watercourses, mill owners diverted water from farmers and destroyed fishing, an important source of income and protein in rural and village America. To protect their customary rights, fishermen and farmers fought the manufacturers in New England state legislatures, but petitions from job seekers in the mill environs supported the manufacturers. The ensuing compromises promoted mill development.

The War of 1812

Though unprepared for war in 1812, the United States seemed unable to avoid it. Having exhausted all efforts to alter British policy, and fearing for the survival of American independence, the United States drifted toward war. The Democratic-Republican "War Hawks," elected to Congress in 1810, cried loudest for war. Britain's response was too little and too late. In spring 1812, the admiralty ordered British ships to avoid clashes with the American navy and to avoid searches and seizures of American ships. Then in June 1812, Britain reopened the seas to American shipping. Hard times had hit the British Isles: the Anglo-French conflict had blocked much British commerce to the European continent, and exports to the United States had fallen 80 percent. But two days after the change in British policy, before word of it had crossed the Atlantic, Congress declared war.

In his message to Congress on June 1, 1812, President Madison enumerated familiar grievances: impressment, interference with neutral commerce, and British alliances with western Indians. More generally, the Democratic-Republicans resolved to defend American independence and honor, and some Americans hoped to conquer and annex British Canada.

The war Congress was a partisan one. Most militant were the War Hawks, land-hungry southerners and westerners, all Democratic-Republicans, led by John C. Calhoun of South Carolina and House Speaker Henry Clay of Kentucky. Most representatives from the coastal states opposed war because

The Vote for War

armed conflict with the Royal Navy would interrupt American shipping. On the vote in Congress, not a single Federalist favored war. However, both houses of Congress voted for war; President Madison signed the bill, and the United States went to war with Britain.

Jefferson's warning that "our constitution is a peace establishment—it is not calculated for war" proved true. Though the U.S. Navy had a corps of experienced officers who had proved their mettle in the Barbary War, it was no match for the Royal Navy. The U.S. Army had neither an able staff nor an adequate force of enlisted men. By 1812 the U.S. Military Academy at West Point, founded in 1802, had produced only eighty-nine regular officers. The American army depended on political leaders and state militias to recruit volunteers, and not all states cooperated. The government offered enlistees a sign-up bonus of $16, monthly pay of $5, a full set of clothes, and a promise of three months' pay and rights to purchase 160 acres of western land upon discharge. Forty-two percent of the enlistees were illiterate.

Recruiting an Army

Canada was tempting, and seemed takeable. The mighty Royal Navy could not reach the Great Lakes separating the United States and Canada because there was no river access to them from the Atlantic. Canada's population of just one-half million was a fraction of the United States's 7.5 million. Canada had seven thousand regulars in uniform; the United States, 12,000. And Americans hoped that the French in Canada might welcome U.S. forces.

Invasion of Canada

Begun with high hopes, the invasion of Canada ended in disaster. The American strategy concentrated on the West, aiming to split Canadian forces and isolate the pro-British Indians. At the outset of the war, Tecumseh joined the British, who promised him in return an Indian nation in the Great Lakes region. U.S. General William Hull, territorial governor of Michigan, marched his troops into Upper Canada, near Detroit. Although he had superior numbers, Hull waged a timid campaign, retreating more than he attacked. His abandonment of Mackinac Island and Fort Dearborn in Chicago and his surrender of Fort Detroit left the entire Midwest exposed to the enemy. The only bright spot was the September 1812 defense of Fort Harrison in Indiana Territory by Captain Zachary Taylor, who provided the Americans with their first land victory. By the winter of 1812–1813, the British controlled about half of the Old Northwest.

The United States had no greater success on the Niagara front, where New York borders Canada. At the Battle of Queenstown, Canada, north of Niagara, the U.S. Army met defeat because the New York militia refused to leave New York. This frustrating scenario was repeated near Lake Champlain when the New York militia's refusal to cross the border into Canada foiled American plans to attack Montreal.

The navy provided the only good news in the first year of the war. The U.S.S. *Constitution*, the U.S.S. *Wasp*, and the U.S.S. *United States* all

Naval Battles

bested British warships on the Atlantic Ocean. However, in the first year of war the Americans lost 20 percent of their ships, while in defeat the British lost just 1 percent of their vessels. With only seventeen ships in 1812, the United States could not fight the British in a general naval war.

The Royal Navy blockaded the Chesapeake and Delaware Bays in December 1812, and by 1814 the blockade covered nearly all American ports along the Atlantic and Gulf coasts. After 1811, American trade overseas had declined nearly 90 percent, and the decline in revenues from customs duties threatened to bankrupt the federal government and prostrate New England.

The contest for control of the Great Lakes, the key to the war in the Northwest, evolved as a ship-building race. Under Master Com-

Great Lakes Campaign

mandant Oliver Hazard Perry and shipbuilder Noah Brown, the United States outbuilt the British on Lake Erie and defeated them at the bloody Battle of Put-in-Bay on September 10, 1813. With this costly victory, the Americans gained control of Lake Erie.

General William Henry Harrison then began the offensive that proved to be among the United States's most successful land campaigns in the war. Harrison's force of forty-five hundred men attacked and took De-

troit. Then they crossed to Canada, defeating the British, Shawnee, and Chippewa forces on October 5 at the Battle of the Thames. The United States regained control of the Old Northwest. Moreover, Tecumseh died in the battle, and with his death expired Native American unity. When the Battle of the Thames was over, the Americans razed the Canadian capital of York (now Toronto).

After defeating Napoleon in Europe in April 1814, the British launched a land counteroffensive against the United States, concentrating on the Chesapeake Bay region. In retaliation for the burning of York—and to divert American troops from Lake Champlain, where the British planned a new offensive—royal troops occupied Washington, D.C., in August and set it ablaze. The attack on the capital was only a diversion, however. The major battle occurred in September 1814 at Baltimore, where the Americans held firm. Francis Scott Key, detained on a British ship, watched the bombardment of Fort McHenry from Baltimore harbor and the next morning wrote the verses of "The Star-Spangled Banner" (which became the national anthem in 1931). Although the British inflicted heavy damage both materially and psychologically, they achieved little militarily. Their offensive at Lake Champlain proved equally unsuccessful. The British halted their offense, and the war was stalemated.

The last campaigns of the war took place in the South, against the Creeks along the Gulf of Mexico and against the British around New

Campaign Against the Creeks

Orleans. The Creeks had responded to Tecumseh's call to resist U.S. expansion. In December 1812 General Andrew Jackson raised his Tennessee militia to fight the Creeks. By late 1813 his anti-Creek campaign had stalled for lack of supplies. His men, who had signed up for a year, muttered about going home. Jackson refused to discharge them. In March 1814 Jackson executed John Woods, a militiaman, for disobedience and mutiny. This act broke the opposition within the ranks, and Jackson's men defeated the Creek nation at the Battle of Horseshoe Bend in Mississippi Territory in March 1814. As a result, the Creeks ceded two-thirds of their land and withdrew to the southern and western part of Mississippi Territory (what is now Alabama); the removal of Indians from the South had begun. Jackson became a major general in the regular army and continued south toward the Gulf of Mexico. After seizing Pensacola in Spanish Florida and securing Mobile, he marched to New Orleans.

The Battle of New Orleans was the last campaign of the war. Early in December the British fleet landed fifteen hundred men east of the city,

Battle of New Orleans

hoping to seize the mouth of the Mississippi River and thus strangle the lifeline of the American West. They faced American regulars, Tennessee and Kentucky volunteers, and two companies of free African American volunteers from New Orleans. For three weeks the British and the Americans played cat-and-mouse. Finally, on January 8, 1815, the two forces met head-on. In fortified positions, Jackson's poorly trained army held its ground against two frontal assaults from a British contingent of six thousand. At day's end, more than two thousand British soldiers lay dead or wounded; the Americans suffered only twenty-one casualties. Andrew Jackson emerged a national hero, and Americans memorialized the battle in song and paintings. The Battle of New Orleans actually took place two weeks after the end of the war. Unknown to the participants, a treaty had been signed in Ghent, Belgium, two weeks before the battle.

Ballou's Pictorial Drawing-Room Companion depicts the Battle of New Orleans, the last campaign of the War of 1812. Andrew Jackson's troops—army regulars, Tennessee and Kentucky volunteers, and two companies of African American volunteers from New Orleans—held off the better-trained British troops in January 1815. The battle made Andrew Jackson a national hero.   (Historic New Orleans Collection)

Peace and Consequences

 The Ghent treaty ignored the issues that had led to war. The United States received no satisfaction on impressment, blockades, or other maritime rights for neutrals. British demands for an independent Indian nation in the Northwest and territorial cessions from Maine to Minnesota likewise went unsatisfied. The Treaty of Ghent essentially restored the prewar status quo. It provided for an end to hostilities, release of prisoners, restoration of conquered territory, and arbitration of boundary disputes.

Why did the negotiators settle for so little? Events in Europe had made peace and the status quo acceptable at the end of 1814, as they had not been in 1812. Napoleon's defeat allowed the United States to abandon its demands, since peace in Europe made impressment and interference with American commerce moot issues. Similarly, war-weary Britain—its treasury nearly depleted—stopped pressing for a military victory.

The War of 1812 affirmed the independence of the American republic. Although conflict with Great Britain over trade and territory continued, it never again led to war. The experience strengthened America's resolve to steer clear of European politics because it was the Anglo-French conflagration that had drawn the United States into war. At the same time, with Indian resistance broken, U.S. expansion would spread south and west, not north to Canada.

Consequences of the War of 1812

The war carried disastrous results for most Native Americans. The ninth article of the Treaty of Ghent pledged the United States to end hostilities and to restore "all the possessions, rights, and privileges" that Indians had enjoyed before the war. Midwestern Indians signed more than a dozen treaties with the United States in 1815, but they had little meaning. With the death of Tecumseh, the Indians had lost their most powerful political and military leader; with the withdrawal of the British, they had lost their strongest ally. The Shawnees, Potawatomis, Chippewas, and others had lost the means to resist American expansion.

The war also exposed weaknesses in defense and transportation at home. American generals had found U.S. roads inadequate to move troops and supplies. Thus improved transportation and a well-equipped army became national priorities in the postwar years. In 1815 Congress voted a standing army of ten thousand men—three times the size of the army during Jefferson's administration. In 1818 the National Road reached Wheeling, Virginia (now West Virginia), from its Cumberland, Maryland, beginning.

Perhaps most important of all, the war stimulated economic growth. The embargo, the Non-Importation and Non-Intercourse Acts, and the war itself spurred the production of manufactured goods because New England capitalists began to invest in home manufactures. The effects of these changes were far-reaching.

Finally, the war sealed the fate of the Federalists. Realizing that they could not win a presidential election in wartime, the Federalists joined renegade Democratic-Republicans in supporting New York City mayor DeWitt Clinton in September 1812. Federalist organization peaked at the state level as the Younger Federalists campaigned hard. Clinton nevertheless lost to President Madison. The Federalists gained some congressional seats, but extremism, in the form of the Hartford Convention, undermined them.

Hartford Convention

During the war Federalists had revived talk of secession. With the war stalemated, delegates from New England met in Hartford, Connecticut in the winter of 1814–1815 to discuss revising the national compact or pulling out of the republic. Moderates prevented a resolution of secession, but convention members condemned the war and the embargo and endorsed radical changes in the Constitution. They wanted to restrict the presidency to one term, require a two-thirds congressional vote to admit new states to the Union, and prohibit naturalized citizens from holding office. It was a fruitless attempt to preserve New England Federalist political power as electoral strength shifted to the South and West.

The timing of the Hartford Convention proved lethal. The victory at New Orleans and news of the peace treaty made the convention, with its talk of secession and constitutional amendments, look ridiculous if not treasonous. Though the Federalists survived in a handful of states until the 1820s, the faction dissolved.

Summary

 The 1800 election marked the peaceful transition in power from the Federalists to the opposition Democratic-Republicans. Thomas Jefferson replaced John Adams as president and sought both to unify the nation and to solidify Democratic-Republican control of the government. Jeffersonians favored frugal government.

The Supreme Court under Chief Justice John Marshall remained a Federalist bastion. Marshall would ensure, until 1835, the dominance of Federalist principle: federal supremacy over the states and the protection of commerce and capital. In *Marbury v. Madison* (1803), the Supreme Court established its great power of judicial review.

Jefferson considered the acquisition of Louisiana Territory and the commissioning of Lewis and Clark's expedition among his significant presidential accomplishments. In a single act the United States doubled its size. Increasingly Americans looked westward.

The Democratic-Republicans won every presidential election in this period. Though the electorate was limited only to males and mostly to whites, both the Federalists and the Democratic-Republicans competed at the grassroots level for popular support.

Despite internal divisions, the greatest threats came from abroad. In both the war with the Barbary states and the War of 1812, the United States sought to guard its commerce and ships on the high seas. The Treaty of Ghent reaffirmed American independence. The War of 1812 also dealt a serious blow to Indian resistance in the West and South. At the same time, embargoes and war forced Americans to look toward building domestic markets and jump-started American manufacturing.

Smith. Afterward she wrote: "The changes of administration, which in every government and in every age have most generally been epochs of confusion, villainy and bloodshed, in this happy country take place without any species of distraction, or disorder." It need not have been so.

John Adams was so bitter over his loss that he exited the city before sunrise that morning. Adams had lost by a narrow margin in the electoral college, but Aaron Burr, Jefferson's running mate, threw the election into turmoil when he unsuccessfully tried to grab the presidency for himself. The campaign of 1800 had been particularly nasty and personal, and candidates hinted that were their opponents elected, chaos would ensue.

Why didn't it? After all, what would plague most new states in the nineteenth and twentieth centuries was the unwillingness of regimes to hand over power peacefully to legitimate successors. Coups, bloodshed, and military rule seemed to be most common.

In later years Jefferson called his election to the presidency the "Revolution of 1800." He meant that the Federalists were turned out and the republican principles of the Revolution were about to be restored.

The real revolution, however, was that the Federalists had relinquished power to the Democratic-Republicans, without confusion or villainy or bloodshed. It established the precedent that political battles would be waged not in the streets but at the polls, in Congress, and before the courts. The "revolution" of 1800 established a unique legacy for a people and a nation that would define governance in the United States: the transfer of governmental power based on the ballot, not on arms.

LEGACY FOR A PEOPLE AND A NATION
The Peaceful Transfer of Power

Among those in attendance at Jefferson's inauguration on March 4, 1801, was novelist Margaret Bayard

For Further Reading, see the Appendix. For Web resources, go to history.college.hmco.com/students.

10

NATIONALISM, EXPANSION, AND THE MARKET ECONOMY

1816–1845

Postwar Nationalism
The Market Economy and Government's Economic Role
Transportation Links
Commercial Farming
The Rise of Manufacturing and Commerce
Workers and the Workplace
Americans on the Move
Native American Resistance and Removal

LEGACY FOR A PEOPLE AND A NATION
A Mixed Economy

The Hutchinson Family from rural New Hampshire, also known as the Tribe of Jesse, was the most popular singing group in nineteenth-century America. Abby, Asa, Jesse, John, and Judson Hutchinson performed the patriotic, religious, and sentimental songs that had dominated popular music since the Revolution. Unlike most musical groups, the Tribe of Jesse not only sang but also presented well-rehearsed and elaborately produced performances. They used folk tunes, but their lyrics explored controversial topics such as abolition and temperance.

The Hutchinson Family traveled by rail, performing across the expanding United States, but drawing their largest audiences in the growing cities of the North. The family's fee for a single night in the 1840s reached $1,000, about 400 times a worker's daily wage. They had an entourage of managers, agents, and publishers. Hawkers sold sheet music, portraits, and songbooks at the Hutchinsons' concerts. The Hutchinson Family made a business of music and entertainment, selling nostalgia and reform.

The Hutchinsons' concert tours exemplified the market economy, in which goods and services sold in cash or credit transactions created a network of exchange that bound distant enterprises together. The family performed in western areas in the 1840s that had had no American settlements twenty years before. The canals and railroads that carried them also in-

IMPORTANT EVENTS

1815 Madison proposes internal improvements

1816 Second Bank of the United States chartered
Tariff of 1816 imposes first substantial duties
Monroe elected president

1817 Rush-Bagot Treaty

1819 *McCulloch v. Maryland* establishes supremacy of federal over state law
Adams-Onís Treaty with Spain gives Florida to U.S. and defines Louisiana territorial border

1819–23 Hard times bring unemployment

1820 Missouri Compromise creates formula for admitting slave and free states
Monroe reelected

1820s New England textile mills expand

1823 Monroe Doctrine closes Western Hemisphere to European intervention

1824 *Gibbons v. Ogden* affirms federal over state authority in interstate commerce

1825 Erie Canal completed

1830 Railroad era begins
Congress passes Indian Removal Act

1830s–40s Cotton production shifts to Mississippi valley

1831 Cherokees turn to courts to defend treaty rights in *Cherokee Nation v. Georgia*

1832 Marshall declares Cherokee nation a distinct political community in *Worcester v. Georgia*

1834 Women workers strike at Lowell textile mills

1835–42 Seminoles successfully resist removal in Second Seminole War

1836 Second Bank of the United States closes

1837 *Charles River Bridge v. Warren Bridge* encourages new enterprises

1839–43 Hard times strike again

1842 *Commonwealth v. Hunt* declares strikes lawful

creasingly linked the nation's regions after the War of 1812. People moved inland from the seacoast. Grain went east to coastal cities, cotton went to Europe, and ready-made men's garments from New York and Cincinnati sold across the nation. Increasingly, farmers turned to staple-crop agriculture and city people worked not for themselves but for others, for wages. These large-scale enterprises needed capital, and new financial institutions amassed and loaned it. Mechanization took hold; factories and precision-made machinery put home workshops and handcrafters out of business. In turn, the increased specialization in agriculture, manufacturing, transportation, and finance further fired the engines of the new nationwide, capitalist, market-oriented economy.

The end of the War of 1812 unleashed this growth. A new nationalist spirit encouraged the economy and promoted western expansion at home, trade abroad, and assertiveness throughout the Western Hemisphere. Economic growth and territorial expansion, however, generated new problems. Sectional conflicts over slavery and economic development created divisions. Migration, shifts in occupations, and changes in the ways people worked created new tensions. Journeyman tailors, displaced by retailers and cheaper labor, found their trades disappearing. New England farm daughters who became wage workers found their world changing no less radically. Moreover, nationwide boom-and-bust cycles wrenched livelihoods and lives.

Everywhere Americans were on the move. Settlement moved to the interior, and farms and cities, linked first by rivers, then by roads, canals, and railroads, stretched to the Ohio and Mississippi River valleys and beyond. The Indian inhabitants attempted to hold their ground but were in the end removed to the West. ▪

Postwar Nationalism

 Nationalism surged after the War of 1812. Self-confident, the nation asserted itself at home and abroad as Democratic-Republicans borrowed a page from the Federalists' agenda and encouraged economic growth. James Madison inspired the postwar wave of nationalism. In his December 1815 message to Congress, he recommended economic development and military expansion. His agenda included a national bank (the charter of the first bank had expired in 1811) and improved transportation. To raise government revenues and foster manufacturing, Madison called for a protective tariff—a tax on imported goods designed to protect American manufactures. Yet his program acknowledged Jeffersonian republicanism: only a constitutional amendment, Madison argued, could authorize the federal government to build local roads and canals.

A new generation of congressional leaders saw Madison's program as a way of unifying the country.

Nationalist Program   Democratic-Republican John C. Calhoun of South Carolina and House Speaker Henry Clay of Kentucky believed that the tariff would stimulate industry. The agricultural South and West would sell cotton to the churning mills of New England and food to its millworkers. New roads and canals would transport the goods, and tariff revenues would provide money to build them. A national bank would handle the transactions.

In 1816 Congress enacted much of the nationalist program. It chartered the Second Bank of the United States, which, like its predecessor, mixed public and private ownership: the government provided one-fifth of the bank's capital and appointed one-fifth of its directors. Congress also passed a protective tariff to aid industries. The Tariff of 1816 levied taxes on imported woolens and cottons and on iron, leather, hats, paper, and sugar, in effect raising their prices in the United States. Foreshadowing a growing trend, support for the tariff divided along sectional lines: New England and the western and Middle Atlantic states stood to benefit and applauded it, but the South did not.

The South did press for better transportation. It was Calhoun who promoted roads and canals to "bind the republic together." However, Madison vetoed Calhoun's internal improvements bill as unconstitutional. The president did approve funds for extending the National Road to Ohio, deeming it a military necessity.

James Monroe, Madison's successor, continued Madison's domestic program, supporting tariffs and vetoing internal improvements. Among

James Monroe   the nation's founders, Monroe was a most ordinary and colorless man who rarely had an original idea. But in 1816 he easily defeated the last Federalist presidential nominee, Rufus King. The American people were "one great family." A Boston newspaper dubbed this one-party period the "Era of Good Feelings."

Led by Federalist chief justice John Marshall, the Supreme Court became the bulwark of a nationalist point of view. In *McCulloch v. Mary-*

McCulloch v. Maryland   *land* (1819), the Court struck down a Maryland law taxing a branch of the federally chartered Second Bank of the United States. Maryland had imposed the tax in an effort to destroy the bank's Baltimore branch. The issue was thus one of state versus federal jurisdiction. Speaking for a unanimous Court, Marshall asserted the supremacy of the federal government over the states.

The Court went on to consider whether Congress could issue a bank charter. The Constitution did not spell out such power, but Marshall noted that Congress had the authority to pass "all laws which shall be necessary and proper for carrying into execution" the enumerated powers of the government. Marshall ruled that Congress could legally exercise "those great powers on which the welfare of the nation essentially depends." The bank charter was declared legal.

McCulloch v. Maryland thus joined nationalism and economics. By asserting federal supremacy, Marshall protected the commercial and industrial interests that favored a national bank. The decision was only one in a series of rulings that cemented the federalist view. In *Fletcher v. Peck* (1810), the Court had voided a Georgia law that violated individuals' rights to make contracts. In *Dartmouth College v. Woodward* (1819), the Court nullified a New Hampshire act altering the charter of Dartmouth College. Marshall ruled that the charter was a contract, and in protecting such contracts he thwarted state interference in commerce and business.

Monroe's secretary of state, John Quincy Adams, matched the self-confident Marshall Court in assertiveness and nationalism. From 1817 to 1825 he brilliantly managed the nation's foreign policy, stubbornly pushing for expansion, fishing rights for Americans in Atlantic waters, political distance from the Old World, and peace. An ardent expansionist, he nonetheless believed that expansion must come about through negotiations, not war, and that newly acquired territories must bar slavery.

John Quincy Adams as Secretary of State

Although an Anglophobe, Adams nonetheless worked to strengthen the peace with Great Britain negotiated at Ghent (1814). In 1817 the two nations agreed in the Rush-Bagot Treaty to limit their naval forces to one ship each on Lake Champlain and Lake Ontario and to two ships each on the four other Great Lakes. This first disarmament treaty of modern times led to the demilitarization of the border between the United States and Canada. Adams then pushed for the Convention of 1818, which fixed the United States–Canadian border from Lake of the Woods in Minnesota westward to the Rockies along the 49th parallel (see Map 10.1). When agreement could not be reached on the territory west of the Rockies, Britain and the United States settled on joint occupation of Oregon for ten years (renewed indefinitely in 1827).

Adams next moved to settle long-term disputes with Spain. During the War of 1812 the United States had seized Mobile and the remainder of West Florida. After the war, Adams took advantage of Spain's preoccupation with domestic and colonial troubles to negotiate for the purchase of East Florida. During the 1818 talks, General Andrew Jackson took it upon himself to occupy much of present-day Florida on the pretext of

Map 10.1   Missouri Compromise and the State of the Union, 1820   The compromise worked out by House Speaker Henry Clay established a formula that avoided debate over whether new states would allow or prohibit slavery. In the process, it divided the United States into northern and southern regions.

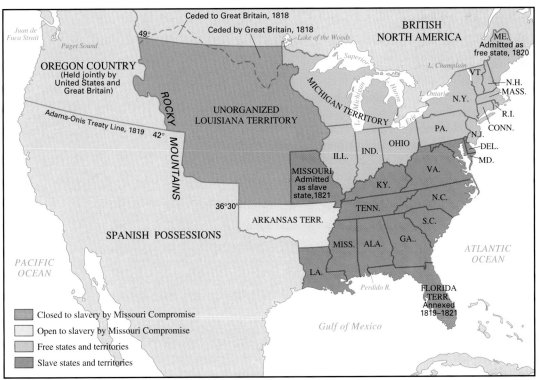

suppressing Seminole raids against American settlements across the border. Adams was furious with Jackson but defended his brazen act.

The following year, Don Luís de Onís, the Spanish minister to the United States, agreed to cede Florida to the United States without payment. The Adams-Onís, or Transcontinental, Treaty also defined the southwestern boundary of the Louisiana Purchase and set the southern border of Oregon at the 42nd parallel (see Map 10.1). The U.S. government assumed $5 million of claims by American citizens against Spain and gave up its dubious claim to northern Mexico (Texas). Expansion was achieved at little cost and without war.

Adams-Onís Treaty

When the Spanish flag was last lowered over Florida, residents differed in how they greeted the United States. Some planter-slaveholders and traders welcomed the American flag. Creeks and Seminoles, free blacks, runaway slaves, and Spanish-speaking town dwellers did not.

Conflict between the United States and European nations was temporarily resolved by the Rush-Bagot Treaty, the Convention of 1818, and the Adams-Onís Treaty, but events to the south still threatened American interests. John Quincy Adams's desire to insulate the United States and the Western Hemisphere from European conflict brought about his greatest achievement: the Monroe Doctrine.

The immediate issue was the recognition of new governments in Latin America. Between 1808 and 1822, the United Provinces of the Río de la Plata (present-day northern Argentina, Paraguay, and Uruguay), Chile, Peru, Colombia, and Mexico all broke free from Spain. Monroe and Adams moved cautiously, seeking to avoid conflict with Spain and to be assured of the stability of the new regimes. In 1822, shortly after the Adams-Onís Treaty was ratified, the United States became the first nation outside Latin America to recognize the new states.

Independent States in Latin America

Soon events in Europe again threatened the stability of the New World. Spain suffered a domestic revolt, and France, to bolster the weak Spanish monarchy against the rebels, occupied Spain. The United States feared that France would return the new Latin American states to colonial rule. Great Britain,

similarly distrustful of France, proposed a joint United States–British declaration against European intervention in the Western Hemisphere and a joint disavowal of territorial ambitions in the region. Adams rejected the British overture. Following George Washington's admonition to avoid foreign entanglements, he insisted that the United States act independently.

President Monroe presented the American position—the Monroe Doctrine—to Congress in December 1823. His message called for noncolonization of the Western Hemisphere by European nations, a principle that addressed American anxiety not only about Latin America but also about Russian expansion beyond Alaska and its settlements in California. He also demanded nonintervention by Europe in the affairs of independent New World nations, and he pledged noninterference by the United States in European affairs, including those of Europe's existing New World colonies.

Monroe Doctrine

Monroe's words, however, carried no force. Indeed, the policy could not have succeeded without the support of the British, who were committed to keeping other European nations out of the hemisphere to protect their dominance in the Atlantic trade. Europeans ignored the Monroe Doctrine; it was the Royal Navy they respected, not American policy.

While nationalism brought Americans together, the question of slavery divided them. Since the drafting of the Constitution, political leaders had tried to avoid the issue. The one exception was an act ending the foreign slave trade after January 1, 1808, which passed without much opposition. In 1819, however, slavery crept onto the political agenda when Missouri residents petitioned Congress for admission to the Union as a slave state. For two and a half years the issue dominated Congress.

The Slavery Issue

The debate transcended slavery in Missouri. Five new states had joined the Union since 1812: Louisiana (1812), Indiana (1816), Mississippi (1817), Illinois (1818), and Alabama (1819). Of these, Louisiana, Mississippi, and Alabama permitted slavery. Because Missouri was on the same latitude as free Illinois, Indiana, and Ohio (a state since 1803), its admission as a slave state would thrust slavery farther northward. It would also tilt the uneasy political balance in the Senate toward the slave states. In 1819 the Union consisted of eleven slave and eleven free states. If Missouri joined as a slave state, slave states would have a two-vote edge in the Senate.

The moral issues made slavery an explosive question. Settlers from slave states—Kentuckians and Tennesseans—made up most of the new Missourians. But many northerners had concluded that slavery was evil. When Representative James Tallmadge, Jr., of New York proposed gradual emancipation in Missouri, a passionate and sometimes violent debate ensued. The House, which had a northern majority, passed the Tallmadge amendment, but the Senate rejected it. The two sides were deadlocked.

A compromise emerged in 1820 under pressure from House Speaker Henry Clay. Maine would enter as a free state, carved out of Massa-

Missouri Compromise

chusetts, while Missouri entered as a slave state. In the rest of the Louisiana Territory north of latitude 36°30' (Missouri's southern boundary), slavery was prohibited forever (see Map 10.1). The compromise carried, but the agreement almost unraveled in November when Missouri submitted a constitution that barred free blacks from entering the state. Clay then produced a second compromise: Missouri guaranteed that none of its laws would discriminate against citizens of other states. (Once admitted, however, Missouri twice banned free blacks.)

The Market Economy and Government's Economic Role

In the years after the War of 1812, Americans increasingly became involved in the market economy—growing crops and producing goods specifically for cash sale and using the cash to purchase items produced by other people. Farms and slave plantations produced crops for market sales. Farm women gave up spinning and weaving and purchased fabric made by wage-earning farm girls in Massachusetts textile mills. Nonfarm men and women sold not goods but their labor for cash, working for wages. Most free farmers and workers bought in stores, increasing the amount of goods produced in workshops and factories. Such a system encouraged specialization. It also energized transportation.

Mechanization, the division of labor, new methods of financing, and improvements in transportation all fueled the expansion of the econ-

Boom-and-Bust Cycles

omy. Goods and services multiplied. This growth, in turn, prompted new improvements and greater opportunities for wage labor. The pace of economic growth, however, was uneven. Prosperity reigned during two long periods, from 1823 to 1835 and from 1843 to 1857. But there were long stretches of economic contraction as well. Contraction and deflation (decline in the general price level) occurred during the hard times of 1819–1823 and 1839–1843. During these periods banks collapsed, businesses went under, wages and prices declined, and jobs were hard to find or to keep.

In 1819 the postwar boom collapsed. Expansion had been built on easy credit; state banks had printed notes freely, fueling speculative buying of western land. When manufacturing fell in 1818, prices spiraled downward. The Second Bank of the United States cut back on loans, thus further shrinking the economy. With urban workers, farmers, and southern planters having less money to spend, the economy declined.

Such contractions devastated workers and their families. As a Baltimore physician noted in 1819, working people felt hard times "a thousand fold more than the merchants." In the 1839 contraction in Baltimore, tailors, shoemakers, milliners, and shipyard and construction workers lost their jobs. Ninety miles to the north, Philadelphia took on an eerie aura. "The streets seemed deserted," Sidney George Fisher observed in 1842. "The largest [merchant] houses are shut up and to rent, there is no business . . . no money, no confidence." In Philadelphia and other cities, soup societies fed the hungry. In smaller cities like Lynn, Massachusetts, the poor became scavengers, digging for clams and harvesting dandelions.

What caused the boom-and-bust cycles that brought about such suffering? Generally speaking, they were a direct result of the mar-

Cause of the Boom-and-Bust Cycles

ket economy. Prosperity stimulated demand for manufactured goods. Increased demand, in turn, led not only to higher prices and still higher production, but also, because of business optimism and expectation of higher prices, to speculation in land. Then, as with the hard times of 1819,

E. Didier painted *Auction in Chatham Street* in 1834. Auction houses in New York and other cities boomed during hard times. (Museum of the City of New York)

production surpassed demand, causing prices and wages to fall; in response, land and stock values collapsed.

Some considered this process beneficial—a self-adjusting cycle that eliminated unprofitable economic ventures. In theory, people concentrated on the activities they did best, and the economy as a whole became more efficient. Advocates of the system also argued that it enhanced individual freedom, since theoretically each seller, whether of goods or of labor, determined the price. But in fact the system tied workers to a perpetual roller coaster; they became dependent on wages—and on the availability of jobs—for their very existence.

The market economy also ushered in another type of boom-and-bust cycle: harvest and destruction. Canals and railroads spurred demand for distant resources, then accelerated the destruction of forests, natural waterways, and any landscape features that represented obstacles. Railroads made possible large-scale lumbering of pinewood forests in Michigan and Wisconsin. During the 1840s, lumber companies deforested millions of acres, leaving most of that land unfit even for agriculture. The process of harvest and destruction would eventually change the ecology of the United States.

The idea of a market economy drew on eighteenth-century republicanism. It emphasized economic liberty and individualism. Limited government, adherents argued, fostered economic expansion because individuals pursuing their own private interests benefited the nation as a whole.

Government Economic Role

Nonetheless, the federal government played an active role in technological and industrial growth. Federal arsenals pioneered new manufacturing techniques and helped to develop the machine-tool industry. The United States Post Office fostered the circulation of information, a critical element in a market economy. The post office also played a brief but crucial role in the development of the telegraph, financing the first telegraph line, from Washington to Baltimore, in 1844. To create an atmosphere conducive to economic growth and individual creativity, the government protected inventions and domestic industries. Patent laws gave inventors a seventeen-year monopoly on their inventions, and tariffs protected American industry from foreign competition.

Government policy also fostered farm life. Republicanism associated farming with virtue, independence, and productivity, essential values in the new republic, and the federal government surveyed public land and opened it to settlement. Internal improvements such as harbors, roads, and canals—some underwritten by government—linked new farms in the West to markets in the East. When Indians got in the way of expansion, the federal government moved them across the Mississippi River.

The federal judiciary validated government promotion of the economy and encouraged business enterprise and risk taking. In *Gibbons v. Ogden* (1824), the Supreme Court overturned a New York State law that gave Robert Fulton and Robert Livingston a monopoly on the New York–New Jersey steamboat trade. Aaron Ogden, their successor, lost the monopoly when Chief Justice John Marshall ruled that the congressional prerogative of licensing new enterprises took precedence over New York's grant of monopoly rights to Fulton and Livingston. Marshall declared that Congress's power under the commerce clause of the Constitution extended to "every species of commercial intercourse," including transportation systems. In defining interstate commerce broadly, the Marshall Court expanded federal powers over the economy while restricting the ability of states to control economic activity within their borders.

Legal Foundations of Commerce

Federal and state courts, in conjunction with state legislatures, also encouraged the proliferation of corporations—organizations entitled to hold property and transact business as if they were individuals. Corporation owners, called shareholders, were granted *limited liability*, or freedom from responsibility for the company's debts beyond their original

Corporations

investments. In 1800 the United States had three hundred incorporated firms; by 1830 the New England states alone had issued nineteen hundred charters. At first each firm needed a special legislative act to incorporate, but after the 1830s applications became so numerous that states established routine procedures allowing firms to incorporate easily.

Though legislative action created corporations, the courts played a crucial role in extending their powers and protecting them. The Supreme Court in particular encouraged corporate development and free enterprise by ruling, in *Charles River Bridge v. Warren Bridge* (1837), that new enterprises could not be restrained by implied privileges under old charters. The case involved issues of great importance: should a new interest be allowed to compete against existing enterprises, and should the state protect existing privilege or encourage innovation and the growth of commerce through competition?

Charles River Bridge Case

The Massachusetts legislature had chartered the Charles River Bridge Company in 1785 and six years later extended its charter for seventy years. In return for assuming the risk of building a bridge between Charlestown and Boston, the owners received the right to collect tolls. In 1828 the legislature chartered another company to build the Warren Bridge across the Charles nearby; the owner would have the right to collect tolls for six years, after which the bridge would be turned over to the state and be free of tolls. The Charles River Bridge Company sued in 1829, claiming that the new bridge breached the earlier charter.

Speaking for the Court majority, Marshall's successor Roger Taney declared that the original charter did not confer the privilege of monopoly and that exclusivity could not therefore be implied. Taney further ruled that charter grants should be interpreted narrowly and that ambiguities would be decided in favor of the public interest. New enterprises should not be restricted by old charters.

In promoting the economy, state governments far surpassed the federal government. From 1815 through the 1840s, for example, government money, mostly from the states, financed three-fourths of the nearly $200 million invested in canals. In the 1830s the states started to invest in rail construction. Though the federal government

States' Support for the Economy

played a larger role in constructing railroads than in building canals, state and local governments provided more than half of the capital for southern rail lines. State governments also invested in corporate and bank stocks, providing corporations and banks with much-needed capital. In fact, states' investments actually equaled or exceeded those of private enterprise.

Political controversy raged over questions of state versus federal activity—especially with regard to internal improvements and banking—but all parties agreed on the general goal of economic expansion. Indeed, during these years the major restraint on government action was not philosophical but financial: the public purse was small. As the private sector grew more vigorous, entrepreneurs looked less to government for financial support, and the states played less of a role in investment.

Transportation Links

 Improved transportation facilitated economic growth. Northern, Middle Atlantic, and western states invested heavily in roads, canals, and railroads, with much of the financing borrowed from Europe. With regional and national financial institutions increasingly concentrated in New York, Boston, and Philadelphia, northeastern seaboard cities became the center of American commerce. New York financial and commercial houses dominated the American export trade, not only of New England textiles but also of southern cotton. The Deep South, with most of its capital invested in slave labor and land, built fewer canals, railroads, and factories and remained mostly rural.

Water routes provided the cheapest and most available transportation. Increasingly, however, settlement extended beyond the river links, and the federal and state governments, followed by private corporations, invested heavily in alternative transportation modes.

In the 1820s new arteries opened up east-west travel. The National Road, which originated in Cumberland, Maryland, reached Columbus, Ohio, in 1833. More important, the Erie Canal, completed in 1825, linked the Great Lakes with New York City and the Atlantic Ocean. Railroads and later

East-West Links

the telegraph would solidify these east-west links. Other than for carrying cotton, links between the Deep South and the North were rarer.

The 363-mile-long Erie Canal was a visionary enterprise. When the state of New York authorized its construction in 1817, the longest American canal was only 28 miles long. Vigorously promoted by Governor DeWitt Clinton, the Erie shortened the journey between Buffalo and New York City from twenty to six days and reduced freight charges from $100 to $5 a ton. By 1835 traffic was so heavy that the canal had to be widened and deepened.

Canals

The success of the Erie Canal triggered an explosion of canal building. By 1840 canals crisscrossed the Northeast and Midwest, and total canal mileage reached 3,300. Unfortunately for investors, none of these canals enjoyed the financial success achieved by the Erie. As the high cost of construction combined with an economic contraction, investment in canals began to slump in the 1830s. By midcentury more miles were being abandoned than built; the canal era had ended.

Meanwhile, railroad construction boomed. The railroad era in the United States began in 1830 when Peter Cooper's locomotive, "Tom Thumb," first steamed along 13 miles of Baltimore and Ohio Railroad track. In 1833 the nation's second railroad ran 136 miles from Charleston to Hamburg in South Carolina. By 1850 the United States had nearly 9,000 miles of railroad track.

Railroads

The earliest railroads connected nearby cities; not until the 1850s did railroads offer long-distance service at reasonable rates. The early lines had to overcome technical problems. In addition, the lack of a standard gauge for the width of track inhibited distance travel. A journey from Philadelphia to Charleston, South Carolina, illustrates the gauge problem. This trip involved eight different gauges, which meant that passengers and freight had to change trains seven times.

Technology and investments in transportation dramatically reduced travel time and shipping. Before 1815 river transportation was the only feasible route for long-distance journeys. In 1815 a traveler took four days to go by stagecoach from New York City to Baltimore. By 1830 the journey took a day and a half, while the Erie Canal reduced the New York–Detroit journey from four weeks to two. Before the War of 1812 wagon transportation cost 30 to 70 cents per ton per mile. By midcentury railroads had brought the cost of land transportation down 95 percent and reduced the journey to one-fifth the time.

Commercial Farming

Although manufacturing increased steadily, agriculture remained the backbone of the economy and American exports. But increasingly the market economy altered farming. Self-sufficient household and plantation economies gave way to market-oriented farming. Equally important, the center of commercial farming moved westward. In the 1830s and after, the plantation South shifted to the Mississippi River valley, while commercial farming came to dominate the Old Northwest and the Ohio River valley, then moved even farther westward to the prairies.

After the 1820s, northeastern agriculture began to decline. Eastern farmers had already cultivated all the
land available to them. Moreover, small New England farms, with their uneven terrains, did not lend themselves to the new labor-saving farm implements introduced in the 1830s— mechanical sowers, reapers, threshers, and balers. As a result, many northern farmers either moved west or gave up farming for jobs in the merchant houses and factories.

The farmers who remained in New England, as well as those in the Middle Atlantic, adapted to the changed environment. By the 1850s many of these farm families had abandoned the commercial production of wheat and corn. Instead, they improved their livestock, especially cattle, and specialized in vegetable and fruit production and dairy farming. They financed these initiatives through land sales and debt. In fact, their greatest potential profit was from increasing land values, not from farming itself.

Farm women had a distinctive role in the market economy. Many sold eggs, dairy products, and garden

produce in local markets, and their earnings became essential to household incomes. Butter and cheese making replaced spinning and weaving; farm women now sold commodities and bought cloth. The work was physically demanding and did not replace regular home and farm chores but added to them. Yet women took pride in their work, often gaining from it a sense of independence that was as valuable as their profits.

Women's success at butter and cheese making led some farms to specialize in dairy production. After the Erie Canal opened, Ohio dairy farms had access to New York's export trade. Ohio entrepreneurs turned cheese into factory production in the 1840s. Canals and railroads took the cheese to eastern ports, where wholesalers sold it around the world.

Most farm families welcomed the opportunities offered by the market economy. While continuing to take pride in self-sufficiency, they shifted toward specialization and market-oriented production. The rewards for such flexibility were great. Produce sold at market financed land and equipment purchases and made credit arrangements possible.

Meanwhile, the economic distance widened between farm owners on the one hand and tenants and hired hands on the other. The rising cost of land and of farming made it harder to start up. By the 1840s it took more than ten years for a rural laborer to save enough money to farm for himself. Thus the number of tenant farmers increased.

Individually and collectively, Americans still valued agrarian life. State governments energetically promoted commercial agriculture to spur economic growth and sustain the values of an agrarian-based republic. Massachusetts in 1817 and New York in 1819 began to subsidize agricultural prizes and county fairs. New York required contestants to submit written descriptions of how they grew their prize crops; the state then published the essays to encourage new methods and specialization. The post office circulated farm journals that helped familiarize farmers with developments in agriculture.

Gradually the Old Northwest replaced the Northeast as the center of American family agriculture. Farms in the Old Northwest were much larger, flatter, and better suited to the new mechanized farming implements than were their northeastern counterparts.

Mechanization of Agriculture

Cyrus McCormick had invented the reaper in 1831. In one continuous motion, a revolving drum on the horse-drawn reaper positioned grain stalks in front of a blade and the cut grain fell onto a platform. McCormick built a factory in Chicago that by 1847 sold a thousand reapers a year. Midwestern farmers bought reapers on credit and paid for them with the profits from their high yields. Similarly, John Deere's steel plow, invented in 1837, replaced the traditional iron plow; steel blades kept the soil from sticking and were tough enough to break the roots of prairie grass.

And just in time. The Midwest was becoming one of the leading agricultural regions of the world. Midwestern farms fed the growing cities in the East, bursting with growing immigrant populations, and still produced enough to export to Europe.

At the end of the eighteenth century, southern agriculture was diverse. Indeed, cotton was profitable only for planters in the Sea Islands of South Carolina and Georgia, where slaves grew the long and silky variety. Whitney's cotton gin (1793), by efficiently removing the seeds from short-staple cotton, made possible the South's cotton boom.

The Cotton South

After 1800 the cultivation of short-staple cotton spread rapidly. By the 1820s there were cotton plantations in the fertile lands of Louisiana, Mississippi, Alabama, Arkansas, and Tennessee. Each decade after 1820, the total crop doubled. By 1825 the South was the world's dominant supplier of cotton, and the white fibers were America's largest export. Southerners with capital bought more land and more slaves and planted ever more cotton.

No region was more tied to international markets than the South, yet the region seemed immune to the market economy's transforming power. It produced cotton exclusively as a market crop. In many ways the cotton economy resembled a colonial economy. Planters depended on distant agents, some in southern cities, many in the North, and even some in Europe, to represent them and handle their finances, which often included loans. Thus critical market decisions were made by bankers, financiers, and brokers, all outside the South. The South was engaged in the new market economy, but at a distance.

The cotton boom, dependent on slave labor, fixed the slave system to the land as it spread westward.

Slaveholders sought profits, just as did commercial farmers, merchants, and entrepreneurs in the North. But they did not pay wages for labor; they bought laborers. Ultimately this "peculiar" system (see pages 217–220) would separate the South from the national economy and the nation.

The Rise of Manufacturing and Commerce

British visitors to the 1851 London Crystal Palace Exhibition, the first modern world's fair, were impressed by American design and fine tooling of working parts. American companies displayed hundreds of American machines and wares. Most impressive to the Europeans were three simple machines: Alfred C. Hobb's unpickable padlocks, Samuel Colt's revolvers, and Robbins and Lawrence's rifles fashioned with completely interchangeable parts. All were machine-tooled rather than handmade, products of what the British called the American system of manufacturing.

American System of Manufacturing

The American system of manufacturing used precision machinery to produce interchangeable parts that did not require individual adjustment to fit. Eli Whitney had promoted the idea of interchangeable parts in 1798 when he contracted with the federal government to make ten thousand rifles in twenty-eight months. By the 1820s the United States Ordnance Department had contracted with private firms to introduce machine-made interchangeable parts for firearms. The American system quickly spread beyond the arsenals, giving birth to the machine-tool industry—the manufacture of machines for the purposes of mass production. One outcome was an explosion in consumer goods that were inexpensive yet of uniformly high quality.

Textile Mills

Even larger than the machine-tool industry was the textile industry. New England mills began processing and weaving southern cotton in the same decade that Whitney patented his gin. Boosted by embargo and war, then protected by the tariff, the textile industry boomed with the expansion of cotton cultivation after the war. By the 1840s a cotton mill resembled a modern factory and textiles were the most important industry in the nation. The industry employed around eighty thousand workers in the mid-1840s, more than half of them women.

Textile manufacturing changed New England and had its greatest impact on Lowell, Massachusetts. The population of Lowell, the "city of spindles" and the prototype of early American industrialization, grew from twenty-five hundred to thirty-three thousand between 1826 and midcentury. The largest of the cotton-mill towns and the front runner in technological change, Lowell boasted the biggest work force, the greatest output, and the most capital invested.

The success of the textile factories spawned the ready-made clothing industry. Before the 1820s, women sewed most clothing at home. Some people purchased used clothing, and tailors and seamstresses made wealthy men's and women's clothing to order. By the 1820s and 1830s, much clothing was mass-produced. Manufacturers used two methods. In one, the clothing was made in a factory; in the other, at home, through the putting-out system. In this arrangement, a journeyman tailor—a trained craftsman employed by a master tailor who owned the workshop—cut the fabric panels in the factory, and the masters "put out" the sewing at piece rates to women working in their own homes.

Ready-made Clothing

Most of the early mass-produced clothes, crudely made and limited to a few loose-fitting sizes, were produced for and purchased by men who lived in city boarding houses and rooming houses. Most women made their own clothes, but those who could afford to do so employed seamstresses. Improvements in fit and changes in men's fashion eventually made ready-to-wear apparel more acceptable to clerks and professional men. In the 1840s men began wearing the short sack coat. This forerunner of the modern suit jacket fit loosely and needed little custom tailoring. Now even upper-class men were willing to consider ready-made apparel.

Retail clothing stores well stocked with ready-made clothes appeared in the 1820s. Their owners often bought goods wholesale, though many manufactured shirts and trousers in their own factories. Lewis and Hanford of New York City boasted of cutting more than one hundred

Retail Merchants

thousand garments in the winter of 1848–1849. The New York firm sold most of its clothing in the South and owned its own retail outlet in New Orleans. In the West, Cincinnati became the center of the new men's clothing industry. By midcentury, Cincinnati's ready-to-wear apparel industry employed fifteen hundred men and ten thousand women.

Commerce expanded hand in hand with manufacturing. Cotton, for instance, had once been traded by plantation agents, who sold the raw cotton and bought manufactured goods that they then sold to plantation owners, extending them credit when necessary. Cotton exports rose from 83 million pounds in 1815 to more than a billion pounds in 1849. Gradually, some agents came to specialize in finance alone: they were cotton brokers, who for a commission brought together buyers and sellers. Similarly, wheat and hog brokers sprang up in the West—in Cincinnati, Louisville, and St. Louis. The distribution of finished goods also became more specialized as wholesalers bought large quantities of particular items from manufacturers, and jobbers broke down the wholesale lots for retail stores and country merchants.

Specialization of Commerce

Commercial specialization transformed some traders in big cities, especially New York, into virtual merchant princes. After the Erie Canal opened, New York City became a stop on every major trade route from Europe, the southern ports, and the West. New York traders were the middlemen for southern cotton and western grain. Merchants in other cities played a similar role within their own regions. Some traders, in turn, invested their profits in factories, further stimulating urban manufacturing. Some cities specialized: Rochester became a milling center, and Cincinnati—"Porkopolis"—became the first meatpacking center.

Financial institutions, which played a significant role in the expansion of manufacturing and commerce, also became a leading industry. Banks, insurance companies, and corporations linked savers—those who deposited money in banks—with producers and speculators who wished to borrow money. After 1816, the Second Bank of the United States injected a national perspective into finance, but many farmers, local bankers, and politicians denounced the bank as a monster, blaming it for serving national, not local, interests. Western

Banking and Credit Systems

landowners suffered severe losses when the Second Bank reduced loans in the western states during the Panic of 1819. In 1836 critics finally succeeded in killing the bank (see page 189).

The closing of the Second Bank in 1836 caused a nationwide credit shortage, which, in conjunction with the Panic of 1837, led to fundamental reforms in banking. Michigan and New York introduced charter laws promoting what was called *free banking*. Previously, every new bank had needed a special legislative charter before it could open for business; thus each bank incorporation was in effect a political decision. Under the new laws, any proposed bank that met certain minimum conditions—amount of capital invested, number of notes issued, and types of loans to be offered—would receive a state charter automatically. Banks in Michigan, New York, and, soon, other states were thus freer to incorporate, although the legislatures placed some restrictions on their operations to reduce the risk of bank failure.

Free banking proved to be a significant stimulus to the economy in the late 1840s and 1850s. New banks sprang up everywhere, providing merchants and manufacturers with the credit they needed. The free-banking laws also served as a precedent for general incorporation statutes that allowed manufacturing firms to receive state charters without special acts of the state legislature.

Workers and the Workplace

Loud the morning bell is ringing,
   Up, up sleepers, haste away;
Yonder sits the redbreast singing,
   But to list we must not stay.

. . .

Sisters, haste, the bell is tolling,
   Soon will close the dreadful gate;
Then, alas! We must go strolling,
   Through the counting-room too late.

. . .

Now the sun is upward climbing,
   And the breakfast hour has come;
Ding, dong, ding, the bell is chiming,
   Hasten, sisters, hasten home.

The poet, writing in 1844 in the *Factory Girl's Garland*, uses the sound of the factory bell as a refrain to emphasize its incessant control, announcing when the workers are to wake, eat, begin work, stop work, and go to sleep. Night and day the millworkers felt the stress of factory schedules.

But the first generation of young single women who left New England villages and farms to work in the mills had come with great optimism. The mills offered steady work and good pay, plus airy boarding houses, prepared meals, and cultural activities. Sisters and cousins often worked in the same mill and lived in the same boarding house. They helped each other adjust, and their letters home drew kin to the mills. Most arrivals were sixteen and stayed only about five years. When they left the mills to marry, other younger women interested in earning a wage took their places.

In the hard times from 1837 to 1842, most mills ran only part-time. Subsequently managers pressured workers by means of the speed-up, the stretch-out, and the premium system. The speed-up increased the speed of the machines; the stretch-out increased the number of machines each worker had to operate; and premiums paid to the overseers whose departments produced the most cloth encouraged them to pressure workers for greater output. Thus, in the race for profits, owners lengthened hours, cut wages, tightened discipline, and packed the boarding houses. Some millworkers began to think of themselves as slaves.

Boom and Bust in the Textile Mills

New England millworkers responded to their deteriorating working conditions by organizing and striking. In 1834, in reaction to a 25 percent wage cut, they unsuccessfully "turned out" (struck) against the Lowell mills. Two years later, when boarding house fees increased, they turned out again. In the 1840s, Massachusetts mill women adopted a new means of resistance: they joined other workers to press for state legislation mandating a ten-hour day. They also aired their complaints in worker-run newspapers.

Protests

The women's labor organizations were weakened by the short tenure of most workers. Few of the militant native-born millworkers stayed on to fight the managers and owners, and gradually there were fewer New England daughters to enter the mills. They were replaced, in the 1850s, by Irish immigrant women who lived at home. Technological improvements in the looms and other machinery had made the work less skilled and more routine. The mills could thus pay lower wages and draw from a reservoir of unskilled labor.

A growing gender division in the workplace, especially in the textile, clothing, and shoemaking

Gender Divisions in Work

industries, was one important outcome of large-scale manufacturing. Although women and men in traditional agricultural and artisan households tended to perform different tasks, they worked as a family unit. As wage work spread, however, men's and women's work cultures became increasingly separate. The women and girls who left home for jobs in textile mills worked and lived in a mostly female world. In the clothing and shoemaking industries, whose male artisans had once worked at home assisted by unpaid family labor, men began working outside the home while women continued to work at home through the putting-out system. Tasks and wages, too, became rigidly differentiated: women sewed, whereas men shaped materials and finished products, receiving higher wages in shops employing men only.

The market economy had an impact on unpaid household labor as well. As home and workplace became separate and labor came to be defined in terms of wages (what could be sold in the marketplace) rather than production (what could be made by hand), the unpaid labor of women was devalued. Yet the family depended on women's work within the household, ever more so as sons and even daughters sought wage work outside the home and had less time for household tasks. Thus gender defined household labor, and in the market economy it went unrecorded, seemed to be worth little, and was taken for granted.

The new textile mills, shoe factories, iron mills, and railroads were the antithesis of traditional work-

Changes in the Workplace

shop and household production. In factory workplaces, authority was hierarchically organized. Factory workers lost their sense of autonomy as impersonal market forces seemed to dominate their lives. Their jobs were insecure, as competition frequently led to layoffs and replacement by cheaper, less-skilled workers or children. Moreover, the formal rules of the factory contrasted sharply with

the more relaxed atmosphere of artisan shops and farm households. When master craftsmen turned their workshops into small factories, master and journeyman were distanced. In large factories, the distance was greater, as supervisors represented owners whom workers never saw. The division of labor and the use of machines narrowed the skills required. There was also the quickening pace of work between the bells, wage reductions, speed-ups, the roar of the looms, and the risk of being maimed or killed while working with power machines. Perhaps most demoralizing, opportunities for advancement in the new system were virtually nil.

In response, some workers organized to resist the changes wrought by the market economy and factories

Labor Parties

and to regain control of their work and their lives. Women textile workers organized into unions and demonstrated for better wages and conditions or lobbied legislatures for relief. Male workers also organized and protested, but because they were eligible to vote, they also organized political parties. Labor parties formed in Pennsylvania, New York, and Massachusetts in the 1820s, and later spread to other states; they advocated free public education and an end to imprisonment for debt and opposed banks and monopolies.

Organized labor's greatest achievement during this period was to gain relief from the threat of con-

Emergence of a Labor Movement

spiracy laws. When journeyman shoemakers organized during the first decade of the century, their employers accused them of criminal conspiracy. The cordwainers' (shoemakers') cases between 1806 and 1815 left labor organizations in a tenuous position. Although the courts acknowledged the journeymen's right to organize, judges ruled unlawful any coercive action by workers that would harm other businesses or the public. In other words, strikes were ruled illegal. Eventually a Massachusetts case, *Commonwealth v. Hunt* (1842), effectively reversed this status when Chief Justice Lemuel Shaw ruled that Boston journeyman bootmakers could strike "in such manner as best to subserve their own interests." Conspiracy laws no longer thwarted unionization.

Yet permanent labor organizations were difficult to sustain. Most workers outside the crafts were unskilled or semiskilled at best. Moreover, religion, race, ethnicity, and gender divided workers. The first unions arose among urban journeymen in printing, woodworking, shoemaking, and tailoring. These early unions tended to be local; the strongest resembled medieval guilds in that members sought to protect themselves against the competition of inferior workmen by regulating apprenticeship and establishing minimum wages. They also excluded women and African Americans. Umbrella organizations composed of individual craft unions, like the National Trades Union (1834), arose in several cities in the 1820s and 1830s, but failed during hard times. Labor organizations remained weak, and after 1830 workers' share of the national wealth declined.

Americans on the Move

Growth in the years following the War of 1812 was not economic only. The Louisiana Purchase (1803) doubled the land area of the United States, and acquisitions in the 1840s nearly doubled it again. Population soared, increasing by a third in each decade. Between 1820 and 1845, the population increased from 9.6 million to 20.2 million.

In land and population the United States expanded outward, mostly westward, from its original seaboard base (see Map 10.2). The admission

Westward Movement

of new states tells the story: Indiana (1816), Mississippi (1817), Illinois (1818), Alabama (1819), Maine (1820), and Missouri (1821) brought the union to twenty-four states in the 1820s. Arkansas (1836) and Michigan (1837) soon followed, as did Florida and Texas (1845), Iowa (1846), and Wisconsin (1848) in the following decade.

During the first two decades of the century, Americans poured into the Ohio River valley; then, starting in the 1820s, they moved into the Mississippi River valley and beyond, doubling the population living beyond the Appalachians. By midcentury two-thirds of Americans lived west of the Appalachians. Mostly young and hard-working, they had visions of establishing family farms and achieving economic security.

After the 1820s the heart of cotton cultivation and the plantation system shifted from the coastal states to Alabama and the newly settled Mississippi valley—

The South

Tennessee, Louisiana, Arkansas, and Mississippi. Southerners brought their institutions with them; slaves moved with planters to the newer areas of the South, and yeoman farmers followed.

The shift was dramatic. The population of Mississippi soared from 73,000 in 1820 to 607,000 in 1850, with African American slaves in the majority. Across the Mississippi River, the population of Arkansas went from 14,000 in 1820 to 210,000 in 1850. And while Texas was still part of Mexico in 1835, 35,000 Americans, including 3,000 slaves, lived there. Texas independence in 1836 spurred further American immigration. By 1845 "Texas fever" had boosted the Anglo population to 125,000. Statehood that year opened the floodgates.

Not all moves were westward. A steady stream drifted from the Upper South to the Ohio valley, from slave to free states. Though northern

Moves North and South

black people moved westward as well, thousands of free people of color moved to northern states and Canada in the 1830s following the adoption of black codes and mob violence in the South (see pages 213–214). Fugitives from slavery too went north. Hispanics in the Southwest continued to move north into areas of Texas and present-day New Mexico and Utah. After the United States acquired Florida and attempted to colonize and suppress the Indian peoples there, southerners poured into the new territory.

Settlers needed land and credit. Reflecting the nationalist outlook, the federal government hoped to fill the West with non-Indian peoples

Land Grants and Sales

and thus promote republican virtue. Some public lands were granted as rewards for military service: veterans of the War of 1812 received 160 acres. Until 1820 civilians could buy government land at $2 an acre (a relatively high price) on a liberal four-year payment plan, but the minimum purchase had been reduced in 1817 to 80 acres. After 1819 the government discontinued credit sales but reduced the price to an affordable $1.25 an acre.

Some eager pioneers settled land before it had been surveyed and offered for sale. Such illegal settlers, or squatters, then had to buy the land at auction and faced the risk of being unable to purchase it. In

Map 10.2   Settled Areas of the United States, 1820 and 1840   Removal of Indians and a growing transportation network opened up land to white and black settlers in the West and in the Southeast, as the U.S. population grew from 9.6 million in 1820 to 17.1 million in 1840.

1841, to facilitate settlement and end property disputes, Congress passed the Pre-emption Act, which legalized settlement prior to surveying.

Since most settlers needed to borrow money, private credit systems arose. Nearly all economic activity in the West involved credit, from land sales to produce shipments to railroad construction. In 1816 and 1836 easy credit boosted land prices. When tight credit,

Credit

high interest, low prices, or destructive weather squeezed farmers' income, land values collapsed, ending the speculative bubble. Mortgage bankers and speculators then purchased land cheaply. As a consequence, many farmers became renters instead of owners of land; tenancy became more common in the West than it had been in New England.

Henry Lewis's *St. Louis in 1846* depicts a pioneer family stopping to view the great Missouri city across the river. The contrast between the towering city, surrounded by modern steamboats and dominating the Mississippi and Missouri Rivers, and the pioneer family, with their wagons and horses, highlights the role cities played in western settlement and growth. (St. Louis Art Museum, Eliza McMillan Fund)

From the start, newly settled western areas depended on their links with towns and cities. Ohio River cities—Louisville and Cincinnati—and the old French settlements—Detroit on the Great Lakes, St. Louis on the Mississippi River—predated and promoted the earliest western settlements. So too in the South, from New Orleans to Natchez to Memphis, towns spearheaded settlement and economic growth. Steamboats connected the river cities with eastern markets and ports, carrying grain east and returning with finished goods. Like cities in the Northeast, these western cities eventually developed into manufacturing centers.

Frontier Cities

Native American Resistance and Removal

Indians were also on the move, but their migrations were more forced than voluntary. Indian removal made white expansion possible, but it uprooted the indigenous cultures of the eastern and southern woodlands. Perhaps 100,000 eastern and southern Indian people were removed between 1820 and 1850; about 30,000 died in the process. Those who remained became virtually invisible.

The U.S. Constitution acknowledged Indian distinctiveness by recognizing Indian sovereignty and by giving the federal government responsibility for dealing with Native Americans. In its relations with Indian leaders, the government followed international protocol and received delegations with pomp and ceremony. Agreements between an Indian nation and the United States were signed, sealed, and ratified like any other international treaty.

Treaty Making

In practice, however, treaty making and Indian sovereignty were fictions. Protocol appeared to signify mutual respect and independence, but treaty negotiations exposed the sham. The American government used treaty making as a tactic to acquire Indian land. Instead of being bargains struck by two equal nations, treaties often were imposed by the victor on the vanquished. Old treaties gave way to new ones requiring

Native Americans to cede their traditional holdings in exchange for other land in the West.

To maintain their independence and preserve their ways of life, many Indian nations tried to accommodate to the expanding market

Indians in the Market Economy

economy. In the first three decades of the century, the Choctaw, Chickasaw, and Creek peoples in the lower Mississippi responded to the growing cotton economy by becoming suppliers and traders. Under treaty provisions, Indian commerce took place through trading posts and stores that provided Indians with supplies and purchased or bartered Indian-produced goods. The trading posts extended credit to chiefs, and increasingly they fell into debt. With pelt prices falling, the debts grew enormously and often could be paid off only by selling land to the federal government. By 1822, for instance, the Choctaw nation had sold 13 million acres but still carried a debt of $13,000. The Indians struggled to adjust, but with the loss of land came dependency. The Choctaws came to rely on Europeans not only for manufactured goods but also for food.

Dependency facilitated the removal of Native American peoples to western lands. While the population of other groups increased by leaps and bounds, the Indian population fell. War, forced removal, disease (especially smallpox), and malnutrition reduced many Indian nations by 50 percent. More than half of the Pawnees, Omahas, Otoes, Missouris, and Kansas died in the 1830s alone.

The wanderings of the Shawnees illustrate the uprooting of Indian people. After giving up 17 million acres in Ohio in the 1795 Treaty

Shawnees

of Greenville (see page 120), the Shawnees scattered to Indiana and eastern Missouri. After the War of 1812, Prophet's Indiana group withdrew to Canada under British protection. In 1822 other Shawnees sought Mexican protection and moved from Missouri to present-day eastern Texas. As the U.S. government promoted removal to Kansas, Prophet returned from Canada to lead a group to the new Shawnee lands in eastern Kansas in 1825. When Missouri achieved statehood in 1821, Shawnees living there were also forced to move to Kansas, where in the 1830s other Shawnees removed from Ohio or expelled from Texas

joined them. By 1854, however, Kansas was open to white settlement, and the Shawnees had to cede seven-eighths of their land, or 1.4 million acres.

Removal had a profound impact on all Shawnees. The men lost their traditional role as providers; their methods of hunting and their knowledge of woodland animals were useless on the prairies of Kansas. As grain became the tribe's dietary staple, Shawnee women played a greater role as providers, supplemented by government aid under treaty provisions. Remarkably, the Shawnees preserved their language and culture in the face of these drastic changes.

Ever since the early days of European colonization, whites had sought the assimilation of Native Americans through education and

Assimilation and Education

Christianity. This goal took on renewed urgency as the United States expanded westward. In 1819, in response to missionary lobbying, Congress appropriated $10,000 annually for "civilization of the tribes adjoining the frontier settlements." Protestant missionaries administered the "civilizing fund" and established mission schools.

Within five years thirty-two boarding schools enrolled Indian students. They substituted English for Native American languages and taught agriculture alongside the Christian Gospel. But to settlers eyeing Indian land, assimilation through education seemed too slow a process. At the program's peak, schools across the United States enrolled fewer than fifteen hundred students; at that rate it would take centuries to assimilate all the Indians. Thus wherever Native Americans lived, illegal settlers disrupted their lives. Though obligated to protect the integrity of treaty lands, the federal government did so only halfheartedly. With government supporting westward expansion, legitimate Indian claims had to give way to the advance of white civilization.

In the 1820s it became apparent that neither economic dependency, education, nor Christianity could persuade Native Americans to cede enough land to satisfy the expansionists. Attention focused on southeastern tribes—Cherokees, Creeks, Choctaws, Chickasaws, and Seminoles—because much of their land remained intact after the War of 1812 and because they aggressively resisted white encroachment.

In his last annual message to Congress in late 1824, President James Monroe suggested that all Indians

Indian Removal as Federal Policy

be moved beyond the Mississippi River. Three days later he sent a special message to Congress proposing removal. Monroe's proposition targeted the Cherokees, Creeks, Choctaws, and Chickasaws, and they unanimously rejected it.

Pressure from Georgia had prompted Monroe's policy. The Cherokees and Creeks lived in northwestern Georgia, and in the 1820s the state accused the federal government of not fulfilling its 1802 promise to remove the Indians in return for the state's renunciation of its claim to western lands. Georgia was satisfied neither by Monroe's removal messages nor by further cessions by the Creeks. In 1826, under federal pressure, the Creek nation ceded all but a small strip of its Georgia acreage. But Georgia still was not satisfied. Only the removal of the Georgia Creeks to the West could resolve the conflict between the state and the federal government.

Adapting to American ways seemed no more successful than resistance in forestalling removal. No

Cherokees

people met the challenge of civilizing themselves by American standards more thoroughly than the Cherokees. Between 1819 and 1829 the tribe became economically self-sufficient and politically self-governing; during this Cherokee renaissance the twelve to fifteen thousand adult Cherokees came to think of themselves as a nation, not a collection of villages. Between 1820 and 1823 the Cherokees created a formal government with a bicameral legislature, a court system, and a salaried bureaucracy. In 1827 they adopted a written constitution, modeled after that of the United States. Cherokee land laws, however, differed from U.S. law. The tribe collectively owned all Cherokee land and forbade land sales to outsiders. Nonetheless, the Cherokees assimilated American cultural patterns. By 1833 they held fifteen hundred black slaves, whose legal status was the same as that of slaves held by southern whites. Moreover, missionaries had been so successful that the Cherokees could be considered a Christian community.

Although the Cherokees developed a political system similar to that of an American state, they failed to win respect or acceptance from southerners. In the 1820s, Georgia pressed them to sell the 7,200 square

miles of land they held in the state, but the Cherokees preferred not to sell. Impatient with their refusals to negotiate cession, Georgia annulled the Cherokees' constitution, extended the state's sovereignty over them, prohibited the Cherokee National Council from meeting except to cede land, and ordered their lands seized.

Backed by sympathetic whites but not by the new president, Andrew Jackson, the Cherokees under Chief John Ross turned to the federal

Cherokee Nation v. Georgia

courts to defend their treaty with the United States and to disarm new threats by Georgia to seize their land. In *Cherokee Nation v. Georgia* (1831), Chief Justice John Marshall ruled that under the federal Constitution an Indian tribe was neither a foreign nation nor a state and therefore had no standing in federal courts. Nonetheless, said Marshall, the Indians had an unquestionable right to their lands; they could lose title only by voluntarily giving it up. A year later, in *Worcester v. Georgia*, Marshall defined the Cherokee position more clearly. The Indian nation was, he declared, a distinct political community in which "the laws of Georgia can have no force" and into which Georgians could not enter without permission or treaty privilege. Georgia refused to comply.

President Andrew Jackson refused to interfere because the case involved a state action. Keen to open up new lands for settlement, Jackson favored expelling the Cherokees. In the Removal Act of 1830 Congress had provided Jackson with the funds he needed to negotiate new treaties and resettle the resistant tribes west of the Mississippi (see Map 10.3).

The Choctaws went first; they made the forced journey from Mississippi and Alabama to the West in the winter of 1831 and 1832. Other

Trail of Tears

tribes soon joined the forced march. The Creeks in Alabama resisted removal until 1836, when the army pushed them westward. A year later the Chickasaws followed.

Having fought removal in the courts, the Cherokees were divided. Some believed that further resistance was hopeless and accepted removal as the only chance to preserve their civilization. The leaders of this minority agreed in 1835 to exchange their southern home for western land in the Treaty of New Echota. Most, though, wanted to stand firm. John

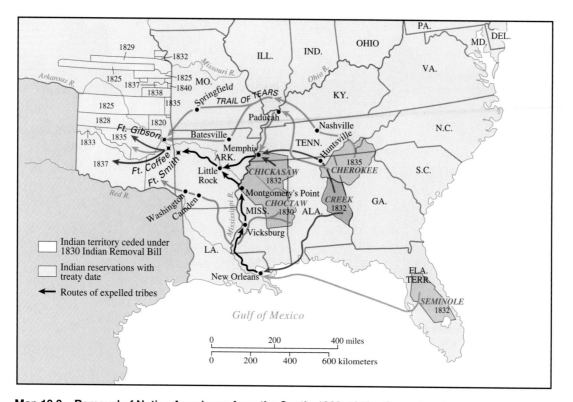

Map 10.3   Removal of Native Americans from the South, 1820–1840   Over a twenty-year period, the federal government and southern states forced Native Americans to exchange their traditional homes for western land. Some tribal groups remained in the South, but most settled in the alien western environment.   (Source: Reprinted from *American History Atlas* by Martin Gilbert [London: Weidenfeld & Nicolson, 1968] by permission of Routledge Ltd.)

Ross, with petitions signed by fifteen thousand Cherokees, lobbied the Senate against ratification of the treaty. They lost. But when the time for evacuation came in 1838, most Cherokees refused to move. President Martin Van Buren sent federal troops to round them up. About twenty thousand Cherokees were evicted, held in detention camps, and marched to Indian Territory in present-day Oklahoma under military escort. Nearly one-quarter of them died of disease and exhaustion on what came to be known as the Trail of Tears.

When the forced march to the West ended, the Indians had traded about 100 million acres east of the Mississippi for 32 million acres west of the river plus $68 million. Only a few scattered remnants, among them the Seminoles in Florida and the Cherokees in

the southern Appalachian Mountains, remained in the East and South.

Forced removal had a disastrous impact on the displaced tribes. In the West they encountered an alien environment; lacking traditional ties, few felt at peace with the land. The animals and plants they found were unfamiliar. Unable to live off the land, many became dependent on government payments for survival. Removal also brought new internal conflicts. The Cherokees in particular struggled over their tribal government. Moreover, conflict arose between Native American groups migrating from the South and East and Indians already living in the West, as they were forced to share land and scarce resources.

In Florida a small band of Seminoles continued to resist. Some Seminole leaders agreed in the 1832

The Trail of Tears, by twentieth-century Pawnee artist Brummet Echohawk. About twenty thousand Cherokees were evicted in 1838–1839, and about one-quarter of them died on the forced march to present-day Oklahoma. (Thomas Gilcrease Institute of American History and Art)

Second Seminole War Treaty of Payne's Landing to relocate to the West within three years, but others opposed the treaty. A minority under Osceola, a charismatic leader, refused to vacate their homes and fought the protreaty group. When federal troops were sent to impose removal in 1835, Osceola waged a fierce guerrilla war against them. Osceola was captured under a white flag of truce and died in an army prison in 1838, but the Seminoles continued the fight. In 1842 the United States abandoned the removal effort. Most of Osceola's followers agreed to move west to Indian Territory in 1858, but many Seminoles remained in the Florida Everglades, proud of having resisted conquest.

Summary

Nationalism and self-confidence accompanied the end of the War of 1812. Under the Democratic-Republicans the federal government fostered expansion and economic growth through internal improvements, tariffs, the Second Bank of the United States, land sales, and In-

dian removal. The Supreme Court and American diplomats, too, asserted nationalism.

But sectionalism accompanied nationalism and geographical expansion. Conflicts over tariffs, economic hard times, and slavery brought discord. The Missouri Compromise was a stopgap measure to avoid the explosive issue of slavery.

From 1816 through 1845 the United States experienced explosive population growth. People moved westward. New farms grew cotton and grain for the market, and cities followed. In the process, Indians and Hispanics were pushed aside.

Agriculture remained the dominant industry, though by midcentury a booming manufacturing sector challenged farming. And agriculture itself was becoming market-oriented and mechanized. The market economy brought sustained growth, but it also ushered in cycles of boom and bust. Hard times and unemployment became frequent occurrences.

Large-scale manufacturing also altered traditional patterns of production and consumption. Farm families began to purchase goods formerly made at home, and geared production to faraway markets. Farm women increasingly contributed income from market sales to the household purse. In New England many young women left the family farm to become the first factory workers in the new textile industry. In the new mills and factories, workplace relations became more impersonal, working conditions grew harsher, and men's and women's work became increasingly dissimilar. Industrial jobs began to attract large numbers of immigrants, and some workers organized labor unions.

LEGACY FOR A PEOPLE AND A NATION
A Mixed Economy

How active should the U.S. government be? Should it run, regulate, or leave to the market system healthcare, Social Security and private pensions, corporate concentration, and stock trading and investments? In other words, to what degree should the government be responsible for the well-being of the economy and individuals?

The Articles of Confederation limited government, the Constitution empowered it, and the Bill of Rights restricted it in specific areas. While Americans have continuously debated the appropriate role of government, the United States has generally occupied a middle ground.

In the early nineteenth century, government played an active role in economic and social expansion. Federal and state governments built roads and canals, developed harbors, and operated post offices and the early telegraph. More commonly the government intervened to stimulate and regulate the private sector.

In the late nineteenth century advocates of laissez-faire or hands-off government challenged the pre–Civil War tradition of active government. Laissez faire dominated briefly until the 1880s and 1890s, when large corporations and trusts accumulated so much power that governments stepped in to regulate railroads and business concentration. After the turn of the century, the federal government extended regulation to food, drugs, the environment, working conditions, and fair business practices. In the 1930s, the crisis of the Great Depression, followed in the 1940s by World War II, would lead the federal government to establish the modern welfare state, which operates through a mixed public/private structure.

As the United States begins the twenty-first century, its people are again debating the appropriate role of government. Conservatives view government as the problem rather than the solution, arguing that government regulation hampers individual freedom and distorts the law of supply and demand. Advocates of an activist government argue that only the government has the power and resources to check economic concentration and to protect health, safety, and the environment. The framework of this debate is a legacy from before the Civil War.

For Further Reading, see the Appendix. For Web resources, go to history.college.hmco.com/students.

REFORM AND POLITICS IN THE AGE OF JACKSON

1824–1845

From Revival to Reform
Antimasonry
Abolitionism and the Women's Movement
Jacksonianism and Party Politics
Federalism at Issue: The Nullification and Bank Controversies
The Whig Challenge and the Second Party System
Manifest Destiny and Expansionism

LEGACY FOR A PEOPLE AND A NATION
The Bible Belt

I proceed, Gentlemen, briefly to call your attention to the present state of Insane persons confined within this Commonwealth," Dorothea Dix petitioned the Massachusetts legislature in 1843, "in cages, closets, stalls, pens! Chained, naked, beaten with rods and lashed into obedience."

A year earlier, in a surprise visit to a Newburyport Almshouse, Dix had discovered one man residing in a shed whose door opened to the local "dead room," or morgue; his only companions were corpses. Shocked, she heard from an attendant about another insane inmate of whom no one spoke openly: "a woman in a cellar." Dix asked to see the woman. The superintendent warned Dix that the woman "was dangerous to be ap-

proached." Dix pressed on. They unlocked the doors and entered an underground cell. Beneath the staircase was a tiny door. In the shadows Dix saw "a female apparently wasted to a skeleton, partially wrapped in blankets." She was withered, wrote Dix, "not by age, but by suffering." When the inmate saw the visitors, she wailed with despair: "Why am I consigned to hell? I used to pray, I used to read the Bible. . . . I had friends; why have all forsaken me!—my God! my God! why hast thou forsaken me?"

Dix described in the most personal and vivid terms her visits to jails, almshouses, and private homes, and the cruel treatment of the insane. Her petition to the General Court of Massachusetts was so graphic

IMPORTANT EVENTS

1790s–1840s	Second Great Awakening spreads religious fervor
1824	No presidential candidate wins a majority in the electoral college
1825	House of Representatives elects Adams president
1826	American Society for the Promotion of Temperance founded Morgan affair is catalyst for Antimasonry movement
1828	Tariff of Abominations passed Jackson elected president
1830	Webster-Hayne debate explores the nature of the Union
1830s–40s	Democratic-Whig competition gels in second party system
1831	Garrison begins abolitionist newspaper *The Liberator* First national Antimason convention
1832	Jackson vetoes rechartering of the Second Bank of the United States Jackson reelected president
1832–33	South Carolina nullifies tariffs of 1828 and 1832, prompting nullification crisis
1836	Republic of Texas established Specie Circular ends credit purchase of public lands Van Buren elected president
1837	Financial panic ends boom of the 1830s
1838–39	United States and Canada mobilize their militias over Maine–New Brunswick border dispute
1839–43	Hard times spread unemployment and deflation
1840	Whigs win presidency under Harrison
1841	Tyler assumes the presidency after Harrison's death "Oregon fever" attracts settlers to the Northwest and intensifies expansionism
1843	Dix petitions Massachusetts legislature regarding deplorable condition of insane asylums
1844	Polk elected president
1845	Texas admitted to the Union
1848	Woman's Rights Convention at Seneca Falls, New York, calls for women's suffrage

and shocking that the legislature voted to reprint it as a government pamphlet. Part petition, part sermon, and part autobiography, it made riveting reading.

Dix epitomized much of early-nineteenth-century reform. She started with a religious belief in individual self-improvement and human perfectibility that led her to advocate collective responsibility, especially on behalf of those dependent on the kindness of others. She made reform her career, fearlessly entering the public arena at a time when women of her class were circumscribed to private life. In investigating asylums, in petitioning the Massachusetts legislature, and in lobbying other states and Congress, Dix moved from reform to politics, and she helped create a new public role for women, in the process broadening the base of political participation.

The religious and reform fervor of the period arose both as part of the spiritual renewal known as the Second Great Awakening and as a response to the enormous transformation that the United States experienced after the War of 1812. Immigration, the spread of a market economy, growing inequality, the westward advance of settlement, and territorial expansion all contributed to remaking the United States.

Anxieties wrought by rapid change drove the impulse to reform society. Men and women organized to end the abuses of alcohol and prostitution, to improve conditions in prisons and asylums, to oppose secret and antidemocratic societies, to end slavery, and to achieve equal rights for women. Inevitably reform movements pushed men and women into politics, though only men voted. Opponents of reform were equally concerned about social problems. They were, however, skeptical about human perfectibility and distrustful of the exercise of power.

Two issues in particular bridged reform and politics: the short-lived Antimasonry frenzy against secret societies, and the intense, uncompromising crusade for immediate emancipation. Though Antimasons organized the first third-party movement, abolition eventually overrode all other concerns. No single issue evoked the passion that slavery did.

The Jacksonians, too, saw themselves as reformers. They opposed special privileges and the Second Bank of the United States. President Jackson believed that a strong federal government restricted individual freedom by favoring one group over another. Social and religious reformers disagreed. Wanting a more active federal role, they rallied around the new Whig Party, which became the vehicle of humanitarian reform. Democrats and Whigs constituted a new party system, characterized by strong organizations, intensely loyal followings, and energetic religious and ethnic competition.

Both parties eagerly promoted expansionism during the prosperous 1840s. Democrats saw the agrarian West as an antidote to urbanization and industrialization; Whigs focused on the new commercial opportunities it offered. Expanding the nation all the way to the Pacific seemed to be the manifest destiny of the United States. ■

From Revival to Reform

 Religion was probably the prime motivating force behind organized benevolence and reform. Beginning in the late 1790s religious revivals galvanized Protestants, especially women, into social action. At camp meetings, sometimes lasting a week and attended by thousands of people, preachers exhorted sinners to repent and become genuine Christians. They offered salvation to all through personal conversion. At a time when only a minority could read and write, these itinerant evangelists were democratizing American religion, making it available to all.

Resembling the Great Awakening of the eighteenth century (see pages 72–73), the movement came to be called the Second Great Awakening. Under its

Second Great Awakening

influence, the role of churches and ministers in community life diminished as lay participation increased, and Christians in all parts of the country tried to right the wrongs of the world.

In the South, huge numbers of people regularly attended revivals, but they especially drew women and African Americans, free and slave. The call to personal repentance and conversion invigorated Protestantism, giving southern churches an evangelical base and giving evangelicalism a southern accent. In essence, the Second Great Awakening turned the South into the Bible belt. In the North, New York lawyer Charles G. Finney led the revival movement. After his 1821 soul-shaking conversion, Finney abandoned the law to convert souls. Salvation could be achieved, Finney preached, through spontaneous conversion like his own. He mesmerized his audiences and in everyday language preached that "God has made man a moral free agent." In other words, evil was avoidable: Christians were not doomed by original sin, and anyone could achieve salvation.

The Second Great Awakening raised people's hopes for the Second Coming of the Christian messiah and the establishment of the Kingdom of God on earth. Revivalists resolved to speed the Second Coming by combating the forces of evil and darkness. Some revivalists even believed that the United States had a special mission in God's design and therefore a unique role in eliminating evil.

Regardless of theology, all revivalists shared a belief in individual self-improvement. Thus the Second Great Awakening bred reform. Wherever they preached, evangelists generated new religious groups and voluntary reform societies. New sects like the Mormons arose out of this ferment. So did associations that addressed the pressing issues of the day: temperance, education, Sabbath observance, dueling, and later slavery.

More women than men answered the call of Christianity, sustaining the Second Great Awakening and invigorating local churches. Pious middle-class women in Rochester, New York, for instance, responded to Finney by spreading the word to other women during the day while their husbands were at work. Gradually women brought their families and sometimes their husbands into church and reform.

Role of Women

Women, more than men, tended to feel personally responsible for counteracting the increasingly secular orientation of the expanding market economy. The emotionally charged conversion experience could return women to what they believed was the right path. It also offered them communal ties with other women.

Everywhere prayer groups and female missionary societies motivated organized religious and benevolent activity on an unprecedented scale. For women and some men, reform represented their first political involvement at a time when women did not cast votes. In reform organizations women represented themselves; by participating directly in service activities, they pioneered new, visible, public roles for women.

An exposé of prostitution in New York City illustrates how reform led to political action and dissent.

The Plight of Prostitutes

In response to an 1830 report documenting the prevalence of prostitution in New York City, New York businessmen and politicians defended the city's good name against "those base slanders." Women, moved by the plight of "fallen women," organized to fight against prostitution. But whereas male reformers made the prostitutes the target of their zeal, the newly organized Female Moral Reform Society focused on the men who victimized young women, publicizing the names of clients who entered brothels in New York City.

During the 1830s, the New York society expanded its activities and geographical scope, calling itself the American Female Moral Reform Society. By 1840 it had 555 affiliated chapters across the nation. The society also entered the political sphere. In New York State in the 1840s, the movement successfully crusaded for criminal sanctions against the men who seduced women into prostitution, as well as against the prostitutes themselves.

One of the most successful reform efforts was the campaign against alcohol. American men gathered in public houses and rural inns to gossip, talk politics, play cards, escape work and home, and drink whiskey, rum, and hard cider. Respectable women did not drink in public, but many regularly tippled alcohol-based patent medicines promoted as cure-alls. Why then did temperance become such a vi-

Temperance

tal issue? And why were women especially active in the movement? Like all nineteenth-century reform, temperance had a strong religious foundation.

Evangelicals considered drinking a sin, and forsaking alcohol was part of conversion. The sale of whiskey often violated the Sabbath, for workers commonly labored for six days and spent Sunday at the public house drinking and socializing. Equally important, alcoholism destroyed families. In the early 1840s thousands of ordinary women formed Martha Washington societies to protect families by reforming alcoholics, raising children as teetotalers, and spreading the temperance message. Employers complained that drinkers took "St. Monday" as a holiday to recover from Sunday. In the new world of the factory, drinking was unacceptable.

As the temperance movement gained momentum, its goal shifted from moderate use of alcohol to voluntary abstinence and finally to prohibition. The American Society for the Promotion of Temperance, organized in 1826 to sign drinkers to a pledge of abstinence, became a pressure group for state prohibition legislation. By the mid-1830s five thousand state and local temperance societies touted teetotalism, and more than a million people had taken the pledge. As the movement spread, per capita consumption of alcohol fell from 5 gallons in 1800 to 2 gallons in the 1840s. Moreover, a number of northern states followed Maine and outlawed the sale of alcohol except for medicinal purpose.

Temperance Societies

As the career of Dorothea Dix demonstrated, moral reform also stimulated the construction of asylums and other institutions to house prisoners, the mentally ill, orphans, delinquent children, and the poor. Such institutions were needed, reformers argued, to shelter victims of society's turbulence and impose on them a familial discipline. Through discipline, and the banning of idleness, inmates might become self-reliant and responsible.

Penitentiaries and Asylums

In the 1820s New York and Pennsylvania rejected incarceration simply to punish criminals or to remove them from society, advocating instead that disciplined regimens would rehabilitate them. New York's Auburn prison isolated prisoners in individual cells but brought

The evils of drinking and the bliss of temperance were a major theme in popular culture. Deacon Robert Peckham illustrated the contrast in two paintings from the 1840s: *The Woes of Liquor (Intemperance)* and *The Happy Abstemious Family (Temperance).*
(Worcester Historical Museum)

them together in common workshops. Pennsylvania's prisons isolated prisoners completely, forcing them to eat, sleep, and work in their individual cells and allowing them contact only with guards and visitors. Both systems sought to separate criminals from evil influences and to expose them to a regimen of order and discipline.

Similar approaches were employed in insane asylums, hospitals, and orphanages. Formerly the prescribed treatment had removed disturbed individuals from society and isolated them among strangers; many were incarcerated with criminals. Dorothea Dix argued that this treatment was inhumane. The new asylums were clean and orderly. In response to Dix's crusade and reform societies, twenty-eight of the thirty-three states had public institutions for the mentally ill by 1860.

Antimasonry

 More intense than the asylum movement but of shorter duration was the crusade against Freemasonry, a secret fraternity that had come to the United States from Eng-

land in the eighteenth century. Sons of the Enlightenment such as Benjamin Franklin and George Washington were attracted to Masonry, with its emphasis on individual belief in a deity (as opposed to organized religion) and on brotherhood (as opposed to one church). In the early nineteenth century Freemasonry spread, attracting men prominent in commerce and civic affairs.

Opponents of Masonry charged that the order's secrecy and appeal to elites were antidemocratic and antirepublican. Publications such as the *Anti Masonic Almanac* attacked Masonic initiation rites. Evangelicals labeled the order satanic. Antimasons argued that Masonry threatened the family because it excluded women and encouraged men to neglect their families for alcohol and ribald entertainments at Masonic lodges. The political arena quickly absorbed Antimasonry, and its short life illustrates the close association of politics and reform in the 1820s and after.

The catalyst for Antimasonry as an organized movement was the suspected murder of William Morgan, a disillusioned Mason who published an exposé in 1826. Even before the book appeared, a group of

Morgan Affair Masons abducted Morgan in Canandaigua, New York. It was widely believed that his kidnappers murdered him, though his body was never found.

Events seemed to confirm Masonry's antidemocratic character. Prosecutors who were Masons appeared to obstruct the investigation of Morgan's abduction. The public pressed for justice, and the series of notorious trials that ensued from 1827 through 1831 led many to suspect a conspiracy. The cover-up became as much of an issue as Masonry itself, and the movement spread to other states. Antimasonry coalesced overnight in western New York, and it quickly became a political movement.

With a growing popular following and a call for public morality and republican principles, the Antimasons held conventions in 1827 to select candidates to oppose Masons running for office. The next year the conventions supported the National Republican candidate, John Quincy Adams, and opposed Andrew Jackson because he was a Mason. The Antimasons held the first national political convention in Baltimore in 1831, and a year later they nominated William Wirt as their presidential candidate. Thus the Antimasons became a rallying point for those opposed to President Andrew Jackson.

Convention System

By the mid-1830s, Antimasonry had lost momentum as a moral and political phenomenon. A single-issue party, the Antimasons declined along with Freemasonry. Yet the movement left its mark on the politics of the era. As a moral crusade focused on public officeholders, it inspired broad participation in the political process. The Antimasons also changed party organization by pioneering the convention, rather than the caucus, for nominating candidates for office and by introducing the party platform.

Abolitionism and the Women's Movement

 Antimasonry foreshadowed and had much in common with abolitionism. To abolitionist William Lloyd Garrison, both slavery and Masonry undermined republican values. Eventually the issue of slavery became so com-

pelling that it consumed all other reforms and threatened the nation itself. Those who advocated immediate emancipation saw slavery as, above all, a moral issue—a flaw in the character of the American nation.

Before the 1830s few whites in either the Northeast or the Old Northwest advocated the abolition of slavery or even took an interest in the issue. Antislavery sentiment appeared strongest in the Upper South, though northern involvement grew after the War of 1812. The American Colonization Society, founded in 1816 in Washington, D.C., advocated gradual, voluntary emancipation and resettlement of former slaves in Africa. Society members did not believe that free blacks had a place in the United States. In the 1830s, however, the immediatists—those who demanded immediate, complete, and uncompensated emancipation—surpassed the gradualists as the dominant strand of abolitionism.

Women played an activist role in reform, especially in abolitionism. A rare daguerreotype from August 1850 shows women and men, including Frederick Douglass, on the podium at an abolitionist rally in Cazenovia, New York. (Collection of J. Paul Getty Museum, Los Angeles, California)

At first only African Americans demanded an immediate end to slavery. David Walker's *Appeal . . . to the Colored Citizens* (1829) was a clarion call read by northern black people. Walker, a southern-born free black, was Boston's leading abolitionist until his death in 1830. When Walker died, there were fifty black abolitionist societies in the United States assisting fugitive slaves, lobbying for emancipation, exposing the evils of slavery, and reminding the nation that its mission as defined in the Declaration of Independence remained unfulfilled. A free black press spread the word, as did the writings and speeches of Frederick Douglass and Sojourner Truth. Douglass and Underground Railroad champion Harriet Tubman joined forces in the 1840s with white reformers in the American Anti-Slavery Society.

Black Abolitionists

In the 1830s a small number of white reformers, driven by moral urgency, also crusaded for immediate emancipation. The most prominent and uncompromising immediatist was the incendiary William Lloyd Garrison, a talented journalist who broke with moderate abolitionists in 1831. That year he began publishing *The Liberator*, in whose first issue Garrison declared, "I am in earnest— I will not equivocate—I will not excuse—I will not retreat a single inch—and *I will be heard*."

William Lloyd Garrison

Garrison's staunch refusal to work with anyone who tolerated the delay of emancipation isolated him from other opponents of slavery. Still, by his actions and rhetorical power, Garrison helped to push antislavery onto the agenda, though he had no specific plan for abolishing slavery.

It is difficult to differentiate between those who became immediatists and those who did not. Immediatists were often young evangelicals active in benevolent societies in the 1820s; many became ordained ministers or started out intending ministry as a career; and many had personal contact with free blacks and were sympathetic to African American rights. They were convinced that slaveholding was a sin. They also shared great moral intensity and were unwilling to compromise.

Immediatists

Most benevolent workers and reformers kept their distance from the immediatists. They shared with immediatists the view that slavery was a sin but believed in gradual emancipation. They feared that if they moved too fast or attacked sinners too harshly, they would destroy the harmony and order they sought.

Immediatists' greatest recruitment successes resulted from defending their own constitutional rights, not the rights of slaves. Wherever they went, immediatists found their civil rights, especially free speech, at risk, threatened by hostile crowds. Mob violence peaked in 1835 with more than fifty riots aimed at abolitionists or African Americans. In 1837 in Alton, Illinois, a mob murdered abolitionist editor Elijah P. Lovejoy. Public outrage at Lovejoy's murder broadened the base of antislavery support in the North.

Opposition to Abolitionists

In the South, mobs blocked the distribution of antislavery tracts. They destroyed pamphlets that the American Anti-Slavery Society (founded in 1833) sent out by the millions. The state of South Carolina intercepted and burned abolitionist literature. In 1835 proslavery assailants killed four abolitionists in South Carolina and Louisiana and forty supposed insurrectionists in Mississippi and Louisiana that summer.

At a rally in Boston's Faneuil Hall in 1835, former Federalist Harrison Gray Otis portrayed abolitionists as subversives. Abolitionists, he predicted, would turn to politics, causing unforeseeable calamity. "What will become of the union?" Otis asked.

But the furor between the abolitionists and their opponents was already being played out in the House of Representatives. Abolitionists were bombarding Congress with petitions to abolish slavery and the slave trade in the District of Columbia, which Congress governed. The House in 1836 adopted what abolitionists immediately labeled the "gag rule," which automatically tabled abolitionist petitions, effectively preventing debate on them. In a dramatic defense of the right of petition, former president John Quincy Adams, now a representative from Massachusetts, took to the floor again and again to speak against the gag rule. (Its repeal in 1844 was anticlimactic.)

Gag Rule

The Missouri Compromise, censorship of the mails, and the gag rule represented attempts to keep the issue of slavery out of the political arena. Yet the more national leaders, especially Democrats, worked to avoid the matter, the more they hardened the resolve of the antislavery forces.

At the outset abolition was highly factionalized, and its adherents fought one another as often as they fought the defenders of slavery. They were divided between Garrison's emphasis on "moral suasion"—winning over the hearts of slaveowners rather than coercing them—and the practical politics of James G. Birney, the Liberty Party's candidate for president in 1840 and 1844. Abolitionists also disagreed about the place of free people of color in American society. And the movement split over support for other reforms, especially the rights of women.

Women had been prominent in the antislavery movement from the first, and in many antislavery organizations women were as active and politically involved as men. Ly-

Women Abolitionists

dia Maria Child, Maria Chapman, and Lucretia Mott served on the American Anti-Slavery Society's executive committee; Child edited its official paper, the *National Anti-Slavery Standard*, from 1841 to 1843, and Chapman coedited it from 1844 until 1848. Garrison's moral suasion attracted many women because it gave them a platform from which to oppose slavery. Yet some politically active societies excluded women because they could not vote.

Opposition to women's prominent roles in reform movements led some women to reexamine their position in society at large. In the 1830s Angelina and Sarah Grimké challenged slavery and women's right to speak out. Born into a slaveholding family in Charleston, South Carolina, both sisters experienced conversion and independently became Quakers. When in 1834 they became activists, they found in Garrison's immediatism a home. Yet they were soon attacked for speaking before mixed groups of men and women. This reaction turned the Grimkés' attention from slavery to women's condition. They attacked the concept of "subordination to man," insisting that men and women had the "same rights and same duties." Sarah Grimké's *Letters on the Equality of the Sexes and the Condition of Women* (1838) and her sister's *Letters to Catharine E. Beecher* (1838) were the opening volleys in the long war over the legal and social inequality of women.

In July 1848 three hundred women and men reformers gathered at the Woman's Rights Convention

Women's Rights

at Seneca Falls, New York, to demand political, social, and economic equality for women. Led by Elizabeth Cady Stanton, Lucretia Mott, and Lucy Stone, they protested women's legal disabilities—inability to vote, limited property rights—and their social restrictions—exclusion from advanced schooling and from most occupations. Their Declaration of Sentiments indicted the injustices suffered by women and launched the women's rights movement. "All men and women are created equal," the declaration proclaimed. If women had the vote, participants argued, they could protect themselves and realize their full potential as moral and spiritual leaders.

Advocates of women's rights were slow to garner support, especially from men, who held most of the political and legal power. Even within the antislavery movement, most men opposed women's rights. Still,

Elizabeth Cady Stanton posed in 1848 with two of her sons, Henry Jr. (*left*), and Neil. Stanton, one of the organizers of the Seneca Falls Woman's Rights Convention, traveled widely and agitated for women's equality while raising five children.   (Collection of Rhoda Jenkins)

some men joined the ranks, notably Garrison and Frederick Douglass.

Jacksonianism and Party Politics

 In the 1820s, reform pushed its way into politics. No less than reformers, politicians sought to control the direction of change in the expanding nation. The 1824 presidential election ignited a political fire that reformers, abolitionists, and expansionists would continuously stoke. By the 1830s, politics had become the great American pastime.

The election of 1824, in which John Quincy Adams and Andrew Jackson faced off for the first time, heralded a more open political system. From 1800 through 1820 the system in which a congressional caucus chose the Democratic-Republican nominees (Jefferson, Madison, and Monroe) had worked well. That it limited voters' involvement in choosing candidates was not an anomaly because in 1800 only five of the sixteen states selected presidential electors by popular vote. In most of the others, state legislatures selected the electors who voted for president. By 1824, however, eighteen out of twenty-four states chose electors by popular vote.

End of the Caucus System

The Democratic-Republican caucus in 1824 chose William H. Crawford of Georgia, secretary of the treasury, as its presidential candidate. But other Democratic-Republicans, emboldened by the chance to appeal directly to voters, put themselves forward as sectional candidates. John Quincy Adams drew support from New England, while westerners backed House Speaker Henry Clay of Kentucky. Secretary of War John C. Calhoun looked to the South for support and hoped to win Pennsylvania as well. The Tennessee legislature nominated Andrew Jackson, a popular military hero whose political views were unknown. Jackson had the most widespread support. By boycotting the caucus and attacking it as undemocratic, these men and their supporters ended the role of Congress in nominating presidential candidates.

In the four-way presidential election of 1824, Andrew Jackson led in both electoral and popular votes, but no candidate received a majority in the elec-

Election of 1824

toral college. Adams finished second, and Crawford and Clay trailed far behind (Calhoun had dropped out of the race before the election). As required by the Constitution, the House of Representatives, voting by state delegation, one vote to a state, selected the next president from among the leaders in electoral votes. Clay, who had received the fewest votes, was dropped. Crawford, a stroke victim, never received serious consideration. The influential Clay backed Adams, who received the votes of thirteen of the twenty-four state delegations to win. Clay then became Adams's secretary of state, the traditional steppingstone to the presidency.

Angry Jacksonians denounced the outcome of the election as a "corrupt bargain" that had stolen the office. The Democratic-Republican Party split. The Adams wing emerged as the National Republicans, and the Jacksonians became the Democrats; they immediately began planning a reversal for 1828.

After taking the oath of office, Adams proposed a strong nationalist policy incorporating Henry Clay's "American System," a program of protective tariffs, a national bank, and internal improvements. Brilliant as a diplomat and secretary of state, Adams was an inept president. He underestimated the lingering effects of the Panic of 1819 and the resulting staunch opposition to a national bank and protective tariffs. Meanwhile, supporters of Andrew Jackson sabotaged Adams's administration at every opportunity.

The 1828 election pitted Adams against Jackson in a rowdy campaign. The contest was also intensely personal. Mudslinging was the order of the day. Anti-Jacksonians published reports that Rachel Jackson had had an affair with Jackson and married the young officer before her first husband divorced her in 1793; she was, they sneered, an adulterer and a bigamist. After the election Rachel Jackson discovered a pamphlet defending her, and she was mortified by the extent of the charges. In December 1828 she died of a heart attack. Jackson never forgave her "murderers."

Election of 1828

Jackson swamped Adams, carrying 56 percent of the popular vote and winning in the electoral college by 178 to 83 votes. He and his supporters believed that the will of the people had finally been served. Through a lavishly financed coalition of state parties, political leaders, and newspaper editors, a popular movement had elected the president, and an era had ended. The Democratic Party became the first well-organized national political party in the United States, and tight party organization became the hallmark of nineteenth-century American politics.

Nicknamed "Old Hickory" after the toughest of American hardwoods, Andrew Jackson was a rough-and-tumble, ambitious man. He rose

Andrew Jackson

from humble beginnings to become a wealthy planter and slaveholder and the first president from the West. Though vindictive and given to violent displays of temper, he could charm opposition into assent. He had an instinct for politics and picked both issues and supporters shrewdly.

Jackson and his supporters offered an alternative to the strong federal government advocated by John Quincy Adams. The Democrats rep-

Democrats

resented a wide range of views but shared a fundamental commitment to the Jeffersonian concept of an agrarian society. They distrusted a powerful central government as the enemy of individual liberty.

Jacksonians feared the concentration of economic and political power. They believed that government intervention in the economy benefited special-interest groups and created corporate monopolies, which favored the rich. They sought to restore the independence of the individual—the artisan and the yeoman farmer—by ending federal support of banks and corporations and restricting the use of paper currency, which they distrusted.

Jackson and his supporters also opposed reform as a movement. Reformers eager to turn their programs into legislation called for a more activist government. But Democrats tended to oppose programs like educational reform and the establishment of a public education system. They believed, for instance, that public schools restricted individual liberty by interfering with parental responsibility and undermined freedom of religion by replacing church schools. Nor did Jackson share reformers' humanitarian concerns.

Jacksonians considered themselves reformers in a different way. By restraining government and emphasizing individualism, they sought to restore traditional

Jacksonians as Reformers

republican virtues, such as prudence and economy. Jackson sought to encourage self-discipline and self-reliance and to restore the harmony that he saw disrupted by economic and social change.

Like Jefferson, Jackson strengthened the executive branch of government even as he weakened the federal role. Given his popularity and the strength of his personality, this concentration of power in the presidency was perhaps inevitable, but in combining the roles of party leader and chief of state, he centralized power in the White House. Jackson relied on political friends, his "Kitchen Cabinet," for advice; he rarely consulted his official cabinet. By rotating officeholders, Jackson introduced a spoils system that rewarded his followers handsomely and thereby strengthened party organization and loyalty.

Jackson stressed rejection of elitism and special favors, rotation of officeholders, and belief in popular government. Time and again he declared that sovereignty resided with the people, not with the states or the courts. In this respect Jackson was a reformer; he returned government to majority rule. Yet it is hard to distinguish between Jackson's belief in himself as the instrument of the people and demagogic arrogance.

Animosity between President Jackson's supporters and opponents grew year by year. Massachusetts senator Daniel Webster feared the men around the president; Henry Clay most feared Jackson himself. Rotation in office, they contended, corrupted government. Opponents mocked Jackson as "King Andrew I," charging him with abuse of power by ignoring the Supreme Court's ruling on Cherokee rights, by using the spoils system, and by consulting his Kitchen Cabinet. Critics also accused him of recklessly destroying the economy.

Amid all the agitation, Jackson invigorated the philosophy of limited government. In 1830 he vetoed the Maysville Road bill, which would have funded construction of a 60-mile turnpike from Maysville to Lexington, Kentucky. A federally subsidized internal improvement confined to one state was unconstitutional, he charged; such projects were properly a state responsibility. The veto undermined Henry Clay's nationalist program and personally embarrassed Clay because the project was in his home district.

Federalism at Issue: The Nullification and Bank Controversies

 Soon Jackson had to face directly the question of the proper division of sovereignty between state and central governments. The slave South feared federal power, no state more so than South Carolina. Southerners also resented protectionist tariffs.

To protect manufactures, Congress in 1828 imposed high import duties on manufactured cloth and iron. But in protecting northern factories, the tariff raised the costs of these goods to southerners, who quickly labeled it the Tariff of Abominations.

Tariff of Abominations

To articulate their interests, South Carolina's political leaders turned to the doctrine of nullification, according to which a state had the right to overrule, or nullify, federal legislation. Nullification was based on the idea expressed in the Virginia and Kentucky resolutions of 1798 (see pages 135–136)—that the states, representing the people, have a right to judge the constitutionality of federal actions. Jackson's vice president, John C. Calhoun of South Carolina, argued in his unsigned *Exposition and Protest* that in any disagreement between the federal government and a state, a special state convention—like the conventions called to ratify the Constitution—should decide the conflict by either nullifying or affirming the federal law. Only the power of nullification, Calhoun asserted, could protect the minority against the tyranny of the majority.

In public, Calhoun let others take the lead in advancing nullification. He hoped to avoid embarrassing the Democratic ticket and to win Jackson's support as the Democratic presidential heir apparent. Thus in early 1830 Calhoun presided silently over the Senate and its packed galleries when Senator Daniel Webster of Massachusetts and Senator Robert Y. Hayne of South Carolina debated states' rights. The debate started over a resolution to restrict western land sales and engaged the tariff issue by exploring sectional differences. It quickly turned to the nature of the Union, with nullification a subtext. At

Webster-Hayne Debate

the climax of the debate, Webster invoked two powerful images. One was the outcome of nullification: "states dissevered, discordant, belligerent; on a land rent with civil feuds, or drenched . . . in fraternal blood!" The other was a patriotic vision of a great nation flourishing under the motto "Liberty and Union, now and forever, one and inseparable."

Though sympathetic to states' rights and distrustful of the federal government, Jackson rejected the idea of state sovereignty. He strongly believed that sovereignty rested with the people. Deeply loyal to the Union, he shared Webster's dread of nullification. Soon after the Webster-Hayne debate, the president made his position clear at a Jefferson Day dinner with the toast "Our Federal Union, it must and shall be preserved." Vice President Calhoun, when his turn came, toasted "The Federal Union—next to our liberty the most dear." Calhoun thus revealed his adherence to states' rights.

Tensions did not subside when Congress passed a new tariff in 1832 reducing some duties but retaining high taxes on imported iron, cottons, and woolens. Though a majority of southern representatives supported the new tariff, South Carolinians refused to go along. More than the duties, they feared that the act could set a precedent for congressional legislation on slavery. In November 1832 a South Carolina state convention nullified both tariffs, making it unlawful for federal officials to collect duties in the state.

Nullification Crisis

Old Hickory was quick to respond. In December he issued a proclamation opposing nullification. He moved troops to federal forts in South Carolina and prepared U.S. marshals to collect the required duties. At Jackson's request, Congress passed the Force Act, which gave the president authority to call up troops but also offered a way to avoid using force by collecting duties before foreign ships reached Charleston's harbor. At the same time, Jackson extended an olive branch by recommending tariff reductions.

Calhoun, disturbed by South Carolina's drift toward separatism, resigned as vice president and soon won election to represent South Carolina in the U.S. Senate. There he worked with Henry Clay to draw up the compromise Tariff of 1833. Quickly passed by Congress and signed by the president, the new tariff lengthened the list of duty-free items and reduced duties over nine years. Satisfied, South Carolina's convention repealed its nullification law. In a final salvo, it also nullified Jackson's Force Act. Jackson ignored the gesture.

Nullification offered a genuine debate on the nature and principles of the republic. Each side believed it was upholding the Constitution. Neither side won a clear victory, though both claimed to have done so. It took another crisis, over a central bank, to define the powers of the federal government more clearly.

At stake was the survival of the Second Bank of the United States, whose twenty-year charter was scheduled to expire in 1836. Among the

Second Bank of the United States

bank's functions were to serve as a depository for federal funds and to act as a clearing-house for state banks, keeping them honest by refusing to accept the bank notes of any state bank lacking sufficient gold reserves. Most state banks resented the central bank's police role: by presenting a state bank's notes for redemption all at once, the Second Bank could easily ruin a state bank. Moreover, with less money in reserve, state banks found themselves unable to compete on an equal footing with the Second Bank.

Many state governments also regarded the national bank as unresponsive to local needs. Westerners and urban workers remembered with bitterness the bank's conservative credit policies during the Panic of 1819. As a private, profit-making institution, its policies reflected the interest of its owners. Its president was an eastern patrician who symbolized all that westerners found wrong with the bank.

Rechartering was a volatile issue in the 1832 presidential campaign. The bank's charter was valid until 1836, but Henry Clay, the National Republican presidential candidate, persuaded Biddle to ask Congress to approve an early rechartering. This strategy was designed to pressure Jackson to sign the rechartering bill or to override his veto of it. The plan backfired, however. The president vetoed the bill, and the Senate failed to override. Jackson's veto message was an emotional attack on the undemocratic nature of the bank. The bank thus became the prime issue in the presidential campaign of 1832, with Jackson denouncing special privilege and economic power.

After his sweeping victory and second inauguration, Jackson moved in 1833 to dismantle the Second Bank of the United States. He

Jackson's Second Term

deposited federal funds in state-chartered banks (critics called them his "pet banks"). Without federal money, the Second Bank shriveled. When its federal charter expired in 1836, it became just another Pennsylvania-chartered private bank. Five years later it closed its doors.

In conjunction with the demise of the Bank of the United States, Congress passed the Deposit Act of 1836. The act authorized the secretary of the treasury to designate one bank in each state and territory to provide the services formerly performed by the Bank of the United States. The act also provided that the federal surplus in excess of $5 million be distributed to the states as interest-free loans beginning in 1837.

The surplus had derived from wholesale speculation in public lands: speculators borrowed money to

Specie Circular

purchase public land, used the land as collateral for credit to buy additional acreage, and repeated the cycle. The state banks providing the loans issued bank notes. Jackson, an opponent of paper money, feared that the speculative craze threatened the stability of state banks and undermined the interests of settlers, who could not compete with speculators in bidding for the best land.

In keeping with his hard-money instincts and opposition to paper currency, the president ordered Treasury Secretary Levi Woodbury to issue the Specie Circular. It provided that after August 1836 only specie—gold or silver—or Virginia scrip (paper money) would be accepted as payment for land. By ending credit sales, it significantly reduced purchases of public land and the federal budget surplus. As a result, the government suspended payments to the states soon after they began.

The policy was a disaster. Although federal land sales were sharply reduced, speculation continued as available land for sale became scarce. The increased demand for specie squeezed banks, and many suspended the redemption of bank notes for specie. Credit contracted further as banks issued fewer notes and made fewer loans. In the waning days of Jackson's administration, Congress voted to repeal the circular, but the president pocket-vetoed the bill by holding it unsigned until Congress adjourned. Finally in mid-1838, a joint resolution of Congress overturned the circular. Restrictions on land sales ended, but the speculative fervor was over.

From George Washington to John Quincy Adams, the first six presidents had vetoed nine bills; Jackson alone vetoed twelve. Previous presidents had believed that vetoes were justified only on constitutional grounds, but Jackson considered policy disagreement legitimate grounds as well. He made the veto an effective weapon for controlling Congress. In effect, Jackson made the executive for the first time a rival branch of government, equal in power to Congress.

Use of the Veto

The Whig Challenge and the Second Party System

Most historians view the 1830s and 1840s as an age of reform and popularly based political parties. Only when the passions of reformers and abolitionists spilled over into politics did party differences become paramount and party loyalties solidify. For the first time in American history, grassroots political groups, organized from the bottom up, set the tone of political life.

Opponents of the Democrats found shelter under a common umbrella, the Whig Party, in the 1830s. Resentful of Jackson's domination of Congress, the Whigs borrowed the name of the British party that had opposed the tyranny of Hanoverian monarchs in the eighteenth century. From 1834 through the 1840s, the Whigs and the Democrats competed on a nearly equal footing. They fought at the city, county, state, and national levels and achieved a stability previously unknown in American politics. The political competition of this period—known as the second party system—was more intense and well organized than that of the first party system of Democratic-Republicans versus Federalists.

Increasingly the parties diverged. Whigs favored economic expansion through an activist government, Democrats through limited central government. Whigs supported corporate charters, a national bank,

Whigs and Reformers

and paper currency; Democrats were opposed to all three. Whigs also favored more humanitarian reforms than did Democrats, including public schools, abolition of capital punishment, prison and asylum reform, and temperance. Whigs were more optimistic than Democrats, generally speaking, and more enterprising. They did not object to helping a specific group if doing so would promote the general welfare. The chartering of corporations, they argued, expanded economic opportunity for everyone, laborers and farmers alike. Democrats, distrustful of concentrated economic power and of moral and economic coercion, held fast to the Jeffersonian principle of limited government.

Religion and ethnicity, not economics and class, most influenced party affiliation. The Whigs won the favor of evangelical Protestants and the small number of free black voters. Democrats, by contrast, tended to be foreign-born Catholics and nonevangelical Protestants, both of whom preferred to keep religion and politics separate.

The Whig Party was the vehicle of revivalist Protestantism. In many locales the membership rolls of reform societies overlapped those of the party. Indeed, Whigs practiced a kind of political revivalism. Their rallies resembled camp meetings; in their speeches they employed pulpit rhetoric; their programs embodied the perfectionist beliefs of reformers.

In their appeal to evangelicals, Whigs alienated members of other faiths. The evangelicals' ideal Christian state had no room for Catholics, Mormons, Unitarians, Universalists, or religious freethinkers. Those groups opposed Sabbath laws and temperance legislation in particular and state interference in moral and religious questions in general. As a result, more than 95 percent of Irish Catholics, 90 percent of Reformed Dutch, and 80 percent of German Catholics voted Democratic.

Vice President Martin Van Buren, handpicked by Jackson, headed the Democratic ticket in the 1836 presidential election. The Whigs, who in 1836 had not yet coalesced into a national party, entered three sectional candidates: Daniel Webster of New England, Hugh White of the South, and

Election of 1836

William Henry Harrison of the West. By splintering the vote, they hoped to throw the election into the House of Representatives. Van Buren, however, comfortably captured the electoral college even though he had only a 25,000-vote edge out of a total of 1.5 million votes cast.

Van Buren and Hard Times

Van Buren took office just weeks before the American credit system collapsed. In response to the impact of the Specie Circular, New York banks stopped redeeming paper currency with gold in mid-1837. Soon all banks suspended payments in hard coin. Thus began a downward economic spiral that curtailed bank loans and strangled business confidence. Hard times persisted from 1839 until 1843.

Ill-advisedly, Van Buren followed Jackson's hard-money policies. He cut federal spending, which caused prices to drop further, and he opposed a national bank, which would have expanded credit. Even worse, the president proposed a new regional treasury system for government deposits. The proposed treasury branches would accept and pay out only gold and silver coin; they would not accept paper currency or checks drawn on state banks. Van Buren's independent treasury bill became law in 1840. By increasing the demand for hard coin, it deprived banks of gold and further accelerated price deflation.

William Henry Harrison and the Election of 1840

With the nation in the grip of hard times, the Whigs prepared confidently for the election of 1840. Their strategy was simple: hold on to loyal supporters and win over independents by blaming hard times on the Democrats. The Whigs rallied behind a military hero, General William Henry Harrison, conqueror of the Shawnees at Tippecanoe Creek in 1811. The Democrats renominated President Van Buren.

Harrison, or "Old Tippecanoe," and his running mate, John Tyler of Virginia, ran a "log cabin and hard cider" campaign—a people's crusade—against the aristocratic president in "the Palace." In a huge turnout, 80 percent of eligible voters cast ballots. Harrison won the popular vote by a narrow margin but swept the electoral college by 234 to 60.

Within a month of his inauguration, Harrison died of pneumonia. His successor, John Tyler, was a former Democrat who had left the party to protest Jackson's nullification proclamation. Tyler turned out to be more of a Democrat than a Whig. He repeatedly vetoed Henry Clay's protective tariffs, internal improvements, and bills aimed at reviving the Bank of the United States. The only important measures that became law during his term were repeal of the independent treasury system and passage of a higher tariff. Two days after Tyler's second veto of a bank bill, the entire cabinet except Secretary of State Daniel Webster resigned; Webster, busy negotiating a new treaty with Great Britain, left shortly thereafter. Tyler became a president without a party, and the Whigs lost the presidency without losing an election.

Anglo-American Tensions

Hard times in the late 1830s and early 1840s deflected attention from a renewal of Anglo-American tensions that had multiple sources: northern commercial rivalry with Britain, the default of state governments and corporations on British-held debts during the Panic of 1837, rebellion in Canada, boundary disputes, southern alarm over West Indian emancipation, and American expansionism.

One problem disrupting Anglo-American relations was an old border dispute between Maine and New Brunswick. Great Britain had accepted an 1831 arbitration decision fixing a new boundary, but the U.S. Senate had rejected it. Thus when Canadian lumbermen cut trees in the disputed region in the winter of 1838–1839, the citizens of Maine attempted to expel them. The lumbermen captured a Maine land agent and posse, both sides mobilized their militias, and Congress authorized a call-up of fifty thousand men. Ultimately, no blood was spilled. General Winfield Scott was dispatched to Aroostook, Maine, where he arranged a truce. The two sides compromised on their conflicting land claims in the Webster-Ashburton Treaty (1842).

The border dispute with Great Britain prefigured the conflicts that were to erupt in the 1840s over the expansion of the United States. With Tyler's succession to power in 1841 and James K. Polk's Democratic victory in the presidential election of 1844, federal activism in the domestic sphere ended for the rest of the decade, as attention turned to territorial expansion.

Manifest Destiny and Expansionism

 The belief that American expansion westward and southward was inevitable, just, and divinely ordained was first labeled manifest destiny by John L. O'Sullivan, editor of the *United States Magazine and Domestic Review*. The annexation of Texas, O'Sullivan wrote in 1845, was "the fulfillment of our manifest destiny to overspread the continent allotted by Providence for the free development of our yearly multiplying millions."

Since colonial days Americans had hungered for more land. As the proportion of Americans living west of the Appalachians grew, both national parties joined the popular clamor for expansion. Agrarian Democrats sought western land to balance urbanization. Enterprising Whigs looked to the new commercial opportunities the West offered. Southerners envisioned the extension of slavery and more slave states.

Fierce national pride spurred the quest for land. Americans were convinced that theirs was the greatest country on earth, with a special role to play in the world. To Americans, expansionism promised to extend the benefits of a republican system of government to the unfortunate and the inferior.

In part, racism contributed to manifest destiny as well. The impulse to colonize and develop the West was based on the belief that Euro-Americans could use the land more productively than Native Americans or Hispanics. Euro-Americans viewed Native Americans and Hispanics as inferior peoples, best controlled or conquered. Thus the same racial attitudes that justified discrimination against black people and slavery supported expansion in the West.

Among the long-standing objectives of expansionists was Texas, which in addition to present-day Texas

Republic of Texas

included parts of Oklahoma, Kansas, Colorado, Wyoming, and New Mexico (see Map 11.1). After winning its independence from Spain in 1821, Mexico encouraged the development of its remote northern province, offering large tracts of land virtually free to U.S. settlers called *empresarios*. The settlers in turn agreed to become Mexican citizens, adopt the Catholic religion, and bring hundreds of American families into the area.

By 1835 thirty-five thousand Americans, including many slaveholders, lived in Texas. As the new settlers' numbers and power grew, they tended to ignore their commitments to the Mexican government. In response, the dictatorship of General Antonio López de Santa Anna tightened control over the region. In turn, the Anglo immigrants and *Tejanos*—Mexicans living in Texas—rebelled. At the Alamo mission in San Antonio in 1836, fewer than two hundred Texans made a heroic but unsuccessful stand against three thousand Mexicans under General Santa Anna. "Remember the Alamo" became the Texans' rallying cry. By the end of the year the Texans had won independence.

Texas established the independent Lone Star Republic but soon sought annexation to the United States. The issue, however, quickly became politically explosive. Southerners favored annexing proslavery Texas; abolitionists, many northerners, and most Whigs opposed annexation. In recognition of the political dangers, President Jackson reneged on his promise to recognize Texas, and President Van Buren ignored annexation. Texans then talked about closer ties with the British and extending their republic to the Pacific coast. President Tyler, concerned that a Texas alliance with Britain might threaten American independence and also hoping to gain southern support for an 1844 election bid, pressed for annexation.

Just as southerners sought expansion to the Southwest, so northerners looked to the Northwest. "Oregon fever" struck thousands in 1841.

Oregon Fever

Lured by the glowing reports of missionaries, migrants in wagon trains took to the Oregon Trail. The 2,000-mile journey took six months or more, but within a few years five thousand settlers had arrived in the fertile Willamette valley.

Britain and the United States had jointly occupied the disputed Oregon Territory since the Convention of 1818 (see page 160). Beginning with the administration of President John Quincy Adams, the United States had tried to fix the boundary at the 49th parallel, but Britain had refused. Time only increased the American appetite. In 1843 a Cincinnati convention of expansionists demanded the entire Oregon Country for the United States, up to its northernmost border at latitude 54°40'. Soon "Fifty-four Forty or Fight" became the rallying cry of American expansionists.

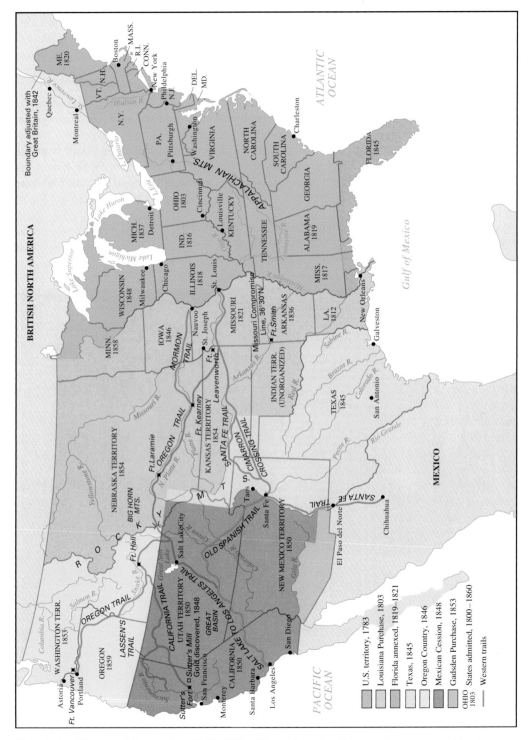

Map 11.1 Westward Expansion, 1800–1860 Through exploration, purchase, war, and treaty, the United States became a continental nation, stretching from the Atlantic to the Pacific.

Expansion into Oregon and rejection of the annexation of Texas, both favored by antislavery forces, worried southern leaders. Anxious

James K. Polk and the Election of 1844

about their diminishing ability to control the debate over slavery, they persuaded the 1844 Democratic convention to adopt a rule requiring the presidential nominee to receive two-thirds of the convention votes. In effect, the southern states acquired a veto, and they wielded it to block Van Buren as the nominee; most southerners objected to his opposition to slavery and Texas annexation. Instead, the party chose House Speaker James K. Polk, a hard-money Jacksonian, avid expansionist, and slaveholding cotton planter from Tennessee. Henry Clay, the Whig nominee, argued that the Democrats' belligerent nationalism would lead the nation into war with Great Britain or Mexico or both. Clay favored expansion through negotiation.

With a well-organized campaign, Polk won the election by 170 electoral votes to 105. (He won the popular vote by just 38,000 out of 2.7 million votes

An unknown artist depicted, in rich detail, the election campaign of 1844. A team of Polk supporters offers a campaign handbill to the seated voter. Passions were so high and party organization was so extensive that door-to-door politicking became the norm. (Courtesy, Nathan Liverant & Son)

cast.) Polk won New York's 36 electoral votes by just 6,000 popular votes. Abolitionist James G. Birney, the Liberty Party candidate, had drawn almost 16,000 votes away from Clay, handing New York and the election to Polk.

Interpreting Polk's victory as a mandate for annexation, President Tyler proposed in his final days in office that Texas be admitted by joint resolution of Congress. The resolution passed, and three days before leaving office, Tyler signed it. Mexico immediately broke relations with the United States. In October the citizens of Texas ratified annexation, and Texas joined the Union in December 1845.

Summary

 Religion, reform, and expansionism shaped politics from 1824 through the 1840s. As the Second Great Awakening spread through villages and towns, the converts, especially women, organized to reform a rapidly changing society. Religion imbued men and women with zeal to right the wrongs of American society and the world. Reformers pursued perfectionism and republican virtue by battling with the evils of slavery, prostitution, and alcohol. In the process, women entered public arenas as advocates of reform. Two issues elicited particular intensity: the comet of Antimasonry and the smoldering fire of abolitionism. The passions they aroused transformed moral crusades into political movements.

Reform remade politics and politics remade public discourse. So too did American nationalism and economic cycles. As did reformers, President Adams raised expectations about an expanded governmental role. The organized parties of the 1820s and the struggles between the National Republicans and the Democrats, then between the Democrats and the Whigs, stimulated even greater interest in campaigns and political issues. The Democrats, who rallied around Andrew Jackson, and Jackson's opponents, who found shelter under the Whig tent, competed almost equally for the loyalty of voters. Both parties favored economic expansion. Their world-views, however, were fundamentally different. Whigs were more optimistic and favored greater centralized government initiative. Democrats harbored a deep-seated belief in limited government.

No less than reform and politics, American people and communities experienced dramatic change in this period. As the nation became larger and its inhabitants more diverse, its manifest destiny divided rather than united, for along with expanding territories went the issue of slavery.

LEGACY FOR A PEOPLE AND A NATION
The Bible Belt

Had an eighteenth-century visitor to North America asked for the Bible belt, she would have been directed to New England. By the 1830s, however, the South was the most churched region. The Second Great Awakening spread like wildfire through the South. By the 1830s more than half of white and one-quarter of black southerners had undergone a conversion experience, and religion and the South formed a common identity. Embracing the Bible as the revealed word of God, the South became known as the Bible belt.

Religion helped define southern distinctiveness. Southern Protestant liturgy and cadences were as much African as European; thus southern and northern denominations grew apart. They formally separated in the 1840s when Southern Baptists and Methodists withdrew from the national organizations that had barred slaveowners from church offices. Presbyterians withdrew later. After the Civil War evangelical denominations remained divided into northern and southern organizations.

Southern religion maintained tradition and resisted modern ways. Mostly evangelical, it emphasized conversion and a personal battle against sin. By the twentieth century, fundamentalism, which stressed a literal reading of the Bible, reinforced resistance to modernism. Yet southern Protestantism lost ground as a political force in opposing evolution and in alliances with nativist groups.

But evangelicalism rose again in the 1960s, especially after a Catholic—John F. Kennedy—won the Democratic nomination for president. Many evangelicals began to vote their religion, moving to the Republican Party, and in 1964 Republican Barry Goldwater won the Bible belt states, breaking up the solid Democratic block. His conservative rhetoric resonated with southerners concerned about desegregation and erosion of religious values.

died of consumption only five weeks later. Then brother Gottlieb assumed the role of head of the family. Gottlieb and Daniel settled in Albany near Anna Maria and rode the roller coaster of the economy, prospering in good times, unemployed in hard times. Barbara moved to Indiana, where she married, became a widow, remarried, and raised seven "Christian children." Katharina married a prosperous grocer and lost contact with the family. Rosina moved to Canada but later returned to New York with her tinsmith husband and "a whole brood of children."

The Klingers represented both the old values of traditional culture and the new values of the market system. Anna Maria worked hard, saved money, and found success in Albany even though widowhood twice threatened her security. Barbara, an unwed mother, lived a hardscrabble life before finding peace in a German American rural community. Even after years in the United States, the Klinger siblings were only partially Americanized. They always lived in German neighborhoods, and they socialized almost exclusively with family and fellow German immigrants.

The Klinger family's experiences were similar to those of many immigrants. From the 1830s through the 1850s, millions of Europeans arrived on America's shores. Immigration added to the rapidly growing population and transformed the nation's character. Within large cities and in the countryside, whole districts became enclaves of ethnic and religious groups.

What it meant to be an American was obviously changing. European immigrants, slaves, free people of color, Hispanics, and Indians had cultural traditions different from those of the American colonial past. Increasingly some white Americans came to see the differences as racial rather than cultural. And as society became increasingly more diverse and complex, conflict became common.

The market economy both energized and accentuated the differences among Americans. In the nation's cities, both wealth and poverty reached extremes unknown in agrarian communities. As in the past, Americans sought community in their neighborhoods, not in the nation, but ethnic background, race, religion, and class divided Americans. Farm families attempted to maintain cohesive rural villages, while utopians and groups like the Mormons sought to create self-governing communal havens.

The market economy altered family life too. With the growth of commerce and industry, the home began to lose its function as a workplace. Goods formerly made at home were now mass-manufactured in factories and bought in stores. Public schools took over much of the family's traditional role as prime educator. Leisure, too, became a commodity to be purchased by those who could afford it. Families shrank in size, and more people lived outside family units. ◼

Country Life

 Rural life changed significantly in the first half of the nineteenth century. Established rural communities lost population as families went west in search of more fertile and cheaper land. New communities in the West arose almost overnight, linked by the new transportation networks to the markets of the East. European immigrants and free people of color from the East and Upper South joined the population stream seeking farmland in the prairies.

The farm village, with its churches, post office, general store, railroad or wagon depot, and tavern, remained the center of rural life. Com-

Farm Communities

munal values still ruled. Families gathered on one another's farms to accomplish as a community what they could not manage individually. Barn-raisings regularly brought people together. A farm family, with the help of an itinerant carpenter, would prepare the walls. The neighbors would come by buggy to help the family raise the walls into position and build a roof. Afterward everyone celebrated with a hearty communal feast and sang, danced, and played games. Similar gatherings took place at harvest time and on special occasions.

Farm men and women had active social lives. Men met frequently at general stores, weekly markets, and taverns, and hunted and fished together. Some women also attended market, especially those engaged in dairy farming. More typically they met at after-church dinners, prayer groups, sewing and corn-husking bees, and quilting parties. These were cherished opportunities to exchange experiences, thoughts, and spiritual support, and to swap letters, books, and news.

Traditional country bees had their town counterparts. Fredrika Bremer, a Swedish visitor, described a

IMPORTANT EVENTS

1830	Smith founds Mormon Church
	First National Negro Convention
1830s–50s	Urban riots commonplace
1832	Rice debuts in New York minstrel show
1835	Arkansas passes first women's property law
1837	Boston employs paid policemen
1837–48	Mann heads the Massachusetts Board of Education
1838	Mormons driven out of Missouri
1841–47	Brook Farm combines spirituality, work, and play in a utopian rural community
1842	Knickerbocker baseball club formed
1844	Smith brothers murdered in Illinois
1845	Irish potato blight begins
	Narrative of the Life of Frederick Douglass appears
1846–47	Mormon trek to the Great Salt Lake
1847–57	Immigration at peak pre–Civil War levels
1848	U.S. acquires Alta California in Treaty of Guadalupe Hidalgo
	Gold discovered in California
1849	California gold rush transforms the West Coast
1852	Stowe's *Uncle Tom's Cabin* published
1854	Large-scale Chinese immigration begins
1855	New York establishes Castle Garden as immigrant center

sewing bee in Cambridge, Massachusetts, in 1849, at which neighborhood women made clothes for "a family who had lost all their clothing by fire." Yet town bees were not the all-day family affairs of the countryside, and those who moved from farm to town missed the country gatherings. In town, people were wage earners and consumers, and the market economy shaped and controlled their daily lives.

Americans were increasingly conscious of such changes, and a few resisted, seeking to avoid the untamed growth of cities and, in utopian rural communities, to restore traditional work tasks and social cohesion. The religious ferment of the Second Great Awakening (see pages 179–180) promoted new religious communities as well. Virtually all these communities broke with tradition by experimenting with communal living, innovative (sometimes shocking) family arrangements, and more egalitarian gender roles in a cooperative rather than competitive environment.

The Shakers, the largest of the communal utopian experiments, reached their peak between 1820 and 1860. During those years, six thousand members lived in twenty settlements in eight states. Founder Ann Lee had brought the sect to America in 1774. Named for the way they danced at worship

Shakers

services, the Shakers believed that the end of the world was near and that sin entered the world through sexual intercourse. They viewed the Shaker community as the instrument of salvation.

Though economically conservative, the Shakers were social radicals. They abolished individual families, practiced celibacy, and elected women leaders. During its period of greatest growth, Lucy Wright headed the Shaker ministry.

The most widespread communitarian group was the Church of Jesus Christ of Latter-day Saints, known as the Mormons. During the religious ferment of the 1820s, Joseph Smith, a young farmer in western New York, reported that an angel called Moroni had visited him and given him engraved divine gold plates. Smith published his revelations as the *Book of Mormon* and organized a church in western New York in 1830. The next year they moved west to Ohio to await the second coming of Jesus. Angry mobs drove them from Ohio, and in 1838 the governor of Missouri gathered evidence to indict Smith and other Mormon leaders for treason.

Mormon Community of Saints

Joseph Smith and his followers then resettled in Nauvoo, Illinois. The state legislature gave them a city charter, which made them self-governing, and

The Lackawanna Valley (1855) by George Inness. Hired by the Lackawanna Railroad to paint a picture showing the company's new roundhouse at Scranton, in northeastern Pennsylvania, Inness combined landscape and locomotive technology into an organic whole. Industrialism, Inness seems to say, belonged to the American landscape; it would neither overpower nor obliterate the land.   (Gift of Mrs. Huttleston Rogers, © Board of Trustees, National Gallery of Art, Washington, D.C.)

authorized a local militia. After 1841, when Smith introduced the practice of polygamy, opponents became furious. In 1842 Smith became mayor, and this consolidation of religious and political power antagonized opponents further. They faced their worst fears when in 1843 Nauvoo petitioned the federal government to be a self-governing territory. In 1844 the authorities indicted Smith and others for plotting to murder their opponents, but the Nauvoo courts released them. Then Joseph and his brother Hyrum were arrested for treason and jailed in Carthage, Illinois. The militia from Warsaw, Nauvoo's neighbor, stormed the jail and killed the two brothers. The next year the Mormons began a trek westward and found a home in the Great Salt Lake valley. There, under Brigham Young, head of the Twelve Apostles (the Mormons' governing body), they established a patriarchal, cooperative "community of saints." They found in the distant desert West both religious freedom and political autonomy.

In Utah the Mormons distributed agricultural land according to family size. An extensive irrigation system, constructed by men who contributed their labor in proportion to the quantity of land they received and the amount of water they expected to use, transformed the arid valley into a rich oasis. As the colony developed, the church elders gained control of water, trade, industry, and eventually the territorial government of Utah.

Not all utopian communities gravitated to the wilderness. The Brook Farm cooperative in West Roxbury, Massachusetts, near Boston,

Brook Farm

had a lasting impact, although its achievements were more artistic than economic. Inspired by transcendentalism—the belief that the physical world is secondary to the spiritual realm—Brook Farm's members rejected materialism in favor of rural communalism, combining spirituality, manual labor, intellectual life, and play.

Though short-lived (1841–1847), Brook Farm played a significant role in the flowering of a national literature. During these years Nathaniel Hawthorne, Ralph Waldo Emerson, and *Dial* (the leading transcendentalist journal) editor Margaret Fuller joined Henry David Thoreau, Herman Melville, and others in a literary outpouring known today as the American Renaissance. In philosophical intensity and moral idealism, their work was both distinctively American and an outgrowth of the European romantic movement. Their themes were universal, their settings and characters American.

The essayist Ralph Waldo Emerson was the prime mover of the American Renaissance and a pillar of the transcendental movement. "We live

Ralph Waldo Emerson

in succession, in division, in parts, in particles," Emerson wrote. "We see the world piece by piece, as the sun, the moon, the animal, the tree; but the whole, of which these are the shining parts, is the soul." Intuitive experience of God is attainable, insisted Emerson, because "the Highest dwells" within every individual in the form of the "Over-soul."

Utopian communities can be seen as attempts to recapture the cohesiveness of traditional agricultural and artisan life in reaction to the competitive pressures of the market economy and urbanization. Utopians resembled Puritan perfectionists; like the Separatists of seventeenth-century New England (see page 32), they sought to begin anew in their own colonies.

The West

In the 1840s a trickling stream of migrants followed the Oregon Trail to the West Coast. Then, in 1848, gold was discovered in California. The next year a pioneer observed that the Oregon Trail "bore no evidence of having been much traveled." Traffic flowed south instead, and California became the new population center on the Pacific slope.

When the United States acquired Alta California from Mexico in the 1848 Treaty of Guadalupe Hidalgo,

Discovery of Gold

the province was inhabited mostly by Indians, with some Mexicans living on large estates. A chain of small settlements surrounded military forts (*presidios*) and missions. That changed almost overnight after James Marshall, a carpenter, spotted gold particles in the millrace at Sutter's Mill (now Coloma, California, northwest of Sacramento) in January 1848. Word of the discovery spread, and Californians rushed to scrabble for instant fortunes.

By 1849 the news had sped around the world, and hundreds of thousands of fortune seekers, mostly young men, streamed into California. Gold mining seemed to offer them instant riches, and indeed, some made fortunes. Most "forty-niners," however, never found enough gold to pay their expenses. "The stories you hear frequently in the States," one gold seeker wrote home, "are the most extravagant lies imaginable—the mines are a humbug." Another gold seeker called gold mining "Nature's Great Lottery scheme." Many found work in California's cities and agricultural districts more profitable. Meanwhile, enterprising merchants rushed to supply, feed, and clothe the new settlers. One such merchant was Levi Strauss, a German Jewish immigrant, whose tough mining pants found a ready market among the prospectors.

The forty-niners had to be fed. Thus began the great California agricultural boom. Farmers preferred

Farming

wheat; it required minimal investment, was easily planted, and offered a quick return at the end of a relatively short growing season. California farmers eagerly imported horse-drawn machines, since labor was scarce (and expensive). By the mid-1850s, California exported wheat and had become firmly linked, through commerce, to the rest of the United States. Farmers on the West Coast cleared the land and, because success often depended on their access to water, sought to divert streams and rivers to irrigate their land.

In contrast to the Midwest, where family farms were the basic unit of production, in California men

Women Settlers dominated mining, grazing, and large-scale wheat farming. Most men came alone, drawn by a sense of adventure and personal opportunity. Women who accompanied their husbands—only one-seventh of the travelers on the overland trails were women—experienced the migration differently. Their lives drastically changed as they left behind networks of friends and kin to journey, often with children, along an unknown and hazardous path to a strange environment. Yet in the West their domestic skills were in great demand. They received high fees for cooking, laundering, and sewing, and they ran boarding houses and hotels.

City Life

 When Anna Maria Klinger arrived in America in 1849, she was part of an urbanizing trend. Between 1830 and 1860, cities expanded geometrically. Europeans spread westward, and small rural settlements quickly became towns. In 1830 the nation had only 23 cities with 10,000 or more people and only 7 with more than 25,000. By 1860, 93 towns exceeded 10,000, 35 towns had more than 25,000, and 9 exceeded 100,000 (see Map 12.1).

Some cities became great metropolitan centers. By 1830 New York City had been the nation's most populous city and major commercial center for twenty years. At midcentury Baltimore and New Orleans dominated the South, and San Francisco was the leading West Coast city. In the Midwest, the new lake cities (Chicago, Detroit, and Cleveland) began to pass the frontier river cities (Cincinnati, Louisville, and Pittsburgh) founded a generation earlier.

As the nation's premier city, New York grew from 202,000 people in 1830 to over 814,000 in 1860. The **New York City** immigrant port city was mostly Irish and German by the 1850s. Across the East River, Brooklyn tripled in size between 1850 and 1860, becoming the nation's third-largest city, with a population of 279,000. Many people were short-term residents of the two cities; the majority did not stay ten years. Thus New York was ever changing, full of energy, reeking of sweat, horse dung, and garbage—and above all, teeming with people.

By modern standards nineteenth-century cities were disorderly, unsafe, and unhealthy. Expansion occurred so rapidly that few cities could **Urban Problems** handle the problems it brought. For example, migrants from rural areas were accustomed to relieving themselves outside and throwing refuse in any vacant area. In the city, such waste smelled, spread disease, and polluted water. New York City partially solved the problem in the 1840s by abandoning wells in favor of reservoir water piped into buildings and outdoor fountains. In some districts, scavengers and refuse collectors carted away garbage and human waste, but in much of the city it just rotted on the ground. Only one-quarter of New York City's streets had sewers by 1857.

New York and other cities lacked adequate taxing power to provide services for all. The best the city could do was to tax property adjoining new sewers, paved streets, and water mains. Thus basic services depended on residents' ability to pay. As a result, those most in need of services got them last. Another solution was to charter private companies to sell basic services. This plan worked well with gas service used for lights. Baltimore first chartered a private gas company in 1816; by midcentury every major city was lit by a private gas supplier. The private sector, however, lacked the economic means to build adequate water systems. City governments therefore had to assume that responsibility.

Cities led in offering public education. In 1800 there were no public schools outside New England; by 1860 every state offered some public **Horace Mann and Public Schools** education to whites. Under Horace Mann, secretary of the state board of education from 1837 to 1848, Massachusetts led the way. It established a minimum school year of six months and formalized the training of teachers.

Mann's preaching on behalf of free, state-sponsored education changed schooling throughout the nation. "If we do not prepare children to become good citizens," Mann argued, "if we do not develop their capacities, . . . then our republic must go down to destruction." Universal education, Mann proposed, would end misery, crime, and suffering. Mann and others were responding to the changes wrought by the market economy, urbanization, and immigration. The

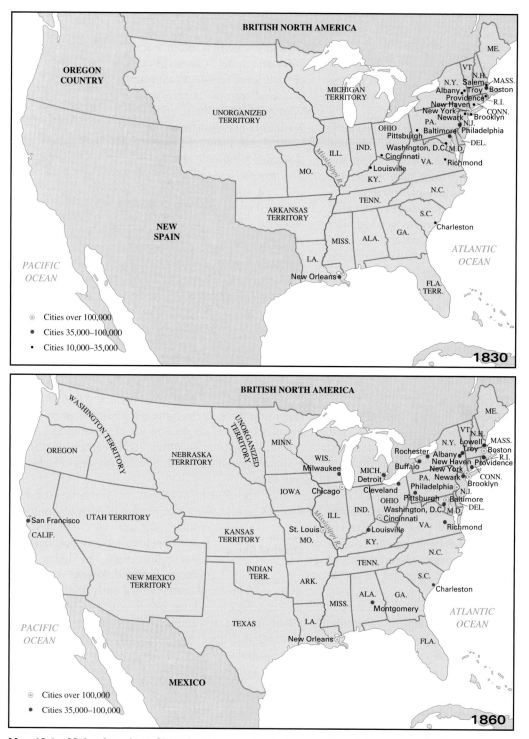

Map 12.1 Major American Cities in 1830 and 1860 The number of Americans who lived in cities increased rapidly between 1830 and 1860, and the number of large cities grew as well. In 1830 only New York City had a population exceeding one hundred thousand; thirty years later, eight more cities had surpassed that level.

typical city dweller was a newcomer, whether from abroad or from the country. Public schools would take the children of strangers and give them shared values. But the system was distinctly racialized; few states included free black children in public schools.

Free public schools altered the scope of education. Schooling previously had focused on literacy, religious training, and discipline. Under Mann's leadership, the curriculum became more secular and appropriate for future clerks, farmers, and workers of America. Students studied geography, American history, arithmetic, and science. Schools retained moral education, but they dropped direct religious indoctrination.

Catholics, immigrants, blacks, and working-class people sought to control their own schools, but the state legislatures established secular statewide standards under Protestant educators. Catholics in New York responded by building their own educational system over the next half-century. When Los Angeles became a city in 1850, it attempted to establish bilingual Spanish-English instruction, but the idea was dropped because trained bilingual teachers could not be found.

Towns and cities created new patterns of leisure as well as work. In rural society both social activities and work often took place at home. But

Leisure

in cities, dedicated spaces—streets, theaters, sports fields—constituted a social sphere where people could come together away from home. Through the sale of admission tickets or membership in associations, leisure became a commodity to be purchased. Even in cities, however, some traditional rural pursuits continued. Fishing remained popular, men played games of strength and skill in taverns, and churches served as social centers.

Americans also read more. Thanks to the expansion of public education, the vast majority of native-born white Americans were literate

Reading

by the 1850s. For the reading public, fiction and autobiographies competed with religious tracts as popular literature. Newspapers and magazines printed fiction, and bookstores and stationers in large cities sold novels and autobiographies. Frederick Douglass's powerful attack on slavery in the *Narrative of the Life of Frederick Douglass, an American Slave, Written by Himself* (1845) sold widely. Many popular novels, some

written by women, often for women, were set in the home and upheld Christian values. Yet in their support of traditional female moral roles, they also can be read as a challenge to prevailing values. Although Susan Warner's *The Wide, Wide, Wide World* (1850), Nathaniel Hawthorne's *The House of the Seven Gables* (1851), and Fanny Fern's *Ruth Hall* (1855) did not challenge women's traditional domestic roles, they gave women a special moral bearing. In giving a positive cast to notions of community and republican virtue, they implicitly criticized the growing market economy. By the 1850s popular fiction circulated widely. Harriet Beecher Stowe's antislavery novel, *Uncle Tom's Cabin, or Life Among the Lowly* (1852), sold 300,000 copies in book form in its first year.

A theater was often the second public building constructed in a town—after a church. Large cities boasted two or more theaters catering

Theater

to different classes. Some plays cut across class lines. Shakespeare was performed so often and appreciated so widely that even illiterate theatergoers knew his plays well. In the 1840s musical and dramatic presentations took on a more professional tone; newly popular minstrel shows and traveling circuses offered carefully rehearsed routines. Dancing and music remained popular and took new forms, as in blackfaced minstrelsy.

By the 1840s hundreds of traveling minstrel troupes presented a white version of African American culture. Minstrel acts had first appeared twenty or thirty years earlier,

Minstrel Show

when white men, in burnt cork makeup, imitated African Americans in song, dance, and patter. In the early 1830s Thomas D. Rice of New York became famous for his role as Jim Crow, an old southern slave. In ill-fitting patched clothing and torn shoes, the blackface Rice shuffled, danced, and sang on stage.

Minstrelsy stereotyped black people by exaggerating physical features. It also portrayed African Americans as being sensual and lazy. The fictional representation of blacks on stage not only defined "blackness" but also defined "whiteness." Whiteness as a racial category took on meaning as laughing white audiences distinguished themselves from the black characters.

The net effect was to stoke the fires of racism and thereby further the growing racial tensions in the United States.

Increasingly, urban recreation and sports became more formal commodities to be purchased. One had to buy a ticket to go to the theater, the circus, the racetrack, or the ballpark.

Sports

Spectator sports became increasingly popular. In addition to horseracing, boxing and baseball became popular spectator sports. News of an 1849 Maryland boxing match was so much in demand that a round-by-round account of the fight was telegraphed throughout the East. And in the 1850s, baseball began to attract large urban male crowds. In 1845 the rules for the game were drawn up by the Knickerbocker Club.

Ironically, public leisure soon developed a private dimension. Exclusive private associations arose to provide space and occasions for leisure set apart from the crowds and rowdiness of public events. At the same time that old-stock middle- and upperclass Americans were isolating themselves, members of various ethnic, racial, and religious groups formed their own associations. The Irish formed the Hibernian Society, the Germans brought Turnvereine physical-cultural clubs across the Atlantic, Jews founded B'nai B'rith, and African Americans started chapters of the Prince Hall Masons in their communities.

City Culture

A youth culture emerged on New York's Bowery, an entertainment strip, in the 1840s. Older New Yorkers feared the "Bowery boys and gals," whose ostentatious dress and behavior seemed threatening to them. A Bowery boy had long hair, often greased into a roll. He wore a broad-brimmed black hat and as much jewelry as he could afford. His swaggering gait, especially when he had a girlfriend on his arm, frightened many in the middle class. Equally disturbing to old New Yorkers were the young working women who strolled the Bowery. Unlike more genteel ladies, who wore modest veils or bonnets, Bowery "gals" drew attention to themselves with outlandish costumes and ornate hats.

Most working people spent much of their lives outdoors; they worked in the streets as laborers, shopped in open markets, and paraded on special occasions. Young people courted, neighbors argued, and ethnic and racial groups defended their turf on the streets. Increasingly, urban streets served as a political arena as crowds formed to listen to speakers, to respond and to demonstrate, and sometimes to take mob action.

In the 1830s riots became commonplace as professionals, merchants, craftsmen, and laborers vented their rage against political and economic rivals. "Gentlemen of property and standing," unnerved by antislavery proponents, sacked abolitionist and antislavery organizations, even murdering newspaper editor Elijah Lovejoy in Alton, Illinois, in 1837. In the 1840s "respectable" citizens drove the Mormons out of Missouri and Illinois. In Philadelphia native-born workers attacked Irish weavers in 1828, and whites and blacks fought on the docks in 1834 and 1835. Philadelphia's riots came to a head in 1844 when mostly Protestant skilled workers attacked Irish Catholics. Smaller cities, too, became battlegrounds as nativist riots peaked in the 1850s. By 1840 more than 125 people had died in urban riots, and by 1860 fatalities exceeded 1,000.

Urban Riots

As public disorder spread, Boston hired uniformed policemen in 1837 to supplement its part-time watchmen and constables, and New York in 1845 established a uniformed force. Nonetheless, middle-class city dwellers did not venture out alone at night. Ironically, in the midst of so much noise, crime, and conflict, the lavish uptown residences of the very rich rose like an affront to those struggling to survive.

Extremes of Wealth

The French nobleman Alexis de Tocqueville in the 1830s characterized the United States as primarily a place of equality and opportunity for white males. Tocqueville attributed American equality—the relative fluidity of the social order—to Americans' mobility and restlessness. Geographic mobility, he felt, offered people a chance to start anew regardless of where they came from or who they were.

Others disagreed with this egalitarian view of American life. *New York Sun* publisher Moses Yale Beach believed a new aristocracy based on wealth and power was forming. Author of twelve editions of *Wealth and Biography of the Wealthy Citizens of New York*

"If Not an Aristocracy"

City, Beach listed 750 New Yorkers with assets of $100,000 or more in 1845. John Jacob Astor, with a fortune of $25 million, led the list of nineteen millionaires. Ten years later, Beach reported more than a thousand New Yorkers worth $100,000, among them twenty-eight millionaires. Tocqueville himself, sensitive to conflicting trends in American life, had described the new industrial wealth. The rich and well educated "come forward to exploit industries," Tocqueville wrote, and become "more and more like the administrators of a huge empire. . . . What is this if not an aristocracy?"

Wealth throughout the United States was becoming concentrated in the hands of a relatively small number of people. In New York City between 1828 and 1845, the richest 4 percent of the city's population increased their holdings from an estimated 63 percent to 80 percent of all individual wealth. By 1860 the top 5 percent of American families owned more than half of the nation's wealth.

A cloud of uncertainty hovered over working men and women. Many feared hard times and resented the competition of immigrant and slave labor. They dreaded poverty, chronic illness, disability, old age, widowhood, and desertion. Women feared raising a family without a spouse. And they had good reason: few women could find a job that paid enough to support a family.

Urban Poverty

Poverty dogged the urban working class. Newly arrived immigrants, free blacks, the working poor, and thieves, beggars, and prostitutes eked out a living in urban slums. New York City's Five Points reflected the worst of urban life. The predominantly immigrant Irish and black neighborhood lacked running water and sewers and was notorious for its squalor. More than a thousand people lived in the rooms, cellars, and

A visible sign of urban poverty in the 1850s was the homeless and orphaned children, most of them immigrants, who wandered the streets of New York City. The Home for the Friendless Orphanage, at Twenty-ninth Street and Madison Avenue, provided shelter for some of the orphan girls. (© Collection of The New-York Historical Society)

John Lewis Krimmel painted this portrait of himself and his sister-in-law and her children around 1812. It shows a prosperous middle-class Philadelphia German family that had been in the United States around five years. The dress and home of the Krimmel children stand in sharp contrast to the homeless and orphaned children of New York City.   (The Warner Collection of Gulf States Paper Corporation, Tuscaloosa, Alabama. Photo courtesy of The Schwarz Gallery, Philadelphia)

subcellars of the converted Old Brewery, which dominated the neighborhood. Throughout the city, houses for two families often held four; tenements built for six families held twelve.

A world apart from Five Points and the people of the streets, though only a short walk away, lived the upper-class elite society of Philip Hone, one-time mayor of New York. Hone's diary, meticulously kept from 1826 until his death in 1851, records the life of an American aristocrat. On February 28, 1840, for instance, Hone attended a masked ball at the Fifth Avenue mansion of Henry Breevoort, Jr., and Laura Carson Breevoort. The ball began at the fashionable hour of 10 P.M., and the five hundred invited ladies and gentlemen wore costumes adorned with er-

The Urban Elite

mine and gold. Similar parties were held in Boston, Philadelphia, Baltimore, and Charleston.

Much of this wealth was inherited. For every John Jacob Astor who made millions in the western fur trade, ten others had inherited or married money. Many of the wealthiest New Yorkers bore the names of the colonial commercial elite: Breevoort, Roosevelt, Van Rensselaer, and Whitney. These rich New Yorkers were not idle; they worked at increasing their fortunes and power by investing in commerce and manufacturing. Wealth begat wealth, and marriage cemented family ties.

Meanwhile, a distinct middle class appeared on the urban scene, and the growth and specialization of trade rapidly increased their numbers. Middle-class families enjoyed the new consumer items: wool carpeting, fine

The Middle Class wallpaper, rooms full of furniture, and indoor toilets. They filled the family pews in church on Sundays; their children pursued whatever educational opportunities were available. They were as distant from Philip Hone's world as they were from the milieu of the working class and the poor. Increasingly they looked to the family and home as the core of middle-class life.

Women, Families, and the Domestic Ideal

 Men dominated American families. English common law gave husbands absolute control over the family. The men owned their wives' personal property; they were legal guardians of the children; and they owned whatever family members produced or earned. Married women, however, began making modest gains in property and spousal rights in the 1830s. Arkansas in 1835 passed the first married women's property law, and by 1860 sixteen more states had followed suit. In those states, women—single, married, or widowed—could own and convey property. When a wife inherited, earned, or acquired property, it was hers, not her husband's; and she could write a will. In the 1830s states began to liberalize divorce, adding cruelty and desertion as grounds for divorce. Nonetheless divorce was rare.

As the urban workplace and home became separate entities, men worked for wages outside the home, and so did their offspring. In New England daughters left farms to work in textile mills, sons to work in urban commerce. In the 1840s the new urban department stores hired young women as clerks and cash runners. Many women worked for a time as teachers, usually for two to five years. But paid employment typically represented a brief stage in women's lives before they left their parental households and entered their marital households.

Supporting Families

Working-class women—the poor, widows, and free blacks—worked to support themselves and their families. Leaving their parental homes as early as age twelve, they earned wages most of their lives, with only short respites for bearing and rearing children. But unlike men and New England farm daughters, most of these women did not work in the new shops and factories. Instead, they worked as domestic servants and as laundresses, seamstresses, and cooks. Few of these occupations enabled them to support themselves or a family at a respectable level.

Most women continued to perform unpaid labor in the home. As the urban family lost its role in the production of goods, household upkeep and child rearing claimed women's full-time attention. Religion, morality, domestic arts, and music and literature filled the void left by the decline in the economic functions of the family; these realms came to be known as woman's sphere. A woman who achieved mastery in these areas lived up to the middle-class ideal of the cult of domesticity.

Middle-class Americans idealized the family as a moral institution characterized by selflessness and cooperation. The world of work—the market economy—was seen as an arena of conflict increasingly identified with men and dominated by base self-interest. In a rapidly changing world, the family represented stability and traditional values. The domestic ideal restricted the range of paying jobs available to middle-class women. One occupation was considered consonant with the genteel female role: teaching. In 1823 the Beecher sisters, Catharine and Mary, established the Hartford Female Seminary and offered history and science in addition to the traditional women's curriculum of domestic arts and religion. A decade later Catharine Beecher successfully campaigned for teacher-training schools for women. By 1850 school teaching had become a woman's profession. Most urban teachers were unmarried women, who earned about half the salary of male teachers.

Idealizing the Family

Meanwhile, family size was shrinking. In 1830 American women bore an average of five or six children; by 1860 the figure had dropped to five. This decline occurred even though many immigrants with large-family traditions were settling in the United States; thus the birth rate among native-born women declined even more steeply.

Decline in Family Size

A number of factors reduced family size. Small families were viewed as increasingly desirable in an economy in which the family was a unit of consumption rather than production. Children in smaller families would have greater opportunities: parents could give them more attention, better education, and more financial help. Evidence suggests many wives and husbands made deliberate decisions to limit the size of families.

How did men and women limit their families in the early nineteenth century? Average age at marriage rose, thus shortening the period of potential childbearing. Women also bore their last child at a younger age, dropping from around forty in the mid-eighteenth century to around thirty-five in the mid-nineteenth. This change suggests family planning. Many couples used traditional forms of birth control, such as coitus interruptus (withdrawal of the male before completion of the sexual act) and breast-feeding, which makes some women temporarily infertile. Some couples used the rhythm method—attempting to confine intercourse to a woman's infertile periods. Awareness of the "safe period," however, was uncertain, even among physicians. Others used cheap rubber condoms. If all else failed, women resorted to abortions, especially after 1830. By 1860, however, twenty states either restricted or outlawed abortions.

Limiting Families

Significantly, the birth-control methods that women themselves controlled—the rhythm method, abstinence, and abortion—became increasingly common. The new emphasis on domesticity encouraged women's autonomy in the home and by extension gave them greater control over their own bodies. Women ruled the household, including the bedroom, with refinement and purity.

Urban life always offered a place for men outside families. Rooming and boarding houses provided them with places to live. The expansion of cities and the market economy offered independence for women outside families as well. Single women departed from the centuries-old pattern in which a woman moved from her father's to her husband's household. Louisa May Alcott (1832–1888), the author of *Little Women* (1868), sought independence and financial security for herself. Alcott worked as a seamstress, governess, teacher, and housemaid before her writing brought her success. "I think I shall

Single Men and Women

come out right, and prove that . . . I can support myself," she wrote her father in 1856. "I like the independent feeling; and though not an easy life, it is a free one, and I enjoy it."

Louisa May Alcott forswore marriage. She and other unmarried women pursued careers and lives defined by female relationships. Given the difficulty women had finding ways to support themselves, they undertook independence at great risk. Nonetheless, the proportion of single women in the population increased significantly in the nineteenth century. Independent white women, in sum, were taking advantage of new opportunities offered by the market economy and urban expansion.

Immigrant Lives in America

The 5 million immigrants who came to the United States between 1830 and 1860 outnumbered the entire population of the country recorded in the first census in 1790. The vast majority were European (see Figure 12.1). During the peak period of pre–Civil War immigration, from 1847 through 1857, 3.3 million immigrants entered the United States; 1.3 million were from Ireland and 1.1 million, like the Klingers, came from the German states. By 1860, 15 percent of the white population was foreign-born.

This massive migration had been set in motion decades earlier. At the turn of the nineteenth century, the Napoleonic wars gave rise to one of the greatest population shifts in history; ultimately it lasted more than a century. War, revolution, famine, religious persecution, and the lure of industrialization led many Europeans to leave home. From the other side of the world, 41,000 Chinese, nearly all men, entered the United States from 1854 through 1860 to work mostly in heavy construction. The United States attracted immigrants as its economy offered jobs and its Constitution protected religious freedom.

The market economy needed workers. Large construction projects and massive mining operations sought strong young men, and textile mills sought young women. Both private firms and governments recruited European immigrants. Midwestern and western states lured potential settlers

Promotion of Immigration

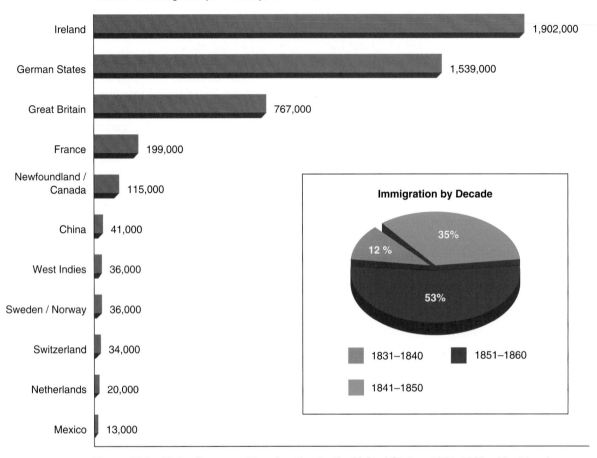

Figure 12.1 Major Sources of Immigration to the United States, 1831–1860 Most immigrants came from two areas: Great Britain, of which Ireland was a part, and the German states. These two areas sent more immigrants between 1830 and 1860 than the inhabitants of the United States enumerated at the first census in 1790. By 1860, 15 percent of the white population was of foreign birth. (Source: Data from Stephan Thernstrom, ed., *Harvard Encyclopedia of American Ethnic Groups* [Cambridge, Mass., and London: Harvard University Press, 1980], 1047.)

to promote economic growth. In the 1850s Wisconsin appointed a commissioner of emigration, who advertised the state's advantages in European newspapers. Wisconsin also opened an office in New York and hired European agents to compete with other states and with firms like the Illinois Central Railroad in recruiting immigrants. Europeans' awareness of the United States grew as employers, states, and shipping companies promoted opportunities across the Atlantic. Often the message was stark: work and prosper in America or starve in Europe. The price of a ticket on the regularly scheduled sailing ships crossing the ocean after 1848 was within easy reach of millions of Europeans.

These immigrants endured the hardships of travel and of living in a strange land. The average transatlantic crossing took six weeks; in bad weather it could take three months. Disease spread unchecked among people packed together like cattle in steerage. More than seventeen thousand immigrants, mostly Irish, died from "ship fever" in 1847. On arrival, con artists and swindlers preyed on the newcomers. In response, New York State established Castle Garden as an immigrant center in 1855. There, at the tip of Manhattan Island, the major port for European entry, immigrants were somewhat sheltered from fraud. Authorized transportation companies maintained offices in the large rotunda and assisted new arrivals with their travel plans.

Most immigrants gravitated toward cities, and many stayed in New York City itself. By 1855, 52 percent of its 623,000 inhabitants were immigrants, 28 percent from Ireland and 16 percent from the German states. Boston also took on a European tone; throughout the 1850s the city was about 35 percent foreign-born, of whom more than two-thirds were Irish. In the West, St. Louis's population was 61 percent foreign-born and San Francisco had a foreign-born majority.

Settling In

Some immigrants settled in rural areas. German, Dutch, and Scandinavian farmers, in particular, headed toward the Midwest. Greater percentages of Scandinavians and Netherlanders took up farming than did other nationalities; both groups came mostly as religious dissenters and migrated in family units. The Dutch who founded colonies in Michigan and Wisconsin, for instance, had seceded from the official Reformed Church of the Netherlands, fleeing persecution in their native land to establish new and more pious communities such as Holland and Zeeland in Michigan.

Not all immigrants found success in the United States; hundreds of thousands returned to their homelands disappointed. Before the famines of the late 1840s hit Ireland, American recruiters had lured many Irish to swing picks and shovels on American canals and railroads and to work in construction. The promise that "he should soon become a wealthy man" lured Michael Gaugin, who had worked for thirteen years as an assistant engineer in the construction of a Dublin canal. The Irish agent for a New York firm convinced him to quit his job, which included a house and an acre of ground, to come to America. But Gaugin landed in New York City during the financial panic of 1837. He could not find work,

Immigrant Disenchantment

and within two months he was broke, struggling to find the means to return to Ireland.

Before the great famine, caused by a blight that turned the potato crop—Ireland's food staple—rotten and inedible, there had been a small but steady stream of migration from Ireland to the United States. From 1845 to 1849, death from starvation, malnutrition, and typhus spread in Ireland. In all, 1 million died and about 1.5 million fled, two-thirds of them to the United States. Ireland's major export became its people. In every year but one between 1830 and 1854, the Irish constituted the largest group of immigrants.

Irish Immigrants

Most of the new immigrants from Ireland were young, female, poor, from rural counties, and Roman Catholic. In America, the women found work in textile mills and households. Young Irishmen worked in transportation and construction. The Irish supported their families back home and in Irish enclaves in cities, built Catholic churches and schools, and established networks of charitable and social organizations.

This wave of Irish immigrants, descended from the ancient Celts who spoke Gaelic, differed greatly from the Irish who had migrated earlier to the American colonies. In the eighteenth century, the Protestant Scots-Irish predominated; they were considered British. But the Celts were considered inferior. The British had thought them barbaric, and colonists carried those views to America. Dr. Robert Knox of the Edinburgh College of Surgeons believed the British stood for liberty, whereas "the source of all evil lies in the race, the Celtic race of Ireland." Many Americans agreed. They talked about Celtic racial characteristics: a small upturned nose, high forehead, and black tint of skin. As scientists like Knox began to classify peoples into biological types, scientific theory buttressed the developing notion of race.

Racial Ideas

With the immigration of new groups to the United States—Celts, Jews, and Catholics, for instance—with the black population expanding, and with territorial expansion bringing Hispanics and more Indians into the United States as well, native-born white Americans were increasingly confronted with people who did not look like them. Many considered these non-British, non-European, non-Protestant people separate races, distinct from their own. Ralph Waldo Emerson asserted the importance of race in *English Traits* (1856). To Emerson, as a son inherits his ancestors' "every mental and moral property," so too does a race pass on to its members its physical, intellectual, and moral characteristics. "Race avails . . . that all Celts are Catholics," Emerson wrote. "Race is a controlling influence in the Jew. . . . Race in the negro (sic) is of appalling importance."

Closely related to racial stereotyping in its causes and nasty effects was anti-Catholicism, which became strident in the 1830s and was most

Anti-Catholicism

overt and cruel in Boston, where a great many Irish had settled. Anti-Catholic riots were almost commonplace. In Lawrence, Massachusetts, for instance, a mob leveled the Irish neighborhood in 1854.

The native-born whites who rejected the Irish and hated Catholics were motivated in part by economic competition and anxiety. Competition was stiffest among the lowest paid and least desirable jobs. To apprehensive workers, racializing the Irish as Celts was a way of keeping them out of the running. Irish Catholics were also blamed for nearly every social problem, from immorality and alcoholism to poverty and economic upheaval. Impoverished native-born workers complained to the Massachusetts legislature in 1845 that the Irish displaced "the honest and respectable laborers of the State." American workers, they claimed, "not only labor for the body but for the mind, the soul, and the State."

In emphasizing "the soul, and the State," native-born workers added a political dimension to their racial expression. Republicanism depended on broad participation and the consent of the governed, and it seemed to American nativists that the Irish, a non-white, non-British "race," were not fit to participate.

The experience of German immigrants differed from that of the Irish. By and large Americans viewed most Germans, especially the major-

German Immigrants

ity Protestant group, as white. They shared a racial stock with the English. Americans stereotyped Germans as hard working, self-reliant, and intelligent, attributes also applied to white people. Many believed that Germans fit more easily into American culture.

In 1854 Germans replaced the Irish as the largest group of new arrivals. Potato blight also prompted emigration from the German states in the 1840s; other hardships added to the steady stream. Many people came from regions where small landholdings made it hard to eke out a living. Craftsmen displaced by the industrial revolution sought jobs in the American expanding market economy. Political refugees—liberals, freethinkers, socialists, communists, and anarchists—fled to the United States after the abortive revolutions of 1848.

In the South they were peddlers and merchants; in the North and West they worked as farmers, urban laborers, and businessmen. Their tendency to migrate as families and groups helped them maintain German customs and institutions. Many settled in small towns and rural areas where they could preserve their language and regional German cultures. In larger cities immigrants from the same German states tended to cluster together. Their presence transformed the tone of cities like Cincinnati and Milwaukee.

Non-Protestant Germans did not fare so well, frequently encountering religious and racial prejudice. A significant number of German immigrants were Jewish, and Jews were considered a separate race. Anti-Catholics attacked the German immigrants who were Catholic. The Sunday tradition of urban German families gathering at beer gardens to eat and drink, to dance and sing, and sometimes to play cards outraged Protestants, who viewed this behavior as violating the sanctity of the Lord's day.

From Florida to Texas and the Southwest to California, Hispanic inhabitants of the borderlands became "immigrants" without actually

Hispanics

moving; treaties placed them in the United States. Some Mexicans were unhappy to find themselves in a new country, while others welcomed the political self-government that the United States seemed to promise.

But reality did not live up to promise. In Nueces County, Texas, at the time of the Texas Revolution (1836), Mexicans held all the land; twenty years later, they had lost it. The new Anglo owners produced crops for the market economy; *rancheros* and *vaqueros*—cowboys—became obsolete. Although many Mexicans, called *Tejanos*, had fought for Texas's independence, new Anglo settlers tended to treat them as inferiors and foreigners. They became second-class citizens on land where they had lived for generations. Still they retained their culture. They held fast to their language, Roman Catholic religion, and cultural traditions.

In California—unlike in Texas, New Mexico, and Arizona—Hispanic society and political power quickly gave way to American and European culture. *Californios*, the Mexican population, numbered 10,000 in 1848, or two-thirds of the non-Indian population. By the end of the century the Hispanic population was 15,000 out of 1.5 million, and Hispanic culture was only a remnant.

White Americans considered Hispanics, a group descended from Indians and Spaniards, as a separate, nonwhite race. Anglo-Americans also inherited the British view of Spaniards as sneaky, cowardly, lazy, and decadent, stereotypes they applied to Hispanics. Racializing Hispanics helped to justify the attitudes and actions of aggressive whites.

Free People of Color

 African Americans were the most visible nonwhite group in the early nineteenth century. As their numbers grew, from 2.3 million in 1830 to 4.4 million in 1860, they were increasingly viewed solely as a racial group. In law and society most black people found themselves outsiders in the land of their birth.

The free African American population rose from 320,000 in 1820 to almost 500,000 in 1860. Nearly half lived in the North, some in rural settlements but far more in cities such as Philadelphia, New York, and Cincinnati. Baltimore, in the border state of Maryland, had the largest community. Despite differences in occupation, wealth, education, religion, and social status, the necessity of self-defense promoted solidarity among free blacks.

Ex-slaves constantly increased the ranks of free people of color. Some, like Frederick Douglass and Harriet Tubman, were fugitives. Douglass, a Baltimore ship caulker, escaped in 1838. Tubman, a slave in Maryland, escaped to Philadelphia in 1849 when it was rumored that she would be sold out of the state. Over the next two years she returned twice to free her two children, her sister, her mother, and her brother and his family. Some slaves received freedom in owners'

wills. And at times, owners released elderly slaves rather than support them in old age.

Free people of color forged cohesive communities and created autonomous institutions within them. Swept up by the Second Great Awakening, blacks turned to religion and reform. Black churches were the center of community life, and pastors became political leaders. Pastors taught religious and secular classes, and their chapels and social halls functioned as town halls, housing schools, political forums and conventions, protest meetings, and benevolent and self-help associations.

African American Communities

A network of voluntary associations became the hallmark of black communities. Besides the churches, men and women organized fraternal and benevolent associations, literary societies, and schools. In Philadelphia in the 1840s, more than half of the black population belonged to mutual beneficiary societies, and female benevolent societies and schools flourished. The Prince Hall Masons had more than fifty lodges in seventeen states by 1860. Many black leaders believed that these mutual aid societies would encourage thrift, industry, and morality, thus assisting their members to improve their lot. But no amount of effort could counteract the burden of white racism, which impinged on every aspect of their lives.

In the majority of states where free blacks were excluded from the ballot, they formed protest organizations to fight for equal rights. Among the early efforts to organize for self-defense was the Negro Convention movement. From 1830 to 1835, and irregularly thereafter, free blacks held national conventions with delegates drawn from city and state organizations. Under the leadership of the small black middle class, which included the Philadelphia sail manufacturer James Forten and the orator Reverend Henry Highland Garnet, the convention movement served as a forum to attack slavery and agitate for equal rights. Militant new black newspapers joined the struggle.

Activists fought the relegation of blacks to second-class status. The Bill of Rights seemed to apply to free African Americans. The Fifth Amendment specified that "no person shall . . . be deprived of life, liberty, or property, without due process of law." But eighteenth-century political theory had defined the republic as being for whites only (see page 112), and early federal legislation excluded blacks from common rights. The first naturalization law in 1790 limited citizenship to "free white persons." And after 1821, every new state admitted until the Civil War, free and slave, banned blacks from voting. Finally, when Congress organized the Oregon and New Mexico Territories, it reserved public land grants for whites. Clearly free people of color were defined as an alien race.

Even in the North, states attempted to exclude African Americans. Many states barred free blacks or required them to post bonds ranging from $500 to $1,000 to guarantee their good conduct. Only in Massachusetts, New Hampshire, Vermont, and Maine could blacks vote on an equal basis with whites throughout the early nineteenth century. In 1842 African Americans gained the right to vote in Rhode Island, but they had lost it earlier in Pennsylvania and Connecticut. Only Massachusetts permitted blacks to serve on juries. Four midwestern states and California did not allow African Americans to testify against whites. In Oregon blacks could not own real estate, make contracts, or sue in court. And throughout the United States white social custom became more rigid in excluding or segregating free people of color. Hotels and restaurants barred them, as did most theaters and white churches.

Racial Exclusion and Segregation

Economic discrimination solidified social segregation. Black people were banned from the jobs opening up in the expanding market economy. Counting-houses, retail stores, and factories refused to hire black men except as janitors and handymen. New England mills hired only whites. Except for a small professional and skilled elite, free black men in the North toiled mostly as unskilled daily laborers.

African American women found jobs more easily than men did. Their domestic skills were in great demand in the cities; they worked as servants, cooks, laundresses, and seamstresses, and kept boarding houses. Unlike their white counterparts, these women did not view paid employment as a temporary phase in their lives; around 40 percent of black women worked for wages during their child-rearing years.

African American Women

But gender roles also restricted black women. In religious organizations they participated regularly but rarely held leadership positions. And black women in the abolitionist movement, like their white sisters, were discouraged from speaking in public. Black women also had to deal with black men's needs to be strong and to protect women, roles men found impossible in slavery and difficult in freedom. Both men and women carried the burden of refuting racial stereotypes, but black women bore the additional burden of gender stereotypes.

The mood of free blacks turned pessimistic in the late 1840s and 1850s. Many felt frustrated by the failure of the abolitionist movement and angered by the passage of the stringent Fugitive Slave Act of 1850 (see page 239). Some fled to Canada. Many more were swept up in a wave of black nationalism that stressed racial solidarity, self-help, and a growing interest in Africa. Before this time, efforts to send African Americans "back to Africa" had originated with whites seeking to rid the United States of blacks. But in the 1850s blacks held emigrationist conventions of their own under the leadership of abolitionists Henry Bibb and Martin Delany. With the coming of the Civil War, the status of blacks would move onto the national political agenda, and African Americans would focus on their position at home.

Black Nationalism

Summary

The American people and communities in the North and West were far more diverse and turbulent in the 1850s than they had been in the 1820s. The market economy and westward movement altered farm life, city life, and class structure; heavy immigration, growing racial ideas, and the anguished position of free people of color added to the tensions. Inequality increased, as did the gap between the haves and the have-nots. As the nation grew more populous and the market economy upset work and social relations, many felt a loss of tradition and community. Some longed to return to old values. Utopians like the Shakers, Mormons, and Brook Farmers sought to counter isolation and individualism.

In the midst of these changes, middle-class families sought to insulate their homes from the competition of the market economy. Many women found fulfillment in the domestic ideal; others found "woman's sphere" confining. Middle-class urban women became associated with nurturing roles, first in homes and schools, then in churches and reform societies. Working-class women had more modest goals: escaping poverty and winning respect. Most Americans found some comfort in religion.

Famine and oppression in Europe propelled millions of people across the Atlantic. American expansion added Hispanics to the nation. Diversity, competition, and religious and scientific thought fueled racial ideas. Many European descendants began to view the Irish, Hispanics, and African Americans as inferior races.

LEGACY FOR A PEOPLE AND A NATION

White Fascination with and Appropriation of Black Culture

White Americans' fascination with and appropriation of black culture blossomed in the early nineteenth century. Whites performed songs and dances from blackface minstrel reviews, while urban young people imitated black language, dress, and hairstyles. In the 1850s white songwriter Stephen Foster's "Old Folks at Home," "Susanna," and "Camptown Races" were enormously popular.

American popular culture combined African, European, and African American traditions. Its emphasis on performance, improvisation, strong rhythms, vernacular language, multiple meanings, and integration into everyday life is evidence of strong African ties. These elements appealed to whites because of their expressive power. Whites also believed that black cultural forms were "exotic" and offered "natural" forms of expression.

Black traditions continue to influence twentieth-century popular culture. Minstrelsy turned into vaudeville and Broadway theater. Popular dance and music, performed mostly by whites, drew heavily on black gospel, slave spirituals, the blues, and jazz. Black traditions influenced the swing bands of the 1930s, and after World War II, they shaped rhythm and blues, rock 'n' roll, and, later, rap, hip-hop, and ska.

Until recently, most whites experienced black culture as appropriated by whites. But in the late twentieth century, a synthesis of black and white traditions became notable. In the early 1950s Bill Haley and the Comets, a white country-western group, combined black rhythm and blues with white country and western music. Their 1954 sensation, "Shake, Rattle & Roll," for instance, was a sanitized version of Big Joe Turner's rhythm and blues hit. White audiences responded enthusiastically, and when Haley and the Comets played "Rock Around the Clock" in the 1955 movie *Blackboard Jungle*, rock 'n' roll took off. Elvis Presley too synthesized rhythm and blues and gospel with country music and middle-of-the-road popular music. Rap and hip-hop built on the talking blues, call and response, and urban black and Chicano/a dance styles of the 1970s. White suburban youth made them dominant popular forms.

Popular music and dance, with its African American roots, is uniquely American. Young people fostered this popular culture and used its expressive elements to define themselves. Thus African American culture has given the people and the nation a unique cultural legacy.

For Further Reading, see the Appendix. For Web resources, go to history.college.hmco.com/students.

PEOPLE AND COMMUNITIES IN A SLAVE SOCIETY: THE SOUTH

1830–1860

Pierce Butler was broke. It was late winter of 1859, fear of disunion dominated national life, and Butler's slave auction had all of coastal Georgia and South Carolina talking. Butler had divided his time between the family's ostentatious home in Philadelphia and 1,500 acres of cotton plantations on Butler Island and St. Simons Island in Georgia, worked by eight hundred slaves. By 1859 Butler had squandered a fortune of $700,000 through speculation and gambling.

Most of Butler's properties and possessions in Philadelphia were sold to satisfy his creditors. Then came the largest slave auction in American history. In the last week of February, 436 Butler slaves were taken to Savannah by railroad and steamboat. People of all ages—infants, husbands, wives, children, grandparents—huddled in fearful expectation. Among the planters and speculators who were there to buy was an undercover *New York Tribune* reporter. The auction lasted an agonizing two days in a driving rainstorm.

If possible, families were sold intact for group prices; thus the old and infirm could still be liquidated, while the closest kin stayed together. A seventeen-year-old "Prime woman" and her three-month-old son went for $2,200. A nineteen-year-old "prime young man" netted $1,295. Some families of four brought only $1,600 together. At the end of the second day of what blacks in the region called the "weeping time," Butler had amassed $303,850 by selling 436 human beings.

Many northerners remained undisturbed during the antebellum era by the growth of human bondage, even its worst elements such as the Butler auction. But

IMPORTANT EVENTS

1810–20	137,000 slaves are forced to move from North Carolina and the Chesapeake to Alabama, Mississippi, and other western regions
1822	Vesey's plot is discovered in South Carolina
1831	Turner leads a violent slave rebellion in Virginia
1832	Virginia holds the last serious debate in the South about the future of slavery
1832 and after	Legislators in several states increase restrictions on slaves
1830s	Class tensions lead to electoral reforms in much of the South The cotton trade provides much of the export capital to finance northeastern economic growth
1836	Arkansas gains admission to the Union
1839	Mississippi's Married Women's Property Act gives married women some property rights
1840s	Southern slave economy prospers, but northern, urban economic growth is less dependent on it
1845	Florida and Texas gain admission to the Union Publication of Douglass's *Narrative of the Life of Frederick Douglass, An American Slave*
1850–60	Of some 300,000 slaves who migrate from Upper to Lower South, 60–70% go by outright sale
1857	Helper denounces the slave system in *The Impending Crisis*

a growing number came to see it as threatening and immoral. By the 1830s the North was an emerging market economy embarking on an industrial revolution.

Meanwhile, the South, with a different kind of growth and prosperity, also participated in the market revolution. New lands were settled and new states peopled, and steadily the South emerged as the world's most extensive and vigorous slave economy, linked to an international cotton trade and textile industry. Slavery had a far-reaching influence on the whole society. The Old South's wealth came from export crops, land, and slaves; and its population was almost wholly rural. ■

The "Peculiar" South?

There has long been a tendency to equate certain American values such as materialism, individualism, and faith in progress with the North in the nineteenth century, and to equate values such as tradition, conservatism, and family loyalty with the South. The South, so the stereotype has it, was static, and the North dynamic. Indeed, the great fact of secession and the Confederacy will al-

ways give the South a distinct place in American history. But there are many measures of just how different the South was from the North in the antebellum era. It depends on which measures one chooses.

The South was peculiar because of its commitment to slavery, but it was also much like the rest of the

South-North Similarity

nation. The geographic sizes of the South and the North were roughly the same. By the 1830s southerners shared a heritage from the era of the American Revolution with their fellow free citizens in the North. Southerners spoke the same language and worshiped the same Protestant God as northerners. White Americans in the South lived under the same cherished Constitution as northerners, and they shared a common mixture of nationalism and localism in their attitudes toward government. Down to the 1840s, northerners and southerners both invoked the doctrine of states' rights against federal authority. A faith in the future fueled by a sense of American mission, and the dreams inspired by the westward movement were as much a part of southern as of northern experience. But as slavery and the plantation economy expanded, the South did not become a land of individual opportunity in quite the same manner as the North.

During the thirty years before the Civil War, the South shared in the nation's economic booms and busts. Research has shown that slavery was a profitable labor system for planters. Southerners and northerners shared an expanding capitalist economy. As it grew, the slave-based economy of money-crop agriculture reflected the rational choices of planters. More land and more slaves generally converted into more wealth. By the eve of the Civil War in 1860, the distribution of wealth and property in the two sections was almost identical: 50 percent of free adult males owned only 1 percent of real and personal property, while the richest 1 percent owned 27 percent of the wealth. Both North and South had ruling classes, and entrepreneurs in both sections, whether planters in the Mississippi Delta or factory owners in New England, sought their fortunes in an expanding market economy.

But there were also important differences between the North and the South. The South's climate and longer growing season gave it an unmistakable rural and agricultural destiny. Its people, white and black, developed an intense attachment to place, to the ways people were related to the land and to one another. It developed as a biracial society of brutal inequality, where the liberty of one race directly depended on the enslavement of another.

South-North Dissimilarity

In this agrarian society, cotton growers spread out over as large an area as possible to maximize production and income. Population density was low in the older plantation states and extremely low in the frontier areas. By 1860 there were only 2.3 people per

Eastman Johnson's *Fiddling His Way* (1866) depicts rural life by representing the visit of an itinerant black musician to a farm family. Expressions and gestures suggest remarkable ease between the races at the yeoman level of southern society. (The Chrysler Museum of Art, Norfolk, Virginia. Bequest of Walter P. Chrysler, Jr.)

square mile in vast and largely unsettled Texas and 18.0 in Georgia. By contrast, population density in the nonslaveholding states east of the Mississippi River was almost three times higher. The Northeast had an average of 65.4 people per square mile. Massachusetts had 153.1 people per square mile, and New York City compressed 86,400 people into each square mile.

Where people were scarce, it was difficult to finance and operate schools, churches, libraries, or even inns and restaurants. Southerners were strongly committed to their churches, and some believed in the importance of universities, but all such institutions were far less developed than those in the North. Factories were rare because planters invested most of their capital in slaves. And despite concerted efforts, the South had only 35 percent of the nation's railroad mileage in 1860.

The South did have urban centers, especially ports like New Orleans and Charleston, which became bustling crossroads of commerce and small-scale manufacturing. But slavery slowed urban growth. Likewise, the South did not attract immigrants as readily as the North.

Like northerners, antebellum southerners were adherents to evangelical Christianity. But southern evangelicalism was distinct from the northern practice. In the South, Baptists and Methodists concentrated on personal rather than social improvement. By the 1830s in the North, evangelicalism was a major wellspring of reform movements; but in the states where blacks were so numerous and unfree, religion, as one scholar has written, preached "a hands-off policy concerning slavery." The only reform movements that did take hold in the emerging Bible belt of the South, such as temperance, focused on personal behavior, not social reform.

Perhaps in no way was the South more peculiar than in its embrace of a particular world-view, a system of thought and meaning held especially by the planter class, but also influencing all groups of whites. At the heart of the proslavery argument was a deep and abiding racism. The persistence of modern racism in all sections of the United States is all the more reason to comprehend antebellum southerners' justifications for human slavery, from which so many modern racial assumptions are derived.

A Southern World-view and the Proslavery Argument

By 1830 white southerners defended slavery as a "positive good," not merely a "necessary evil." They used the Bible and its many references to slaveholding, as well as the ancient roots of slavery, to foster a historical argument for bondage. They arrayed a variety of assumptions about the superiority and inferiority of races in support of slavery as the natural status of blacks. Whites were the more intellectual race and blacks the race more inherently physical, and therefore destined for labor.

Some southerners defended slavery in practical terms; they simply saw their bondsmen as an economic necessity and as symbols of their quest for prosperity. Others argued that slaveholding was essentially a matter of property rights. James Henry Hammond of South Carolina spoke for many southerners in his unwillingness to "deal in abstractions" about the "right and wrong" of slavery: property was sacred, and slaves were legal property—end of argument.

The deepest root of the proslavery argument was a conservative, hierarchical view of human relations, a concern for social order as slavery's defenders believed God or nature had prescribed it. Southerners cherished stability, duty, and honor, believing social change should come only in slow increments, if at all. As the Virginia legislature debated the gradual abolition of slavery in 1832, Thomas R. Dew contended, "There is a time for all things, and nothing in this world should be done before its time."

Southern defenders of slavery held views decidedly different from those of northern reformers on the concepts of freedom, progress, and equality. They turned natural law doctrine to their favor, arguing that the natural state of mankind was inequality of ability and condition, not equality. Proslavery writers believed that people were born to certain stations or purposes in life; they stressed dependence over autonomy, and duty over rights, as the human condition.

Hence, however differently their slaves may have interpreted the relationship, many slaveholders believed that their ownership of people bound them, by honor, to a set of paternal obligations. They saw themselves as guardians of a familial relationship between masters and slaves given to them by fate and heritage. Although contradicted by countless examples of slave resistance and escape, planters needed to believe in, and exerted great energy in constructing, the idea of the faithful, contented slave.

What the South had become by the 1830s, and grew even more fully into by 1860, was not merely a

A Slave Society society with slaves, but a slave society (see pages 48–49). In this way, the region was most distinct within the larger American nation. Slavery and race affected everything in the Old South. Whites and blacks alike grew up, were socialized, married, reared children, and honed their most basic habits of behavior under the influence of slavery. Slavery shaped the social structure of the South, fueled almost anything meaningful in its economy, and came to dominate its politics.

This does not mean that the Old South did not share a common culture, political system, and economy with the North, and with Europe. The South was interdependent with the North and the West in a growing capitalist market system. Southerners relied on northern banks, northern steamship companies, and northern merchants to keep the cotton trade flowing. But there were elements of that system that southerners increasingly rejected during the antebellum era, especially urbanism, the wage labor system, a broadening right to vote, and any threats to the racial and class order on which they so depended. Although enmeshed in a national economy, the Old South became antimodern.

Just how peculiar the South was will always be debated. Culturally, the South developed a proclivity to tell its own story. Its ruralness and its sense of tradition may have given southerners a special habit of telling tales. "Southerners . . . love a good tale," said Mississippi writer Eudora Welty. The South's tragic and distinct story begins in the Old South. The story was peculiar and national all at once.

Free Southerners: Farmers, Planters, and Free Blacks

 A large majority of white southern families (three-quarters in 1860) owned no slaves. Some lived in towns, but most were yeoman farmers who owned their own land and grew their own food. The social distance between different groups of whites was great. Still greater was the distance between whites and blacks.

Most slaveowners lived in comfortable country homes rather than in stately mansions. This rare daguerreotype, dating from about 1853, shows a family in front of their home. Notice the presence of a male slave in the left background. (The J. Paul Getty Museum, Los Angeles, California)

These farmers were individualistic and hard working. Unlike their northern counterparts, their lives were not being transformed by improvements in transportation. They could be independent thinkers as well, but their status as a numerical majority did not mean that they set the political or economic direction of the slave society. Often isolated, always absorbed in the work of their farms, they operated both apart from and within the slave-based staple-crop economy. They valued their self-reliance and freedom from others' control.

Yeoman Farmers

Yeomen pioneered the southern wilderness, moving into undeveloped regions and building log cabins. After the War of 1812 they moved in successive waves down the southern Appalachians into new Gulf lands, first as herders of livestock and then as farmers. In large sections of the South, small, self-sufficient farms that grew staple crops were the norm. Lured by stories of good land, many men uprooted their wives and children repeatedly.

On the southern frontier men worked hard to clear fields and establish farms, while their wives labored in the household economy and patiently re-created the social ties—to relatives, neighbors, fellow churchgoers—that enriched everyone's experience. Women seldom shared the men's excitement about moving. They dreaded the isolation and loneliness of the frontier.

Some yeomen acquired large tracts of level land, purchased slaves, and became planters. These people made up part of the new wealth of the boom states of Mississippi and Louisiana, the region to which the southern political power base had shifted by the 1840s and 1850s. Others clung to familiar mountainous areas or kept moving as independent farmers.

The yeomen enjoyed a folk culture based on family, church, and local region. Their speech patterns and inflections recalled their Scots-Irish and Irish backgrounds. They flocked to religious revivals called camp meetings, and in between they got together for house-raisings, logrollings, quilting bees, corn-shuckings, and hunting for both food and sport. Such occasions combined work with fun and provided welcome fellowship to isolated rural dwellers.

Yeoman Folk Culture

A demanding round of work and family responsibilities shaped women's lives in the home. At harvest they helped in the fields, and throughout the year the care and preparation of food consumed much of their time. Household tasks continued during frequent pregnancies and childcare. Primary nursing and medical care also fell to the mother, who might have a book of remedies to aid her but often relied on folk wisdom.

Among the men there were many who aspired to wealth, eager to join the race for slaves and cotton profits. Others were content with their independence, family, religion, and recreation. All worked hard.

Yeoman Livelihoods

Ferdinand L. Steel, who as a young man moved from North Carolina to Tennessee to work as a river boatman but eventually took up farming in Mississippi, was a typical yeoman. Steel rose every day at five and worked until sundown. With the help of his family he raised corn, wheat, pork, and vegetables. Cotton was his cash crop: he sold five or six bales (about 2,000 pounds) a year to obtain money for sugar, coffee, salt, calico, gunpowder, and a few other store-bought goods.

Thus Steel entered the market economy as a small farmer, but with mixed results. When cotton prices fell, a small grower like Steel could be driven into debt and lose his farm. In fact, he wanted to grow less cotton. "We are too weak handed" to manage it, he noted in his diary. "We had better . . . raise corn and keep out of debt and we will have no necessity of raising cotton."

Steel's life in Mississippi in the 1840s retained much of the flavor of the frontier. He made all the family's shoes; his wife and sister sewed dresses, shirts, and "pantiloons." The Steel women also rendered their own soap and spun and wove cotton into cloth; the men hunted game. As the nation fell deeper into crisis over the future of free or slave labor, this independent southern farmer never came close to owning a slave.

The focus of Steel's life was family and religion. Family members prayed together daily, and Steel studied Scripture for an hour after lunch. He borrowed histories and religious books from his church. Eventually he became a traveling Methodist minister. "My life is one of toil," he reflected, "but blessed be God that it is as well with me as it is."

Toil with even less security was the lot of two other groups of free southerners: landless whites and

Landless Whites free blacks. A sizable minority of white southern workers—from 25 to 40 percent—were unskilled laborers who owned no land and worked for others in the countryside and towns. Their property consisted of a few household items and some animals—usually pigs—that could feed themselves on the open range. The landless included some immigrants, especially Irish, who did heavy and dangerous work such as building railroads and digging ditches.

In the countryside, white farm laborers struggled to purchase land in the face of low wages or, if they rented, unpredictable market prices for their crops. By scrimping and saving and finding odd jobs, some managed to climb into the ranks of yeomen. When James and Nancy Bennitt of North Carolina succeeded in their ten-year struggle to buy land, they decided to avoid the unstable market in cotton; thereafter they raised extra corn and wheat as sources of cash.

Herdsmen who viewed pigs and livestock as a major economic asset always had a desperate struggle to succeed. By 1860, as the South anticipated war to preserve its society, between 300,000 and 400,000 white people in the four states of Virginia, North and South Carolina, and Georgia lived in genuine poverty, approximately one-fifth of the total white population. Their lives were harsh to say the least.

For the nearly quarter-million free blacks in the South in 1860, conditions were often little better than the slaves'. They usually did not own **Free Blacks** land and had to labor in someone else's fields, often beside slaves. By law free blacks could not own a gun, buy liquor, violate curfew, assemble except in church, testify in court, or (throughout the South after 1835) vote. Despite these obstacles, a minority bought land, and others found jobs as skilled craftsmen.

A few free blacks prospered and bought slaves, most of them purchasing their own wives and children (whom they could not free, since laws required newly emancipated blacks to leave their states). In 1830 there were 3,775 free black slaveholders in the South; 80 percent lived in the four states of Louisiana, South Carolina, Virginia, and Maryland, and approximately one-half of the total lived in the two cities of New Orleans and Charleston.

In the cotton and Gulf regions, a large proportion of free blacks were mulattos, the privileged offspring of wealthy white planters. Not all **Free Black Communities** planters freed their mixed-race offspring, but those who did often recognized a moral obligation and gave their children a good education and financial backing. In a few cities like New Orleans, Charleston, and Mobile, extensive interracial sex, as well as migrations from the Caribbean, had produced a mulatto population that was recognized as a distinct class.

In many southern cities by the 1840s, free black communities formed, especially around an expanding number of churches. By the late 1850s, Baltimore had fifteen churches, Louisville nine, and Nashville and St. Louis four each, and most of them were African Methodist Episcopal. Class and race distinctions were important to southern free blacks, but outside a few cities, which developed fraternal orders of skilled craftsmen and fellowships of light-skinned people, most mulattos experienced more disadvantages than benefits. In the United States, "one drop" of black "blood" made them black, and potentially enslaveable.

At the top of the southern social pyramid were slaveholding planters. As a group they lived well and enjoyed luxuries. But most lived in **Planters** comfortable farmhouses, not on the opulent scale that legend suggests. A few statistics tell the fuller story: in 1850, 50 percent of southern slaveholders had fewer than five slaves; 72 percent had fewer than ten; 88 percent had fewer than twenty. Thus the average slaveholder was not a wealthy aristocrat but an aspiring farmer, usually a person of humble origins, with little formal education.

The richest planters used their wealth to model genteel sophistication. Extended visits, parties, and balls to which women wore the latest fashions provided opportunities for friendship, courtship, and display. Such parties were held during the Christmas holidays, but also on such occasions as a molasses stewing, a Bachelor's Ball, a horse race, or the crowning of the May Queen. These entertainments were especially important as diversions for plantation women. Young women relished social events to break the monotony of their domestic lives.

Some old Virginia and South Carolina families were represented among the proud new "cotton snobs" of Alabama and Mississippi, but most of the planters in these cotton boom states were newly rich by the 1840s. As one historian put it, "a number of men mounted from log cabin to plantation mansion on a stairway of cotton bales, accumulating slaves as they climbed." And many did not live like rich men. Some lived for decades in their original log cabins, improved only by clapboards or a frame addition. They put their new wealth into cotton acreage and slaves even as they sought refinement and high social status.

Slaveholding men dominated society and, especially among the wealthiest and oldest families, justified their dominance through a paternalistic ideology. Instead of stressing the profitable aspects of commercial agriculture, they focused on their obligations, viewing themselves as custodians of the welfare of society in general and of the black families they owned in particular. The paternalistic planter saw himself not as an oppressor but as the benevolent guardian of an inferior race. He developed affectionate feelings toward his slaves (as long as they knew their place) and was genuinely shocked at criticism of his behavior.

Southern Paternalism

Paul Carrington Cameron, who was North Carolina's largest slaveholder, exemplifies this mentality. After a period of sickness among his one thousand North Carolina slaves (he had hundreds more in Alabama and Mississippi), Cameron wrote, "I fear the Negroes have suffered much from the want of proper attention and kindness under this late distemper . . . no love of lucre shall ever induce me to be cruel. . . ."

It was comforting to rich planters to see themselves in this way, and slaves—accommodating to the realities of power—encouraged their masters to think their benevolence was appreciated. Paternalism also served as a defense against abolitionist criticism. Still, paternalism was often a matter of style, covering harsher assumptions. As talk of paternalistic duties increased, theories about the complete and permanent inferiority of blacks multiplied. In reality, paternalism grew as a give-and-take relationship between masters and slaves, each extracting from the other as much as they could of what they desired—labor from the bondsmen, a measure of autonomy and living space from the slaveowners. But it also evolved as a theory of black slavery and white dominance.

Even Paul Cameron's benevolence vanished with changed circumstances. After the Civil War, he bris-

tled at African Americans' efforts to be free and made sweeping economic decisions without regard to their welfare. Writing on Christmas Day 1865, Cameron showed little Christian charity (but a healthy profit motive) when he declared, "I am convinced that the people who gets rid of the free negro first will be the first to advance in improved agriculture. Have made no effort to retain any of mine [and] will not attempt a crop beyond the capacity of 30 hands." With that he turned off his land nearly a thousand black people, rented his fields to several white farmers, and invested in industry.

Relations between men and women in the planter class were similarly paternalistic. The upper-class southern woman was raised and educated to be a wife, mother, and subordinate companion to men. South Carolina's Mary Boykin Chesnut wrote of her husband, "He is master of the house. To hear is to obey. . . . All the comfort of my life depends upon his being in a good humor." In a social system based on the coercion of an entire race, women were not allowed to challenge society's rules on sexual or racial relations.

Plantation Mistresses

Planters' daughters usually attended one of the South's rapidly multiplying boarding schools. There they formed friendships with other girls and received an education that emphasized grammar, composition, penmanship, geography, literature, and languages. Typically the young woman could entertain suitors whom her parents approved. But very soon she had to choose a husband and commit herself for life to a man whom she generally had known for only a brief time. Young women were often alienated and emotionally unfulfilled. They had to follow the wishes of their families, especially fathers. "It was for me best that I yielded to the wishes of papa," wrote a young North Carolinian in 1823. "I wonder when my best will cease to be painful and when I shall begin to enjoy life instead of enduring it."

Upon marriage, a planter class woman ceded to her husband most of her legal rights, becoming part of his family. Most of the year she was isolated on a large plantation, where she had to oversee the cooking and preserving of food, manage the house, supervise care of the children, and attend sick slaves. It is not surprising that a perceptive

Marriage and Family

young woman sometimes approached marriage with anxiety. Women could hardly help viewing their wedding days, as one put it in 1832, as "the day to fix my fate."

Childbearing often involved grief, poor health, and death. In 1840 the birth rate for white southern women in their childbearing years was almost 30 percent higher than the national average. The average southern white woman could expect to bear eight children in 1800; by 1860 the figure had decreased to only six, with one or more miscarriages likely. For those women who wanted to plan their families, methods of contraception and medical care were uncertain. Complications of childbirth were a major cause of death, occurring twice as often in the hot, humid South as in the Northeast.

Slavery was another source of problems that white women had to endure but were not supposed to notice. "Violations of the moral law . . . made mulattoes as common as blackberries," protested a woman in Georgia, but wives had to play "the ostrich game." "A magnate who runs a hideous black harem," wrote Mrs. Chesnut, ". . . poses as the model of all human virtues to these poor women whom God and the laws have given him."

Southern men tolerated little discussion by women of the slavery issue. In the 1840s and 1850s, as abolitionist attacks on slavery increased, southern men published a barrage of articles stressing that women should restrict their concerns to the home. The *Southern Quarterly Review* declared, "The proper place for a woman is at home. One of her highest privileges, to be politically merged in the existence of her husband."

But some southern women were beginning to seek a larger role. A study of women in Petersburg, Virginia, revealed behavior that valued financial autonomy. Over several decades before 1860, the proportion of women who never married, or did not remarry after the death of a spouse, grew to exceed 33 percent. Likewise the number of women who worked for wages, controlled their own property, and ran millinery or dressmaking businesses increased. In managing property, these and other women benefited from legal changes; to protect families from the husband's indebtedness during business panics and recessions, reforms gave married women some property rights.

Slave Life and Labor

 For African Americans, slavery was a burden that destroyed some people and forced others to develop modes of survival. Slaves knew a life of poverty, coercion, toil, and resentment. They provided the physical strength, and much of the know-how, to build a burgeoning agricultural empire. But their daily lives embodied the nation's most basic contradiction: in the world's model republic, they were on the wrong side of a brutally unequal power relationship between masters and slaves.

Southern slaves enjoyed few material comforts beyond the bare necessities. Although they generally had enough to eat, their diet was plain and monotonous. Clothing too was plain, coarse, and inexpensive. Few slaves received more than one or two changes of clothing for hot and cold seasons and one blanket each winter. Children of both sexes ran naked in hot weather and wore long cotton shirts in winter. Many slaves had to go without shoes until December. The shoes they received were uncomfortable brass-toed brogans or stiff wraparounds made from tanned leather.

Slaves' Everyday Conditions

Summer and winter, slaves typically lived in small one-room cabins, possibly with a window opening but no glass. Some of the richer plantations provided more substantial houses, but the average slave lived in crude accommodations, where dirt was the only floor. The gravest drawback of slave cabins was their unhealthfulness. Each small cabin housed one or two entire families. Crowding and lack of sanitation fostered the spread of infection and contagious diseases such as typhoid fever, malaria, and dysentery.

Hard work was the central fact of slaves' existence. The long hours and large work gangs that characterized Gulf Coast cotton districts operated almost like factories in the field. Overseers rang the morning bell before dawn—so early that some slaves remembered being "afraid to start work for fear that they would cover the cotton plants with dirt because they couldn't see clearly." Slaves who cultivated tobacco in the Upper South worked long hours picking the sticky, sometimes noxious, tobacco leaves under harsh discipline.

Slaves' Work Routines

Working "from sun to sun" became a norm in much of the South. Long hours and hard work were among the advantages that slave labor gave southern planters. As one planter put it, slaves were the best labor because "you could command them and make them do what was right." Profit took precedence over paternalism. Slave women did heavy fieldwork, often as much as the men and even during pregnancy. Old people—of whom there were few—were kept busy caring for young children, doing light chores, or carding, ginning, and spinning cotton. Children had to gather kindling, carry water to the fields, or sweep the yard.

Different jobs, talents, and circumstances created variations in status and rivalries among slaves. But only one-quarter of all slaves lived on plantations of fifty or more blacks, so few experienced a wide chasm separating house servants and lowly field hands. Many slaves did both housework and fieldwork, depending on their age and the season, and this arrangement helped create a sense of group unity.

But incentives had to be part of the labor regime and the master-slave relationship as well. Planters in the South Carolina and Georgia low country used a task system whereby slaves were assigned measured amounts of work to be performed in a given amount of time. So much cotton on a daily basis was to be picked from a designated field; so many rows were to be hoed or plowed in a particular slave's specified section. By the 1830s slaveowners found that labor could be regulated and motivated by the clock. When their task and "clock time" was up, slaves' time was their own, for working in garden plots, tending to hogs, or even hiring out their own extra labor.

Slaves could not demand too much autonomy, of course, because the owner enjoyed a monopoly on force and violence. Whites throughout the South believed that slaves "can't be governed except with the whip." Evidence suggests that whippings were less frequent on small farms than on large plantations. But beatings symbolized authority to the master and tyranny to the slaves, who made them a benchmark for evaluating a master. In the words of former slaves, a good owner was one who did not "whip too much," whereas a bad owner "whipped till he's bloodied you and blistered you."

Violence Against Slaves

As these reports suggest, terrible abuses could and did occur. The master wielded virtually absolute authority on his plantation, and courts did not recognize the word of chattel. Pregnant women were whipped, and there were burnings, mutilations, tortures, and murders. Yet physical cruelty may have been less prevalent in the United States than in other slaveholding parts of the New World. In sugar-growing operations in Brazil and mining regions in Peru in the 1800s, slaves were regarded as an expendable resource to be replaced after several years. In some of the sugar islands of the Caribbean, treatment was so poor and death rates were so high that the heavily male slave population shrank in size. In the United States, by contrast, the slave population experienced a steady natural increase as births exceeded deaths and each generation grew larger.

The worst evil of American slavery was not its physical cruelty but the nature of slavery itself: coercion, lack of freedom, belonging to another person, virtually no hope for mobility or change. A woman named Delia Garlic made the essential point: "It's bad to belong to folks that own you soul an' body. I could tell you 'bout it all day, but even then you couldn't guess the awfulness of it."

The great majority of American slaves retained their mental independence and self-respect despite their bondage. Contrary to popular belief at the time, they were not loyal partners in their own oppression. They had to be subservient and speak honeyed words to their masters, but they talked and behaved quite differently among themselves. The evidence of their resistant attitudes comes from their actions and their own life stories. In his *Narrative* (1845), Frederick Douglass wrote that most slaves, when asked about "their condition and the character of their masters, almost universally say they are contented, and that their masters are kind." Slaves did this, said Douglass, because they were governed by the maxim that "a still tongue makes a wise head," especially in the presence of unfamiliar people.

Some former slaves remembered warm feelings between masters and slaves, but the prevailing attitudes were distrust and antagonism. Slaves saw through acts of kindness. One woman said her mistress was "a mighty good somebody to belong to" but only "'cause she was raisin' us to work for her." A man recalled that

Slave-Master Relationships

his owners took good care of their slaves, "and Grandma Maria say, 'Why shouldn't they—it was their money.'" Slaves also resented being used as beasts of burden. One man observed that his master "fed us reg'lar on good, 'stantial food, just like you'd tend to your horse, if you had a real good one."

Slaves were alert to the thousand daily signs of their degraded status. One man recalled the general rule that slaves ate cornbread and owners ate biscuits. If blacks did get biscuits, "the flour that we made the biscuits out of was the third-grade sorts." A former slave recalled, "Us catch lots of 'possums," but "the white folks ate 'em." If the owner took his slaves' garden produce to town and sold it for them, the slaves often suspected him of pocketing part of the profits.

Suspicion often grew into hatred. When a yellow fever epidemic struck in 1852, many slaves saw it as God's retribution. An elderly ex-slave named Minnie Fulkes cherished the conviction that God was going to punish white people for their cruelty to blacks. She described the whippings that her mother had to endure, and then she exclaimed, "Lord, Lord, I hate white people and the flood waters goin' to drown some more."

Slave Culture

A people is always "more than the sum of its brutalization," wrote the African American novelist Ralph Ellison in 1967. What people create in the face of hard luck and oppression is what provides hope. The resource that enabled slaves to maintain such defiance was their culture: a body of beliefs, values, and practices born of their past and maintained in the present. As best they could, they built a community knitted together by stories, music, a religious world-view, leadership, the smells of their cooking, the sounds of their own voices, and the tapping of their feet. That slaves endured and found loyalty and strength among themselves is a tribute to their courage.

Slave culture changed significantly after 1800, as fewer and fewer slaves were African-born. For a few years South Carolina reopened the international slave trade, but after 1808 Congress banned further importations. By the 1830s, the vast majority of slaves in the South were native-born Americans.

Despite lack of firsthand memory, African influences remained strong, especially in appearance and

African Cultural Survival

forms of expression. Some slave men plaited their hair into rows and fancy designs; slave women often wore their hair "in string"—tied in small bunches secured by a string or piece of cloth. A few men and many women wrapped their heads in kerchiefs of the styles and colors of West Africa.

Music, religion, and folktales were parts of daily life for most slaves. Borrowing partly from their African background, as well as forging new American folkways, they developed what scholars have called a "sacred world-view" that affected all aspects of work, leisure, and self-understanding. Slaves made musical instruments with carved motifs that resembled African stringed instruments. Their drumming and dancing followed African patterns that made whites marvel. One visitor to Georgia in the 1860s described a ritual dance of African origin: "A ring of singers is formed. . . . They then utter a kind of melodious chant, which gradually increases in strength, and in noise, until it fairly shakes the house, and it can be heard for a long distance."

Many slaves continued to believe in spirit possession. Their belief resembled the African concept of the living dead—the idea that deceased relatives visit the earth for many years until the process of dying is complete. Slaves also practiced conjuration, voodoo, and quasi-magical root medicine. By the 1850s the most notable conjurers and root doctors were reputed to live in South Carolina, Georgia, Louisiana, and other isolated coastal areas with high slave populations.

These cultural survivals provided slaves with a sense of their separate past and their own special ways. Such practices and beliefs were not static "Africanisms" or mere "retentions." They were cultural adaptations, living traditions reformed in the Americas in response to new experience.

As they became African Americans, slaves also developed a sense of racial identity. In the colonial period, Africans had arrived in America from many different states and kingdoms, represented by distinctive languages, body markings, and traditions. Planters had used ethnic differences to create occupational hierarchies. By the early antebellum period, however, old ethnic identities were giving way as American slaves increasingly saw themselves as a single group unified by race. Africans had arrived in the New World with virtually no concept of "race"; by the antebellum era, their descendants had learned that race was now the defining feature of their lives.

With the maturing of African American culture, more and more slaves adopted Christianity. But they fashioned Christianity into an instrument of support and resistance. Theirs was a religion of justice and deliverance, quite unlike their masters' religious propaganda directed at them. "You ought to have heard that preachin'," said one man. "'Obey your master and mistress, don't steal chickens and eggs and meat,' but nary a word about havin' a soul to save." Slaves believed that Jesus cared about their souls and their plight. For them, Christianity was a religion of personal and group salvation. Many slaves nurtured an unshakable belief that God would enter history and end their bondage. This faith—and the joy and emotional release that accompanied worship—sustained them.

Slaves' Religion and Music

Slaves also adapted Christianity to African practices. In West African belief, devotees are possessed by a god so thoroughly that the god's own personality replaces the human personality. In the late antebellum era, Christian slaves experienced possession by the Protestant "Holy Spirit." The combination of shouting, singing, and dancing that seemed to overtake black worshipers formed the heart of their religious faith. "The old meeting house caught fire," recalled an ex-slave preacher. "The spirit was there. . . . God saw our need and came to us." And out in brush arbors or in meetinghouses, slaves took in the presence of God and sang away their woes.

Rhythm and physical movement were crucial to slaves' religious experience. In their own preachers' chanted sermons, which reached out to gather the sinner into a narrative of meanings and cadences along the way to conversion, an American tradition was born. The chanted sermon was both a message from Scripture and a patterned form that required audience response punctuated by "yes sirs!" and "amens!" But it was in song that the slaves left their most sublime gift to American culture.

Tension and sudden change between sorrow and joy animates many of the slave songs: "Sometimes I feel like a motherless chile . . . / Sometimes I feel like an eagle in the air, / Spread my wings and fly, fly, fly!" Many of these songs also express a sense of intimacy and closeness with God. Some songs display an unmistakable rebelliousness, such as the enduring "He said, and if I had my way / If I had my way, if I had my way, / I'd tear this building down!" And some spirituals reached for a collective sense of hope in the black community as a whole:

O, gracious Lord! When shall it be,
That we poor souls shall all be free;
Lord, break them slavery powers—
Will you go along with me?
Lord break them slavery powers,
Go sound the jubilee!

In many ways, American slaves converted the Christian God to themselves. They sought an alternative world in which they could live. In a thousand variations on the 'Brer Rabbit folktales, in which power and success could be reversed, and in the countless refrains of their songs, they fashioned survival and resistance out of their own cultural imagination.

The main source of support for individuals was the family, which faced severe pressures. Many families were separated by the forced migration and sale of an estimated 2 million slaves between 1820 and 1860 into the region extending from western Georgia to eastern Texas. When the Union Army registered thousands of black marriages in Mississippi and Louisiana in 1864 and 1865, fully 25 percent of the men over forty reported that they had been forcibly separated from a previous wife.

The Slave Trade and Separation

Many antebellum white southerners made their livings from the slave trade. In South Carolina alone, by the 1850s there were over one hundred slave-trading firms selling an annual average of approximately 6,500 slaves to southwestern states. Although southerners often denied it, vast numbers of slaves moved west by outright sale and not by migrating with their owners.

Slave traders were practical, roving businessmen. They were sometimes considered degraded by white planters, but many became prominent citizens, and whatever their status, many slaveowners did business with them. Traders did their utmost to make their slaves appear young, healthy, and happy, cutting gray whiskers off men and forcing people to dance and sing as buyers arrived for an auction. When transported to the southwestern markets, slaves were often chained together in "coffles," which made journeys of 500 miles or more on foot.

The complacent mixture of racism and business among traders is evident in their own language. "I refused a girl 20 year[s] old at 700 yesterday," one trader wrote to another in 1853. "If you think best to take her at 700 I can still get her. She is very badly whipped but good teeth." Some sales were transacted at owners' requests. "Bought a cook yesterday that was to go out of state," wrote a trader; "she just made the people mad that was all."

But separation did not mean that slave families could not endure. American slaves clung tenaciously to the personal relationships that gave meaning to life. Although American law did not recognize slave families, masters permitted them; in fact, slaveowners expected slaves to form

The Black Family in Slavery

families and have children. As a result, even along the rapidly expanding edge of the cotton kingdom, there was a normal ratio of men to women, young to old.

Following African kinship traditions, African Americans avoided marriage between cousins. Adapting West African customs, they did not condemn unwed mothers but did expect a young woman to enter a monogamous relationship after one pregnancy, if not before. By naming their children after relatives of past generations, African Americans emphasized their family histories. If they chose to bear the surname of a slaveowner, it was often the name not of their current master but of the owner under whom their family had begun their bondage in America.

Sexual abuse and rape by white masters of slave women were ever-present threats. Harriet Jacobs spent much of her youth and early adult years dodging her owner's relentless sexual pursuit. In recollecting

This photograph of five generations of a slave family, taken in Beaufort, South Carolina, in 1862, is silent but powerful testimony to the importance that enslaved African Americans placed on their ever-threatened family ties.   (Library of Congress)

her desperate effort to protect her children, Jacobs asked a haunting question that many slave women carried with them to their graves: "Why does the slave ever love? Why allow the tendrils of the heart to twine around objects which may at any moment be wrenched away by the hand of violence?"

Slaves hated interference in their family lives. Indeed, some individuals refused separations and struggled for years to keep their children together and reestablish contact with lost loved ones. Kinship networks, indeed, were often what held family life together in many slave communities.

Slave Resistance and Rebellion

 Slaves brought to their efforts at resistance the same common sense and determination that characterized their family lives. The scales were weighted heavily against overt revolution, and the slaves knew it. But they seized opportunities to alter their work and life conditions.

Sometimes slaves slacked off work when they were not being watched. Sometimes their discontentment was manifested through the sabotage of equipment, theft of food, or wanton carelessness about work. Many male, and some female, slaves acted out their defiance by violently attacking overseers or even their owners. Southern court records and newspapers are full of accounts of these resistant slaves who gave the lie to the syrupy image of the docile bondsmen. The price they paid was high. Such lonely rebels were customarily secured and flogged, sold away, or hanged.

Strategies of Resistance

Many individual slaves attempted to run away to the North, and some received assistance from the loose network known as the Underground Railroad (see page 240). But it was more common for slaves to run off temporarily and hide in the woods. Fear, disgruntlement over treatment, family separation, and a hundred other complaints might motivate slaves to try to stay at large in the Upper South states for weeks or months at a time. Only a minority of those who tried such escapes ever made it to freedom in the North.

American slavery produced some fearless revolutionaries. Gabriel's Rebellion involved as many as a thousand slaves when it was discovered in 1800 (see page 138). A similar conspiracy in Charleston in 1822, led by a free black named Denmark Vesey, involved many of the prominent whites' most trusted slaves. And the most famous rebel of all, Nat Turner, struck for freedom in Southampton County, Virginia, in 1831.

The son of an African woman who passionately hated her enslavement, Nat Turner was a precocious child who learned to read when he was very young. Encouraged by his first owner to study the Bible, he enjoyed certain privileges but also endured hard work and changes of masters. His father successfully escaped to freedom.

Nat Turner's Insurrection

Eventually young Nat became a preacher with a reputation for eloquence and a tendency toward mysticism. After nurturing his plan for several years, Turner led a band of rebels from farm to farm in the predawn darkness of August 22, 1831. The group severed limbs and crushed skulls with axes or killed their victims with guns. Before they were stopped, Turner and his followers had slaughtered sixty whites of both sexes and all ages in forty-eight hours. The rebellion was put down, Turner hanged, and an estimated two hundred African Americans, including innocent victims, killed by vengeful whites. In the wake of the insurrection, many states stiffened legal codes prohibiting black education and religious practices.

Harmony and Tension in a Slave Society

 From 1830 to 1860, slavery impinged on laws and customs, individual values, and, increasingly, every aspect of southern politics.

In all things, from their workaday movements to Sunday worship, slaves fell under the supervision of whites. State courts held that a slave "has no civil right" and could not hold property "except at the will and pleasure of his master." Revolts like Nat Turner's tightened the legal straitjacket even more. As political conflicts between North and South deepened, fears of slave revolt grew, and restrictions on slaves increased accordingly.

State and federal laws aided the capture of fugitive slaves and required nonslaveholders to support the slave system. All white male citizens had a legal duty to participate in slave patrols. Ship captains, harbor masters, and other whites in strategic positions in both

North and South were required to scrutinize the papers of African Americans who might be attempting to escape bondage.

Slavery deeply affected southern values precisely because it was the main determinant of wealth. Own-

Slavery, Wealth, and Social Standing

ership of slaves guaranteed the labor to produce cotton and other crops on a large scale. Slaves were therefore vital to the acquisition of a fortune. Beyond that, they were a commodity and an investment, much like gold; people bought them on speculation, hoping for a steady rise in their market values.

Wealth in slaves also translated into political power: a solid majority of political officeholders were slaveholders, and the most powerful were usually large-scale planters. Lawyers and newspaper editors were sometimes influential, but they were dependent on planters for business and support.

Slavery's influence spread throughout the social system until even the values and mores of nonslaveholders bore its imprint. The availability of slave labor tended to devalue free labor: where strenuous work under supervision was reserved for an enslaved race, few free people relished it. When Alexis de Tocqueville crossed from Ohio into Kentucky in his celebrated travels of 1831, he observed that on "the right bank of the Ohio [River] everything is activity, industry; labor is honoured; there are no slaves. Pass to the left bank and . . . the enterprising spirit is gone. There, work is not only painful; it is shameful. . . ." Tocqueville's own class impulses, however, were at home in the South, where he found a "veritable aristocracy."

The values of the aristocrat—lineage, privilege, pride, and refinement of person and manner—com-

Aristocratic Values and Frontier Individualism

manded respect throughout the South. Many of those qualities were in short supply, however, in the recently settled portions of the cotton kingdom, where the frontier values of courage and self-reliance ruled. Independence and defense of one's honor became highly valued traits for planter and frontier farmer alike. Thus, instead of gradually disappearing as it did in the North, dueling, which required men to defend their honor through violence, lasted much longer in the South.

Other aristocratic values of the planter class were less acceptable to the average voter. Planters believed they were better than other people. In their pride, they expected not only to wield power but also to receive deference from poorer whites. Independent and proud, the yeoman class resented infringements of their rights. And being aware of national democratic ideals, yeomen sometimes challenged or rejected the aristocratic pretensions of planters.

Class tensions emerged in the western, nonslaveholding parts of the seaboard states by the 1830s.

Yeoman Demands for Political Reform

There yeoman farmers resented their underrepresentation in state legislatures and the corruption in local government. After vigorous debate, the reformers won many battles. Voters in more recently settled areas—Alabama, Mississippi, Tennessee, Arkansas, and Texas—adopted white manhood suffrage and other electoral reforms, including popular election of governors, legislative apportionment based on white population only, and locally chosen county government. Kentucky, Georgia, Florida, Louisiana, Maryland, and North Carolina adopted most or some of these measures. Only South Carolina and Virginia effectively defended property qualifications for office, legislative malapportionment, and selection of the governor by state legislatures. The structure of southern government thus became more democratic than planters wished.

Slaveowners knew that a more open government structure could permit troubling issues to arise. In Virginia, it was nonslaveholding westerners who petitioned and initiated an 1832 debate over the gradual abolition of slavery in the wake of Nat Turner's Rebellion. The pro-abolition measure failed by a vote of 73 to 58. It was the last public debate on slavery in the antebellum South.

Given such tensions, it was perhaps remarkable that slaveholders and nonslaveholders did not experi-

Antebellum White Class Relations

ence more overt conflict. Why were class confrontations among whites so infrequent? One of the most important factors was race. The South's racial ideology stressed the superiority of all whites to blacks. Thus slavery became the basis of equality among whites, and racism inflated the status of poor whites and gave them a common interest with the rich. Family ties also linked some nonslaveholders to wealthy planters, especially on the expanding frontier. And the westward expansion of the cotton kingdom gave yeomen the hope of rising in status through the acquisition of land and slaves.

Most importantly, in their daily lives yeomen and slaveholders were seldom in conflict. Before the Civil War most yeomen were able to pursue their independent lifestyle unhindered. They worked their farms, avoided debt, and marked progress for their families that in their rural habitats was unrelated to slaveholding. Likewise, slaveholders pursued their goals quite independently of yeomen.

Suppression of dissent also played an increasing role. After 1830 white southerners who criticized the slave system out of moral conviction or class resentment were intimidated, attacked, or legally prosecuted. (Some, like James Birney, went north and joined the antislavery movement.) By the 1850s the defense of slavery's interests exerted an ever more powerful influence on southern politics and society.

Still, there were signs that the relative lack of conflict between slaveholders and nonslaveholders was coming to an end in the late antebellum period. As cotton lands filled up, nonslaveholders saw their opportunities beginning to narrow; meanwhile, wealthy planters enjoyed expanding profits. The risks of entering cotton production were becoming too great and the cost of slaves too high for many yeomen to rise in society. From 1830 to 1860 the percentage of white southern families holding slaves declined steadily from 36 to 25 percent. At the same time, the monetary gap between the classes was widening.

Hardening of Class Lines

Urban artisans and mechanics felt the pinch acutely. Their numbers were few, and in bad times they were often the first to lose work as markets collapsed. Moreover, they faced stiff competition from urban slaves, whose masters wanted to hire them out to practice trades. White workers protested, demanding that economic competition from slaves be forbidden, but they were ignored. However, the angry protests of white workers resulted in harsh restrictions on free African American laborers and craftsmen.

Pre–Civil War politics reflected these tensions as well. Anticipating possible secession and the prospect of a war to defend slavery, slaveowners expressed growing fear about the loyalty of nonslaveholders. Schemes to widen the ownership of slaves were discussed, including reopening the African slave trade. In North Carolina, a prolonged and increasingly bitter controversy erupted over the combination of high taxes on land and low taxes on slaves. When nonslaveholder Hinton R. Helper denounced the slave system in *The Impending Crisis*, published in 1857, discerning planters feared the eruption of such controversies in every southern state.

But for the moment slaveowners stood secure. In the 1850s they occupied from 50 to 85 percent of the seats in state legislatures and a similarly high percentage of the South's congressional seats. Planters had established their point of view in all the other major social institutions. Professors who criticized slavery had been dismissed from colleges and universities; schoolbooks that contained "unsound" ideas had been replaced. And almost all the Methodist and Baptist clergy had become slavery's most vocal defenders.

Summary

During the thirty years before the Civil War, the South grew as part of America's westward expansion. Ideologically and economically, the southern states developed in many distinctive ways; at the same time, they were also deeply enmeshed in the nation's heritage and political economy. Far more than the North, the antebellum South was a biracial society; whites grew up directly influenced by black folkways and culture, and blacks, the vast majority of whom were slaves, became predominantly native-born Americans and the cobuilders with whites of a rural, agricultural society.

With the sustained cotton boom, the South grew fatefully into a much larger slave society than it had been early in the century. The coercive influence of slavery affected virtually every element of southern life and politics. Despite the white supremacy that united them, the democratic values of yeomen often clashed with the profit motives of aristocratic planters. The benevolent self-image and paternalistic ideology of slaveholders had to ultimately stand the test of the slaves' own judgments. African American slaves responded by fashioning over time a rich expressive folk culture and a religion of personal and group deliverance.

From the Old South on to modern times, white and black southerners have always shared a tragic, mutual history. By 1850, through their own wits and on the backs of African labor, white southerners had aggressively built one of the last profitable, expanding slave societies on earth. North of them, deeply intertwined with them in the same nation, market economy, constitutional system, and history, a different kind of society had grown even faster—one driven by industrialism and individualistic free labor. The clash of these two deeply connected, yet divided societies was about to explode in political storms over how the nation would define its future.

LEGACY FOR A PEOPLE AND A NATION
The Black Family

In the late 1830s Virginia slaveholder Robert Bruce prepared a list of the slaves on his plantation. He noted that three maternal grandmothers performed the primary care of small children whose mothers either were dead or had been sold away. Bruce made no mention of slave fathers.

Bruce's list illustrates one of slavery's deepest legacies—its impact on family life. The questions are still with us. Can poverty and broken families since emancipation be attributed to the slave experience? Does slavery's heritage require persistent redistributive justice in our current society?

Slavery put unbearable pressures on black family life, and ever since emancipation, popular lore has supported the idea that a nuclear family could not survive the masters' economic and sexual power. In 1939 the black sociologist E. Franklin Frazier argued that "no social organization" survived from African heritage among American slaves, and that the family "went to pieces." In the 1960s Daniel Patrick Moynihan conducted a study that concluded that blacks had plunged into urban poverty because of a set of behaviors drawn from the past (a "culture of poverty") that eroded stable families.

Historians challenged the "damage" thesis in the 1970s, revealing evidence of strong families both during and after slavery. Moreover, sociologists argued that it is the fact of poverty, not a "culture" developed from it, that severs marriages and families. But even these new theses are challenged by studies of widespread family separation during slavery, the women-centered character of slave life, and the ravages of sharecropping and segregation.

Much damage was done by slavery to black family life. Discussions of exactly what the long-term effects are may never produce a consensus. But this question drives nearly every policy debate Americans face over the relationships among race, history, and social welfare. Many single black women raise well-adjusted children, and kin networks are still crucial in African American family life. But troubling facts remain: a majority of black children still live in families that include their mothers but not their fathers, whereas about four of five white children under eighteen live with both parents.

For Further Reading, see the Appendix. For Web resources, go to history.college.hmco.com/students.

SLAVERY AND AMERICA'S FUTURE: THE ROAD TO WAR

1845–1861

The War with Mexico and Its Consequences
1850: Compromise or Armistice?
Slavery Expansion and Collapse of the Party System
Slavery and the Nation's Future
Disunion
LEGACY FOR A PEOPLE AND A NATION
Revolutionary Violence

As the delegates filed into the Musical Fund Hall in Philadelphia on June 17, 1856, they knew they had created something special in American politics. The first national nominating convention of the Republican Party was meeting to approve a platform and select their presidential ticket. Formed just two years earlier, the party had drawn together a broad coalition of northern politicians who opposed both the expansion of slavery and the growing power of the South in the federal government.

Their coalition combined men who had been former Democrats; men who had been founding members of the American Party, a group that wanted to prohibit foreigners, especially Catholics, from settling in the United States; and many former Whigs, whose party had been shattered by the crisis over slavery and

its expansion. They consisted of conservatives, moderates, and radicals; some believed slavery and all its influences a moral evil, while others saw it as a political problem.

At this convention, a radical temper prevailed. The convention was only minutes old when the temporary chairman, Robert Emmet of New York, brought the delegates to their feet by using the Declaration of Independence to label slavery a great political danger to the nation's future. Speaker after speaker declared that their party would render "freedom national" and "slavery sectional" by using the power of Congress to outlaw human bondage in all western territories.

The convention's platform committee was chaired by David Wilmot, a former Democrat who was no friend of black civil and political rights. But Wilmot, like the others, was firmly opposed to slavery's expansion and just as firmly endorsed the protection of free white men's labor and land ownership across the continent. At the heart of the platform was the short, direct credo calling upon Congress to "prohibit in the territories those twin relics of barbarism—polygamy and slavery."

The Republicans nominated John C. Frémont, the famous western explorer and former California senator, for president. In the election that followed, Americans began to vote by section and not by party as never before. The Republican coalition began to unify the North around keeping the West free and alarmed the South, which now saw the future of its slave society endangered by a political movement determined to limit if not destroy slavery. Frémont lost the 1856 election, but the Republicans made the best showing ever in American history of a newly born party in its first presidential bid.

Meanwhile, a larger drama of conflict and violence had begun to envelop the nation. In Kansas territory, open warfare had exploded between proslavery and antislavery settlers. On the floor of the U.S. Senate a southern representative beat a northern senator senseless. A new fugitive slave law sent thousands of blacks fleeing into Canada in fear for their liberty and their lives. The tradition of compromise on political problems related to slavery teetered on the brink of complete collapse. Within a year the Supreme Court had issued a dramatic decision about slavery, its constitutionality in westward expansion, and the status of African American citizenship—to the delight of most southerners and the dread of most northerners. And abolitionist John Brown was planning a raid into Virginia to start a slave rebellion.

The political culture of the American republic was disintegrating. As the 1850s advanced, slavery pulled Americans, North and South, into a maelstrom of dispute that its best statesmen, ultimately, could not subdue. The prosperous model republic, riven by stark contradictions, was on the road to a terrible war.

Slavery had aroused passions that could be neither contained nor resolved. What began as a dark cloud over the territories became a storm engulfing the nation. Between 1845 and 1853 the United States added Texas, California, Oregon Country, and the Southwest to its domain and launched the settlement of the Great Plains. Each time the nation expanded, it confronted a thorny issue: should new territories and states be slave or free?

The ensuing political storms gave rise to a feeling in both North and South that America's future was at stake. The new Republican Party believed that America's future depended on the unbounded labor of free men, whose rights were protected by a government devoted to liberty. They charged southerners with using the power of the federal government to make slavery legal throughout the Union. Southern leaders defended slavery and charged the North with unconstitutional efforts to destroy it. To these southerners, a government that failed to protect slavery was unworthy of their loyalty. For blacks, the growing dispute brought hope and despair. They could take heart that the country's political strife over slavery might somehow lead to their liberation. But with the nation now trying to define its future, blacks had to wonder whether they had a future at all in America. ■

The War with Mexico and Its Consequences

In the 1840s, territorial expansion surged forward under the leadership of President James K. Polk. The annexation of Texas just before his inauguration did not necessarily make war with Mexico inevitable, but by design and through a series of calculated decisions, Polk made the conflict all but unavoidable. Polk was determined to fulfill the nation's "manifest destiny" to rule the continent. He wanted Mexico's territory all the way to the Pacific, and all of Oregon Country as well.

During the 1844 campaign, Polk's supporters had threatened war with Great Britain to gain all of Oregon. As president, however, Polk turned first to diplomacy. Not wanting to fight Mexico and Great Britain at the same time, he tried to avoid bloodshed in the Northwest, where America and Britain had since 1818 jointly occupied disputed territory. Dropping the demand for a boundary at latitude 54°40', he pressured the British to accept the 49th parallel. In 1846 Great Britain agreed. The Oregon Treaty gave the United States all of present-day Oregon, Washington, and Idaho and parts of Wyoming and Montana.

Oregon

IMPORTANT EVENTS

1846 War with Mexico begins
Oregon Treaty negotiated
Wilmot Proviso inflames sectional divisions

1847 Cass proposes idea of popular sovereignty

1848 Treaty of Guadalupe Hidalgo gives United
States new territory in the Southwest
Free-Soil Party formed
Taylor elected president

1849 Gold discovered in California, which applies
for admission to Union as free state

1850 Compromise of 1850 passed in separate bills

1852 Stowe publishes *Uncle Tom's Cabin*
Pierce elected president

1854 Publication of "Appeal of the Independent
Democrats"
Kansas-Nebraska Act wins approval and
ignites controversy
Republican Party formed
Return of fugitive Burns from Boston to
slavery in Virginia

1856 Bleeding Kansas troubles nation
Brooks attacks Sumner in Senate chamber
Buchanan elected president

1857 *Dred Scott v. Sandford* endorses southern
views on black citizenship and slavery in
territories
Economic panic and widespread unemployment begins

1858 Kansas voters reject Lecompton Constitu-
tion
Lincoln-Douglas debates attract attention
Douglas proposes Freeport Doctrine

1859 Brown raids Harpers Ferry

1860 Democratic Party splits in two; southern
Democrats demand "Slave Code for the
Territories"
Lincoln elected president
Crittenden Compromise fails
South Carolina secedes from Union

1861 Six more Deep South states secede
Confederacy established at Montgomery,
Alabama
Attack on Fort Sumter begins Civil War
Four states in the Upper South join the
Confederacy

Toward Mexico, Polk was more aggressive. In early 1846, he ordered American troops to march south and defend the contested bor-

"Mr. Polk's War"

der of the Rio Grande. Polk had earlier encouraged Texas to claim the Rio Grande as its southern and western border. Polk especially desired California as the prize in his expansionist strategy, and to that end he attempted to buy from the angry Mexicans a huge tract of land extending to the Pacific. The effort failed. Meanwhile, negotiations between troops on the Rio Grande proved fruitless. The situation became increasingly tense, and on April 24, 1846, Mexican cavalry ambushed a U.S. cavalry unit on the north side of the river; eleven Americans were killed and sixty-three taken captive.

Polk now drafted a message to Congress: Mexico had "passed the boundary of the United States, had invaded our territory and shed American blood on American soil." Polk deceptively declared that "war exists by the act of Mexico itself" and summoned the nation to arms. Two days later, on May 13, the House recognized a state of war with Mexico by a vote of 174 to 14, and the Senate by 40 to 2, with numerous abstentions. Some antislavery Whigs had tried to oppose the war but were barely allowed to gain the floor of Congress to speak. Since Polk withheld key facts, the full reality of what had happened on the distant Rio Grande was not known. But the theory and practice of manifest destiny had launched the United States into its first war on foreign territory.

The idea of war unleashed great public celebrations. Huge crowds gathered in southern cities to

Foreign War and the Popular Imagination

voice support for the war effort. Twenty thousand Philadelphians and even more New Yorkers rallied in the same spirit. After news came of General Zachary Taylor's first two battlefield victories at Palo Alto and Resaca de la Palma, volunteers swarmed recruiting stations.

Here was an adventurous war of conquest in a far-off, exotic land. Here was the fulfillment of Anglo-Saxon–Christian destiny to expand and possess the North American continent and to take "civilization" to the "semi-Indian" Mexicans. For many, racism fueled the expansionist spirit. In 1846 an Illinois newspaper justified the war on the basis that Mexicans were "reptiles in the path of progressive democracy."

The war spawned an outpouring of poetry, song, drama, travel literature, and lithographs that captured the popular imagination and glorified the war. Most of the war-inspired flowering in the popular arts was patriotic. But not everyone cheered. The abolitionist James Russell Lowell considered the war a "national crime committed in behoof of slavery, our common sin." Even proslavery spokesman John C. Calhoun saw the perils of expansionism. Mexico, he said, was "the forbidden fruit; the penalty of eating it would be to subject our institutions to political death."

Conquest

Early in the war U.S. forces made significant gains. In May 1846 Colonel Stephen Kearny and a small detachment invaded the remote and thinly populated provinces of New Mexico and California. Taking Santa Fe without opposition, Kearny pushed into California, where he joined forces with rebellious American settlers led by Captain John C. Frémont and with a couple of U.S. naval units. General Zachary Taylor's forces attacked and occupied Monterrey, which surrendered in September, securing northeastern Mexico (see Map 14.1). American soldiers established dominion over distant California before the end of 1846.

Because losses on the periphery of their large country had not broken Mexican resistance, General Winfield Scott carried the war to the enemy's heartland. Landing at Veracruz, he led fourteen thousand men toward Mexico City. After a series of hard-fought battles, U.S. troops captured the Mexican capital.

Treaty of Guadalupe Hidalgo

Representatives of both countries signed the Treaty of Guadalupe Hidalgo in February 1848. The United States gained California and New Mexico (including present-day Nevada, Utah, and Arizona, and parts of Colorado and Wyoming) and recognition of the Rio Grande as the southern boundary of Texas. In return, the American government agreed to settle the claims of its citizens against Mexico ($3.2 million) and to pay Mexico a mere $15 million.

The costs of the war included the deaths of thirteen thousand Americans and fifty thousand Mexicans. It also sharply divided public opinion in the United States. Southwesterners were enthusiastic about the war, as were most southern planters; New Englanders strenuously opposed it. Whigs in Congress charged that Polk, a Democrat, had "provoked" an unnecessary war and "usurped the power of Congress." The aged John Quincy Adams denounced the war; and a tall, young Illinois Whig named Abraham Lincoln called Polk's justifications the "half insane mumbling of a fever-dream." Abolitionists and a small minority of antislavery Whigs charged that the war was no less than a plot to extend slavery.

"Slave Power Conspiracy"

These charges fed northern fear of the so-called Slave Power. Abolitionists had long warned of a slaveholding oligarchy that controlled the South and intended to dominate the nation through its hold on federal power. These dangerous aristocrats had forced the gag rule on Congress in 1836 and threatened northern liberties. To many white northerners, even those who saw nothing wrong with slavery, it was the battle over free speech and the right of petition that first made the idea of a Slave Power credible. The War with Mexico deepened such fears. Why, asked antislavery northerners, had claims to part of Oregon been abandoned and a questionable war begun for vast new slave territory?

Northern opinion on the expansion of slavery began to shift, but the impact of events on southern opinion was even more dramatic. At first some southern leaders criticized the War with Mexico. Southern Whigs attacked the Democratic president for causing the war. Even John C. Calhoun—despite his earlier schemes to annex Texas for slavery—strongly opposed the seizure of large amounts of land from Mexico. Many whites in both North and South feared that large land seizures would bring thousands of nonwhite Mexicans into the United States and upset the racial order. An Indiana politician did not want "any mixed races in our Union, nor men of any color except white, unless they be slaves." Despite their racism, however, many statesmen soon saw other prospects in the outcomes of a war of conquest in the Southwest.

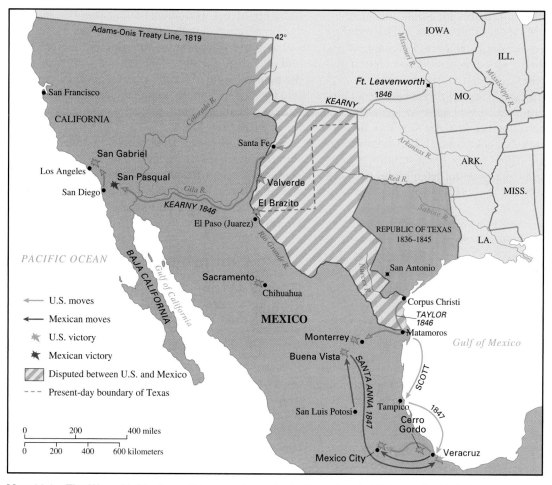

Map 14.1   The War with Mexico   This map shows the territory disputed between the United States and Mexico. After U.S. gains in northeastern Mexico and in New Mexico and California, General Winfield Scott captured Mexico City in the decisive campaign of the war.

The War with Mexico proved generally popular with southern voters, and no southern Whig could oppose it once slavery became the central issue. That happened in August 1846, when David Wilmot, a Pennsylvania Democrat, proposed an amendment, or proviso, to a military appropriations bill: that "neither slavery nor involuntary servitude shall ever exist" in any territory gained from Mexico. Although the proviso never passed both houses of Congress, it transformed the debate.

Wilmot Proviso

Southerners suddenly circled their wagons to protect the future of a slave society. John C. Calhoun asserted a radical new southern position. The territories, Calhoun insisted, belonged to all the states, and the federal government could do nothing to limit the spread of slavery there. Southern slaveholders had a constitutional right rooted in the Fifth Amendment, Calhoun claimed, to take their slaves (as property) anywhere in the territories.

This position, often called "state sovereignty," which quickly became a test of orthodoxy among southern politicians, was a radical reversal of history. In 1787 the Confederation Congress had excluded slavery from the Northwest Territory (see pages 118–119); Article IV of the federal Constitution had authorized Congress to make "all needful rules and regulations" for the territories; and the Missouri Compromise had barred slavery from most of the Louisiana Purchase. Now, however, southern leaders demanded protection and future guarantees for slavery.

In the North, the Wilmot Proviso became a rallying cry for abolitionists. Eventually the legislatures of fourteen northern states endorsed it—and not because all its supporters were abolitionists. David Wilmot, significantly, was neither an abolitionist nor an anti-slavery Whig. His goal was to defend "the rights of white freemen" and to obtain California "for free white labor."

Fear of the Slave Power, however, was building a potent antislavery movement that united abolitionists and antiblack voters. The latter's concern was to protect from the Slave Power an abiding version of the American Dream: the free, individual, immigrant farmer's access to social mobility through acquisition of land and jobs in the West. This sacred ideal of free labor, and the dread of concentrated power, fueled a new political persuasion in America.

The slavery question divided northerners and southerners in both parties and could not be kept out of national politics. After Polk renounced a second term as president, the Democrats nominated Senator Lewis Cass of Michigan for president. Cass, a party loyalist, had devised in 1847 the idea of "popular sovereignty" for the territories—letting residents in the territories decide the question of slavery for themselves. His party's platform declared that Congress lacked the power to interfere with slavery and criticized those who pressed the question. The Whigs nominated General Zachary Taylor, a southern slaveholder and war hero. The Whig convention similarly refused to assert that Congress had power over slavery in the territories.

The Election of 1848 and Popular Sovereignty

Among northerners, concern over slavery led to the formation of a new party. New York Democrats committed to the Wilmot Proviso rebelled against Cass and nominated former president Martin Van Buren. Antislavery Whigs and former supporters of the Liberty Party then joined them to organize the Free-Soil Party, with Van Buren as its candidate. This party, whose slogan was "Free Soil, Free Speech, Free Labor, and Free Men," won almost 300,000 northern votes. Taylor polled 1.4 million votes to Cass's 1.2 million and won the White House, but the results were more ominous than decisive. The War with Mexico made the political issue of slavery expansion into a moral issue. Politics split along sectional lines as never before. Religious denominations, too, were splitting into northern and southern wings.

The conflicts of 1848 would dominate politics throughout the 1850s, as slavery in the territories colored every other national issue. The nation's uncertain attempts to deal with economic and social change gave way to more pressing questions about the nature of the Union itself.

1850: Compromise or Armistice?

The first sectional battle of the new decade involved California. More than eighty thousand Americans flooded into California during the gold rush of 1849. With Congress unable to agree on a formula to govern the territories, President Taylor urged these settlers to apply directly for admission to the Union. They promptly did so, proposing a state constitution that banned slavery. Southern politicians objected because California's admission as a free state would upset the equal balance of free states and slave states in the Senate. At a minimum, southerners wanted the Missouri Compromise line extended to the Pacific.

Henry Clay, the venerable Whig leader, sensed that the Union was in peril. Twice before—in 1820 and 1833—Clay had taken the lead in shaping sectional compromise; now he struggled one last time to preserve the nation. To hushed Senate galleries Clay presented a series of compromise measures in the winter of 1850. Over the weeks that followed, he and Senator Stephen A. Douglas of Illinois steered their omnibus bill, or compromise package, through debate and amendment.

The problems to be solved were numerous and difficult. Would California, or part of it, become a free state? How should the territory acquired from Mexico be organized? Texas, which allowed slavery, claimed large portions of the new land as far west as Santa Fe, so that claim, too, had to be settled. Southerners complained that fugitive slaves were not being returned as the Constitution required, and northerners objected to the sale of human beings in the nation's capital. But most troublesome of all was the status of slavery in the territories.

Clay and Douglas hoped to avoid a specific formula, for Lewis Cass's idea of popular sovereignty possessed what one historian called the "charm of ambiguity" that appealed to practical politicians. Ultimately Congress would have to approve statehood for a territory, but "in the meantime," said Cass, it should allow the people living there "to regulate their own concerns in their own way."

Those simple words proved all but unenforceable. When could settlers prohibit slavery? To avoid dissension within their party, northern and southern Democrats explained Cass's statement to their constituents in two incompatible ways. Southerners claimed that neither Congress nor a territorial legislature could bar slavery. Only late in the territorial process, when settlers were ready to draft a state constitution, could they take that step. Northerners, however, insisted that Americans living in a territory were entitled to local self-government and thus could outlaw slavery at any time.

The cause of compromise gained a powerful supporter when Senator Daniel Webster committed his prestige and eloquence to Clay's bill. "I wish to speak today," Webster declaimed on March 7 in a scene of high drama, "not as a Massachusetts man, nor as a Northern man, but as an American. I speak today for the preservation of the Union. Hear me for my cause." Yet Webster's influence and rising fear of disunion were not enough. After months of labor, Clay and Douglas finally brought their legislative package to a vote, and lost. Then, with Clay sick and absent from Washington, Douglas reintroduced the compromise measures one at a time. Though there was no majority for compromise, Douglas shrewdly realized that different majorities might be created for the separate measures. The strategy worked, and the Compromise of 1850 became law.

The compromise had five essential measures: California became a free state; the Texas boundary was set at its present limits (see Map 14.2 on page 242) and the United States paid Texas $10 million in compensation for the loss of New Mexico territory; the territories of New Mexico and

Compromise of 1850

Utah were organized on a basis of popular sovereignty; the fugitive slave law was strengthened; and the slave trade was abolished in the District of Columbia. Jubilation greeted passage of the compromise; crowds in Washington and other cities celebrated the happy news.

In reality, there was less cause for celebration than people hoped. The compromise had two basic flaws. The first concerned the ambiguity of territorial legislation: how exactly was popular sovereignty to be enforced? During debate, southerners insisted there would be no prohibition of slavery during the territorial stage, and northerners declared that settlers could bar slavery whenever they wished. The compromise even allowed for the appeal of a territorial legislature's action to the Supreme Court.

The second flaw lay in the Fugitive Slave Act, which gave new—and controversial—protection to slavery. The law empowered slaveowners to go into court in their own states to present evidence that a slave who owed them service had escaped. The resulting transcript and a description of the fugitive would then serve as legal proof of a person's slave status, even in free states and territories. Specially appointed court officials would adjudicate the identity of the person described, not whether he or she was indeed a slave. Penalties made it a felony to harbor fugitives. Moreover, the fees paid to U.S. marshals favored slaveholders: $10 if the alleged fugitive was returned to the slaveowner, $5 if not returned.

Fugitive Slave Act

Abolitionist newspapers quickly attacked the Fugitive Slave Act as a violation of fundamental American rights. Why were alleged fugitives denied a trial by jury? Why were they given no chance to present evidence or cross-examine witnesses? Why did the law give authorities a financial incentive to send suspected fugitives into bondage? These haunting questions led to protest meetings all over the North.

Between 1850 and 1854, violent resistance to slave catchers occurred in dozens of northern towns. Sometimes a captured fugitive was broken out of jail or from the clutches of slave agents by abolitionists, as in the case of Shadrach Minkins in 1851 in Boston, who was spirited by a series of wagons and trains across Massachusetts, up through Vermont, to Montreal, Canada. Also in 1851, the small black community in Lancaster County, Pennsylvania, rose up in arms to defend four escaped slaves from a federal posse charged with reenslaving them. At this "Christiana riot," the fugitives shot and killed Edward Gorsuch, the Maryland slaveowner who sought the return of his "property."

At this point a novel portrayed the humanity and suffering of slaves in a way that touched millions of northerners. Harriet Beecher Stowe, whose New England family had produced many prominent ministers, wrote *Uncle Tom's Cabin* out of deep moral conviction. Her story, serialized in 1851 and published as a book in 1852, conveyed the agonies faced by slave families. Stowe also portrayed slavery's evil effects on slaveholders, indicting the institution itself more harshly than she indicted the southerners caught in its web. By mid-1853 over a million copies of *Uncle Tom's Cabin* had been sold. Through her book, Stowe brought home the evil of slavery to many who had never given it much thought.

Uncle Tom's Cabin

The popularity of *Uncle Tom's Cabin* alarmed anxious southern whites. In politics and now in popular literature they saw threats to their way of life. Behind the South's aggressive claims about territorial rights lay the fear that if nearby areas became free soil, they would be used as bases from which to spread abolitionism into the slave states. To most white southerners, a moral condemnation of slaveholding anywhere meant the same thing everywhere.

Slaveholders were especially disturbed by the 1850s over what was widely called the Underground Railroad. This loose, illegal network of abolitionist stations all over the border state region (the area all along the Ohio River and the boundaries between Pennsylvania and Maryland and Virginia), spiriting runaways to freedom in safe houses, secret hideouts, and wagons, was never very organized. Thousands of slaves did escape by these routes, but largely through their own wits and courage, and through the assistance of black vigilance committees in some northern cities.

The Underground Railroad

Moreover, Harriet Tubman, herself an escapee in 1848, returned to her native Maryland and to Virginia nearly twenty times, and through clandestine measures helped as many as three hundred slaves to freedom. Maryland planters were so outraged at her heroic success that they offered a $40,000 reward for her capture.

The Underground Railroad also had numerous maritime routes, as coastal slaves escaped aboard ship out of Virginia or the Carolinas, or from a major port like New Orleans. This constant, dangerous flow of humanity was a testament to human courage, good luck, and the will for freedom. It never reached the scale that some angry slaveholders believed, but in reality and in legend it applied pressure to the slavery crisis and served as a symbol and a national conscience against oppression.

The 1852 election gave southern leaders hope that slavery would be secure under the administration of a new president. Franklin Pierce, a Democrat from New Hampshire, won an easy victory over the Whig presidential nominee, General Winfield Scott. Pierce defended each section's rights as essential to the nation's unity, and southerners hoped that his firm support for the Compromise of 1850 might end the season of crisis. His victory suggested widespread support for the compromise.

Election of 1852 and the Collapse of Compromise

Pierce's victory, however, derived less from his strengths than from the Whig Party's weakness. The Whigs were a congressional and state-based party that never had achieved much success in presidential politics. Sectional discord was splitting the party in two, further undermining its national competitiveness, and the deaths of President Taylor, Daniel Webster, and Henry Clay had deprived the Whigs of decisive leadership. In 1852 the Whig Party was all but dead.

President Pierce's embrace of the compromise appalled many northerners. His vigorous enforcement of the Fugitive Slave Act provoked outrage and fear of the Slave Power, especially in the case of the fugitive slave Anthony Burns. Burns had fled Virginia by stowing away on a ship. In Boston, thinking he was safe in a city known for abolitionism, Burns began a new life. But in 1854 federal marshals found and placed him under guard in Boston's courthouse. An interracial crowd of abolitionists attacked the courthouse, killing a jailor, in an unsuccessful attempt to free Burns.

Pierce moved decisively to enforce the Fugitive Slave Act. He telegraphed local officials to "incur any expense to insure the execution of the law" and sent marines, cavalry, and artillery to Boston. When Burns's owner seemed willing to sell his property, the U.S. attorney blocked the sale and won a decision that Anthony Burns must return to slavery. U.S. troops marched Burns to Boston harbor through streets draped in black and hung with American flags at half-mast. At a cost of $100,000, a single black man was returned to slavery through the power of federal law.

This demonstration of federal support for slavery radicalized opinion. Textile manufacturer Amos A. Lawrence observed that "we went to bed one night old fashioned, conservative, Compromise Union Whigs & waked up stark mad Abolitionists." In New England, states began to pass personal-liberty laws designed to impede or block federal enforcement of the Fugitive Slave Act. Before the end of the 1850s, nine northern states had passed such laws. Where northerners now saw evidence of a dominating Slave Power, outraged slaveholders saw the legal defense of their rights.

Pierce seemed unable to avoid sectional conflict in other arenas as well. His proposal for a transcontinental railroad derailed when congressmen fought over its location, North or South. His attempts to acquire foreign territory stirred more trouble. An annexation treaty with Hawai'i failed because southern senators would not vote for another free state, and efforts to acquire slaveholding Cuba angered northerners. Then another territorial bill threw Congress and the nation into even greater turmoil, and the Compromise of 1850 fell into complete collapse.

Slavery Expansion and Collapse of the Party System

The new controversy began in a surprising way. Stephen A. Douglas, one of the architects of the Compromise of 1850, introduced a bill to establish the Kansas and Nebraska Territories. Talented and ambitious, Douglas was known for compromise, but he was willing to risk some controversy to win economic benefits for Illinois, his home state. A transcontinental railroad would encourage settlement of the Great Plains and stimulate the economy of Illinois; but no company would build such a railroad before Congress organized the territories it would cross. Thus interest in promoting the construction of such a railroad drove Douglas to introduce a bill that inflamed sectional passions.

The Kansas-Nebraska bill exposed the first flaw of the Compromise of 1850—the conflicting interpreta-

The Kansas-Nebraska Bill

tions of popular sovereignty. Douglas's bill left "all questions pertaining to slavery in the Territories . . . to the people residing therein." Northerners and southerners, however, still disagreed violently over what territorial settlers could constitutionally do. Moreover, the Kansas and Nebraska Territories lay within the Louisiana Purchase, and the Missouri Compromise prohibited slavery in all that land from latitude 36°30' north to the Canadian border. If popular sovereignty were to mean anything in Kansas and Nebraska, it had to mean that the Missouri Compromise was no longer in effect and that settlers could establish slavery there.

Southern congressmen, anxious to establish slaveholders' right to take slaves into any territory, pressed Douglas to concede this point. They demanded an explicit repeal of the 36°30' limitation as the price of their support. During a carriage ride with Senator Archibald Dixon of Kentucky, Douglas debated the point at length. Finally he made an impulsive decision: "By God, Sir, you are right. I will incorporate it in my bill, though I know it will raise a hell of a storm."

His bill thus threw open to slavery land from which it had been prohibited for thirty-four years. Opposition from Free-Soilers and antislavery forces was immediate and enduring. The titanic struggle in Congress lasted three and a half months. Douglas eventually prevailed: the bill became law in May 1854 by a vote that demonstrated the dangerous sectionalization of American politics (see Map 14.2).

But the storm was just beginning. Abolitionists charged sinister aggression by the Slave Power, and northern fears of slavery's influence deepened. Opposition to the Fugitive Slave Act grew dramatically; between 1855 and 1859 Connecticut, Rhode Island, Massachusetts, Michigan, Maine, Ohio, and Wisconsin passed personal-liberty laws. These laws enraged southern leaders by providing counsel for alleged fugitives and requiring trial by jury. More important was the devastating impact of the Kansas-Nebraska Act on political parties. The weakened Whig Party broke apart into northern and southern wings that could no longer cooperate nationally. One of the two foundations of the second party system (see pages 190–191) was now gone. The Democrats survived, but their support in the North fell drastically in the 1854 elections.

The beneficiary of northern voters' wrath was a new political party. During the summer and fall of

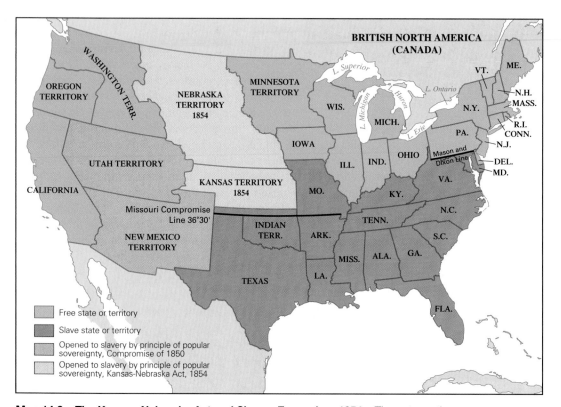

Map 14.2 The Kansas-Nebraska Act and Slavery Expansion, 1854 The vote on the Kansas-Nebraska Act in the House of Representatives demonstrates the sectionalization of American politics due to the slavery question.

Birth of the Republican Party

1854, antislavery Whigs and Democrats, Free-Soilers, and other reformers throughout the Old Northwest met to form the new Republican Party, dedicated to keeping slavery out of the territories. The influence of the Republicans rapidly spread to the East, and they won a stunning victory in the 1854 elections: in their first appearance on the ballot, Republicans captured a majority of northern House seats. Antislavery sentiment had created a new party and caused roughly a quarter of northern Democrats to desert their party.

For the first time, too, a sectional party had gained significant power in the political system. Now the Whigs were gone, and only the Democrats struggled to maintain national membership. The Republicans absorbed the Free-Soil Party and grew rapidly in the North. Indeed, the emergence of the Republican coalition of antislavery interests is the most rapid transformation in party allegiance and voter behavior in American history. This fact alone attests to the centrality of slavery expansion in the causation of the Civil War.

And Republicans were not the only new party. For a brief period, an anti-immigrant organization, the American Party, blossomed. This party, popularly known as the Know-Nothings (because its first members kept their purposes secret, answering "I know nothing" to all questions), exploited nativist fear of foreigners and Catholics. Between 1848 and 1860, nearly 3.5 million immigrants entered the United States—proportionally the heaviest inflow of foreigners ever in American history.

In 1854 anti-immigrant fears gave the Know-Nothings spectacular success in some northern states.

Know-Nothings

They triumphed especially in Massachusetts, electing 11 congressmen, a governor, all state officers, all state senators, and all but 2 of 378 state representatives. The temperance movement also gained new strength early in the 1850s with its promises to stamp out the evils associated with liquor and immigrants (a particularly anti-Irish campaign). In this context the Know-Nothings strove to reinforce Protestant morality and to restrict voting and officeholding to the native-born. But, like the Whigs, the Know-Nothings could not keep their northern and southern wings together, and they dissolved after 1856.

With nearly half of the old electorate up for grabs, the demise of the Whig Party ensured a major realignment of the political system. To win over these homeless Whigs, the remaining parties made appeals to various segments of the electorate. Immigration, temperance, homestead bills, the tariff, internal improvements—all played important roles in attracting voters during the 1850s. The Republicans appealed strongly to those interested in the economic development of the West. Commercial agriculture was booming in the Ohio–Mississippi–Great Lakes area, but residents of that region desired more canals, roads, and river and harbor improvements to reap the full benefit of their labors. They also favored a homestead program through which western land would be made available free to individual farmers. Seizing their opportunity, the Republicans added internal improvements and land-grant planks to their platform. They also backed higher tariffs as an enticement to industrialists and businessmen.

Party Realignment and the Republicans' Appeal

Partisan ideological appeals became the currency of the realigned political system. As Republicans preached "Free Soil, Free Labor, Free Men," they captured a self-image of many northerners. These phrases resonated with traditional ideals of equality, liberty, and opportunity.

"Free Soil, Free Labor, Free Men" seemed an appropriate motto for a northern economy that was energetic, expanding, and prosperous. The key to progress appeared, to many people, to be free labor—the dignity of work and the incentive of opportunity. Any hard-working and virtuous man, it was thought, could improve his condi-

Republican Ideology

tion and achieve economic independence by seizing opportunities that the country had to offer. Republicans argued that the South, with little industry and its slave labor system, was backward and retrograde by comparison, and their arguments captured much of the spirit of the age in the North.

Traditional republicanism hailed the virtuous common man as the backbone of the country. In Abraham Lincoln, a man of humble origins who had become a successful lawyer and political leader, Republicans had a symbol of that tradition. They portrayed their party as the guardian of economic opportunity, giving individuals a chance to work, acquire land, and attain success.

At stake in the enveloping crises of the 1850s were thus two competing definitions of "liberty": southern planters' claims to protection of their liberty in the possession and transport of their slaves anywhere in the land, and northern workers' and farmers' claims to protection of their liberty to seek a new start on free land, unimpeded by a system that defined labor as slave and black. Thus, a growing number of northerners expressed the fear that the rising political storm was an "irrepressible conflict."

Opposition to the extension of slavery had brought the Republicans into being, but party members wisely broadened their appeal by adopting the causes of other groups. As the editor Horace Greeley wrote in 1860, "an Anti-Slavery man per se cannot be elected." But, he added, "a Tariff, River-and-Harbor, Pacific Railroad, Free Homestead man, may succeed although he is Anti-Slavery." As these elements joined the Republican Party, they also grew to fear slavery even more.

In the South, the disintegration of the Whig Party had left many southerners at loose ends politically. Some gravitated to the American Party, but not for long. In the increasingly tense atmosphere of sectional crisis, these people were highly susceptible to strong states' rights positions and defense of slavery. In the 1850s, Democratic leaders managed to convert most of the formerly Whig slaveholders, who responded to their class interests.

Southern Democrats

Most southern Democrats, however, were not slaveholders. Since Andrew Jackson's day, small farmers had been the heart of the Democratic Party. Democratic politicians, though often slaveowners themselves, lauded the common man and argued that their policies advanced his interests. According to the southern version of republicanism, white citizens in a slave society enjoyed liberty and social equality because black people were enslaved. As Jefferson Davis put it in 1851, slavery elevated every white person's status and allowed the nonslaveholder to "stand upon the broad level of equality with the rich man." Southern Democrats warned that the issue was "shall negroes govern white men, or white men govern negroes?" They also portrayed the well-ordered South as the true defender of constitutional principles.

Racial fears and traditional political loyalties helped keep the political alliance between yeoman farmers and planters largely intact through the 1850s. Across class lines, white southerners joined together; potential conflicts between slaveholders and nonslaveholders were not discussed, and no viable party emerged to replace the Whigs. The result was a one-party system that emphasized sectional issues and loyalty. In the South as in the North, political realignment sharpened sectional identities.

Political leaders of both sections used race in their arguments about opportunity. The *Montgomery* (Alabama) *Mail* warned southern whites in 1860 that the Republicans intended "to free the negroes and force amalgamation between them and the children of the poor men of the South." Republicans warned northern workers that if slavery entered the territories, the great reservoir of opportunity for ordinary citizens would be poisoned.

In the territory of Kansas a succession of events, like hammer blows, deepened the conflict. The Kansas-Nebraska Act spawned hatred and violence. Abolitionists and religious groups sent in armed Free-Soil settlers; southerners sent in their reinforcements to establish slavery and prevent "northern hordes" from stealing Kansas away. Conflicts led to bloodshed, and soon the whole nation was talking about "Bleeding Kansas."

Politics in the territory resembled war more than democracy. During elections for a territorial legislature in 1855, thousands of proslavery

Bleeding Kansas

Missourians invaded the polls and ran up a large but fraudulent majority for slavery candidates. The resulting legislature legalized slavery, and in response Free-Soilers held an unauthorized convention at which they created their own government and constitution. In the spring of 1856, a proslavery posse sent to arrest the Free-Soil leaders sacked the Kansas town of Lawrence, killing several people. In revenge John Brown, a radical abolitionist who saw himself as God's instrument to destroy slavery, murdered five proslavery settlers living along Pottawatomie Creek. Soon, armed bands of guerrillas roamed the territory.

These passions brought violence to the U.S. Senate in May 1856, when Charles Sumner of Massachusetts denounced "the Crime against Kansas." Radical in his antislavery views, Sumner bitterly assailed the president, the South, and Senator Andrew P. Butler of South Carolina. Soon thereafter Butler's cousin, Representative Preston Brooks, approached Sumner at the latter's Senate desk, raised his cane, and began to beat Sumner on the head.

Shocked northerners recoiled from what they saw as another southern assault on free speech and the South's readiness to use violence to have its way. And while popular opinion in Massachusetts supported Sumner, voters in South Carolina reelected Brooks and sent him dozens of commemorative canes. The country was becoming polarized.

The election of 1856 showed how extreme that polarization had become. The Democrats chose James Buchanan of Pennsylvania, whose chief virtue was that for the past four years he had been ambassador to Britain and so had been uninvolved in territorial controversies. This anonymity and superior party organization helped Buchanan win the election, but he owed his victory to southern support. The Republican candidate, John C. Frémont, won eleven of sixteen free states; Republicans had become the dominant party in the North. The Know-Nothing candidate, Millard Fillmore, won almost 1 million votes, but this election was to be his party's last hurrah. The coming battle would pit a sectional Republican Party against an increasingly divided Democratic Party.

Slavery and the Nation's Future

For years the issue of slavery in the territories had convulsed Congress, and for years Congress had tried to settle the issue with vague formulas. In 1857 a different branch of government stepped into the fray. The Supreme

Dred Scott, a slave who brought suit in Missouri for his freedom, and Chief Justice Roger Taney, a descendant of Maryland's slaveholding elite, were principal figures in the most controversial Supreme Court decision of the nineteenth century. (Scott: Missouri Historical Society; Taney: Maryland Historical Society, Baltimore)

Court took up this emotionally charged subject and attempted to silence controversy with a definitive verdict.

A Missouri slave named Dred Scott had sued his owner for his freedom. Scott based his claim on the fact that his former owner, an army surgeon, had taken him for several years into Illinois, a free state, and into the Wisconsin Territory, from which slavery had been barred by the Missouri Compromise. Scott first won and then lost his case as it moved on appeal through the state courts, into the federal system, and finally to the Supreme Court.

Dred Scott Case

This case involved substantive, and very controversial issues: Was a black person like Dred Scott a citizen of the United States and thus eligible to sue in federal court? Had residence in a free state or territory made him free? Did Congress have the power to prohibit slavery in a territory or to delegate that power to a territorial legislature?

In March 1857, Chief Justice Roger B. Taney of Maryland addressed these questions when he delivered the majority opinion of a divided Court. Taney declared that Scott was not a citizen of either the United States or Missouri; that residence in free territory did not make Scott free; and that Congress had no power to bar slavery from any territory. The decision not only overturned a sectional compromise (the Missouri Compromise of 1820) that had been honored for years; it also invalidated the basic ideas of the Wilmot Proviso and probably popular sovereignty as well.

The Slave Power seemed to have won a major constitutional victory. African Americans were especially dismayed, for Taney's decision asserted that the founders had never intended for black people to be citizens. At the nation's founding, the chief justice wrote, blacks had been regarded "as beings of an inferior order" with "no rights which the white man was bound to respect." Taney was mistaken; African Americans had been citizens in several of the original states. Nevertheless, the ruling seemed to shut the door permanently on African Americans' hopes for justice and equal rights.

A storm of angry reaction broke in the North. The decision seemed to confirm every charge against the aggressive Slave Power. "There is such a thing as the slave power," warned the *Cincinnati Daily Commercial*. "It has marched over and annihilated the boundaries of the states. We are now one great homogenous slaveholding community." "Where will it end?" asked the *Atlantic Monthly*. "Is the success of this conspiracy to be final and eternal?"

To Abraham Lincoln, the territorial question affected every citizen. "The whole nation," he had declared as early as 1854, "is interested

Abraham Lincoln on the Slave Power

that the best use shall be made of these Territories. We want them for homes of free white people. This they cannot be, to any considerable extent, if slavery shall be planted within them." The territories must be reserved, he insisted, "as an outlet for free white people everywhere."

More importantly, Lincoln warned of slavery's increasing control over the nation. The founders had created a government dedicated to freedom, Lincoln insisted. Admittedly they had recognized slavery's existence, but the public mind, he argued in 1858, had always rested in the belief that slavery would die either naturally or by legislation. The next step in the unfolding Slave Power conspiracy, Lincoln alleged, would be a Supreme Court decision "declaring that the Constitution does not permit a State to exclude slavery from its limits. . . ." This charge was not pure hyperbole, for lawsuits soon challenged state laws that freed slaves brought within their borders.

Lincoln's most eloquent statement against the Slave Power was his famous "House Divided" speech, in which he declared:

> "A house divided against itself cannot stand." I believe this government cannot endure, permanently half slave and half free. I do not expect the Union to be dissolved—I do not expect the House to fall—but I do expect it to cease to be divided. It will become all one thing or all the other. Either the opponents of slavery will arrest the further spread of it, and place it where the public mind shall rest in the belief that it is in the course of ultimate extinction; or its advocates will push it forward, till it shall become alike lawful in all the States, old as well as new, North as well as South.

Politically, these forceful Republican arguments offset the difficulties that the *Dred Scott* decision posed. By endorsing the South's doctrine of state sovereignty, the Court had in effect declared that the central position of the Republican Party—no extension of slavery—was unconstitutional. Republicans could only

repudiate the decision, appealing to a "higher law," or hope to change the personnel of the Court. They did both and gained politically.

For northern Democrats like Stephen Douglas, the Court's decision posed an awful

The Lecompton Constitution

dilemma. Northern voters were alarmed by the prospect that the territories would be opened to slavery. To retain their support, Douglas had to find some way to reassure them. Yet, given his ambitions to lead the national Democratic Party and become president, Douglas could not afford to alienate southern Democrats.

Douglas chose to stand by his principle of popular sovereignty, even if the result angered southerners. In 1857 Kansans voted on a proslavery constitution that had been drafted at Lecompton. It was defeated by more than ten thousand votes. The evidence was overwhelming that Kansans did not want slavery, yet President Buchanan tried to force the Lecompton Constitution through Congress. Breaking with the administration, Douglas threw his weight against the Lecompton Constitution. He gauged opinion in Kansas correctly, for in 1858 voters there rejected the constitution again. But his action infuriated southern Democrats.

Douglas further alienated the southern wing of his party in his well-publicized debates with Abraham Lincoln, who challenged him for the

Stephen Douglas and the Freeport Doctrine

Illinois Senate seat in 1858. Speaking at Freeport, Illinois, Douglas attempted to revive the concept of popular sovereignty with some tortured arguments. Asserting that the Supreme Court had ruled only on the powers of Congress, not on the powers of a territorial legislature, Douglas claimed that citizens in a territory could still bar slavery either by passing a law against it or by doing nothing. Without the patrol laws and police regulations that supported slavery, he reasoned, the institution could not exist. This argument, called the Freeport Doctrine, temporarily shored up Douglas's crumbling position in the North. But it gave southern Democrats further evidence that Douglas was unreliable. Southerners studied the trend in northern opinion and concluded that southern rights and slavery would be safe only in a separate nation.

The immediate consequence for politics, however, was the likelihood of a split in the Democratic Party. Northern Democrats could not support the territorial protection for slavery that southern Democrats insisted was theirs as a constitutional right. Thus, in the North and in the South the issue of slavery in the territories continued to destroy moderation and promote militancy.

Disunion

 It is worth remembering that in the late 1850s most Americans were not caught up daily in the slavery crisis. They were preoccupied with personal affairs, especially with coping with the effects of the economic panic that had begun in the spring of 1857. They were worried about widespread unemployment, a sick cow, the plummeting price of wheat, the declining wages at a textile mill, or a son who wanted to marry and needed land.

By 1858 Philadelphia had 40,000 unemployed workers, and New York City nearly 100,000. Fear of bread riots and class warfare gripped many cities in the North. True to form, blame for such economic woe became sectionalized, as southerners saw their system justified by the temporary collapse of industrial prosperity, and northerners feared even more the incursions of the Slave Power on an insecure future.

Soon, however, the entire nation's focus would be thrown again on a new dimension of the slavery question—armed rebellion. John Brown had been raised by staunchly religious and antislavery parents. He relied on an Old Testament conception of justice—"an eye for an eye"—and he had a puritanical obsession with the wickedness of others, especially southern slaveowners. Brown believed that violence in a righteous cause was a holy act. To Brown, the destruction of slavery in America required revolutionary ideology and revolutionary acts.

John Brown's Raid on Harpers Ferry

On October 16, 1859, Brown led a small band of whites and blacks (eighteen men in all) in an attack on the federal arsenal at Harpers Ferry, Virginia. Hoping to trigger a slave rebellion, Brown failed miserably and was quickly captured, tried, and executed. Yet his attempted insurrection struck fear into the South. Then

it became known that Brown had received financial backing from several prominent abolitionists. When northern intellectuals such as Emerson and Henry David Thoreau praised Brown as a holy warrior who "would make the gallows as glorious as the cross," white southerners' outrage multiplied.

Many Americans believed that the election of 1860 would decide the fate of the Union. Only the Democratic Party remained as an organization that was truly national in scope. "One after another," wrote a Mississippi editor, "the links which have bound the North and South together, have been severed . . . [but] the Democratic party looms gradually up . . . and waves the olive branch over the troubled waters of politics." But at its 1860 convention in Charleston, South Carolina, the Democratic Party split.

Election of 1860

Stephen A. Douglas wanted his party's presidential nomination, but he could not afford to alienate northern voters by accepting the southern position on the territories. Southern Democrats, however, insisted on recognition of their rights and moved to block Douglas's nomination. When Douglas obtained a majority for his version of the platform, delegates from eight slave states walked out of the convention. After efforts at compromise failed, the Democrats presented two nominees: Douglas for the northern wing, and Vice President John C. Breckinridge of Kentucky for the southern. The Republicans nominated Abraham Lincoln, and a Constitutional Union Party, formed to preserve the nation but strong only in the Upper South, nominated John Bell of Tennessee.

Bell's only issue in the ensuing campaign was the urgency of preserving the Union, and Douglas desperately wanted to hold his northern and southern supporters together. Even Breckinridge quickly backed away from the appearance of extremism, and his supporters in several states stressed his unionism. Although Lincoln and the Republicans denied any intent to interfere with slavery in the states where it existed, they stood firm against the extension of slavery into the territories.

The election of 1860 was sectional in character. Lincoln won, but Douglas, Breckinridge, and Bell together received most of the votes. Douglas had broad-based support but won few states. Breckinridge carried nine southern states, all in the Deep South. Bell won pluralities in Virginia, Kentucky, and Tennessee. Lincoln prevailed in the North, but in the four border states that ultimately remained loyal to the Union (Missouri, Kentucky, Maryland, and Delaware) he gained only a plurality, not a majority. Lincoln's victory was won in the electoral college.

Opposition to slavery's extension was the core issue of the Republican Party, and Lincoln's alarm over slavery's growing political power was genuine. Moreover, abolitionists and supporters of free soil in the North worked to keep the Republicans from compromising on their territorial stand. Meanwhile, in the South, proslavery advocates and secessionists whipped up public opinion and demanded that state conventions assemble to consider secession.

On February 18, 1861, in Montgomery, Alabama, Jefferson Davis took an oath as president of the Confederate States of America. Davis later recalled that he foresaw "troubles innumerable" but was committed to seek independence as his paramount goal.   (Boston Athenaeum)

Lincoln made the crucial decision not to soften his party's position on the territories. His refusal to compromise derived both from conviction and from concern for the unity of the Republican Party. Although many conservative Republicans—eastern businessmen and former Whigs who did not feel strongly about slavery—hoped for a compromise, the original and most committed Republicans—antislavery voters and "conscience Whigs"—were adamant for free soil. Lincoln chose to stand firm against slavery's extension.

Southern leaders in the Senate were willing, conditionally, to accept a compromise drawn up by Senator John J. Crittenden of Kentucky. Crittenden proposed that the two sections divide the territories between them at latitude 36°30'. But the southerners would agree to this only if the Republicans did, too. When Lincoln ruled out concessions on the territorial issue, Crittenden's peacemaking effort collapsed.

Meanwhile, the Union was being destroyed. On December 20, 1860, South Carolina passed an ordinance of secession. This step marked the inauguration of separate-state secession. Recognizing the difficulty of persuading all the southern states to challenge the federal government simultaneously, secessionists concentrated their efforts on the most extreme proslavery state. They hoped South Carolina's secession would induce other states to follow, with each decision building momentum for disunion.

Secession

Southern extremists soon got their way in the Deep South. They called separate state conventions and passed secession ordinances in Mississippi, Florida, Alabama, Georgia, Louisiana, and Texas. By February 1861 these states had joined South Carolina to form a new government in Montgomery, Alabama: the Confederate States of America. The delegates at Montgomery chose Jefferson Davis as their president, and the Confederacy began to function independently of the United States.

The Confederate States of America

This apparent unanimity of action was deceiving. Confused and dissatisfied with the alternatives, many southerners who in 1860 had voted in the U.S. presidential election stayed home a few months later rather than vote for delegates who would decide on secession. Even so, in some state conventions the vote to secede was close, with secession decided by overrepresenta-

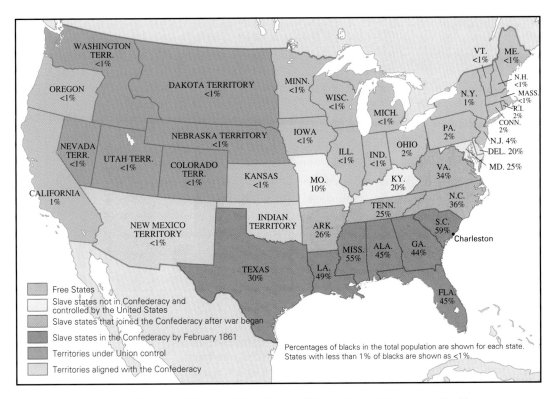

Map 14.3   The Divided Nation—Slave and Free Areas, 1861   After fighting began, the Upper South joined the Deep South in the Confederacy. How does the nation's pattern of division correspond to the distribution of slavery and the percentage of blacks in the population?

tion of plantation districts. Furthermore, the conventions were noticeably unwilling to let voters ratify their acts. Four states in the Upper South—Virginia, North Carolina, Tennessee, and Arkansas—flatly rejected secession and did not join the Confederacy until after fighting had begun. In the border states, popular sentiment was deeply divided; minorities in Kentucky and Missouri tried to secede, but these slave states ultimately came under Union control, along with Maryland and Delaware (see Map 14.3).

Such misgivings were not surprising. Secession raised the possibility of war and the question of who would die. Analysis of election returns from 1860 and 1861 indicates that slaveholders and nonslaveholders were beginning to part company politically. Heavily slaveholding counties strongly supported secession, but most counties with few slaves took an antisecession stance (see Figure 14.1). Thus, with war on the horizon, nonslaveholders were beginning to consider their

class interests and to ask themselves how far they would go to support slavery and slaveowners.

The dilemma facing President Lincoln on inauguration day in March 1861 was how to maintain the authority of the federal government without provoking war. Proceeding cautiously, he sought only to hold on to forts in the states that had left the Union, reasoning that in this way he could assert federal sovereignty while waiting for a restoration of relations. But Jefferson Davis, who could not claim to lead a sovereign nation if the Confederate ports were under foreign (that is, United States) control, was unwilling to be so patient. A collision was inevitable.

It arrived in the early morning hours of April 12, 1861, at Fort Sumter in Charleston harbor. A federal garrison there ran low on food, and Lincoln notified the South Carolinians that he was sending a ship to

Fort Sumter and Outbreak of War

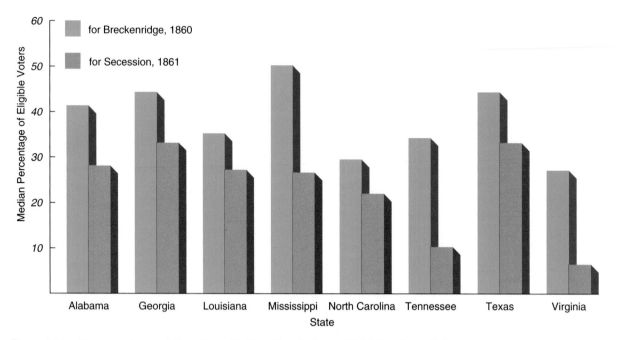

Figure 14.1 Voting Returns of Counties with Few Slaveholders, Eight Southern States, 1860 and 1861 This graph depicts voting in counties whose percentage of slaveholders ranked them among the lower half of the counties in their state. How does voters' support for secession in 1861 compare with their support for John Breckinridge, the southern Democratic candidate in 1860? Why was their support for secession so weak? At this time counties with many slaveholders were giving increased support to secession.

resupply the fort. For the Montgomery government, the alternatives were to attack the fort or to acquiesce to Lincoln's authority. After the Confederate cabinet met, the secretary of war ordered local commanders to obtain a surrender or attack the fort. After two days of heavy bombardment, the federal garrison finally surrendered. Confederates permitted the U.S. troops to sail away on unarmed vessels while Charlestonians celebrated wildly. The Civil War had begun.

Summary

 Throughout the 1840s and 1850s, many able leaders had worked diligently to avert this outcome. Most people, North and South, had hoped to keep the nation together. As late as 1858 even Jefferson Davis had declared, "This great country will continue united," saying that "to the innermost fibers of my heart I love it all, and every part."

Why had war broken out? Why had all efforts to prevent it failed? The conflict slavery generated was fundamental and beyond adjustment. The emotions bound up in attacking and defending it were too powerful, and the interests it affected too vital, for compromise. Because it was deeply entwined with major policy questions of the present and the foreseeable future, each section ultimately regarded slavery as too important to be put aside.

North and South had fundamentally different attitudes toward the institution. The logic of Republican ideology tended in the direction of abolishing slavery, even though Republicans denied any such intention. The logic of southern arguments led toward establishing slavery everywhere, though southern leaders too denied such a motive. Lincoln put these facts succinctly. In a postelection letter to his old friend Alexander Stephens of Georgia, Lincoln wrote, "You think slavery is right and ought to be expanded; while we think it is wrong and ought to be restricted. That I suppose is the rub."

Territorial expansion generated disputes so frequently that the nation never enjoyed a breathing space. Every southern victory increased fear of the Slave Power, and each new expression of Free-Soil sentiment made alarmed slaveholders more insistent in their demands. Eventually even those opposed to war could see no way to avoid it. In the profoundest sense, slavery was the root of the war. But as the fighting began, this, the war's central issue, was shrouded in confusion. How would the Civil War affect slavery, its place in the law, and African Americans' place in society?

LEGACY FOR A PEOPLE AND A NATION
Revolutionary Violence

The greatest significance of John Brown's raid on Harpers Ferry in 1859 rests in its long aftermath in American memory. Brown is as important as a symbol as he is for his deeds. He has been at once one of the most beloved and most loathed figures in American history. In the song that bears his name, "John Brown's Body," a popular marching tune during the Civil War, his "soul goes marching on."

In the wake of his execution, in painting, song, and poetry, people constructed a John Brown mythology. Was he the Christ-like figure who died for the nation's sins? Or was he the terrorist thief who murdered in the name of his own peculiar vision of God's will? Brown can be disturbing and inspiring, majestic and foolish, a monster or a warrior saint. He represented the highest ideals and ruthless deeds. He killed for justice.

Brown forces us to ask when and how revolutionary violence—violence in the name of a political or spiritual end—is justified. The 1850s and the turn of the twenty-first century are two different contexts. But in today's world, terrorist, revolutionary violence is commonplace: an airliner is blown up over Lockerbie, Scotland; buses are strafed in Jerusalem; a federal building explodes in Oklahoma City; the Irish Republican Army plants bombs in London subways; American embassies are attacked in Africa and Europe. In the contemporary world, as at the time of John Brown's raid, people must confront the question of when revolutionary violence is right or wrong.

For Further Reading, see the Appendix. For Web resources, go to history.college.hmco.com/students.

15

TRANSFORMING FIRE:
THE CIVIL WAR

1861–1865

He was an ordinary twenty-seven-year-old store clerk from a New England town. But he went off to war. In the spring of 1861, Charles Brewster left his mother and two sisters behind and joined Company C of the Tenth Massachusetts Volunteers. At that moment, Brewster had no idea of his capacity for leadership or his ability to uphold such values as courage and manliness.

In more than two hundred sometimes lyrical letters to his mother and sisters, Brewster, who rose to lieutenant and adjutant of his regiment, left a trove of commentary on the meaning of war, the character of slavery and why it had to be destroyed, and especially

the values of common, mid-nineteenth-century American men. Brewster was as racist as many southerners in his perceptions of blacks. He was no "desperate hero" about battlefield courage, and he nearly died of dysentery more than once. He was personally eager for rank and recognition, and he eventually held only contempt for civilians who stayed at home. He was often miserably lonely and homesick, and he described battlefield carnage with an honest realism.

Most tellingly, Brewster grew in his attitudes about race. In 1862 he defied orders and took in a seventeen-year-old ex-slave as his personal servant. In 1864, after surviving some of the worst battles of the war in Vir-

IMPORTANT EVENTS

1861 Battle of Bull Run
McClellan organizes Union Army
Union blockade begins
U.S. Congress passes first confiscation act
Trent affair
Some slaves admitted to Union lines as
"contraband" of war

1862 Union captures Fort Henry and
Fort Donelson
U.S. Navy captures New Orleans
Battle of Shiloh shows the war's
destructiveness
Confederacy enacts conscription
McClellan's Peninsula Campaign fails
to take Richmond
U.S. Congress passes second confiscation
act, initiating emancipation
Confederacy mounts offensive in Maryland
and Kentucky
Battle of Antietam ends Lee's drive into
Maryland in September
British intervention in the war on
Confederate side is averted by events
and northern diplomacy

1863 Emancipation Proclamation takes effect
U.S. Congress passes National Banking Act
Union enacts conscription
African American soldiers join Union Army
Food riots occur in southern cities

Battle of Chancellorsville ends in
Confederate victory but Jackson's death
Union wins key victories at Gettysburg
and Vicksburg
Draft riots take place in New York City
Battle of Chattanooga leaves South vulnerable
to Sherman's march into Georgia

1864 Battles of the Wilderness and Spotsylvania
produce heavy casualties on both sides in
the effort to capture and defend Richmond
Battle of Cold Harbor continues carnage in
Virginia
Lincoln requests Republican Party plank
abolishing slavery
Sherman captures Atlanta
Confederacy begins to collapse on the home
front, as southern hardship destroys morale
Lincoln wins reelection, eliminating any Con-
federate hopes for a negotiated end to war
Jefferson Davis proposes emancipation within
the Confederacy
Sherman marches through Georgia to the sea

1865 Sherman marches through Carolinas
U.S. Congress approves Thirteenth
Amendment
Lee abandons Richmond and Petersburg
Lee surrenders at Appomattox Court House
Lincoln assassinated
Death toll in war reaches 620,000

ginia, which destroyed his regiment, and frightened of civilian life, Brewster reenlisted to be a recruiter of black troops. In this new role, Brewster worked from an office in Norfolk, Virginia, where his principal job was writing "love letters" for illiterate black women to their soldier husbands at the front. In imagining Brewster sitting at a table with a lonely freedwoman, swallowing his prejudices toward blacks and women, and repeatedly writing or reciting the phrases "give my love to . . ." and "your Husband untall Death," we can glimpse the enormous potential for human transformation at work in this war.

The Civil War brought astonishing, unexpected changes not only to Charles Brewster but everywhere in both North and South. Countless southern soldiers experienced similar transformations. But they, and their families, also experienced what few other groups of Americans have—utter defeat. Contrasts abounded between noble and crass motives. Even the South's slaves, who hoped that they were witnessing God's "Holy War," encountered unsympathetic liberators. When a Yankee soldier ransacked a slave woman's cabin, stealing her best quilts, she denounced him as a "nasty, stinkin' rascal" who had betrayed his cause of freedom. Angrily the soldier contradicted her, saying, "I'm fightin' for $14 a month and the Union."

Northern troops were not the only ones to feel anger over their sacrifices. Impoverished by the war, one southern farmer had endured inflation, taxes, and shortages to support the Confederacy. Then an impressment agent arrived to take still more from him—grain and meat, horses and mules, and wagons. In return, the agent offered only a certificate promising repayment sometime in the future. Bitter and disgusted, the farmer spoke for many by declaring, "The sooner this damned Government falls to pieces, the better it will be for us."

For millions, the Civil War was a life-changing event. It obliterated the normal patterns and circumstances of life. Millions of men were swept away into training camps and battle units. Armies numbering in the hundreds of thousands marched over the South, devastating once-peaceful countrysides. Families struggled to survive without their men; businesses tried to cope with the loss of workers. Women in both North and South took on extra responsibilities in the home and moved into new jobs in the work force.

Change was most drastic in the South, where the leaders of the secession movement had feared that a peacetime government of Republicans would interfere with slavery and upset the routine of plantation life. Instead, their own actions led to a war that turned southern life upside down, imperiled the very existence of slavery, and resulted in policies more objectionable to the elite than any proposed by President-elect Lincoln. Life in the Confederacy proved to be a shockingly unsouthern experience.

War altered the North as well, but less sharply. Because most of the fighting took place on southern soil, northern farms and factories remained virtually unscathed. The drafting of workers and the changing need for products slowed the pace of industrialization somewhat, but factories and businesses remained busy. Workers lost ground to inflation, but the economy hummed. A new pro-business atmosphere dominated Congress. To the alarm of many, the powers of the federal government and of the president increased during the war.

Ultimately, the Civil War forced on the nation a social and political revolution regarding race. Its greatest effect was to compel leaders and citizens to deal directly with the issue they had struggled over but had been unable to resolve: slavery. ∎

America Goes to War, 1861–1862

 Few Americans understood what they were getting into when the war began. The onset of hostilities sparked patriotic sentiments and joyous ceremonies in both North and South. Northern communities raised companies of volunteers eager to save the Union. In the South, confident recruits boasted of whipping the Yankees and returning home at least before Christmas.

Through the spring of 1861 both sides scrambled to organize and train their undisciplined armies. On July 21, 1861, the first battle took place outside Manassas Junction, Virginia, near a stream called Bull Run. General Irvin McDowell and 30,000 Union troops attacked General P. G. T. Beauregard's 22,000 southerners (see Map 15.1 on page 257). As the raw recruits struggled amid the confusion of their first battle, federal forces began to gain ground. Then they ran into a line of Virginia troops under General Thomas Jackson. "There is Jackson standing like a stone wall," shouted one Confederate. "Stonewall" Jackson's line held, and the arrival of 9,000 Confederate reinforcements won the day for the South. The Union troops fled back to Washington.

First Battle of Bull Run

The unexpected rout at Bull Run gave northerners their first hint of the nature of the war to come. While the United States enjoyed an enormous advantage in resources, victory would not be easy. Pro-Union feeling was growing in western Virginia, and loyalties were divided in the four border slave states—Missouri, Kentucky, Maryland, and Delaware. But the rest of the Upper South, the states of North Carolina, Virginia, Tennessee, and Arkansas, had joined the Confederacy. Moved by an outpouring of regional loyalty, half a million southerners volunteered to fight.

Lincoln gave command of the army to General George B. McClellan, an officer who proved to be better at organization and training than at fighting. McClellan put his growing army into camp and devoted the fall and winter of 1861 to readying a formidable force of a quarter-million men whose mission would be to take Richmond, established as the Confederate capital by July 1861.

While McClellan prepared, the Union began to implement other parts of its overall strategy, which

In *Departure of the Seventh Regiment* (1861), flags and the spectacle of thousands of young men from New York marching off to battle give a deceptively gay appearance to the beginning of the Civil War. (Museum of Fine Arts, Boston; M. and M. Karolik Collection)

Grand Strategy called for a blockade of southern ports and eventual capture of the Mississippi River. Like a constricting snake, this "Anaconda plan" would strangle the Confederacy. At first the Union Navy had too few ships to patrol 3,550 miles of coastline and block the Confederacy's avenues of commerce and supply. Gradually, however, the navy increased the blockade's effectiveness, though it never stopped southern commerce completely.

Confederate strategy was essentially defensive. A defensive posture not only was consistent with the South's claim of independence, but acknowledged the North's advantage in resources (see Figure 15.1). Jefferson Davis, however, wisely rejected a static or wholly defensive strategy. The South would pursue an "offensive defensive," taking advantage of opportunities to attack and using its interior lines of transportation to concentrate troops at crucial points.

Strategic thinking on both sides slighted the importance of "the West," that vast expanse of territory between Virginia and the Mississippi River. When the war began, both sides were unprepared for large-scale operations in the West, but before the end of the war these operations would prove to be decisive.

The last half of 1861 brought no major land battles, but the North made gains by sea. Late in the summer Union naval forces captured **Union Naval Campaign** Cape Hatteras and then seized Hilton Head, one of the Sea Islands off Port Royal, South Carolina. A few months later, similar operations secured vital coastal points in North Carolina, as well as Fort Pulaski, which defended Savannah. The coastal victories off South Carolina frightened planters, who abandoned their lands and fled. But thousands of slaves greeted what they hoped to be freedom with rejoicing and broke the hated cotton gins. Their jubilation and the growing stream of runaways who poured into the Union lines eliminated any doubt about which side slaves would support. The Union government, unwilling at first to wage a war against slavery, did not acknowledge the slaves' freedom. It began, however, to use their labor in the Union cause.

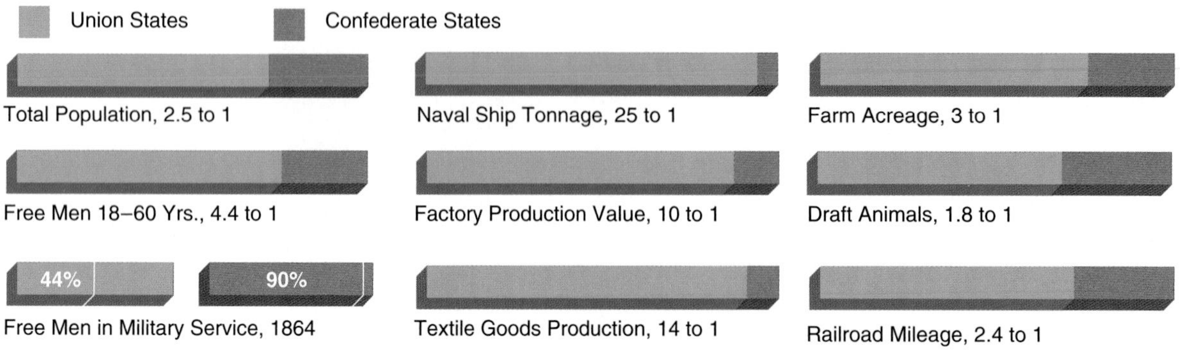

Union States **Confederate States**

Total Population, 2.5 to 1

Naval Ship Tonnage, 25 to 1

Farm Acreage, 3 to 1

Free Men 18–60 Yrs., 4.4 to 1

Factory Production Value, 10 to 1

Draft Animals, 1.8 to 1

44% 90%

Free Men in Military Service, 1864

Textile Goods Production, 14 to 1

Railroad Mileage, 2.4 to 1

Figure 15.1 Comparative Resources, Union and Confederate States, 1861 The North had vastly superior resources. Although the North's advantages in manpower and industrial capacity proved very important, the South still had to be conquered, its society and its will crushed. (Source: *The Times Atlas of World History.* Time Books, London, 1978. Used with permission.)

The coastal incursions worried southerners, but the spring of 1862 brought even stronger evidence of the war's gravity. In April Union ships commanded by Admiral David Farragut smashed through log booms blocking the Mississippi River and fought their way upstream to capture New Orleans. Farther west a Union victory at Elkhorn Tavern, Arkansas, shattered southern control of Indian Territory.

In February 1862 land and river forces in northern Tennessee won significant victories for the Union.

Grant's Tennessee Campaign and the Battle of Shiloh

There a hard-drinking Union commander named Ulysses S. Grant captured Fort Henry and Fort Donelson, and thereby secured two prime routes to the heartland of the Confederacy. A path into Tennessee, Alabama, and Mississippi now lay open before the Union Army.

Grant moved on into southern Tennessee and the first of the war's shockingly bloody encounters, the Battle of Shiloh. On April 6 Confederate general Albert Sidney Johnston caught federal troops with their backs to the Tennessee River. The Confederates attacked early in the morning and inflicted heavy damage all day. Close to victory, General Johnston was shot from his horse and killed. Southern forces almost achieved a breakthrough, but Union reinforcements arrived that night. The next day the tide of battle turned, and after ten hours of terrible combat, the Confederates withdrew. Neither side won a victory at Shiloh, yet the losses were staggering. Northern troops

lost 13,000 men (killed, wounded, or captured) out of 63,000; southerners sacrificed 11,000 out of 40,000. The true nature of the war was emerging.

Meanwhile, on the Virginia front, President Lincoln had a different problem. General McClellan was slow to

McClellan and the Peninsula Campaign

move. Habitually overestimating the size of enemy forces, McClellan called repeatedly for reinforcements and ignored Lincoln's directions to advance. Finally he chose to move by a water route, sailing his troops down the Chesapeake, landing them on the peninsula between the York and James Rivers, and advancing on Richmond from the east (see Map 15.1).

After a bloody but indecisive battle at Fair Oaks on May 31–June 1, the federal armies moved to within 7 miles of the Confederate capital. The Confederate commanding general, Joseph E. Johnston, was badly wounded at Fair Oaks, and President Jefferson Davis placed his chief military adviser, Robert E. Lee, in command. Lee soon foiled McClellan's legions.

First, he sent Stonewall Jackson's corps of 17,000 into the Shenandoah valley behind Union forces, where they threatened Washington, D.C., and thereby drew some federal troops away from Richmond to protect their own capital. Then, in a series of engagements known as the Seven Days Battles, June 26–July 1, Lee struck at McClellan's army. Lee never managed to close his pincers around the retreating Union forces, but he forced McClellan to retreat toward the James River. By August 3 McClellan withdrew his

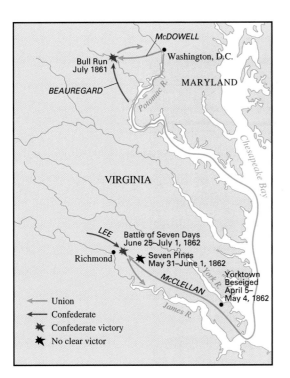

Map 15.1   McClellan's Campaign   The water route chosen by McClellan to threaten Richmond during the peninsular campaign.

army to the Potomac; Richmond remained safe for another two years.

Buoyed by these results, Jefferson Davis conceived an ambitious plan to turn the tide of the war and gain recognition of the Confederacy by European nations. He ordered a general offensive, sending Lee north into Maryland and Generals Kirby Smith and Braxton Bragg into Kentucky. Calling on residents of Maryland and Kentucky to make a separate peace with his government, Davis also invited northwestern states like Indiana, which sent much of their trade down the Mississippi to New Orleans, to leave the Union.

Confederate Offensive in Maryland and Kentucky

The plan was promising, but every part of the offensive failed. In the bloodiest day of the entire war, September 17, 1862, McClellan turned Lee back in the Battle of Antietam near Sharpsburg, Maryland. In Kentucky Generals Smith and Bragg secured Lexington and Frankfurt, but their effort to force the Yankees back to the Ohio River was stopped at the Battle of

Perryville on October 8. Bragg's army retreated back into Tennessee. Confederate leaders had marshaled all their strength for a breakthrough but had failed. Tenacious defense and stoic endurance now seemed the South's only long-range hope.

But 1862 also brought painful lessons to the North. Confederate general J. E. B. Stuart executed a daring cavalry raid into Pennsylvania in October. Then on December 13 Union general Ambrose Burnside, now in command of the Army of the Potomac, unwisely ordered his soldiers to attack Lee's army, which held fortified positions on high ground at Fredericksburg, Virginia. Lee's men performed so coolly and controlled the engagement so thoroughly that Lee was moved to say, "It is well that war is so terrible. We should grow too fond of it."

War Transforms the South

The war caused tremendous disruptions in civilian life and altered southern society beyond all expectations. One of the first traditions to fall was the southern preference for local and limited government. States' rights had been a formative ideology for the Confederacy, but to withstand the massive power of the North, the South needed to centralize. No one saw the necessity of centralization more clearly than Jefferson Davis.

Promptly Davis moved to bring all arms, supplies, and troops under his control. But by early 1862 the scope and duration of the conflict required something more. When the states failed to provide sufficient numbers of troops, Davis secured passage in April 1862 of the first national conscription (draft) law in American history. Davis also adopted a firm leadership role toward the Confederate Congress, which raised taxes and later passed a tax-in-kind—paid in farm products. When opposition arose, the government suspended the writ of habeas corpus (which prevented individuals from being held without trial) and imposed martial law. In the face of political opposition that cherished states' rights, Davis proved unyielding.

The Confederacy and Centralization of Power

Soon the Confederate administration in Richmond gained virtually complete control over the southern economy. Because it controlled the supply of labor

In October 1862 in New York City, photographer Mathew Brady opened an exhibition of photographs from the Battle of Antietam. Although few knew it, Brady's vision was very poor, and this photograph of Confederate dead was actually made by his assistants, Alexander Gardner and James F. Gibson.   (Library of Congress)

through conscription, the administration could compel industry to work on government contracts and supply the military's needs. The Confederate Congress also gave the central government almost complete control of the railroads. New statutes even limited corporate profits and dividends. A large bureaucracy sprang up to administer these operations. By the war's end, the southern bureaucracy was larger in proportion to population than its northern counterpart.

Clerks and subordinate officials crowded the towns and cities where Confederate departments set up their offices. The sudden population booms that resulted overwhelmed the housing supply and stimulated new construction. The pressure was especially great in Richmond, whose population increased 250 percent.

Wartime Southern Cities and Industry

As the Union blockade disrupted imports of manufactured products, the traditionally agricultural South forged industries. Many planters shared Davis's hope that industrialization would bring "deliverance, full and unrestricted, from all commercial dependence" on the North or the world. Indeed, beginning almost from scratch, the Confederacy achieved tremendous feats of industrial development. The government also constructed new railroad lines to improve the efficiency of the South's transportation system. Much of the labor on railroads and ironworks consisted of slaves relocated from farms and plantations.

White women, restricted to narrow roles in antebellum society, gained substantial new responsibilities in wartime. The wives and mothers of soldiers now headed households and performed men's work. Women in nonslaveowning families cultivated fields them-

Changing Roles of Women

selves, while wealthier women suddenly had to manage field hands unaccustomed to female overseers. In the cities, white women—who had been virtually excluded from the labor force—found a limited number of respectable new paying jobs. Clerks had always been males, but the war changed that, too. "Government girls" staffed the Confederate bureaucracy, and female schoolteachers appeared in the South for the first time. Some women gained confidence from their new responsibilities, but others resented their new burdens. Many among the wealthy found their war-imposed tasks difficult and their changed situation distasteful.

For millions of ordinary southerners, change brought privation and suffering. Mass poverty descended for the first time on a large minority of the white population.

Human Suffering and Inflation

Many yeoman families had lost their breadwinners to the army. As a South Carolina newspaper put it, "The duties of war have called away from home the sole supports of many, many families. . . . Help must be given, or the poor will suffer." The poor sought help from relatives, neighbors, friends, anyone. Sometimes they pleaded their cases to the Confederate government.

Other factors aggravated the effect of the labor shortage. The South was in many places so sparsely populated that the conscription of one skilled craftsman could work a hardship on the people of an entire county. Often these people begged in unison for the exemption or discharge of the local miller, a wheelwright, or especially a blacksmith. As a petition from Alabama explained, "Our Section of County [is] left entirely Destitute of any man that is able to keep in order any kind of Farming Tules."

Inflation raged out of control, fueled by the Confederate government's heavy borrowing and inadequate taxes, until prices had increased almost 7,000 percent. Inflation particularly imperiled urban dwellers without their own sources of food. As early as 1861 and 1862, newspapers reported that "want and starvation are staring thousands in the face." Some families came to the aid of their neighbors, and "free markets," which disbursed goods as charity, sprang up in various cities. But other people would not cooperate. And private charity,

as well as a rudimentary relief program organized by the Confederacy, failed to meet the need.

As their fortunes declined, people of once-modest means looked around and found abundant evidence that all classes were not sacrificing equally.

Inequities of the Confederate Draft

And they noted that the Confederate government enacted policies that favored the upper class. Until the last year of the war, for example, prosperous southerners could avoid military service by hiring substitutes. Prices for substitutes skyrocketed until it cost a man $5,000 or $6,000 to send someone to the front in his place. Well over 50,000 upper-class southerners purchased such substitutes.

Anger at such discrimination exploded in October 1862 when the Confederate Congress exempted from military duty anyone who was supervising at least twenty slaves. Protests poured in from every corner of the Confederacy, and North Carolina's legislators formally condemned the law. Its defenders argued, however, that the exemption preserved order and aided food production, and the statute remained on the books.

Dissension spread, and alert politicians and newspaper editors warned of class warfare. The bitterness of letters to Confederate officials suggests the depth of the people's anger. One swore to the secretary of war that unless help was provided to poverty-stricken wives and mothers "an allwise god . . . will send down his fury and judgment in a very grate manar . . . [on] those that are in power." War magnified existing social tensions in the Confederacy, and created a few new ones.

Wartime Northern Economy and Society

With the onset of war, a tidal wave of change rolled over the North as well. Factories and citizens' associations geared up to support the war, and the federal government and its executive branch gained new powers. The energies of an industrializing, capitalist society were harnessed to serve the cause of the Union. Idealism and greed flourished together, and the northern economy proved its awesome productivity.

At first the war was a shock to business. Northern firms lost their southern markets, and many companies

Northern Business, Industry, and Agriculture

had to change their products and find new customers in order to remain open. Southern debts became uncollectible, jeopardizing not only northern merchants but also many western banks. In farming regions, families struggled with an aggravated shortage of labor.

But certain entrepreneurs, such as wool producers, benefited from shortages of competing products, and soaring demand for war-related goods swept some businesses to new success. Secretary of War Edwin M. Stanton's list of the supplies needed by the Ordnance Department indicates the scope of government demand: "7,892 cannon, 11,787 artillery carriages, 4,022,130 small-arms, . . . 1,022,176,474 cartridges for small-arms, 1,220,555,435 percussion caps, . . . 26,440,054 pounds of gunpowder, 6,395,152 pounds of niter, and 90,416,295 pounds of lead." Stanton's list covered only weapons; the government also purchased huge quantities of uniforms, boots, food, camp equipment, saddles, ships, and other necessities.

War aided some heavy industries in the North, especially iron and steel production. Although new railroad construction slowed, repairs helped the manufacture of rails to increase. Of considerable significance for the future was the railroad industry's adoption of a standard gauge (width) for track, which eliminated the unloading and reloading of boxcars and created a unified transportation system.

The northern economy also grew because of a complementary relationship between agriculture and industry. Mechanization of agriculture had begun before the war. Wartime recruitment and conscription, however, gave western farmers an added incentive to purchase labor-saving machinery. The shift from human labor to machines created new markets for industry and expanded the food supply for the urban industrial work force. The boom in the sale of agricultural tools was tremendous. Mechanization in agriculture also meant that northern farm families whose breadwinners went to war did not suffer as much as did their counterparts in the South.

Northern industrial and urban workers did not fare as well. After the initial slump, jobs became plentiful, but inflation ate up much of a worker's paycheck. Between 1860 and 1864 consumer prices rose at least 76 percent, while daily wages rose only 42 percent.

New Militancy Among Northern Workers

Workers' families consequently suffered a substantial decline in their standard of living.

As their real wages shrank, industrial workers lost job security. To increase production, some employers were replacing workers with labor-saving machines. Other employers urged the government to promote immigration to secure cheap labor. Workers responded by forming unions and sometimes by striking. Skilled craftsmen organized to combat the loss of their jobs and status to machines; women and unskilled workers, who were excluded by the craftsmen, formed their own unions. In recognition of the increasingly national scope of business activity, thirteen occupational groups—including tailors, coal miners, and railway engineers—formed national unions during the Civil War.

Employers reacted with hostility to this new labor independence. Manufacturers viewed labor activism as a threat to their freedom of action and accordingly formed statewide or craft-based associations to cooperate and pool information. These employers shared blacklists of union members and required new workers to sign "yellow dog" contracts (promises not to join a union). To put down strikes, they hired strikebreakers from among blacks, immigrants, and women, and sometimes used federal troops to break the will of unions.

Despite the unions' emerging presence, they did not prevent employers from making profits or from profiteering on government contracts. Unscrupulous businessmen took advantage of the suddenly immense demand for army supplies by selling clothing and blankets made of "shoddy"—wool fibers reclaimed from rags or worn cloth. Shoddy goods often came apart in the rain; most of the shoes purchased in the early months of the war were worthless. Contractors sold inferior guns for double the usual price and passed off tainted meat as good.

Legitimate enterprises also made healthy profits. The output of woolen mills increased so dramatically that dividends in the industry nearly tripled. Some cotton mills made record profits on what they sold, even though they reduced their output. Railroads carried immense quantities of freight and passengers, increasing

Government and Business Partnership

their business to the point that railroad stocks doubled and tripled in value.

Railroads also were a leading beneficiary of government largesse. With the South absent from Congress, the northern, rather than southern, route of the transcontinental railroad quickly prevailed. In 1862 and 1864 Congress chartered two corporations, the Union Pacific Railroad and the Central Pacific Railroad, and assisted them financially in connecting Omaha, Nebraska, with Sacramento, California. Overall, the two corporations gained approximately 20 million acres of land and nearly $60 million in loans.

Other businessmen benefited handsomely from the Morrill Land Grant Act (1862). To promote public education in agriculture, engineer-

Economic Nationalism

ing, and military science, Congress granted each state 30,000 acres of federal land for each of its congressional districts. The law eventually fostered sixty-nine colleges and universities, but one of its immediate effects was to enrich a few prominent speculators. Hard-pressed to meet wartime expenses, some states sold their land cheaply to wealthy entrepreneurs.

Before the war, there was no national banking, taxation, or currency. Banks operating under state charters issued no fewer than seven thousand different kinds of notes, which were difficult to distinguish from forgeries. During the war, Congress and the Treasury Department established a national banking system empowered to issue national bank notes. At the close of the war in 1865, Congress forced most state banks to join the national system. This process created a sounder currency, but also inflexibility in the money supply and an eastern-oriented financial structure.

In response to the war, the Republicans created an activist federal government. Indeed, with agricultural legislation, the land grant colleges, higher tariffs, and railroad subsidies, the federal government entered the economy forever. Moreover, Republican economic policies bonded people to the nation as never before.

The powers of the federal government and the president grew steadily during the crisis. Abraham Lincoln, like Jefferson Davis, found

Expansion of Presidential Power

that war required active presidential leadership. At the beginning of the conflict, Lincoln launched a major shipbuilding program without wait-

ing for Congress to assemble. The lawmakers later approved his decision, and Lincoln continued to act in advance of Congress when he deemed such action necessary. In one striking exercise of executive power, Lincoln, in order to ensure the loyalty of Maryland, suspended the writ of habeas corpus for everyone living between Washington, D.C., and Philadelphia. Later in the war, with congressional approval, Lincoln repeatedly suspended habeas corpus and invoked martial law, mainly in the border states.

On occasion Lincoln used his wartime authority to bolster his own political fortunes. He and his generals proved adept at furloughing soldiers so they could vote in close elections. Those whom Lincoln furloughed, of course, usually voted Republican.

In thousands of self-governing towns and communities, northern citizens felt a personal connection to representative government. Secession

The Union Cause

threatened to destroy their system, and northerners rallied to its defense. Secular and church leaders supported the cause, and in the first two years of the war, northern morale remained remarkably high.

But social attitudes on the northern home front evolved in directions that would have shocked the soldiers in the field. In the excitement of moneymaking, an eagerness to display one's wealth flourished in the largest cities. *Harper's Monthly* reported that "the suddenly enriched contractors, speculators, and stock-jobbers . . . are spending money with a profusion never before witnessed in our country. . . . The men button their waistcoats with diamonds . . . and the women powder their hair with gold and silver dust." The *New York Herald* noted that this "war has entirely changed the American character. . . . The individual who makes the most money—no matter how—and spends the most—no matter for what—is considered the greatest man."

Yet idealism coexisted with ostentation. Abolitionists campaigned to turn the war into a crusade against slavery. Free black communities and churches both black and white responded to the needs of slaves who flocked to the Union lines, sending clothing, ministers, and teachers to aid the freedpeople.

Northern women, like their southern counterparts, took on new roles. Those who stayed home organized over ten thousand soldiers' aid societies, rolled bandages, and raised $3 million to aid injured

Northern Women

troops. Women were instrumental in pressing for the first trained ambulance corps in the Union armies, and they formed the backbone of the U.S. Sanitary Commission. The Sanitary Commission provided crucial nutritional and medical aid to soldiers. Women also organized elaborate "Sanitary Fairs" all across the North to raise money and awareness for soldiers' health and hygiene.

Approximately 3,200 women also served as nurses in frontline hospitals, where they pressed for better care of the wounded. Yet women were only about one-quarter of all nurses, and they had to fight for a chance to serve at all. The professionalization of medicine since the Revolution had created a medical system dominated by men, and many male physicians did not want women's aid. Even Clara Barton, famous for her persistence in working in the worst hospitals at the front, was ousted from her post in 1863.

Thus northern society embraced strangely contradictory tendencies. Materialism and greed flourished alongside idealism, religious conviction, and self-sacrifice. While some soldiers risked their lives willingly out of a desire to preserve the Union or extend freedom, many others openly sought to avoid service. Under the law, a draftee could stay at home by providing a substitute or paying a $300 commutation fee. In all, 118,000 substitutes were provided and 87,000 commutations paid before Congress ended the commutation system in 1864.

The Advent of Emancipation

 Despite the sense of loyalty to cause that animated soldiers and civilians on both sides, the governments of the United States and the Confederacy lacked clarity about the purpose of the war. Throughout the first several months of the struggle, both Davis and Lincoln studiously avoided references to slavery. Davis, realizing that emphasis on the issue could increase class conflict, told southerners that they were fighting for constitutional liberty.

Lincoln had his own reasons for not mentioning slavery. It was crucial at first not to antagonize the Union's border slave states, whose loyalty was tenuous. Also for many months Lincoln hoped that a pro-Union majority would assert itself in the South. It might be possible, he thought, to coax the South back into the Union and stop the fighting. And not all Republicans burned with moral outrage over slavery. A forthright stand by Lincoln on the subject of slavery could split the party, gratifying some groups and alienating others. No northern consensus on what to do about slavery existed early in the war.

Lincoln first broached the subject of slavery in a substantive way in March 1862, when he proposed that the states consider emancipation on their own. He asked Congress to promise aid to any state that decided to emancipate, appealing especially to border state representatives. What Lincoln proposed was gradual emancipation, with compensation for slaveholders and colonization of the freed slaves outside the United States. To a delegation of free blacks he explained that "it is better for us both . . . to be separated."

Lincoln and Emancipation

Until well into 1864 Lincoln's administration promoted a wholly impractical scheme to colonize blacks in Central America or the Caribbean. Lincoln saw colonization as one option among others in dealing with the impending freedom of America's 4.2 million slaves. He was not yet convinced that America had any prospect as a truly biracial society.

Other politicians had different ideas. A group of Republicans in Congress, known as the Radicals, dedicated themselves to a war for emancipation. In August 1861, at the Radicals' instigation, Congress passed its first confiscation act. Designed to punish the Confederates, the law confiscated all property used for "insurrectionary purposes." Thus if the South used slaves in a hostile action, those slaves were declared seized and liberated. A second confiscation act (July 1862) went much further: it confiscated the property of anyone who supported the rebellion, even those who merely resided in the South and paid Confederate taxes. Their slaves were declared "forever free of their servitude." Let the government use its full powers, free the slaves, and crush the insurrection, urged the Radicals.

Confiscation Acts

Lincoln refused to adopt that view in the summer of 1862. He stood by his proposal of voluntary gradual emancipation by the states and made no effort to enforce the second confiscation act. His stance provoked a public protest from Horace Greeley, editor of the powerful *New York Tribune*. In an open letter to the president entitled "The Prayer of Twenty Millions," Greeley pleaded with Lincoln to "execute the laws" and declared, "On the face of this wide earth, Mr. President, there is not one disinterested, determined, intelligent champion of the Union cause who does not feel that all attempts to put down the Rebellion and at the same time uphold its inciting cause are preposterous and futile." Lincoln's reply was an explicit statement of his calculated approach to the question. "I would save the Union," announced Lincoln. "If I could save the Union without freeing any slave I would do it, and if I could save it by freeing all the slaves I would do it; and if I could save it by freeing some and leaving others alone I would also do that. What I do about slavery, and the colored race, I do because I believe it helps to save the Union."

When he wrote those words, Lincoln had already decided to boldly issue a presidential Emancipation Proclamation. He was waiting, however, for a Union victory so that it would not appear to be an act of desperation.

On September 22, 1862, shortly after Union success at the Battle of Antietam, Lincoln issued the first part of his two-part proclamation.

Emancipation Proclamation

Invoking his powers as commander-in-chief of the armed forces, he announced that on January 1, 1863, he would emancipate the slaves in the states "in rebellion against the United States." Thus his September proclamation was less a declaration of the right of slaves to be free than a threat to southerners: unless they put down their arms, they would lose their slaves. Lincoln had little expectation that southerners would give up their effort, but he was careful to offer them the option, thus trying to put the onus of emancipation on them.

In the fateful January 1 proclamation, Lincoln excepted (as areas in rebellion) every Confederate county or city that had fallen under Union control. Those areas, he declared, "are, for the present, left precisely as if this proclamation were not issued." Nor did Lincoln liberate slaves in the border slave states that remained in the Union. "The President has purposely made the proclamation inoperative in all places where . . . the slaves [are] accessible," charged the anti-administration *New York World*. "He has proclaimed emancipation only where he has notoriously no power to execute it."

Thus the Emancipation Proclamation was an ambiguous document that said less than it seemed to say. But if as a legal document it was wanting, as a moral and political document it had great meaning. Because the proclamation defined the war as a war against slavery, radicals could applaud it, even if the president had not gone as far as Congress. Yet at the same time it protected Lincoln's position with conservatives, leaving him room to retreat if he chose and forcing no immediate changes on the border slave states.

Most important, though, thousands of slaves had already reached Union lines in various sections of the South. They had "voted with their feet" for emancipation, as many said, well before the proclamation. And now every advance of federal forces into slave society was a liberating step. This Lincoln knew in taking his own initially tentative, and then forthright, steps toward emancipation.

The need for men soon convinced the administration to recruit northern and southern blacks for the Union Army. By the spring of 1863, African American troops were answering the call of a dozen or more black recruiters barnstorming the cities and towns of the North. Lincoln came to see black soldiers as "the great available and yet unavailed of force for restoring the Union." African American leaders hoped that military service would secure equal rights for their people. Once the black soldier had fought for the Union, wrote Frederick Douglass, "there is no power on earth which can deny that he has earned the right of citizenship in the United States."

In June 1864 Lincoln gave his support to a constitutional ban on slavery. On the eve of the Republican national convention, Lincoln called the party's chairman to the White House and instructed him to have the party "put into the platform as the keystone, the amendment of the Constitution abolishing and prohibiting slavery forever." The party promptly called for the Thirteenth Amendment. Lincoln demonstrated his commitment by lobbying Congress for quick approval of the measure. The proposed amendment passed in early 1865 and was sent to the states for ratification. The war to save the Union had also become the war to free the slaves.

It has long been debated whether Abraham Lincoln deserved the label of "Great Emancipator." Was Lincoln ultimately a reluctant emancipator, following rather than leading Congress and public opinion? Or

Who Freed the Slaves?

did Lincoln give essential presidential leadership to the most transformative and sensitive aspect of the war by going slow on emancipation, but once moving, never backpedaling on the main issue—black freedom? Once Lincoln decided to prosecute the war to the unconditional surrender of the Confederates, he made the destruction of slavery central to the conflict's purpose.

Others have argued, however, that the slaves themselves are the central story in the achievement of their own freedom. When they were in proximity to the war zones or had opportunities as traveling laborers, slaves fled for their freedom by the thousands. Some worked as camp laborers for the Union armies, and eventually more than 180,000 black men served in the Union Army and Navy.

However freedom came to individuals, emancipation was a historical confluence of two essential forces: one, a policy directed by and dependent on the military authority of the president in his effort to win the war; and two, the will and courage necessary for acts of self-emancipation.

Before the war was over, the Confederacy, too, addressed the issue of emancipation. Jefferson Davis himself offered a proposal for black freedom of a kind. He was dedicated to independence and was willing to sacrifice slavery to achieve that goal. Davis concluded late in 1864 that the military situation of the Confederacy was so desperate that independence with emancipation was preferable to defeat with emancipation. He proposed that the Confederate government purchase forty thousand slaves to work for the army as laborers, with a promise of freedom at the end of their service. Soon Davis upgraded the idea, calling for the recruitment and arming of slaves as soldiers, who likewise would gain their freedom at war's end. The wives and children of these soldiers, he made plain, must also receive freedom from the states.

Bitter debate over Davis's plan resounded through the Confederacy. When the Confederate Congress approved slave enlistments without the promise of freedom in March 1865, Davis insisted on more. He issued an executive order to guarantee that owners would emancipate slave soldiers, and his allies in the states started to work for emancipation of the soldiers' families.

A Confederate Plan of Emancipation

The war ended before much could come of these desperate policy initiatives on the part of the Confederacy. By contrast, Lincoln's Emancipation Proclamation stimulated a vital infusion of forces into the Union armies. Before the war was over, 134,000 slaves (and 52,000 free African Americans) had fought for freedom and the Union. Their participation aided northern victory while it discouraged recognition of the Confederacy by foreign governments.

The Soldiers' War

The intricacies of policymaking and social revolution were far from the minds of most ordinary soldiers. Military service completely altered their lives. Army life meant tedium, physical hardship, and separation from loved ones. Yet the military experience had powerful attractions as well. It molded men on both sides so thoroughly that they came to resemble one another far more than they resembled civilians back home. Many soldiers forged amid war a bond with their fellows and a connection to a noble purpose that they cherished for years afterward.

Soldiers benefited from certain new products, such as canned condensed milk, but blankets, clothing, and arms were often of poor quality. Vermin abounded. Hospitals were badly managed at first. Rules of hygiene in large camps were scarcely enforced; latrines were poorly made or carelessly used. Water supplies were unsafe and typhoid epidemics common. About 57,000 men died from dysentery and diarrhea; in fact, 224,000 Union troops died from disease or accidents, far more than the 140,000 who died as a result of battle.

Hospitals and Camp Life

On both sides troops quickly learned that soldiering was far from glorious. Before the war, few had seen violent death. Now the war exposed them to the blasted bodies of their friends and comrades. "Any one who goes over a battlefield after a battle," wrote one Confederate, "never cares to go over another. . . . It is a sad sight to see the dead and if possible more sad to see the wounded—shot in every possible way you can imagine." Much of the carnage resulted from tactics that made little sense.

Advances in technology made the Civil War particularly deadly. By far the most important were the ri-

The Rifled Musket

fle and the "minie ball." Bullets fired from a smoothbore musket tumbled and wobbled as they flew through the air and thus were not accurate at distances over 80 yards. Cutting spiraled grooves inside the barrel gave the projectile a spin and much greater accuracy, but rifles remained difficult to load and use until the Frenchman Claude Minie and the American James Burton developed a new kind of bullet. Civil War bullets were sizable lead slugs with a cavity at the bottom that expanded upon firing so that the bullet "took" the rifling and flew accurately. With these bullets, rifles were accurate at 400 yards and useful up to 1,000 yards.

This meant, of course, that soldiers assaulting a position defended by riflemen were in greater peril than ever before. Even though Civil War rifles were cumbersome to load, the defense gained a significant advantage. Advancing soldiers were repeatedly exposed to accurate rifle fire. Because medical knowledge was rudimentary, even minor wounds often led to amputation, and to death through infection. Never before in Europe or America had such massive forces pummeled each other with weapons of such destructive power.

Still, Civil War soldiers developed deep commitments to each other and to their task. The bonding may have been most dramatic among officers and men in the northern black regiments, for there white and black troops took their first steps toward bridging a deep racial divide. Racism in the Union Army was strong. Most white soldiers wanted nothing to do with black people and regarded them as inferior. "I never came out here for to free the black devils," wrote one soldier. For many, acceptance of black troops grew only because they could do heavy labor and "stop Bullets as well as white people."

The Black Soldier's Fight for Manhood

But among some a change occurred. White officers who volunteered to lead black units only to gain promotion found that experience altered their opinions. After just one month with black troops, a white captain informed his wife, "I have a more elevated opinion of their abilities than I ever had before. I know that many of them are vastly the superiors of those . . . who would condemn them all to a life of brutal degradation." One general reported that his "colored regi-

ments" possessed "remarkable aptitude for military training"; another observer said, "They fight like fiends."

Black troops created this change through their own dedication. They had a mission to destroy slavery and demonstrate their equality. Corporal James Henry Gooding of Massachusetts's black Fifty-fourth Regiment explained that his unit intended "to live down all prejudice against its color, by a determination to do well in any position it is put." After an engagement he was proud that "a regiment of white men gave us three cheers as we were passing them," because "it shows that we did our duty as men should."

African American soldiers displayed courage despite persistent discrimination. Off-duty black soldiers were sometimes attacked by northern mobs; on duty, they did most of the "fatigue duty," or heavy labor. The Union government, moreover, paid white privates $13 per month plus a clothing allowance of $3.50, whereas black privates earned only $10 per month less $3 for clothing.

1863: The Tide of Battle Turns

The fighting in the spring and summer of 1863 did not settle the war, but it began to suggest the outcome. The campaigns began in a deceptively positive way for Confederates, as their Army of Northern Virginia performed brilliantly in the Battle of Chancellorsville.

On May 2 and 3, west of Fredericksburg, Virginia, some 130,000 members of the Union Army of the Potomac bore down on fewer than 60,000 Confederates.

Battle of Chancellorsville

Boldly, as if they enjoyed being outnumbered, Generals Robert E. Lee and Stonewall Jackson divided their forces, ordering 30,000 men under Jackson on a day-long march westward to gain position for a flank attack. Jackson's seasoned "foot cavalry" found unprepared Union troops laughing, smoking, and playing cards. The Confederate attack drove the entire right side of the Union Army back in confusion. Eager to press his advantage, Jackson rode forward with a few officers to study the ground. As they returned at twilight, southern troops mistook them for federals and fired, fatally wounding their commander. The next day Union forces left in defeat. Chancellorsville was a remarkable southern victory but costly because of the loss of Stonewall Jackson.

July brought crushing defeats for the Confederacy in two critical battles—Vicksburg and Gettysburg—that severely damaged Confederate hopes for independence. Vicksburg was a vital western citadel, the last major fortification on the Mississippi River in southern hands. After months of searching through swamps and bayous, General Ulysses S. Grant found an advantageous approach to the city. He laid siege to Vicksburg in May, bottling up the defending forces. If Vicksburg fell, Union forces would control the river, cutting the Confederacy in two and gaining an open path into its interior. Meanwhile, General Lee proposed a Confederate invasion of the North.

Siege of Vicksburg

Lee's troops streamed through western Maryland and into Pennsylvania, threatening both Washington and Baltimore. As his emboldened army advanced, the possibility of a major battle near the Union capital became more and more likely. Confederate prospects along the Mississippi, however, darkened. Davis repeatedly wired General Joseph E. Johnston, urging him to concentrate his forces and attack Grant's army. Johnston, however, did little. Grant's men, meanwhile, were supplying themselves from the abundant crops of the Mississippi River valley and could continue their siege indefinitely.

In such circumstances the fall of Vicksburg was inevitable, and on July 4, 1863, its commander surrendered. The same day a battle that had been raging for three days concluded at Gettysburg, Pennsylvania. On July 1 Confederate forces hunting for a supply of shoes had collided with part of the Union Army. Heavy fighting on the second day over two steep hills left federal forces in possession of high ground along Cemetery Ridge. There they enjoyed the protection of a stone wall and a clear view of their foe across almost a mile of open field.

Battle of Gettysburg

Undaunted, Lee believed his reinforced troops could break the Union line, and on July 3 he ordered a direct assault. Full of foreboding, General James Longstreet warned Lee that "no 15,000 men ever arrayed for battle can take that position." But Lee stuck to his plan. Virginians under General George E. Pickett and North Carolinians under General James Pettigrew methodically marched up the slope in a doomed assault known as Pickett's Charge. For a moment a few hundred Confederates breached the enemy's line, but most fell in heavy slaughter. On July 4 Lee had to withdraw, having suffered almost 4,000 dead and about 24,000 missing and wounded.

Southern troops displayed unforgettable courage and dedication at Gettysburg, and the Union Army, which suffered 23,000 casualties (nearly one-quarter of the force), under General George G. Meade exhibited the same bravery in stopping the Confederate invasion. But the results there and at Vicksburg were disastrous for the South. The Confederacy was split in two and its heartland lay exposed to invasion. Lee's defeat spelled the end of major southern offensive actions. Too weak to prevail in attack, the Confederacy henceforth would have to conserve its limited resources and rely on a prolonged defense.

Disunity, South and North

Both northern and southern governments waged the final two years of the war in the face of increasing opposition at home. The gigantic costs of a civil war that neither side seemed able to win fed the unrest. But protest also arose from fundamental stresses in the social structures of North and South.

The Confederacy's problems were both more serious and more deeply rooted than the North's. One ominous development was the planters' increasing opposition to their own government. Not only did the Richmond government impose new taxes and the tax-in-kind, but Confederate military authorities also impressed slaves to build fortifications. And when Union forces advanced on plantation areas, Confederate commanders burned stores of cotton that lay in the enemy's path. Such interference with plantation routines and financial interests was not what planters had expected of their government, and they complained bitterly.

Disintegration of Confederate Unity

Nor were the centralizing policies of the Davis administration popular. The increasing size and power of the Richmond government startled and alarmed planters. The Confederate constitution had in fact granted substantial powers to the central government, especially in time of war. But many planters had assumed with R. B. Rhett, editor of the *Charleston Mer-*

cury, that the Confederate constitution "leaves the States untouched in their Sovereignty, and commits to the Confederate Government only a few simple objects, and a few simple powers to enforce them."

Years of opposition to the federal government within the Union had frozen southerners in a defensive posture. Now they erected the barrier of states' rights as a defense against change. Planters sought, above all, a guarantee that their plantations and their lives would remain untouched; many were not deeply committed either to building a southern nation or to winning independence. If the Confederacy had been allowed to depart from the Union in peace and continue as a semideveloped cotton-growing region, they would have been content. When secession revolutionized their world, they could not or would not adjust.

Meanwhile, for ordinary southerners, the dire predictions of hunger and suffering were becoming a reality. Food riots occurred in the spring of 1863 in Atlanta, Macon, Columbus, and Augusta, Georgia, and in Salisbury and High Point, North Carolina. On April 2 a crowd assembled in Richmond to demand relief. A passerby, noticing the excitement, asked a young girl, "Is there some celebration?" "We celebrate our right to live," replied the girl. "We are starving. As soon as enough of us get together we are going to the bakeries and each of us will take a loaf of bread." Soon they did just that, sparking a riot that Davis himself had to quell at gunpoint.

Food Riots in Southern Cities

Throughout the rural South, ordinary people resisted more quietly—by refusing to cooperate with conscription, tax collection, and impressments of food. "In all the States impressments are evaded by every means which ingenuity can suggest, and in some openly resisted," wrote a high-ranking commissary officer. Farmers who did provide food for the army refused to accept payment in certificates of credit or government bonds, as required by law. Conscription officers increasingly found no one to draft—men of draft age were hiding out in the forests.

Such discontent was certain to affect the Confederate armies. Worried about their loved ones and resentful of what they saw as a rich man's war, large numbers of men deserted. The problem became especially acute after 1862. In mid-1863 it was estimated

Desertions from the Confederate Army

that 40,000 to 50,000 troops were absent without leave and that 100,000 were evading duty in some way. By November 1863 Secretary of War James Seddon admitted that one-third of the army could not be accounted for. The situation would worsen.

The defeats at Gettysburg and Vicksburg dealt a heavy blow to Confederate morale. In desperation President Davis and several state governors resorted to threats and racial scare tactics to drive southern whites to further sacrifice. Despite such tactics, the internal disintegration of the Confederacy quickened. A few newspapers even began to call openly for peace.

In North Carolina a peace movement grew under the leadership of William W. Holden, a popular Democratic politician and editor. Over one hundred public meetings took place in the summer of 1863 in support of peace negotiations. In Georgia early in 1864, Governor Joseph E. Brown and Alexander H. Stephens, vice president of the Confederacy, led a similar effort. Ultimately these movements came to naught, but that the movement existed at all demonstrates deep disaffection.

Southern Peace Movements

By 1864 much of the opposition to the war had moved entirely outside the political sphere. Southerners were simply giving up the struggle and withdrawing their cooperation from the government. Deserters dominated whole towns and counties. Secret societies favoring reunion sprang up. Active dissent was particularly common in upland and mountain regions. The government was losing the support of its citizens.

In the North opposition to the war was similar but less severe. Alarm intensified over the growing centralization of government, and by 1863 war-weariness was widespread. Resentment of the draft sparked protest, especially among poor citizens, and the Union Army struggled with a desertion rate as high as the Confederates'. But the Union was so much richer in human resources than the South that fresh recruits were always available, and there were no shortages of food and other necessities.

Antiwar Sentiment in the North

Also, Lincoln possessed a talent that Davis lacked: he knew how to stay in touch with the ordinary citizen.

Through letters to newspapers and to soldiers' families, he reached the common people and demonstrated that he had not forgotten them. The daily carnage, the tortuous political problems, and the ceaseless criticism weighed heavily on him. But this self-educated man of humble origins was able to communicate his suffering with words that helped to contain northern discontent.

Much of the wartime protest in the North was political in origin. The Democratic Party fought to regain power by blaming Lincoln for the war's death toll, the expansion of federal powers, inflation and the high tariff, and the emancipation of blacks. Appealing to tradition, its leaders called for an end to the war and reunion on the basis of "the Constitution as it is and the Union as it was." The Democrats denounced conscription and martial law and defended states' rights and the interests of agriculture. In the 1862 congressional elections, the Democrats made a strong comeback, and peace Democrats, who would go much further than others in the party to end the war, had influence in New York State and majorities in the legislatures of Illinois and Indiana.

Peace Democrats

Led by outspoken men like Representative Clement L. Vallandigham of Ohio, the peace Democrats made themselves highly visible. Vallandigham criticized Lincoln as a dictator who had suspended the writ of habeas corpus without congressional authority and had arrested thousands of innocent citizens. Like other Democrats, he condemned both conscription and emancipation. Vallandigham stayed carefully within legal bounds, but his attacks seemed so damaging to the war effort that military authorities arrested him for treason after Lincoln suspended habeas corpus. Lincoln wisely decided against punishment—and martyr's status—for the Ohioan and exiled him to the Confederacy.

Lincoln believed that antiwar Democrats were linked to secret organizations that harbored traitorous ideas. These societies, he feared, encouraged draft resistance, discouraged enlistment, sabotaged communications, and plotted to aid the Confederacy. Likening such groups to a poisonous snake, Republicans sometimes branded them—and by extension the peace Democrats—as "Copperheads." Though Democrats were connected with these organizations, most engaged in politics rather than treason.

More violent opposition to the government arose from ordinary citizens facing the draft, which became law in 1863. The urban poor and immigrants in strongly Democratic areas were especially hostile to conscription. Many men, including some of modest means, managed to avoid the army by hiring a substitute or paying commutation, but the poor viewed the commutation fee as discriminatory, and many immigrants suspected (wrongly, on the whole) that they were called in disproportionate numbers.

New York City Draft Riots

As a result, there were scores of disturbances and melees. Enrolling officers received rough treatment in many parts of the North, and riots occurred in New Jersey, Ohio, Indiana, Pennsylvania, Illinois, and Wisconsin. By far the most serious outbreak of violence occurred in New York City in July 1863. New York was a Democratic stronghold, and racial, ethnic, and class tensions ran high. Working-class New Yorkers feared an inflow of black labor from the South and regarded blacks as the cause of the war. Poor Irish workers resented being forced to serve in the place of others who could afford to avoid the draft. When these tensions led to violence, seventy-four people died during three days of rioting.

Discouragement and war-weariness reached a peak in the summer of 1864, when the Democratic Party nominated the popular General George B. McClellan for president and inserted a peace plank into its platform. The plank, written by Vallandigham, condemned "four years of failure to restore the Union by the experiment of war," called for an armistice, and spoke vaguely about preserving the Union. Lincoln, running with Tennessee's Andrew Johnson on a "National Union" ticket, concluded that it was "exceedingly probable that this Administration will not be reelected." However, the fortunes of war soon changed the electoral situation.

1864–1865: The Final Test of Wills

During the final year of the war, the Confederates could still have won their version of victory if military stalemate and northern antiwar sentiment had forced a negotiated settlement to end the war. But events, northern determination, and Lincoln's insistence on the unconditional surrender of Confederate forces prevailed.

From the outset, the North had pursued one paramount diplomatic goal: to prevent recognition of the

Northern Diplomatic Strategy

Confederacy by European nations. Foreign recognition would belie Lincoln's claim that the United States was fighting an illegal rebellion and would open the way to financial and military aid. The British elite, however, felt considerable sympathy for southern planters, whose aristocratic values were similar to their own. And both England and France stood to benefit from a divided and weakened America. Thus, to achieve their goal, Lincoln and Secretary of State William H. Seward needed to avoid both serious military defeats and controversies with the European powers.

Aware that the textile industry employed one-fifth of the British population directly or indirectly, southerners banked on British recognition of the Confederacy. But at the beginning of the war, British mills had a 50 percent surplus of cotton on hand; later on, new sources of supply in India, Egypt, and Brazil helped to meet Britain's needs. Refusing to be stampeded into recognition of the Confederacy, the British government kept its eye on the battlefield. France, though sympathetic to the South, was unwilling to act independently of Britain.

More than once the Union strategy nearly broke down. An acute crisis occurred in 1861 when the overzealous commander of an American frigate stopped the British steamer *Trent* and removed two Confederate ambassadors. The British interpreted this action as a violation of freedom of the seas and demanded the prisoners' release. Lincoln and Seward waited until northern public opinion cooled and then released the two southerners.

Another issue that sparked vigorous protest was the sale to the Confederacy of warships constructed in England. A few English-built ships, notably the *Alabama*, reached open water to serve the South. Over a period of twenty-two months, the *Alabama* destroyed or captured more than sixty Union ships. But the British government, as a neutral power, soon barred delivery of warships such as the Laird rams, formidable vessels whose pointed prows were designed to end the blockade by battering the Union ships.

On the battlefield, the northern victory was far from won in 1864. General Nathaniel Banks's Red River campaign, designed to capture more of Louisiana and Texas, quickly fell apart, and the capture of Mobile Bay in August did not cause the fall of Mobile. Union

Battlefield Stalemate and a Union Strategy for Victory

general William Tecumseh Sherman commented that the North had to "keep the war South until they are not only ruined, exhausted, but humbled in pride and spirit."

Military authorities throughout history have agreed that deep invasion is very risky: the farther an army penetrates enemy territory, the more vulnerable its own communications and supply lines. General Grant, by now in command of all the federal armies, decided to test this assertion—and southern will—with a strategic innovation of his own: raids on a massive scale. Grant proposed to use whole armies, not just cavalry, to destroy Confederate railroads, thus ruining the enemy's transportation and damaging the South's economy. Abandoning their lines of support, Union troops would live off the land while laying to waste all resources useful to the military and to the civilian population of the Confederacy. After General George H. Thomas's troops won the Battle of Chattanooga in November 1863 by ignoring orders and charging up Missionary Ridge, the heartland of Georgia lay open. Moving to Virginia, Grant entrusted General Sherman with 100,000 men for an invasion deep into the South, toward the rail center of Atlanta.

Jefferson Davis countered by positioning the army of General Joseph E. Johnston in Sherman's path.

Atlanta

Davis's entire political strategy for 1864 was based on demonstrating Confederate military strength and successfully defending Atlanta. The U.S. presidential election of 1864 was approaching, and Davis hoped that southern resolve would lead to the defeat of Lincoln and the election of a president who would sue for peace. When General Johnston slowly but steadily fell back toward Atlanta, Davis grew anxious and sought assurances that Atlanta would be held. From a purely military point of view, Johnston maneuvered skillfully, but the president of the Confederacy could not take a purely military point of view. When Johnston provided no information and continued to retreat, Davis replaced him with the one-legged General John Hood, who knew his job was to fight. Hood attacked but was beaten, and Sherman's army occupied Atlanta on September 2, 1864. The victory buoyed northern spirits, ensured Lincoln's reelection, and cleared the way for Sherman's march from Atlanta to the sea (see Map 15.2).

Sherman's army was an unusually formidable force, composed almost entirely of battle-tested veterans and officers who had risen through the

Sherman's March to the Sea

ranks. Tanned, bearded, tough, and unkempt, the remaining veterans were determined, as one put it, "to Conquer this Rebelien or Die." As Sherman's men moved across Georgia, they cut a path 50 to 60 miles wide and more than 200 miles long. The totality of the destruction they caused was awesome. A Georgia woman described the "Burnt Country" this way: "The fields were trampled down and the road was lined with carcasses of horses, hogs, and cattle that the invaders, unable either to consume or to carry with them, had wantonly shot down to starve our people and prevent them from making their crops. The stench in some places was unbearable." Such devastation diminished the South's material resources and sapped its will to resist. Indeed, the lack of popular resistance in Georgia and South Carolina indicated that southern whites had lost the will to continue the struggle.

In Virginia, too, the path to victory proved protracted and ghastly. Throughout the spring and summer of 1864, intent on capturing Richmond, Grant hurled his troops at

Virginia's Bloody Soil

Lee's army in Virginia and suffered appalling losses: almost 18,000 casualties in the Battle of the Wilderness, where skeletons poked out of the shallow graves dug one year before; more than 8,000 at Spotsylvania; and 12,000 in the space of a few hours at Cold Harbor.

Before the assault at Cold Harbor (which Grant later admitted was a grave mistake), Union troops pinned scraps of paper bearing their names and addresses to their backs, certain they would be mowed down as they rushed Lee's trenches. In four weeks in May and June, Grant lost as many men as were en-

Map 15.2 Sherman's March to the Sea   The West proved a decisive theater at the end of the war. From Chattanooga, Union forces drove into Georgia, capturing Atlanta. Then General Sherman embarked on his march of destruction through Georgia to the coast and then northward through the Carolinas.

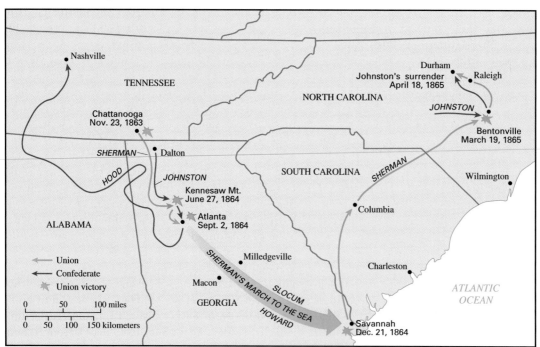

At the war's end, the U.S. flag flew over the state capitol in Richmond, Virginia, which bore many marks of destruction. (National Archives)

rolled in Lee's entire army. Though costly, and testing northern morale to its limits, these battles prepared the way for eventual victory: Lee's army shrank until offensive action was no longer possible, while Grant's army kept replenishing its forces with new recruits.

The end finally came in the spring of 1865. Grant kept battering Lee, who tried but failed to break through the Union line. With the numerical superiority of Grant's army now greater than two to one, Confederate defeat was inevitable. On April 2 Lee abandoned Richmond and Petersburg. On April 9, hemmed in by Union troops, short of rations, and with fewer than thirty thousand men left, Lee surrendered at Appomattox Court House. Grant treated his rival with respect and paroled the defeated troops. The war was over at last. Within weeks, Confederate forces under Johnston surrendered and Davis was captured in Georgia.

Surrender at Appomattox

With Lee's surrender, Lincoln knew that the Union had been preserved, yet he lived to see but a few days of the war's aftermath. On the evening of Good Friday, April 14, he accompanied his wife to Ford's Theatre in Washington to enjoy a popular comedy. There John Wilkes Booth, an embittered southern sympathizer, shot the president in the head at point-blank range. The Union had lost its wartime leader, and millions publicly mourned the martyred chief executive. Relief at the war's end mingled hauntingly with a renewed sense of loss and anxiety about the future.

Property damage and financial costs were enormous, though difficult to tally. U.S. loans and taxes during the conflict totaled almost $3 billion, and interest on the war debt was $2.8 billion. The Confederacy borrowed over $2 billion but lost far more in the destruction of homes, crops, livestock, and other property. In southern war zones the landscape was desolated. Over wide regions fences and crops were destroyed; houses, barns, and bridges burned; and fields abandoned and left to erode. Visitors to the countryside were struck by how empty and impoverished it looked.

Financial Tally

Estimates of the total cost of the war exceed $20 billion—five times the total expenditures of the federal government from its creation to 1861. The northern government increased its spending by 700 percent in the first full year of the war; by the last year its spending had soared to twenty times the prewar level. By 1865 the federal government accounted for over 26 percent of the gross national product.

Many of these changes were more or less permanent. In the 1880s, interest on the war debt still accounted for approximately 40 percent of the federal budget and Union soldiers' pensions for as much as 20 percent. The federal government had used its power to support manufacturing and business interests by means of tariffs, loans, and subsidies, and wartime measures left the government more deeply involved in the banking and transportation systems. If southerners had hoped to remove government from the economy, the war had now irrepressibly bound them together.

The human costs of the Civil War were especially staggering. The total number of military casualties on both sides exceeded 1 million—a

Death Toll

frightful toll for a nation of 31 million people. Approximately 360,000 Union soldiers died. Another 275,175 Union soldiers were wounded but survived. On the Confederate side, an estimated 260,000 lost their lives, and almost as many suffered wounds. More men died in the Civil War than in all other American wars combined until Vietnam.

Summary

 The Civil War altered American society forever. During the war, in both North and South, women had taken on new roles. Industrialization and large economic enterprises grew in power. The character and extent of government power changed markedly. Under Republican leadership, the federal government had expanded its power not only to preserve the Union but also to extend freedom. A social revolution and government authority emancipated the slaves. A republic desperately divided against itself had survived, yet in new constitutional forms yet to take shape under tremendous political strife during Reconstruction.

It was unclear, however, how or whether the nation would use its power to protect the rights of the former slaves. Secession was dead, but whether Americans would continue to embrace a centralized nationalism remained to be seen. How would white southerners, embittered and impoverished, respond to efforts to reconstruct the nation? How long would military occupation last in the South, and who would rule its civil society? How would the country care for the maimed, the orphans, the farming women without men to work their land, and all the dead who had to be properly found and buried? And of central importance: what would be the place of black men and women in American life? Black veterans and former slaves eagerly sought an answer. They would find it during Reconstruction.

LEGACY FOR A PEOPLE AND A NATION

The Confederate Battle Flag

The most widespread and controversial symbol to emerge from the Civil War era is the Confederate flag. Rather than the official flag of the Confederacy, it was a battle flag that soldiers carried to mark the center of a unit's position in the confusion of combat. Over time, this flag has taken on powerful emotional meanings.

At Confederate veterans' reunions and parades from the 1870s to well into the twentieth century, the flag was an emblem of the South's Lost Cause. After extended controversy, many captured Confederate flags were returned by the federal government to southern states in 1905 as a gesture of reconciliation. Increasingly, Confederate remembrance merged with white supremacy at the turn of the twentieth century, and African Americans resented the flag's appearance.

In the late 1940s the flag became a fixture of popular culture with heightened racial meanings. In 1948 it was a symbol of the States' Rights ("Dixiecrat") Party. By the 1950s waving the Confederate flag became a demonstration of defiance among southern whites against the civil rights revolution.

What does this flag mean as a symbol? Some southern whites argue that it is merely a marker of regional pride and identity. But to most blacks and to many whites, it expresses racism. The flag is loaded with coded meanings that can be interpreted in opposite ways. Some claim it represents the "nobility" of southern military tradition; others conclude that it stands for the hatred embodied in the history of the Ku Klux Klan.

In recent times, the Confederate flag has been the center of legal and political controversy. Disputes have emanated from city councils, high schools, and universities over public and private uses of the flag. Most visible of all have been the debates in the states of Georgia, South Carolina, and Alabama over whether to cease flying the Confederate flag at official sites. At issue are important questions and traditions: free speech, equal protection under law, perception versus reality, official government endorsement of collective symbols, the significance of race and racism in our national memory, and the meaning of the Civil War itself.

For Further Reading, see the Appendix. For Web resources, go to history.college.hmco.com/students.

RECONSTRUCTION:
AN UNFINISHED REVOLUTION
1865–1877

In 1861 Robert Smalls was a slave in South Carolina, while Wade Hampton was a South Carolina legislator and one of the richest planters in the South. The events of the next fifteen years turned each man's world upside down more than once.

Robert Smalls became a Union hero in 1862 when he stole a Confederate ship from Charleston harbor and piloted it to the blockading federal fleet. After the war, Smalls began a career in politics and served in both the South Carolina legislature and Congress. There he worked for educational and economic opportunity for his people. But Smalls was helpless to prevent the return of white control in South Carolina in 1877.

Wade Hampton joined the Confederate Army in 1861 and soon became a general. The South's defeat profoundly shocked him. The postwar years brought further painful changes, including forced bankruptcy. By 1876, though, Hampton's fortunes were again on the rise: the Democrats nominated him for governor, promising that he would "redeem" South Carolina from Republican misrule. Among Hampton's white supporters were the paramilitary Red Shirts, who pledged to "control the vote of at least one Negro, by intimidation, purchase," or other means. Hampton won the governor's chair, then a seat in the U.S. Senate.

As the careers of Smalls and Hampton suggest, Reconstruction was revolutionary. Robert Smalls rose from bondage to experience glory, emancipation, political power, and, ultimately, disappointment. Wade Hampton fell from privilege to endure defeat, failure, bankruptcy, and, eventually, a return to leadership in his state. Unprecedented changes took place in American society, but the underlying realities of economic power, racial prejudice, and judicial conservatism limited Reconstruction's revolutionary potential.

Nowhere was the turmoil of Reconstruction more evident than in national politics. Lincoln's successor, Andrew Johnson, fought bitterly with Congress over the shaping of a plan for Reconstruction. Though a southerner, Johnson had always been a foe of the South's wealthy planters, and his first acts as president suggested that he would be tough on "traitors." Before the end of 1865, however, Johnson's policies changed direction. Jefferson Davis stayed in prison for two years, but Johnson quickly pardoned other rebel leaders and allowed them to occupy high offices. He also ordered the return of plantations to their original owners, including abandoned Georgia and South Carolina coastal lands on which forty thousand freed men and women had settled as a result of General William Tecumseh Sherman's Field Order Number 15 of February 1865.

Johnson imagined a lenient and rapid "restoration" of the South to the Union rather than the fundamental "reconstruction" that Republican congressmen favored. Between 1866 and 1868, the president and the Republican leadership in Congress engaged in a bitterly antagonistic power struggle over how to put the United States back together again.

Before these struggles were over, Congress had impeached the president, enfranchised the freedmen, and given them a role in reconstructing the South. The nation also adopted the Fourteenth and Fifteenth Amendments. Yet little was done to open the doors of economic opportunity to black southerners. Moreover, by 1869 the Ku Klux Klan was employing extensive violence and terror to thwart Reconstruction and undermine black freedom.

As the 1870s advanced, industrial growth accelerated, creating new opportunities and raising new priorities. A new economic depression after 1873 refocused northerners' attention. Political corruption became a nationwide scandal, bribery a way of doing business. "Money has become the God of this country," wrote one disgusted observer, "and men, otherwise good men, are almost compelled to worship at her shrine."

Thus Reconstruction became a revolution eclipsed. White southerners' desire to take back control of their states and of race relations overwhelmed the national interest in stopping them. But Reconstruction left enduring legacies the nation has struggled with ever since. ■

Wartime Reconstruction

 Civil wars leave immense challenges of healing, justice, and physical rebuilding. Anticipating that process, Reconstruction of the Union was an issue as early as 1863. The very idea of Reconstruction raised many questions: How would the nation be restored? How would southern states and leaders be treated? What was the constitutional basis for readmission of states to the Union? More specifically, four vexing problems compelled early thinking and would haunt the country throughout the Reconstruction era. One, *who* would rule in the South once it was defeated? Two, *who* would rule in the federal government, Congress or the president? Three, what were the dimensions of *black freedom*, and what rights under law would the freedmen enjoy? And four, would Reconstruction be a preservation of the *old* republic or a second revolution, a re-invention of a *new* republic?

Abraham Lincoln had never been antisouthern. He planned early for a swift and moderate Reconstruction process. In his Second Inaugural Address, Lincoln promised "malice toward none; with charity for all" as Americans strove to "bind up the nation's wounds."

Lincoln's 10 Percent Plan

In his "Proclamation of Amnesty and Reconstruction," issued in December 1863, Lincoln proposed to replace majority rule with "loyal rule" as a means of reconstructing southern state governments. He proposed pardoning all ex-Confederates except the highest-ranking military and civilian officers. Then, as soon as 10 percent of the voting population in the 1860 election had taken an oath and established a government, that government would be recognized. Lincoln did not consult Congress in these plans, and "loyal" assemblies (known as "Lincoln governments") were created in Louisiana, Tennessee, and Arkansas in 1864, states largely occupied by Union troops.

Congress responded with great hostility to Lincoln's moves to readmit southern states in what seemed such a premature manner. Many Radical Republicans considered the 10 percent plan a "mere

IMPORTANT EVENTS

1865 Johnson begins rapid and lenient
Reconstruction
Confederate leaders regain power
White southern governments pass
restrictive black codes
Congress refuses to seat southern
representatives
Thirteenth Amendment ratified

1866 Congress passes Civil Rights Act and
renewal of Freedmen's Bureau over
Johnson's veto
Congress approves Fourteenth Amendment
Most southern states reject Fourteenth
Amendment
In *Ex parte Milligan* the Supreme Court
reasserts its influence
In congressional elections, Republicans
win more than two-thirds majority, a
renunciation of Johnson's plan of
Reconstruction

1867 Congress passes Reconstruction Acts and
Tenure of Office Act
Secretary of State William Seward arranges
purchase of Alaska
Constitutional conventions called in
southern states

1868 House impeaches Johnson; Senate
acquits him
Most southern states gain readmission to
the Union under Radical plan
Fourteenth Amendment ratified
Grant elected president

1869 Congress approves Fifteenth Amendment
(ratified in 1870)

1870 Congress passes first Enforcement Act

1871 Congress passes Ku Klux Klan Act

1872 Amnesty Act frees almost all remaining
Confederates from restrictions on holding
office
Liberal Republicans organize and oppose
Grant
Debtors urge government to keep greenbacks
in circulation
Grant reelected

1873 *Slaughter-House* cases limit power of
Fourteenth Amendment
Panic of 1873 sends economy into extended
depression, leading to widespread
unemployment and labor strife

1874 Grant vetoes increase in supply of paper
money
Democrats win majority in House of
Representatives

1875 Several Grant appointees indicted for
corruption
Congress passes weak Civil Rights Act
Congress requires that after 1878 greenbacks
be convertible into gold
Democratic Party continues to "redeem"
control of southern states with white
supremacy campaigns

1876 *U.S. v. Cruikshank* and *U.S. v. Reese* further
weaken Fourteenth Amendment
Presidential election disputed

1877 Congress elects Hayes president
Exodusters migrate to Kansas
"Home rule" returns to three remaining
southern states not yet controlled by
Democrats; Reconstruction over

Congress and the Wade-Davis Bill

mockery" of democracy. Thaddeus Stevens of Pennsylvania advocated a "conquered provinces" theory, and Charles Sumner of Massachusetts employed an argument of "state suicide." Both contended that by seceding, southern states had destroyed their status as states. They there-

fore must be treated as "conquered foreign lands" and revert to the status of "unorganized territories" before Congress could entertain any process of readmission.

In July 1864, the Wade-Davis bill, named for its sponsors, Senator Benjamin Wade of Ohio and Congressman Henry W. Davis of Maryland, emerged from Congress with three specific conditions for southern readmission: one, it demanded a "majority" of white male citizens participating in the creation of a new government; two, to vote or be a delegate to constitutional conventions, men had to take an "iron-clad" oath (declaring they had never aided the Confederate war effort); and three, all officers above the rank of lieutenant, and all civil officials in the Confederacy, would be disfranchised and deemed "not a citizen of the United States." Lincoln pocket-vetoed the bill and issued a conciliatory proclamation of his own, announcing that he would not be inflexibly committed to any "one plan" of Reconstruction.

The timing of this exchange came during Grant's bloody campaign in Virginia against Lee. The outcome of the war and Lincoln's reelection were still in doubt. Radical members of his own party, indeed, were organizing a dump-Lincoln campaign for the 1864 election. What emerged in 1864–1865 was a clear-cut debate and a potential constitutional crisis. Lincoln saw Reconstruction as a means of weakening the Confederacy and winning the war; the Radicals saw it as a longer-term transformation of the political and racial order of the country.

In early 1865, Congress and Lincoln joined in passing two important measures that recognized slavery's centrality to the war. On January 31, with strong administration backing, Congress passed the Thirteenth Amendment, which had two provisions: it abolished involuntary servitude everywhere in the United States, and it declared that Congress shall have power to enforce this outcome by "appropriate legislation."

Thirteenth Amendment and the Freedmen's Bureau

Potentially as significant, on March 3, 1865, Congress created the Bureau of Refugees, Freedmen, and Abandoned Lands—the Freedmen's Bureau, an unprecedented agency of social uplift, necessitated by the ravages of the war. In the mere four years of its existence, the Freedmen's Bureau supplied food and medical services, built several thousand schools and some colleges, negotiated several hundred thousand employment contracts between freedmen and their former masters, and tried to manage confiscated land.

The Bureau would be a controversial aspect of Reconstruction, both within the South, where whites generally hated it, and within the federal government, where politicians divided over its constitutionality.

The war had forced into the open an eternal question of republics: What are the social welfare obligations of the state toward its people, and what do people owe their governments in return?

The Meanings of Freedom

 Black southerners entered into life after slavery with hope and circumspection. Expecting hostility from southern whites, freed men and women tried to gain as much as they could from their new circumstances. Often the changes they valued the most were personal—alterations in location, employer, or living arrangements.

For America's former slaves, Reconstruction had one paramount meaning: a chance to explore freedom.

The Feel of Freedom

Former slaves remembered singing far into the night after federal troops, who confirmed rumors of their emancipation, reached their plantations. The slaves on a Texas plantation shouted for joy, their leader proclaiming, "We is free—no more whippings and beatings." One man recalled that he and others "started on the move," either to search for family members or just to exercise the human right of mobility.

Many freed men and women reacted more cautiously and shrewdly, taking care to test the boundaries of their new condition. As slaves they had learned to expect hostility from white people, and they did not presume it would instantly disappear. Life in freedom might still be a matter of what was allowed, not what was right. One sign of their caution was the way freedpeople evaluated potential employers. "Most all the Negroes that had good owners stayed with 'em, but the others left. Some of 'em come back and some didn't," explained one man. After considerable wandering in search of better circumstances, a majority of blacks eventually settled as agricultural workers back on their former farms or plantations. But they relocated their houses and did their utmost to control the conditions of their labor.

The search for family members who had been sold away during slavery was awe-inspiring. With only shreds of information to guide them, thousands of freedpeople embarked on odysseys in search of a husband, wife, child, or parent. Some succeeded in their quest, sometimes almost miraculously. Others trudged through several states and never found loved ones.

Parents in African American Families

Husbands and wives who had belonged to different masters established homes together for the first time, and parents asserted the right to raise their own children. A mother bristled when her old master claimed a right to whip her children. She informed him that "he warn't goin' to brush none of her chilluns no more." The freed men and women were too much at risk to act recklessly, but, as one man put it, they were tired of punishment and "sure didn't take no more foolishment off of white folks."

Many black people wanted to minimize contact with whites. To avoid contact with overbearing whites who were used to supervising them,

Blacks' Search for Independence

blacks abandoned the slave quarters and fanned out to distant corners of the land they worked. Some described moving "across the creek to [themselves]" or building a "saplin house . . . back in the woods." Others established small all-black settlements that still exist today along the back roads of the South.

In addition to a fair employer, what freed men and women most wanted was the ownership of land. Land

African Americans' Desire for Land

represented their chance to enjoy the independence that self-sufficient farmers value. It represented compensation for generations of travail in bondage. A northern observer noted that slaves freed in the Sea Islands of South Carolina and Georgia made "plain, straightforward" inquiries as they settled the land set aside for them by General Sherman. They wanted to be sure the land "would be theirs after they had improved it."

But how much of a chance would whites give to blacks? Most members of both political parties opposed genuine land redistribution to the freedmen. Even northern reformers showed little sympathy for black aspirations. The former Sea Island slaves wanted to establish small, self-sufficient farms. Northern soldiers, officials, and missionaries insisted that they grow cotton.

"The Yankees preach nothing but cotton, cotton!" complained one Sea Island black. "We wants land," wrote another, but tax officials "make the lots too big, and cut we out." Indeed, the U.S. government sold thousands of acres in the Sea Islands for nonpayment

African Americans of all ages eagerly pursued the opportunity in freedom to gain an education. This young woman in Mt. Meigs, Alabama, is helping her mother learn to read. (Smithsonian Institute, photo by Rudolf Eickemeyer)

of taxes, but 90 percent of the land went to wealthy investors from the North.

Ex-slaves reached out for valuable things in life that had been denied them. One of these was education. Blacks of all ages hungered for

The Black Embrace of Education

the knowledge in books that had been permitted only to whites. With freedom, they started schools and filled classrooms both day and night. On log seats and dirt floors, freed men and women studied their letters in old almanacs and discarded dictionaries. Young children brought infants to school with them, and adults attended at night or after "the crops were laid by."

The federal government and northern reformers of both races assisted this pursuit of education. In its brief life, the Freedmen's Bureau founded over four thousand schools, and idealistic men and women from the North established and staffed others founded by private northern philanthropy. Thus did African Americans seek a break from their pasts through learning. The results included the beginnings of a public school system in each southern state and the enrollment of over six hundred thousand African Americans in elementary school by 1877.

Blacks and their white allies also saw the need for colleges and universities to train teachers, ministers, and professionals for leadership. The American Missionary Association founded seven colleges, including Fisk and Atlanta Universities, between 1866 and 1869. The Freedmen's Bureau helped to establish Howard University in Washington, D.C., and northern religious groups supported dozens of seminaries and teachers' colleges. By the late 1870s black churches had joined in the effort, founding numerous colleges despite limited resources.

During Reconstruction, African American leaders often were highly educated individuals; many of them came from the prewar elite of free people of color. This group had benefited from its association with wealthy whites, many of whom were blood relatives; some planters had given their mulatto children an outstanding education. Francis Cardozo, who held various offices in South Carolina, had attended universities in Scotland and England. The two black senators from Mississippi, Blanche K. Bruce and Hiram Revels, possessed privileged educations. These men and many self-educated former slaves brought to political office their experience as artisans, businessmen, lawyers, teachers, and preachers.

Freed from the restrictions and regulations of slavery, blacks could build their own institutions as they saw fit. The secret churches of slavery came into the open; throughout the South, ex-slaves "started a brush arbor." A brush arbor was merely "a sort of . . . shelter with leaves for a roof," but the freed men and women worshiped in it enthusiastically. Within a few years, however, independent branches of the Methodist and Baptist denominations had attracted the great majority of black Christians in the South.

Growth of Black Churches

The desire to gain as much independence as possible also shaped the former slaves' economic arrangements. Since most of them lacked the money to buy land, they preferred the next best thing: renting the land they worked. But the South had a cash-poor economy with few sources of credit. Therefore, black farmers and white landowners turned to sharecropping, a system in which farmers kept part of their crop and gave the rest to the landowner while living on his property. The landlord or a merchant "furnished" food and supplies needed before the harvest, and he received payment from the crop. Although landowners tried to set the laborers' share at a low level, black farmers had some bargaining power, at least at first. Sharecroppers would hold out, or move and try to switch employers from one year to another.

Rise of the Sharecropping System

The sharecropping system originated as a desirable compromise. It eased landowners' problems with cash and credit, and provided them a permanent, dependent labor force; blacks accepted it because it gave them more freedom from daily supervision. Instead of working under a white overseer, as in slavery, they farmed a plot of land on their own in family groups. But sharecropping later proved to be a disaster. Owners and merchants developed a monopoly of control over the agricultural economy, and sharecroppers found themselves riveted into ever-increasing debt. Coinciding with the emergence of a southern economy based on sharecropping was the nation's struggle to put its political house back in order.

Johnson's Reconstruction Plan

 When Reconstruction began under President Andrew Johnson, many expected his policies to be harsh. Throughout his career in Tennessee he had criticized the wealthy planters and championed the small farmers. When an assassin's bullet thrust Johnson into the presidency, many former slaveowners, as well as northern Radicals, had reason to believe that Johnson would deal sternly with the South. When one Radical suggested the exile or execution of ten or twelve leading rebels to set an example, Johnson replied, "How are you going to pick out so small a number?"

Like his martyred predecessor, Johnson followed a path in antebellum politics from obscurity to power. With no formal education, he became a tailor's apprentice. But from 1829, while in his early twenties, he held nearly every office in Tennessee politics: alderman, state representative, congressman, two terms as governor, and U.S. senator by 1857. Although elected as a southern Democrat, Johnson was the only senator from a seceded state who refused to follow his state out of the Union. Lincoln appointed him war governor of Tennessee in 1862, and hence, his symbolic place on the ticket in the president's bid for reelection in 1864.

Who Was Andrew Johnson?

Although a staunch Unionist, Johnson was also an ardent states' rightist. And while he vehemently opposed secession, Johnson advocated limited government. Above all, when it came to race, Johnson was a thoroughgoing white supremacist. He accepted emancipation as a result of the war, but he did not favor black civil and political rights. His philosophy toward Reconstruction may be summed up in the slogan he adopted: "The Constitution as it is, and the Union as it was."

Through 1865 Johnson alone controlled Reconstruction policy, for Congress recessed shortly before he became president and did not reconvene until December. In the following eight months, Johnson put into operation his own plan, forming new state governments in the South by using his power to grant pardons. But what role, if any, would blacks have in these governments?

Johnson's Leniency and Racial Views

Johnson held that black suffrage could never be imposed on a southern state by the federal government. His racism put him on a collision course with the Radicals. In perhaps the most blatantly racist official statement ever delivered by an American president, Johnson declared in his annual message of 1867 that blacks possessed less "capacity for government than any other race of people. No independent government of any form has ever been successful in their hands."

This racial conservatism had an enduring effect on Johnson's policies. Where whites were concerned, however, Johnson seemed to be pursuing changes in class relations. He proposed rules that would keep the wealthy planter class at least temporarily out of power. White southerners were required to swear an oath of loyalty as a condition of gaining amnesty or pardon, but Johnson barred several categories of people from taking the oath: former federal officials, high-ranking Confederate officers, and political leaders or graduates of West Point or Annapolis who had violated their oaths to support the United States by aiding the Confederacy. To this list Johnson added another important group: all southerners who aided the rebellion and whose taxable property was worth more than $20,000. These individuals had to apply personally to the president for pardon and restoration of their political rights. It thus appeared that the leadership class of the Old South would be removed from power and replaced by deserving yeomen.

Johnson appointed provisional governors who began the Reconstruction process by calling constitutional conventions. The delegates chosen for these conventions had to draft new constitutions that eliminated slavery and invalidated secession.

Johnson's Pardon Policy

After ratification of these constitutions, new governments could be elected, and the states would be restored to the Union with full congressional representation. But only those southerners who had taken the oath of amnesty and been eligible to vote on the day the state seceded could participate in this process. Thus unpardoned whites and former slaves were not eligible.

If Johnson intended to strip the old elite of its power, he did not hold to his plan. Surprisingly, he helped to subvert his own plan by pardoning aristocrats and leading rebels. These pardons, plus the rapid return of planters' abandoned lands, restored the old elite to power.

Why did Johnson allow the planters to regain power? Part of the answer is tied to his determination to implement a rapid Reconstruction in order to deny the Radicals the opportunity for the more thorough racial and political changes they desired in the South. Another reason was Johnson's need for southern support in the 1866 elections. Such factors led him to endorse the new governments and declare Reconstruction complete only eight months after Appomattox. Thus in December 1865 many Confederate leaders, including the vice president of the Confederacy, traveled to Washington to claim seats in the U.S. Congress.

The election of such prominent rebels troubled many northerners. So did other results of Johnson's program. Some of the state conven-

Black Codes

tions were slow to repudiate secession; others admitted only grudgingly that slavery was dead. Furthermore, to define the status of freed men and women and control their labor, some legislatures merely revised large sections of the slave codes by substituting the word *freedmen* for *slaves*. The new black codes compelled the former slaves to carry passes, observe a curfew, live in housing provided by a landowner, and give up hope of entering many desirable occupations. Stiff vagrancy laws and restrictive labor contracts bound supposedly free laborers to plantations.

It seemed to northerners that the South was intent on returning African Americans to servility. Thus the Republican majority in Congress decided to call a halt to the results of Johnson's plan. On reconvening, the House and Senate considered the credentials of the newly elected southern representatives and decided not to admit them. Instead, they bluntly challenged the president's authority and established a joint committee to study and investigate a new direction for Reconstruction.

The Congressional Reconstruction Plan

Northern congressmen were hardly unified, but they did not doubt their right to shape Reconstruction policy. The Constitution mentioned neither secession nor reunion, but it gave Congress the primary role in the admission of states. Moreover, the Constitution declared that the United States shall guarantee to each state a republican form of government. This provision, legislators believed, gave them the authority to devise policies for Reconstruction.

They soon found that other constitutional questions affected their policies. What, for example, had rebellion done to the relationship between southern states and the Union? Lincoln had always insisted that states could not secede—they had engaged in an "in-

surrection"—and that the Union remained intact. Johnson also argued that the Union had endured, though individuals had erred. In contrast, congressmen who favored vigorous Reconstruction measures argued that the war had broken the Union, and that the South was subject to the victor's will. Moderate congressmen held that the states had forfeited their rights through rebellion and thus had come under congressional supervision.

These theories mirrored the diversity of Congress itself. Northern Democrats denounced any idea of racial equality and supported John-

The Radicals

son's policies. Conservative Republicans favored a limited federal role in Reconstruction. The Radical Republicans wanted to transform the South. Although they were a minority within their party, they had the advantage of a clearly defined goal. They believed it was essential to democratize the South, establish public education, and ensure the rights of freedpeople. They favored black suffrage, often supported land confiscation and redistribution, and were willing to exclude the South from the Union for several years if necessary to achieve their goals. A large group of moderate Republicans did not want to go as far as the Radicals but believed some reworking of Johnson's policies was necessary.

Ironically, Johnson and the Democrats sabotaged the possibility of a conservative coalition. They refused to cooperate with conservative or moderate Republicans and insisted that Reconstruction was over, that the new state governments were legitimate, and that southern representatives should be admitted to Congress. To devise a Republican program, conservative and moderate elements in the party had to work with the Radicals, whose influence grew in proportion to Johnson's intransigence.

Trying to work with Johnson, Republicans believed a compromise had been reached in the spring of 1866. Under its terms Johnson would

Congress Wrests Control from Johnson

agree to two modifications of his program: extension of the life of the Freedmen's Bureau for another year and passage of a civil rights bill to counteract the black codes. This bill would force southern courts to practice equality before the law by allowing federal judges to remove from state courts cases in which blacks were treated unfairly.

Its provisions applied to public, not private, acts of discrimination. The civil rights bill of 1866 was the first statutory definition of the rights of American citizens.

Johnson destroyed the compromise, however, by vetoing both bills (they later became law when Congress overrode the president's veto). All hope of presidential-congressional cooperation was now dead. In 1866 newspapers reported daily violations of blacks' rights in the South and carried alarming accounts of antiblack violence. In Memphis, for instance, forty blacks were killed and twelve schools burned by white mobs. Such violence convinced Republicans, and the northern public, that more needed to be done. A new Republican plan took the form of a proposed amendment to the Constitution, forged out of a compromise between radical and conservative elements of the party. The Fourteenth Amendment, passed and sent to the states in June 1866, was Congress's alternative to Johnson's program of Reconstruction.

Of the four parts of the Fourteenth Amendment, the first was to have the greatest legal significance in

The Fourteenth Amendment

later years. It conferred citizenship on the freedmen and prohibited states from abridging their constitutional "privileges and immunities." It also barred any state from taking a person's life, liberty, or property "without due process of law" and from denying "equal protection of the laws." These resounding phrases became powerful guarantees of African Americans' civil rights—indeed, of the rights of all citizens—in the twentieth century.

Nearly universal agreement emerged among Republicans on the amendment's second and third provisions. The second declared the Confederate debt null and void and guaranteed the war debt of the United States. The third provision barred Confederate leaders from holding state and federal office. Only Congress, by a two-thirds vote of each house, could remove the penalty.

The fourth part of the amendment dealt with representation and embodied the compromises that produced the document. Emancipation made every former slave a full person rather than three-fifths of a person, which would increase southern representation. Thus the postwar South stood to gain power in Congress, and if white southerners did not allow blacks to vote, former secessionists would derive the political benefit from emancipation. So Republicans determined that if a southern state did not grant black men the vote, its representation would be reduced proportionally. If a state did enfranchise black men, its representation would be increased proportionally. This compromise avoided a direct enactment of black suffrage, but would deliver future black voters to the Republican Party.

The Fourteenth Amendment paved the way for black male suffrage but ignored female citizens, black and white. For this reason it provoked a strong reaction from the women's rights movement. When legislators defined women as nonvoting citizens, prominent leaders such as Elizabeth Cady Stanton and Susan B. Anthony decided that it was time to end their alliance with abolitionists and fight more determinedly for themselves. Thus the amendment infused new life into the women's rights movement and caused considerable strife among old allies.

In 1866, however, the major question in Reconstruction politics was how the public would respond to

The South's and Johnson's Defiance, 1866

the congressional initiative. Johnson did his best to block the Fourteenth Amendment in both North and South. Condemning Congress for its refusal to seat southern representatives, the president urged state legislatures in the South to vote against ratification. Every southern legislature except Tennessee's rejected the amendment by a wide margin.

To present his case to northerners, Johnson organized a National Union Convention and took to the stump himself. In an age when active personal campaigning was rare for a president, Johnson boarded a special train for a "swing around the circle" that carried his message deep into the Northeast, the Midwest, and then back to Washington. In city after city, he criticized the Republicans in a ranting, undignified style. Increasingly, audiences rejected his views and hooted and jeered at him.

The elections of 1866 were a resounding victory for Republicans in Congress. Radicals and moderates whom Johnson had denounced won reelection by large margins, and the Republican majority grew to two-thirds of both houses of Congress. The North had spoken clearly: Johnson's policies were prematurely giving the advantage to rebels and traitors. Thus Republican congressional leaders won a mandate to pursue their Reconstruction plan.

After some embittered debate, Congress, in March 1867, passed the First Reconstruction Act. This plan, under which the southern states were actually readmitted to the Union, incorporated only a part of the Radical program. Union generals, commanding small garrisons of troops and charged with supervising all elections, assumed control in five military districts in the South (see Map 16.1). Confederate leaders designated in the Fourteenth Amendment were barred from voting until new state constitutions were ratified. The act guaranteed freedmen the right to vote in elections for state constitutional conventions and in subsequent elections. In addition, each southern state was required to ratify the

The Reconstruction Acts of 1867–1868

Fourteenth Amendment, to ratify its new constitution by majority vote, and to submit that constitution to Congress for approval. The Second, Third, and Fourth Reconstruction Acts, passed between March 1867 and March 1868, provided for the details of operation of voter registration boards, the adoption of constitutions, and the administration of "good faith" oaths on the part of white southerners.

In the words of one historian, the Radicals succeeded in "clipping Johnson's wings." But they had hoped Congress could do much more. Thaddeus Stevens, for example, argued that economic opportunity was essential to the freedmen. Stevens therefore drew up a plan for extensive confiscation and redistribu-

The Failure of Land Redistribution

Map 16.1   The Reconstruction   This map shows the five military districts established when Congress passed the Reconstruction Act of 1867. As the dates within each state indicate, conservative Democratic forces quickly regained control of government in four southern states. So-called Radical Reconstruction was curtailed in most of the others as factions within the weakened Republican Party began to cooperate with conservative Democrats.

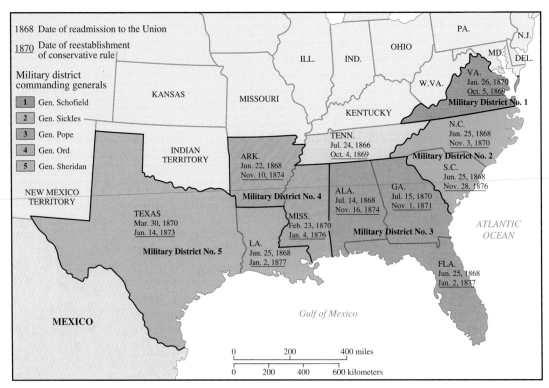

tion of land. Only one-tenth of the land affected by his plan was earmarked for freedmen, in 40-acre plots. The rest was to be sold to generate money for Union veterans' pensions, compensation to loyal southerners for damaged property, and payment of the federal debt.

By these means Stevens hoped to win support for a basically unpopular measure. But he failed. Northerners were accustomed to a limited role for government, and the business community staunchly opposed any interference with private property rights, even for former Confederates.

Congress's role as the architect of Reconstruction was not quite over. To restrict Johnson's influence and safeguard its plan, Congress passed a

Constitutional Crisis

number of controversial laws. First, it set the date for its own reconvening—an unprecedented act, for the president traditionally summoned legislators to Washington. Then it limited Johnson's power over the army by requiring the president to issue military orders through the General of the Army, Ulysses S. Grant, who could not be dismissed without the Senate's consent. Finally, Congress passed the Tenure of Office Act, which gave the Senate power to approve changes in the president's cabinet. Designed to protect Secretary of War Edwin M. Stanton, who sympathized with the Radicals, this law violated the tradition that a president controlled appointments to his own cabinet. All of these measures, as well as each of the Reconstruction Acts, were passed by a two-thirds override of presidential vetoes.

Johnson took several belligerent steps of his own. He issued orders to military commanders in the South limiting their powers and increasing the powers of the civil governments he had created in 1865. Then he removed military officers who were conscientiously enforcing Congress's new law, preferring commanders who allowed disqualified Confederates to vote. Finally, he tried to remove Secretary of War Stanton. With that attempt the confrontation reached its climax.

Twice in 1867, the House Judiciary Committee had considered impeachment of Johnson, rejecting the idea once and then recommending it

Impeachment of President Johnson

by only a 5-to-4 vote. That recommendation was decisively defeated by the House. After Johnson tried to remove Stanton, however, a third attempt to impeach the president car-

ried easily. The indictment concentrated on his violation of the Tenure of Office Act, though modern scholars regard his efforts to impede enforcement of the Reconstruction Act of 1867 as a far more serious offense.

Johnson's trial in the Senate began promptly and lasted more than three months. The prosecution attempted to prove that Johnson was guilty of "high crimes and misdemeanors." But they also argued that the trial was a means to judge Johnson's performance, not a judicial determination of guilt or innocence. The Senate ultimately rejected such reasoning, which could have made removal from office a political weapon against any chief executive who disagreed with Congress. Although a majority of senators voted to convict Johnson, the prosecution fell one vote short of the necessary two-thirds majority. Johnson remained in office, politically weakened and with only a few months left in his term.

In the 1868 presidential election Ulysses S. Grant, running as a Republican, defeated Horatio Seymour, a

Election of 1868

New York Democrat. Grant was not a Radical, but his platform supported congressional Reconstruction and endorsed black suffrage in the South. (Significantly, Republicans stopped short of endorsing it in the North.) The Democrats vigorously denounced Reconstruction. For the first time African Americans participated in a presidential election on a wide scale; they voted en masse for General Grant.

In office Grant acted as an administrator of Reconstruction but not as its enthusiastic advocate. He vacillated in his dealings with the southern states, sometimes defending Republican regimes and sometimes currying favor with Democrats. On occasion Grant called out federal troops to stop violence or enforce acts of Congress. But he never imposed a true military occupation on the South. The later legend of "military rule," so important to southern claims of victimization during Reconstruction, was steeped in myth.

In 1869, in an effort to write democratic principles into the Constitution, the Radicals passed the Fifteenth Amendment. This measure

Fifteenth Amendment

forbade states to deny the right to vote "on account of race, color, or previous condition of servitude." Such wording did not guarantee the right to vote. It deliberately left states free to restrict suffrage on other grounds so that northern states could continue to deny suffrage to women and certain groups of men—Chinese immigrants, illiterates, and those too poor to pay poll taxes. Ironically, the votes of four uncooperative southern states—compelled by Congress to approve the amendment as an added condition to rejoining the Union—proved necessary to impose even this language on parts of the North. Although several states outside the South refused to ratify, three-fourths of the states approved the measure, and the Fifteenth Amendment became law in 1870.

With passage of the Fifteenth Amendment, many Americans, especially supportive northerners, considered Reconstruction essentially completed. "Let us have done with Reconstruction," pleaded the *New York Tribune* in April 1870. "The country is tired and sick of it. . . . Let us have Peace!"

Reconstruction Politics in the South

From the start, Reconstruction encountered the resistance of white southerners. In the black codes and in private attitudes, many whites stubbornly opposed emancipation, and the former planter class proved especially unbending. In 1866 a Georgia newspaper frankly observed that "most of the white citizens believe that the institution of slavery was right, and . . . they will believe that the condition, which comes nearest to slavery, that can now be established will be the best."

Fearing loss of control over their slaves, some planters attempted to postpone freedom by denying or misrepresenting events. Former slaves reported that their owners "didn't tell them it was freedom" or "wouldn't let [them] go." To hold onto their workers, some landowners claimed control over black children and used guardianship and apprentice laws to bind black families to the plantation. Whites also blocked blacks from acquiring land.

White Resistance

After President Johnson encouraged the South to resist congressional Reconstruction, white conservatives worked hard to capture the new state governments. Many whites also boycotted the polls in an attempt to defeat Congress's plans; by sitting out the

Thomas Nast, in this 1868 cartoon, pictured the combination of forces that threatened the success of Reconstruction: southern opposition and the greed, partisanship, and racism of northern interests. (Library of Congress)

elections, whites might block the new constitutions, which had to be approved by a majority of registered voters. This tactic was tried in North Carolina and succeeded in Alabama, forcing Congress to base ratification of the Fourteenth Amendment and of new state constitutions on a majority of "votes cast."

Very few black men stayed away from the polls. Enthusiastically and hopefully, they voted Republican. Most agreed with one man who felt he should "stick to the end with the party that freed me." Illiteracy did not prohibit blacks (or uneducated whites) from making intelligent choices. A Mississippi black testified that he and his friends had no difficulty selecting the Republi-

Black Voters and Emergence of a Southern Republican Party

can ballot. "We stood around and watched," he explained. "We saw D. Sledge vote; he owned half the county. We knowed he voted Democratic so we voted the other ticket so it would be Republican."

Thanks to a large black turnout and the restrictions on prominent Confederates, a new southern Republican Party came to power in the constitutional conventions of 1868–1870. Republican delegates consisted of a sizable contingent of blacks (265 out of the total of just over 1,000 delegates throughout the South), some northerners who had moved to the South, and native southern whites who favored change. Together these Republicans brought the South into line with progressive reforms adopted earlier in the rest of the nation. The new constitutions were more democratic. They eliminated property qualifications for voting and holding office, and they turned many appointed offices into elective posts. They provided for public schools and institutions to care for the mentally ill, the blind, the deaf, the destitute, and the orphaned.

The conventions broadened women's rights in property holding and divorce. Usually, the goal was not to make women equal with men but to provide relief to thousands of suffering debtors. In families left poverty-stricken by the war and weighed down by debt, it was usually the husband who had contracted the debts. Thus giving women legal control over their own property provided some protection to their families. The goal of some delegates, however, was to elevate women. Blacks in particular called for laws to provide for woman suffrage, but they were ignored by their white colleagues.

Under these new constitutions the southern states elected Republican-controlled governments. For the first time, the ranks of state legislators in 1868 included some black southerners. These new biracial regimes appreciated the realities of power and the depth of racial enmity. In most states, whites were in the majority and former slaveowners controlled the best land and other sources of economic power. James Lynch, a leading black politician from Mississippi, explained why African Americans shunned the "folly" of disfran-

Triumph of Republican Governments

chisement of ex-Confederates. Unlike northerners who "can leave when it becomes too uncomfortable," landless former slaves "must be in friendly relations with the great body of the whites in the state."

Blacks also believed in the principle of universal suffrage and the Christian goal of reconciliation. Far from being vindictive toward the race that had enslaved them, they treated leading rebels with generosity and appealed to white southerners to adopt a spirit of fairness and cooperation. In this way the South's Republican Party condemned itself to defeat if white voters would not cooperate. Within a few years Republicans were reduced to the embarrassment of making futile appeals to whites while ignoring the claims of their strongest supporters, blacks. But for a time both Republicans and their opponents, who called themselves Conservatives or Democrats, moved to the center and appealed for support from a broad range of groups. Some propertied whites accepted congressional Reconstruction as a reality and declared themselves willing to compete under the new rules. All sides found an area of agreement in economic policies.

Reflecting northern ideals and southern necessity, the Reconstruction governments enthusiastically promoted industry. Confederates had seen how industry aided the North during the war. Accordingly, Reconstruction legislatures encouraged investment with loans, subsidies, and exemptions from taxation for periods up to ten years. The southern railroad system was rebuilt and expanded, and coal and iron mining made possible Birmingham's steel plants. Between 1860 and 1880, the number of manufacturing establishments in the South nearly doubled. This emphasis on big business, however, produced higher state debts and taxes, drew money away from schools and other programs, and multiplied possibilities for corruption.

Industrialization

Policies appealing to African American voters never went beyond equality before the law. In fact, the whites who controlled the southern Republican Party were reluctant to allow blacks a share of offices proportionate to their electoral strength. Aware of their weakness, black leaders did not push very far for revolutionary economic or social change. In every southern

Republican Policies on Racial Equality

state, they led efforts to establish public schools, although they did not press for integrated facilities.

Economic progress was uppermost in the minds of most freedpeople. Black southerners needed land, but only a few promoted confiscation. In fact, much land did fall into state hands for nonpayment of taxes and was offered for sale in small lots. But most freedmen had too little cash to bid against investors or speculators, and few acquired land in this way. Any widespread redistribution of land had to arise from Congress, which never supported such action. The lack of genuine land redistribution remained the significant lost opportunity of Reconstruction.

Within a few years, as centrists in both parties met with failure, white hostility to congressional Reconstruction began to dominate. Some conservatives had always desired to fight Reconstruction through pressure and racist propaganda. Charging that the South had been turned over to ignorant blacks, conservatives deplored "black domination," which became a rallying cry for a return to white supremacy.

The Myth of "Negro Rule"

Such attacks were inflammatory propaganda, and part of the growing myth of "Negro rule." African Americans participated in politics but hardly dominated or controlled events. They were a majority in only two out of ten state constitution–writing conventions (transplanted northerners were a majority in one). In the state legislatures, only in the lower house in South Carolina did blacks ever constitute a majority; among officeholders, their numbers generally were far fewer than their proportion in the population. Sixteen blacks won seats in Congress before Reconstruction was over, but none was ever elected governor. Only eighteen served in a high state office such as lieutenant governor, treasurer, superintendent of education, or secretary of state. However, elected officials, such as Robert Smalls in South Carolina, labored tirelessly for cheaper land prices, better healthcare, access to schools, and the enforcement of civil rights for their people.

Conservatives also assailed the allies of black Republicans. Their propaganda denounced whites from the North as "carpetbaggers," greedy crooks planning to pour stolen tax revenues into their sturdy luggage made of carpet material. In fact, most northerners who settled in the South had come seeking business oppor-

Carpetbaggers and Scalawags

tunities or a warmer climate and never entered politics. Those who did enter politics generally wanted to democratize the South and to introduce northern ways, such as industry, public education, and the spirit of enterprise.

In addition to tagging northern interlopers as carpetbaggers, Conservatives invented the term *scalawag* to discredit any native white southerner who cooperated with the Republicans. A substantial number of southerners did so. Most scalawags were yeoman farmers, men from mountain areas and nonslaveholding districts who saw that they could benefit from the education and opportunities promoted by Republicans. Banding together with freedmen, they pursued common class interests and hoped to make headway against the power of long-dominant planters. A majority of scalawags, however, did not support racial equality. The black-white coalition was thus vulnerable on the race issue. Republican tax policies also cut into upcountry yeoman support because reliance on the property tax hit many small landholders hard.

Taxation was a major problem for the Reconstruction governments. Republicans wanted to maintain prewar services, repair the war's destruction, stimulate industry, and support important new ventures such as public schools. But the Civil War had destroyed much of the South's tax base. Thus an increase in taxes was necessary even to maintain traditional services, and new ventures required still higher taxes.

Tax Policy and Corruption as Political Wedges

Corruption was another serious charge levied against the Republicans. Unfortunately, it often was true. Many carpetbaggers and black politicians engaged in fraudulent schemes, sold their votes, or padded expenses, taking part in what scholars recognize was a nationwide surge of corruption. Corruption carried no party label, but the Democrats successfully pinned the blame on unqualified blacks and greedy carpetbaggers among southern Republicans.

All these problems hurt the Republicans, but in many southern states the deathblow came through violence. The Ku Klux Klan began in Tennessee in 1866; it spread through the South and rapidly evolved into a terrorist organization. Violence against African Americans occurred from the first days of Re-

Ku Klux Klan

construction but became far more organized and purposeful after 1867. Klansmen rode to frustrate Reconstruction and keep the freedmen in subjection. Nighttime harassment, whippings, beatings, and murder became common, and terrorism dominated some counties and regions.

The Klan's main purpose was political. Lawless nightriders made active Republicans the target of their attacks. Leading white and black Republicans were killed in several states. After freedmen who worked for a South Carolina scalawag started voting, terrorists visited the plantation and, in the words of one victim, "whipped every nigger man they could lay their hands on." Klansmen also attacked Union League clubs—Republican organizations that mobilized the black vote—and schoolteachers who were aiding the freedmen.

Klan violence was not a spontaneous outburst of racism; very specific social forces shaped and directed it. In North Carolina, for example, Alamance and Caswell Counties were the sites of the worst Klan violence. Slim Republican majorities there rested on cooperation between black voters and white yeomen. Together, these black and white Republicans had ousted officials long entrenched in power. The wealthy and powerful men in Alamance and Caswell who had lost their accustomed political control then organized a deliberate campaign of terror. The campaign weakened the Republican coalition and restored a Democratic majority.

Klan violence injured Republicans across the South. No fewer than one-tenth of the black leaders who had been delegates to the 1867–1868 state constitutional conventions were attacked, seven fatally. A single attack on Alabama Republicans in the town of Eutaw left four blacks dead and fifty-four wounded. In South Carolina five hundred masked Klansmen lynched eight black prisoners at the Union County jail. According to historian Eric Foner, the Klan "made it virtually impossible for Republicans to campaign or vote in large parts of Georgia."

Thus a combination of difficult fiscal problems, Republican mistakes, racial hostility, and terror brought down the Republican regimes. In most southern states, "Radical Reconstruction" lasted only a few years (see Map 16.1). The most enduring failure of Reconstruction, however, was not political; it was social and economic. Recon-

Failure of Reconstruction

struction failed to alter the South's social structure or its distribution of wealth and power. Without land of their own, freed men and women were dependent on white landowners, who could and did use their economic power to compromise blacks' political freedom. Armed only with the ballot, freedmen in the South had little chance to effect major changes.

Reconstruction Reversed

 Northerners had always been more interested in suppressing rebellion than in aiding southern blacks, and by the early 1870s the North's commitment to bringing about change in the South was weakening. Criticism of the southern governments grew, new issues captured public attention, and sentiment for national reconciliation gained popularity in politics. In one southern state after another, Democrats regained control. And for one of only a few times in American history, violence and terror emerged as a tactic in normal politics.

In 1870 and 1871 the violent campaigns of the Ku Klux Klan forced Congress to pass two Enforcement Acts and an anti-Klan law. These laws made actions by individuals against the civil and political rights of others a federal criminal offense for the first time. They also provided for election supervisors and permitted martial law and suspension of the writ of habeas corpus to combat murders, beatings, and threats by the Klan. Federal prosecutors used the laws rather selectively. In 1872 and 1873 Mississippi and the Carolinas saw many prosecutions; but in other states where violence flourished, the laws were virtually ignored. Southern juries sometimes refused to convict Klansmen.

Political Implications of Klan Terrorism

Some conservative but influential Republicans opposed the anti-Klan laws. Rejecting other Republicans' arguments that the Thirteenth, Fourteenth, and Fifteenth Amendments had made the federal government the protector of the rights of citizens, these dissenters echoed an old Democratic charge that Congress was infringing on states' rights. This opposition foreshadowed a more general revolt within Republican ranks in 1872.

Disenchanted with Reconstruction, a group calling itself the Liberal Republicans bolted the party in 1872 and nominated Horace Greeley, the well-known

The Liberal Republican Revolt

editor of the *New York Tribune*, for president. The Liberal Republicans were a varied group, including civil service reformers, foes of corruption, and advocates of a lower tariff. Normally such disparate elements would not cooperate with one another, but two popular and widespread attitudes united them: distaste for federal intervention in the South and an elitist desire to let market forces and the "best men" determine events, both in the South and in Washington. The Democrats also gave their nomination to Greeley in 1872. The combination was not enough to defeat Grant, who won reelection, but it reinforced Grant's desire to avoid confrontation with white southerners.

Dissatisfaction with Grant's administration grew during his second term. Strong-willed but politically naive, Grant made a series of poor appointments. His secretary of war, his private secretary, and officials in the Treasury and Navy Departments were involved in bribery or tax-cheating scandals. Instead of exposing the corruption, Grant defended some of the culprits. In 1874, as Grant's popularity and his party's prestige declined, the Democrats recaptured the House of Representatives.

The effect of Democratic gains in Congress was to weaken legislative resolve on southern issues. Congress had already lifted the political disabilities of the Fourteenth Amendment from many former Confederates. In 1872 it had adopted a sweeping Amnesty Act, which pardoned most of the remaining rebels and left only five hundred barred from political officeholding. In 1875 Congress passed a Civil Rights Act purporting to guarantee black people equal accommodations in public places, such as inns and theaters, but the bill was watered down and contained no effective provisions for enforcement. And by 1876 the Democrats had regained control in all but three southern states. Meanwhile, new concerns were capturing the public's attention.

A General Amnesty

Both industrialization and immigration were surging, hastening the pace of change in national life. Within only eight years, postwar industrial production increased by an impressive 75 percent. For the first time, nonagricultural workers outnumbered farmers, and only Britain's industrial output was greater than

Reconciliation and Industrial Expansion

that of the United States. Many of those finding employment in the expanding economy were among the 3 million immigrants who entered the country between 1865 and 1873.

Then the Panic of 1873 ushered in over five years of economic contraction. Three million people lost their jobs, and the clash between labor and capital became the major issue of the day. Class attitudes diverged, especially in the large cities. Debtors and the unemployed sought easy money policies to spur economic expansion. Businessmen, disturbed by the widespread strikes and industrial violence that accompanied the panic, became increasingly concerned about the defense of property.

Class conflict fueled a monetary issue: whether paper money—the Civil War greenbacks—should be kept in circulation. In 1872 Democratic farmers and debtors urged this policy to expand the money supply and raise prices, but businessmen, bankers, and creditors overruled them. Now hard times swelled the ranks of the "greenbackers"—voters who favored easy money.

Greenbacks Versus Sound Money

Congress voted in 1874 to increase the number of greenbacks in circulation, but Grant vetoed the bill in deference to the opinions of financial leaders. The next year, "sound money" interests prevailed in Congress, winning passage of a law requiring that greenbacks be convertible into gold after 1878. The chasm between farmers and workers and wealthy industrialists grew even wider.

Meanwhile, the Supreme Court played its part in the northern retreat from Reconstruction. During the Civil War the Court had been cautious and inactive. Reaction to the *Dred Scott* decision (1857) had been so violent, and the Union's wartime emergency so great, that the Court avoided interference with government actions. In 1866, however, *Ex parte Milligan* reached the Court.

Judicial Retreat from Reconstruction

Lambdin P. Milligan of Indiana had plotted to free Confederate prisoners of war and overthrow state governments. For these acts a military court sentenced Milligan, a civilian, to death. Milligan challenged the authority of the military tribunal, claiming that he had a right to a civil trial. The Supreme Court declared that military trials were illegal when civil courts were open and functioning, and its language indicated that the Court intended to reassert its authority.

In the 1870s the Court successfully renewed its challenge to Congress's actions when it narrowed the meaning and effectiveness of the Fourteenth Amendment. The *Slaughter-House* cases (1873) began in 1869, when the Louisiana legislature granted one company a monopoly on the slaughtering of livestock in New Orleans. Rival butchers in the city promptly sued. Their attorney, former Supreme Court justice John A. Campbell, argued that the Fourteenth Amendment had revolutionized the constitutional system by bringing individual rights under federal protection. Campbell thus articulated an original goal of the Republican Party: to nationalize civil rights and guard them from state interference.

The Court rejected Campbell's argument and thus dealt a stunning blow to the scope and vitality of the Fourteenth Amendment. Indeed, it interpreted the "privileges and immunities" of citizens so narrowly that it reduced them almost to trivialities. State citizenship and national citizenship were separate, the Court declared. National citizenship involved only matters such as the right to travel freely from state to state and to use the navigable waters of the nation, and only these narrow rights were protected by the Fourteenth Amendment.

The Supreme Court also concluded that the butchers who sued had not been deprived of their rights or property in violation of the due-process clause of the amendment. The Court's majority declared that the framers of the recent amendments had not intended to "destroy" the federal system, in which the states exercised "powers for domestic and local government, including the regulation of civil rights." Thus the justices severely limited the amendment's potential for securing and protecting the rights of black citizens—its original intent.

The next day the Court decided *Bradwell v. Illinois*, a case in which Myra Bradwell, a female attorney, had been denied the right to practice law in Illinois on account of her gender. Pointing to the Fourteenth Amendment, Bradwell's attorneys contended that the state had unconstitutionally abridged her "privileges and immunities" as a citizen. The Supreme Court rejected her claim, alluding to women's traditional role in the home.

In 1876 the Court weakened the Reconstruction era amendments even further by emasculating the enforcement clause of the Fourteenth Amendment and revealing deficiencies inherent in the Fifteenth Amendment. In *U.S. v. Cruikshank* the Court overruled the conviction under the 1870 Enforcement Act of Louisiana whites who had attacked a meeting of blacks and conspired to deprive them of their rights. The justices ruled that the Fourteenth Amendment did not give the federal government power to act against these whites. The duty of protecting citizens' equal rights, the Court said, "rests alone with the States." In *U.S. v. Reese* the Court noted that the Fifteenth Amendment did not guarantee the right to vote but merely listed certain impermissible grounds for denying suffrage. The decision opened the door for southern states to deny blacks the vote on grounds other than "race, color, or previous condition of servitude." Such judicial conservatism had profound impact down through the next century, as the revolutionary potential in the Civil War amendments was blunted, if not destroyed.

Disputed Election of 1876 and the Compromise of 1877

As the 1876 elections approached, most political observers saw that the North was no longer willing to pursue the goals of Reconstruction. The results of a disputed presidential election confirmed this fact. Samuel J. Tilden, the Democratic governor of New York, ran strongly in the South and needed only one more electoral vote to triumph over Rutherford B. Hayes, the Republican nominee. Nineteen electoral votes from Louisiana, South Carolina, and Florida (the only southern states yet "unredeemed" by Democratic rule) were disputed; both Democrats and Republicans claimed to have won in those states despite fraud committed by their opponents. One vote from Oregon was undecided because of a technicality (see Map 16.2).

To resolve this unprecedented situation Congress established a fifteen-member electoral commission. In the interest of impartiality, membership on the commission was to be balanced between Democrats and Republicans. But one independent Republican, Supreme Court Justice David Davis, refused appointment in

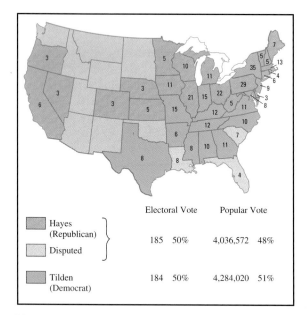

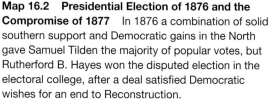

	Electoral Vote	Popular Vote
Hayes (Republican)	185 50%	4,036,572 48%
Disputed		
Tilden (Democrat)	184 50%	4,284,020 51%

Map 16.2   Presidential Election of 1876 and the Compromise of 1877   In 1876 a combination of solid southern support and Democratic gains in the North gave Samuel Tilden the majority of popular votes, but Rutherford B. Hayes won the disputed election in the electoral college, after a deal satisfied Democratic wishes for an end to Reconstruction.

order to accept his election as a senator. A regular Republican took his place, and the Republican Party prevailed 8 to 7 on every attempt to count the returns, along strict party lines. Hayes would become president if Congress accepted the commission's findings.

Congressional acceptance was not certain, and many citizens worried that the nation had entered a major constitutional crisis and would slip once again into civil war. The crisis was resolved when Democrats acquiesced in the election of Hayes based on a "deal" cut in a Washington hotel. Negotiations took place between Hayes's supporters and southerners who wanted federal aid to railroads, internal improvements, federal patronage, and removal of troops from southern states. Neither party was well enough organized to implement and enforce the various parts of this bargain between the sections. Northern and southern Democrats simply decided they could not win and did not contest the election of a Republican

who was not going to continue Reconstruction. Thus Hayes became president.

Southern Democrats rejoiced, but African Americans grieved over the betrayal of their hopes for equality. In the minds of many of these people, the only hope lay outside the South. Thus from South Carolina, Louisiana, Mississippi, and other southern states, thousands gathered up their possessions and migrated to Kansas. They were known as Exodusters, disappointed people still searching for their share in the American dream. Even in Kansas they met disillusionment, as the welcome extended by the state's governor soon gave way to hostile public reactions.

Betrayal of Black Rights and the Exodusters

Summary

Reconstruction left a contradictory record. It was an era of tragic aspirations and failures, but also of unprecedented legal, political, and social change. The Union victory brought about an increase in federal power, stronger nationalism, sweeping federal intervention in the southern states, and landmark amendments to the Constitution. But northern commitment to make these changes endure had eroded, and the revolution remained unfinished.

The North embraced emancipation, black suffrage, and constitutional alterations strengthening the central government. But it did so to defeat the rebellion and secure the peace. As the pressure of these crises declined, strong underlying continuities emerged and placed their mark on Reconstruction. The American people and the courts maintained a preference for state authority and a distrust of federal power. The ideology of free labor dictated that property should be respected and that individuals should be self-reliant. Racism endured and was transformed into the even more virulent forms of Klan terror. Concern for the human rights of African Americans was strongest when their plight threatened to undermine the interests of whites, and reform frequently had less appeal than moneymaking in an individualistic, enterprising society.

In the wake of the Civil War Americans faced two profound tasks—the achievement of healing and the dispensing of justice. Both had to occur, but they never developed in historical balance. Making sectional re-union compatible with black freedom and equality overwhelmed the imagination in American political culture, and the nation still faced much of this dilemma more than a century later.

LEGACY FOR A PEOPLE AND A NATION
The Fourteenth Amendment

Before the Civil War, no definition of civil rights ex-isted in America. Reconstruction legislation, especially the Fourteenth Amendment, changed that forever. Approved by Congress in 1866, the Fourteenth Amendment enshrined in the Constitution the ideas of birthright citizenship and equal rights. The Four-teenth Amendment was designed to secure and protect the rights of the freedpeople. But over time, the "equal protection of the law" clause has been used at times to support the rights of states, cities, corporations, immi-grants, women, religious organizations, gays and les-bians, students, and labor unions. It has advanced both tolerance and intolerance, affirmative action and anti–affirmative action programs. It provides the legal well-spring for the generations-old civil rights movement in the United States.

The amendment as originally written required in-dividuals to pursue grievances through private litiga-tion, alleging state denial of a claimed federal right. At first the Supreme Court interpreted it conservatively, especially on racial matters, and by 1900 the idea of color-blind liberty in America was devastated by Jim Crow laws, disfranchisement, and unpunished mob vi-olence.

But Progressive reformers used the equal protec-tion clause to advocate government support of health, union organizing, municipal housing, and the protec-tion of woman and child laborers. In the 1920s and 1930s, a judicial defense of civil liberties and free speech took hold. The Supreme Court expanded the amendment's guarantee of equality by a series of deci-sions upholding the rights of immigrant groups to re-sist "forced Americanization," especially Catholics in their creation of parochial schools. And, from its in-ception in 1910, the NAACP waged a long campaign to reveal the inequality of racial segregation in school-ing and every other kind of public facility. Led by Charles Houston and Thurgood Marshall, this epic le-gal battle culminated in the *Brown v. Board of Education* desegregation decision of 1954. In the Civil Rights Act of 1964, the equal protection tradition was reen-shrined into American law. Since 1964 Americans have lived in a society where the Fourteenth Amendment's legacy is the engine of expanded liberty for women and all minorities, as well as a political battleground for defining the nature and limits of human equality, and for redistributing justice long denied.

For Further Reading, see the Appendix. For Web resources, go to history.college.hmco.com/students.

APPENDIX

Suggestions for Further Reading

Chapter 1

General

Noble D. Cook, *Born to Die: Disease and New World Conquest, 1492-1650* (1998); Alfred W. Crosby, *The Columbian Exchange: Biological and Cultural Consequences of 1492* (1972); Bernard Lewis, *Cultures in Conflict: Christians, Muslims, and Jews in the Age of Discovery* (1995).

Mesoamerican Civilizations

Michael Coe, *Mexico from the Olmecs to the Aztecs* (1994); Brian Fagan, *Kingdoms of Gold, Kingdoms of Jade: The Americas Before Columbus* (1991); John S. Henderson, *The World of the Ancient Maya* (1997); Eduardo Matos Moctezuma and David Carrasco, *Moctezuma's Mexico: Visions of the Aztec World* (1992).

North American Indians

Brian Fagan, *Ancient North America: The Archaeology of a Continent* (1991); Francis Jennings, *The Founders of America: From the Earliest Migrations to the Present* (1993); Alvin Josephy, Jr., ed., *America in 1492* (1992); Elsa Redmond, ed., *Chiefdoms and Chieftaincy in the Americas* (1999); Colin F. Taylor, ed., *The Native Americans: The Indigenous People of North America* (1992); Bruce Trigger and Wilcomb Washburn, eds., *The Cambridge History of the Native Peoples of the Americas*, vol. 1: *North America* (1996).

Africa

Jacob Ade Ajayi and Michael Crowder, *History of West Africa* (1985); Philip Curtin et al., eds., *African History: From Earliest Times to Independence*, rev. ed. (1995); John Iliffe, *Africans: The History of a Continent* (1996); Paul Lovejoy, *Transformations in Slavery: A History of Slavery in Africa* (1983); John Thornton, *Africa and Africans in the Making of the Atlantic World, 1400–1680* (1992).

Europe in the Age of Discovery

Christopher Allmand, *The Hundred Years' War: England and France at War, ca. 1300–ca. 1450* (1988); G. R. Elton, ed., *The Reformation* (1990); Anthony Grafton, *New Worlds, Ancient Texts: The Power of Tradition and the Shock of Discovery* (1992); Denys Hay, *Europe in the Fourteenth and Fifteenth Centuries*, 2d ed. (1989); H. G. Koenigsberger et al., *Europe in the Sixteenth Century*, 2d ed. (1989); John Larner, *Marco Polo and the Discovery of the World* (1999); Anthony Pagden, *Lords of All the World: Ideologies of Empire in Spain, Britain and France, 1500–1800* (1995); J. R. S. Phillips, *The Medieval Expansion of Europe* (1988); Philip Ziegler, *The Black Death* (1982).

Exploration and Discovery

Emerson Baker et al., eds., *American Beginnings: Exploration, Culture, and Cartography in the Land of Norumbega* (1994); Felipe Fernández-Armesto, *Before Columbus: Exploration and Colonization from the Mediterranean to the Atlantic, 1229–1492* (1987); Charles Hudson, *Knights of Spain, Warriors of the Sun: Hernando de Soto and the South's Ancient Chiefdoms* (1997); Samuel Eliot Morison, *The European Discovery of America: The Northern Voyages*, A.D. *1500–1600* (1971); Samuel Eliot Morison, *The European Discovery of America: The Southern Voyages*, A.D. *1492–1616* (1974); J. H. Parry, *The Age of Reconnaissance* (1963); J. H. Parry, *The Discovery of the Sea* (1974); William and Carla Phillips, *The Worlds of Christopher Columbus* (1992); David B. Quinn, *North America from Earliest Discovery to First Settlements* (1977); P. E. Russell, *Portugal, Spain, and the African Atlantic* (1995).

Early European Conquest and Settlements

Kenneth Andrews, *Trade, Plunder and Settlement: Maritime Enterprise and the Genesis of the British Empire, 1480-1630* (1984); Charles Gibson, *Spain in America* (1966); Ross Hassig, *Mexico and the Spanish Conquest* (1994); Paul E. Hoffman, *A New Andalucia and a Way to the Orient: The American Southeast during the Sixteenth Century* (1990); Karen O. Kupperman, *Roanoke, the Abandoned Colony* (1984); A. J. R. Russell-Wood,

A World on the Move: The Portuguese in Africa, Asia, and America, 1415–1808 (1993); Hugh Thomas, *Conquest: Montezuma, Cortés, and the Fall of Old Mexico* (1993).

Chapter 2

General

David Hackett Fischer, *Albion's Seed: Four British Folkways in America* (1989); D. W. Meinig, *Atlantic America, 1492–1800* (1986); Gary B. Nash, *Red, White, and Black: The Peoples of Early America*, 4th ed. (2000); Mary Beth Norton, *Founding Mothers & Fathers: Gendered Power and the Forming of American Society* (1996); John E. Pomfret, *Founding the American Colonies, 1583–1660* (1970); Paula Treckel, *To Comfort the Heart: Women in Seventeenth-Century America* (1996); Alden T. Vaughan, *Roots of American Racism* (1994).

New Spain, New Netherland, New France, and the Caribbean

Karen Anderson, *Chain Her by One Foot: The Subjugation of Native Women in Seventeenth-Century New France* (1991); Charles R. Boxer, *The Dutch Seaborne Empire, 1600–1800* (1965); Denys Delage, *Bitter Feast: Amerindians and Europeans in Northeastern North America, 1600–64* (1993); Richard S. Dunn, *Sugar and Slaves: The Rise of the Planter Class in the English West Indies, 1624–1713* (1972); William J. Eccles, *France in America*, rev. ed. (1990); Carol Hoffecker et al., eds., *New Sweden in America* (1995); Jonathan Israel, *Dutch Primacy in World Trade, 1585–1740* (1989); Donna Merwick, *Possessing Albany, 1630–1710* (1990); David J. Weber, *The Spanish Frontier in North America* (1992).

England

Susan Dwyer Amussen, *An Ordered Society: Gender and Class in Early Modern England* (1988); A. G. Dickens, *The English Reformation*, 2d ed. (1989); Ralph Houlbrooke, *The English Family, 1450–1700* (1984); Peter Laslett, *The World We Have Lost*, 3d ed. (1984); J. P. Sommerville, *Politics and Ideology in England, 1603–1640* (1986); Keith Wrightson, *English Society, 1580–1680* (1982).

Early Contact Between Europeans and Indians

James Axtell, *The Invasion Within: The Contest of Cultures in Colonial North America* (1985); Philip Barbour, *Pocahontas and Her World* (1970); Alfred Cave, *The Pequot War* (1997); Frederic W. Gleach, *Powhatan's World and Colonial Virginia: A Conflict of Cultures* (1997); Daniel Richter, *The Ordeal of the Longhouse: The Peoples of the Iroquois League in the Era of European Colonization* (1992); Helen C. Rountree, *Pocahontas's People: The Powhatan Indians of Virginia Through Four Centuries* (1990); Neal Salisbury, *Manitou and Providence: Indians, Europeans, and the Making of New England, 1500–1643* (1982); Timothy Silver, *A New Face on the Countryside: Indians, Colonists, and Slaves in South Atlantic Forests, 1500–1800* (1990); Peter Wood et al., eds., *Powhatan's Mantle: Indians in the Colonial Southeast* (1989).

Chesapeake Society and Politics

David Galenson, *White Servitude in Colonial America: An Economic Analysis* (1981); James Horn, *Adapting to a New World: English Society in the Seventeenth-Century Chesapeake* (1994); Ivor Noël Hume, *The Virginia Adventure: Roanoke to James Towne* (1994); A. J. Leo Lemay, *The American Dream of Captain John Smith* (1991); Gloria L. Main, *Tobacco Colony: Life in Early Maryland, 1650–1720* (1983); Edmund S. Morgan, *American Slavery, American Freedom: The Ordeal of Colonial Virginia* (1975); Darrett Rutman and Anita Rutman, *A Place in Time: Middlesex County, Virginia, 1650–1750* (1984); Alden T. Vaughan, *American Genesis: Captain John Smith and the Founding of Virginia* (1975).

New England Communities, Politics, and Religion

David Grayson Allen, *In English Ways: The Movement of Societies and the Transferral of English Law and Custom to Massachusetts Bay in the 17th Century* (1981); Virginia DeJohn Anderson, *New England's Generation: The Great Migration and the Formation of Society and Culture in the 17th Century* (1991); David D. Hall, *Worlds of Wonder, Days of Judgment: Popular Religious Belief in Early New England* (1989); Stephen Innes, *Creating the Commonwealth: The Economic Culture of Puritan New England* (1995); Sydney V. James, *Colonial Rhode Island* (1975); George Langdon, *Pilgrim Colony: A History of New Plymouth, 1620–1691* (1966); Kenneth A. Lockridge, *A New England Town: The First Hundred Years (Dedham, Massachusetts, 1636–1736)* (1970); John Frederick Martin, *Profits in the Wilderness: Entrepreneurship and the Founding of New England Towns in the 17th Century* (1991); Edmund S. Morgan, *The Puritan Dilemma: The Story of John Winthrop* (1958); Darrett Rutman, *Winthrop's Boston* (1965).

New England Women and Family Life

James and Patricia Deetz, *The Times of Their Lives* (2000); John P. Demos, *A Little Commonwealth: Family Life in Plymouth Colony* (1970); Edmund S. Morgan, *The Puritan Family*, rev. ed. (1966); Amanda Porterfield, *Female Piety in Puritan New England* (1992); Roger Thompson, *Sex in Middlesex: Popular Mores in a Massachusetts County, 1649–1699* (1986); Laurel Thatcher Ulrich, *Good Wives: Image and Reality in the Lives of Women in Northern New England, 1650–1750* (1982).

Chapter 3

General

Colin Calloway, *New Worlds for All: Indians, Europeans, and the Remaking of Early America* (1997); Wesley Frank Craven, *The Colonies in Transition, 1660–1713* (1968); Jack P. Greene and J. R. Pole, eds., *Colonial British America* (1984).

New Netherland and the Restoration Colonies

Edwin Bronner, *William Penn's "Holy Experiment": The Founding of Pennsylvania, 1681–1701* (1962); Wesley Frank Craven, *New Jersey and the English Colonization of North America* (1964); Joyce Goodfriend, *Before the Melting Pot: Society and Culture in Colonial New York City, 1664–1730* (1992); Donna Merwick, *Death of a Notary: Conquest and Change in Colonial New York* (1999); Oliver Rink, *Holland on the Hudson: An Economic and Social History of Dutch New York* (1986); Robert C. Ritchie, *The Duke's Province: A Study of Politics and Society in Colonial New York, 1660–1691* (1977); Robert M. Weir, *Colonial South Carolina: A History* (1983).

Imperial Trade and Administration

Robert M. Bliss, *Revolution and Empire: English Politics and the American Colonies in the Seventeenth Century* (1991); Marcus Rediker, *Between the Devil and the Deep Blue Sea: Merchant Seamen, Pirates, and the Anglo-American Maritime World, 1700–1750* (1987); Robert C. Ritchie, *Captain Kidd and the War Against the Pirates* (1986); Stephen Saunders Webb, *Lord Churchill's Coup: The Anglo-American Empire and the Glorious Revolution Reconsidered* (1995); Stephen Saunders Webb, *1676: The End of American Independence* (1984); Stephen Saunders Webb, *The Governors-General: The English Army and the Definition of the Empire, 1569–1681* (1979).

Africa and the Slave Trade

Robin Blackburn, *The Making of New World Slavery: From the Baroque to the Modern, 1492–1800* (1997); Philip D. Curtin, *The Atlantic Slave Trade: A Census* (1969); David Eltis, *The Rise of African Slavery in the Americas* (1999); Joseph Inikori and Stanley Engerman, eds., *The Atlantic Slave Trade* (1992); Robin Law, *The Slave Coast of West Africa, 1550–1750: The Impact of the Atlantic Slave Trade on an African Society* (1991); James Rawley, *The Transatlantic Slave Trade: A History* (1981); Barbara Solow, ed., *Slavery and the Rise of the Atlantic System* (1991).

Africans in America

Ira Berlin, *Many Thousands Gone: The First Two Centuries of Slavery in North America* (1998); Douglas Deal, *Race and Class in Colonial Virginia: Indians, Englishmen, and Africans on the Eastern Shore During the Seventeenth Century* (1993); Michael A. Gomez, *Exchanging Our Country Marks: The Transformation of African Identities in the Colonial and Antebellum South* (1998); Graham R. Hodges, *Root & Branch: African Americans in New York and East Jersey, 1613–1863* (1999); Allan Kulikoff, *Tobacco and Slaves: The Development of Southern Cultures in the Chesapeake, 1680–1800* (1986); Jane Landers, *Black Society in Spanish Florida* (1999); Edgar J. McManus, *Black Bondage in the North* (1973); Lorena S. Walsh, *From Calabar to Carter's Grove: The History of a Virginia Slave Community* (1997); Betty Wood, *The Origins of American Slavery* (1997); Peter H. Wood, *Black Majority: Negroes in Colonial South Carolina from 1670 Through the Stono Rebellion* (1974).

European-Native American Relations in the North

Russell Bourne, *The Red King's Rebellion: Racial Politics in New England, 1675–1678* (1991); John Demos, *The Unredeemed Captive: A Family Story from Early America* (1994); Matthew Dennis, *Cultivating a Landscape of Peace: Iroquois-European Encounter in Seventeenth-Century America* (1993); Francis Jennings, *The Ambiguous Iroquois Empire* (1984); Jill Lepore, *The Name of War: King Philip's War and the Origins of American Identity* (1998); Peter Mancall, *Deadly Medicine: Indians and Alcohol in Early America* (1995); Daniel Richter, *The Ordeal of the Longhouse: The Peoples of the Iroquois League in the Era of European Colonization* (1992); Daniel Richter and James Merrell, eds., *Beyond the Covenant Chain: The Iroquois and Their Neighbors in Indian America, 1600–1800* (1987); Richard White, *The Middle Ground: Indians, Empires, and Republics in the Great Lakes Region, 1650–1815* (1991).

European-Native American Relations in the South and West

David H. Corkran, *The Creek Frontier, 1540–1783* (1967); Carl Ekberg, *French Roots in the Illinois Country: The Mississippi Frontier in Colonial Times* (1998); Ramón Gutiérrez, *When Jesus Came, the Corn Mothers Went Away: Marriage, Sexuality, and Power in New Mexico, 1500–1846* (1991); Elizabeth A. H. John, *Storms Brewed in Other Men's Worlds: The Confrontation of Indians, Spanish, and French in the Southwest, 1540–1795* (1975); Andrew Knaut, *The Pueblo Revolt of 1680* (1995); Jim Norris, *After the Year Eighty* (2000); Daniel H. Usner, Jr., *Indians, Settlers, and Slaves in a Frontier Exchange Economy: The Lower Mississippi Valley Before 1783* (1992).

Colonial Politics

Patricia U. Bonomi, *The Lord Cornbury Scandal: The Politics of Reputation in British America* (1998); Lois Green Carr and David W. Jordan, *Maryland's Revolution of Government, 1689–1692*

(1974); Richard P. Johnson, *Adjustment to Empire: The New England Colonies, 1675–1715* (1981); David S. Lovejoy, *The Glorious Revolution in America* (1972); Jack M. Sosin, *English America and Imperial Inconstancy: The Rise of Provincial Autonomy, 1696–1715* (1985); Jack M. Sosin, *English America and the Restoration Monarchy of Charles II* (1980); Jack M. Sosin, *English America and the Revolution of 1688* (1982).

New England

Bernard Bailyn, *The New England Merchants in the Seventeenth Century* (1955); Richard Bushman, *From Puritan to Yankee: Character and the Social Order in Connecticut, 1690–1765* (1967); Christine Heyrman, *Commerce and Culture: The Maritime Communities of Colonial Massachusetts, 1690–1750* (1984); Richard Melvoin, *New England Outpost: War and Society in Colonial Deerfield* (1990); Amanda Porterfield, *Female Piety in Puritan New England* (1991); Laurel Thatcher Ulrich, *Good Wives: Image and Reality in the Lives of Women in Northern New England, 1650–1750* (1982).

New England Witchcraft

Paul Boyer and Stephen Nissenbaum, *Salem Possessed: The Social Origins of Witchcraft* (1974); Elaine Breslaw, *Tituba, Reluctant Witch of Salem: Devilish Indians and Puritan Fantasies* (1996); John Demos, *Entertaining Satan: Witchcraft and the Culture of Early New England* (1982); Richard Godbeer, *The Devil's Dominion: Magic and Religion in Early New England* (1992); Peter Hoffer, *The Devil's Disciples: Makers of the Salem Witchcraft Trials* (1996); Carol Karlsen, *The Devil in the Shape of a Woman: Witchcraft in Early New England* (1987); Bernard Rosenthal, *Salem Story: Reading the Witch Trials of 1692* (1993).

Chapter 4

General

Carol R. Berkin, *First Generations: Women in Colonial America* (1996); Jack P. Greene, *Pursuits of Happiness: The Social Development of the Early Modern British Colonies and the Formation of American Culture* (1988); Stephanie G. Wolf, *As Various as Their Land: The Everyday Lives of 18th Century Americans* (1992).

New France and New Spain

Ramón Gutiérrez, *When Jesus Came, the Corn Mothers Went Away: Marriage, Sexuality, and Power in New Mexico, 1500–1846* (1991); Gwendolyn Midlo Hall, *Africans in Colonial Louisiana: The Development of Afro-Creole Culture in the Eighteenth Century* (1992); Dale Miquelon, *New France, 1701–1744* (1987); G. F. G. Stanley, *New France, 1744–1760* (1968); Daniel H. Usner, Jr., *Indians, Settlers, and Slaves in a Frontier Exchange Economy: The Lower Mississippi Valley Before 1783* (1992); David J. Weber, *The Spanish Frontier in North America* (1992).

Anglo-American Society

T. H. Breen, *Tobacco Culture* (1985); Lois Green Carr et al., eds., *Colonial Chesapeake Society* (1988); David Conroy, *In Public Houses: Drink and the Revolution of Authority in Colonial Massachusetts* (1995); Rhys Isaac, *The Transformation of Virginia, 1740–1790* (1982); Sung Bok Kim, *Landlord and Tenant in Colonial New York: Manorial Society, 1664–1775* (1978); Gary B. Nash, *The Urban Crucible: Social Change, Political Consciousness, and the Origins of the American Revolution* (1979); Michael Rozbicki, *The Complete Colonial Gentleman: Cultural Legitimacy in Plantation America* (1998); David S. Shields, *Civil Tongues and Polite Letters in British America* (1997).

American Economic Development

Richard Bushman, *The Refinement of America: Persons, Houses, Cities* (1992); Cary Carson et al., eds., *Of Consuming Interests: The Style of Life in the Eighteenth Century* (1994); Marc Egnal, *New World Economies: The Growth of the Thirteen Colonies and Early Canada* (1999); David Hancock, *Citizens of the World: London Merchants and the Integration of the British Atlantic Community, 1735–1785* (1995); Stephen Innes, ed., *Work and Labor in Early America* (1988); Alice Hanson Jones, *Wealth of a Nation to Be: The American Colonies on the Eve of the Revolution* (1980); Cathy Matson, *Merchants and Empire: Trading in Colonial New York* (1998); John J. McCusker and Russell R. Menard, *The Economy of British America, 1607–1789* (1985); Margaret E. Newell, *From Dependency to Independence: Economic Revolution in Colonial New England* (1998).

Anglo-American Politics

Bernard Bailyn, *The Origins of American Politics* (1968); Patricia U. Bonomi, *A Factious People: Politics and Society in Colonial New York* (1971); Richard Bushman, *King and People in Provincial Massachusetts* (1985); Edward M. Cook, Jr., *The Fathers of the Towns: Leadership and Community Structure in Eighteenth-Century New England* (1976); Jack P. Greene, *The Quest for Power: The Lower Houses of Assembly in the Southern Royal Colonies, 1689–1776* (1963); John Gilman Kolp, *Gentlemen and Freeholders: Electoral Politics in Colonial Virginia* (1998).

Immigration to British America

Bernard Bailyn, *The Peopling of British North America* (1986); Bernard Bailyn, *Voyagers to the West* (1986); Bernard Bailyn and Philip Morgan, eds., *Strangers Within the Realm* (1991); Marilyn Baseler, *"Asylum for Mankind": America 1607–1800* (1998); Jon Butler, *The Huguenots in America* (1983); R. J. Dickson, *Ulster Immigration to Colonial America, 1718–1775* (1966); David Dobson, *Scottish Immigration to Colonial America, 1607–1785* (1994); A. Roger Ekirch, *Bound for America: The Transportation of British Convicts to the Colonies, 1718–1775* (1987); Ned Landsman, *Scotland and Its First American Colony* (1985); A. G. Roeber, *Palatines, Liberty, and Property: German Lutherans in Colonial British America* (1993).

African Americans

Ira Berlin, *Many Thousands Gone: The First Two Centuries of Slavery in North America* (1998); Graham R. Hodges, *Root & Branch: African Americans in New York and East Jersey, 1613–1863* (1999); Marvin L. Michael Kay and Lorin Lee Cary, *Slavery in North Carolina, 1748–1775* (1995); Allan Kulikoff, *Tobacco and Slaves: The Development of Southern Cultures in the Chesapeake, 1680–1800* (1986); Michael Mullin, *Africa in America: Slave Acculturation and Resistance in the American South and the British Caribbean, 1736–1834* (1992); Robert Olwell, *Masters, Slaves, and Subjects* (1998); William Pierson, *Black Yankees: The Development of an Afro-American Subculture in Eighteenth-Century New England* (1988); Mechal Sobel, *The World They Made Together: Black and White Values in Eighteenth-Century Virginia* (1987); Betty Wood, *Women's Work, Men's Work: The Informal Slave Economies of Low Country Georgia* (1995).

Anglo-American Women, Men, and Families

Kathleen M. Brown, *Good Wives, Nasty Wenches, and Anxious Patriarchs: Gender, Race, and Power in Colonial Virginia* (1996); Cornelia Hughes Dayton, *Women Before the Bar: Gender, Law, and Society in Connecticut, 1639–1789* (1995); Joan Gundersen, *To Be Useful to the World: Women in Eighteenth-Century America* (1996); Barry J. Levy, *Quakers and the American Family* (1988); June Namias, *White Captives: Gender and Ethnicity on the American Frontier* (1993); Marylynn Salmon, *Women and the Law of Property in Early America* (1986); Daniel Blake Smith, *Inside the Great House: Planter Family Life in Eighteenth-Century Chesapeake Society* (1980); Merril D. Smith, *Breaking the Bonds: Marital Discord in Pennsylvania, 1730–1830* (1992); Lisa Wilson, *Ye Heart of a Man: The Domestic Life of Men in Colonial New England* (1999).

Anglo-American Education, Science, and the Enlightenment

Lawrence A. Cremin, *American Education: The Colonial Experience, 1607–1783* (1970); Richard Beale Davis, *Intellectual Life in the Colonial South, 1585–1763* (1978); Kenneth Lock-ridge, *Literacy in Colonial New England* (1974); Henry F. May, *The Enlightenment in America* (1976); Amy R. W. Meyers and Margaret Beck Pritchard, eds., *Nature's Empire: Mark Catesby's New World Vision* (1998); Thomas P. Slaughter, *The Natures of John and William Bartram* (1996); William Sloan and Julie Williams, *The Early American Press, 1690–1783* (1994); Raymond P. Stearns, *Science in the British Colonies of America* (1970).

Religion and the Great Awakening

Catherine Brekus, *Strangers and Pilgrims: Female Preaching in America, 1740–1845* (1998); Patricia U. Bonomi, *Under the Cope of Heaven: Religion, Society, and Politics in Colonial America* (1986); Jon Butler, *Awash in a Sea of Faith: Christianizing the American People* (1990); Michael Crawford, *Seasons of Grace: Colonial New England's Revival Tradition in Its British Context* (1991); Frank Lambert, *Inventing the "Great Awakening"* (1999); David S. Lovejoy, *Religious Enthusiasm in the New World* (1985); Harry S. Stout, *The Divine Dramatist: George Whitefield and the Rise of Modern Evangelicalism* (1991); Patricia Tracy, *Jonathan Edwards, Pastor* (1980).

Chapter 5

General

Marc Egnal, *A Mighty Empire: The Origins of the American Revolution* (1988); Merrill Jensen, *The Founding of a Nation: A History of the American Revolution, 1763–1776* (1968); John Phillip Reid, *The Constitutional History of the American Revolution* (1995); Robert W. Tucker and David C. Hendrickson, *The Fall of the First British Empire: Origins of the War of American Independence* (1982).

Colonial Warfare and the British Empire

Fred Anderson, *A People's Army: Massachusetts Soldiers and Society in the Seven Years' War* (1984); Fred Anderson, *Crucible of War* (2000); Frank W. Brecher, *Losing a Continent: France's North American Policy, 1753–1763* (1998); William Pencak, *War, Politics, and Revolution in Provincial Massachusetts* (1981); Timothy Shannon, *Indians and Colonists at the Crossroads of Empire: The Albany Congress of 1754* (1999); John Shy, *Toward Lexington: The Role of the British Army in the Coming of the American Revolution* (1965); Ian K. Steele, *Warpaths: Invasions of North America* (1994).

British Politics and Policy

Colin Bonwick, *English Radicals and the American Revolution* (1977); James E. Bradley, *Popular Politics and the American Revolution in England* (1986); John Brooke, *King George III*

(1972); John L. Bullion, *A Great and Necessary Measure: George Grenville and the Genesis of the Stamp Act, 1763–1765* (1981); P. D. G. Thomas, *Tea Party to Independence* (1991); P. D. G. Thomas, *The Townshend Duties Crisis* (1987); P. D. G. Thomas, *British Politics and the Stamp Act Crisis* (1975).

Native Americans and the West

Andrew Cayton and Fredrika Teute, eds., *Contact Points: American Frontiers from the Mohawk Valley to the Mississippi, 1750–1830* (1998); Gregory Dowd, *A Spirited Resistance: The North American Indian Struggle for Unity, 1745–1815* (1992); Tom Hatley, *The Dividing Paths: Cherokees and South Carolinians Through the Revolutionary Era* (1995); Francis Jennings, *Empire of Fortune: Crowns, Colonies and Tribes in the Seven Years' War in America* (1988); Howard H. Peckham, *Pontiac and the Indian Uprising* (1947); Richard White, *The Middle Ground: Indians, Empires and Republics in the Great Lakes Region, 1650–1815* (1991).

Political and Economic Thought

Bernard Bailyn, *The Ideological Origins of the American Revolution* (1967); J. C. D. Clark, *The Language of Liberty, 1660–1832: Political Discourse and Social Dynamics in the Anglo-American World* (1994); J. E. Crowley, *This Sheba, Self: The Conceptualization of Economic Life in Eighteenth-Century America* (1974); Jay Fliegelman, *Prodigals and Pilgrims: The American Revolution Against Patriarchal Authority, 1750–1800* (1982).

American Resistance

Joseph Albert Ernst, *Money and Politics in America, 1755–1775: A Study in the Currency Act of 1764 and the Political Economy of Revolution* (1973); David Conroy, *Drink and the Revolution of Authority in Colonial Massachusetts* (1995); Woody Holton, *Forced Founders: Indians, Debtors, Slaves, and the Making of the American Revolution in Virginia* (1999); Benjamin W. Labaree, *The Boston Tea Party* (1964); Pauline R. Maier, *From Resistance to Revolution: Colonial Radicals and the Development of American Opposition to Britain, 1765–1776* (1972); Edmund S. Morgan and Helen M. Morgan, *The Stamp Act Crisis: Prologue to Revolution* (1953); Gary B. Nash, *The Urban Crucible: Social Change, Political Consciousness, and the Origins of the American Revolution* (1979); Bruce A. Ragsdale, *A Planters' Republic: The Search for Economic Independence in Revolutionary Virginia* (1996); Peter Thompson, *Rum Punch & Revolution: Taverngoing & Public Life in Eighteenth-Century Philadelphia* (1999); John W. Tyler, *Smugglers and Patriots: Boston Merchants and the Advent of the American Revolution* (1986); Richard Walsh, *Charleston's Sons of Liberty: A Study of the Artisans, 1763–1789* (1959).

Chapter 6

General

Colin Bonwick, *The American Revolution* (1991); Edward Countryman, *The American Revolution* (1985); Theodore Draper, *A Struggle for Power: The American Revolution* (1996); Elizabeth Fenn, *Pox Americana* (2001); Harry M. Ward, *The American Revolution: Nationhood Achieved, 1763–1788* (1995); Alfred F. Young, ed., *Beyond the American Revolution* (1993); Alfred F. Young, ed., *The American Revolution: Explorations in the History of American Radicalism* (1976).

Continental Congress, Committees, and the Declaration of Independence

David Ammerman, *In the Common Cause: American Response to the Coercive Acts of 1774* (1974); Richard D. Brown, *Revolutionary Politics in Massachusetts: The Boston Committee of Correspondence and the Towns, 1772–1774* (1970); Jay Fliegelman, *Declaring Independence: Jefferson, Natural Language, & the Culture of Performance* (1993); Pauline Maier, *American Scripture: Making the Declaration of Independence* (1997); Jerrilyn Marston, *King and Congress: The Transfer of Political Legitimacy, 1774–1776* (1987); Garry Wills, *Inventing America: Jefferson's Declaration of Independence* (1978); Ann Withington, *Toward a More Perfect Union: Virtue and the Formation of American Republics* (1992).

Military Affairs

Richard Buel, *In Irons: Britain's Naval Supremacy and the American Revolutionary Economy* (1999); E. Wayne Carp, *To Starve the Army at Pleasure: Continental Army Administration and American Political Culture, 1775–1783* (1984); Stephen Conway, *The War of American Independence, 1775–1783* (1995); Don Higginbotham, *The War of American Independence: Military Attitudes, Policies, and Practice, 1763–1789* (1971); Ronald Hoffman and Peter Albert, eds., *Arms and Independence: The Military Character of the American Revolution* (1984); Piers Mackesy, *The War for America, 1775–1783* (1964); James K. Martin, *Benedict Arnold, Revolutionary Hero* (1997); Holly Mayer, *Belonging to the Army* (1996); Charles Niemeyer, *America Goes to War: A Social History of the Continental Army* (1997); Charles Royster, *A Revolutionary People at War: The Continental Army and American Character, 1775–1783* (1980).

Local and Regional Studies

Michael Bellesiles, *Revolutionary Outlaws: Ethan Allen and the Struggle for Independence on the Early American Frontier* (1993); Richard Buel, *Dear Liberty: Connecticut's Mobilization for the Revolutionary War* (1980); Edward Countryman, *A People in*

Revolution: The American Revolution and Political Society in
New York, 1760–1790 (1981); Jeffrey Crow and Larry Tise,
eds., The Southern Experience in the American Revolution
(1978); Thomas Doerflinger, A Vigorous Spirit of Enterprise:
Merchants and Economic Development in Revolutionary Philadel-
phia (1986); John Mack Faragher, Daniel Boone (1992); David
Hackett Fischer, Paul Revere's Ride (1994); Robert A. Gross,
The Minutemen and Their World (1976); Ronald Hoffman,
Thad W. Tate, and Peter Albert, eds., An Uncivil War: The
Southern Backcountry During the American Revolution (1985);
Jean B. Lee, The Price of Nationhood: The American Revolution
in Charles County (1994); Stephen Rosswurm, Arms, Country,
and Class: The Philadelphia Militia and the "Lower Sort" Dur-
ing the American Revolution (1988).

Indians and African Americans

Colin Calloway, The American Revolution in Indian Country
(1995); Sylvia Frey, Water from the Rock: Black Resistance in a
Revolutionary Age (1991); Barbara Graymont, The Iroquois in the
American Revolution (1972); Isabel T. Kelsey, Joseph Brant,
1743–1807: Man of Two Worlds (1984); James H. O'Donnell III,
Southern Indians in the American Revolution (1973); Anthony
F. C. Wallace, The Death and Rebirth of the Seneca (1969).

Loyalists

Bernard Bailyn, The Ordeal of Thomas Hutchinson (1974);
Robert McCluer Calhoon, The Loyalists in Revolutionary Amer-
ica, 1760–1781 (1973); Mary Beth Norton, The British-Ameri-
cans: The Loyalist Exiles in England, 1774–1789 (1972); Janice
Potter, The Liberty We Seek: Loyalist Ideology in Colonial New
York and Massachusetts (1983); Paul H. Smith, Loyalists and Red-
coats: A Study in British Revolutionary Policy (1964); James W.
St. G. Walker, The Black Loyalists: The Search for a Promised
Land in Nova Scotia and Sierra Leone, 1783–1870 (1976).

Women

Richard Buel and Joy Buel, The Way of Duty: A Woman and
Her Family in Revolutionary America (1984); Ronald Hoffman
and Peter Albert, eds., Women in the Age of the American Revolution (1989); Linda K. Kerber, Women of the Republic: Intellect and Ideology in Revolutionary America (1980); Mary Beth
Norton, Liberty's Daughters: The Revolutionary Experience of
American Women, 1750–1800 (1980).

Foreign Policy

Jonathan Dull, A Diplomatic History of the American Revolution
(1985); Ronald Hoffman and Peter Albert, eds., Peace and the
Peacemakers: The Treaty of 1783 (1986); Ronald Hoffman and
Peter Albert, eds., Diplomacy and Revolution: The Franco-

American Alliance of 1778 (1981); Jan Willem Schulte Nord-
holt, The Dutch Republic and American Independence (1982).

Patriot Leaders

Fawn M. Brodie, Thomas Jefferson: An Intimate History (1974);
Joseph Ellis, American Sphinx (1997); Founding Brothers (2000);
John E. Ferling, The First of Men: A Life of George Washington
(1988); Eric Foner, Tom Paine and Revolutionary America
(1976); Norman Risjord, Thomas Jefferson (1994); John
Rhodehamel, The Great Experiment: George Washington and
the American Republic (1998); Charles Royster, Light-Horse
Harry Lee and the Legacy of the American Revolution (1981); Pe-
ter Shaw, The Character of John Adams (1976); Sheila Skemp,
Benjamin and William Franklin: Father and Son, Patriot and
Loyalist (1994); Esmond Wright, Franklin of Philadelphia
(1986).

Chapter 7

General

Richard Beeman et al., eds., Beyond Confederation: Origins of
the Constitution and American National Identity (1987); Ronald
Hoffman et al., eds., The Economy of Early America: The Revolutionary Period, 1763–1790 (1988); Ronald Hoffman and
Peter Albert, eds., The Transforming Hand of Revolution: Re-
considering the American Revolution as a Social Movement
(1995); Mark E. Kann, A Republic of Men: The American
Founders, Gendered Language, and Patriarchal Politics (1998);
Cathy Matson and Peter S. Onuf, A Union of Interests: Political and Economic Thought in Revolutionary America (1990); Edmund S. Morgan, Inventing the People: The Rise of Popular
Sovereignty in England and America (1988); David Wald-
streicher, In the Midst of Perpetual Fetes: The Making of American Nationalism, 1776–1820 (1997); Gordon S. Wood, The
Radicalism of the American Revolution (1992); Gordon S. Wood,
The Creation of the American Republic, 1776–1787 (1969).

Continental Congress and Articles of Confederation

E. James Ferguson, The Power of the Purse: A History of American Public Finance, 1776–1790 (1961); H. James Henderson,
Party Politics in the Continental Congress (1974); Richard B.
Morris, The Forging of the Union, 1781–1789 (1987); Peter S.
Onuf, Statehood and Union: A History of the Northwest Ordinance (1987); Jack N. Rakove, The Beginnings of National Politics: An Interpretive History of the Continental Congress (1979).

State Politics

Willi Paul Adams, The First American Constitutions: Republican Ideology and the Making of the State Constitutions in the Rev-

olutionary Era (1980); Robert Gross, ed., In Debt to Shays (1992); Ronald Hoffman and Peter Albert, eds., Sovereign States in an Age of Uncertainty (1981); Donald Lutz, Popular Consent and Popular Control: Whig Political Theory in the Early State Constitutions (1980); Jackson Turner Main, Political Parties Before the Constitution (1973); Jackson Turner Main, The Sovereign States, 1775–1783 (1973); David P. Szatmary, Shays' Rebellion: The Making of an Agrarian Insurrection (1980).

The Constitution

Thornton Anderson, Creating the Constitution: The Convention of 1787 and the First Congress (1993); Lance Banning, The Sacred Fire of Liberty: James Madison and the Founding of the Federal Republic (1995); Roger H. Brown, Redeeming the Republic: Federalists, Taxation, and the Origins of the Constitution (1993); Saul Cornell, Anti-Federalism & the Dissenting Tradition in America, 1788–1828 (1999); Christopher Duncan, The Anti-Federalists and Early American Political Thought (1995); Frederick W. Marks III, Independence on Trial: Foreign Affairs and the Making of the Constitution (1973); Jack N. Rakove, Original Meanings: Politics and Ideas in the Making of the Constitution (1996); Robert A. Rutland, The Ordeal of the Constitution: The Antifederalists and the Ratification Struggle of 1787–88 (1966); Abraham Sofaer, War, Foreign Affairs, and Constitutional Power, vol. 1: The Origins (1976).

Education and Culture

Cathy N. Davidson, Revolution and the Word: The Rise of the Novel in America (1987); Joseph M. Ellis, After the Revolution: Profiles of Early American Culture (1979); Carl F. Kaestle, Pillars of the Republic: Common Schools and American Society, 1780–1860 (1983); Kenneth Silverman, A Cultural History of the American Revolution (1976).

Women

Susan Branson, These Fiery Frenchified Dames (2001); Edith Gelles, Portia: The World of Abigail Adams (1992); Susan Juster, Disorderly Women: Sexual Politics and Evangelicalism in Revolutionary New England (1994); Linda K. Kerber, Women of the Republic: Intellect and Ideology in Revolutionary America (1980); Mary Beth Norton, Liberty's Daughters: The Revolutionary Experience of American Women, 1750–1800 (1980); Sheila Skemp, Judith Sargent Murray (1998); Rosemarie Zagarri, A Woman's Dilemma: Mercy Otis Warren and the American Revolution (1995).

African Americans and Slavery

Ira Berlin and Ronald Hoffman, eds., Slavery and Freedom in the Age of the American Revolution (1983); Patricia Bradley, Slavery, Propaganda, and the American Revolution (1998);

David Brion Davis, The Problem of Slavery in the Age of Revolution, 1770–1823 (1975); Paul Finkelman, Slavery and the Founders: Race and Liberty in the Age of Jefferson (2002); Gary Nash, Forging Freedom: The Formation of Philadelphia's Black Community, 1720-1840 (1988); Donald L. Robinson, Slavery in the Structure of American Politics, 1765–1820 (1971); Shane White, Somewhat More Independent: The End of Slavery in New York City, 1770–1810 (1991).

Indians

Harvey L. Carter, The Life and Times of Little Turtle (1987); Gregory E. Dowd, A Spirited Resistance: The North American Indian Struggle for Unity, 1745–1815 (1992); Wiley Sword, President Washington's Indian War: The Struggle for the Old Northwest, 1790–1795 (1985); Anthony F. C. Wallace, The Death and Rebirth of the Seneca (1969); Richard White, The Middle Ground: Indians, Empires, and Republics in the Great Lakes Region, 1650–1815 (1991).

Chapter 8

National Government and Administration

Kenneth Bowling, The Creation of Washington, D.C. (1991); Ralph Adams Brown, The Presidency of John Adams (1975); William Casto, The Supreme Court in the Early Republic: The Chief Justiceships of John Jay and Oliver Ellsworth (1995); Stanley Elkins and Eric McKitrick, The Age of Federalism, 1788–1800 (1993); Morton Frisch, Alexander Hamilton and the Political Order (1991); Ronald Hoffman and Peter J. Albert, eds., Launching the "Extended Republic": The Federalist Era (1998); Forrest McDonald, The Presidency of George Washington (1974); John R. Nelson, Jr., Liberty and Property: Political Economy and Policymaking in the New Nation, 1789–1812 (1987); James R. Sharp, American Politics in the Early Republic: The New Nation in Crisis (1993).

Partisan Politics

Lance Banning, The Jeffersonian Persuasion: Evolution of a Party Ideology (1978); Richard Buel, Securing the Revolution: Ideology in American Politics, 1789–1815 (1972); Richard Hofstadter, The Idea of a Party System: The Rise of Legitimate Opposition in the United States, 1780–1840 (1970); John Zvesper, Political Philosophy and Rhetoric: A Study of the Origins of American Party Politics (1977).

Economics in Thought and Practice

Joyce Appleby, Capitalism and a New Social Order: The Republican Vision of the 1790s (1984); Christopher Clark, The Roots of Rural Capitalism: Western Massachusetts, 1780–1860 (1990); Paul Gilje, ed., Wages of Independence: Capitalism in the Early

American Republic (1997); James A. Henretta, *The Origins of American Capitalism* (1991); Allan Kulikoff, *The Agrarian Origins of American Capitalism* (1992); Curtis Nettels, *The Emergence of a National Economy, 1775–1815* (1962); Winifred Rothenberg, *From Market-Places to Market Economy: The Transformation of Rural Massachusetts, 1750–1850* (1992) .

Foreign Relations

Harry Ammon, *The Genet Mission* (1973); Samuel F. Bemis, *Jay's Treaty*, 2d ed. (1962); Samuel F. Bemis, *Pinckney's Treaty*, 2d ed. (1960); Jerald A. Combs, *The Jay Treaty* (1970); Alexander DeConde, *The Quasi-War: Politics and Diplomacy of the Undeclared War with France, 1797–1801* (1966); Alexander DeConde, *Entangling Alliance: Politics and Diplomacy Under George Washington* (1958); Reginald Horsman, *The Diplomacy of the New Republic, 1776–1815* (1985); Lawrence Kaplan, *"Entangling Alliances with None": American Foreign Policy in the Age of Jefferson* (1987); Conor Cruise O'Brien, *The Long Affair: Thomas Jefferson and the French Revolution, 1785–1800* (1996); Bradford Perkins, *The First Rapprochement: England and the United States, 1795–1805* (1967); Matthew Spalding and Patrick J. Garrity, *A Sacred Union of Citizens: George Washington's Farewell Address and American Character* (1996); William Stinchcombe, *The XYZ Affair* (1981).

Civil Liberties

Ronald Hoffman and Peter Albert, eds., *The Bill of Rights: Government Proscribed* (1997); Leonard W. Levy, *Emergence of a Free Press* (1985); Leonard W. Levy, *Origins of the Fifth Amendment* (1968); Robert A. Rutland, *The Birth of the Bill of Rights, 1776–1791*, rev. ed. (1983); James Morton Smith, *Freedom's Fetters: The Alien and Sedition Laws and American Civil Liberties* (1956).

Indians and African Americans

Douglas Egerton, *Gabriel's Rebellion: The Virginia Slave Conspiracies of 1800 and 1802* (1993); Dorothy Jones, *License for Empire: Colonization by Treaty in Early America* (1982); Frederick Hoxie, et al., eds., *Native Americans and the Early Republic* (2000); Francis Paul Prucha, *American Indian Policy in the Formative Years: The Indian Trade and Intercourse Acts, 1790–1834* (1962); James Sidbury, *Ploughshares into Swords: Race, Rebellion, and Identity in Gabriel's Virginia, 1730–1810* (1997); Anthony F. C. Wallace, *The Death and Rebirth of the Seneca* (1969).

Chapter 9

General

Noble E. Cunningham, Jr., *The United States in 1800: Henry Adams Revisited* (1988); Jean V. Matthews, *Toward a New Society: American Thought and Culture, 1800–1830* (1991); John Mayfield, *The New Nation, 1800–1845* (1981); Marshall Smelser, *The Democratic Republic, 1801–1815* (1968).

Party Politics

Noble E. Cunningham, Jr., *The Jeffersonian Republicans in Power: Party Operations, 1801–1809* (1963); Linda K. Kerber, *Federalists in Dissent* (1970); Milton Lomask, *Aaron Burr*, 2 vols. (1979, 1983); Richard P. McCormick, *The Presidential Game: The Origins of American Presidential Politics* (1982); Drew McCoy, *The Elusive Republic* (1980); Arnold A. Rogow, *A Fatal Friendship: Alexander Hamilton and Aaron Burr* (1998); James Roger Sharp, *American Politics in the Early Republic: The New Nation in Crisis* (1993); James Sterling Young, *The Washington Community, 1800–1828* (1966).

Jefferson and Madison

Noble E. Cunningham, Jr., *The Process of Government Under Jefferson* (1978); Joseph J. Ellis, *American Sphinx: The Character of Thomas Jefferson* (1996); Annette Gordon-Reed, *Thomas Jefferson and Sally Hemings: An American Controversy* (1997); Ralph Ketcham, *Presidents Above Party: The First American Presidency, 1789–1829* (1984); Drew R. McCoy, *The Last of the Fathers: James Madison and the Republican Legacy* (1989); Peter S. Onuf, ed., *Jeffersonian Legacies* (1993); Norman K. Risjord, *Thomas Jefferson* (1994); Robert Allen Rutland, *The Presidency of James Madison* (1990); Robert W. Tucker and David C. Hendrickson, *Empire of Liberty: The Statecraft of Thomas Jefferson* (1990).

The Supreme Court and the Law

Robert Lowry Clinton, *Marbury v. Madison and Judicial Review* (1989); Morton J. Horowitz, *The Transformation of American Law, 1780–1860* (1977); Herbert A. Johnson, *The Chief Justiceship of John Marshall, 1801–1835* (1997); R. Kent Newmyer, *The Supreme Court Under Marshall and Taney* (1968); Thomas C. Shevory, *John Marshall's Law: Interpretation, Ideology, and Interest* (1994).

Louisiana and Lewis and Clark

Stephen E. Ambrose, *Undaunted Courage: Meriwether Lewis, Thomas Jefferson, and the Opening of the American West* (1996); Alexander De Conde, *This Affair of Louisiana* (1976); Donna J. Kessler, *The Making of Sacagawea: A Euro-American Legend* (1996); James P. Ronda, ed., *Thomas Jefferson and the Changing West* (1997); James P. Ronda, ed., *Voyage of Discovery: Essays on the Lewis and Clark Expedition* (1998).

Expansionism, the War of 1812, and Foreign Relations

Robert J. Allison, *The Crescent Obscured: The United States and the Muslim World, 1776–1815* (1995); Paul Baepler, ed.,

White Slaves, African Masters: An Anthology of American Barbary Captivity Narratives (1999); R. David Edmunds, *Tecumseh and the Quest for Indian Leadership* (1984); R. David Edmunds, *The Shawnee Prophet* (1983); Clifford L. Egan, *Neither Peace nor War: Franco-American Relations, 1803–1812* (1983); Donald R. Hickey, *The War of 1812: A Short History* (1995); Bradford Perkins, *The Creation of a Republican Empire, 1776–1865* (1993); Robert V. Remini, *The Battle of New Orleans: Andrew Jackson and America's First Military Victory* (1999); J. C. A. Stagg, *Mr. Madison's War: Politics, Diplomacy, and Warfare in the Early Republic, 1783–1830* (1983); David J. Weber, *The Spanish Frontier in North America* (1992); J. Leitch Wright, Jr., *Creeks and Seminoles* (1986).

Chapter 10

General

Jack Larkin, *The Reshaping of Everyday Life, 1790–1840* (1988); D. W. Meinig, *The Shaping of America: A Geographical Perspective on 500 Years of History*, vol. 2: *Contininental America, 1800–1867* (1993); Charles G. Sellers, Jr., *The Market Revolution: Jacksonian America, 1815–1840* (1991); Melvyn Stokes and Stephen Conway, eds., *The Market Revolution in America: Social, Political, and Religious Expressions, 1800–1860* (1996).

Postwar Nationalism

Noble E. Cunningham, *The Presidency of James Monroe* (1996); Mary W. M. Hargreaves, *The Presidency of John Quincy Adams* (1985); Ralph Ketcham, *Presidents Above Party: The First American Presidency, 1789–1829* (1984); Walter LaFeber, ed., *John Quincy Adams and American Continental Empire* (1965); Ernest R. May, *The Making of the Monroe Doctrine* (1976); Paul C. Nagel, *John Quincy Adams: A Public Life, a Private Life* (1997); R. Kent Newmyer, *The Supreme Court Under Marshall and Taney* (1968); Dexter Perkins, *Hands Off: A History of the Monroe Doctrine* (1941).

The Market Economy, Manufacturing, and Commerce

Stuart Bruchey, *Enterprise: The Dynamic Economy of a Free People* (1990); William Cronon, *Nature's Metropolis: Chicago and the Great West* (1991); Paul A. Gilje, ed., *Wages of Independence: Capitalism in the Early American Republic* (1997); David A. Hounshell, *From the American System to Mass Production, 1800–1932: The Development of Manufacturing Technology in the United States* (1984); Herbert A. Johnson, *The Chief Justiceship of John Marshall, 1801–1835* (1997); David Klingaman and Richard Vedder, eds., *Essays in Nineteenth-Century History* (1975); Walter Licht, *Industrializing America:*

The Nineteenth Century (1995); Douglass C. North, *Economic Growth of the United States, 1790–1860* (1966); Theodore Steinberg, *Nature Incorporated: Industrialization and the Waters of New England* (1991).

Transportation

Carter Goodrich, *Government Promotion of American Canals and Railroads, 1800–1890* (1960); Richard R. John, *Spreading the News: The American Postal System from Franklin to Morse* (1995); Ronald E. Shaw, *Canals for a Nation: The Canal Era in the United States, 1790–1860* (1990); Carol Sheriff, *The Artificial River: The Erie Canal and the Paradox of Progress, 1817–1862* (1996); George R. Taylor, *The Transportation Revolution, 1815–1860* (1951); James A. Ward, *Railroads and the Character of America, 1820–1887* (1986).

Commercial Farming

"American Agriculture, 1790–1840, A Symposium," *Agricultural History* 46 (January 1972); Jeremy Atack and Fred Bateman, *To Their Own Soil: Agriculture in the Antebellum North* (1987); Clarence Danhof, *Change in Agriculture: The Northern United States, 1820–1870* (1969); Paul W. Gates, *The Farmer's Age: Agriculture, 1815–1860* (1962); Joan M. Jensen, *Loosening the Bonds: Mid-Atlantic Farm Women, 1750–1850* (1986); Peter D. McClelland, *Sowing Modernity: America's First Agricultural Revolution* (1999); Sally McMurry, *Transforming Rural Life: Dairying Families and Agricultural Change, 1820–1885* (1995); Gavin Wright, *The Political Economy of the Cotton South* (1978).

Workers

Mary H. Blewett, *Men, Women, and Work: Class, Gender, and Protest in the New England Shoe Industry, 1780–1910* (1988); Jeanne Boydston, *Home and Work: Housework, Wages, and the Ideology of Labor in the Early Republic* (1990); Thomas Dublin, *Transforming Women's Work: New England Lives in the Industrial Revolution* (1994); Thomas Dublin, *Women at Work: The Transformation of Work and Community in Lowell, Massachusetts, 1826–1860* (1979); Bruce Laurie, *Artisans into Workers: Labor in Nineteenth-Century America* (1989); Sean Wilentz, *Chants Democratic: New York City and the Rise of the American Working Class, 1788–1850* (1984).

Americans on the Move

Joan Cashin, *A Family Venture: Men and Women on the Southern Frontier* (1991); James E. Davis, *Frontier America 1800–1840: A Comparative Demographic Analysis of the Frontier Process* (1977); Julie Roy Jeffrey, *Frontier Women: The Trans-Mississippi West, 1840–1880* (1979); Peter D. McClelland and Richard J. Zeckhauser, eds., *Demographic Dimensions of the New Republic* (1982); Gerald McFarland, *A Scattered People: An American Family Moves West* (1985); Malcom J. Rohrbough, *The Trans-Appalachian Frontier: People, Societies, and Institutions, 1775–1850* (1978); Russell Thornton, *American Indian Holocaust and Survival: A Population History Since 1492* (1987); David J. Weber, *The Spanish Frontier in North America* (1992); Richard White, *"It's Your Misfortune and None of My Own": A History of the American West* (1991).

Native American Resistance and Removal

Paul H. Carlson, *The Plains Indians* (1998); Michael D. Green, *The Politics of Indian Removal: Creek Government and Society in Crisis* (1982); Stanley W. Hoig, *The Cherokees and Their Chiefs in the Wake of Empire* (1998); Theda Perdue, *Slavery and the Evolution of Cherokee Society, 1540–1866* (1979); Ronald N. Satz, *American Indian Policy in the Jacksonian Era* (1975); Daniel H. Usner, Jr., *American Indians in the Lower Mississippi Valley* (1998); Anthony F. C. Wallace, *The Long, Bitter Trail: Andrew Jackson and the Indians* (1993); Richard White, *The Roots of Dependency: Subsistence, Environment, and Social Change Among the Choctaws, Pawnees, and Navajos* (1983).

Chapter 11

General

George Dangerfield, *The Awakening of American Nationalism, 1815–1828* (1965); Daniel Feller, *The Jacksonian Promise: America, 1815–1840* (1995); Jean V. Matthews, *Toward a New Society: American Thought and Culture, 1800–1830* (1991); Charles Sellers, *The Market Revolution: Jacksonian America, 1815–1846* (1991).

Religion, Revivalism, and Reform

Robert H. Abzug, *Cosmos Crumbling: American Reform and the Religious Imagination* (1994); Michael Barkun, *Crucible of the Millennium: The Burned-over District of New York in the 1840s* (1986); Clifford S. Griffen, *Their Brothers' Keepers: Moral Stewardship in the United States, 1800–1865* (1960); Keith J. Hardman, *Charles Grandison Finney, 1792–1875: Revivalist and Reformer* (1987); Nathan O. Hatch, *The Democratization of American Christianity* (1989); Christine Leigh Heyrman, *Southern Cross: The Beginnings of the Bible Belt* (1997); Paul E. Johnson, *A Shopkeeper's Millennium: Society and Revivals in Rochester, New York, 1815–1837* (1978); Steven Mintz, *Moralists and Modernizers: America's Pre–Civil War Reformers* (1995); Ronald G. Walters, *American Reformers, 1815–1860*, rev. ed. (1997).

Temperance, Asylums, and Antimasonry

Thomas J. Brown, *Dorothea Dix: New England Reformer* (1998); Paul Goodman, *Towards a Christian Republic: Antimasonry and the Great Transition in New England, 1826–1836* (1988); Gerald N. Grob, *Mental Institutions in America: Social Policy to 1875* (1973); W. J. Rorabaugh, *The Alcoholic Republic: An American Tradition* (1979); Ian R. Tyrrell, *Sobering Up: From Temperance to Prohibition in Antebellum America, 1800–1860* (1979); William Preston Vaughn, *The Antimasonic Party in the United States, 1826–1843* (1983).

Women and Reform

Barbara J. Berg, *The Remembered Gate: Origins of American Feminism: The Woman and the City, 1800–1860* (1977); Ellen C. Du Bois, *Feminism and Suffrage: The Emergence of an Independent Woman's Movement in America, 1848–1869* (1978); Lori D. Ginzberg, *Women and the Work of Benevolence: Morality, Politics, and Class in the Nineteenth-Century United States* (1990); Nancy A. Hewitt, *Women's Activism and Social Change: Rochester, New York, 1822–1872* (1984); Sylvia D. Hoffert, *When Hens Crow: The Woman's Rights Movement in Antebellum America* (1995); Nancy Isenberg, *Sex and Citizenship in Antebellum America* (1998); Gerda Lerner, *The Grimké Sisters of South Carolina* (1967); Mary P. Ryan, *Women in Public: Between Banners and Ballots, 1825–1880* (1990); Shirley J. Yee, *Black Women Abolitionists: A Study in Activism, 1828–1860* (1992); Jean Fagan Yellin, *Women & Sisters: The Antislavery Feminists in American Culture* (1989).

Antislavery and Abolitionism

James Brewer Stewart, *Holy Warriors: The Abolitionists and American Slavery*, rev. ed. (1996); Frederick Douglass, *Life and Times of Frederick Douglass* (1881); George M. Fredrickson, *The Black Image in the White Mind: The Debate on Afro-American Character and Destiny, 1817–1914* (1971); Paul Goodman, *Of One Blood: Abolitionism and the Origins of Racial Equality* (1998); David Grimsted, *American Mobbing, 1828–1861* (1998); Henry Mayer, *All on Fire: William Lloyd Garrison and the Abolition of Slavery* (1998); William H. Pease and Jane H. Pease, *They Who Would Be Free: Blacks' Search for Freedom, 1830–1861* (1974); Benjamin Quarles, *Black Abolitionists* (1969); Ronald G. Walters, *The Antislavery Appeal: American Abolitionism After 1830* (1976).

Politics and Diplomacy, 1816–1828

Noble E. Cunningham, *The Presidency of James Monroe* (1996); Mary W. M. Hargreaves, *The Presidency of John Quincy Adams* (1985); Ralph Ketcham, *Presidents Above Party: The First American Presidency, 1789–1829* (1984); Walter

LaFeber, ed., *John Quincy Adams and American Continental Empire* (1965); Ernest R. May, *The Making of the Monroe Doctrine* (1976); Paul C. Nagel, *John Quincy Adams: A Public Life, a Private Life* (1997); Thomas C. Shevory, *John Marshall's Law: Interpretation, Ideology, and Interest* (1994); William Earl Weeks, *John Quincy Adams and American Global Empire* (1992).

Andrew Jackson and the Jacksonians

Donald B. Cole, *Martin Van Buren and the American Political System* (1984); Michael F. Holt, *Political Parties and American Political Development from the Age of Jackson to the Age of Lincoln* (1992); Marvin Meyers, *The Jacksonian Persuasion* (1960); John Niven, *Martin Van Buren* (1983); Edward Pessen, *Jacksonian America: Society, Personality, and Politics*, rev. ed. (1979); Robert V. Remini, *The Life of Andrew Jackson* (1988); Harry L. Watson, *Liberty and Power: The Politics of Jacksonian America* (1990).

Democrats and Whigs

William J. Cooper, *The South and the Politics of Slavery, 1828–1856* (1978); Daniel Walker Howe, *The Political Culture of the American Whigs* (1979); Lawrence Frederick Kohl, *The Politics of Individualism: Parties and the American Character in the Jacksonian Era* (1989); Richard P. McCormick, *The Second American Party System: Party Formation in the Jacksonian Era* (1966); Merrill D. Peterson, *The Great Triumvirate: Webster, Clay, and Calhoun* (1987); Norman Lois Peterson, *The Presidencies of William Henry Harrison and John Tyler* (1989).

Manifest Destiny and Foreign Policy

John M. Belohlavek, *"Let the Eagle Soar!" The Foreign Policy of Andrew Jackson* (1985); Thomas R. Hietala, *Manifest Destiny: Anxious Aggrandizement in Late Jacksonian America* (1985); Reginald Horsman, *Race and Manifest Destiny* (1981); Michael Hunt, *Ideology and U.S. Foreign Policy* (1987); Bradford Perkins, *The Creation of a Republican Empire, 1776–1865* (1993); David M. Pletcher, *The Diplomacy of Annexation: Texas, Oregon, and the Mexican War* (1973); Anders Stephanson, *Manifest Destiny: American Expansionism and the Empire of Right* (1995); Paul A. Varg, *United States Foreign Relations, 1820–1860* (1979); David J. Weber, *The Spanish Frontier in North America* (1992).

The Supreme Court and the Law

Leonard Baker, *John Marshall: A Life in Law* (1974); Francis N. Stites, *John Marshall: Defender of the Constitution* (1981).

Chapter 12

Rural and Utopian Communities

Priscilla J. Brewer, *Shaker Communities, Shaker Lives* (1986); David B. Danbom, *Born in the Country: A History of Rural America* (1995); John Mack Faragher, *Sugar Creek: Life on the Illinois Prairie* (1986); Steven Hahn and Jonathan Prude, eds., *The Countryside in the Age of Capitalist Transformation* (1985); Joan M. Jensen, *Loosening the Bonds: Mid-Atlantic Farm Women, 1750–1850* (1986); Anthony F. C. Wallace, *Rockdale: The Growth of an American Village in the Early Industrial Revolution* (1978); Kenneth H. Winn, *Exiles in a Land of Liberty: Mormons in America, 1830–1846* (1989).

The West

John Mack Faragher, *Women and Men on the Overland Trail* (1979); Julie Roy Jeffrey, *Frontier Women: The Trans-Mississippi West, 1840–1880* (1979); Malcolm J. Rohrbough, *Days of Gold: The California Gold Rush and the American Nation* (1997); Quintard Taylor, *In Search of the Racial Frontier: African Americans in the American West, 1528–1990* (1998); David J. Weber, *The Spanish Frontier in North America* (1992); Richard White, *"It's Your Misfortune and None of My Own": A History of the American West* (1991).

Urban Communities

Stuart M. Blumin, *The Emergence of the Middle Class: Social Experience in the American City, 1760–1900* (1989); Edwin G. Burrows and Mike Wallace, *Gotham: A History of New York City to 1898* (1999); Timothy J. Gilfoyle, *City of Eros: New York City, Prostitution, and the Commercialization of Sex, 1790–1920* (1992); Karen V. Hansen, *A Very Social Time: Crafting Community in Antebellum New England* (1994); Jack Larkin, *The Reshaping of Everyday Life, 1790–1840* (1988); Edward Pessen, *Riches, Class and Power Before the Civil War* (1973); Christine Stansell, *City of Women: Sex and Class in New York, 1789–1860* (1986); Richard B. Stott, *Workers in the Metropolis: Class, Ethnicity, and Youth in Antebellum New York City* (1990); Alexis de Tocqueville, *Democracy in America*, 2 vols. (1835, 1840).

Women and American Families

Janet Farrell Brodie, *Contraception and Abortion in Nineteenth-Century America* (1994); Lee Virginia Chambers-Schiller, *Liberty, A Better Husband: Single Women in America: The Generations of 1780–1840* (1984); Nancy F. Cott, *The Bonds of Womanhood: "Woman's Sphere" in New England, 1780–1835* (1977); Joan Hoff, *Law, Gender and Injustice: A Legal History of U.S. Women* (1991); Glenda Riley, *Divorce: An American Tradition* (1991); Mary P. Ryan, *Cradle of the Middle Class: The Family in Oneida County, New York, 1790–1865* (1981); Kathryn Kish

Sklar, *Catharine Beecher: A Study in American Domesticity* (1973); Robert V. Wells, *Revolutions in Americans' Lives* (1982); Barbara Welter, "The Cult of True Womanhood, 1820–1860," *American Quarterly* 18 (Summer 1966): 151–174.

Immigrants and Hispanics

Thomás Almaguer, *Racial Fault Lines: The Historical Origins of White Supremacy in California* (1994); Gunther Barth, *Bitter Strength: A History of Chinese in the United States, 1850–1870* (1964); Arnoldo De León, *The Tejano Community, 1836–1900* (1982); Hasia R. Diner, *Erin's Daughters in America: Irish Immigrant Women in the Nineteenth Century* (1983); Noel Ignatiev, *How the Irish Became White* (1995); Matthew Frye Jacobson, *Whiteness of a Different Color: European Immigrants and the Alchemy of Race* (1998); Walter D. Kamphoefner et al., eds., *News from the Land of Freedom: German Immigrants Write Home* (1991); Timothy M. Matovina, *Tejano Religion and Ethnicity: San Antonio, 1821–1860* (1995); Kerby A. Miller, *Emigrants and Exiles: Ireland and the Irish Exodus to North America* (1985); Stanley Nadel, *Little Germany: Ethnicity, Religion, and Class in New York City, 1845–80* (1990); David Roediger, *The Wages of Whiteness: Race and the Making of the Working Class* (1991); David J. Weber, *The Spanish Frontier in North America* (1992).

Free People of Color and Race

Ira Berlin, *Slaves Without Masters: The Free Negro in the Antebellum South* (1974); Thomas F. Gossett, *Race: The History of an Idea in America* (1963); James O. Horton and Lois E. Horton, *In Hope of Liberty: Culture, Community and Protest Among Northern Free Blacks, 1700–1860* (1996); David M. Katzman, *Before the Ghetto: Black Detroit in the Nineteenth Century* (1973); W. T. Lhamon, Jr., *Raising Cain: Blackface Performance from Jim Crow to Hip Hop* (1998); Leon Litwack, *North of Slavery: The Negro in the Free States, 1790–1860* (1961); Eric Lott, *Love and Theft: Blackface Minstrelsy and the American Working Class* (1995); Floyd J. Miller, *The Search for a Black Nationality: Black Colonization and Emigration, 1787–1863* (1975); Gary B. Nash, *Forging Freedom: The Formation of Philadelphia's Black Community, 1720–1840* (1988); Quintard Taylor, *In Search of the Racial Frontier: African Americans in the American West, 1528–1990* (1998).

Chapter 13

The Peculiar South

Wilbur J. Cash, *The Mind of the South* (1939); Carl N. Degler, *Place Over Time* (1977); Drew G. Faust, "The Peculiar South Revisited," in John B. Boles and Evelyn T. Nolen, eds., *Interpreting Southern History* (1987); C. Vann Woodward, *The Burden of Southern History* (1960).

Southern Society

Edward L. Ayers, *Vengeance and Justice* (1984); Bradley G. Bond, *Political Culture in the Nineteenth-Century South* (1995); Randolph B. Campbell, "Planters and Plain Folks," in John B. Boles and Evelyn T. Nolen, eds., *Interpreting Southern History* (1987); William J. Cooper, *The South and the Politics of Slavery, 1828–1856* (1978); William W. Freehling, *Prelude to Civil War* (1965); Peter Kolchin, *Unfree Labor: American Slavery and Russian Serfdom* (1987); Christine L. Heyrman, *Southern Cross* (1997); James Hebron Moore, *The Emergence of the Cotton Kingdom in the Old Southwest: Mississippi, 1770–1860* (1987); Larry E. Tise, *Proslavery* (1987); Ralph A. Wooster, *Politicians, Planters, and Plain Folk* (1975); Gavin Wright, *The Political Economy of the Cotton South* (1978); Bertram Wyatt-Brown, *Southern Honor* (1982).

Slaveholders and Nonslaveholders

Edward L. Ayers and John C. Willis, eds., *The Edge of the South* (1991); Ira Berlin, *Slaves Without Masters* (1974); Joan E. Cashin, *A Family Venture* (1991); Charles B. Dew, *Bond of Iron* (1995); Everett Dick, *The Dixie Frontier* (1948); Paul D. Escott, ed., *North Carolina Yeoman* (1996); Drew Faust, *A Sacred Circle: The Dilemma of the Intellectual in the Old South* (1977); Drew Faust, ed., *The Ideology of Slavery* (1981); J. Wayne Flynt, *Dixie's Forgotten People* (1979); John Hope Franklin, *The Militant South, 1800–1861* (1956); John Inscoe, *Mountain Masters* (1989); Michael P. Johnson and James L. Roark, *Black Masters* (1984); Kenneth S. Greenberg, *Masters and Statesmen* (1985); Stephanie McCurry, *Masters of Small Worlds* (1995); James Oakes, *The Ruling Race* (1982); Loren Schweninger, *Black Property Owners in the South, 1790–1915* (1990); J. Mills Thornton III, *Politics and Power in a Slave Society: Alabama, 1800–1860* (1978).

Southern Women

Carol Bleser, *In Joy and in Sorrow* (1990); Carol Bleser, ed., *Tokens of Affection* (1995); Victoria Bynum, *Unruly Women* (1992); Catherine Clinton, *The Plantation Mistress* (1982); Elizabeth Fox-Genovese, *Within the Plantation Household* (1988); Jean E. Friedman, *The Enclosed Garden* (1985); Harriet Jacobs, *Incidents in the Life of a Slave Girl*, ed. Jean Fagan Yellin (1987); Jacqueline Jones, *Labor of Love, Labor of Sorrow* (1985); Suzanne Lebsock, *Free Women of Petersburg* (1984); Sally McMillen, *Motherhood in the Old South* (1990); Patricia Morton, ed., *Discovering the Women in Slavery* (1995); Mary D. Robertson, ed., *Lucy Breckinridge of Grove Hill* (1979); Deborah G. White, *Ar'n't I a Woman?* (1985).

Conditions of Slavery

Larry E. Hudson, Jr., *To Have and to Hold* (1997); Wilma King, *Stolen Childhood* (1995); Peter Kolchin, *American Slavery, 1619–1877* (1993); Randall M. Miller and John David Smith, eds., *Dictionary of Afro-American Slavery* (1997); Randall M. Miller, ed., *The Afro-American Slaves: Community or Chaos* (1981); Orlando Patterson, *Rituals of Blood* (1998); Mark M. Smith, *Mastered by the Clock* (1997); Kenneth M. Stampp, *The Peculiar Institution* (1956); Brenda E. Stevenson, *Life in Black and White: Family and Community in the Slave South* (1996); Michael Tadman, *Speculators and Slaves* (1989).

Slave Culture and Resistance

John W. Blassingame, *The Slave Community* (1979); John Blassingame, ed., *Slave Testimony* (1977); Frederick Douglass, *Narrative of the Life of Frederick Douglass*, ed. David W. Blight (1993); Dena J. Epstein, *Sinful Tunes and Spirituals* (1977); Paul D. Escott, *Slavery Remembered: A Record of Twentieth-Century Slave Narratives* (1979); John Hope Franklin and Loren Schweninger, *Runaway Slaves* (1999); Eugene D. Genovese, *Roll, Jordan, Roll* (1974); Michael A. Gomez, *Exchanging Our Country Marks* (1998); Kenneth Greenberg, ed., *The Confessions of Nat Turner and Related Documents* (1996); Herbert G. Gutman, *The Black Family in Slavery and Freedom, 1750–1925* (1976); Charles Joyner, *Down by the Riverside* (1984); Lawrence W. Levine, *Black Culture and Black Consciousness* (1977); Albert J. Raboteau, *Slave Religion* (1978); James Sidbury, *Plowshares into Swords: Gabriel's Virginia* (1997); Sterling Stuckey, *Slave Culture* (1987).

Chapter 14

General

Tyler Anbinder, *Nativism and Slavery* (1992); Paul Bergeron, *The Presidency of James K. Polk* (1987); Stanley W. Campbell, *The Slave Catchers* (1968); Richard J. Carwardine, *Evangelicals and Politics in Antebellum America* (1997); Don E. Fehrenbacher, *The Dred Scott Case* (1978); George M. Fredrickson, *The Black Image in the White Mind* (1971); William W. Freehling, *The Road to Disunion* (1990); Michael F. Holt, *Political Parties and American Political Development* (1992); Michael F. Holt, *The Political Crisis of the 1850s* (1978); Daniel Walker Howe, *The Political Culture of the American Whigs* (1979); William Lee Miller, *Arguing About Slavery* (1996); Merrill D. Peterson, *The Great Triumvirate: Webster, Clay, and Calhoun* (1987); David M. Potter, *The Impending Crisis, 1848–1861* (1976); James A. Rawley, *Race and Politics* (1969); Robert V. Remini, *Henry Clay: Statesman for the Union* (1991); Richard H. Sewell, *A House Divided: Sectionalism and the Civil War, 1848–1865* (1988); Joel H. Silbey, *The Transformation of American Politics, 1840–1960* (1967); Joel H. Silbey, ed., *The American Party Battle*, 2 vols. (1999); Kenneth M. Stampp, *America in 1857* (1991); Kenneth M. Stampp, *And the War Came* (1950).

The South and Slavery

William L. Barney, *The Secessionist Impulse* (1974); Steven A. Channing, *A Crisis of Fear: Secession in South Carolina* (1970); William J. Cooper, Jr., *The South and the Politics of Slavery, 1828–1856* (1978); Daniel W. Crofts, *Reluctant Confederates: Upper South Unionists in the Secession Crisis* (1989); Merton L. Dillon, *Slavery Attacked* (1991); Drew G. Faust, *The Ideology of Slavery* (1981); Lacy K. Ford, Jr., *Origins of Southern Radicalism* (1988); Eugene D. Genovese, *The World the Slaveholders Made* (1969); Michael P. Johnson, *Toward a Patriarchal Republic: The Secession of Georgia* (1977); John Niven, *John C. Calhoun and the Price of Union* (1988); James Oakes, *Slavery and Freedom* (1991); David M. Potter, *The South and the Sectional Conflict* (1968); J. Mills Thornton III, *Politics and Power in a Slave Society* (1978).

The North and Antislavery

Eugene H. Berwanger, *The Frontier Against Slavery* (1967); Gary Collison, *Shadrach Minkins: From Fugitive Slave to Citizen* (1997); Paul Finkelman, ed., *His Soul Goes Marching On: Responses to John Brown and the Harpers Ferry Raid* (1995); Eric Foner, *Free Soil, Free Labor, Free Men* (1970); William E. Gienapp, *The Origins of the Republican Party, 1852–1856* (1986); Joan D. Hedrick, *Harriet Beecher Stowe* (1994); James O. and Lois E. Horton, *In Hope of Liberty* (1997); Robert W. Johannsen, *Stephen A. Douglas* (1973); Aileen S. Kraditor, *Means and Ends in American Abolitionism* (1969); Stephen B. Oates, *To Purge This Land with Blood*, 2d ed. (1984); Benjamin Quarles, *Black Abolitionists* (1969); C. Peter Ripley et al., ed., *Witness for Freedom: African American Voices on Race, Slavery and Freedom* (1993); Richard Sewell, *Ballots for Freedom: Antislavery Politics in the United States, 1837–1860* (1976); John Stauffer, *The Black Hearts of Men: Radical Abolitionists and the Transformation of Race* (2002); James B. Stewart, *Holy Warriors: The Abolitionists and American Slavery*, 2d ed. (1996); Albert J. Von Frank, *The Trials of Anthony Burns* (1998).

The War with Mexico and Foreign Policy

Gene M. Brack, *Mexico Views Manifest Destiny, 1821–1846* (1976); Richard Griswold del Castillo, *The Treaty of Guadalupe Hidalgo* (1990); Reginald Horsman, *Race and Manifest Destiny* (1981); Robert W. Johannsen, *To the Halls of the Montezumas: The Mexican War and the American Imagination* (1985); Ernest M. Lander, Jr., *Reluctant Imperialists: Calhoun, the South Carolinians, and the Mexican War* (1980); Robert E. May, *The Southern Dream of a Caribbean Empire, 1854–1861* (1973); Frederick Merk, *Manifest Destiny and Mission in*

American History (1963); John H. Schroeder, *Mr. Polk's War: American Opposition and Dissent* (1973); Anders Stephanson, *Manifest Destiny* (1995); David J. Weber, *The Mexican Frontier, 1821–1846* (1982).

Chapter 15

The War and the South

Stephen Ash, *When the Yankees Came* (1995); Richard E. Beringer et al., *Why the South Lost the Civil War* (1986); William A. Blair, *Virginia's Private War: Feeding Body and Soul in the Confederacy* (1998); Gabor S. Boritt, ed., *Why the Confederacy Lost* (1992); William C. Davis, *Jefferson Davis* (1991); Robert F. Durden, *The Gray and the Black: The Confederate Debate on Emancipation* (1972); Paul D. Escott, *After Secession: Jefferson Davis and the Failure of Confederate Nationalism* (1978); Eli N. Evans, *Judah P. Benjamin* (1987); Drew Gilpin Faust, *The Creation of Confederate Nationalism* (1988); Mark Grimsley, *The Hard Hand of War* (1995); Mary Elizabeth Massey, *Refugee Life in the Confederacy* (1964); Alan T. Nolan, *Lee Considered* (1991); Harry P. Owens and James J. Cooke, eds., *The Old South in the Crucible of War* (1983); James L. Roark, *Masters Without Slaves* (1977); Daniel Sutherland, *Seasons of War* (1995); Emory M. Thomas, *The Confederate Nation* (1979); Bell Irvin Wiley, *The Plain People of the Confederacy* (1943).

The War and the North

Iver Bernstein, *The New York City Draft Riots* (1990); Robert Cruden, *The War That Never Ended* (1973); David Donald, ed., *Why the North Won the Civil War* (1960); J. Matthew Gallman, *The North Fights the Civil War* (1994); James W. Geary, *We Need Men* (1991); Randall C. Jimerson, *The Private Civil War* (1988); Frank L. Klement, *The Copperheads in the Middle West* (1960); James M. McPherson, *Battle Cry of Freedom* (1988); James H. Moorhead, *American Apocalypse* (1978); Phillip S. Paludan, *"A People's Contest": The Union and the Civil War, 1861–1865* (1989); Anne C. Rose, *Victorian America and the Civil War* (1992); *George Templeton Strong, Diary*, 4 vols., ed. Allan Nevins and Milton Hasley Thomas (1952); Maris A. Vinovskis, ed., *Toward a Social History of the American Civil War* (1990); Bell Irvin Wiley, *The Life of Billy Yank* (1952).

Women

John Q. Anderson, ed., *Brokenburn: The Journal of Kate Stone* (1955); John R. Brumgardt, ed., *Civil War Nurse: The Diary and Letters of Hannah Ropes* (1980); Catherine Clinton and Nina Silber, eds., *Divided Houses: Gender and the Civil War* (1992); Drew Gilpin Faust, *Mothers of Invention* (1996); George C. Rable, *Civil Wars: Women and the Crisis of Southern Nationalism* (1989); Lee Ann Whites, *The Civil War as a*

Crisis in Gender (1995); C. Vann Woodward and Elisabeth Muhlenfeld, eds., *Mary Chesnut's Civil War* (1981).

African Americans

Virginia M. Adams, ed., *On the Altar of Freedom: A Black Soldier's Civil War Letters from the Front* (1991); Ira Berlin, ed., *Freedom: A Documentary History of Emancipation, 1861–1867*, Series I, *The Destruction of Slavery* (1979), and Series II, *The Black Military Experience* (1982); Richard M. Blackett, ed., *Thomas Morris Chester: Black Civil War Correspondent* (1989); David W. Blight, *Frederick Douglass' Civil War* (1989); Joseph T. Glatthaar, *Forged in Battle* (1990); Leon Litwack, *Been in the Storm So Long* (1979); James M. McPherson, *The Negro's Civil War* (1965); Clarence L. Mohr, *On the Threshold of Freedom* (1986); Lynda J. Morgan, *Emancipation in Virginia's Tobacco Belt, 1850–1870* (1992); Benjamin Quarles, *The Negro in the Civil War* (1953); Edwin S. Redkey, ed., *A Grand Army of Black Men* (1992).

Military History

Albert Castel, *Decision in the West* (1992); Bruce Catton, *Grant Takes Command* (1969); Bruce Catton, *A Stillness at Appomattox* (1953); Peter Cozzens, *This Terrible Sound* (1992); Michael Fellman, *Citizen Sherman* (1995); Shelby Foote, *The Civil War, a Narrative*, 3 vols. (1958–1974); Douglas Southall Freeman, *Lee's Lieutenants*, 3 vols. (1942–1944); Gary W. Gallagher, *The Confederate War* (1997); Gary W. Gallagher, *Lee and His Generals in War and Memory* (1998); Joseph T. Glatthaar, *The March to the Sea and Beyond* (1985); Herman Hattaway and Archer Jones, *How the North Won* (1983); Laurence M. Hauptman, *Between Two Fires: American Indians in the Civil War* (1995); Alvin M. Josephy, Jr., *The Civil War in the American West* (1991); Gerald F. Linderman, *Embattled Courage* (1989); Thomas L. Livermore, *Numbers and Losses in the Civil War in America* (1957); Reid Mitchell, *Civil War Soldiers* (1988); Roy Morris, Jr., *Sheridan* (1992); Charles Royster, *The Destructive War* (1991); Stephen W. Sears, *To the Gates of Richmond* (1992); Stephen W. Sears, *George B. McClellan* (1988); Brooks D. Simpson, *Ulysses S. Grant* (2000); Emory M. Thomas, *Robert E. Lee* (1995); Steven E. Woodworth, *Jefferson Davis and His Generals* (1990).

Foreign Relations

Stuart L. Bernath, *Squall Across the Atlantic: American Civil War Prize Cases and Diplomacy* (1970); R. J. M. Blackett, *Divided Hearts: Britain and the American Civil War* (2001); David P. Crook, *The North, the South, and the Powers, 1861–1865* (1974); Charles P. Cullop, *Confederate Propaganda in Europe* (1969); Howard Jones, *Union in Peril* (1992); Frank L. Owsley and Harriet Owsley, *King Cotton Diplomacy* (1959);

Gordon H. Warren, *Fountain of Discontent: The Trent Affair and Freedom of the Seas* (1981).

Abraham Lincoln and the Union Government

Allan G. Bogue, *The Earnest Men: Republicans of the Civil War Senate* (1981); Gabor S. Borit, ed., *The Historian's Lincoln* (1989); Richard N. Current, *The Lincoln Nobody Knows* (1958); Christopher Dell, *Lincoln and the War Democrats* (1975); David Donald, *Lincoln* (1995); James M. McPherson, *Abraham Lincoln and the Second American Revolution* (1990); Mark Neely, *The Fate of Liberty* (1991); Philip S. Paludan, *The Presidency of Abraham Lincoln* (1994); Heather Cox Richardson, *The Greatest Nation of the Earth: Republican Economic Policies During the Civil War* (1997); Joel Silbey, *A Respectable Minority: The Democratic Party in the Civil War Era* (1977); Benjamin P. Thomas, *Abraham Lincoln* (1952); Hans L. Trefousse, *The Radical Republicans* (1969); Michael Vorenberg, *Final Freedom: The Civil War, The Abolition of Slavery, and the Thirteenth Amendment* (2001); T. Harry Williams, *Lincoln and His Generals* (1952).

Chapter 16

National Policy, Politics, and Constitutional Law

Herman Belz, *Emancipation and Equal Rights* (1978); Michael Les Benedict, *A Compromise of Principle: Congressional Republicans and Reconstruction, 1863–1869* (1974); Michael Les Benedict, *The Impeachment and Trial of Andrew Johnson* (1973); Adrian Cook, *The Alabama Claims* (1975); David Donald, *Charles Sumner and the Rights of Man* (1970); Harold M. Hyman, *A More Perfect Union* (1973); William S. McFeely, *Grant* (1981); William S. McFeely, *Yankee Stepfather: General O. O. Howard and the Freedmen* (1968); Eric L. McKitrick, *Andrew Johnson and Reconstruction* (1966); Joel Silbey, *A Respectable Minority: The Democratic Party in the Civil War Era* (1977); Brooks D. Simpson, *The Reconstruction Presidents* (1998); Kenneth M. Stampp, *The Era of Reconstruction* (1965); Hans L. Trefousse, *Andrew Johnson* (1989).

The Freed Slaves

Ira Berlin, ed., *Freedom: A Documentary History of Emancipation, 1861–1867* (1984); Orville Vernon Burton, *In My Father's House Are Many Mansions* (1985); Edmund L. Drago, *Black Politicians and Reconstruction in Georgia* (1982); Eric Foner, *One Kind of Freedom* (1983); Gerald Jaynes, *Branches Without Roots: The Genesis of the Black Working Class in the American South, 1862–1882* (1986); Leon Litwack, *Been in the Storm So Long* (1979); Edward Magdol, *A Right to the Land* (1977); Robert Morris, *Reading, 'Riting and Reconstruction* (1981); Howard Rabinowitz, ed., *Southern Black Leaders*

in Reconstruction (1982); Emma Lou Thornbrough, ed., *Black Reconstructionists* (1972).

Politics and Reconstruction in the South

Robert W. Coakley, *The Role of Federal Military Forces in Domestic Disorders, 1789–1878* (1988); Richard N. Current, *Those Terrible Carpetbaggers* (1988); W. E. B. Du Bois, *Black Reconstruction* (1935); Paul D. Escott, *Many Excellent People: Power and Privilege in North Carolina, 1850–1900* (1985); Michael W. Fitzgerald, *The Union League Movement in the Deep South* (1989); Eric Foner, *Reconstruction: America's Unfinished Revolution, 1863–1877* (1988); William C. Harris, *The Day of the Carpetbagger* (1979); Thomas Holt, *Black over White: Negro Political Leadership in South Carolina During Reconstruction* (1977); J. Morgan Kousser and James M. McPherson, eds., *Region, Race and Reconstruction* (1982); Michael Perman, *The Road to Redemption* (1984); George C. Rable, *But There Was No Peace* (1984); James Roark, *Masters Without Slaves* (1977); Mark W. Summers, *Railroads, Reconstruction, and the Gospel of Prosperity* (1984); Allen Trelease, *White Terror* (1967); Ted Tunnell, *Crucible of Reconstruction* (1984); Michael Wayne, *The Reshaping of Plantation Society* (1983).

Women, Family, and Social History

Virginia I. Burr, ed., *The Secret Eye* (1990); Ellen Carol Dubois, *Feminism and Suffrage* (1978); Elizabeth Jacoway, *Yankee Missionaries in the South* (1979); Jacqueline Jones, *Soldiers of Light and Love* (1980); Robert C. Kenzer, *Kinship and Neighborhood in a Southern Community* (1987); Mary P. Ryan, *Women in Public* (1990); Rebecca Scott, "The Battle over the Child," *Prologue* 10 (Summer 1978): 101–113.

The End of Reconstruction

Michael Les Benedict, "Southern Democrats in the Crisis of 1876–1877," *Journal of Southern History* 66 (November 1980): 489–524; William Gillette, *Retreat from Reconstruction, 1869–1879* (1980); John G. Sproat, *"The Best Men": Liberal Reformers in the Gilded Age* (1968); C. Vann Woodward, *Reunion and Reaction* (1951).

Reconstruction's Legacy for the South and the Nation

Edward L. Ayers, *The Promise of the New South* (1992); David W. Blight, *Race and Reunion: The Civil War in American Memory, 1863–1915* (2001); Norman L. Crockett, *The Black Towns* (1979); Steven Hahn, *The Roots of Southern Populism* (1983); Jay R. Mandle, *The Roots of Black Poverty* (1978); Nell Irvin Painter, *Exodusters* (1976); Howard Rabinowitz, *Race Relations in the Urban South, 1865–1890* (1978); Roger L. Ransom and Richard Sutch, *One Kind of Freedom* (1977); Jonathan M. Wiener, *Social Origins of the New South* (1978).

Historical Reference Books by Subject:
Encyclopedias, Dictionaries, Atlases, Chronologies, and Statistics

American History: General

Gorton Carruth, ed., *The Encyclopedia of American Facts and Dates* (1997); *Dictionary of American History* (1976) and Joan Hoff and Robert H. Ferrell, eds., *Supplement* (1996); John M. Farragher, ed., *The American Heritage Encyclopedia of American History* (1998); Eric Foner and John A. Garraty, eds., *The Reader's Companion to American History* (1991); Bernard Grun, *The Timetables of History* (1991); *International Encyclopedia of the Social Sciences* (1968–); Richard B. Morris and Jeffrey B. Morris, eds., *Encyclopedia of American History* (1996); Harry Ritter, *Dictionary of Concepts in History* (1986); Lawrence Urdang, ed., *The Timetables of American History* (1996); U.S. Bureau of the Census, *Historical Statistics of the United States* (1975).

American History: General, Twentieth Century

John D. Buenker and Edward R. Kantowicz, eds., *Historical Dictionary of the Progressive Era, 1890–1920* (1988); David Farber and Beth Bailey, *The Columbia Guide to America in the 1960s* (2001); Robert H. Ferrell and John S. Bowman, eds., *The Twentieth Century: An Almanac* (1984); George H. Gallup, *The Gallup Poll: Public Opinion, 1935–1971* (1972), *1972–1977* (1978), and annual reports (1979–); Lois Gordon and Alan Gordon, *American Chronicles: Year by Year Through the Twentieth Century* (1999): Stanley Hochman, *The Penguin Dictionary of Contemporary American History* (1997); Stanley I. Kutler, ed., *Encyclopedia of the United States in the Twentieth Century* (1995); Peter B. Levy, *Encyclopedia of the Reagan-Bush Years* (1996); James S. Olson, *Historical Dictionary of the 1920s* (1988), and *Historical Dictionary of the 1950s* (2000); Thomas Parker and Douglas Nelson, *Day by Day: The Sixties* (1983).

American History: General Atlases and Gazetteers

Geoffrey Barraclough, ed., *The Times Atlas of World History* (1994); Rodger Doyle, *Atlas of Contemporary America* (1994);
Robert H. Ferrell and Richard Natkiel, *Atlas of American History* (1997); Edward W. Fox, *Atlas of American History* (1964); Archie Hobson, *The Cambridge Gazetteer of the United States and Canada* (1996); Eric Homberger, *The Penguin Historical Atlas of North America* (1995); National Geographic Society, *Historical Atlas of the United States* (1994); U.S. Department of the Interior, *National Atlas of the United States* (1970). Other atlases are listed under specific categories.

American History: General Biographies

Lucian Boia, ed., *Great Historians of the Modern Age* (1991); John S. Bowman, *The Cambridge Dictionary of American Biography* (1995); *Current Biography* (1940–); *Dictionary of American Biography* (1928–); John A. Garraty and Mark C. Carnes, eds., *American National Biography* (1999); John Garraty and Jerome L. Sternstein, eds., *The Encyclopedia of American Biography* (1996); *National Cyclopedia of American Biography* (1898–). Other biographical works appear under specific categories.

African Americans

Molefi Asante and Mark T. Mattson, *Historical and Cultural Atlas of African-Americans* (1991); James Ciment, *Atlas of African-American History* (2001); Jonathan Earle, *The Routledge Atlas of African American History* (2000); John N. Ingham, *African-American Business Leaders* (1993); Rayford W. Logan and Michael R. Winston, eds., *The Dictionary of American Negro Biography* (1983); Sharon Harley, *The Timetables of African-American History* (1995); Darlene C. Hine et al., eds., *Black Women in White America* (1994); Charles D. Lowery and John F. Marszalek, eds., *Encyclopedia of African-American Civil Rights* (1992); Larry G. Murphy et al., eds., *Encyclopedia of African American Religions* (1993); Jack Salzman et al., eds., *Encyclopedia of African-American Culture and History* (1996); Jessie Carney Smith, ed., *Notable Black American Women* (1992). See also "Slavery."

American Revolution and Colonies

Ian Barnes, *The Historical Atlas of the American Revolution* (2000); Richard Blanco and Paul Sanborn, eds., *The American Revolution* (1993); Lester J. Cappon, ed., *Atlas of Early American History: The Revolutionary Era, 1760–1790* (1976); Jacob E. Cooke, ed., *Encyclopedia of the American Colonies* (1993); John M. Faragher, ed., *The Encyclopedia of Colonial and Revolutionary America* (1990); Jack P. Greene and J. R. Pole, eds., *The Blackwell Encyclopedia of the American Revolution* (1991); Gregory Palmer, ed., *Biographical Sketches of Loyalists of the American Revolution* (1984); John W. Raimo, ed., *Biographical Directory of American Colonial and Revolutionary Governors, 1607–1789* (1980); *Rand-McNally Atlas of the American Revolution* (1974); Seymour I. Schwartz, *The French and Indian War, 1754–1763* (1995).

Architecture

William D. Hunt, Jr., ed., *Encyclopedia of American Architecture* (1980).

Asian Americans

Monique Avakian, *Atlas of Asian-American History* (2001); Hyung-Chan Kim, ed., *Dictionary of Asian American History* (1986); Brian Niiya, ed., *Japanese American History* (1993); Lynn Pan, ed., *The Encyclopedia of the Chinese Overseas* (1999). See also "Immigration and Ethnic Groups."

Business and the Economy

Christine Ammer and Dean S. Ammer, *Dictionary of Business and Economics* (1983); Douglas Auld and Graham Bannock, *The American Dictionary of Economics* (1983); Michael J. Freeman, *Atlas of World Economy* (1991); John N. Ingham, *Biographical Dictionary of American Business Leaders* (1983); John N. Ingham and Lynne B. Feldman, *Contemporary American Business Leaders* (1990); Neil A. Hamilton, *American Business Leaders* (1999); William H. Mulligan, Jr., ed., *A Historical Dictionary of American Industrial Language* (1988); Paul Paskoff, ed., *Encyclopedia of American Business History and Biography* (1989); Glenn Porter, *Encyclopedia of American Economic History* (1980); Richard Robinson, *United States Business History, 1602–1988* (1990); Malcolm Warner, ed., *International Encyclopedia of Business and Management* (1996). See also "African Americans," "Native Americans and Indian Affairs," and "Transportation."

Cities and Towns

John L. Androit, ed., *Township Atlas of the United States* (1979); David J. Bodenhamer and Robert J. Barrows, eds., *The Encyclopedia of Indianapolis* (1994); *The Comparative Guide to American Suburbs* (2001); Gary A. Goreham, ed., *Encyclopedia of Rural America* (1997); Melvin G. Holli and Peter d'A. Jones, eds., *Biographical Dictionary of American Mayors, 1820–1980: Big City Mayors* (1981); Eric Homberger and Alice Hudson, *The Historical Atlas of New York City* (1998); Kenneth T. Jackson, ed., *Encyclopedia of New York City* (1995); John E. Kleber et al., eds., *The Encyclopedia of Louisville* (2000); George T. Kurian, *World Encyclopedia of Cities* (1994); Ory M. Nergal, ed., *The Encyclopedia of American Cities* (1980); Neil Larry Shumsky, ed., *Encyclopedia of Urban America* (1998); David D. Van Tassel and John J. Grabowski, eds., *The Dictionary of Cleveland Biography* (1996); David D. Van Tassel and John J. Grabowski, eds., *The Encyclopedia of Cleveland History* (1987). See also "Politics and Government."

Civil War and Reconstruction

Mark M. Boatner III, *The Civil War Dictionary* (1988); Richard N. Current, ed., *Encyclopedia of the Confederacy* (1993); John T. Hubbell and James W. Geary, eds., *Biographical Dictionary of the Union* (1995); Kenneth C. Martis, *The Historical Atlas of the Congresses of the Confederate States of America: 1861–1865* (1994); James M. McPherson, ed., *The Atlas of the Civil War* (1994); Mark E. Neely, Jr., *The Abraham Lincoln Encyclopedia* (1982); Craig L. Symonds, *A Battlefield Atlas of the Civil War* (1983); Hans L. Trefousse, *Historical Dictionary of Reconstruction* (1991); U.S. War Department, *The Official Atlas of the Civil War* (1958); Jon L. Wakelyn, ed., *Biographical Dictionary of the Confederacy* (1977); Ezra J. Warner and W. Buck Yearns, *Biographical Register of the Confederate Congress* (1975); Steven E. Woodworth, ed., *The American Civil War* (1996). See also "South" and "Politics and Government."

The Cold War

Thomas S. Arms, *Encyclopedia of the Cold War* (1994); Michael Kort, *The Columbia Guide to the Cold War* (1998); Thomas Parrish, *The Cold War Encyclopedia* (1996); Richard A. Schwartz, *Cold War Culture: The Media and the Arts* (1998); Joseph Smith and Simon Davis, *Historical Dictionary of the Cold War* (2000); Brandon Toropov, *Encyclopedia of Cold War Politics* (2000). See also "Foreign Relations" and "Military and Wars."

Constitution, Supreme Court, and Judiciary

David Bradley and Shelly F. Fishkin, eds., *The Encyclopedia of Civil Rights* (1997); Congressional Quarterly, *The Supreme Court A to Z* (1994); Kermit L. Hall, ed., *The Oxford Companion to the Supreme Court of the United States* (1992); Kermit L. Hall, ed., *The Oxford Guide to United States Supreme Court Decisions* (1999); Richard F. Hixson, *Mass Media and the Con-*

stitution (1989); Robert J. Janosik, ed., *Encyclopedia of the American Judicial System* (1987); John W. Johnson, ed., *Historic U.S. Court Cases* (2001); Leonard W. Levy et al., eds., *Encyclopedia of the American Constitution* (1986); Fred R. Shapiro, *The Oxford Dictionary of American Legal Quotations* (1993); Melvin I. Urofsky, ed., *The Supreme Court Justices* (1994). See also "Politics and Government" and "Sexuality."

Crime, Violence, Police, and Prisons

William G. Bailey, *Encyclopedia of Police Science* (1994); Marilyn D. McShane and Frank P. Williams III, eds., *Encyclopedia of American Prisons* (1995); Michael Newton and Judy Ann Newton, *Racial and Religious Violence in America* (1991); Michael Newton and Judy Newton, *The Ku Klux Klan* (1990); Carl Sifakis, *Encyclopedia of Assassinations* (2001); Carl Sifakis, *The Encyclopedia of American Crime* (2000); Carl Sifakis, *The Mafia Encyclopedia* (1999).

Culture and Folklore

Jan Harold Brunvald, *American Folklore* (1996); Mary K. Cayton and Peter W. Williams, eds., *Encyclopedia of American Cultural and Intellectual History* (2001); Hennig Cohen and Tristam Potter Coffin, eds., *The Folklore of American Holidays* (1987); Richard M. Dorson, ed., *Handbook of American Folklore* (1983); Robert L. Gale, *A Cultural Encyclopedia of the 1850s in America* (1993); Robert L. Gale, *The Gay Nineties in America* (1992); M. Thomas Inge, ed., *Handbook of American Popular Culture* (1979–1981); Wolfgang Mieder et al., eds., *A Dictionary of American Proverbs* (1992); J. F. Rooney, Jr., et al., eds., *This Remarkable Continent: An Atlas of United States and Canadian Society and Cultures* (1982); Jane Stern and Michael Stern, *Encyclopedia of Pop Culture* (1992); Justin Wintle, ed., *Makers of Nineteenth Century Culture, 1800–1914* (1982). See also "The Cold War," "Entertainment and the Arts," "Mass Media and Journalism," "Music," and "Sports."

Education and Libraries

Lee C. Deighton, ed., *The Encyclopedia of Education* (1971); Joseph C. Kiger, ed., *Research Institutions and Learned Societies* (1982); John F. Ohles, ed., *Biographical Dictionary of American Educators* (1978); Wayne A. Wiegard and Donald E. Davis, Jr., eds., *Encyclopedia of Library History* (1994).

Entertainment and the Arts

Tim Brooks and Earle Marsh, *The Complete Directory to Prime Time Network and Cable TV Shows, 1946–Present* (1999); Barbara N. Cohen-Stratyner, *Biographical Dictionary of Dance* (1982); John Dunning, *Tune in Yesterday* (radio)

(1967); Larry Langman and Edgar Borg, *Encyclopedia of American War Films* (1989); Larry Langman and David Ebner, *Encyclopedia of American Spy Films* (1990); Don Rubin, *World Encyclopedia of Contemporary Theatre: The Americas* (2000); Andrew Sarris, *The American Cinema: Directors and Directions, 1929–1968* (1968); Anthony Slide, *The American Film Industry* (1986); Anthony Slide, *The Encyclopedia of Vaudeville* (1994); Evelyn M. Truitt, *Who Was Who on Screen* (1984); Don B. Wilmeth and Tice L. Miller, eds., *The Cambridge Guide to American Theatre* (1993). See also "The Cold War," "Culture and Folklore," "Mass Media and Journalism," "Music," and "Sports."

Environment and Conservation

André R. Cooper, ed., *Cooper's Comprehensive Environmental Desk Reference* (1996); Forest History Society, *Encyclopedia of American Forest and Conservation History* (1983); Irene Franck and David Brownstone, *The Green Encyclopedia* (1992); Robert J. Mason and Mark T. Mattson, *Atlas of United States Environmental Issues* (1990); Robert Paehlke, ed., *Conservation and Environmentalism* (1995); World Resources Institute, *Environmental Almanac* (1992).

Exploration: From Columbus to Space

Silvio A. Bedini, ed., *The Christopher Columbus Encyclopedia* (1992); Michael Cassutt, *Who's Who in Space* (1987); W. P. Cumming et al., *The Discovery of North America* (1972); William Goetzmann and Glyndwr Williams, *The Atlas of North American Exploration* (1992); Clive Holland, *Arctic Exploration and Development* (1993); Adrian Johnson, *America Explored* (1974); Kenneth Nebenzahl, *Atlas of Columbus and the Great Discoveries* (1990). See also "Science and Technology."

Foreign Relations

Gérard Chaliand and Jean-Pierre Rageau, *Strategic Atlas* (1990); Alexander DeConde, ed., *Encyclopedia of American Foreign Policy* (1978); Margaret B. Denning and J. K. Sweeney, *Handbook of American Diplomacy* (1992); Graham Evans and Jeffrey Newnham, *The Penguin Dictionary of International Relations* (1999); John E. Findling, *Dictionary of American Diplomatic History* (1989); Chas. W. Freeman, Jr., *The Diplomat's Dictionary* (1999); Don Smith and Michael Kidron, *The State of the World Atlas* (1995); Bruce W. Jentleson and Thomas G. Paterson, eds., *Encyclopedia of U.S. Foreign Relations* (1997); Warren F. Kuehl, ed., *Biographical Dictionary of Internationalists* (1983); Edward Lawson, *Encyclopedia of Human Rights* (1991); Jack C. Plano and Roy Olton, eds., *The International Relations Dictionary* (1988). See also "The Cold War," "Peace Movements and Pacifism,"

"Politics and Government," "Military and Wars," and specific wars.

Hispanics

Nicolás Kanellos, ed., *The Hispanic-American Almanac* (1993); Nicolás Kanellos, ed., *Reference Library of Hispanic America* (1993); Francisco Lomelí, ed., *Handbook of Hispanic Cultures in the United States* (1993); Matt S. Meier, *Mexican-American Biographies* (1988); Matt S. Meier, *Notable Latino Americans* (1997); Matt S. Meier and Feliciano Rivera, *Dictionary of Mexican American History* (1981); Joseph C. Tardiff and L. Mpho Mabunda, eds., *Dictionary of Hispanic Biography* (1996). See also "Immigration and Ethnic Groups."

Immigration and Ethnic Groups

James P. Allen and Eugene J. Turner, *We the People: Atlas of America's Ethnic Diversity* (1988); Gerald Chaliand and Jean-Pierre Rageau, *The Penguin Atlas of Diasporas* (1995); Francesco Cordasco, ed., *Dictionary of American Immigration History* (1990); Salvatore J. LaGumina et al., eds., *The Italian American Experience* (2000); David Levinson and Melvin Ember, eds., *American Immigrant Cultures* (1997); Judy B. Litoff and Judith McDonnell, eds., *European Immigrant Women in the United States* (1994); Sally M. Miller, ed., *The Ethnic Press in the United States* (1987); Stephan Thernstrom, ed., *Harvard Encyclopedia of American Ethnic Groups* (1980); Rudolph J. Vecoli et al., eds., *Gale Encyclopedia of Multicultural America* (1995). See also "Asian Americans," "Jewish Americans," and "Hispanics."

Jewish Americans

American Jewish Yearbook (1899–); Jack Fischel and Sanford Pinsker, eds., *Jewish-American History and Culture* (1992); E. Paula Hyman and Deborah Dash Moore, eds., *Jewish Women in America* (1998); Geoffrey Wigoder, *Dictionary of Jewish Biography* (1991). See also "Immigration and Ethnic Groups."

Labor

Ronald L. Filippelli, *Labor Conflict in the United States* (1990); Gary M. Fink, ed., *Biographical Dictionary of American Labor* (1984); Gary M. Fink, ed., *Labor Unions* (1977); Philip S. Foner, *First Facts of American Labor* (1984).

Literature

James T. Callow and Robert J. Reilly, *Guide to American Literature* (1976–1977); *Dictionary of Literary Biography* (1978–); Eugene Ehrlich and Gorton Carruth, *The Oxford Illustrated Literary Guide to the United States* (1992); Jon Tuska and Vicki Piekarski, *Encyclopedia of Frontier and Western Fiction* (1983). See also "Culture and Folklore," "The South," and "Women."

Mass Media and Journalism

Robert V. Hudson, *Mass Media* (1987); Joseph P. McKerns, ed., *Biographical Dictionary of American Journalism* (1989); Michael D. Murray, ed., *Encyclopedia of Television News* (1998); William H. Taft, ed., *Encyclopedia of Twentieth-Century Journalists* (1986). See also "The Cold War," "Constitution, Supreme Court, and Judiciary," "Entertainment and the Arts," and "Immigration and Ethnic Groups."

Medicine and Nursing

Rima D. Apple, ed., *Women, Health, and Medicine in America* (1990); Vern L. Bullough et al., eds., *American Nursing: A Biographical Dictionary* (1988); Martin Kaufman et al., eds., *Dictionary of American Nursing Biography* (1988); Martin Kaufman et al., eds., *Dictionary of American Medical Biography* (1984); George L. Maddox, ed., *The Encyclopedia of Aging* (1995).

Military and Wars

William M. Arkin et al., *Encyclopedia of the U.S. Military* (1990); Charles D. Bright, ed., *Historical Dictionary of the U.S. Air Force* (1992); John W. Chambers, ed., *Oxford Companion to United States Military History* (2000); Andre Corvisier, ed., *A Dictionary of Military History* (1994); R. Ernest Dupuy and Trevor N. Dupuy, *The Harper Encyclopedia of Military History* (1993); David S. Frazier, ed., *The United States and Mexico at War* (1998); John E. Jessup, ed., *Encyclopedia of the American Military* (1994); Kenneth Macksey and William Woodhouse, *The Penguin Encyclopedia of Modern Warfare* (1992); Franklin D. Margiotta, ed., *Brassey's Encyclopedia of Naval Forces and Warfare* (1996); David F. Marley, *Pirates and Privateers of the Americas* (1994); James I. Matray, ed., *Historical Dictionary of the Korean War* (1991); Stanley Sandler, ed., *The Korean War* (1995); Roger J. Spiller and Joseph G. Dawson III, eds., *Dictionary of American Military Biography* (1984); Jerry K. Sweeney, ed., *A Handbook of American Military History* (1996); Peter G. Tsouras et al., *The United States Army* (1991); U.S. Military Academy, *The West Point Atlas of American Wars, 1689–1953* (1959); Bruce W. Watson et al., eds., *United States Intelligence* (1990); Bruce W. Watson and Susan M. Watson, *The United States Air Force* (1992); Bruce W. Watson and Susan M. Watson, *The United States Navy* (1991). See also "American Revolution and Colonies," "Civil War and Reconstruction," "The Cold War," "Vietnam War," and "World War II."

Music

John Chilton, *Who's Who of Jazz* (1985); Donald Clarke et al., eds., *The Penguin Encyclopedia of Popular Music* (1999); Edward Jablonski, *The Encyclopedia of American Music* (1981); Ellen Koskoff, *Garland Encyclopedia of World Music: The United States and Canada* (2000); Roger Lax and Frederick Smith, *The Great Song Thesaurus* (1989); Philip D. Morehead, *The New International Dictionary of Music* (1993); Austin Sonnier, Jr., *A Guide to the Blues* (1994). See also "Culture and Folklore" and "Entertainment and the Arts."

Native Americans and Indian Affairs

Gretchen M. Bataille, ed., *Native American Women* (1992); Michael Coe et al., *Atlas of Ancient America* (1986); Mary B. Davis, ed., *Native America in the Twentieth Century* (1994); Rayna Green, *The British Museum Encyclopedia of Native North America* (1999); *Handbook of North American Indians* (1978–); Sam D. Gill and Irene F. Sullivan, *Dictionary of Native American Mythology* (1992); J. Norman Heard et al., *Handbook of the American Frontier: Four Centuries of Indian–White Relationships* (1987–); Bruce E. Johansen, ed., *The Encyclopedia of Native American Economic History* (1999); Bruce E. Johansen, ed., *The Encyclopedia of Native American Legal Tradition* (1998); Bruce E. Johansen et al., eds., *The Encyclopedia of Native American Biography* (1997); Barry Klein, ed., *Reference Encyclopedia of the American Indian* (1993); Richard B. Lee and Richard Daly, eds., *The Cambridge Encyclopedia of Hunters and Gatherers* (2000); Barry M. Plitzker, ed., *A Native American Encyclopedia* (2000); Francis P. Prucha, *Atlas of American Indian Affairs* (1990); Carl Waldman, *Encyclopedia of Native American Tribes* (1988); Carl Waldman, *Atlas of the North American Indian* (2000).

The New Deal and Franklin D. Roosevelt

Otis L. Graham, Jr., and Meghan R. Wander, eds., *Franklin D. Roosevelt: His Life and Times* (1985); James S. Olson, ed., *Historical Dictionary of the New Deal* (1985). See also "Politics and Government."

Peace Movements and Pacifism

Harold Josephson et al., eds., *Biographical Dictionary of Modern Peace Leaders* (1985); Ervin Laszlo and Jong Y. Yoo, eds., *World Encyclopedia of Peace* (1986); Robert S. Meyer, *Peace Organizations Past and Present* (1988); Nancy L. Roberts, *American Peace Writers, Editors, and Periodicals* (1991). See also "Foreign Relations," "Military and Wars," and specific wars.

Politics and Government: General

J. Clark Archer et al., *Atlas of American Politics, 1960–2000* (2001); Erik W. Austin and Jerome M. Clubb, *Political Facts of the United States Since 1789* (1986); *The Columbia Dictionary of Political Biography* (1991); Jack P. Greene, ed., *Encyclopedia of American Political History* (1984); Leon Hurwitz, *Historical Dictionary of Censorship in the United States* (1985); George T. Kurian, ed., *A Historical Guide to the U.S. Government* (1998); John J. Patrick et al., *The Oxford Guide to the United States Government* (2001); Jack Plano, *The American Political Dictionary* (2001); Philip Rees, *Biographical Dictionary of the Extreme Right Since 1890* (1991); Charles R. Ritter et al., *American Legislative Leaders, 1850–1910* (1989); William Safire, *Safire's Political Dictionary* (1993); Robert Scruton, *A Dictionary of Political Thought* (1982); Jay M. Shafritz, *The HarperCollins Dictionary of American Government and Politics* (1992). See also "Cities and Towns," "Constitution, Supreme Court, and Judiciary," "States," and the following sections.

Politics and Government: Congress

American Enterprise Institute, *Vital Statistics on Congress* (1980–); Donald C. Brown et al., eds., *The Encyclopedia of the United States Congress* (1995); Stephen G. Christianson, *Facts About the Congress* (1996); Congressional Quarterly, *Biographical Directory of the American Congress, 1774–1996* (1997); Congressional Quarterly, *Congress and the Nation* (1965–); Kenneth C. Martis, *Historical Atlas of Political Parties in the United States Congress, 1789–1989* (1989); Kenneth C. Martis, *Historical Atlas of United States Congressional Districts, 1789–1983* (1982); Joel H. Silbey, ed., *Encyclopedia of the American Legislative System* (1994).

Politics and Government: Election Statistics

Congressional Quarterly, *Guide to U.S. Elections* (1994); Congressional Quarterly, *Presidential Elections, 1789–1996* (1997); L. Sandy Maisel, ed., *Political Parties and Elections in the United States* (1991); Yanek Mieczkowski, *The Routledge Historical Atlas of Presidential Elections* (2001); Svend Petersen and Louis Filler, *A Statistical History of the American Presidential Elections* (1981); Richard M. Scammon et al., eds., *America Votes* (1956–); Harold W. Stanley and Richard G. Niemi, *Vital Statistics on American Politics* (1988–); Lyn Ragsdale, *Vital Statistics on the Presidency* (1998); G. Scott Thomas, *The Pursuit of the White House* (1987).

Politics and Government: Parties

Earl R. Kruschke, *Encyclopedia of Third Parties in the United States* (1991); George T. Kurian, ed., *The Encyclopedia of the Republican Party* and *The Encyclopedia of the Democratic Party* (1996); Edward L. Schapsmeier and Frederick H. Schapsmeier, eds., *Political Parties and Civic Action Groups* (1981). See also other listings for "Politics and Government."

Politics and Government: Presidency and Executive Branch

Alan Brinkley and Davis Dyer, eds., *The Reader's Companion to the American Presidency* (2000); Henry F. Graff, *The Presidents* (1996); Mark Grossman, *Encyclopedia of the United States Cabinet* (2000); Bernard S. Katz and C. Daniel Vencill, eds., *Biographical Dictionary of the United States Secretaries of the Treasury, 1789–1995* (1996); Richard S. Kirkendall, ed., *The Harry S Truman Encyclopedia* (1989); Leonard W. Levy and Louis Fisher, eds., *Encyclopedia of the American Presidency* (1993); Merrill D. Peterson, ed., *Thomas Jefferson* (1986); Lyn Ragsdale, *Vital Statistics on the Presidency* (1998); Robert A. Rutland, ed., *James Madison and the American Nation* (1995); Robert Sobel, ed., *Biographical Directory of the United States Executive Branch, 1774–1977* (1977). See other categories for various presidents.

Politics and Government: Radicalism and the Left

Mari Jo Buhle et al., eds., *The American Radical* (1994); Mari Jo Buhle et al., eds., *Encyclopedia of the American Left* (1998); David DeLeon, ed., *Leaders of the 1960s* (1994); Bernard K. Johnpoll and Harvey Klehr, eds., *Biographical Dictionary of the American Left* (1986).

Religion and Cults

Henry Bowden, *Dictionary of American Religious Biography* (1993); S. Kent Brown et al., eds., *Historical Atlas of Mormonism* (1995); Bret Carroll, *The Routledge Historical Atlas of Religion in America* (2001); Edwin Gaustad and Philip L. Barlow, *New Historical Atlas of Religion in America* (1998); Michael Glazier and Thomas J. Shelley, eds., *The Encyclopedia of American Catholic History* (1997); Bill J. Leonard, *Dictionary of Baptists in America* (1994); Donald Lewis, ed., *A Dictionary of Evangelical Biography* (1995); Charles H. Lippy and Peter W. Williams, eds., *Encyclopedia of the American Religious Experience* (1988); J. Gordon Melton, *The Encyclopedia of American Religions* (1992); J. Gordon Melton, *The Encyclopedic Handbook of Cults in America* (1992); Mark A. Noll and Nathan O. Hatch, eds., *Eerdman's Handbook to Christianity in America* (1983); Stephen R. Prothero et al., *The Encyclopedia of American Religious History* (1996); Wade C. Roof, ed., *Contemporary American Religion* (2000); Paul J. Weber and W. Landis Jones, *U.S. Religious Interest Groups* (1994). See also "African Americans" and "South."

Science and Technology

James W. Cortada, *Historical Dictionary of Data Processing* (1987); Clark A. Elliott, *Biographical Index to American Science: The Seventeenth Century to 1920* (1990); Charles C. Gillespie et al., eds., *Dictionary of Scientific Biography* (1970–); National Academy of Sciences, *Biographical Memoirs* (1877–); Roy Porter, ed., *The Biographical Dictionary of Scientists* (1994). See also "Exploration."

Sexuality

Robert T. Francoeur, ed., *The International Encyclopedia of Sexuality* (1998); Wayne R. Dynes, ed., *Encyclopedia of Homosexuality* (1990); Steve Hogan and Lee Hudson, *Completely Queer: The Gay and Lesbian Encyclopedia* (1998); Arthur S. Leonard, ed., *Sexuality and the Law* (1993); Neil Schlager, ed., *Gay & Lesbian Almanac* (1998); Michael J. Tyrkus, ed., *Gay & Lesbian Biography* (1997); Bonnie Zimmerman and George Haggerty, eds., *Encyclopedia of Lesbian and Gay Histories and Cultures* (1999). See also "Social History and Reform."

Slavery

Seymour Drescher and Stanley L. Engerman, eds., *A Historical Guide to World Slavery* (1998); Paul Finkelman and Joseph C. Miller, eds., *Macmillan Encyclopedia of World Slavery* (1998); Randall M. Miller and John D. Smith, eds., *Dictionary of Afro-American Slavery* (1997); Junius P. Rodriguez, ed., *The Historical Encyclopedia of World Slavery* (1997). See also "African Americans."

Social History and Reform

Mary K. Cayton et al., eds., *Encyclopedia of American Social History* (1993); Louis Filler, *Dictionary of American Social Change* (1982); Robert S. Fogarty, *Dictionary of American Communal and Utopian History* (1980); Joseph M. Hawes and Elizabeth I. Nybakken, eds., *American Families* (1991); David Hey, ed., *The Oxford Companion to Local and Family History* (1996); Harold M. Keele and Joseph C. Kiger, eds., *Foundations* (1984); Mark E. Lender, *Dictionary of American Temperance Biography* (1984); Patricia M. Melvin, ed., *American Community Organizations* (1986); Randall M. Miller and Paul A. Cimbala, eds., *American Reform and Reformers* (1996); Roger S. Powers and William B. Vogele, eds., *Protest, Power, and Change* (1996); Alvin J. Schmidt, *Fraternal Organizations* (1980); Peter N. Stearns, ed., *Encyclopedia of Social History* (1993); Walter I. Trattner, *Biographical Dictionary of Social Welfare in America* (1986). See also "Crime, Violence, Police, and Prisons" and "Sexuality."

South

Edward L. Ayers and Brad Mittendorf, eds., *The Oxford Book of the American South* (1997); Robert Bain et al., eds., *Southern Writers* (1979); Kenneth Coleman and Charles S. Gurr, eds., *Dictionary of Georgia Biography* (1983); Andrew Frank, *The Routledge Historical Atlas of the American South* (1999);

Samuel S. Hill, ed., *Encyclopedia of Religion in the South* (1998); William S. Powell, ed., *Dictionary of North Carolina Biography* (1979–1996); David C. Roller and Robert W. Twyman, eds., *The Encyclopedia of Southern History* (1979); A. Ray Stephens and William M. Holmes, *Historical Atlas of Texas* (1990); James M. Volo and Dorothy D. Volo, *Encyclopedia of the Antebellum South* (2000); Walter P. Webb et al., eds., *The Handbook of Texas* (1952, 1976); Charles R. Wilson et al., eds., *Encyclopedia of Southern Culture* (1989). See also "Civil War and Reconstruction," "Politics and Government," and "States."

Sports

Peter C. Bjarkman, ed., *Encyclopedia of Major League Baseball Team Histories* (1991); Ralph Hickok, *A Who's Who of Sports Champions* (1995); Ralph Hickok, *The Encyclopedia of North American Sports History* (1991); David Levinson and Karen Christensen, eds., *Encyclopedia of World Sport* (1996); Jonathan F. Light, *The Cultural Encyclopedia of Baseball* (1997); David L. Porter, *Biographical Dictionary of American Sports: Baseball* (2000), *Basketball and Other Indoor Sports* (1989), *Football* (1987), and *Outdoor Sports* (1988); Victoria Sherrow, *Encyclopedia of Women and Sports* (1996); David Wallechinsky, *The Complete Book of the Summer Olympics* (1996); David Wallechinsky, *The Complete Book of the Winter Olympics* (1993). See also "Culture and Folklore."

States

Gary Alampi, ed., *Gale State Rankings Reporter* (1994); Roy R. Glashan, comp., *American Governors and Gubernatorial Elections, 1775–1978* (1979); John Hoffmann, ed., *A Guide to the History of Illinois* (1991); Edith R. Hornor, *Almanac of the Fifty States* (1997); Joseph E. Kallenback and Jessamine S. Kallenback, *American State Governors, 1776–1976* (1977); Joseph N. Kane et al., eds., *Facts About the States* (1994); John E. Kleber et al., eds., *The Kentucky Encyclopedia* (1992); Thomas A. McMullin and Marie Mullaney, *Biographical Directory of the Governors of the United States, 1983–1987* (1988) and *1988–1993* (1994); Marie Mullaney, *Biographical Directory of the Governors of the United States, 1988–1994* (1994); Thomas J. Noel, *Historical Atlas of Colorado* (1994); John W. Raimo, ed., *Biographical Directory of the Governors of the United States, 1978–1983* (1985); James W. Scott and Ronald L. De Lorme, *Historical Atlas of Washington* (1988); Benjamin F. Shearer and Barbara S. Shearer, *State Names, Seals, Flags, and Symbols* (1994); Robert Sobel and John W. Raimo, eds., *Biographical Directory of the Governors of the United States, 1789–1978* (1978); Richard W. Wilkie and Jack Tager, eds., *Historical Atlas of Massachusetts* (1991). See also "Politics and Government," "South," and "West and Frontier."

Transportation

Keith L. Bryant, ed., *Railroads in the Age of Regulation, 1900–1980* (1988); Rene De La Pedraja, *A Historical Dictionary of the U.S. Merchant Marine and Shipping Industry* (1994); Robert L. Frey, ed., *Railroads in the Nineteenth Century* (1988); John Stover, *The Routledge Historical Atlas of the American Railroads* (1999). See also "Business and the Economy."

Vietnam War

John S. Bowman, ed., *The Vietnam War: An Almanac* (1986); Stanley I. Kutler, ed., *Encyclopedia of the Vietnam War* (1996); James S. Olson, ed., *Dictionary of the Vietnam War* (1988); Harry G. Summers, Jr., *Vietnam War Almanac* (1985); Spencer C. Tucker, ed., *Encyclopedia of the Vietnam War* (2000). Also see "Peace Movements and Pacifism" and "Military and Wars."

West and Frontier

William A. Beck and Ynez D. Haase, *Historical Atlas of the American West* (1989); Doris O. Dawdy, *Artists of the American West* (1974–1984); J. Norman Heard, *Handbook of the American Frontier* (1987); Howard R. Lamar, ed., *The New Encyclopedia of the American West* (1998); Clyde A. Milner III et al., eds., *The Oxford History of the American West* (1994); Jay Robert Nash, *Encyclopedia of Western Lawmen and Outlaws* (1992); Doyce B. Nunis, Jr., and Gloria R. Lothrop, eds., *A Guide to the History of California* (1989); Charles Phillips and Alan Axelrod, eds., *Encyclopedia of the American West* (1996); Dan L. Thrapp, *The Encyclopedia of Frontier Biography* (1988–1994); David Walker, *Biographical Directory of American Territorial Governors* (1984). See also "Cities and Towns," "Literature," and "Native Americans and Indian Affairs."

Women

Anne Gibson and Timothy Fast, *The Women's Atlas of the United States* (1986); Karen Greenspan, *The Timetables of Women's History* (1996); Maggie Humm, *The Dictionary of Feminist Theory* (1990); Edward T. James et al., *Notable American Women, 1607–1950* (1971); Lina Mainiero, ed., *American Women Writers* (1979–1982); Wilma Mankiller et al., *The Reader's Companion to U.S. Women's History* (1998); Kirstin Olsen, *Chronology of Women's History* (1994); Sandra Opdycke, *The Routledge Historical Atlas of Women in America* (2000); Barbara G. Shortridge, *Atlas of American Women* (1987); Barbara Sicherman and Carol H. Green, eds., *Notable American Women, The Modern Period* (1980); Helen Tierney, ed., *Women's Studies Encyclopedia* (1991); James Trager, *The Women's Chronology* (1994); Angela H. Zophy and Frances M. Kavenik, eds., *Handbook of American*

Women's History (1990). See also "African Americans," "Immigration and Ethnic Groups," "Medicine and Nursing," "Native Americans and Indian Affairs," and "Sports."

World War I

David F. Burg and L. Edward Purcell, *Almanac of World War I* (1998); Martin Gilbert, *Atlas of World War I* (1994); Holger H. Herwig and Neil M. Heyman, *Biographical Dictionary of World War I* (1982); George T. Kurian, *Encyclopedia of the First World War* (1990); Stephen Pope and Elizabeth-Anne Wheal, *The Dictionary of the First World War* (1995); U.S. Military Academy, *The West Point Atlas of American Wars: 1900–1918* (1997); Anne C. Venzon, *The United States in the First World War* (1995). See also "Military and Wars."

World War II

David G. Chandler and James Lawton Collins, Jr., eds., *The D-Day Encyclopedia* (1993); I. C. B. Dear and M. R. D. Foot, eds., *The Oxford Companion to World War II* (1995); Simon Goodenough, *War Maps: Great Land Battles of World War II* (1988); Robert Goralski, *World War II Almanac* (1981); John Keegan, ed., *The Times Atlas of the Second World War* (1989); George T. Kurian, *Encyclopedia of the Second World War* (1991); Norman Polmer and Thomas B. Allen, *World War II: America at War* (1991); U.S. Military Academy, *Campaign Atlas to the Second World War: Europe and the Mediterranean* (1980); Peter Young, ed., *The World Almanac Book of World War II* (1981). See also "Military and Wars."

Documents

_____

DECLARATION OF INDEPENDENCE IN CONGRESS, JULY 4, 1776

When, in the course of human events, it becomes necessary for one people to dissolve the political bonds which have connected them with another, and to assume, among the powers of the earth, the separate and equal station to which the laws of nature and of nature's God entitle them, a decent respect to the opinions of mankind requires that they should declare the causes which impel them to the separation.

We hold these truths to be self-evident: That all men are created equal; that they are endowed by their Creator with certain unalienable rights; that among these are life, liberty, and the pursuit of happiness; that, to secure these rights, governments are instituted among men, deriving their just powers from the consent of the governed; that whenever any form of government becomes destructive of these ends, it is the right of the people to alter or to abolish it, and to institute new government, laying its foundation on such principles, and organizing its powers in such form, as to them shall seem most likely to effect their safety and happiness. Prudence, indeed, will dictate that governments long established should not be changed for light and transient causes; and accordingly all experience hath shown that mankind are more disposed to suffer, while evils are sufferable, than to right themselves by abolishing the forms to which they are accustomed. But when a long train of abuses and usurpations, pursuing invariably the same object, evinces a design to reduce them under absolute despotism, it is their right, it is their duty, to throw off such government, and to provide new guards for their future security. Such has been the patient sufferance of these colonies; and such is now the necessity which constrains them to alter their former systems of government. The history of the present King of Great Britain is a history of repeated injuries and usurpations, all having in direct object the establishment of an absolute tyranny over these states. To prove this, let facts be submitted to a candid world.

He has refused his assent to laws, the most wholesome and necessary for the public good.

He has forbidden his governors to pass laws of immediate and pressing importance, unless suspended in their oper-

ation till his assent should be obtained; and, when so suspended, he has utterly neglected to attend to them.

He has refused to pass other laws for the accommodation of large districts of people, unless those people would relinquish the right of representation in the legislature, a right inestimable to them, and formidable to tyrants only.

He has called together legislative bodies at places unusual, uncomfortable, and distant from the depository of their public records, for the sole purpose of fatiguing them into compliance with his measures.

He has dissolved representative houses repeatedly, for opposing, with manly firmness, his invasions on the rights of the people.

He has refused for a long time, after such dissolutions, to cause others to be elected; whereby the legislative powers, incapable of annihilation, have returned to the people at large for their exercise; the state remaining, in the mean time, exposed to all the dangers of invasions from without and convulsions within.

He has endeavored to prevent the population of these states; for that purpose obstructing the laws for naturalization of foreigners; refusing to pass others to encourage their migration hither, and raising the conditions of new appropriations of lands.

He has obstructed the administration of justice, by refusing his assent to laws for establishing judiciary powers.

He has made judges dependent on his will alone, for the tenure of their offices, and the amount and payment of their salaries.

He has erected a multitude of new offices, and sent hither swarms of officers to harass our people and eat out their substance.

He has kept among us, in times of peace, standing armies, without the consent of our legislatures.

He has affected to render the military independent of, and superior to, the civil power.

He has combined with others to subject us to a jurisdiction foreign to our constitution, and unacknowledged by our laws, giving his assent to their acts of pretended legislation:

For quartering large bodies of armed troops among us;

For protecting them, by a mock trial, from punishment for any murders which they should commit on the inhabitants of these states;

For cutting off our trade with all parts of the world;

For imposing taxes on us without our consent;

For depriving us, in many cases, of the benefits of trial by jury;

For transporting us beyond seas, to be tried for pretended offenses;

For abolishing the free system of English laws in a neighboring province, establishing therein an arbitrary government, and enlarging its boundaries, so as to render it at once an example and fit instrument for introducing the same absolute rule into these colonies;

For taking away our charters, abolishing our most valuable laws, and altering fundamentally the forms of our governments;

For suspending our own legislatures, and declaring themselves invested with power to legislate for us in all cases whatsoever.

He has abdicated government here, by declaring us out of his protection and waging war against us.

He has plundered our seas, ravaged our coasts, burned our towns, and destroyed the lives of our people.

He is at this time transporting large armies of foreign mercenaries to complete the works of death, desolation, and tyranny already begun with circumstances of cruelty and perfidy scarcely paralleled in the most barbarous ages, and totally unworthy the head of a civilized nation.

He has constrained our fellow-citizens, taken captive on the high seas, to bear arms against their country, to become the executioners of their friends and brethren, or to fall themselves by their hands.

He has excited domestic insurrection among us, and has endeavored to bring on the inhabitants of our frontiers the merciless Indian savages, whose known rule of warfare is an undistinguished destruction of all ages, sexes, and conditions.

In every stage of these oppressions we have petitioned for redress in the most humble terms; our repeated petitions have been answered only by repeated injury. A prince, whose character is thus marked by every act which may define a tyrant, is unfit to be the ruler of a free people.

Nor have we been wanting in our attentions to our British brethren. We have warned them, from time to time, of attempts by their legislature to extend an unwarrantable jurisdiction over us. We have reminded them of the circumstances of our emigration and settlement here. We have appealed to their native justice and magnanimity; and we have conjured them, by the ties of our common kindred, to disavow these usurpations, which would inevitably interrupt our connections and correspondence. They, too, have been deaf to the voice of justice and of consanguinity. We must, therefore, acquiesce in the necessity which denounces our separation, and hold them, as we hold the rest of mankind, enemies in war, in peace friends.

We, therefore, the representatives of the United States of America, in General Congress assembled, appealing to the Supreme Judge of the world for the rectitude of our intentions, do, in the name and by the authority of the good people of these colonies, solemnly publish and declare, that these United Colonies are, and of right ought to be, FREE AND INDEPENDENT STATES; that they are absolved from all allegiance to the British crown, and that all political connection between them and the state of Great Britain is, and ought to be, totally dissolved; and that, as free and independent states, they have full power to levy war, conclude peace, contract alliances, establish commerce, and do all other acts and things which independent states may of right do. And for the support of this declaration, with a firm reliance on the protection of Divine Providence, we mutually pledge to each other our lives, our fortunes, and our sacred honor.

ARTICLES OF CONFEDERATION

(The text of the Articles of Confederation can be found at college.hmco.com.)

CONSTITUTION OF THE UNITED STATES OF AMERICA AND AMENDMENTS*

Preamble

We the people of the United States, in order to form a more perfect union, establish justice, insure domestic tranquillity, provide for the common defense, promote the general welfare, and secure the blessings of liberty to ourselves and our posterity, do ordain and establish this Constitution for the United States of America.

Article I

Section 1 All legislative powers herein granted shall be vested in a Congress of the United States, which shall consist of a Senate and a House of Representatives.

Section 2 The House of Representatives shall be composed of members chosen every second year by the people of the several States, and the electors in each State shall have the qualifications requisite for electors of the most numerous branch of the State Legislature.

----

*Passages no longer in effect are printed in italic type.

No person shall be a Representative who shall not have attained to the age of twenty-five years, and been seven years a citizen of the United States, and who shall not, when elected, be an inhabitant of that State in which he shall be chosen.

Representatives and direct taxes shall be apportioned among the several States which may be included within this Union, according to their respective numbers, *which shall be determined by adding to the whole number of free persons, including those bound to service for a term of years and excluding Indians not taxed, three-fifths of all other persons.* The actual enumeration shall be made within three years after the first meeting of the Congress of the United States, and within every subsequent term of ten years, in such manner as they shall by law direct. The number of Representatives shall not exceed one for every thirty thousand, but each State shall have at least one Representative; *and until such enumeration shall be made, the State of New Hampshire shall be entitled to choose three, Massachusetts eight, Rhode Island and Providence Plantations one, Connecticut five, New York six, New Jersey four, Pennsylvania eight, Delaware one, Maryland six, Virginia ten, North Carolina five, South Carolina five, and Georgia three.*

When vacancies happen in the representation from any State, the Executive authority thereof shall issue writs of election to fill such vacancies.

The House of Representatives shall choose their Speaker and other officers; and shall have the sole power of impeachment.

Section 3 The Senate of the United States shall be composed of two Senators from each State, *chosen by the legislature thereof,* for six years; and each Senator shall have one vote.

Immediately after they shall be assembled in consequence of the first election, they shall be divided as equally as may be into three classes. The seats of the Senators of the first class shall be vacated at the expiration of the second year, of the second class at the expiration of the fourth year, and of the third class at the expiration of the sixth year, so that one-third may be chosen every second year; and if vacancies happen by resignation or otherwise, during the recess of the legislature of any State, the Executive thereof may make temporary appointments until the next meeting of the legislature, which shall then fill such vacancies.

No person shall be a Senator who shall not have attained to the age of thirty years, and been nine years a citizen of the United States, and who shall not, when elected, be an inhabitant of that State for which he shall be chosen.

The Vice-President of the United States shall be President of the Senate, but shall have no vote, unless they be equally divided.

The Senate shall choose their other officers, and also a President *pro tempore*, in the absence of the Vice-President, or when he shall exercise the office of President of the United States.

The Senate shall have the sole power to try all impeachments. When sitting for that purpose, they shall be on oath or affirmation. When the President of the United States is tried, the Chief Justice shall preside: and no person shall be convicted without the concurrence of two-thirds of the members present.

Judgment in cases of impeachment shall not extend further than to removal from the office, and disqualification to hold and enjoy any office of honor, trust or profit under the United States: but the party convicted shall nevertheless be liable and subject to indictment, trial, judgment and punishment, according to law.

Section 4 The times, places and manner of holding elections for Senators and Representatives shall be prescribed in each State by the legislature thereof; but the Congress may at any time by law make or alter such regulations, except as to the places of choosing Senators.

The Congress shall assemble at least once in every year, and such meeting *shall be on the first Monday in December, unless they shall by law appoint a different day.*

Section 5 Each house shall be the judge of the elections, returns and qualifications of its own members, and a majority of each shall constitute a quorum to do business; but a smaller number may adjourn from day to day, and may be authorized to compel the attendance of absent members, in such manner, and under such penalties, as each house may provide.

Each house may determine the rules of its proceedings, punish its members for disorderly behavior, and with the concurrence of two-thirds, expel a member.

Each house shall keep a journal of its proceedings, and from time to time publish the same, excepting such parts as may in their judgment require secrecy; and the yeas and nays of the members of either house on any question shall, at the desire of one-fifth of those present, be entered on the journal.

Neither house, during the session of Congress, shall, without the consent of the other, adjourn for more than three days, nor to any other place than that in which the two houses shall be sitting.

Section 6 The Senators and Representatives shall receive a compensation for their services, to be ascertained by law and paid out of the treasury of the United States. They shall in all cases except treason, felony and breach of the peace, be privileged from arrest during their attendance at the session of their respective houses, and in going to and returning from the same; and for any speech or debate in either house, they shall not be questioned in any other place.

No Senator or Representative shall, during the time for which he was elected, be appointed to any civil office under the authority of the United States, which shall have been created, or the emoluments whereof shall have been increased, during such time; and no person holding any office under the United States shall be a member of either house during his continuance in office.

Section 7   All bills for raising revenue shall originate in the House of Representatives; but the Senate may propose or concur with amendments as on other bills.

Every bill which shall have passed the House of Representatives and the Senate, shall, before it become a law, be presented to the President of the United States; if he approve he shall sign it, but if not he shall return it with objections to that house in which it originated, who shall enter the objections at large on their journal, and proceed to reconsider it. If after such reconsideration two-thirds of that house shall agree to pass the bill, it shall be sent, together with the objections, to the other house, by which it shall likewise be reconsidered, and, if approved by two-thirds of that house, it shall become a law. But in all such cases the votes of both houses shall be determined by yeas and nays, and the names of the persons voting for and against the bill shall be entered on the journal of each house respectively. If any bill shall not be returned by the President within ten days (Sundays excepted) after it shall have been presented to him, the same shall be a law, in like manner as if he had signed it, unless the Congress by their adjournment prevent its return, in which case it shall not be a law.

Every order, resolution, or vote to which the concurrence of the Senate and House of Representatives may be necessary (except on a question of adjournment) shall be presented to the President of the United States; and before the same shall take effect, shall be approved by him, or being disapproved by him, shall be repassed by two-thirds of the Senate and House of Representatives, according to the rules and limitations prescribed in the case of a bill.

Section 8   The Congress shall have power

To lay and collect taxes, duties, imposts, and excises, to pay the debts and provide for the common defense and general welfare of the United States; but all duties, imposts and excises shall be uniform throughout the United States;

To borrow money on the credit of the United States;

To regulate commerce with foreign nations, and among the several States, and with the Indian tribes;

To establish an uniform rule of naturalization, and uniform laws on the subject of bankruptcies throughout the United States;

To coin money, regulate the value thereof, and of foreign coin, and fix the standard of weights and measures;

To provide for the punishment of counterfeiting the securities and current coin of the United States;

To establish post offices and post roads;

To promote the progress of science and useful arts by securing for limited times to authors and inventors the exclusive right to their respective writings and discoveries;

To constitute tribunals inferior to the Supreme Court;

To define and punish piracies and felonies committed on the high seas and offenses against the law of nations;

To declare war, grant letters of marque and reprisal, and make rules concerning captures on land and water;

To raise and support armies, but no appropriation of money to that use shall be for a longer term than two years;

To provide and maintain a navy;

To make rules for the government and regulation of the land and naval forces;

To provide for calling forth the militia to execute the laws of the Union, suppress insurrections, and repel invasions;

To provide for organizing, arming, and disciplining the militia, and for governing such part of them as may be employed in the service of the United States, reserving to the States respectively the appointment of the officers, and the authority of training the militia according to the discipline prescribed by Congress;

To exercise exclusive legislation in all cases whatsoever, over such district (not exceeding ten miles square) as may, by cession of particular States, and the acceptance of Congress, become the seat of government of the United States, and to exercise like authority over all places purchased by the consent of the legislature of the State, in which the same shall be, for erection of forts, magazines, arsenals, dockyards, and other needful buildings; —and

To make all laws which shall be necessary and proper for carrying into execution the foregoing powers, and all other powers vested by this Constitution in the government of the United States, or in any department or officer thereof.

Section 9   *The migration or importation of such persons as any of the States now existing shall think proper to admit shall not be prohibited by the Congress prior to the year 1808; but a tax or duty may be imposed on such importation, not exceeding $10 for each person.*

The privilege of the writ of habeas corpus shall not be suspended, unless when in cases of rebellion or invasion the public safety may require it.

No bill of attainder or ex post facto law shall be passed.

No capitation, or other direct, tax shall be laid, unless in proportion to the census or enumeration herein before directed to be taken.

No tax or duty shall be laid on articles exported from any State.

No preference shall be given by any regulation of commerce or revenue to the ports of one State over those of another; nor shall vessels bound to, or from, one State, be obliged to enter, clear, or pay duties in another.

No money shall be drawn from the treasury, but in consequence of appropriations made by law; and a regular statement and account of the receipts and expenditures of all public money shall be published from time to time.

No title of nobility shall be granted by the United States: and no person holding any office of profit or trust under them, shall, without the consent of the Congress, accept of any present, emolument, office, or title, of any kind whatever, from any king, prince, or foreign state.

Section 10 No State shall enter into any treaty, alliance, or confederation; grant letters of marque and reprisal; coin money; emit bills of credit; make anything but gold and silver coin a tender in payment of debts; pass any bill of attainder, ex post facto law, or law impairing the obligation of contracts, or grant any title of nobility.

No State shall, without the consent of Congress, lay any imposts or duties on imports or exports, except what may be absolutely necessary for executing its inspection laws: and the net produce of all duties and imposts, laid by any State on imports or exports, shall be for the use of the treasury of the United States; and all such laws shall be subject to the revision and control of the Congress.

No State shall, without the consent of Congress, lay any duty of tonnage, keep troops or ships of war in time of peace, enter into any agreement or compact with another State, or with a foreign power, or engage in war, unless actually invaded, or in such imminent danger as will not admit of delay.

Article II

Section 1 The executive power shall be vested in a President of the United States of America. He shall hold his office during the term of four years, and, together with the Vice-President, chosen for the same term, be elected as follows:

Each State shall appoint, in such manner as the legislature thereof may direct, a number of electors, equal to the whole number of Senators and Representatives to which the State may be entitled in the Congress; but no Senator or Representative, or person holding an office of trust or profit under the United States, shall be appointed an elector.

The electors shall meet in their respective States, and vote by ballot for two persons, of whom one at least shall not be an inhabitant of the same State with themselves. And they shall make a list of all the persons voted for, and of the number of votes for each; which list they shall sign and certify, and transmit sealed to the seat of government of the United States, directed to the President of the Senate. The President of the Senate shall, in the presence of the Senate and House of Representatives, open all the certificates, and the votes shall then be counted. The person having the greatest number of votes shall be the President, if such number be a majority of the whole number of electors appointed; and if there be more than one who have such majority, and have an equal number of votes, then the House of Representatives shall immediately choose by ballot one of them for President; and if no person have a majority, then from the five highest on the list said house shall in like manner choose the President. But in choosing the President the votes shall be taken by States, the representation from each State having one vote; a quorum for this purpose shall consist of a member or members from two-thirds of the States, and a majority of all the States shall be necessary to a choice. In every case, after the choice of the President, the person having the greatest number of votes of the electors shall be the Vice-President. But if there should remain two or more who have equal votes, the Senate shall choose from them by ballot the Vice-President.

The Congress may determine the time of choosing the electors and the day on which they shall give their votes; which day shall be the same throughout the United States.

No person except a natural-born citizen, *or a citizen of the United States at the time of the adoption of this Constitution,* shall be eligible to the office of President; neither shall any person be eligible to that office who shall not have attained to the age of thirty-five years, and been fourteen years a resident within the United States.

In cases of the removal of the President from office or of his death, resignation, or inability to discharge the powers and duties of the said office, the same shall devolve on the Vice-President, and the Congress may by law provide for the case of removal, death, resignation, or inability, both of the President and Vice-President, declaring what officer shall then act as President, and such officer shall act accordingly, until the disability be removed, or a President shall be elected.

The President shall, at stated times, receive for his services a compensation, which shall neither be increased nor diminished during the period for which he shall have been elected, and he shall not receive within that period any other emolument from the United States, or any of them.

Before he enter on the execution of his office, he shall take the following oath or affirmation:—"I do solemnly swear (or affirm) that I will faithfully execute the office of President of the United States, and will to the best of my ability preserve, protect and defend the Constitution of the United States."

Section 2 The President shall be commander in chief of the army and navy of the United States, and of the militia of the several States, when called into the actual service of the United States; he may require the opinion, in writing, of the principal officer in each of the executive departments, upon any subject relating to the duties of their respective offices, and he shall have power to grant reprieves and pardons for offenses against the United States, except in cases of impeachment.

He shall have power, by and with the advice and consent of the Senate, to make treaties, provided two-thirds of the Senators present concur; and he shall nominate, and by and with the advice and consent of the Senate, shall appoint ambassadors, other public ministers and consuls, judges of the Supreme Court, and all other officers of the United States, whose appointments are not herein otherwise provided for, and which shall be established by law: but Congress may by law vest the appointment of such inferior officers, as they think proper, in the President alone, in the courts of law, or in the heads of departments.

The President shall have power to fill up all vacancies that may happen during the recess of the Senate, by granting commissions which shall expire at the end of their next session.

Section 3   He shall from time to time give to the Congress information of the state of the Union, and recommend to their consideration such measures as he shall judge necessary and expedient; he may, on extraordinary occasions, convene both houses, or either of them, and in case of disagreement between them, with respect to the time of adjournment, he may adjourn them to such time as he shall think proper; he shall receive ambassadors and other public ministers; he shall take care that the laws be faithfully executed, and shall commission all the officers of the United States.

Section 4   The President, Vice-President and all civil officers of the United States shall be removed from office on impeachment for, and on conviction of, treason, bribery, or other high crimes and misdemeanors.

Article III

Section 1   The judicial power of the United States shall be vested in one Supreme Court, and in such inferior courts as the Congress may from time to time ordain and establish. The judges, both of the Supreme and inferior courts, shall hold their offices during good behavior, and shall, at stated times, receive for their services a compensation which shall not be diminished during their continuance in office.

Section 2   The judicial power shall extend to all cases, in law and equity, arising under this Constitution, the laws of the United States, and treaties made, or which shall be made, under their authority;—to all cases affecting ambassadors, other public ministers and consuls;—to all cases of admiralty and maritime jurisdiction;—to controversies to which the United States shall be a party;—to controversies between two or more States;—*between a State and citizens of another State;*—between citizens of different States;—between citizens of the same State claiming lands under grants of different States, and between a State, or the citizens thereof, and foreign states, citizens or subjects.

In all cases affecting ambassadors, other public ministers and consuls, and those in which a State shall be party, the Supreme Court shall have original jurisdiction. In all the other cases before mentioned, the Supreme Court shall have appellate jurisdiction, both as to law and fact, with such exceptions, and under such regulations, as the Congress shall make.

The trial of all crimes, except in cases of impeachment, shall be by jury; and such trial shall be held in the State where said crimes shall have been committed; but when not committed within any State, the trial shall be at such place or places as the Congress may by law have directed.

Section 3   Treason against the United States shall consist only in levying war against them, or in adhering to their enemies, giving them aid and comfort. No person shall be convicted of treason unless on the testimony of two witnesses to the same overt act, or on confession in open court.

The Congress shall have power to declare the punishment of treason, but no attainder of treason shall work corruption of blood, or forfeiture except during the life of the person attainted.

Article IV

Section 1   Full faith and credit shall be given in each State to the public acts, records, and judicial proceedings of every other State. And the Congress may by general laws prescribe the manner in which such acts, records, and proceedings shall be proved, and the effect thereof.

Section 2   The citizens of each State shall be entitled to all privileges and immunities of citizens in the several States.

A person charged in any State with treason, felony, or other crime, who shall flee from justice, and be found in another State, shall on demand of the executive authority of the State from which he fled, be delivered up, to be removed to the State having jurisdiction of the crime.

No person held to service or labor in one State, under the laws thereof, escaping into another, shall, in consequence of any law or regulation therein, be discharged from such service or labor, but shall be delivered up on claim of the party to whom such service or labor may be due.

Section 3   New States may be admitted by the Congress into this Union; but no new State shall be formed or erected within the jurisdiction of any other State; nor any State be formed by the junction of two or more States, or parts of States, without the consent of the legislatures of the States concerned as well as of the Congress.

The Congress shall have power to dispose of and make all needful rules and regulations respecting the territory or other property belonging to the United States; and nothing in this Constitution shall be so construed as to prejudice any claims of the United States, or of any particular State.

Section 4   The United States shall guarantee to every State in this Union a republican form of government, and shall protect each of them against invasion; and on application of the legislature, or of the executive (when the legislature cannot be convened), against domestic violence.

Article V

The Congress, whenever two-thirds of both houses shall deem it necessary, shall propose amendments to this Constitution, or, on the application of the legislatures of two-thirds of the several States, shall call a convention for proposing amendments, which, in either case, shall be valid to all intents and purposes, as part of this Constitution, when ratified by the legislatures of three-fourths of the several States, or by conventions in three-fourths thereof, as the one or the other mode of ratification may be proposed by the Congress; provided *that no amendments which may be made prior to the year one thousand eight hundred and eight shall in any manner affect the first and fourth clauses in the ninth section of the first article;* and that no State, without its consent, shall be deprived of its equal suffrage in the Senate.

Article VI

All debts contracted and engagements entered into, before the adoption of this Constitution, shall be as valid against the United States under this Constitution, as under the Confederation.

This Constitution, and the laws of the United States which shall be made in pursuance thereof; and all treaties made, or which shall be made, under the authority of the United States, shall be the supreme law of the land; and the judges in every State shall be bound thereby, anything in the Constitution or laws of any State to the contrary notwithstanding.

The Senators and Representatives before mentioned, and the members of the several State legislatures, and all executive and judicial officers, both of the United States and of the several States, shall be bound by oath or affirmation to support this Constitution; but no religious test shall ever be required as a qualification to any office or public trust under the United States.

Article VII

The ratification of the conventions of nine States shall be sufficient for the establishment of this Constitution between the States so ratifying the same.

Done in Convention by the unanimous consent of the States present, the seventeenth day of September in the year of our Lord one thousand seven hundred and eighty-seven and of the Independence of the United States of America the twelfth. In witness whereof we have hereunto subscribed our names.

————

AMENDMENTS TO THE CONSTITUTION*

Amendment I

Congress shall make no law respecting an establishment of religion, or prohibiting the free exercise thereof; or abridging the freedom of speech, or of the press; or the right of the people peaceably to assemble, and to petition the government for a redress of grievances.

Amendment II

A well-regulated militia being necessary to the security of a free State, the right of the people to keep and bear arms shall not be infringed.

Amendment III

No soldier shall, in time of peace, be quartered in any house without the consent of the owner, nor in time of war, but in a manner to be prescribed by law.

Amendment IV

The right of the people to be secure in their persons, houses, papers, and effects, against unreasonable searches and seizures, shall not be violated, and no warrants shall issue but upon probable cause, supported by oath or affirmation, and particularly describing the place to be searched, and the persons or things to be seized.

Amendment V

No person shall be held to answer for a capital, or otherwise infamous crime, unless on a presentment or indictment of a grand jury, except in cases arising in the land or naval forces, or in the militia, when in actual service in time of war or public danger; nor shall any person be subject for the same of-

---

*The first ten Amendments (the Bill of Rights) were adopted in 1791.

fense to be twice put in jeopardy of life or limb; nor shall be compelled in any criminal case to be a witness against himself, nor be deprived of life, liberty, or property, without due process of law; nor shall private property be taken for public use without just compensation.

Amendment VI

In all criminal prosecutions, the accused shall enjoy the right to a speedy and public trial, by an impartial jury of the State and district wherein the crime shall have been committed, which district shall have been previously ascertained by law, and to be informed of the nature and cause of the accusation; to be confronted with the witnesses against him; to have compulsory process for obtaining witnesses in his favor, and to have the assistance of counsel for his defense.

Amendment VII

In suits at common law, where the value in controversy shall exceed twenty dollars, the right of trial by jury shall be preserved, and no fact tried by a jury shall be otherwise reexamined in any court of the United States, than according to the rules of the common law.

Amendment VIII

Excessive bail shall not be required, nor excessive fines imposed, nor cruel and unusual punishments inflicted.

Amendment IX

The enumeration in the Constitution, of certain rights, shall not be construed to deny or disparage others retained by the people.

Amendment X

The powers not delegated to the United States by the Constitution, nor prohibited by it to the States, are reserved to the States respectively, or to the people.

Amendment XI

[Adopted 1798]
The judicial power of the United States shall not be construed to extend to any suit in law or equity, commenced or prosecuted against one of the United States by citizens of another State, or by citizens or subjects of any foreign state.

Amendment XII

[Adopted 1804]

The electors shall meet in their respective States, and vote by ballot for President and Vice-President, one of whom, at least, shall not be an inhabitant of the same State with themselves; they shall name in their ballots the person voted for as President, and in distinct ballots the person voted for as Vice-President, and they shall make distinct lists of all persons voted for as President, and of all persons voted for as Vice-President, and of the number of votes for each, which lists they shall sign and certify, and transmit sealed to the seat of government of the United States, directed to the President of the Senate;—the President of the Senate shall, in the presence of the Senate and House of Representatives, open all the certificates and the votes shall then be counted;—the person having the greatest number of votes for President shall be the President, if such number be a majority of the whole number of electors appointed; and if no person have such majority, then from the persons having the highest numbers not exceeding three on the list of those voted for as President, the House of Representatives shall choose immediately, by ballot, the President. But in choosing the President, the votes shall be taken by States, the representation from each State having one vote; a quorum for this purpose shall consist of a member or members from two-thirds of the States, and a majority of all the States shall be necessary to a choice. And if the House of Representatives shall not choose a President whenever the right of choice shall devolve upon them, before *the fourth day of March* next following, then the Vice-President shall act as President, as in the case of the death or other constitutional disability of the President.

The person having the greatest number of votes as Vice-President shall be the Vice-President, if such number be a majority of the whole number of electors appointed; and if no person have a majority, then from the two highest numbers on the list the Senate shall choose the Vice-President; a quorum for the purpose shall consist of two-thirds of the whole number of Senators, and a majority of the whole number shall be necessary to a choice. But no person constitutionally ineligible to the office of President shall be eligible to that of Vice-President of the United States.

Amendment XIII

[Adopted 1865]

Section 1   Neither slavery nor involuntary servitude, except as a punishment for crime whereof the party shall have been duly convicted, shall exist within the United States, or any place subject to their jurisdiction.

Section 2   Congress shall have power to enforce this article by appropriate legislation.

Amendment XIV

[Adopted 1868]

Section 1 All persons born or naturalized in the United States, and subject to the jurisdiction thereof, are citizens of the United States and of the State wherein they reside. No State shall make or enforce any law which shall abridge the privileges or immunities of citizens of the United States; nor shall any State deprive any person of life, liberty, or property, without due process of law; nor deny to any person within its jurisdiction the equal protection of the laws.

Section 2 Representatives shall be apportioned among the several States according to their respective numbers, counting the whole number of persons in each State, excluding Indians not taxed. But when the right to vote at any election for the choice of Electors for President and Vice-President of the United States, Representatives in Congress, the executive and judicial officers of a State, or the members of the legislature thereof, is denied to any of the male inhabitants of such State, being twenty-one years of age and citizens of the United States, or in any way abridged, except for participation in rebellion, or other crime, the basis of representation therein shall be reduced in the proportion which the number of such male citizens shall bear to the whole number of male citizens twenty-one years of age in such State.

Section 3 No person shall be a Senator or Representative in Congress, or Elector of President and Vice-President, or hold any office, civil or military, under the United States, or under any State, who, having previously taken an oath, as a member of Congress, or as an officer of the United States, or as a member of any State legislature, or as an executive or judicial officer of any State, to support the Constitution of the United States, shall have engaged in insurrection or rebellion against the same, or given aid or comfort to the enemies thereof. Congress may, by a vote of two-thirds of each house, remove such disability.

Section 4 The validity of the public debt of the United States, authorized by law, including debts incurred for payment of pensions and bounties for services in suppressing insurrection or rebellion, shall not be questioned. But neither the United States nor any State shall assume or pay any debt or obligation incurred in aid of insurrection or rebellion against the United States, or any claim for the loss of emancipation of any slave; but all such debts, obligations, and claims shall be held illegal and void.

Section 5 The Congress shall have power to enforce, by appropriate legislation, the provisions of this article.

Amendment XV

[Adopted 1870]

Section 1 The right of citizens of the United States to vote shall not be denied or abridged by the United States or by any State on account of race, color, or previous condition of servitude.

Section 2 The Congress shall have power to enforce this article by appropriate legislation.

Amendment XVI

[Adopted 1913]

The Congress shall have power to lay and collect taxes on incomes, from whatever source derived, without apportionment among the several States, and without regard to any census or enumeration.

Amendment XVII

[Adopted 1913]

Section 1 The Senate of the United States shall be composed of two Senators from each State, elected by the people thereof, for six years; and each Senator shall have one vote. The electors in each State shall have the qualifications requisite for electors of [voters for] the most numerous branch of the State legislatures.

Section 2 When vacancies happen in the representation of any State in the Senate, the executive authority of such State shall issue writs of election to fill such vacancies: Provided, that the Legislature of any State may empower the executive thereof to make temporary appointments until the people fill the vacancies by election as the Legislature may direct.

Section 3 This amendment shall not be so construed as to affect the election or term of any Senator chosen before it becomes valid as part of the Constitution.

Amendment XVIII

[Adopted 1919; Repealed 1933]

Section 1 After one year from the ratification of this article the manufacture, sale, or transportation of intoxicating liquors within, the importation thereof into, or the exportation thereof from the United States and all territory subject to the jurisdiction thereof, for beverage purposes, is hereby prohibited.

Section 2 The Congress and the several States shall have concurrent power to enforce this article by appropriate legislation.

Section 3 This article shall be inoperative unless it shall have been ratified as an amendment to the Constitution by the legislatures of the several States, as provided by the Constitution, within seven years from the date of the submission thereof to the States by the Congress.

Amendment XIX

[Adopted 1920]

Section 1   The right of citizens of the United States to vote shall not be denied or abridged by the United States or by any State on account of sex.

Section 2   The Congress shall have power to enforce this article by appropriate legislation.

Amendment XX

[Adopted 1933]

Section 1   The terms of the President and Vice-President shall end at noon on the 20th day of January, and the terms of Senators and Representatives at noon on the 3rd day of January, of the years in which such terms would have ended if this article had not been ratified; and the terms of their successors shall then begin.

Section 2   The Congress shall assemble at least once in every year, and such meeting shall begin at noon on the 3d day of January, unless they shall by law appoint a different day.

Section 3   If, at the time fixed for the beginning of the term of the President, the President-elect shall have died, the Vice-President–elect shall become President. If a President shall not have been chosen before the time fixed for the beginning of his term, or if the President-elect shall have failed to qualify, then the Vice-President–elect shall act as President until a President shall have qualified; and the Congress may by law provide for the case wherein neither a President-elect nor a Vice-President–elect shall have qualified, declaring who shall then act as President, or the manner in which one who is to act shall be selected, and such persons shall act accordingly until a President or Vice-President shall have qualified.

Section 4   The Congress may by law provide for the case of the death of any of the persons from whom the House of Representatives may choose a President whenever the right of choice shall have devolved upon them, and for the case of the death of any of the persons from whom the Senate may choose a Vice-President whenever the right of choice shall have devolved upon them.

Section 5   Sections 1 and 2 shall take effect on the 15th day of October following the ratification of this article.

Section 6   This article shall be inoperative unless it shall have been ratified as an amendment to the Constitution by the Legislatures of three-fourths of the several States within seven years from the date of its submission.

Amendment XXI

[Adopted 1933]

Section 1   The eighteenth article of amendment to the Constitution of the United States is hereby repealed.

Section 2   The transportation or importation into any State, Territory, or Possession of the United States for delivery or use therein of intoxicating liquors, in violation of the laws thereof, is hereby prohibited.

Section 3   This article shall be inoperative unless it shall have been ratified as an amendment to the Constitution by conventions in the several States, as provided in the Constitution, within seven years from the date of submission thereof to the States by the Congress.

Amendment XXII

[Adopted 1951]

Section 1   No person shall be elected to the office of President more than twice, and no person who has held the office of President, or acted as President, for more than two years of a term to which some other person was elected President shall be elected to the office of President more than once. But this article shall not apply to any person holding the office of President when this article was proposed by the Congress, and shall not prevent any person who may be holding the office of President, or acting as President, during the term within which this article becomes operative from holding the office of President or acting as President during the remainder of such term.

Section 2   This article shall be inoperative unless it shall have been ratified as an amendment to the Constitution by the legislatures of three-fourths of the several States within seven years from the date of its submission to the States by the Congress.

Amendment XXIII

[Adopted 1961]

Section 1   The District constituting the seat of Government of the United States shall appoint in such manner as the Congress may direct:

A number of electors of President and Vice-President equal to the whole number of Senators and Representatives in Congress to which the District would be entitled if it were a State, but in no event more than the least populous State; they shall be in addition to those appointed by the States, but they shall be considered for the purposes of the election of President and Vice-President, to be electors appointed by a State; and they shall meet in the District and perform such duties as provided by the twelfth article of amendment.

Section 2   The Congress shall have the power to enforce this article by appropriate legislation.

Amendment XXIV

[Adopted 1964]

Section 1   The right of citizens of the United States to vote in any primary or other election for President or Vice-President, for electors for President or Vice-President, or for Senator or Representative in Congress, shall not be denied or abridged by the United States or any State by reason of failure to pay any poll tax or other tax.

Section 2   The Congress shall have the power to enforce this article by appropriate legislation.

Amendment XXV

[Adopted 1967]

Section 1   In case of the removal of the President from office or of his death or resignation, the Vice-President shall become President.

Section 2   Whenever there is a vacancy in the office of the Vice-President, the President shall nominate a Vice-President who shall take office upon confirmation by a majority vote of both Houses of Congress.

Section 3   Whenever the President transmits to the President pro tempore of the Senate and the Speaker of the House of Representatives his written declaration that he is unable to discharge the powers and duties of his office, and until he transmits to them a written declaration to the contrary, such powers and duties shall be discharged by the Vice-President as Acting President.

Section 4   Whenever the Vice-President and a majority of either the principal officers of the executive departments or of such other body as Congress may by law provide, transmit to the President pro tempore of the Senate and the Speaker of the House of Representatives their written declaration that the President is unable to discharge the powers and duties of his office, the Vice-President shall immediately assume the powers and duties of the office as Acting President.

Thereafter, when the President transmits to the President pro tempore of the Senate and the Speaker of the House of Representatives his written declaration that no inability exists, he shall resume the powers and duties of his office unless the Vice-President and a majority of either the principal officers of the executive department[s] or of such other body as Congress may by law provide, transmit within four days to the President pro tempore of the Senate and the Speaker of the House of Representatives their written declaration that the President is unable to discharge the powers and duties of his office. Thereupon Congress shall decide the issue, assembling within forty-eight hours for that purpose if not in session. If the Congress, within twenty-one days after receipt of the latter written declaration, or, if Congress is not in session, within twenty-one days after Congress is required to assemble, determines by two-thirds vote of both Houses that the President is unable to discharge the powers and duties of his office, the Vice-President shall continue to discharge the same as Acting President; otherwise, the President shall resume the powers and duties of his office.

Amendment XXVI

[Adopted 1971]

Section 1   The right of citizens of the United States, who are eighteen years of age or older, to vote shall not be denied or abridged by the United States or by any State on account of age.

Section 2   The Congress shall have power to enforce this article by appropriate legislation.

Amendment XXVII

[Adopted 1992]

No law, varying the compensation for the services of the Senators and Representatives, shall take effect, until an election of Representatives shall have intervened.

The American People and Nation: A Statistical Profile

Population of the United States

Year	Number of States	Population	Percent Increase	Population Per Square Mile	Percent Urban/ Rural	Percent Male/ Female	Percent White/ Non-white	Persons Per House-hold	Median Age
1790	13	3,929,214		4.5	5.1/94.9	NA/NA	80.7/19.3	5.79	NA
1800	16	5,308,483	35.1	6.1	6.1/93.9	NA/NA	81.1/18.9	NA	NA
1810	17	7,239,881	36.4	4.3	7.3/92.7	NA/NA	81.0/19.0	NA	NA
1820	23	9,638,453	33.1	5.5	7.2/92.8	50.8/49.2	81.6/18.4	NA	16.7
1830	24	12,866,020	33.5	7.4	8.8/91.2	50.8/49.2	81.9/18.1	NA	17.2
1840	26	17,069,453	32.7	9.8	10.8/89.2	50.9/49.1	83.2/16.8	NA	17.8
1850	31	23,191,876	35.9	7.9	15.3/84.7	51.0/49.0	84.3/15.7	5.55	18.9
1860	33	31,443,321	35.6	10.6	19.8/80.2	51.2/48.8	85.6/14.4	5.28	19.4
1870	37	39,818,449	26.6	13.4	25.7/74.3	50.6/49.4	86.2/13.8	5.09	20.2
1880	38	50,155,783	26.0	16.9	28.2/71.8	50.9/49.1	86.5/13.5	5.04	20.9
1890	44	62,947,714	25.5	21.2	35.1/64.9	51.2/48.8	87.5/12.5	4.93	22.0
1900	45	75,994,575	20.7	25.6	39.6/60.4	51.1/48.9	87.9/12.1	4.76	22.9
1910	46	91,972,266	21.0	31.0	45.6/54.4	51.5/48.5	88.9/11.1	4.54	24.1
1920	48	105,710,620	14.9	35.6	51.2/48.8	51.0/49.0	89.7/10.3	4.34	25.3
1930	48	122,775,046	16.1	41.2	56.1/43.9	50.6/49.4	89.8/10.2	4.11	26.4
1940	48	131,669,275	7.2	44.2	56.5/43.5	50.2/49.8	89.8/10.2	3.67	29.0
1950	48	150,697,361	14.5	50.7	64.0/36.0	49.7/50.3	89.5/10.5	3.37	30.2
1960	50	179,323,175	18.5	50.6	69.9/30.1	49.3/50.7	88.6/11.4	3.33	29.5
1970	50	203,302,031	13.4	57.4	73.6/26.4	48.7/51.3	87.6/12.4	3.14	28.0
1980	50	226,542,199	11.4	64.1	73.7/26.3	48.6/51.4	85.9/14.1	2.75	30.0
1990	50	248,718,301	9.8	70.3	75.2/24.8	48.7/51.3	83.9/16.1	2.63	32.8
2000	50	281,421,906	13.2	75.7	NA	49.1/50.9	75.1/24.9	2.59	35.3

NA = Not available.

Vital Statistics

Year	Birth Rate*	Death Rate*	Total Population	White Females	Nonwhite Females	White Males	Nonwhite Males	Marriage Rate	Divorce Rate
				Life Expectancy in Years					
1790	NA	NA	NA	NA	NA	NA	NA	NA	NA
1800	55.0	NA	NA	NA	NA	NA	NA	NA	NA
1810	54.3	NA	NA	NA	NA	NA	NA	NA	NA
1820	55.2	NA	NA	NA	NA	NA	NA	NA	NA
1830	51.4	NA	NA	NA	NA	NA	NA	NA	NA
1840	51.8	NA	NA	NA	NA	NA	NA	NA	NA
1850	43.3	NA	NA	NA	NA	NA	NA	NA	NA
1860	44.3	NA	NA	NA	NA	NA	NA	NA	NA
1870	38.3	NA	NA	NA	NA	NA	NA	NA	NA
1880	39.8	NA	NA	NA	NA	NA	NA	NA	NA
1890	31.5	NA	NA	NA	NA	NA	NA	NA	NA
1900	32.3	17.2	47.3	48.7	33.5	46.6	32.5	NA	NA
1910	30.1	14.7	50.0	52.0	37.5	48.6	33.8	NA	NA
1920	27.7	13.0	54.1	55.6	45.2	54.4	45.5	12.0	1.6
1930	21.3	11.3	59.7	63.5	49.2	59.7	47.3	9.2	1.6
1940	19.4	10.8	62.9	66.6	54.9	62.1	51.5	12.1	2.0
1950	24.1	9.6	68.2	72.2	62.9	66.5	59.1	11.1	2.6
1960	23.7	9.5	69.7	74.1	66.3	67.4	61.1	8.5	2.2
1970	18.4	9.5	70.8	75.6	69.4	68.0	61.3	10.6	3.5
1980	15.9	8.8	73.7	78.1	73.6	70.7	65.3	10.6	5.2
1990	16.6	8.6	75.4	79.4	75.2	72.7	67.0	9.8	4.7
1998	14.5†	8.8†	76.7	79.9	76.1°	74.6	68.9°	8.3	4.2

Note: Data per one thousand for Birth, Death, Marriage, and Divorce Rates.

NA = Not available. *Data for 1800, 1810, 1830, 1850, 1870, and 1890 for whites only. †Data for 1999. °Data for 1996.

Immigrants to the United States

Years	Number	Years	Number
	Immigration Totals by Decade		
1820–1830	151,824	1911–1920	5,735,811
1831–1840	599,125	1921–1930	4,107,209
1841–1850	1,713,251	1931–1940	528,431
1851–1860	2,598,214	1941–1950	1,035,039
1861–1870	2,314,824	1951–1960	2,515,479
1871–1880	2,812,191	1961–1970	3,321,677
1881–1890	5,246,613	1971–1980	4,493,314
1891–1900	3,687,546	1981–1990	7,338,062
1901–1910	8,795,386	1991–1998	7,605,068
		Total	64,599,082

Major Sources of Immigrants by Country or Region (in thousands)

Period	Asia[a]	Germany	Mexico	Italy	Great Britain (UK)[b]	Ireland	Canada	Austria and Hungary	Soviet Union (Russia)	Caribbean	Central America and South America	Norway and Sweden
1820–1830	—	8	5	—	27	54	2	—	—	4	—	—
1831–1840	—	152	7	2	76	207	14	—	—	12	—	1
1841–1850	—	435	3	2	267	781	42	—	—	14	4	14
1851–1860	42	952	3	9	424	914	59	—	—	11	2	21
1861–1870	65	787	2	12	607	436	154	8	3	9	1	109
1871–1880	124	718	5	56	548	437	384	73	39	14	1	211
1881–1890	70	1,453	2[c]	307	807	655	393	354	213	29	3	568
1891–1900	75	505	1[c]	652	272	388	3	593	505	33	2	321
1901–1910	324	341	50	2,046	526	339	179	2,145	1,597	108	25	440
1911–1920	247	144	219	1,110	341	146	742	896	921	123	59	161
1921–1930	112	412	459	455	340	211	925	64	62	75	58	166
1931–1940	17	114	22	68	32	11	109	11	1	16	14	9
1941–1950	37	227	61	58	139	20	172	28	—	50	43	21
1951–1960	153	478	300	185	203	48	378	104	—	123	136	45
1961–1970	428	191	454	214	214	33	413	26	2	470	359	33
1971–1980	1,588	74	640	129	137	11	170	16	39	741	430	10
1981–1990	2,738	92	2,336	67	160	32	157	25	58	872	930	15
1991–1998	2,347	73	1,932	58	129	55	158	21	386	823	866	15
Total	8,366	7,156	5,820	5,431	5,249	4,780	4,454	4,364	3,830	3,526	2,936	2,161

Notes: Numbers for periods are rounded. Dash indicates less than 1,000. [a]Includes Asia. [a]Includes Middle East. [b]Since 1925, includes England, Scotland, Wales, and Northern Ireland data. [c]No data available for 1886–1894.

The American Worker

Year	Total Number of Workers	Males as Percent of Total Workers	Females as Percent of Total Workers	Married Women as Percent of Female Workers	Female Workers as Percent of Female Population	Percent of Labor Force Unemployed	Percent of Workers in Labor Unions
1870	12,506,000	85	15	NA	NA	NA	NA
1880	17,392,000	85	15	NA	NA	NA	NA
1890	23,318,000	83	17	14	19	4 (1894 = 18)	NA
1900	29,073,000	82	18	15	21	5	3
1910	38,167,000	79	21	25	25	6	6
1920	41,614,000	79	21	23	24	5 (1921 = 12)	12
1930	48,830,000	78	22	29	25	9 (1933 = 25)	11.6
1940	53,011,000	76	24	36	27	15 (1944 = 1)	26.9
1950	62,208,000	72	28	52	31	5.3	31.5
1960	69,628,000	67	33	55	38	5.5	31.4
1970	82,771,000	62	38	59	43	4.9	27.3
1980	106,940,000	58	42	55	52	7.1	21.9
1990	125,840,000	55	45	54	58	5.6	16.1
1999	140,900,000[a]	54[b]	46[b]	53	60	4.2	13.9

[a]Data for 2000.

[b]Data for 1998.

NA = Not available.

The American Economy

Year	Gross National Product (GNP) and Gross Domestic Product (GDP)[a] (in $ billions)	Steel Production (in tons)	Corn Production (millions of bushels)	Automobiles Registered	New Housing Starts	Foreign Trade (in $ millions) Exports	Imports
1790	NA	NA	NA	NA	NA	20	23
1800	NA	NA	NA	NA	NA	71	91
1810	NA	NA	NA	NA	NA	67	85
1820	NA	NA	NA	NA	NA	70	74
1830	NA	NA	NA	NA	NA	74	71
1840	NA	NA	NA	NA	NA	132	107
1850	NA	NA	592[d]	NA	NA	152	178
1860	NA	13,000	839[e]	NA	NA	400	362
1870	7.4[b]	77,000	1,125	NA	NA	451	462
1880	11.2[c]	1,397,000	1,707	NA	NA	853	761
1890	13.1	4,779,000	1,650	NA	328,000	910	823
1900	18.7	11,227,000	2,662	8,000	189,000	1,499	930
1910	35.3	28,330,000	2,853	458,300	387,000 (1918 = 118,000)	1,919	1,646
1920	91.5	46,183,000	3,071	8,131,500	247,000 (1925 = 937,000)	8,664	5,784
1930	90.7	44,591,000	2,080	23,034,700	330,000 (1933 = 93,000)	4,013	3,500
1940	100.0	66,983,000	2,457	27,465,800	603,000 (1944 = 142,000)	4,030	7,433
1950	286.5	96,836,000	3,075	40,339,000	1,952,000	9,997	8,954
1960	506.5	99,282,000	4,314	61,682,300	1,365,000	19,659	15,093
1970	1,016.0	131,514,000	4,200	89,279,800	1,434,000	42,681	40,356
1980	2,819.5	111,835,000	6,600	121,601,000	1,292,000	220,626	244,871
1990	5,764.9	98,906,000	7,933	143,550,000	1,193,000	394,030	485,453
2000	9,256.1[f]	107,395,010[g]	9,970	131,839,000	1,593,000	782,000	1,217,000

[a]In December 1991 the U.S. government began featuring Gross Domestic Product rather than Gross National Product as the primary measure of U.S. production.

[b]Figure is average for 1869–1878.

[c]Figure is average for 1879–1888.

[d]Figure for 1849.

[e]Figure for 1859.

[f]Figure for 1999.

[g]Figure for 1998.

NA = Not available.

Federal Budget Outlays and Debt

Year	Defense[a]	Veterans Benefits[a]	Income Security[a]	Social Security[a]	Health and Medicare[a]	Education[a,d]	Net Interest Payments[a]	Federal Debt (dollars)
1790	14.9	4.1[b]	NA	NA	NA	NA	55.0	75,463,000[c]
1800	55.7	.6	NA	NA	NA	NA	31.3	82,976,000
1810	48.4 (1814: 79.7)	1.0	NA	NA	NA	NA	34.9	53,173,000
1820	38.4	17.6	NA	NA	NA	NA	28.1	91,016,000
1830	52.9	9.0	NA	NA	NA	NA	12.6	48,565,000
1840	54.3 (1847: 80.7)	10.7	NA	NA	NA	NA	.7	3,573,000
1850	43.8	4.7	NA	NA	NA	NA	1.0	63,453,000
1860	44.2 (1865: 88.9)	1.7	NA	NA	NA	NA	5.0	64,844,000
1870	25.7	9.2	NA	NA	NA	NA	41.7	2,436,453,000
1880	19.3	21.2	NA	NA	NA	NA	35.8	2,090,909,000
1890	20.9 (1899: 48.6)	33.6	NA	NA	NA	NA	11.4	1,222,397,000
1900	36.6	27.0	NA	NA	NA	NA	7.7	1,263,417,000
1910	45.1 (1919: 59.5)	23.2	NA	NA	NA	NA	3.1	1,146,940,000
1920	37.1	3.4	NA	NA	NA	NA	16.0	24,299,321,000
1930	25.3	6.6	NA	NA	NA	NA	19.9	16,185,310,000
1940	17.5 (1945: 89.4)	6.0	16.0	.3	.5	20.8	9.4	42,967,531,000
1950	32.2	20.3	9.6	1.8	.6	.6	11.3	256,853,000,000
1960	52.2	5.9	8.0	12.6	.9	1.0	7.5	290,525,000,000
1970	41.8	4.4	8.0	15.5	6.2	4.4	7.3	308,921,000,000
1980	22.7	3.6	14.6	20.1	9.4	5.4	8.9	909,050,000,000
1990	23.9	2.3	11.7	19.8	12.4	3.1	14.7	3,266,073,000,000
2000	16.2	2.6	14.0	22.7	19.9	3.5	12.3	5,686,338,000,000

[a]Figures represent percentage of total federal spending for each category. Not included are transportation, commerce, housing, and various other categories.

[b]1789–1791 figure.

[c]1791 figure.

[d]Includes training, employment, and social services.

NA = Not available.

The Fifty States, District of Columbia, and Puerto Rico

State	Date of Admission (with Rank)	Capital City	Population (2000) (with Rank)	Racial/Ethnic Distribution (1998)	Per Capita Personal Income (1998) (with Rank)	Total Area in Square Miles (with Rank)
Alabama (AL)	Dec. 14, 1819 (22)	Montgomery	4,447,100 (23)	White: 3,141,000; Black: 1,132,000; Hispanic: 36,000; Asian: 28,000; Native American: 15,000	$21,442 (40)	52,423 (30)
Alaska (AK)	Jan. 3, 1959 (49)	Juneau	626,932 (48)	White: 444,000; Black: 24,000; Hispanic: 19,000; Asian: 28,000; Native American: 100,000	$25,675 (20)	656,424 (1)
Arizona (AZ)	Feb. 14, 1912 (48)	Phoenix	5,130,632 (20)	White: 3,182,000; Black: 169,000; Hispanic: 963,000; Asian: 98,000; Native American: 256,000	$23,060 (35)	114,006 (6)
Arkansas (AR)	June 15, 1836 (25)	Little Rock	2,673,400 (33)	White: 2,055,000; Black: 408,000; Hispanic: 44,000; Asian: 19,000; Native American: 14,000	$20,346 (46)	53,182 (29)
California (CA)	Sept. 9, 1850 (31)	Sacramento	33,871,648 (1)	White: 16,511,000; Black: 2,456,000; Hispanic: 9,454,000; Asian: 3,938,000; Native American: 309,000	$27,503 (1)	163,707 (3)
Colorado (CO)	Aug. 1, 1876 (38)	Denver	4,301,261 (24)	White: 3,125,000; Black: 172,000; Hispanic: 541,000; Asian: 96,000; Native American: 37,000	$28,657 (18)	104,100 (8)
Connecticut (CT)	Jan. 9, 1788 (5)	Hartford	3,405,565 (29)	White: 3,125,000; Black: 172,000; Hispanic: 238,000; Asian: 96,000; Native American: 37,000	$37,598 (1)	5,544 (48)
Delaware (DE)	Dec. 7, 1787 (1)	Dover	783,600 (45)	White: 560,000; Black: 144,000; Hispanic: 22,000; Asian: 15,000; Native American: 2,000	$29,814 (6)	2,489 (49)
District of Columbia (DC)	U.S. Capital, Dec. 1, 1800	Washington (coextensive with DC)	572,059 (not ranked)	White: 149,000; Black: 326,000; Hispanic: 30,000; Asian: 16,000; Native American: 2,000	$33,433 (not ranked)	68 (not ranked)
Florida (FL)	Mar. 3, 1845 (27)	Tallahassee	15,982,378 (4)	White: 10,239,000; Black: 2,268,000; Hispanic: 2,080,000; Asian: 271,000; Native American: 58,000	$25,852 (19)	65,756 (22)
Georgia (GA)	Jan. 2, 1788 (4)	Atlanta	8,186,453 (10)	White: 5,100,000; Black: 2,181,000; Hispanic: 193,000; Asian: 149,000; Native American: 18,000	$25,020 (23)	59,441 (24)
Hawai'i (HI)	Aug. 21, 1959 (50)	Honolulu	1,211,537 (42)	White: 344,000; Black: 35,000; Hispanic: 51,000; Asian: 757,000; Native American: 7,000	$26,137 (17)	10,932 (43)
Idaho (ID)	July 3, 1890 (43)	Boise	1,293,953 (39)	White: 1,109,000; Black: 7,000; Hispanic: 82,000; Asian: 14,000; Native American: 17,000	$21,081 (43)	83,574 (14)
Illinois (IL)	Dec. 3, 1818 (21)	Springfield	12,419,293 (5)	White: 8,630,000; Black: 1,840,000; Hispanic: 1,145,000; Asian: 403,000; Native American: 27,000	$28,873 (8)	57,918 (25)

The Fifty States, District of Columbia, and Puerto Rico (continued)

State	Date of Admission (with Rank)	Capital City	Population (2000) (with Rank)	Racial/Ethnic Distribution (1998)	Per Capita Personal Income (1998) (with Rank)	Total Area in Square Miles (with Rank)
Indiana (IN)	Dec. 11, 1816 (19)	Indianapolis	6,080,485 (14)	White: 5,206,000; Black: 491,000; Hispanic: 132,000; Asian: 56,000; Native American: 15,000	$24,219 (29)	36,420 (38)
Iowa (IA)	Dec. 28, 1846 (29)	Des Moines	2,926,324 (30)	White: 2,709,000; Black: 57,000; Hispanic: 52,000; Asian: 36,000; Native American: 8,000	$23,925 (32)	56,276 (26)
Kansas (KS)	Jan. 29, 1861 (34)	Topeka	2,688,418 (32)	White: 2,278,000; Black: 155,000; Hispanic: 137,000; Asian: 46,000; Native American: 23,000	$24,981 (24)	82,282 (15)
Kentucky (KY)	June 1, 1792 (15)	Frankfort	4,041,769 (25)	White: 3,591,000; Black: 285,000; Hispanic: 28,000; Asian: 27,000; Native American: 6,000	$21,506 (39)	40,411 (37)
Louisiana (LA)	Apr. 30, 1812 (18)	Baton Rouge	4,408,976 (22)	White: 2,787,000; Black: 1,407,000; Hispanic: 100,000; Asian: 55,000; Native American: 19,000	$21,346 (41)	51,843 (31)
Maine (ME)	Mar. 15, 1820 (23)	Augusta	1,274,923 (40)	White: 1,215,000; Black: 6,000; Hispanic: 8,000; Asian: 9,000; Native American: 6,000	$22,952 (36)	35,387 (39)
Maryland (MD)	Apr. 28, 1788 (7)	Annapolis	5,296,486 (19)	White: 3,329,000; Black: 1,428,000; Hispanic: 158,000; Asian: 204,000; Native American: 16,000	$29,943 (5)	12,407 (42)
Massachusetts (MA)	Feb. 6, 1788 (6)	Boston	6,349,097 (13)	White: 5,217,000; Black: 395,000; Hispanic: 298,000; Asian: 223,000; Native American: 15,000	$32,797 (3)	10,555 (44)
Michigan (MI)	Jan. 26, 1837 (26)	Lansing	9,938,444 (8)	White: 7,961,000; Black: 1,405,000; Hispanic: 234,000; Asian: 158,000; Native American: 60,000	$25,857 (18)	96,705 (11)
Minnesota (MN)	May 11, 1858 (32)	Saint Paul	4,919,479 (21)	White: 4,328,000; Black: 141,000; Hispanic: 76,000; Asian: 124,000; Native American: 58,000	$27,510 (11)	86,943 (12)
Mississippi (MS)	Dec. 10, 1817 (20)	Jackson	2,844,658 (31)	White: 1,701,000; Black: 1,003,000; Hispanic: 18,000; Asian: 19,000; Native American: 10,000	$18,958 (50)	48,434 (32)
Missouri (MO)	Aug. 10, 1821 (24)	Jefferson City	5,595,211 (17)	White: 4,668,000; Black: 613,000; Hispanic: 77,000; Asian: 60,000; Native American: 21,000	$24,427 (28)	69,709 (21)
Montana (MT)	Nov. 8, 1889 (41)	Helena	902,195 (44)	White: 803,000; Black: 3,000; Hispanic: 13,000; Asian: 5,000; Native American: 56,000	$20,172 (47)	147,046 (4)
Nebraska (NE)	Mar. 1, 1867 (37)	Lincoln	1,711,263 (38)	White: 1,493,000; Black: 67,000; Hispanic: 66,000; Asian: 22,000; Native American: 15,000	$24,754 (27)	77,358 (16)
Nevada (NV)	Oct. 3, 1864 (36)	Carson City	1,998,257 (35)	White: 1,248,000; Black: 133,000; Hispanic: 253,000; Asian: 81,000; Native American: 31,000	$27,200 (14)	110,567 (7)

The Fifty States, District of Columbia, and Puerto Rico (continued)

State	Date of Admission (with Rank)	Capital City	Population (2000) (with Rank)	Racial/Ethnic Distribution (1998)	Per Capita Personal Income (1998) (with Rank)	Total Area in Square Miles (with Rank)
New Hampshire (NH)	June 21, 1788 (9)	Concord	1,235,786 (41)	White: 1,109,000; Black: 9,000; Hispanic: 16,000; Asian: 14,000; Native American: 2,000	$29,022 (7)	9,351 (46)
New Jersey (NJ)	Dec. 18, 1787 (3)	Trenton	8,414,350 (9)	White: 5,586,000; Black: 1,188,000; Hispanic: 866,000; Asian: 453,000; Native American: 22,000	$33,937 (2)	8,722 (47)
New Mexico (NM)	Jan. 6, 1912 (47)	Santa Fe	1,819,046 (36)	White: 834,000; Black: 45,000; Hispanic: 669,000; Asian: 26,000; Native American: 163,000	$19,936 (48)	121,598 (5)
New York (NY)	July 26, 1788 (11)	Albany	18,976,457 (3)	White: 11,895,000; Black: 3,220,000; Hispanic: 1,990,000; Asian: 995,000; Native American: 76,000	$31,734 (4)	54,471 (27)
North Carolina (NC)	Nov. 21, 1789 (12)	Raleigh	8,049,313 (11)	White: 5,545,000; Black: 1,665,000 Hispanic: 139,000; Asian: 100,000; Native American: 98,000	$24,036 (31)	53,821 (28)
North Dakota (ND)	Nov. 2, 1889 (39)	Bismarck	642,200 (47)	White: 593,000; Black: 4,000; Hispanic: 6,000; Asian: 5,000; Native American: 30,000	$21,675 (38)	70,704 (19)
Ohio (OH)	Mar. 1, 1803 (17)	Columbus	11,353,140 (7)	White: 9,610,000; Black: 1,290,000; Hispanic: 158,000; Asian: 129,000; Native American: 23,000	$25,134 (21)	44,828 (34)
Oklahoma (OK)	Nov. 16, 1907 (46)	Oklahoma City	3,450,654 (27)	White: 2,668,000; Black: 262,000; Hispanic: 109,000; Asian: 45,000; Native American: 263,000	$21,072 (44)	69,903 (20)
Oregon (OR)	Feb. 14, 1859 (33)	Salem	3,421,399 (28)	White: 2,888,000; Black: 61,000; Hispanic: 182,000; Asian: 106,000; Native American: 45,000	$24,766 (26)	98,386 (9)
Pennsylvania (PA)	Dec. 12, 1787 (2)	Harrisburg	12,281,054 (6)	White: 10,354,000; Black: 1,166,000; Hispanic: 265,000; Asian: 198,000; Native American: 18,000	$26,792 (16)	46,058 (33)
Puerto Rico (PR)	Ascession 1898; Common-wealth Status 1952	San Juan	3,808,610 (not ranked)	White: <1,000; Black: <1,000; Hispanic: 3,856,000; Asian: <1,000	$7,882* (not ranked)	3,427* (not ranked)
Rhode Island (RI)	May 29, 1790 (13)	Providence	1,048,319 (43)	White: 859,000; Black: 49,000; Hispanic: 52,000; Asian: 23,000; Native American: 5,000	$26,797 (15)	1,545 (50)
South Carolina (SC)	May 23, 1788 (8)	Columbia	4,012,012 (26)	White: 2,603,000; Black: 1,147,000; Hispanic: 42,000; Asian: 34,000; Native American: 9,000	$21,309 (42)	32,008 (40)
South Dakota (SD)	Nov. 2, 1889 (40)	Pierre	754,844 (46)	White: 662,000; Black: 5,000; Hispanic: 7,000; Asian: 5,000; Native American: 59,000	$22,114 (37)	77,121 (17)
Tennessee (TN)	June 1, 1796 (16)	Nashville	5,689,283 (16)	White: 4,413,000; Black: 900,000; Hispanic: 54,000; Asian: 53,000; Native American: 12,000	$23,559 (33)	42,149 (36)

The Fifty States, District of Columbia, and Puerto Rico (continued)

State	Date of Admission (with Rank)	Capital City	Population (2000) (with Rank)	Racial/Ethnic Distribution (1998)	Per Capita Personal Income (1998) (with Rank)	Total Area in Square Miles (with Rank)
Texas (TX)	Dec. 29, 1845 (28)	Austin	20,851,820 (2)	White: 11,038,000; Black: 2,430,000; Hispanic: 5,640,000; Asian: 556,000; Native American: 96,000	$24,957 (25)	268,601 (2)
Utah (UT)	Jan. 4, 1896 (45)	Salt Lake City	2,233,169 (32)	White: 1,866,000; Black: 19,000; Hispanic: 132,000; Asian: 53,000; Native American: 30,000	$21,019 (45)	84,904 (13)
Vermont (VT)	Mar. 4, 1791 (14)	Montpelier	608,827 (49)	White: 577,000; Black: 3,000; Hispanic: 5,000; Asian: 5,000; Native American: 2,000	$24,175 (30)	9,615 (45)
Virginia (VA)	June 25, 1788 (10)	Richmond	7,078,515 (12)	White: 4,943,000; Black: 1,363,000 Hispanic: 220,000; Asian: 247,000; Native American: 19,000	$27,385 (13)	42,777 (35)
Washington (WA)	Nov. 11, 1889 (42)	Olympia	5,894,121 (15)	White: 4,743,000; Black: 198,000; Hispanic: 315,000; Asian: 330,000; Native American: 103,000	$27,961 (11)	71,302 (18)
West Virginia (WV)	June 20, 1863 (35)	Charleston	1,808,344 (37)	White: 1,732,000; Black: 58,000; Hispanic: 9,000; Asian: 9,000; Native American: 3,000	$19,362 (49)	24,231 (41)
Wisconsin (WI)	May 29, 1848 (30)	Madison	5,363,675 (18)	White: 4,687,000; Black: 291,000; Hispanic: 120,000; Asian: 80,000; Native American: 56,000	$25,079 (22)	65,499 (23)
Wyoming (WY)	July 10, 1890 (44)	Cheyenne	493,782 (50)	White: 435,000; Black: 4,000; Hispanic: 27,000; Asian: 4,000; Native American: 11,000	$23,167 (34)	97,818 (10)

*1996 figure.

Presidential Elections

Year	Number of States	Candidates	Parties	Popular Vote	% of Popular Vote	Electoral Vote	% Voter Participation[a]
1789	10	**George Washington**	No party			69	
		John Adams	designations			34	
		Other candidates				35	
1792	15	**George Washington**	No party			132	
		John Adams	designations			77	
		George Clinton				50	
		Other candidates				5	
1796	16	**John Adams**	Federalist			71	
		Thomas Jefferson	Democratic-Republican			68	
		Thomas Pinckney	Federalist			59	
		Aaron Burr	Democratic-Republican			30	
		Other candidates				48	
1800	16	**Thomas Jefferson**	Democratic-Republican			73	
		Aaron Burr	Democratic-Republican			73	
		John Adams	Federalist			65	
		Charles C. Pinckney	Federalist			64	
		John Jay	Federalist			1	
1804	17	**Thomas Jefferson**	Democratic-Republican			162	
		Charles C. Pinckney	Federalist			14	
1808	17	**James Madison**	Democratic-Republican			122	
		Charles C. Pinckney	Federalist			47	
		George Clinton	Democratic-Republican			6	
1812	18	**James Madison**	Democratic-Republican			128	
		DeWitt Clinton	Federalist			89	
1816	19	**James Monroe**	Democratic-Republican			183	
		Rufus King	Federalist			34	
1820	24	**James Monroe**	Democratic-Republican			231	

Presidential Elections (continued)

Year	Number of States	Candidates	Parties	Popular Vote	% of Popular Vote	Electoral Vote	% Voter Partici- pation[a]
		John Quincy Adams	Independent Republican			1	
1824	24	**John Quincy Adams**	Democratic- Republican	108,740	30.5	84	26.9
		Andrew Jackson	Democratic- Republican	153,544	43.1	99	
		Henry Clay	Democratic- Republican	47,136	13.2	37	
		William H. Crawford	Democratic- Republican	46,618	13.1	41	
1828	24	**Andrew Jackson**	Democratic	647,286	56.0	178	57.6
		John Quincy Adams	National Republican	508,064	44.0	83	
1832	24	**Andrew Jackson**	Democratic	701,780	54.2	219	55.4
		Henry Clay	National Republican	484,205	37.4	49	
		Other candidates		107,988	8.0	18	
1836	26	**Martin Van Buren**	Democratic	764,176	50.8	170	57.8
		William H. Harrison	Whig	550,816	36.6	73	
		Hugh L. White	Whig	146,107	9.7	26	
1840	26	**William H. Harrison**	Whig	1,274,624	53.1	234	80.2
		Martin Van Buren	Democratic	1,127,781	46.9	60	
1844	26	**James K. Polk**	Democratic	1,338,464	49.6	170	78.9
		Henry Clay	Whig	1,300,097	48.1	105	
		James G. Birney	Liberty	62,300	2.3		
1848	30	**Zachary Taylor**	Whig	1,360,967	47.4	163	72.7
		Lewis Cass	Democratic	1,222,342	42.5	127	
		Martin Van Buren	Free Soil	291,263	10.1		
1852	31	**Franklin Pierce**	Democratic	1,601,117	50.9	254	69.6
		Winfield Scott	Whig	1,385,453	44.1	42	
		John P. Hale	Free Soil	155,825	5.0		
1856	31	**James Buchanan**	Democratic	1,832,955	45.3	174	78.9
		John C. Frémont	Republican	1,339,932	33.1	114	
		Millard Fillmore	American	871,731	21.6	8	
1860	33	**Abraham Lincoln**	Republican	1,865,593	39.8	180	81.2
		Stephen A. Douglas	Democratic	1,382,713	29.5	12	
		John C. Breckinridge	Democratic	848,356	18.1	72	
		John Bell	Constitutional Union	592,906	12.6	39	
1864	36	**Abraham Lincoln**	Republican	2,206,938	55.0	212	73.8
		George B. McClellan	Democratic	1,803,787	45.0	21	

Presidential Elections (continued)

Year	Number of States	Candidates	Parties	Popular Vote	% of Popular Vote	Elec-toral Vote	% Voter Partici-pation[a]
1868	37	**Ulysses S. Grant**	Republican	3,013,421	52.7	214	78.1
		Horatio Seymour	Democratic	2,706,829	47.3	80	
1872	37	**Ulysses S. Grant**	Republican	3,596,745	55.6	286	71.3
		Horace Greeley	Democratic	2,843,446	43.9	[b]	
1876	38	**Rutherford B. Hayes**	Republican	4,036,572	48.0	185	81.8
		Samuel J. Tilden	Democratic	4,284,020	51.0	184	
1880	38	**James A. Garfield**	Republican	4,453,295	48.5	214	79.4
		Winfield S. Hancock	Democratic	4,414,082	48.1	155	
		James B. Weaver	Greenback-Labor	308,578	3.4		
1884	38	**Grover Cleveland**	Democratic	4,879,507	48.5	219	77.5
		James G. Blaine	Republican	4,850,293	48.2	182	
		Benjamin F. Butler	Greenback-Labor	175,370	1.8		
		John P. St. John	Prohibition	150,369	1.5		
1888	38	**Benjamin Harrison**	Republican	5,447,129	47.9	233	79.3
		Grover Cleveland	Democratic	5,537,857	48.6	168	
		Clinton B. Fisk	Prohibition	249,506	2.2		
		Anson J. Streeter	Union Labor	146,935	1.3		
1892	44	**Grover Cleveland**	Democratic	5,555,426	46.1	277	74.7
		Benjamin Harrison	Republican	5,182,690	43.0	145	
		James B. Weaver	People's	1,029,846	8.5	22	
		John Bidwell	Prohibition	264,133	2.2		
1896	45	**William McKinley**	Republican	7,102,246	51.1	271	79.3
		William J. Bryan	Democratic	6,492,559	47.7	176	
1900	45	**William McKinley**	Republican	7,218,491	51.7	292	73.2
		William J. Bryan	Democratic; Populist	6,356,734	45.5	155	
		John C. Wooley	Prohibition	208,914	1.5		
1904	45	**Theodore Roosevelt**	Republican	7,628,461	57.4	336	65.2
		Alton B. Parker	Democratic	5,084,223	37.6	140	
		Eugene V. Debs	Socialist	402,283	3.0		
		Silas C. Swallow	Prohibition	258,536	1.9		
1908	46	**William H. Taft**	Republican	7,675,320	51.6	321	65.4
		William J. Bryan	Democratic	6,412,294	43.1	162	
		Eugene V. Debs	Socialist	420,793	2.8		
		Eugene W. Chafin	Prohibition	253,840	1.7		
1912	48	**Woodrow Wilson**	Democratic	6,296,547	41.9	435	58.8
		Theodore Roosevelt	Progressive	4,118,571	27.4	88	
		William H. Taft	Republican	3,486,720	23.2	8	
		Eugene V. Debs	Socialist	900,672	6.0		

Presidential Elections (continued)

Year	Number of States	Candidates	Parties	Popular Vote	% of Popular Vote	Electoral Vote	% Voter Participation[a]
		Eugene W. Chafin	Prohibition	206,275	1.4		
1916	48	**Woodrow Wilson**	Democratic	9,127,695	49.4	277	61.6
		Charles E. Hughes	Republican	8,533,507	46.2	254	
		A. L. Benson	Socialist	585,113	3.2		
		J. Frank Hanly	Prohibition	220,506	1.2		
1920	48	**Warren G. Harding**	Republican	16,143,407	60.4	404	49.2
		James M. Cox	Democratic	9,130,328	34.2	127	
		Eugene V. Debs	Socialist	919,799	3.4		
		P. P. Christensen	Farmer-Labor	265,411	1.0		
1924	48	**Calvin Coolidge**	Republican	15,718,211	54.0	382	48.9
		John W. Davis	Democratic	8,385,283	28.8	136	
		Robert M. La Follette	Progressive	4,831,289	16.6	13	
1928	48	**Herbert C. Hoover**	Republican	21,391,993	58.2	444	56.9
		Alfred E. Smith	Democratic	15,016,169	40.9	87	
1932	48	**Franklin D. Roosevelt**	Democratic	22,809,638	57.4	472	56.9
		Herbert C. Hoover	Republican	15,758,901	39.7	59	
		Norman Thomas	Socialist	881,951	2.2		
1936	48	**Franklin D. Roosevelt**	Democratic	27,752,869	60.8	523	61.0
		Alfred M. Landon	Republican	16,674,665	36.5	8	
		William Lemke	Union	882,479	1.9		
1940	48	**Franklin D. Roosevelt**	Democratic	27,307,819	54.8	449	62.5
		Wendell L. Wilkie	Republican	22,321,018	44.8	82	
1944	48	**Franklin D. Roosevelt**	Democratic	25,606,585	53.5	432	55.9
		Thomas E. Dewey	Republican	22,014,745	46.0	99	
1948	48	**Harry S Truman**	Democratic	24,179,345	49.6	303	53.0
		Thomas E. Dewey	Republican	21,991,291	45.1	189	
		J. Strom Thurmond	States' Rights	1,176,125	2.4	39	
		Henry A. Wallace	Progressive	1,157,326	2.4		
1952	48	**Dwight D. Eisenhower**	Republican	33,936,234	55.1	442	63.3
		Adlai E. Stevenson	Democratic	27,314,992	44.4	89	
1956	48	**Dwight D. Eisenhower**	Republican	35,590,472	57.6	457	60.6
		Adlai E. Stevenson	Democratic	26,022,752	42.1	73	
1960	50	**John F. Kennedy**	Democratic	34,226,731	49.7	303	62.8
		Richard M. Nixon	Republican	34,108,157	49.5	219	
1964	50	**Lyndon B. Johnson**	Democratic	43,129,566	61.1	486	61.7
		Barry M. Goldwater	Republican	27,178,188	38.5	52	
1968	50	**Richard M. Nixon**	Republican	31,785,480	43.4	301	60.6
		Hubert H. Humphrey	Democratic	31,275,166	42.7	191	

Presidential Elections (continued)

Year	Number of States	Candidates	Parties	Popular Vote	% of Popular Vote	Electoral Vote	% Voter Participation[a]
		George C. Wallace	American Independent	9,906,473	13.5	46	
1972	50	**Richard M. Nixon**	Republican	47,169,911	60.7	520	55.2
		George S. McGovern	Democratic	29,170,383	37.5	17	
		John G. Schmitz	American	1,099,482	1.4		
1976	50	**James E. Carter**	Democratic	40,830,763	50.1	297	53.5
		Gerald R. Ford	Republican	39,147,793	48.0	240	
1980	50	**Ronald W. Reagan**	Republican	43,904,153	50.7	489	52.6
		James E. Carter	Democratic	35,483,883	41.0	49	
		John B. Anderson	Independent	5,720,060	6.6	0	
		Ed Clark	Libertarian	921,299	1.1	0	
1984	50	**Ronald W. Reagan**	Republican	54,455,075	58.8	525	53.3
		Walter F. Mondale	Democratic	37,577,185	40.6	13	
1988	50	**George H. W. Bush**	Republican	48,886,097	53.4	426	50.1
		Michael S. Dukakis	Democratic	41,809,074	45.6	111[c]	
1992	50	**William J. Clinton**	Democratic	44,909,326	43.0	370	55.2
		George H. W. Bush	Republican	39,103,882	37.4	168	
		H. Ross Perot	Independent	19,741,048	18.9	0	
1996	50	**William J. Clinton**	Democratic	47,402,357	49.2	379	49.1
		Robert J. Dole	Republican	39,196,755	40.7	159	
		H. Ross Perot	Reform	8,085,402	8.4	0	
		Ralph Nader	Green	684,902	0.7	0	
2000	50	**George W. Bush**	Republican	50,455,156	47.87	271	51.2
		Albert Gore	Democratic	50,992,335	48.38	266	

Candidates receiving less than 1 percent of the popular vote have been omitted. Thus the percentage of popular vote given for any election year may not total 100 percent.

Before the passage of the Twelfth Amendment in 1804, the Electoral College voted for two presidential candidates; the runner-up became vice president.

Before 1824, most presidential electors were chosen by state legislatures, not by popular vote.

[a]Percent of voting-age population casting ballots.

[b]Greeley died shortly after the election; the electors supporting him then divided their votes among minor candidates.

[c]One elector from West Virginia cast her Electoral College presidential ballot for Lloyd Bentsen, the Democratic Party's vice-presidential candidate.

Presidents and Vice Presidents

1. President	**George Washington**	1789–1797		18. President	**Ulysses S. Grant**	1869–1877
Vice President	John Adams	1789–1797		Vice President	Schuyler Colfax	1869–1873
2. President	**John Adams**	1797–1801		Vice President	Henry Wilson	1873–1877
Vice President	Thomas Jefferson	1797–1801		19. President	**Rutherford B. Hayes**	1877–1881
3. President	**Thomas Jefferson**	1801–1809		Vice President	William A. Wheeler	1877–1881
Vice President	Aaron Burr	1801–1805		20. President	**James A. Garfield**	1881
Vice President	George Clinton	1805–1809		Vice President	Chester A. Arthur	1881
4. President	**James Madison**	1809–1817		21. President	**Chester A. Arthur**	1881–1885
Vice President	George Clinton	1809–1813		Vice President	None	
Vice President	Elbridge Gerry	1813–1817		22. President	**Grover Cleveland**	1885–1889
5. President	**James Monroe**	1817–1825		Vice President	Thomas A. Hendricks	1885–1889
Vice President	Daniel Tompkins	1817–1825		23. President	**Benjamin Harrison**	1889–1893
6. President	**John Quincy Adams**	1825–1829		Vice President	Levi P. Morton	1889–1893
Vice President	John C. Calhoun	1825–1829		24. President	**Grover Cleveland**	1893–1897
7. President	**Andrew Jackson**	1829–1837		Vice President	Adlai E. Stevenson	1893–1897
Vice President	John C. Calhoun	1829–1833		25. President	**William McKinley**	1897–1901
Vice President	Martin Van Buren	1833–1837		Vice President	Garret A. Hobart	1897–1901
8. President	**Martin Van Buren**	1837–1841		Vice President	Theodore Roosevelt	1901
Vice President	Richard M. Johnson	1837–1841		26. President	**Theodore Roosevelt**	1901–1909
9. President	**William H. Harrison**	1841		Vice President	Charles Fairbanks	1905–1909
Vice President	John Tyler	1841		27. President	**William H. Taft**	1909–1913
10. President	**John Tyler**	1841–1845		Vice President	James S. Sherman	1909–1913
Vice President	None			28. President	**Woodrow Wilson**	1913–1921
11. President	**James K. Polk**	1845–1849		Vice President	Thomas R. Marshall	1913–1921
Vice President	George M. Dallas	1845–1849		29. President	**Warren G. Harding**	1921–1923
12. President	**Zachary Taylor**	1849–1850		Vice President	Calvin Coolidge	1921–1923
Vice President	Millard Fillmore	1849–1850		30. President	**Calvin Coolidge**	1923–1929
13. President	**Millard Fillmore**	1850–1853		Vice President	Charles G. Dawes	1925–1929
Vice President	None			31. President	**Herbert C. Hoover**	1929–1933
14. President	**Franklin Pierce**	1853–1857		Vice President	Charles Curtis	1929–1933
Vice President	William R. King	1853–1857		32. President	**Franklin D. Roosevelt**	1933–1945
15. President	**James Buchanan**	1857–1861		Vice President	John N. Garner	1933–1941
Vice President	John C. Breckinridge	1857–1861		Vice President	Henry A. Wallace	1941–1945
16. President	**Abraham Lincoln**	1861–1865		Vice President	Harry S Truman	1945
Vice President	Hannibal Hamlin	1861–1865		33. President	**Harry S Truman**	1945–1953
Vice President	Andrew Johnson	1865		Vice President	Alben W. Barkley	1949–1953
17. President	**Andrew Johnson**	1865–1869		34. President	**Dwight D. Eisenhower**	1953–1961
Vice President	None			Vice President	Richard M. Nixon	1953–1961

Presidents and Vice Presidents (continued)

35. President	**John F. Kennedy**	1961–1963		40. President	**Ronald W. Reagan**	1981–1989
Vice President	Lyndon B. Johnson	1961–1963		Vice President	George H. W. Bush	1981–1989
36. President	**Lyndon B. Johnson**	1963–1969		41. President	**George H. W. Bush**	1989–1993
Vice President	Hubert H. Humphrey	1965–1969		Vice President	J. Danforth Quayle	1989–1993
37. President	**Richard M. Nixon**	1969–1974		42. President	**William J. Clinton**	1993–2001
Vice President	Spiro T. Agnew	1969–1973		Vice President	Albert Gore	1993–2001
Vice President	Gerald R. Ford	1973–1974		43. President	**George W. Bush**	2001–
38. President	**Gerald R. Ford**	1974–1977		Vice President	Richard Cheney	2001–
Vice President	Nelson A. Rockefeller	1974–1977				
39. President	**James E. Carter**	1977–1981				
Vice President	Walter F. Mondale	1977–1981				

For a complete list of Presidents, Vice Presidents, and Cabinet Members, go to college.hmco.com.

Party Strength in Congress

Period	Congress	House Majority Party		House Minority Party		Others	Senate Majority Party		Senate Minority Party		Others	Party of President	
1789–91	1st	Ad	38	Op	26		Ad	17	Op	9		F	Washington
1791–93	2nd	F	37	DR	33		F	16	DR	13		F	Washington
1793–95	3rd	DR	57	F	48		F	17	DR	13		F	Washington
1795–97	4th	F	54	DR	52		F	19	DR	13		F	Washington
1797–99	5th	F	58	DR	48		F	20	DR	12		F	J. Adams
1799–1801	6th	F	64	DR	42		F	19	DR	13		F	J. Adams
1801–03	7th	DR	69	F	36		DR	18	F	13		DR	Jefferson
1803–05	8th	DR	102	F	39		DR	25	F	9		DR	Jefferson
1805–07	9th	DR	116	F	25		DR	27	F	7		DR	Jefferson
1807–09	10th	DR	118	F	24		DR	28	F	6		DR	Jefferson
1809–11	11th	DR	94	F	48		DR	28	F	6		DR	Madison
1811–13	12th	DR	108	F	36		DR	30	F	6		DR	Madison
1813–15	13th	DR	112	F	68		DR	27	F	9		DR	Madison
1815–17	14th	DR	117	F	65		DR	25	F	11		DR	Madison
1817–19	15th	DR	141	F	42		DR	34	F	10		DR	Monroe
1819–21	16th	DR	156	F	27		DR	35	F	7		DR	Monroe
1821–23	17th	DR	158	F	25		DR	44	F	4		DR	Monroe
1823–25	18th	DR	187	F	26		DR	44	F	4		DR	Monroe
1825–27	19th	Ad	105	J	97		Ad	26	J	20		C	J. Q. Adams
1827–29	20th	J	119	Ad	94		J	28	Ad	20		C	J. Q. Adams
1829–31	21st	D	139	NR	74		D	26	NR	22		D	Jackson
1831–33	22nd	D	141	NR	58	14	D	25	NR	21	2	D	Jackson
1833–35	23rd	D	147	AM	53	60	D	20	NR	20	8	D	Jackson
1835–37	24th	D	145	W	98		D	27	W	25		D	Jackson
1837–39	25th	D	108	W	107	24	D	30	W	18	4	D	Van Buren
1839–41	26th	D	124	W	118		D	28	W	22		D	Van Buren
1841–43	27th	W	133	D	102	6	W	28	D	22	2	W	W. Harrison
												W	Tyler
1843–45	28th	D	142	W	79	1	W	28	D	25	1	W	Tyler
1845–47	29th	D	143	W	77	6	D	31	W	25		D	Polk
1847–49	30th	W	115	D	108	4	D	36	W	21	1	D	Polk
1849–51	31st	D	112	W	109	9	D	35	W	25	2	W	Taylor
												W	Fillmore
1851–53	32nd	D	140	W	88	5	D	35	W	24	3	W	Fillmore
1853–55	33rd	D	159	W	71	4	D	38	W	22	2	D	Pierce
1855–57	34th	R	108	D	83	43	D	40	R	15	5	D	Pierce
1857–59	35th	D	118	R	92	26	D	36	R	20	8	D	Buchanan
1859–61	36th	R	114	D	92	31	D	36	R	26	4	D	Buchanan

Party Strength in Congress (continued)

Period	Congress	House Majority Party		House Minority Party		House Others	Senate Majority Party		Senate Minority Party		Senate Others	Party of President	
1861–63	37th	R	105	D	43	30	R	31	D	10	8	R	Lincoln
1863–65	38th	R	102	D	75	9	R	36	D	9	5	R	Lincoln
1865–67	39th	U	149	D	42		U	42	D	10		R	Lincoln
												R	A. Johnson
1867–69	40th	R	143	D	49		R	42	D	11		R	A. Johnson
1869–71	41st	R	149	D	63		R	56	D	11		R	Grant
1871–73	42nd	R	134	D	104	5	R	52	D	17	5	R	Grant
1873–75	43rd	R	194	D	92	14	R	49	D	19	5	R	Grant
1875–77	44th	D	169	R	109	14	R	45	D	29	2	R	Grant
1877–79	45th	D	153	R	140		R	39	D	36	1	R	Hayes
1879–81	46th	D	149	R	130	14	D	42	R	33	1	R	Hayes
1881–83	47th	D	147	R	135	11	R	37	D	37	1	R	Garfield
												R	Arthur
1883–85	48th	D	197	R	118	10	R	38	D	36	2	R	Arthur
1885–87	49th	D	183	R	140	2	R	43	D	34		D	Cleveland
1887–89	50th	D	169	R	152	4	R	39	D	37		D	Cleveland
1889–91	51st	R	166	D	159		R	39	D	37		R	B. Harrison
1891–93	52nd	D	235	R	88	9	R	47	D	39	2	R	B. Harrison
1893–95	53rd	D	218	R	127	11	D	44	R	38	3	D	Cleveland
1895–97	54th	R	244	D	105	7	R	43	D	39	6	D	Cleveland
1897–99	55th	R	204	D	113	40	R	47	D	34	7	R	McKinley
1899–1901	56th	R	185	D	163	9	R	53	D	26	8	R	McKinley
1901–03	57th	R	197	D	151	9	R	55	D	31	4	R	McKinley
												R	T. Roosevelt
1903–05	58th	R	208	D	178		R	57	D	33		R	T. Roosevelt
1905–07	59th	R	250	D	136		R	57	D	33		R	T. Roosevelt
1907–09	60th	R	222	D	164		R	61	D	31		R	T. Roosevelt
1909–11	61st	R	219	D	172		R	61	D	32		R	Taft
1911–13	62nd	D	228	R	161	1	R	51	D	41		R	Taft
1913–15	63rd	D	291	R	127	17	D	51	R	44	1	D	Wilson
1915–17	64th	D	230	R	196	9	D	56	R	40		D	Wilson
1917–19	65th	D	216	R	210	6	D	53	R	42		D	Wilson
1919–21	66th	R	240	D	190	3	R	49	D	47		D	Wilson
1921–23	67th	R	301	D	131	1	R	59	D	37		R	Harding
1923–25	68th	R	225	D	205	5	R	51	D	43	2	R	Coolidge
1925–27	69th	R	247	D	183	4	R	56	D	39	1	R	Coolidge
1927–29	70th	R	237	D	195	3	R	49	D	46	1	R	Coolidge
1929–31	71st	R	267	D	167	1	R	56	D	39	1	R	Hoover
1931–33	72nd	D	220	R	214	1	R	48	D	47	1	R	Hoover
1933–35	73rd	D	310	R	117	5	D	60	R	35	1	D	F. Roosevelt
1935–37	74th	D	319	R	103	10	D	69	R	25	2	D	F. Roosevelt
1937–39	75th	D	331	R	89	13	D	76	R	16	4	D	F. Roosevelt

Party Strength in Congress (continued)

Period	Congress	House Majority Party		House Minority Party		Others	Senate Majority Party		Senate Minority Party		Others	Party of President	
1939–41	76th	D	261	R	164	4	D	69	R	23	4	D	F. Roosevelt
1941–43	77th	D	268	R	162	5	D	66	R	28	2	D	F. Roosevelt
1943–45	78th	D	218	R	208	4	D	58	R	37	1	D	F. Roosevelt
1945–47	79th	D	242	R	190	2	D	56	R	38	1	D	Truman
1947–49	80th	R	245	D	188	1	R	51	D	45		D	Truman
1949–51	81st	D	263	R	171	1	D	54	R	42		D	Truman
1951–53	82nd	D	234	R	199	1	D	49	R	47		D	Truman
1953–55	83rd	R	221	D	211	1	R	48	D	47	1	R	Eisenhower
1955–57	84th	D	232	R	203		D	48	R	47	1	R	Eisenhower
1957–59	85th	D	233	R	200		D	49	R	47		R	Eisenhower
1959–61	86th	D	284	R	153		D	65	R	35		R	Eisenhower
1961–63	87th	D	263	R	174		D	65	R	35		D	Kennedy
1963–65	88th	D	258	R	117		D	67	R	33		D	Kennedy
												D	L. Johnson
1965–67	89th	D	295	R	140		D	68	R	32		D	L. Johnson
1967–69	90th	D	246	R	187		D	64	R	36		D	L. Johnson
1969–71	91st	D	245	R	189		D	57	R	43		R	Nixon
1971–73	92nd	D	254	R	180		D	54	R	44	2	R	Nixon
1973–75	93rd	D	239	R	192	1	D	56	R	42	2	R	Nixon
1975–77	94th	D	291	R	144		D	60	R	37	3	R	Ford
1977–79	95th	D	292	R	143		D	61	R	38	1	D	Carter
1979–81	96th	D	276	R	157		D	58	R	41	1	D	Carter
1981–83	97th	D	243	R	192		R	53	D	46	1	R	Reagan
1983–85	98th	D	269	R	166		R	54	D	46		R	Reagan
1985–87	99th	D	253	R	182		R	53	D	47		R	Reagan
1987–89	100th	D	258	R	177		D	55	R	45		R	Reagan
1989–91	101st	D	259	R	174		D	55	R	45		R	Bush
1991–93	102nd	D	267	R	167	1	D	56	R	44		R	Bush
1993–95	103rd	D	258	R	176	1	D	57	R	43		D	Clinton
1995–97	104th	R	230	D	204	1	R	52	D	48		D	Clinton
1997–99	105th	R	227	D	207	1	R	55	D	45		D	Clinton
1999–2001	106th	R	223	D	211	1	R	55	D	45		D	Clinton
2001–2003	107th	R	221	D	212	2	D	50	R	49	1	R	Bush

AD = Administration; AM = Anti-Masonic; C = Coalition; D = Democratic; DR = Democratic-Republican; F = Federalist; J = Jacksonian; NR = National Republican; Op = Opposition; R = Republican; U = Unionist; W = Whig. Figures are for the beginning of the first session of each Congress, except the 93rd, which are for the beginning of the second session.

Justices of the Supreme Court

	Term of Service	Years of Service	Life Span		Term of Service	Years of Service	Life Span
John Jay	1789–1795	5	1745–1829	Joseph P. Bradley	1870–1892	22	1813–1892
John Rutledge	1789–1791	1	1739–1800	Ward Hunt	1873–1882	9	1810–1886
William Cushing	1789–1810	20	1732–1810	*Morrison R. Waite*	1874–1888	14	1816–1888
James Wilson	1789–1798	8	1742–1798	John M. Harlan	1877–1911	34	1833–1911
John Blair	1789–1796	6	1732–1800	William B. Woods	1880–1887	7	1824–1887
Robert H. Harrison	1789–1790	—	1745–1790	Stanley Mathews	1881–1889	7	1824–1889
James Iredell	1790–1799	9	1951–1799	Horace Gray	1882–1902	20	1828–1902
Thomas Johnson	1791–1793	1	1732–1819	Samuel Blatchford	1882–1893	11	1820–1893
William Paterson	1793–1806	13	1745–1806	Lucius Q. C. Lamar	1888–1893	5	1825–1893
*John Rutledge**	1795	—	1739–1800	*Melville W. Fuller*	1888–1910	21	1833–1910
Samuel Chase	1796–1811	15	1741–1811	David J. Brewer	1890–1910	20	1837–1910
Oliver Ellsworth	1796–1800	4	1745–1807	Henry B. Brown	1890–1906	16	1836–1913
Bushrod Washington	1798–1829	31	1762–1829	George Shiras, Jr.	1892–1903	10	1832–1924
Alfred Moore	1799–1804	4	1755–1810	Howell E. Jackson	1893–1895	2	1832–1895
John Marshall	1801–1835	34	1755–1835	Edward D. White	1894–1910	16	1845–1921
William Johnson	1804–1834	30	1771–1834	Rufus W. Peckham	1895–1909	14	1838–1909
H. Brockholst Livingston	1806–1823	16	1757–1823	Joseph McKenna	1898–1925	26	1843–1926
Thomas Todd	1807–1826	18	1765–1826	Oliver W. Holmes	1902–1932	30	1841–1935
Joseph Story	1811–1845	33	1779–1845	William D. Day	1903–1922	19	1849–1923
Gabriel Duval	1811–1835	24	1752–1844	William H. Moody	1906–1910	3	1853–1917
Smith Thompson	1823–1843	20	1768–1843	Horace H. Lurton	1910–1914	4	1844–1914
Robert Trimble	1826–1828	2	1777–1828	Charles E. Hughes	1910–1916	5	1862–1948
John McLean	1829–1861	32	1785–1861	Willis Van Devanter	1911–1937	26	1859–1941
Henry Baldwin	1830–1844	14	1780–1844	Joseph R. Lamar	1911–1916	5	1857–1916
James M. Wayne	1835–1867	32	1790–1867	*Edward D. White*	1910–1921	11	1845–1921
Roger B. Taney	1836–1864	28	1777–1864	Mahlon Pitney	1912–1922	10	1858–1924
Philip P. Barbour	1836–1841	4	1783–1841	James C. McReynolds	1914–1941	26	1862–1946
John Catron	1837–1865	28	1786–1865	Louis D. Brandeis	1916–1939	22	1856–1941
John McKinley	1837–1852	15	1780–1852	John H. Clarke	1916–1922	6	1857–1945
Peter V. Daniel	1841–1860	19	1784–1860	*William H. Taft*	1921–1930	8	1857–1930
Samuel Nelson	1845–1872	27	1792–1873	George Sutherland	1922–1938	15	1862–1942
Levi Woodbury	1845–1851	5	1789–1851	Pierce Butler	1922–1939	16	1866–1939
Robert C. Grier	1846–1870	23	1794–1870	Edward T. Sanford	1923–1930	7	1865–1930
Benjamin R. Curtis	1851–1857	6	1809–1874	Harlan F. Stone	1925–1941	16	1872–1946
John A. Campbell	1853–1861	8	1811–1889	*Charles E. Hughes*	1930–1941	11	1862–1948
Nathan Clifford	1858–1881	23	1803–1881	Owen J. Roberts	1930–1945	15	1875–1955
Noah H. Swayne	1862–1881	18	1804–1884	Benjamin N. Cardozo	1932–1938	6	1870–1938
Samuel F. Miller	1862–1890	28	1816–1890	Hugo L. Black	1937–1971	34	1886–1971
David Davis	1862–1877	14	1815–1886	Stanley F. Reed	1938–1957	19	1884–1980
Stephen J. Field	1863–1897	34	1816–1899	Felix Frankfurter	1939–1962	23	1882–1965
Salmon P. Chase	1864–1873	8	1808–1873	William O. Douglas	1939–1975	36	1898–1980
William Strong	1870–1880	10	1808–1895	Frank Murphy	1940–1949	9	1890–1949

Justices of the Supreme Court (continued)

	Term of Service	Years of Service	Life Span		Term of Service	Years of Service	Life Span
Harlan F. Stone	1941–1946	5	1872–1946	Abe Fortas	1965–1969	4	1910–1982
James F. Byrnes	1941–1942	1	1879–1972	Thurgood Marshall	1967–1991	24	1908–1993
Robert H. Jackson	1941–1954	13	1892–1954	*Warren C. Burger*	1969–1986	17	1907–1995
Wiley B. Rutledge	1943–1949	6	1894–1949	Harry A. Blackmun	1970–1994	24	1908–1998
Harold H. Burton	1945–1958	13	1888–1964	Lewis F. Powell, Jr.	1972–1987	15	1907–1998
Fred M. Vinson	1946–1953	7	1890–1953	*William H. Rehnquist*	1972–	—	1924–
Tom C. Clark	1949–1967	18	1899–1977	John P. Stevens III	1975–	—	1920–
Sherman Minton	1949–1956	7	1890–1965	Sandra Day O'Connor	1981–	—	1930–
Earl Warren	1953–1969	16	1891–1974	Antonin Scalia	1986–	—	1936–
John Marshall Harlan	1955–1971	16	1899–1971	Anthony M. Kennedy	1988–	—	1936–
William J. Brennan, Jr.	1956–1990	34	1906–1977	David H. Souter	1990–	—	1939–
Charles E. Whittaker	1957–1962	5	1901–1973	Clarence Thomas	1991–	—	1948–
Potter Stewart	1958–1981	23	1915–1985	Ruth Bader Ginsburg	1993–	—	1933–
Byron R. White	1962–1993	31	1917–	Stephen Breyer	1994–	—	1938–
Arthur J. Goldberg	1962–1965	3	1908–1990				

Note: Chief justices are in italics.

*Appointed and served one term, but not confirmed by the Senate.

INDEX